*The American
Immigration Collection*

The Italian
Emigration of
Our Times

ROBERT F. FOERSTER

Arno Press and *The New York Times*

NEW YORK 1969

THE ITALIAN EMIGRATION
OF OUR TIMES

BY

ROBERT F. FOERSTER, Ph.D.

PROFESSOR OF ECONOMICS
PRINCETON UNIVERSITY

CAMBRIDGE
HARVARD UNIVERSITY PRESS
LONDON: HUMPHREY MILFORD
OXFORD UNIVERSITY PRESS
1924

PRINTED AT THE HARVARD UNIVERSITY PRESS
CAMBRIDGE, MASS., U.S.A.

TO

MY MOTHER

PREFACE

A world engrossed as never before with defining the rights and obligations of nationalities and with mitigating the causes of national and international discord cannot afford to ignore the fertile field for study presented by the great migrations of our day. Among these the Italian easily ranks first in importance, and it is typical in many respects of the rest. The problems it exhibits are fundamental, and they stand forth in such sharpness of relief and such largeness of dimension that there can be no mistaking their nature.

One's interest, however, easily goes further. So embracing has been this emigration that a chronicle of its development must constitute an indispensable chapter in the history of the Italian people, whose gifts to civilization and whose qualities in human intercourse have attached them to men everywhere. So memorable likewise have been the contributions of the emigrants in a number of lands that chapters setting forth their fortunes there must always hold a place in the histories of the several countries themselves. Inevitably such chapters must lack a certain dramatic element possible to narrative or political or biographical writing. For emigration is first of all, and chiefly, a scattering. The steerage of the Atlantic vessel has farmers without lands, builders without bricks, doctors without patients, and the marks that distinguish the *dramatis personae* at every step have to be obliterated in order that the collective experience may be understood. On the other hand, just the fact that a myriad of wills are in question, and the homely types among men — the diggers and hewers, at the best the artisans — brings us nearer to certain great human experiences, to the "still, sad music of humanity," than a study of protagonists could do.

Of an immigration problem we in the United States hear much, and now and then we are warned that in other quarters a problem

v

of emigration exists. We have yet to learn that, strictly speaking, there is only a migration problem. Though no one would pretend that Napoleon can be justly studied as emperor alone or a flower as it blooms in August, it is assumed in most of our writings upon immigration that the causes of emigration may be glossed over, the situation of emigrants in other lands ignored, the policy of the country of emigration passed by, and so forth. Often, even, it is deemed quite sufficient to point out, picturesquely, how Antonio, earning thirty cents at home, dreamed of Eldorado and freedom, found both, and returned to his native hills to rouse his people to higher ways of living.

But anecdote and incident can never be made sufficiently illustrative to do justice to so large a theme. In no one place and at no one moment of time is its rationale completely unfolded. From day to day and land to land the scene changes. The broadest glance of any one man is insufficient. We are like the astronomer who must supplement what he sees through his telescope with what other men have recorded and with what the steadier gaze of the camera reveals. And just because no personal record can ever suffice for such a history, the historian must the more willingly be guided by multifarious evidence.

The bane of social studies has ever been their specious simplification of what is inevitably complex, even their entire contentedness with stating inferences while burking premises. Hence incessant and futile debate, pointless conclusions, inapplicable remedies. For this situation readers themselves are partly to blame. A busy world too easily adopts the fashion of approving interpretation while caring naught for the ordering of fact, and is not even disturbed when the language of the ideal is employed in the description of the actual. It is only when they are put to a false use that facts are inert or that they mislead or confuse. Rightly placed, they alone can give reality to argument. Birds in migration fly high in order to fly far; their view is of large outlines, assuring them of direction, yet they must be able to alight on a branch.

I have dealt more fully with the causes of emigration than have most students because from the first it seemed reasonable to suppose that unwholesome forces might be at work, which no world economy could afford to ignore. At unusual length, again, I have followed the Italians into the countries of their settlement, both to discover the character of their economic and cultural contributions and to learn the nature of their fortunes. Too broad to be taken in at a glance, the picture in so far might be called panoramic, did it not lack the continuity which panoramic views suppose; it is more like a succession of frescoes, each panel complete and marked off from the next, yet each illustrating a single theme in different coloring and circumstance. But there the analogy ends, for another principle is at work. No one would pretend that the comparative method of inquiry can accomplish for social problems what it has done for the natural sciences, even for anthropology and religions. Yet uniformities, repetitions, some counterpart of the " habits " of natural history, exist, and though greatly variable in their degree of fixity, have undeniable significance. In regard to Italian emigration, a rare opportunity for comparative study is at hand, hitherto all but neglected; but the available materials, however tempting, must not be forced, and I have put into Book IV about as much as they have seemed to me to allow.

.The historian of an emigration, I suspect, finds more chaff in his wheat than the historian of a great people; at least, he cannot and often dare not winnow it so far. My own visits to Italy and my observation of Italians in some other countries have been helpful more in providing points of view and standards of criticism than in supplying materials. While a wealth of information is to be had upon many matters, it is frequently necessary to depend on the evidence of consuls and their sort, which is often self-contradictory, often palpably exaggerated, often stupidly cribbed from what their predecessors in office have written, and often filled with patriotic boastfulness or vigilant faultfinding. Even when the attempt has been made to exclude or label such doubtful material, or to interpret it in the light of local report and the observation of travelers, errors have undoubtedly crept into the narrative. But these, I hope, have been compensating, and in any case they would scarcely invalidate the drift of the argument.

A book, Walt Whitman has said, should " go as lightly as the bird flies in the air or a fish swims in the sea." I have made mine carry much luggage: footnotes apologetic or bibliographical. For readers are like countries: some like a sort of free trade, while others care more about examining chattels and credentials than welcoming the visitor. And since the literature of this book is mainly unfamiliar to English readers, I have somewhat freely indicated the pertinent references as I have gone along. These in general are my bibliography, more usefully presented so, I believe, than they would be if detached and detailed at the end.

The book is almost wholly new. Only that part of Book I which attempts to balance the outgoing and returning Italians has hitherto been published (in Volume XXIII of the *Quarterly Journal of Economics*). Among a great many persons whom I have to thank for help at one point or another, I will here name only two: Professor Taussig, who first, years ago, suggested to me the riches of my subject and who has since been unstinting in friendly counsel, and my wife, whose wise and essential criticism has seen the task through.

HARVARD UNIVERSITY
September, 1919

CONTENTS

BOOK I. — MAIN CURRENTS

CHAPTER I

CHAPTER II

BOOK II. — CAUSES

CHAPTER III

CHAPTER IV

BOOK III. — IN FOREIGN LANDS

CHAPTER VIII

CHAPTER IX

CHAPTER X

CHAPTER XI

CHAPTER XII

CHAPTER XIII

CHAPTER XIV

CHAPTER XV

CHAPTER XVI

BOOK IV. — ITALY AMONG THE NATIONS

CHAPTER XXI

CHAPTER XXII

CHAPTER XXIII

ABBREVIATIONS

Boll. Emig.   Bollettino dell' Emigrazione, some twelve to twenty numbers a year, issued since 1902 by the Commissariato dell' Emigrazione.

Emig. e Col.   Emigrazione e Colonie, special reports by diplomatic and consular officials, 1893 and 1903–09.

Inch. Agr.   Atti della Giunta per la Inchiesta Agraria e sulle Condizioni delle Classi Agricole, 15 vols., Rome, 1879–84.

Inch. Parl.   Inchiesta Parlamentare sulle Condizioni dei Contadini nelle Provincie Meridionali e nella Sicilia, 8 vols., Rome, 1909–11.

He abandons the niggardly soil as the swallow forsakes the inclement skies; he returns to his familiar and cherished hut as the bird repairs to its old nest.

E. MORPURGO, 1882

ITALIAN EMIGRATION

BOOK I
MAIN CURRENTS

CHAPTER I

DEPARTURE

WHAT gives importance to an epoch of geographical discovery is the character and consequence of the single voyage. One voyage may even define an epoch; and any voyage that shows persistence in a hard quest or that braves unknown realms finds a world eager to listen to the tale of its adventure. With an epoch of migration a different emphasis appears. The country of destination is known, its wonders have become accepted, even commonplace. The journey thither is no longer unique; it is the experience of the multitude. Then it is not the single traveller, but the comprehensive group alone, which makes history. Or if perchance an emigrant write the tale of his own adventure, the world will peruse it only if pleased to regard his as the typical career, as the miniature representation of the collective whole. Those who compose a great migration may be never so ordinary; *en masse* they arrest attention. The steerage is negligible — but not a thousand times the steerage. So reckoned and tested, a million men outweigh a thousand; and ten millions are a nation. The farther one moves from the experience of the individual, the nearer one approaches to some of the essential traits of the world of men.

Emigration from Italy belongs among the extraordinary movements of mankind. In its chief lineaments it has no like. Through the number of men it has involved and the courses it has pursued, through its long continuance on a great scale and its rôle in other lands, it stands alone. Its overwhelming general character lights up the details of its development, and gives them lasting significance. How it began and grew, what paths it has followed, to what lands it has gone by predilection, these are fit questions for study. Particularly we must ask how commonly it happens that this emigration retraces its ways; with what frequency Italians, once out of Italy, return home, and so for a time or finally put an end to their journeying.

These questions are not new. They have been asked and answered frequently. Yet a casual reading of writings published in Italy and in other countries discloses wide discrepancies in the answers. Where official sources are directly quoted, the differences are not less pronounced than in the more popular writings, where no special regard is had for sources. Inevitably, a study of the validity of the official statistics themselves must precede any unqualified acceptance of figures. In the end, however, it should be possible to attain some fairly definite conception of the volume of the emigrant tide, both in its flux and reflux.

What, first, of the outgoing tide ? What has been the history of emigration from Italy ? It is not enough to understand by emigrant one who expatriates himself for permanent settlement in another country. Such a limited definition has been appropriate in cases where it amply covered the common practice, and it has been persistently current among the nations. By tradition in Italy too it had a vogue, and the opposition to Sig. Bodio was strong when, years ago, he insisted that those also were emigrants who left their country for temporary settlement elsewhere. Fortunately, having regard for the characteristics of the Italian movement, Bodio's wider definition won acceptance; and in time an emigrant became, officially, anyone not travelling for pleasure, health or business, who went abroad either for permanent settlement or temporarily, for a period often less than a year.

It is certain that the modern emigration of Italians was well under way long before the official collection of statistics was undertaken. While in some parts of Italy, notably the South, severe laws barred all emigration during the first decades of the nineteenth century, movement in other parts was relatively free. Duval gives occasional figures for the transoceanic emigration of this earlier period, based on material (gleaned from various sources) in the Emigration Bureau of the French Ministry of the Interior. In the years 1835–42, he says, 7894 Sardinians arrived at Montevideo; in 1856, 2738 Sardinians sailed for Buenos Aires; in June, 1860, there were 12,755 Italians in Algeria; and so forth.[1] In these years, as the American figures show, few Italians came into the United States. When Correnti, in 1858, published a compilation of many sorts of Italian statistics, he estimated that some 30,000 Italians were living in South America. " In these last months an Italian colony was venturesomely planted in Mexico, a mere sapling on the shore of a turbulent sea." Italian laborers, he said, were in Switzerland, Belgium, and England. In France there were 63,000, chiefly seamen, soldiers, and workmen, " many of them among the most intelligent silk workers of the Lyons mills." [2] Little accuracy can be claimed for the figures published in the Italian census of 1861, but they serve for general indications. The temporary emigration of the census year had amounted to nearly 44,000 persons. From various sources it was calculated that the Italian colonies in Switzerland and Germany comprised nearly 14,000 persons each, the colony in England 4500, in France 76,500, in Tunis 6000, and in Alexandria 12,000.[3] What emerges clearly from most of the accounts is that the early emigrants were chiefly from the Alpine slopes of Italy and from the Ligurian coast. Some connection in time there surely has been with the old commercial voyages of the North Italians. Did not an ancient saying hold that " In whatever quarter of the world you open an egg a Genoese will spring from it " ?

In Italy this early emigration appears not to have roused much attention. Serious enough problems of other sorts pressed for solution. Besides, the impulse, though imminent, was yet to come, which would swell the streamlet to the proportions of a flood. From 1860 on, our knowledge begins to be more precise. Leone Carpi, perhaps fairly to be regarded as the first Italian to

---

[1] J. Duval, *Histoire de l'émigration au XIXᵉ siècle* (Paris, 1862), pp. 155 ff., 248 ff.

[2] C. Correnti, *Annuario statistico italiano, Anno I, 1857–1858* (Turin and Milan, 1858), pp. 441 f. Despite its title, this work is not official.

[3] *Censimento generale, 31 dicembre 1861* (3 vols.), i, p. xxix. Part of the census description of the Italians in France is taken almost literally from Correnti. The figure for temporary emigration is the earliest I have found.

study broadly the emigration of his people, wrote, " Numerous provinces which before 1860 made no contribution to the stream sent contingents, from 1861 to 1869, which were annually larger. In other provinces where by tradition emigration had been moderate and wholesome it took on large proportions." [1]   Indeed, by the end of this decade (if not earlier, for no figures apply before 1869) more than a hundred thousand Italians per year were quitting their country, and the proportion to her population was already such as to place Italy beside Germany as a land of emigration.   With the help of the ministries of the Interior and of Foreign Affairs, Carpi compiled a set of annual figures, which, somewhat revised, have been given virtually an official status. They follow:

Year	Total	Temporary	Permanent	Clandestine
1869	119,806	83,565	22,201	14,040
1870	111,459	83,588	16,427	11,444
1871	122,479	96,384	15,027	11,068
1872	146,265	?	?	5,585
1873	151,781	?	?	11,921
1874	108,601	?	?	17,362
1875	103,348	?	?	27,253

The decrease in 1870, Carpi ascribed, not without good ground, to the Franco-Prussian war.   Clandestine emigrants were commonly workmen, clergy, students, and others who departed without a passport, largely to escape military service.   From 1874 to 1876, when restrictions were in force regarding the issuance of passports for America, it is likely that the clandestine emigrants were much more numerous than indicated.   Indeed, a parliamentary commission was unwilling, in 1879, to admit that there had been a decrease in emigration since 1873.[2]   Partly because of difficulties in securing his figures which Carpi himself mentions, partly for

---

[1] See Carpi's chief work: *Delle colonie e dell' emigrazione d'italiani all'estero sotto l'aspetto dell' industria, commercio, agricoltura e con trattazione d'importanti questioni sociali* (4 vols., Milan, 1874), i, p. 17; in an earlier work more specific evidence is given.   See also G. Florenzano, *Della emigrazione italiana in America comparata alle altre emigrazioni europee* (Naples, 1874), ch. 6.   (This work includes results of the author's own inquiry in several provinces.)

[2] I. Sachs, *L'Italie, ses finances et son développement économique depuis l'unification du Royaume* (Paris, 1885), p. 934.

reasons next to be set forth, all of these early statistics for total emigration have probably to be revised upward — no one can say by how much.

In 1876 the Italian Bureau of Statistics [1] began an important collection of figures which has been continued to the present day. It is the only series which covers a long period of years and includes emigration into the countries of Europe and North Africa. It is the only series which gives the emigration by compartments, provinces, and communes.[2] It possesses further the extrinsic importance of having been more widely quoted than any other series; partly for the reasons given, partly — as regards emigration to transoceanic countries — because of ignorance of better statistics. Consider some of the more significant figures of this collection. For quinquennial periods before 1911, I have prepared annual averages:

ANNUAL AVERAGE NUMBER OF EMIGRANTS

Period	All countries	Europe and the Mediterranean basin	Transoceanic countries
1876–1880	108,797	82,201	26,596
1881–1885	154,141	95,146	58,995
1886–1890	221,977	90,694	131,283
1891–1895	256,511	109,067	147,444
1896–1900	310,435	148,533	161,901
1901–1905	554,050	244,808	309,242
1906–1910	651,287	257,593	393,694

NUMBER OF EMIGRANTS

Year			
1906	787,977	276,042	511,935
1907	704,675	288,774	415,901
1908	486,674	248,101	238,573
1909	625,637	226,355	399,282
1910	651,475	248,696	402,779
1911	533,844	271,065	262,779
1912	711,446	308,140	403,306
1913	872,598	313,032	559,566
1914	479,041	245,897	233,144

[1] I shall thus translate Direzione Generale della Statistica. The annual figures are published in reports styled *Statistica della emigrazione*.

[2] The sixteen *compartimenti* embrace the sixty-nine *provincie*. The *compartimento* is not an administrative division, but is maintained in official classifications because it conveniently marks off regional differences.

The total number of recorded emigrants for the thirty-one years 1876–1914 is about fourteen million. In both the overseas emigration and the European a great growth has taken place. The quinquennium 1886–90 marks a turning point: while the total emigration increased much, that into Europe changed slightly, and for the first time in its career was surpassed by the American current. In other words, the stream that had begun to flow so copiously into Europe was now largely diverted into America, more than doubling the earlier volume. In the quarter century that has since elapsed, the emigration into America has apparently remained in excess of that into Europe. In 1901 there was a sharp bound in the movement. The new level was virtually maintained until 1905, when another bound occurred, chiefly in the overseas emigration; and in 1913 the new level was in turn exceeded.

To the ending of the war with Turkey and to the return of conditions of prosperity in the United States the high figure of 1913 must be ascribed. The new exodus was still proceeding when the shock came of the outbreak of the European war. Promptly, on August 6, 1914, a royal decree suspended the emigration of all men of military age. At the point of embarkation, men subject to eventual recall for service were detained; likewise women, children, and the aged going to rejoin men subject to military duty. What with the restrictions upon the issuance of passports, the dangers to navigation, and the suspension of the steamship service, the great movement of Italian emigration, caught almost at its zenith, was violently brought to a stop.

Consider now the figures for emigration into the principal countries of Europe:

ANNUAL AVERAGE NUMBER OF EMIGRANTS

Period	Austria-Hungary	France	Switzerland	Germany
1876–1880.......	19,196	36,256	12,884	7,315
1881–1885.......	25,625	44,500	7,032	6,927
1886–1890.......	34,118	30,114	7,203	10,351
1891–1895.......	36,345	26,897	12,166	15,249
1896–1900.......	46,287	24,960	25,647	30,941
1901–1905.......	54,454	54,299	53,828	56,021
1906–1910.......	37,138	60,224	77,305	62,199

NUMBER OF EMIGRANTS

Year	Austria-Hungary	France	Switzerland	Germany
1906	39,521	62,497	80,019	67,620
1907	41,953	63,105	83,026	75,885
1908	36,998	57,702	76,708	59,780
1909	30,989	56,863	66,931	53,391
1910	36,233	60,956	79,843	53,648
1911	35,099	63,370	88,777	64,950
1912	42,010	74,089	89,258	75,507

Into each of these countries emigration has been much greater than into any other country of Europe. For each it averaged about 54,000 persons a year in 1901–05. From 1876 to 1885 the emigration into European countries was greatest into France; from 1886 to 1900, greatest into Austria-Hungary. Before 1900 the emigration into Hungary was about half that into Austria; since, it has run one-tenth to one-fourth. Emigration into France reached its lowest point in 1896; so sensitively does the barometer of emigration register a period of strained relations. In 1901 the emigration into France suddenly sprang to a new level, which it has maintained. From the middle eighties to 1905 the average annual emigration into Switzerland has, roughly speaking, doubled with each quinquennium; in subsequent years this emigration has been greater than that into any other country of Europe. Since 1890 emigration into Germany has progressed similarly, but not to such heights. Throughout the previous decade Germany was herself still sending forth heavy annual quotas of emigrants, and indeed in the earlier nineties also, so that she could hardly be expected to receive many immigrants, even from such a country as Italy.

These four countries lie very near to Italy. It is simpler for the North Italian to enter Ticino than to migrate to Central Italy. Ventimiglia is at once Vintimille. Belluno and Udine, great reservoirs of temporary emigrants, lie merely across the border from Austria-Hungary.[1] Hence the emigration is in some respects more of a kind with the extraordinary internal migration of Italy than with the transoceanic movement.

[1] Of late years, however, the emigration from these provinces has been more strongly into Germany (especially Bavaria) than into Austria-Hungary.

To the outlying countries of Europe not many emigrants have gone. By hundreds oftener than by thousands, they have moved into Russia, Spain, Portugal, Holland, Belgium, the Scandinavian countries. They have had, however, a long and notable history in Great Britain; since 1900, steadily year by year, 3000–4000 have immigrated, including some hundreds to Ireland. Only the smallness of the territory of Luxemburg justifies inclusion of the grand duchy in the minor countries, for a pronounced immigration, running easily to 2000 a year, has entered there. The Balkan states, one of the older fields, received in 1890–1900 an average of about 14,000 a year, but since 1900 have received less than 3500 a year.

Fluctuating about one or two thousand a year before 1904, Egypt in that year and in 1905 received 4500, soon, however, relapsing to 2000–2500. Before 1900, Algeria and Tunisia received together less than 4000 a year; after 1907, about 4000. Generally Tunisia has received many more than Algeria. In 1911, for the first time, Tripoli received as many as a thousand; in 1912 more than 7400 — a reminder that on November 5, 1911, by royal decree, Tripoli and Cyrenaica were brought under the full sovereignty of Italy. Only fluctuating numbers have gone into western Asia.

What now of the value of these figures? The early official reports made few qualifications. " On the whole," says one of them, " we have reason to believe that our statistics . . . represent with sufficient approximation the departure of our compatriots in search of temporary occupation or of permanent employment." [1] In 1902 a slightly more guarded statement appears: " Although the authorities endeavor to keep as accurate an account as possible of those who emigrate, whether for some months only, or for an indefinite period, yet the official statistics do not succeed in measuring the movement with absolute precision." [2]

Upon the method of collecting the figures we have explicit knowledge. Whoever would emigrate is expected to apply in

---

[1] *Statistica della emigrazione nell' anno 1887*, p. iv.
[2] *Statistica della emigrazione negli anni 1900 e 1901*, p. 5.

person or in writing to the *sindaco* (mayor) of his commune, who after granting the *nulla-osta* (which indicates that there are no legal obstacles to departure) procures the passport from the prefect or sub-prefect of the province, and delivers it to the applicant. Until 1901 the passport for a laborer cost 2.40 lire. Since 1901 it has been free. The sindaco recorded the number of those who had been granted the nulla-osta and the number of those who, by whatever avenues of information, had been reported as having gone without a passport; and the combined numbers he called the emigration from his commune. In 1904 the work of compilation was taken over by the officers of public safety, who every three months, in every *circondario* and province, performed their task upon the basis of passports actually granted.

If all emigrants procured passports, or if all those who did not were registered by the sindaco, and if none that did procure them subsequently stayed at home instead of leaving the country, there would be no reason to question the final totals for emigration. But the if's are momentous. Since 1901 the passport has been obligatory for all emigrants sailing from Italy or enrolled in North Italy to sail by authorized carriers from Havre. But the obligatory provision did not apply before 1901, nor has it ever applied to emigration into countries of Europe or of the Mediterranean basin. Clearly, another test must guide us. Does the usefulness of the passport make it a desirable document to possess ? Undoubtedly, in some countries of Europe, though not even in all of the important ones, the passport materially helps the emigrant to get work. But he may not apprehend its advantages. He may expect to return to Italy soon, and may not think it worth the necessary inconvenience (before the charge was abandoned the outlay equalled from one to three days' wages).

Other considerations are important. At many points of the long land border it is easy to cross afoot.[1] The propertyless *contadino*, migrating from one province to another, and recorded, if at all, merely as an internal migrant, may be induced to join

---

[1] P. Baldioli-Chiorando, *e.g.*, has written (" L'emigrazione in alcuni paesi della provincia di Cuneo," *Riforma Sociale*, October, 1913, p. 853): "A good half (mostly women) make the journey afoot, thus sacrificing a week's wage, but spending almost nothing."

others in going to France or Germany, and may never become known to his sindaco as an emigrant. A man may depart to escape military service [1] or to flee penal justice. He may be induced by agents of steamship companies not recognized by the Italian government as emigrant carriers to leave from a French, German or English port, especially since a lower rate is often charged for an unprotected, unregulated service. Since 1902 the passport has been refused to persons likely to be debarred from foreign ports; yet unauthorized carriers often succeed in enrolling them by promises of admission. Since 1901 the passport has been valid for three years; consequently a man may emigrate thrice in three years, and yet be recorded only once. On the other hand, the paper may get lost and is easily soiled and crumpled, so that application for a new one may be made; the worker may even procure a second, in order to hold one in reserve.[2] Some persons receive the nulla-osta to whom the provincial authorities later refuse the passport; before 1904 they would have been regarded as emigrants.[3]

But one of the greatest sources of error is the general unreliability of the operations of the sindaci who, until recently, compiled the statistics. The Italian commune, in many regions, has never been won over to work in sympathy with national measures. A governmental investigation, held in 1903, showed that " in many communes the registers of the nulla-osta were not regularly kept "; and further, that " more and more rarely were the communal authorities found to have inquired whether persons had emigrated from the locality without providing themselves with the prescribed documents; so that the number of persons recorded as only known through public report to have emigrated had in late years fallen almost to zero, account having been kept of them in only four or five provinces." [4]

[1] Bodio declared this to be the chief source of the secret emigration; see *Di alcuni indici misuratori del movimento economico in Italia* (Rome, 1891), p. 6.

[2] Cf. C. C. Dominioni, " L'immigrazione italiana nel distretto consolare di Innsbruck durante l'anno 1906," *Boll. Emig.*, 1907, No. 5, p. 28.

[3] *Boll. Emig.*, 1907, No. 14, p. 5. They may, however, leave without the passport, unless to go to America.

[4] *Statistica della emigrazione negli anni 1902 e 1903*, p. vi. Cf. also a comment

The emigrants who had departed without passports, and been subsequently reported to the sindaci of their communes, were as follows: [1]

```
1887–1891 (yearly average) .....................    37,287
1892–1896     "          "     .....................    33,850
1897–1901     "          "     .....................    41,745
1902  .........................................    17,290
1903  .........................................    28,278
```

Are the figures veracious ? Is it sufficient to add them to the totals for emigration ? Some evidence can be had to show that neither the early nor the late records for emigration without the passport come close to the truth. In a report of the Society for the Protection of Temporary Emigrants into Europe we read: [2]

When one notes that in 1889 [when 94,823 emigrants were recorded as having gone into European countries] 120,000 emigrant laborers passed through the stations of Basel and Schaffhausen alone, and that the results of investigations repeated for a series of years in ten other centers of the Swiss Confederation show that thirty out of one hundred emigrants possessed no passport — the only means of official record — and that a great number of them had crossed the frontier on foot, one can calculate that our continental emigration in 1899 must have consisted of an army of over 400,000 workmen, while the governmental statistical bureau announced only 177,031.

More explicit are the findings of Dr. Cosattini, appointed by his government to study emigration from the Friuli.[3] He supplemented the official figures — which are " far below the truth " — by personal investigations made in various communes. His most striking facts, however, have reference to the sales of railway tickets, during March, April, and May, for frontier destinations or beyond. A reduced third-class fare for these destinations is granted to groups of five or more men who present a request from the sindaco. To the number of these Cosattini added those third-class passengers who, not departing in groups of at least five per-

by G. Prato, " L'emigrazione temporanea italiana e l'opera di assistenza di Mons. Bonomelli," *Riforma Sociale*, June 15, 1901, p. 552.

[1] Compiled from *Statistica dell' emigrazione* (for 1902 and 1903), p. ix.

[2] Consorzio per la Tutela dell' Emigrazione Temporanea nell' Europa Continentale, *Relazione* (Milan, 1904), p. 6.

[3] G. Cosattini, " L'emigrazione temporanea del Friuli," *Boll. Emig.*, 1904, No. 3.

sons, had paid the full fare. Of this number, some certainly were not emigrants, but the procedure is justified because the departures in these three months are actually four times as numerous as during the other months; and only the temporary emigration movement could explain the concentration. He then made the following comparison:

Railway figures		Bureau of Statistics ("Temporary" emigration)	
1898, 3 months............	65,023	1898, 12 months............	50,598
1899, " "	64,464	1899, " "	55,536
1900, " "	63,350	1900, " "	43,306
1901, " "	63,660	1901, " "	49,448
1902, 2 "	48,534	1902, " "	45,125

Allowing for the reduced emigration during nine months of the year, it would still hold that almost twice as many persons had emigrated from this greatest recruiting ground in Italy as had been officially recorded. It would be hazardous, however, to apply the same proportion to emigration from other parts of Italy.[1]

In recent years the consuls have reported the number of Italians to whom, during residence abroad, they have granted passports. Since special need for the document does not arise commonly, the 20,000–30,000 emigrants a year so added to the figures must include only a fraction of those who might be added.

It is just the fact that emigration today is free or only slightly conditioned by law that makes all documentary registration difficult. If the passport had notable value in foreign countries, it would be a fair measure of emigration. But it is only a rough index. Some persons receive it who do not emigrate, but those who do not receive it and yet emigrate, and those who use it more than once during its three-years' validity, contribute to a total

---

[1] In the reports which the Italian consuls have made to the emigration department there are numerous references to the large number of Italians working without passports in the countries of Europe. Let two or three examples suffice. From Ticino, it was reported that nine-tenths of the temporary immigrants (a conjecture) lacked passports for Switzerland (A. Marazzi, "Il canton Ticino e la immigrazione italiana," *Boll. Emig.*, 1903, No. 11, p. 32). Three-fourths of the immigrants into Germany in 1904 were said to be without a passport (summary of a study by Dr. Stuzke in *Boll. Emig.*, 1904, No. 14, p. 40). In 1912 it was said that a quarter of the numerous furnace workers who came into Bavaria were without a passport (P. Sandicchi, "I fornaciai italiani in Baviera," *Boll. Emig.*, 1912, No. 12, p. 8.)

far higher than that proclaimed. No one can say how far the
official figures for emigration into Europe have fallen below the
truth; unquestionably it is very far.[1]

Procuring a passport, sailing from a port — Italian or other —
landing in America, are so many aspects of a single movement.
There is, perhaps, a fair presumption that the third of these makes
the safest starting-point for a study of the transoceanic movement; it is a bird in hand that is being counted when American
statistics are collected.[2] They follow:

ANNUAL AVERAGE NUMBER OF IMMIGRANTS

Period	United States	Brazil	Argentina
1877–1881	8,217	....	16,553
1882–1886	23,084	12,600	39,088
1887–1891	50,499	68,847	57,089
1892–1896	56,048	94,019	42,587
1897–1901	87,249	41,090	49,513
1902–1906	224,649	19,215	71,714
1907–1911	206,622	16,450	87,598
1912–1916	165,773	....	....

NUMBER OF IMMIGRANTS

Year	United States	Brazil	Argentina
1906	286,814	20,777	127,348
1907	294,061	18,238	90,282
1908	135,247	13,873	93,479
1909	190,398	13,064	93,528
1910	223,453	14,163	102,019
1911	189,950	22,914	58,185
1912	162,273	31,785	80,583
1913	274,147	30,886	114,252
1914	296,414	....	36,122
1915	57,217	....	11,309
1916	38,814	....	....

[1] Even the emigrants have asked for a reorganization of the account-keeping; so
the first *Convegno degli Emigranti Vallellinesi in Tirano* in a vote passed January 12,
1914 (C. A. Aschieri, " Relazione sulle statistiche dell' emigrazione italiana per
l'estero e per l'interno," *Annali di Statistica*, Serie V, viii, p. 119). In 1913 a
commission was appointed by the Minister of Foreign Affairs to study the question of the passport (*Bollettino dell' Ufficio del Lavoro* (ediz. quindicinale), May 16,
1913, p. 94).

[2] For the United States I have used an official compilation, " Immigration into
the United States from 1820 to 1903," published in the *Summary of Commerce and
Finance* for June, 1903, and the reports of the Commissioner-General of Immigra-

Records for the United States began as early as 1820, when 30 Italians arrived. But the great growth has been very recent. In 1887–1906, 2,092,821 were admitted; in 1907–16, 1,892,155. By the census of 1850 the Italians in the United States (3679) were slightly in excess of the Swedes (3559), a minor immigrant people. At each successive census, through that of 1900, the Swedes were decidedly in the majority, though clearly losing ground in the last decade of the century. Twice after 1900 — first when the panic of 1907 struck, next when the war of 1914 broke out — the Italian immigration to the United States fell from the greatest height it had till then attained to its lowest level in many years.[1]

Before 1875 German and Portuguese immigrants into Brazil, especially the latter, were constantly more numerous than Italian immigrants. The Italians first exceeded the Germans in 1875 and thereafter never failed to do so. They first exceeded the Portuguese, their chief rivals, in 1876 and so continued in nearly every year of the quarter century ending in 1903. Since 1820 they have been nearly half of all immigrants into Brazil, having numbered about one and one-third millions. The great period of their coming began in the eighties when passage was commonly supplied free by the Brazilian government. But within a decade's time thereafter a crisis in coffee-growing occurred, and the emigration fell off greatly. In 1898 the Brazilian government ceased to collect statistics of immigration, resigning that function to the states, which have inadequately performed their task.[2] In 1902, after a notable increase in new arrivals had again taken place, an Italian decree put an end to all emigration to Brazil of a subsidized kind. Once more the movement fell off, and a decade elapsed before even a modest revival appeared.

tion. (Before 1906 the figures relate to aliens who came from Italy; since, they are for immigrant Italians.) For Argentina I have used the *Memoria de la Dirección de Inmigración* and the municipal yearbooks of Buenos Aires. The Brazilian statistics have not currently appeared in any one publication, but have been many times officially reproduced (see chapter XV, below).

[1] In the calendar year 1914, Italian immigration was not large. The ending of the fiscal year at June 30 credited to 1915 the reduced arrivals of July–December, 1914.

[2] At first only São Paulo and Minas Geraes published official figures, but latterly annual collections have emanated from Rio de Janeiro.

Statistics for immigration into Argentina were first collected in 1857. In 1873, 26,878 Italians arrived. A larger number came in 1882, when a rise began which culminated in the year 1889 with 88,647 immigrants. Then a severe crisis broke upon the country, and the years 1890 and 1891 brought only 39,122 and 15,511 Italians respectively. After some fluctuation, generally on a low level, the high mark of 1889 was overpassed in 1905 and 1906. In the entire period 1857–1906, 1,605,432 Italian immigrants entered the republic; in 1907–14, 668,947. Except for thirteen months in 1911–12, when the Italian government prohibited emigration to Argentina, the annual movement held close to 100,000 a year until the war brought it emphatically to a stop. The Argentine statistics are based on information contained in the passenger lists of vessels that arrive at Buenos Aires.

The other American countries have been less important destinations. Uruguay has long received 2000–5000 a year, but in 1889 and 1890, by way of striking exception, 15,047 and 12,873. Canada before 1900 received a few hundreds per year; in the next decade, 4000–8000 a year; subsequently even more. Italian emigration has been pushing its way with decision into all parts of America, into Mexico, Cuba, and Central America, as well as Peru, Bolivia, and Chile.

The statistics we have been considering may be compared with those secured by the Italian Bureau of Statistics on the basis of nulla-osta, or of passports granted. Before 1901 the passport was not obligatory. We should therefore expect many persons to have emigrated in this period without it, especially since in neither North nor South America does it possess the same usefulness as in some regions of Europe. Since 1901 many persons must have taken out the passport, which is free, without actually emigrating. The following table would seem to confirm these probabilities. The figures of the first column are the quinquennial totals for Italian immigration according to the appropriate country's records. The figures of the second column represent, according as they are preceded by (+) or (−), the amount by which the American figures are greater or less than those of the Italian Bureau of Statistics:

Period	United States		Brazil		Plata countries [1]	
1877–1881	41,085	+17,584	....	....	82,766	+23,880
1882–1886	115,419	+15,583	62,989	+16,564	233,739	+75,169
1887–1891	252,495	+64,584	344,235	+73,460	330,020	+71,478
1892–1896	280,240	+64,517	470,094	+171,939	240,651	+47,849
1897–1901	436,243	+60,859	205,451	−50,363	264,317	+44,023
1902–1906	1,123,243	−112,539	96,075	−49,677	372,999	+34,141
1907–1911	1,033,109	−130,508	82,252	−15,285	451,524	+60,639

Only nine-tenths of those who in 1902–11 secured passports for the United States actually came to the country. The American figures, it must be borne in mind, refer to the fiscal year which closes in June; and the period July–December, 1901, included in the figures does not compensate for the period July–December, 1911, not included in them. Allowing for this, there would still be many who had secured passports, but not departed. Apparently numerous emigrants who, on applying for the passport, had named Brazil for their destination, actually went to Argentina; and some, also, perhaps, who had named the United States. A third part of the Argentine immigration is probably composed of Italians who, after having lived for a time in Brazil, shifted their abode to Argentina.[2] It is reasonable to conclude that the American figures reflect the actual emigration more truly than do the Italian.[3]

[1] The Bureau of Statistics comprehends in this term Argentina, Uruguay, and Paraguay. The last country receives a very slight immigration, which has not been included in the American figures except in 1907–11.

[2] Apparently no records have been published which measure this immigration fully. In the first nine months of 1914, out of 10,839 Italians recorded as departing from Santos, 1443 gave Argentina and Uruguay as their destination. *Boll. Emig.*, 1914, No. 13, p. 66.

[3] Some interesting data of another sort strengthen this probability materially. In the table which follows, I have compared for five-year periods the number of immigrants actually arrived in America with the emigrants who actually sailed from Europe. I have not given the absolute figures, but have stated, for the sake of comparison, by how much they are greater or less than the figures of the Bureau of Statistics. The figures for sailings are those of the third-class passengers departed from Italian ports according to the records of the port officials; to them I have added the Italian passengers embarked in other European ports. All the principal ports are included. So, likewise, are first and second class passengers, but these are an inconsiderable number, and may be taken to compensate for emigrants embarked in ports not included. The ports represented differ slightly from year to year. All

In 1901 a permanent Commissionership of Emigration (*Commissariato dell' Emigrazione*) was established, which keeps a record of all emigrants who sail from the Italian ports and Havre. Its statistics for number are based on the taxes paid by the steamship companies for emigrants carried. How do these statistics compare with the American ?

By taking the emigrants to the United States, month by month, and grouping them to correspond to our fiscal year, we get a series of figures somewhat comparable with those of our Commissioner-General. Considering that two to three thousand Italians a year are debarred from the United States, that some Italians sail from non-Italian ports and that the Italian figures include a sprinkling of non-Italian emigrants, and finally that the two sets of figures do not refer to quite the same moment of time — a late June, 1905, emigrant being a July immigrant in the fiscal year 1906 — the correspondence is so close as to enhance our confidence in both sets of figures. The following table is for sample years only:

data for sailings have been taken from recent numbers of the *Annuario Statistico Italiano* or of the *Statistica della emigrazione*. The American figures utilized are those for Brazil, Argentina, Uruguay, and the United, States; since 1907, for Paraguay also.

I	II
The American figures are greater or less than the corresponding figures of the Bureau of Statistics according as + or −	The figures for sailings from Europe are greater or less than those of the Bureau of Statistics figures for transoceanic emigration according as + or −
1877–1881................. +41,464	.... +134,309
1882–1886................. +109,088	.... +106,799
1887–1891................. +200,726	.... +188,570
1892–1896................. +149,393	.... +149,636
1897–1901................. +42,477	.... +107,780
1902–1906................. −152,187	.... −120,383
1907–1911................. −85,154	.... −264,651

Plainly, the excess of the American figures before 1901 rests upon fact. Hence here again, for the overseas emigration, as before for the European, the figures collected on the basis of nulla-osta granted appear as understatements. Furthermore, for 1902–11 the figures for sailings confirm the conclusion already reached, that in this period more persons procured the passport than really emigrated.

The closeness of the figures is impressive. That it is not greater in recent years is due to the fact that the sailings from Italy include a small but increasing number of third-class foreign passengers, such as Greeks and Turks; further that the Italian emigration to other countries of America, especially that into Canada, has become more considerable; finally that the fiscal year of the United States ends in June.

Period	Italian figures	United States figures
1904–05................	214,031	221,479
1905–06.:...............	287,523	273,120
1907–08................	135,709	128,503
1908–09................	226,117	183,218
1913–14................	225,516	283,738
1914–15................	44,614	49,688
1915–16 [1].............	28,455	33,665

When, however, the Commissionership figures for Brazil and Argentina are compared with the corresponding American figures, an appreciable and rising excess of the latter is disclosed.[2] Indeed it may be argued on specific grounds that the Italian Commissioner's figures are too low for these countries and perhaps also for the United States. The official reports declare that nearly every ship licensed for transoceanic travel carries some " clandestine " emigrants, and the unlicensed ships carry many. At Milan, in 1913, more than 13,000 such emigrants were held up before they could depart, and the Udine office repatriated 360 who tried to go to Brazil on a free passage; and more than 300 law-breaking steamship agents were prosecuted.[3] Again, no tax has to be paid for second-cabin passengers and they therefore are not embraced in the statistics. Yet among them are many emigrants. From the port of Naples alone such emigrants, departing thus elusively, have been estimated to reach 20,000 a year.[4] Finally, the very limitations placed by the Italian government upon emigration to

[1] The American figures are for the full year, the Italian figures for eleven months only.

[2] A similar excess appears when they are compared with the figures of the Bureau of Statistics.

[3] " Notizie sul movimento dell' emigrazione transoceanica italiana . . . nell' anno 1913," *Boll. Emig.*, 1914, No. 3, pp. 7 f. There is another reason for insufficiency. The Havre statistics recorded by the Commissioner have been only of Italians who had bought their tickets in Italy. When the license with the Compagnie Général Transatlantique was renewed, the company was for the first time called upon to pay the emigrant tax on Italians not enrolled in Italy yet sailing within a month after leaving Italy. In the first seven months of 1914, before sailings were stopped by the war, some 3000 emigrants were accordingly listed, who in a previous year would not have been registered. See " Notizie statistiche riassuntive sulla emigrazione italiana transoceanica negli anni 1914 e 1915," *Boll. Emig.*, 1916, No. 2, p. 11. An Italian who after a season in Germany (for example) sails from Havre is still not included.

[4] Aschieri, p. 120.

Brazil and for a time to Argentina give color to the view that many emigrants for these countries escaped record.

A summary statement is now possible. The most reliable statistics of transoceanic emigration from Italy are those compiled in American ports. The figures of the Italian commissioner, the most widely accepted by Italian writers (so far as recent transatlantic emigration is concerned), err somewhat in understatement, certainly as regards South America. The figures of the Bureau of Statistics, long unduly low, have in the present century erred in excess, many persons having taken out the passport for emigration only to change their minds subsequently; a situation probably commoner since the passport became free, in 1901, than before.

An Italian cobbler in Pennsylvania once told me that before coming to the United States he had worked for several years in Brazil. Is such inter-country migration frequent ? The passport, we know, is valid for any country or at least for several. The emigrant recorded as having gone to Switzerland may presently pass into Germany, perhaps move to and fro. Of statistical measurement of such movements there is little; but of testimony to their existence, an abundance. We read, for example, that common laborers and miners, brick and earth workers, unemployed in Germany, had moved from Germany into France; that hotel workers left summer employment in Switzerland for winter employment in Nice; that laborers at Homécourt had come from New York, Chicago or New Orleans, some making an annual journey to the United States; that many of the later miners in Algeria had first worked in the declining lead mines of Laurium, Greece; that Italians who went to the Panama Canal from France and the United States later scattered to Chile, Peru, Ecuador, and northern Brazil; that of less than 9000 Italians who entered Santos in the first nine months of 1914, 2800 came from Argentina and Uruguay; finally, that five or ten thousand Italian immigrants a year, and even more, have in recent years come into the United States from other countries of the world than Italy.[1]

[1] The reports of the Commissioner-General of Immigration give the figures by countries. For the previous items see *Soziale Praxis*, September 25, 1913, p. 1451,

These are scattered examples only. Why, indeed, should not the Italian move so, from country to country? He is primarily a laborer. The possibility of earning a very little more than the grudging modicum bid by his own country lowers for him those bars of language, nationality, and social life which so effectually maintain the distinctness of communities economically advanced. During the building of the Simplon tunnel, Pasquale Villari asked some Italians there employed whether they loved their country. He says, " They answered me, smiling, as if I had spoken of some stranger, ' Italy is for us whoever gives us our bread.' " [1]

note (cf. December 28, 1911, p. 398, and May 30, 1912, p. 1114); A. Bernardy, "Alcuni aspetti della nostra emigrazione femminile nel distretto consolare di Basilea," *Boll. Emig.*, 1912, No. 6, p. 34; G. Reynaud, "La colonie italienne d'Homécourt," *La Musée Sociale*, June, 1910, pp. 207, 212; E. Bonelli, "Il distretto consolare del Pireo e la immigrazione italiana," *Emig. e Col.*, 1905, i[iii], p. 268; A. Lomonoco, "Il canale di Panama e il lavoro italiano," *Boll. Emig.*, 1909, No. 2, pp. 138 ff.; note in *Boll. Emig.*, 1914, No. 13, p. 66.

[1] "L'emigrazione e le sue conseguenze in Italia," *Nuova Antologia*, January 1, 1907, p. 53.

CHAPTER II

RETURN. CIRCUMSTANCES OF EMIGRATION

EVEN in its beginnings, Italian emigration had a characteristic which marked it off from most modern migrations. It was often impermanent. The Italian who went forth was unwilling to fix his abode in a foreign country. When Carpi asked the prefects of the provinces concerning these repatriations, they generally told him that lasting absence was not usual; but his persistent efforts to learn from them how many returned were unavailing.[1] Recognizing the moment of the question, Italy, in a backward glance — the basis is none too clear — divided the emigrants of 1869–71 into "permanent" and "temporary"; the exact figures have been given above.[2] In the first year of its concern with emigration (1876), and thereafter continuously through 1903, the Bureau of Statistics listed every emigrant either as "permanent" or "temporary" or under an equivalent phrase. Here, in condensed form, are the results:

ANNUAL AVERAGE NUMBER OF EMIGRANTS

Period	Temporary	Permanent
1876–1880	81,170	27,627
1881–1885	91,971	62,166
1886–1890	97,392	125,384
1891–1895	120,077	132,432
1896–1900	158,364	152,070

NUMBER OF EMIGRANTS

Year	Temporary	Permanent
1899	177,031	131,308
1900	199,031	153,209
1901	281,668	251,577
1902	286,292	245,217
1903	277,135	230,841

Apparently in 1869–71 the temporary emigration was four to six times as great as the permanent. Between 1876 and 1885 the

[1] Carpi, i, pp. 10, 32 ff.   [2] See the revised Carpi table above.

excess declined fast, and in 1887 the temporary emigration fell below the permanent. There it generally remained until 1898, when it again surpassed the permanent. Throughout the period, the number of temporary emigrants corresponds rather closely with the number emigrating to countries of Europe, hence of course the number of permanent emigrants corresponds as closely with the number of transoceanic emigrants. Do the figures correspond as closely with the truth ?

Few emigration statistics have had so wide a currency as these. They have passed into the general literature on emigration apparently without a challenge.[1] Yet is it certain that the question of the sindaco, whether the emigrant was leaving for a few months only or permanently, was correctly answered ?

The Italian field laborer, so unskilled that he can be put only to pick and shovel work in another country, whose entire property can often be carried in a bundle, who feels the scantiness of his earnings at home and hears of greater possible wages elsewhere, must often depart without mature or definite planning. He is young and ready for experiment, and he feels that other lands cannot treat him more harshly than his own. He clings to Italy, yes, but — Italy is whatever land will give him his bread. This man must often not know what answer to give to the sindaco.[2] The latter, unless he be an exceptional officer, will not take much trouble even about ascertaining the real state of the man's mind. And even if an answer is given, and is clear, still the emigrant, when he reaches another land, may change his decision. Where most of the man's life is still before him, he often cannot, even if he would, answer the momentous question of the sindaco.

But the most eloquent argument today against these statistics proceeds from the action of the statistical officials themselves.

---

[1] So, *e.g.*, R. Mayo-Smith, *Emigration and Immigration* (New York, 1890), p. 19. Mayo-Smith even identifies the temporary emigration with that to neighboring countries and the permanent with that to countries outside of Europe. Cf. also R. Gonnard, *L'Emigration européenne au XIXᵉ siècle* (Paris, 1906), p. 187, who accepts the figures implicitly.

[2] The Italian consuls in France agreed in inferring that the Italian emigrants do not usually know, when they leave Italy, that their absence will be permanent. Count Tornielli, " La Francia e l'emigrazione italiana," *Emig. e Col.*, 1903, iⁱ, p. 63.

After thirty years of record and tabulation, in 1903, they brought the series to an end — an admitted failure. " These figures," the Parliamentary Commission of Vigilance upon the Emigration Funds reported to the Chamber, ". . . cannot give an exact account of the phenomenon." [1] The governmental investigation already alluded to had found the task of learning the future plans of emigrants " so difficult that in most cases it was neglected, and the officers made the classification by conjecture." [2] Inspection of the registries of passports showed that the distinction had been made "upon uncertain and arbitrary grounds. In some circondari the entire transoceanic emigration had been considered permanent in the absence of information as to opposite intentions. In others, analogous groups had been assigned to the periodic emigration, because it had been found that in preceding years many persons who had gone to America had returned after a brief stay." [3]

The figures, however, are not wholly misleading. The permanent emigration can, for a long period of years, be measured in another and more reliable way, and the results of the two methods compared. If one deducts from the excess of births over deaths in the intercensal period 1882–1901 the actual increase in the population of Italy recorded by the census of 1901, the remainder will represent the true net loss by emigration. The census of 1882 was taken on the first of January; that of 1901 on the tenth of February. I have accordingly estimated the excess of births over deaths January 1–February 10, 1901, as one-ninth of the year's total. Similarly for the permanent emigration of the Bureau of Statistics in January 1–February 10, 1901, I have estimated one-ninth of the total emigration for the year. This seems fair, for the temporary emigrants of these forty days were, like the permanent, not included in the census; nay, it is probably a conservative overstatement, for emigration at this period of the year is slight. My calculation then reads somewhat as follows:

[1] " Relazione della commissione parlamentare di vigilanza sul fondo per l'emigrazione," *Boll. Emig.*, 1904, No. 11, p. 11.

[2] G. Russo, " Emigrazione dell' Europa e immigrazione in America e in Australasia," *Boll. Emig.*, 1907, No. 14, p. 6.

[3] *Loc. cit.*

Excess of births over deaths in the intercensal period January 1,
  1882 to February 10, 1901 6,206,059
Excess census 1901 over census 1882 4,015,625
Loss by emigration, — *i.e.*, net or permanent emigration 2,190,434
" Permanent " emigration of Bureau of Statistics for the same period 2,390,145
Excess of this over calculated permanent emigration 200,021
Percentage of error of Bureau of Statistics 9.13

In effect, 10,000 persons a year on the average, who have been recorded as permanent emigrants, seem actually to have returned to Italy. Or, otherwise put, one person in eleven has been wrongly classified as permanent. Considering the difficulties inevitable in preparing the figures of the Bureau of Statistics, it seems surprising that the error is not greater. But the effective error by no means measures the actual. Since, so far as applicants for passports are concerned, the temporary and permanent emigrants have apparently long been nearly equal in number, there may have been a great compensating misrecord of permanent and temporary emigrants. It would be particularly hazardous to assume that the percentage of error which I have calculated can be applied to the statistics of any single year. What is most of all to be said to the credit of these figures is that, while the temporary emigration changes slightly from year to year, the permanent reveals just such violent fluctuations as the transoceanic emigration shows.

The computed figure 2,190,434 can be taken to measure with some closeness the net or permanent emigration from Italy in the period considered. It includes a few Italians, to be sure, who will still return to Italy. But it gives absolutely no clew to the extent of the temporary emigration. The total recorded emigration for the same period was 4,638,658. The difference between the two numbers, 2,448,224, cannot be taken to represent the temporary emigration, because, as has been shown, the totals of the Bureau of Statistics for emigration are, to an indefinite extent, understatements.

With the twentieth century, still another official basis has been provided for distinguishing permanent and temporary emigration: the communal registry of population. From the local registry is stricken the name of any emigrant who departs for an indefinite term and gives up his residence. In the years 1901–11, 1,984,154 names were cancelled. In the same years, the names of 724,985 Italians were added to the lists who had given up their foreign residence and returned. The difference, 1,259,169, though it includes some Italians who were yet to return home, represents chiefly those who had permanently disappeared, and is 19 per cent of the 6,560,535 who had received passports in the same period.[1]

Yet these figures in turn are open to criticism. They afford us no indication of the number of those who leave without the passport or of those who, receiving the passport, decide to stay at home. And, as the Italian Commissioner wrote of them some years ago, " they have a very dubious value, for it is common knowledge what a want of accuracy and precision in keeping the population records exists in a large part of the communes of the kingdom." [2]

Even if these figures and the classification previously considered were trustworthy, they would help us little in treating the return movement for particular countries of Europe, since no information has been published for countries. For the method which I propose to follow to determine this migration, accuracy cannot be claimed, but the results, I believe, sufficiently reflect the broad facts.

The first step consists in securing the census figures for Italians living in the countries of Europe in the period 1880–1911.[3] Fortunately, the official counts were in nearly every case taken in December, the very month when fewest temporary emigrants were living abroad. The second step consists simply in subtract-

[1] The annual figures for these computations appear in *Boll. Emig.* and *Statistica della emigrazione.*

[2] L. Rossi, " Relazione sui servizi dell' emigrazione per l'anno 1909–1910," *Boll. Emig.*, 1910, No. 18, p. 25.

[3] For 1880–1901, the figures have been reproduced in the " Terza relazione annuale del commissariato generale," *Boll. Emig.*, 1904, No. 7, pp. 210 ff.; in the case of a few unimportant countries, only consular estimates were available. For 1901–11, I have consulted the later censuses of Austria, Germany, France, and Switzerland and a study, " Saggio di una statistica della popolazione italiana all' estero," *Boll. Emig.*, 1912, No. 1, p. 6.

ing each census figure from its successor in the next decade. This gives the increase in the Italian permanent population. The third step consists in deducting this figure from the Italian immigration into the country during the decade, the difference being then the return migration into Italy. The last figure it is convenient to state as a percentage. In the following table the years represent census dates as well as the comprehending years of the emigration period under consideration. The absolute figures are those of temporary or returned emigrants, and the percentages are those of returned emigrants in total emigrants of the period.

	Period	Total returned	Per cent returned
Total, Europe...............	1881–1891	858,978	91.3
France....................	1881–1891	294,992	84.2
Germany..................	1880–1890	75,972	90.1
Switzerland...............	1880–1888	50,734	99.3
Austria-Hungary	1880–1890	354,520	94.9
Total, Europe...............	1891–1901	1,243,305	85.9
France....................	1891–1896	116,944	96.4
Germany..................	1890–1900	176,580	76.4
Switzerland...............	1888–1900	143,754	65.6
Austria....................	1890–1900	270,078	58.3
Hungary..................	1890–1900	123,093	97.4
Total, Europe...............	1901–1911	2,265,496	90.2
France....................	1901–1911	488,846	85.3
Germany..................	1900–1910	556,634	94.1
Switzerland...............	1900–1910	263,414	75.7
Austria....................	1900–1910	396,835	96.1

Qualifications of this table at once suggest themselves. One is that the figures for returned emigrants are indeed not such, but represent rather emigrants disappeared from the country of destination in intercensal years. Some have died, not many probably in the older periods nor a large proportion in the recent periods of increased immigration, for the emigrants are in the best years of life. Some have migrated elsewhere, but the currents, we can assume, are somewhat compensatory; and, even where they are not, the difference would immaterially affect the number of permanent residents, which is at all events small. Some have migrated to America. All the rest have returned to Italy. These are the true temporary emigrants, and undoubtedly they are a great majority of those included in our figures. Unavoidably, in our calculation we have used the emigration figures of the Bureau of Statistics, and these we have found too low. Hence it may be assumed that the backflow is indefinitely greater than the high percentages computed. That it is not less can be stated with assurance.[1]

When we consider the return movement of Italians from the New World, we have little choice of figures. Only since 1908 has the United States kept a record of departing immigrants. The South American countries have likewise kept records, but have not classified their emigrants by nationality. Before 1904, we have seen, the Italians procuring passports for emigration were classified as temporary or permanent emigrants. But the distinction has even less value for the emigration into America than for that into Europe, primarily because emigration overseas is a much more momentous undertaking. Even if the emigrant has made up his mind regarding the term of his absence, his sojourn abroad is contingent upon so many speculative conditions that he may later change his mind. It can hardly be reckoned a loss that the Bureau of Statistics has in only a few instances published the figures of temporary and permanent emigration by countries.

Our chief source of statistics for the return migration into Italy is the record of passengers disembarked in Italian ports. For the reflux over the land frontier, frequently even when that has originated in America, we have no measure. The figures of the following table before 1901 were collected by the Ministry of the Marine, and since that year by the emigration inspectors, upon

---

[1] Still other qualifications of the table deserve mention. The German and Austrian censuses give the *de facto* population; the French and Swiss, the resident population. But these differences do not affect comparisons made within one country. The emigrants of one year do not necessarily return in the same year, but they usually do so. Hence this is, for decennial periods certainly, an inconsiderable factor. The figures given for the total return from Europe are the least reliable; for, while the factor of emigration covers the ten years indicated, the census figures only approximately cover the same ten years; and some consular estimates of population are included. Even here, however, a correction, were it possible, would only slightly affect the units of our percentages.

the basis of passenger lists.[1] They are for third-class passengers
only, and before 1902 include a negligible sprinkling of foreigners.
Many Italians go from the United States to Havre. When they
proceed thence by rail to Italy, they are included (or have been
since 1902) in the statistics. The last column includes more than
emigrants from the specified countries; it would be higher by
about 15,000 a year, in recent years, if immigrants returning by
first-class and second-class passage were included.[2]

ANNUAL AVERAGE NUMBER OF EMIGRANTS RETURNED

Period	From the United States	From Brazil	From the Plata countries	Total
1887–1891	5,371	1,829	29,815	37,097
1892–1896	20,075	11,444	22,555	54,622
1897–1901	26,992	17,122	27,061	72,631
1902–1906	88,012	23,066	26,013	134,457
1906–1911	149,979	14,168	46,733	211,862

NUMBER OF EMIGRANTS RETURNED

Year	From the United States	From Brazil	From the Plata coutnries	Total
1906	109,258	17,236	30,393	157,987
1907	176,727	20,721	49,867	248,428
1908	240,877	14,675	44,196	300,834
1909	73,806	14,071	45,232	134,210
1910	104,459	10,808	42,888	158,902
1911	154,027	10,568	51,483	216,820
1912	129,649	9,031	43,593	182,990
1913	122,589	12,742	51,151	188,978
1914	156,274	12,865	48,413	219,178
1915	104,265	11,489	51,322	167,925

Is the situation quite as extraordinary as these figures pro-
claim ? The only test that can be applied to them is that of
comparison with those of the United States. In 1908 our Commissioner-General began to keep tally of all outgoing aliens. Between July, 1908, and July, 1916, nine fiscal years, the departing
Italians were 1,215,996, or 130,070 more than the number that
(according to the Italian statistics) arrived in Italy, from the
United States, in the eight calendar years 1908–15. Quite apart,
however, from the longer period of time covered in the American
figures cited, the two series are not exactly comparable. In the

[1] *Statistica della emigrazione*, 1900, and following years, and Russo, p. 36. The
Annuario Statistico for 1904, p. 117, gives some earlier figures.

[2] See the table in *Statistica della emigrazione* for 1910 and 1911, p. xxii.

American figures are included Italians departing for any country, even transient Italians bound for Canada — numbering in some years 10,000 or 12,000. And the Italian figures, in turn, embrace American-born children who, in American law, are American citizens.[1] In the circumstances, while it cannot be said that the Italian figures are confirmed by the American, nothing suggests that the two series are irreconcilable.[2]

What we should most like to know regarding the return movement is, What part of those who emigrate return? Of course our answer can only be historical and approximate. In the table which follows I have stated in percentages of total immigrants for five-year periods the number of returned emigrants for the same periods. For the Italian immigration into the several countries I have used the American figures. For the transoceanic total I have used, on the one hand, the sum of the American figures for the United States, Brazil, Argentina, and Uruguay, and, on the other, the total returned emigrants from whatever transoceanic country. How impressive are alike the volume and the fluctuations of this movement![3]

[1] What weight should be given to this factor (which has been courteously brought to my attention by our Commissioner-General) it is difficult to say. The only statistical evidence which I have been able to secure suggests that it should have slight weight. From Professor Beneduce's detailed study of the immigrants returned from the United States in 1905, it appears that there were in that year only 1763 children under twelve months of age and 4867 children between one and fifteen years, many of whom of course had been born in Italy. (A. Beneduce, " Saggio di statistica dei rimpatriati dalle Americhe," *Boll. Emig.*, 1911, No. 11, Table VIII.)

[2] One lacuna of the American statistics is regrettable. The figures tell how many Italians leave the United States for all countries, how many go back to Italy to stay a year or more, and how many go back to Italy after a stay in the United States of less than a year. On the other hand, though they tell how many departing aliens plan to return to the United States in less than a year, they do not specify these departures by nationality nor even by country of destination.

An expected sojourn of a year or more in the United States constitutes a " permanent " residence. Although not strictly a revival of the Italian statistical distinction of " permanent " and " temporary," this attempt at classification is open to objections similar to those which led to the discontinuance of the Italian series.

[3] For the interest of comparison, the figures of the Italian Commissioner may be used as a base:

	1902–06	1907–11	1912–15
United States	38.77	76.63	76.42
Brazil.......................	} 69.08	123.92	81.59
Argentina and Uruguay		67.55	102.12
Total	43.97	74.75	82.32

PERCENTAGE OF RETURNED IMMIGRANTS

	1887–91	1892–96	1897–1901	1902–06	1907–11	1912–15
United States	10.63	42.97	30.93	37.90	72.60	64.90
Brazil	2.65	12.28	42.83	} 60.70	86.12	
Argentina and Uruguay	45.23	46.87	51.19		51.75	
Total	20.01	27.46	40.33	41.87	68.23	

Two striking tendencies of the emigration movement from Italy find expression in these figures. One is that it is very sensitive to changes, especially of an economic sort, in the conditions of the countries to which it moves. Many years ago, by authority of the Bureau of Statistics, the sindaci asked applicants for passports whether they were leaving Italy because driven from it by the hard conditions of life there or because they were seeking better circumstances in other lands. These puzzling questions find a partial answer in our table. Emigration is checked whenever the chance of finding better circumstances elsewhere appears to be insecure; and repatriation is increased. Thus, in 1892–96, for every five Italians who entered the United States, two returned to Italy — eloquent evidence of the conditions then prevailing; the proportion was four times as great as that of the previous quinquennium. The proportion of returned emigrants, which had again fallen off in 1897–1901, rose substantially in 1902–06, and quite prodigiously in the next decade.[1] The low percentage of Brazil in 1887–96 reflects the active period of colonization; very different is the tale subsequently told, due to the accumulated disorders of the coffee *fazendas*, and particularly to the diminished immigration of the next years. The countries of the Plata have long been regurgitating about half their immigrants. Their unprecedented rate in the recent years turns partly upon the Italo-Argentine dispute already referred to, and partly on the prolonged economic disturbance that set in in Argentina after the outbreak of the European war.

Never has there been so embracing and prompt a return of emigrants as that determined by the war. With fearful swiftness

[1] According to the figures of the Italian Commissioner (*Boll. Emig.*, 1908, No. 6, pp. 4, 6) only 5033 persons departed for the United States in December, 1907, while 52,532 returned — so swiftly did the panic spread.

the routine of existence in the countries of Europe was undone. What with sudden stoppage of employment and the collapse of telegraph and postal service, the Italians rushed hither and thither like frantic caged creatures. When German troops entered Luxemburg on the first day of August, thousands of Italians were there. Only with difficulty, it is said, did those in Germany escape being enrolled for the work of military preparation. From France many were expelled as subjects of a member of the Triple Alliance. Everywhere workmen hastened away, leaving baggage behind them and wages uncollected. Into Switzerland they poured, seeking the great highways through the Alps. In the first three days of August, twenty thousand passed through Basel. From Austria they hurried through Bregenz.[1] The throng seemed as endless as it was tempestuous. By mid-September the army of returned workers — for only those aged fifteen or over appear in the special statistics collected — numbered 470,866.[2] How numerous those were who, desiring to return, found all channels blocked — for example, in Roumania [3] — no one can say. Nearly all those who returned by the middle of September came overland. Whatever their speculation as to further chances of employment, they must chiefly have been inspired to their decision by the nearness of war, the terror it instilled, and the sense of being indefinitely cast off from the Italy of family and friends. The shock to business was universal, how-

---

[1] Opera di Assistenza agli Operai Italiani Emigrati in Europa, *Relazione del lavoro compiuto dall' Opera in occasione del rimpatrio (Agosto-Novembre, 1914), compilata a cura di G. Gallavresi,* Milan, 1914 (a vivid and explicit account); F. Calimani, "I profughi di guerra italiani rimpatriati attraverso alla Svizzera," *Boll. Emig.,* 1916, No. 3, pp. 5–35; "L'assistenza agli italiani profughi dai paesi belligeranti (Informazioni del commissariato dell' emigrazione)," *ibid.,* pp. 36–45.

[2] Of these 62,787 were women. By September 15, 280,612 were still unemployed. The official figure admittedly does not include quite all who had returned even by September 15. Figures for repatriation and unemployment are provided for each circondario in a somewhat elaborate report, Ufficio del Lavoro, *Dati statistici sui rimpatriati per causa di guerra e sulla disoccupazione (Pubblicazioni,* Serie B, No. 45), Rome, 1915. A trade-unionist estimate was that one million had returned in the same weeks. See "La guerra e l'emigrazione," in *La Confederazione del Lavoro* (monitore ufficiale della Confederazione Generale del Lavoro), September 16, 1914, pp. 669 f.

[3] See a note in *Boll. Emig.,* 1916, No. 5, pp. 59 f.

ever, exempting no country. A pall fell over wage-earning. No
land seemed hospitable. Italy was the old mother. So in September and October, but much more in November and December,
returned emigrants began to pour in from the Americas. In the
spring, when it became manifest that Italy would enter the war, a
new wave of emigration came from Germany and Austria.[1] War
being declared in May, the July–September repatriations from
overseas again became heavy.[2] From all lands men came to join
the colors.[3] By 1916 the return movement had almost run its
course. Between July, 1914, and December, 1915, for every 100
emigrants who left by Italian ports, 412 returned — an inverse
migration, assuredly, without parallel!

But sensitiveness to foreign changes, acting with astonishing
immediacy and thoroughness, is only the first deduction to be
made from the statistics of return. A second is this: in the last
thirty years Italian emigration has become increasingly of a
temporary nature. Note the high percentage of emigrants returned from the United States in 1897–1901 as compared with
1887–91, and the high percentage in 1902–06, almost as high as in
1892–96, when economic conditions were so radically different;
and note the astonishing rate in the years after 1906. From
Brazil one expects a heavy backflow of the tide, but the Argentine Republic, despite conditions which have brought more immigrants to her shores per year than ever before, has certainly also
sent extraordinary numbers back into Italy.

Some day it should be possible to measure closely the length of
sojourn which the Italians make abroad. On the basis of data not
very explicitly described the Italian Commissioner-General concluded that the stay in the United States, when not permanent,
was terminated in most cases within five years; the stay in Argentina in from two to five years.[4] Very recently the same official

[1] Calimani, p. 17.

[2] " Notizie statistiche reassuntive sulla emigrazione italiana transoceanica negli
anni 1914 e 1915," *Boll. Emig.*, 1916, No. 2, pp. 24 f.; see also pp. 16 f.

[3] Even Egypt, according to an estimate, sent back 2000 for this end. Nisi,
" Lettera dal Cairo," *La Vita Italiana*, August 15, 1915, p. 166.

[4] " Relazione sui servizi," etc., *Boll. Emig.*, 1910, No. 18, p. 40.

has attempted to collect more accurate statistics. Until his results appear we may gratefully study a series of figures which the Commissioner-General of Immigration of the United States has compiled annually since 1908. These show the number of Italians emigrated from the United States after a residence of from one to five years. In the following table I have stated these figures in percentages of all Italians emigrated in the year in question, who do not expect to return to the United States within twelve months: [1]

1908....82.6 per cent	1911....78.0 per cent	1914....68.5 per cent
1909....80.9 "	1912....72.0 "	1915....81.8 "
1910....77.8 "	1913....67.9 "	1916....57.9 "

The figures allow certain inferences. They show beyond question that a heavy majority of those who return do so within five years after their arrival. The returned of 1908 and 1909 were largely of those who had so abundantly come in the preceding prosperous years. With a slackened immigration, the percentage would hardly be so high in ensuing years. The first war months precipitated the departure of the more recent immigrants, those most likely to desire to return to their families and their affairs in Italy. In the second war year, many recent immigrants having already departed, the older residents stood forth more prominently.

How frequently does it happen that those who go back to Italy emigrate again ? Certainly many return to the countries of Europe, but they have never been counted. Many return also to the United States. Nearly half a century ago the Italian consul-general at New York was of the opinion that of the hundreds annually who went back to Italy most returned again to the United States.[2] Much later, during the thirteen years from 1896 to 1908, the immigration reports of the United States gave a count of those immigrants who " had been in the United States before."

---

[1] I have taken no account of the " non-emigrant " Italians who departed, since an indistinguishable though large portion of these go to Canada and other countries after only a brief stay in the United States. My table excludes likewise all Italians who returned to Italy in less than one year after arrival.

[2] Quoted by Carpi, ii, p. 247.

The sum of the Italians was 244,236. In 1904 they were 10 per cent of the Italian immigrants; in the next succeeding years, 21, 14, and 7 per cent. In the decade 1897–1906 they were 41 per cent of the number recorded at Italian ports as having returned from the United States. That is, in effect, two out of every five Italians who had returned from the United States had re-emigrated thither.[1]

No statistics exist to measure the frequency with which Italians, returned to Italy from one country, migrate next to another. The phenomenon seems not even to have come under observation. Yet it is reasonable to suppose that a people that resorts readily to re-immigration to the same foreign country, and one that shows frequent migration directly from one foreign country to another, and in general develops a great temporary emigration, will also vary its destination from year to year. So the emigrant into France one year may become an emigrant into Germany the next. But does the emigrant who has been in America turn to Europe ? This also is likely. A study of the figures for Europe and America, even a study by compartments, shows that it often happens (*e.g.*, in 1910 and 1911) that a decreased emigration in one direction accompanies an increased emigration in another. It is possible that if records of such movements were to be gathered they would reveal an amazing frequency of proletariat globe-trotting, a frequency unequalled by the upper-class travellers of the richer countries.

Still another trait must be considered. Even in countries from which there is little emigration internal seasonal movements commonly take place. In Italy these have had an extraordinary development, involving hundreds of thousands of men, women, and children a year. They go into Emilia for the rice planting and care, into Latium for the grain harvest, and so forth. Those who years ago went down from the uplands of Tuscany to labor in the maremma have even been said to be the direct forerunners

[1] This interesting series of statistics was discontinued because " it was believed the continuation of the . . . figures would be surplusage and lead to confusion in understanding the immigration and emigration tables." (Letter to the author from the Acting Commissioner-General, February 9, 1917.)

of the Tuscan foreign emigration.[1] Much of the emigration into Europe is of this seasonal sort, the same individuals participating for years on end. The extraordinary migration of building workmen out of Venetia is an example; for no sharp distinction, in this regard, is to be drawn between agricultural and industrial workers. If statistics could be had they would doubtless show that many persons who depart for the United States between March and May, returning between October and December, repeat their migration in the following spring. There can be no question at all regarding the existence of a great seasonal movement between Italy and Argentina. The laborer who goes to Argentina in November, and stays till May, can engage in agriculture both at home and in Argentina. It was the known existence of a great seasonal emigration that led the Italian authorities in early days to regard the terms temporary and periodic as interchangeable, who thereby erred only through excess.

Viewed from one angle, the history of emigration from Italy is but the collective histories of the emigration from the sixteen compartments. When the first regional figures were gathered, they revealed a preponderant development in the North. The emigration census of 1871, for whose inaccuracies due allowance must be made, held that a quarter of all emigrants were from Piedmont, that more than a quarter were from Liguria, and that Lombardy and Venetia contributed largely; on the other hand, that Sicily, Calabria, and Basilicata could each claim but from one to three per cent.[2] Carpi found that in 1871 Reggio di Calabria — later a prolific source — had only 48 emigrants, Syracuse 41. Little wonder then that, when Potenza contributed only 369 emigrants in 1869 and as many as 1439 in 1871, he exclaimed, "What an enormous increase!"[3]—but in the latter year Udine in the North yielded 19,321 emigrants. In the decade of the seventies the southern compartments continued greatly to enlarge their

[1] A. Mori, " L'emigrazione dalla Toscana e particolarmente dal Casentino," *Boll. Emig.*, 1910, No. 12, p. 77.

In the Appendix, I have elaborated an account of the Italian internal migration.

[2] *Censimento degli italiani all'estero, 31 dicembre 1871* (Rome, 1874), p. cxxi.

[3] Carpi, i, p. 19.

quotas. How they presently came to outrival the northern can best be read in a table: [1]

	1876–1886 (average)	1887–1900 (average)	1901–1909 (average)	1911	1913
Piedmont	29,529	27,447	55,076	52,335	78,663
Liguria	5,218	4,325	6,793	7,052	9,428
Lombardy	19,622	21,660	50,178	65,069	87,133
Venetia	37,662	98,107	98,765	97,588	123,853
North Italy	92,031	151,539	210,812	222,044	299,077
Emilia	4,966	11,866	33,209	32,459	39,134
Tuscany	8,856	13,764	30,700	37,442	45,599
Marches	945	4,261	21,907	17,232	32,069
Umbria	32	608	9,824	12,098	17,851
Latium	33	1,104	12,273	9,121	25,962
Central Italy	14,832	31,603	107,913	108,352	160,615
Abruzzi and Molise	4,083	14,320	48,744	32,025	62,038
Campania	9,921	29,405	70,766	54,149	78,633
Apulia	618	3,106	20,906	20,318	41,837
Basilicata	5,636	9,245	14,460	10,426	16,153
Calabria	5,542	15,355	43,279	30,382	55,910
Sicily	2,010	14,596	75,265	50,789	146,061
Sardinia	101	501	5,101	5,359	12,274
Southern and Insular Italy	27,911	86,528	278,521	203,448	412,906
Total	134,774	269,670	597,246	533,844	872,598

What proportion of the inhabitants has gone ? During most of the past thirty years, in Venetia, about thirty in the thousand; and in a large part of this period, the same proportion in Calabria, Basilicata, and the Abruzzi and Molise. Only less powerful has been the outward current from Lombardy and Piedmont in the North and Sicily in the South. In the regions given least to emigration in recent years — Liguria and Sardinia — the rate has been about six in the thousand.[2]

Since 1876 the Bureau of Statistics has reported the sex and age of all emigrants and whether they have planned to depart alone

[1] It is based, since we lack other figures, on the compilations of the Bureau of Statistics. See *Boll. Emig.*, 1910, No. 18, p. 3, *Statistica della emigrazione* for 1910 and 1911, and *Bollettino dell' Ufficio del Lavoro, serie quindicinale*, July 14, 1914.

[2] A valuable compilation of statistics is in the Commissioner-General's report, *Boll. Emig.*, 1910, No. 18, p. 5.

or with others of their family. The sheer detail of the record we may here be spared. Suffice it to say that in the earlier years nearly nine-tenths of the emigrants were males,[1] and that pretty steadily, in the thirty-odd years since, four-fifths have been. The case seems the more striking when it is recalled that among the immigrants of all peoples into the United States the average of males has hung about two-thirds. The emigration of children from Italy has been much less than the immigration from all countries into the United States. Only in the depressed period of the nineties did the number of women and children increase, and the number of those who left in company with others of their families. If we knew nothing of Italian emigration save these telling figures we could not fail to infer its strangely temporary character.

This character, we have already said, has been accentuated with the passing years. Has it been so in the sense that more Italians go away for a short time, or in the sense that a larger proportion of those who go leave for a short absence only, or finally that those who go away temporarily stay away for a shorter time ? More do go away for temporary absence. The increasing totals of emigration confirm that. There is no evidence that the temporary emigrants are as individuals a larger percentage of all persons who in one year or another emigrate. Rather, the figures just reviewed encourage the deduction that the percentage has been unchanged. Hence, the meaning of the general tables showing what proportion of emigrants return to Italy must be that the stay abroad, especially the stay in the Americas, is generally briefer than it was. Here essentially is the sense in which Italian emigration is increasingly temporary.

How the emigrants will fare abroad depends to no mean degree on their occupational equipment. What has this been ?

Working upon his data of 1870, Carpi classified the emigrants according to their origin in country or town. The rural he deemed to be about five-sixths of all. When statistics of occupation were first officially collected, in 1878, they indicated, just as their successors have done, that the great mass of emigrants came from the agricultural districts. It is true that those directly employed

---

[1] Carpi inferred a similar fraction for the years 1870 and 1871 (i, pp. 19, 31).

in field undertakings have appreciably declined from the earlier level. But on the other hand, the number of common day laborers has by at least as much increased. The truth is that these two groups have never been securely marked off from one another. Both originate mainly in the country. No alchemy is needed to make over the farm hand into a navvy. It is doubtless the case that when a field laborer has for a season or more outside of Italy worked as a navvy, he tends to be classified as such in his subsequent departures.[1] In this fact chiefly, I venture to suppose, rather than in a change of attitude of the authorities, lies the explanation of the steady and marked increase in the emigration of common laborers.

The great classes of common laborers and workers in agriculture have been two-thirds or more of all emigrants.[2] Particularly heavy has been the agricultural representation in the southern compartments. There the industrial and artisan groups — if from the last named we consent to exclude workers in the building trades — also abound. On the other hand an emphatic predominance in the representation of building workmen has characterized the northern compartments, Venetia (notably), Lombardy, and Piedmont. There have never been more than a few professional persons. Among the occupied women who emigrate, the agricultural stock has largely dominated, especially in the South, but undoubtedly many women accustomed to work occasionally in the fields are listed as of indefinite occupation. From the North many women depart, who in the neighboring countries become factory workers.

Although the backflow into Italy may differ in important respects from the outflow, the Italian government has never attempted to describe it. Once only, and then for just the two years 1905 and 1906, a special analysis was made of the repatriations from overseas. Its results, meager and insufficiently representative though they are, cannot be passed by. They show the women to

---

[1] In the fiscal year 1916, the number of Italian farm laborers admitted to the United States slightly exceeded the number of laborers. Among the Italians departed from the United States, the laborers were about one thousand times as numerous as the farm laborers.

[2] A detailed table of occupations is reproduced in the Appendix.

have fallen slightly under their proportion among outgoing emigrants, those from Brazil being much more numerous relatively than those from the United States. They show the men aged between sixteen and forty-five years to have been over three-fifths of all returning emigrants, a proportion considerably larger than among outgoing emigrants. More than two-thirds of all who returned were unaccompanied by members of their families; of those returning from the United States three-quarters, of those from the Plata countries two-thirds. Indeed, if the return movement from Brazil is excluded, with its notable representation of families, the evidence points convincingly to a return to Italy of men who had planned, on departing, to be gone for only a time. To Calabria the returns were much more frequent, relatively, than to Sicily, and these in turn more frequent than to Basilicata.[1]

Interesting light upon the occupational character of the returning Italians has been provided, since 1908, by the United States. So numerous are the unskilled laborers found to be that they deserve to be set off in a table. I have added together the laborers and farm laborers for each year and determined their percentage of all the emigrants.

1908......83.4	1911......75.4	1914......77.0
1909......74.0	1912......81.5	1915......83.1
1910......67.1	1913......78.7	1916......83.9

Mainly, then, the temporary emigration is made up of unskilled laborers. They expect, in leaving Italy, not to develop ties abroad, but only to lay by dollars. And when the dollars cease to come the return home begins. If a comparison be made of the percentages just stated with the series of figures for the total number of emigrant Italians, it will show that with but one minor exception the percentages actually rise in the years of greater emigration and decline in the years of less.

[1] On the assumption that emigrants generally return after four years of absence, the repatriations were compared with the emigrants of 1901 and 1902. The assumption, however modestly put forth, cannot be substantiated, since the fluctuations in the totals for repatriations do not even remotely follow the same course (four years later) as the totals for emigration. The general results of the analysis of the figures for 1905 and 1906 appear in the cited report *Boll. Emig.*, 1910, No. 18,

Two main purposes have guided us in these statistical chapters: to find the strength of the outflow from Italy and of the backflow into Italy, and to find the strength of the inflow into particular countries and the outflow from them. A word of recapitulation may add definiteness to the picture. Before the unification of Italy the emigration was slight. Since about 1875 it has grown steadily, making a sudden bound in 1901 to a new level, which it has since not only maintained but raised. Official figures for the last four decades show an emigration of fourteen million, but this number probably understates the truth by at least two or three million. About two-thirds of the total emigration is temporary. Of the emigration into Europe at least nine-tenths is such, and that into America has become so increasingly. It is safe to say that annually in the last dozen years (before the war) between 300,000 and 400,000 emigrants have returned to Italy.

The permanent emigration is equally striking. I have already given a figure for the period 1882–1901, calculated as the difference between the excess of births over deaths and the growth of the census population. The following table, compiled by this method, presents the permanent emigration from Italy in the half-century 1862–1911.[1]

Total Net Emigration

1862–1871	16,253
1872–1881	362,335
1882–1901	2,190,434
1901–1911	1,621,266
Entire period	4,190,288

pp. 31–43. Subsequently the details were elaborated by Dr. Beneduce, *op. cit.* It was planned also to analyze the figures later than 1906, but by 1916 no results had been published.

[1] The chief sources I have utilized are the *Annuario Statistico Italiano* for 1884 (pp. 46, 64), that for 1904 (p. 95), that for 1911 (p. 17); and a volume published by the Direzione Generale della Statistica, *Movimento della popolazione nell' anno 1903* (p. ix). To illustrate my procedure: since the census of 1901 was taken on February 10 and that of 1911 on May 10, I have included the excess of births over deaths for eight-ninths of the first year and for four-ninths of the last year, as the entire intervening excess; and I have used the *de facto* census population.

It is true that some emigrants apparently lost in one intercensal period will return to Italy in the next. However, they will then only tend to diminish the total loss for the next period. No considerable deduction has to be made for emigrants returning after the last census date.

Four million emigrants finally disappeared in the half century. This large number would be enough to place Italy among a very few great emigrating nations. What, however, gives to the country its peculiar place among such nations is the accompanying fact of a temporary emigration fully twice as copious as the permanent, creating a situation to which there has never been a parallel.

Writings upon emigration frequently enunciate a law of emigration. The first emigrants are nearly all men; after a while the women and children follow; emigration ceases — the cycle is complete. This generalization does, indeed, with some fairness describe the course of certain completed or lately declining migrations. But there is no necessity in the supposed law. The Italian emigration has, since its infancy, been composed, four parts out of five, of males, and of these chiefly in the productive years of life. It is unsafe to set forth laws of emigration without calculating the possible effects of a cheapened, rapid ocean transportation service and the willingness of great nations to receive men for the strength that is in their arms and their readiness to toil hard. So long as these things continue, so long as there are poverty-burdened Italians whose Italy is whatever country will give them their bread, so long may Italian temporary emigration continue. And, as it has risen, so some day it may decline into insignificance without having ever, for a last step, become characteristically an emigration of families.

BOOK II

CAUSES

CHAPTER III

INTRODUCTORY

HOPES, passions, and calculations, uniquely colored for each individual among the millions who have departed from Italy, have been the immediate precursors of the decision to emigrate. One man gazes ahead, another is driven from behind; one dreams, another measures and weighs his thoughts; one reasons, then follows with his will, while another unquestioningly accepts the decision of a first. In so complex a situation, some loss of verisimilitude and of interest accompanies the attempt to reach behind the concreteness of the surface to a view of general and deeper causes, of whose articulate form the emigrant may be wholly unaware. Yet no other course than this is open to us. In no other way can we apprehend the full strength of the forces which press and are not satisfied till the world highways that cross the horizon have been taken.

To discern the larger causes is no simple matter. And whoever critically scans the innumerable utterances upon the causes of emigration must often shake his head at their abounding misemphases. Cheap and convenient transportation, it seems almost gratuitous to say, is not at bottom a cause. Transportation is as cheap from Argentina to Italy as from Italy to Argentina. Nor do the instigations of the agents of steamship companies for a long time constitute a cause. If a deeper pressure be lacking, the truth will presently be noised about. Nor does the spirit of adventure, so commonly emphasized,[1] and often, no doubt, a concomitant of emigration, really actuate whole bodies of people to migrate. And although it be true that many of the Italian emigrants to the United States come upon steamship tickets purchased in the United States, it cannot be said that the invitations of friends are a cause.

---

[1] *E.g.*, in the *Atti della Giunta per la Inchiesta Agraria e sulle Condizioni delle Classi Agricole*, 15 vols. Rome, 1879-84.

To distinguish the temporary from the long-time causes is quite as important as to differentiate the accidental from the essential. The temporary cause is generally the added burden that makes the other burdens unbearable. Ravages of the phylloxera or the olive-fly, or the failure of the wheat crop, have at various times given a sudden impetus to emigration. But quite apart from the uncertainty which attends any attempt to trace the year-by-year succession of such causes, they cannot pretend themselves to explain a phenomenon which unfolds in several decades. A chronological comparison of the movements in various regions provides no better clew. The fact that emigration from Campania was abundant before it became so in Calabria, and that it only as much as ten or fifteen years later assumed large proportions in Sicily, need signify merely that the occasion which turned a passive into an active cause arose earlier in one compartment than in another. Similarly, the fact that emigration was declining sharply in one section of Calabria while it was rising rapidly in another, need not indicate the disappearance of the actuating cause, but perhaps only a temporary depletion by heavy emigration in the ranks of the people upon whom the cause might act.

The most conspicuous difference of level between the regions of Italy from which emigration proceeds and the countries of immigration is economic. The causes which have sustained an emigration of millions of persons for half a century do in truth constitute a defect or an inadequacy of great magnitude in the Italian economic system. Moral causes also, less conspicuous but very powerful, have acted through the economic. Though some fairly recent developments have been of deep significance, our study will show that emigration from Italy is essentially the final outcome of a chain of causes reaching well into the past and, as such, is a notable historic phenomenon. Is there danger that we may neglect the present ? In Italy, largely, the past is the present.

A full account of the causes of Italian emigration would require an examination of the conditions in each region of the country. Whoever begins such a study, not unmindful of the diverse political pasts of the regions, must note with surprise how commonly economic conditions in them are similar. He will conclude that many words can be saved if he will confine his statement to those things which are typical or general in the principal regions. I have not, I believe, done serious injustice in limiting my analysis to the three compartments of the South in which emigration has had greatest importance — Basilicata, Calabria, Sicily; and to three corresponding compartments in the North — Venetia, Lombardy, Piedmont. Regions adjacent to these need no separate judgment. Central Italy may be passed by, because the conditions there have not, at least till recently, made for much emigration.

In very few countries of the world do the causes of emigration show themselves in such prominence as in the south of Italy. There emigration has been well nigh expulsion; it has been exodus, in the sense of depopulation; it has been characteristically permanent. So the South is a great laboratory in which emigration may be studied in its largest aspects, and it is its own apology for the extended treatment which I have given it. But also, because of this very elaboration, it will be possible to proceed more summarily in our subsequent study of North Italy. Is it not first of all true that throughout Italy the agricultural classes have led in emigration ? In North Italy, let us admit, the proportion has been slightly less than in South Italy, but not to such an extent as to require a different emphasis in the investigation of causes. In a country where manufactures are, even today, in their infancy, where mining is slight, and where actually one-half of the adult male population is engaged in agriculture,[1] the position of the craft and trading population must be mainly dependent upon the fortunes of the agricultural classes.

The general course of agricultural fortunes during the last third of the nineteenth century is reflected in certain available statistical facts. These merit mention here because they reveal a phenomenon which has certainly aggravated the persistent causes

---

[1] This was true at the census of 1901 as well as in 1882. I have seen no figures for 1911, but believe that it is still true.

of emigration. After 1871, while the population was increasing by a quarter, the production of olive oil remained stationary; that of wine, rising at first, became stationary after about 1885. After 1884, the production of wheat, which occupies the greatest acreage in Italian agriculture, rose about 20 per cent, partly under the stimulus since 1888 of a high protective tariff. But the excess of importations of wheat over exportations rose until in recent years it has amounted to a quarter of the home production. Indian corn, of which a quantity one-half as great as that of wheat is annually produced, has been unvaried in amount since 1884, but an importation a fifth as great as the home production has meanwhile grown up. After 1870, a large increase took place in the production of oranges and lemons, but the prices declined by 65–70 per cent. Similar great declines have ruled, since before 1880, in the prices of many other important agricultural products, while the production has in general either remained stationary or declined, and the imports have risen. Since the recent rebound in prices belongs to a different epoch, we may here ignore it.

From this cursory survey the inference is inevitable that a force lying partly without the control of Italy — the competition of other countries in agriculture — has seriously reduced the profit from the leading industry of the country. How far that industry was in a position to sustain the loss, we must try to discover. Our task is complicated, and no atomistic summation of different ills can accomplish it. Whatever independence various forces have had originally, they have later come to interaction and generally to mutual intensification. If we take them up separately in this study, it is only to make clearer their individual bearings.

CHAPTER IV

SOUTH ITALY. I. NATURE AND MAN

THERE is a notion long current, encouraged by the existence of various garden-spots and of certain districts especially fitted for agriculture, that the Mezzogiorno of Italy is a region peculiarly endowed for agriculture. Of far the greater part of its extent this view is inaccurate. Nature is not wholly favorable there, and if man, by means of tillage, irrigation, and fertilizer, has sometimes supplied her deficiencies, he has more generally been powerless to remedy, and has even increased, his disabilities.

One primary requisite of a successful agriculture is lacking. The rainfall is so slight and virtually absent for such long intervals of time that the richest of soils would produce scantily. The situation is worst in Sicily, but serious enough also on the continent. In some years, the summer is almost devoid of rainfall, and the drought may endure for seven months. Though the temperature is seldom higher than during the hot days of a Massachusetts summer, the heat is recurringly great day after day. Whatever rain falls, therefore, quickly evaporates. Within sight of the blue sea the grass of Sicily is a lifeless brown and the road a powder of white. The stifling scirocco may destroy a year's crop. In many regions it is necessary to go long distances to procure drinking water, and a spring rents for a high sum.[1]

The range of products suitable for this climate is narrow, comprising chiefly woody plants whose fruits mature in the spring. Of most crops, especially the herbaceous, it is foreordained that their success will be mediocre. The utility of fertilizer, as is well known, is greatly diminished by an insufficiency of water. Grazing and dairying cannot thrive. Whereas, in the north of Italy

---

[1] Much stress is laid on this inconvenience and much said regarding the devices for transporting water, in the reports of *Inch. Parl.* Cf. *Risultati dell' inchiesta sulle condizioni igieniche e sanitarie nei comuni del regno: relazione generale* (Rome, 1886), ch. v.

the field that has yielded its harvest of grain becomes pasture for cattle, plant growth in the South ceases after the crop has been gathered; at best a few goats and sheep may graze. In turn there is a deficiency of animal manure, and of animals for draft purposes as well.

How vitally the aridity of the climate has involved the entire scheme of land proprietorship in the South has never been sufficiently recognized. When, in the nineties, an agrarian agitation took the shape of a demand for the division of the latifundia, the Marquis di Rudinì — himself the owner of great estates in Sicily — elaborately discussed the causes of the maintenance of the latifundium. He said, " A large cultural unit, and an agrarian rotation which permits the soil to lie fallow: these are the two salient characteristics of the latifundium and of Sicilian graniculture. If the rains were more abundant we should have rich pastures, plenty of manure, and a totally different agrarian rotation. The want of rains and the scarcity of flowing water thus potently and invincibly influence the entire agrarian economy of Sicily." [1] A mixed and intensive cultivation upon small holdings, fundamentally dependent, as it would be, upon a sufficient water supply, could not, he believed, prevail in the great interior of Sicily. Whether the case is really so hopeless we need not now discuss. In the past, certainly, the aridity of the southern climate has been a heavy impediment in the way of a fortunate social economy. [2]

Has this aridity increased within historic times ? Such forests as in ancient days covered the mountains of the South could not, it is often argued, subsist today. Angelo Mosso, impressed by the size of the ancient aqueducts and bathing establishments in Sicily, and by the absence or diminutive size of watercourses where in Roman times had been, according to contemporary accounts, large streams and luxuriant forests, believes that only a decline in the rainfall could explain the change. [3] While climatologists have

[1] A. di Rudinì, "Terre incolte e latifondi," *Giornale degli Economisti*, February, 1895, p. 171.

[2] Cf. also, on the relation of dryness to the size of estates, G. Bruccoleri, *La Sicilia di oggi* (Rome, 1913), pp. 425–428.

[3] A. Mosso, *Vita moderna degli italiani* (Milan, 1906), pp. 234, 372–376, 385–394; cf. I. Giglioli, *Malessere agrario ed alimentare in Italia* (Rome, 1903), p. 354.

been reluctant to hold that any appreciable alterations of climate could take place within the short span of human history, yet some strong arguments, resting on geological and other evidence, have recently been urged, which tend to justify the popular opinion.[1] It is a matter upon which the authoritative word has yet to be spoken.

If dryness of soil and air are among the conditions that explain the narrow productivity of South Italy, at least it may be said that they are purely natural factors and that man is not to blame for them. Unluckily, however, as if these conditions had not been made ill enough, man has intensified them, and has added to them still others which seriously impede agriculture. It is a grave damage that deforestation has wrought, and the penalty of the unwisdom of centuries is still being paid.

In the ancient world, Sicily and the southern Apennines were heavily wooded. Not otherwise can the numerous references and allusions of classical literature be explained.[2] When the Saracens came, they caused the Calabrian coast population to retreat upon the mountains, where considerable felling of trees seems to have taken place; but they probably did not greatly hurt the forests of Sicily. No definite picture of mediaeval deforestation can now be drawn, but it is clear that by the twelfth century the monasterial preserves had begun to be invaded. Undoubtedly the communes cut down forests. In the eighteenth century and early nineteenth, destruction proceeded on a large scale, at first, " with some reserve and moderation, but later with vandalic fury, especially during the constant and frequent succession and restoration of various governments." [3] The pace was quickened again after the

---

[1] See E. Huntington, "Climatic Change and Agricultural Exhaustion as Elements in the Fall of Rome," *Quarterly Journal of Economics*, February, 1917, pp. 173–208.

[2] Mosso has garnered some of the passages; pp. 369–400.

[3] G. Podestà, " Disboscamento," in *Supplemento alla Sesta Edizione della Nuova Enciclopedia Italiana* (Turin, 1893), iii, p. 179. Cf. L. Bianchini, *Della storia delle finanze del Regno di Napoli* (Naples, 1859), pp. 306 f., 419, 423. On the earlier period, see G. Salvioli, *Le nostre origini; estudi sulle condizioni fisiche, economiche e sociali d'Italia nel medio evo prima del mille* (Naples, 1913), pp. 108 ff. and G. Wermert, *Die Insel Sicilien* (Berlin, 1905), pp. 122 ff.

middle of the nineteenth century, to be slackened only in the recent period.

It is curious that the great deforestations of the nineteenth century should have been closely related to two movements in Italy whose intention was in a high degree beneficent. These were the abolition of feudalism and the secularization of ecclesiastical lands. We must stop for a moment to examine both.

Feudalism was abolished in the continental Neapolitan kingdom in 1806, in Sicily in 1812. As a compensation for the cessation of popular rights upon the baronial estates, parts of these estates were given to the communes, as trustees for the people, among whom they were, in the next instance, to be divided. A considerable distribution was made at once; a lull under the restored Bourbons was followed by greater activity after the middle of the century, and all in all a good deal of land was divided.[1]

Half a century after the abolition of feudalism the extensive lands of the Church were secularized. By a series of measures enacted in the period 1855–73, various classes of religious incorporation were suppressed and their lands scattered. In Sicily a law of 1862 compelled the corporations to offer their lands in perpetual emphyteuses. Other laws provided for the final alienation of lands, which presently took place upon a stupendous scale. In the years 1867–1905, 700,000 hectares (say 1,750,000 acres) were

---

[1] In Basilicata, it has been reckoned, 16,161 hectares were distributed from 1806 to 1815, only 8788 from 1815 to 1860; under the new government, however, from 1861 to 1887, 17,238 hectares. See S. Piot, "La Basilicate," *Annales des Sciences Politiques*, January 15, 1907, p. 36; P. Lacava, "La Basilicata," *Nuova Antologia*, May 1, 1903, p. 144. No figures regarding the sum of the transactions are quite reliable, nor do we know how much land the communes in the first place acquired, since litigation, especially under the Bourbons, has not succeeded in defining the status of many lands; on this, see the conclusions of a competent student, F. Arcà, *Calabria vera* (Reggio Calabria, 1907), pp. 45 f.

On some of the changes that followed the abolition of feudalism, see A. Coppi, *Annali d'Italia dal 1750* (Rome), iii (1825), pp. 263–269, and iv (1827), pp. 106–112; G. Salvioli, *Trattato di storia del diritto italiano*, 6th ed. (Turin, 1908), pp. 241–246; Bianchini, pp. 399–411; E. Caselli, "La ripartizione dei demanii nel Mezzogiorno," in *Nuova Antologia*, December 16, 1900, pp. 630–651; E. Ciolfi, *I demani popolari e le leggi agrarie* (Rome, 1906), ch. vi.

sold — half in the first six years, two-thirds by 1877 — and of these a large part were in the south of Italy.[1]

What lends such great significance to the disposal of the feudal and ecclesiastical lands is the circumstance that they were plentifully covered with timber. While the small folk had been clearing their properties for cultivation in preceding centuries the great feudal lords and ecclesiastical corporations had conserved their forests. Indeed, wherever common rights (*usi civici*) existed — and they were peculiarly an institution of the South — the peasants were truly joint-owners of the forests, and neither lord nor peasant could lawfully undertake to fell trees beyond his immediate needs. Moreover, it was not until the nineteenth century that it became commercially profitable to fell more than sufficed for local wants.

The allotment of feudal lands was the signal for deforestation. Since the shares were small, they had to be cleared before being tilled. The Sicilian emphyteuses were essentially improvement leases, and what that implies for deforestation can be inferred from the fact that one-tenth of the area of the island had been subject to the religious bodies, which had placed under cultivation only the eleventh part of their land.

Some blame also rests upon the forestry laws and their administration. The act of 1877, for instance, removed restrictions that had previously protected wide stretches of forest land. Whoever wished to evade the laws had a simple task, and the communes

---

[1] At the end of 1877, the sales in the South stood:

Abruzzi and Molise	12,109	hectares
Campania	33,370	"
Apulia	96,440	"
Basilicata	39,106	"
Calabria	36,387	"
Sicily	17,851	"
Total	235,263	"

With the figures for Sicily should be considered the 192,000 hectares leased under the emphyteusis contract.

Perhaps the best account of the secularization movement is by G. C. Bertozzi, "Notizie storiche e statistiche sul riordinamento dell'asse ecclesiastico nel regno d'Italia" in *Annali di Statistica*, Ser. II, iv (Rome, 1879). Cf. Sachs, pp. 285–296, 300–309. Introducing new material is a discussion, "Di taluni effetti delle nostre leggi sul patrimonio ecclesiastico," in *Bollettino di Statistica e di Legislazione Com-*

themselves are declared to have offended quite as much as private persons. For many years exports of lumber were heavy.[1]

It is not possible to measure with any degree of accuracy the extent of the century's deforestation. Plenty of statistics have been compiled, but they are either far from complete or their terms are indefinite — *bosco*, for example, being sometimes applied to mere scrub, or to lands that goats are content to use for pasture! The Italian official yearbooks used to state the extent of the forest area but their figure declined little with the passing years and finally was abandoned, no doubt having got far out of relation with the facts.

What is the more tangible aftermath of the stripping of the forests ?

In the tertiary exposures of the Apennines, and in some older formations in Sicily, there is a physical predisposition to landslides, which acts with heightened frequency whenever the staying hold of the trees is released. Not more than a third of the area of Sicily is *terreno stabile*. Over vast stretches of country, the surface soils, even when their slope is moderate, become soaked with water during the heavy winter rains, and when their weight becomes over-great, they slide toward a stabler level, bringing disaster to houses and farms and not seldom to human lives as well.[2]

More serious still is the effect of deforestation upon the flow of streams and the morphology of their beds. Here again the con-

parata (Rome, Anno V, 1904–05), fasc. i, pp. 176–211. Excellent for its summary of the financial operations is V. Racca, " La suppression des congrégations religieuses et l'expropriation," in *Journal des Economistes*, March, 1901, pp. 321–343. See also *Inch. Parl.*, v[i], pp. 223–227.

[1] On the progress of deforestation and the motives which governed it, see *Inch. Agr.*, ix, pp. 135, 230; *Inch. Parl.*, v[iii], p. 37, and vi[i], pp. 157–165; D. Taruffi, L. De Nobili, and C. Lori, *La questione agraria e l'emigrazione in Calabria* (Florence, 1908), pp. 238–244; A. De Viti de Marco, *Saggi di economia e finanza* (Rome, 1898), pp. 173 ff.; N. R. D'Alfonso, " Il disboscamento in Calabria," *Nuova Antologia*, October 16, 1913, pp. 622–631; V. Perona, "Le foreste nel presente e nell' avvenire," *L'Italia Economica*, Anno II (1908), pp. 90 f.

[2] A good discussion of this situation is in T. Fischer, *La penisola italiana* (Turin, 1902), pp. 47–51. In *Inch. Parl.*, v[iii], Note ed appendici, pp. 354 f., is a discussion significantly entitled " The journeying communes " (Basilicata).

formation of the country predisposes to harm and intensifies the evil done. It is a comparatively short course which the streams must traverse from mountain altitudes to sea level. A hydrographic map of South Italy, especially of Calabria, shows with what economy of distance they flow to the sea. There is not much winding until the thin margin of coastal plain is reached; diffusion of drainage is secured rather by multiplicity of independent streams. Evidently, their course must be decidedly precipitous. Where natural conditions imply so strong a tendency to rapid erosion and torrential flow, the removal of the great retainers of the soil and conservers of moisture starts havoc. Broad inundations, virtual lakes, abound in the lower courses. In 1878, nearly half the area under water in all Italy in valleys held to be deficient in drainage was in Basilicata, Calabria, and Campania.[1]

" Has there been deforestation ? " the investigators of a government commission inquired, a few years ago, as to all the mountain communes in Calabria. In every instance the reply was "yes"; often further " completely " or " to the last tree," or " as if with fire and sword." [2] In Basilicata the higher mountains are in part still beautifully wooded. In Sicily, in the north and about the shoulders of Etna, there is splendid growth. Yet even the extensive district around the volcano lost two-thirds of its mantle in the last three-quarters of the nineteenth century. And the whole mountainous interior of Sicily, except where the grain is green or gold, is a disheartening picture of stark bareness.

What of the streams themselves ? Many pictures have been drawn of them. The lower valley of the Stilo in Calabria, once very fertile, has been covered with gravel, dry and naked in the summer, showing a few scattered orange trees " left over as documents and memories of former prosperity," as a writer has said, and in the wet season, overflowing with tumultuous waters. Dr. Taruffi has told of the immense damage done by two Calabrian streams in covering fertile farms and prosperous orchards with a solitude of gravel and sand. An official statement a few years ago held that in Calabria alone there were ninety streams

---

[1] *Risultati dell' inchiesta sulle condizioni igieniche*, etc., p. 48.
[2] *Inch. Parl.*, v[ii], p. 204.

whose floods regularly damage the valleys through which they flow. When the prime minister Zanardelli made his much acclaimed southern journey, he said, " I travelled for days through stretches of naked, parched mountains, which were without any cultivation, and had scarcely a blade of grass; and through valleys quite as unproductive. For hours I saw not a single house, and I passed from the desolate silence of the mountains and the valleys to the malarial plain where the streams, breaking their banks, drove off cultivation and spread out in swamps; and I saw, for example, the bed of the Agri coterminous with the valley of the Agri and the listless water with hardly a current in those immense fields." [1]

Such are the fruits of unremitting deforestation. What they mean for agriculture can be briefly told. The damage wrought by landslips and torrents is mainly local; it is their number and the costliness of the repairs they necessitate that make them serious.[2] Similarly the spreading waters of the lower courses are grave because general. They have covered over the most fertile lands of the country. Cultivation is further made difficult in a deforested region because the rainfall is not retained in the soil, and because the absence of trees and therefore of gradual evaporation lessens the humidity of the region. The hilly deforested country had been upon a natural margin of cultivation. Washing away of the soil was considerable even before the trees were felled; with the trees gone it proceeded at a quicker pace. Accounts agree that the cultivators who secured these lands after the middle of the century were able to cultivate them profitably for only a short time. " After a decade of such exhaustive cultivation, and when nothing or very little remained of the primitive covering of plant-bearing soil, the *contadino*, who beheld his labor no longer profitable, promptly abandoned the lot assigned to him in the

---

[1] Cited by P. Lacava, " Sulle condizioni economico-sociali della Basilicata," *Nuova Antologia*, March 1, 1907, p. 108. The *Inchiesta Agraria* held that the lands in Basilicata permanently under stagnant water as a result of deforestation amounted to 10,000 hectares; see ix, pp. 12, 18 (on Sicily, cf. xiii[i], fasc. iii, pp. 2 ff., 571). See also *Inch. Parl.*, v[iii], p. 44; Giglioli, pp. 350 f.; Arcà, pp. 134 ff.; Taruffi, p. 233.

[2] See, for the province of Cosenza alone, *Inch. Parl.*, v[ii], p. 205.

repartition." [1] Referring to the deeply furrowed hills in the central part of the South, another writer says, " fifty times out of a hundred these lands belonged to the domain." [2]

What a curious irony there was in the mid-century movement to extend cultivation! With the decline of newly cleared places, and their abandonment, came the decline, by gravel deposits and inundation, of many fertile lowlands, and their abandonment.

A scourge has ruled in South Italy from immemorial time, sustained by the natural conditions of soil and drainage, aggravated by the consequences of deforestation. This scourge, malaria, having a particularly virulent form in the South, has touched or threatened the homes of millions. Not only has it, in a direct way, hindered the daily work of agriculture, but it has even influenced the very form of agriculture. It stands forth, in truth, as one of the prime forces that have made for emigration.

Whatever its origins,[3] there appears to be no doubt that the area subject to the disease in South Italy has substantially increased since antiquity, and notably in the nineteenth century — Metaponto, Sibari, and Cotrone, seats of the splendor of Magna Graecia, are shunned by men today. In order to flourish, it requires the presence of stagnant water. With six months of heavy rains and six of almost no rain, the floods produced by the winter and spring torrents only gradually vanish in the dry season. In most of Sicily, not large swamps but numerous small pools are the mainstay of the disease. By the increase of the watery area through deforestation in the nineteenth century malaria has been carried into regions hitherto immune, and elsewhere its ravages have been intensified. After 1860 it apparently increased in extraordinary fashion.

[1] Podestà, p. 183.

[2] A. O. Olivetti, " Lo Stato ed il rimboschimento," *Riforma Sociale*, September, 1902, p. 825. Cf. *Inch. Agr.*, ix, p. 115; Lacava, " La Basilicata," p. 128.

[3] Upon evidence of primitive communities in regions historically known to be malarial, Mosso speculates that the early Sicilian peoples did not know malaria; *op. cit.*, pp. 403 ff. It was prevalent in Roman times; *ibid.*, pp. 416 ff.; Fischer, *Penisola italiana*, p. 355; J. J. Blunt, *Vestiges of Ancient Manners and Customs discoverable in Modern Italy and Sicily* (London, 1823), pp. 194 ff. On a later period, see Salvioli, *Le nostre origini*, p. 106.

As late as in the year 1887, 21,000 persons died of malaria in Italy. Steadily thereafter the number declined, till, in 1912, it but little exceeded 3100. In 1902 illnesses began to be reported officially: after reaching a high point of 323,000 in 1905, they have of late years fallen under 200,000. As a rule, these figures for cases of illness exceed those reported for any other infectious malady; and unquestionably they are minima, for the patient can administer quinine without recourse to a physician, and he may in many instances go for cure to the unauthorized physicians who abound in the less advanced regions.[1]

Beyond question, Italy has been the most malarial country of Europe; and within its borders the South has maintained an unenviable primacy. Though Lombardy has had, among northern compartments, a wide prevalence of the disease, the deaths in Basilicata in 1901–05 averaged fifty times as many in proportion to its inhabitants as those of Lombardy.[2] Malaria abounds in the central and coast regions of Basilicata and Calabria, particularly where the gathered waters rest upon a substratum of clay. In the former compartment the entire littoral zone is affected, a region of much fertile soil, and in the central zone the disease is found in every commune. The heavy migrations in the harvest season doubtless have helped to spread it. In Sicily, except in the province of Messina, few communes are devoid of malarial spaces.[3]

---

[1] In a statement of advice issued by the Minister of the Interior to the inhabitants in malarial sections, avoidance of quack physicians is explicitly recommended. See A. Zambler, *Le malattie e gli infortuni del lavoro agricolo* (Casale Monferrato, 1908), p. 115. Zambler's entire account (pp. 94–115 and Appendix) is useful.

[2] These figures (*Annuario Statistico, 1905–07*, i, pp. 186–189) are illustrative:

ANNUAL AVERAGE NUMBER OF DEATHS FROM MALARIA PER 100,000 INHABITANTS

	1887–90	1901–05
Lombardy	10	3
Venetia	15	5
Basilicata	187	155
Calabria	156	69
Catanzaro	186	92
Sicily	132	69
Caltanissetta	200	56
Girgenti	202	62
Trapani	233	102
Syracuse	166	145

[3] See *Inch. Parl.*, v[i], pp. 60, 146, 149, 195, 224; v[iii], pp. 200 f., 356–370; vi[ii], pp. 586–603, 624–631. The *Inchiesta sulle condizioni igieniche* (p. clxxvii) declared that " In Liguria there is not a single commune at all seriously exposed to malaria;

The recent extraordinary decline in deaths for all Italy reflects the equally recent abandonment of Hippocrates' theory of a " principle of malaria floating in the atmosphere of infected places," or rather reflects the discovery that this " principle of fever " is a germ transmitted by the *anopheles* mosquito.[1] Gratuitous distribution of quinine by the State has directly made for the decline in deaths,[2] and a variety of precautionary measures will reduce the rate still further. In a discussion of the causes of emigration, however, the more significant figures are those of the earlier era; and the evil which they disclose is far-reaching.

The character of the interference of malaria with agriculture is not found in the number of deaths, nor even in the far greater number of cases of illness reported. The many attacks and the frequent relapses do indeed withhold a great deal of labor from the land; and anaemia, following the fever, reduces the quality of much other labor. Graver even than these, however, is the nature of the precautions which from time immemorial have been necessary to escape the disease.[3] The peasant may not live upon the field he cultivates. Low-lying land is at once the most fertile and the most malarial. *Anopheles* bites between dusk and dawn. Hence the peasant must pass his night on the higher hills and expend time and energy at morning and evening in going to and from his work — a distance frequently of several miles. There is no precise way of indicating what part of the population passes its nights in non-malarial places, but the census statistics of "agglomerated population " come near to doing so. They show, paradoxi-

in Piedmont the communes are 17 per cent, in Tuscany 19, in the Marches 10, in Emilia 22; and by contrast they are in Apulia 75 per cent, in Sicily 74, in Sardinia 68, in Latium 66, in Basilicatà 62, in Calabria 63." These figures do not pretend to close accuracy. Valuable studies have been published in the annual *Atti della Società per gli Studi della Malaria* (Rome); see, *e.g.*, L. Manfredi and others, " Secondo contributo allo studio della malaria in Sicilia," v (1904), pp. 819–847; and F. Martirano, " La malaria nel Mezzogiorno d'Italia," iv (1903), pp. 440–468.

[1] See the interesting old-fashioned account of L. Simond, *A Tour in Italy and Sicily* (London, 1828), p. 357.

[2] Ministero delle Finanze, *Il chinino dello state da sue origini ad oggi*, Turin, 1911.

[3] Such precautions have recently increased; for a description see A. Celli, *Malaria* (London, 1901), Part II.

cally, that the South, though it is emphatically the non-industrial region of Italy, contains a larger portion of people living in towns than does any other part:[1]

PERCENTAGE OF POPULATION RESIDING

	In centers of 500 or more inhabitants		In centers of less than 500 inhabitants		Scattered on the land		
	1882	1901	1882	1901	1871	1882	1901
Basilicata............	92.4	90.3	0.8	1.2	11.7	6.8	8.5
Calabria..............	79.4	76.9	7.0	5.8		13.6	17.3
Sicily................	89.9	88.0	1.8	1.3	6.8	8.3	10.8
All Italy.............	62.1	63.3	10.6	8.5	26.0	27.3	28.2

Expenditure of time and effort in a region where these are cheap is in turn, however, not the most serious consequence of malaria. Rather, the very cheapness of time and effort itself partly proceeds from the menace of the disease. Intensive agriculture, the form natural in a populous region, cannot well develop where the cultivators must march far to their work. That is the crux of the problem. The tentative erection of farmhouses has in many places failed because malaria has afflicted the occupants. It appears, in other words, that this malady, placing a great premium upon extensive cultivation, has in some measure been responsible for the persistence of the latifundium[2] and so also for the considerable degree of insecurity which still reigns in the rural districts of South Italy. That is, it partly explains the long history of brigandage, which has only come to an end in recent times, the field robberies which continue to be a curse throughout the South and Sicily, the murders in the open country which give to Sicily a position unique in civilized countries; and it partly explains why today one may see the contadini marching to their work with rifles on their shoulders.

[1] See *Censimento, 1901*, v, p. 62, and *Annuario Statistico*, 1881, p. 89. Cf. the description of Sicily in *Inch. Agr.*, xiii[1], fasc. iii, pp. 13–21.

[2] Cf. Taruffi, pp. 258, 314; *Inch. Agr.*, xv, p. 58; F. Maggiore-Perni, *Delle condizioni economiche, politiche e morali della Sicilia dopo il 1860* (Palermo, 1896), p. 38.

Castrovillari and Rossano are *circondarii* in which the latifundium predominates; the percentages of agglomerated population are 93 and 99.15; they are the most malarial circondarii of Calabria and the only ones in that compartment that decreased in population in 1882–1901. See Taruffi, pp. 84, 89, 313.

What the torrential rains have wrought, and the devastating fever, has been by gradual process, day by day and year after year. Though the sum of loss from these agencies is great there is even something calculable in the risk of loss which they impose. How different is the case with earthquakes! Looking back over eight or nine centuries, the historian can indeed count them with some exactness, but the time of their appearance and their magnitude have so far eluded prophecy. It is these uncertainties that have rendered of so slight avail the generalization that certain broad regions are particularly subject to them. To indicate (by way of example) the recent earthquakes of Calabria alone: those of 1854, 1870, 1894, 1905, 1907 and, worst of all, 1908, accomplished a disheartening round of destruction of life and property. Today, ten years after the demolition of Messina, the city, its little wooden suburb notwithstanding, still is a pile of ruins.

Disaster to the crop of a single season is of course the least important effect of earthquakes upon economic activities. The general destruction of capital is pervasive.[1] Of all consequences however the most serious is probably psychological, the creation of a mood of helplessness, or even worse, of apathy, restraining at once the impulse to progress and the energies needed for accomplishment.

[1] A summary account, by Professor G. Mercalli, of the earthquakes of recent centuries is in *Inch. Parl.*, v[iii], pp. 30–32. Evidence of the destructiveness of the earthquake of 1908 may be found in Ministero dei Lavori Pubblici, *L'opera del Ministero dei Lavori Pubblici nei comuni colpiti dal terremoto del 28 dicembre 1908*, (Rome, 1912), 3 vols., especially vol. i. See also A. Caputo, " I disastri del mezzogiorno e i mezzi per ripararli " in *Giornale degli Economisti*, September, 1910, pp. 259–280.

CHAPTER V

SOUTH ITALY. II. THE AGRICULTURAL SYSTEM

WE have dealt thus far with difficulties or adversities originating in nature, but intensified at one point or another by the action of man. They are barriers which lie athwart the way to a successful agriculture; formidable, yet neither wholly irremovable nor wholly insurmountable. We have still before us the heart of our problem. Nothing less than a broad examination of the agricultural system, of the division of land ownership, the forms of agrarian contract, and the relation of these to output and to the incomes and living of the people can discover the forces that depress and constrict the country. Such an examination cannot be brief. Resting inevitably upon an understanding of certain historical vicissitudes, it must follow a train of causes to their final expression in the lives of the people.

Although few countries have had so changeful a political history as the south of Italy, its agricultural annals have exhibited little variety. The Saracens introduced some important new plants. The establishment of feudalism by the Normans, and not infrequent shiftings of jurisdiction or ownership of large properties by towns, barons, and the Church, were movements primarily of significance for the political state. No agricultural revolution took place. Growth of population, though it extended the margin of cultivation by driving back the forest line, brought no innovations in technique. While important changes in the condition of the cultivators can be traced — notably the development of serfdom into villeinage and the decline of the latter — the passing centuries left unchanged the essentials of the ancient agricultural economy: the large estate, extensive cultivation, and the instruments and practices which today we call primitive.

I

Not indefinitely could a country, situated as Italy is in Europe, expect to retain an agriculture of this description and also support a large population.

Even in the eighteenth century steps began to be taken which, if well directed, might have led to an increase in the number of proprietors: Charles III and Ferdinand IV suppressed many monasteries and transferred their lands to the public domain. In 1809 Murat, having already begun to sell some Church estates, annulled ecclesiastical titles to land; but the restored government forbade further sales.[1]

With the abolition of feudalism, a truly magnificent opportunity was opened, for the communes agreed to divide their newly gained lands into lots and grant them to the people, especially the poor. But under the Bourbons, partly because they were reactionary, partly because litigation regarding rival claims was incessant, the distribution followed an uneven course. By fraud, it is alleged, much of the acreage was acquired by the greater proprietors. And what the poor received was soon, because they lacked capital, sold to creditors or seized for failure to pay taxes. One consequence of the abolition of feudalism had been to make the lands the barons retained alienable, so that many barons found themselves at the mercy of their creditors. Yet what lands they were forced to sell did not, it is said, come into the hands of the poor. In sum — for no other conclusion is possible — the abolition of feudalism, considered as a device for extending the ownership of the land among persons of small means, was an almost unqualified failure.[2]

Later, we have seen, came the comprehensive distribution of the lands of the Church. What was its issue? Consider first the

---

[1] P. Colletta, *History of the Kingdom of Naples, 1734–1825* (trans., 2 vols., Edinburgh, 1858), i, pp. 40 f.; Bianchini, pp. 407, 409.

[2] On the history of the changes in ownership of the former feudal lands, see Franchetti in L. Franchetti and S. Sonnino, *La Sicilia nel 1876* (2 vols., Florence, 1877), i, ch. ii, p. 115 (cf. Coppi, iii, p. 269), and Sonnino, ii, p. 290; *Inch. Agr.,* ix, pp. 57, 105, 114 f.; Ciolfi, ch. vi, esp. pp. 81–89; Arcà, p. 107.

law of 1862 for Sicily, providing that the lands should be given in perpetual emphyteuses, redeemable by the tenants. The estates of 1440 ecclesiastical proprietors — forty of whom owned two-thirds of the entire amount — were broken into more than 20,000 lots, generally about ten hectares in extent. These lots were leased at auction for a sum much above their former rental and upon terms that required that if ever the rent payment were in default for three months, the properties must revert to the State. Within eight years all the lands were distributed. To whom ? In the first instance, certainly, to many poor persons, most of whom — by no means all — were agriculturists. But men who were not agriculturists and who already were proprietors of lands — in other words, many persons well off — made up nearly half of the lessees and their lots were worth nearly two-thirds of the total amount. It soon developed that many tenants were forced to renounce their lots and that others were prevented from becoming owners in full, because the clergy threatened excommunication or demanded fees for permitting the transaction. Upon the final outcome Baron Sonnino wrote, in his classic volume,

We travelled through the principal communes of the various provinces of Sicily, interrogating and observing. We have a large number of reports from places whither it was impossible for us to go. Everywhere there was only one response: The ecclesiastical lands fell almost exclusively, and with the rarest exceptions, into the hands of proprietors in easy circumstances, for the most part the great proprietors; and this especially in those regions where the properties were least divided, and where therefore it was the more urgent that a division should take place.[1]

Social motives, thwarted by the outcome, inspired the emphyteusis law. Though such motives were important in the laws of 1865 and thereafter, which suppressed the religious corpora-

[1] Sonnino, ii, p. 286. That the result could not be different was due largely to an organized effort on the part of the wealthy persons at the auctions to secure the lands for themselves (pp. 286 f.). Six years later than Sonnino, the *Inchiesta Agraria* made its study. A search in the volume (xiii[ii], fasc. iv) devoted to a detailed view of the Sicilian circondarii discovers the following pages where it is declared that the lands went to large holders: pp. 46, 55, 67, 122, 133, 142, 161, 191, 226, 235, 249, 262, 279, 302, 330, 348. More favorable are these: pp. 91, 182, 201, 235, 292, 310, 322, 339. See also xiii[i], fasc. i, p. 85 and fasc. iii, p. 574. Cf. "Di taluni effetti," pp. 187, 190.

tions, the primary intention of these was fiscal. The lands were to be broken into small lots and sold at auction. Bids were restricted to persons who deposited in advance one-tènth of the auction minimum. This amount had to be increased within ten days to a tenth of the purchase price, and sundry fees added; the other nine-tenths were to be paid in annual instalments in eighteen years with interest at six per cent. For a cash payment in full, seven per cent was deducted from the selling price. Finally, the ecclesiastical bonds issued by the Treasury were accepted in lieu of cash, and they could be bought at about four-fifths of their par value.[1]

Here was an invitation to the rich and a relative penalty upon the poor. Does it matter that no statistics of buyers are to be had ? Add to this discrimination of the classes the promise of divine punishments for whoever should acquire the Church lands and the low intellectual conditions prevalent in just those regions where the lands to be sold were most plentiful, and then it is clear that the poor could not, in large numbers, have participated in the auctions. The price secured for each hectare, it should be noted, was nearly a thousand lire during the years when most lots were sold. " But this was a matter of the early days, of the better lands, of the time when men thought that buying lots which they could pay for during eighteen years at six per cent interest would open the way to a fortune." [2]

It is probable that lands were bought speculatively for cash and then sold to persons of smaller means who had been deterred from outright purchases. Though the matter is still obscure, it appears that a not inconsiderable acreage came early into the hands of moderate buyers who were later forced to sell to escape the burden of interest charges or taxes. Especially as agricultural prices declined, it became more difficult than it had been to pay charges, and after a while only the well-to-do few remained upon the field.[3]

---

[1] Bertozzi, pp. 56 ff.   [2] " Di taluni effetti," p. 200; see also p. 150.

[3] The *Inch. Agr.* frequently but in insufficient detail noted the consequences of the sales of ecclesiastical lands. Only " the least part," it reported for Basilicata, remained in the hands of the buyers (ix, p. 57). In Catanzaro, the evil of very great estates (*grandissimi latifondi*) was not corrected, because the lands were sold mainly

The last word upon the distribution of the immense lay and ecclesiastical estates in South Italy and Sicily during the nineteenth century is inevitably that a great opportunity was lost. At most some broadening of ownership followed, but even that is doubtful. The great properties remained great properties as they had been in the Middle Ages and in ancient times. In a region where agriculture was the paramount source of wealth, the mere possession of a large estate continued to supply an all-sufficient income to the possessor.

While these momentous experiments were running their course, another force was quietly but insistently giving a special character to the proprietorship of land. As a consequence of the succession provisions of the Civil Code, a parcelling or splitting up of land — *frazionamento* in the expressive Italian word — was taking place. Only half of the testator's property must be equally divided among his children, but in practice all is so divided. Grave consequences have followed. Many properties are economically indivisible; many others might be economically divided but are so apportioned as to give to each heir, particularly in the case of the small estates, an equal share of each kind of land. Excessive division is commoner in some other parts of Italy than in the South and in Sicily, but it everywhere necessitates awkward cultivation of scattered or minute holdings. To remedy the situation, which is particularly bad in Basilicata, no systematic effort has been made; but some proprietors have sold lots inconveniently located and bought adjacent ones.[1]

in large lots and because smaller buyers were unable to retain their holdings for lack of capital (pp. 203, 205). In Reggio and also in Cosenza, " all the property became concentrated in the hands of a few powerful families " (pp. 114 f., 315). The report generally relates under one caption the effects of the distribution of ecclesiastical and the older domain lands. Though this sometimes sacrifices definiteness, it is not entirely to be regretted. More expressly it was indicated that in the provinces of Catania and Syracuse, in the eighteen years in which payments were to be made, lands were "frequently put up at auction again for failure to fulfill the instalment obligations" (xiii[i], fasc. iii, p. 572). By a study of tax lists, the author of the official article, "Di taluni effetti" (p. 202) supports his opinion that the ecclesiastical lands were mainly bought by persons who already owned landed estates. Cf. also the Final Report of *Inch. Agr.*, xv, pp. 53 ff.

[1] See G. Bianchi, *La proprietà fondiaria e le classi rurali* (Pisa, 1891), ch. v, and many passages in *Inch. Parl.*

Have not the inheritance laws effectively broken the great estates ? On the contrary, the estates have rather increased than decreased; and this for several reasons. Malarial conditions and the scarcity of water have tended to preserve or to restore them in many districts. In others, notably in Calabria, it has long been customary to marry only one son in the richer families.[1] In Basilicata the large proprietors have generally bequeathed no land to their daughters, and in Calabria many have followed the same rule. In Sicily, lastly, subdivision upon inheritance has been rare.[2]

Both combination and subdivision of lands there has been then — such is the burden of this chapter. Is the net result, when one considers all sizes of estates, an increase or a decrease of proprietors ? In each one thousand inhabitants the landed proprietors numbered

	In 1882	In 1901
In Basilicata	168	159
In Calabria	121	91
In Sicily	114	94

and the decrease, as it happens, has been not merely relative but absolute. Had persons of small means acquired parts of large estates, or had there been much breaking up by inheritance, an enhancement of the figures would have appeared. As it is, they seem to sustain the common opinion that small estates have been combined into larger ones faster than large ones have been split into small.[3]

One of the fundamental questions to be asked about any agricultural system is, How far is the land cultivated by its owners ?

[1] The Inch. Agr. (ix, p. xxvi) still called this an "unaltered custom." L. A. Caputo declares the custom to be very recently declining; see his essay " Di alcune questioni economiche della Calabria," in Giornale degli Economisti (December, 1907, and March, 1908), p. 1179. Cf., however, Inch. Parl., v[iii], p. 126.

[2] Ibid., v[i], p. 105; vi[i], p. 114; v[ii], pp. 250 f.; v[iii], p. 126. Yet Lorenzoni believes that in Sicily there has been, for whatever reason, an appreciable break-up of the larger estates, but he cannot say how much (ibid., pp. 236 ff.).

[3] The first two censuses were silent on the subject of ownership, and I have found no figures in the volumes so far published of the fifth. For the figures in the text, see Censimento, 1901, v, p. 162.

For South Italy the answer, if we are to grasp its full import, sends us back again into earlier times. How very heavily, in this matter, the hand of the past weighs!

During the Middle Ages and before the rise of the towns, the lords generally lived upon their estates. Even after the rise of towns the need of defense in a region where insecurity reigned kept them upon their lands. Most potent cause of all was, however, the generally exalted position of the feudal lord in the society of a time when towns were unimportant or mostly under feudal jurisdiction, and when the royal power was content or was constrained to play a small rôle in internal affairs.[1] It was the gradual encroachment of the royal power, the desire of the kings to count as the first might in the land, that changed the relation of the lord to his estate. To enfeeble the barons, to detach them from their abodes and bring them to Naples, the Bourbons resorted to such blandishments, such profusion of royal honors, that the barons forgot the humbler autonomy which they possessed on their estates and grew accustomed to live as subjects. The gayety of the life of the capital, music, dancing, spectacle, gambling, luxurious palaces, made attraction easy. This defection of the richer lords had the great disadvantage of rendering them careless of agricultural interests, over which — however occupied they had been with the general tasks of administration and justice — they had at least exercised supervision. Henceforth these interests remained in the charge of avid factors or simple contadini. The latter, through ignorance or the lack of capital, the former in order to grow rich quickly at the expense of proprietors and lesser tenants, far from proceeding to refresh the soil sought instead to exhaust it. To appreciate the breadth of the damage, it is necessary to recall that it was a time when the nobles, the domain, and the religious corporations held most of the land.[2]

[1] When the Bourbon Charles ascended the throne, the communes subject to him contained less than a third as many inhabitants as those subject to the lords.

[2] R. De Cesare, *La fine di un regno* (3 vols., Città di Castello, 1909), ii, pp. 110f., 115; M. Schipa, *Il regno di Napoli al tempo di Carlo di Borbone* (Naples, 1904), p. 661. A good general statement is in *Inch. Agr.*, vii, p. 217. Cf. Salvioli, *Trattato*, p. 320; *idem*, " Il villanaggio in Sicilia e la sua abolizione," *Rivista Italiana di*

Absenteeism, though it did not begin under Bourbon rule —
some Spanish lords, for example, went to Spain when the Spanish
dominion fell — increased greatly in extent under that rule. In
the nineteenth century, with the expanding attractiveness of city
life, it increased further. How far has it gone ?

Here are some figures of great interest prepared for the census
of 1901: [1]

	Basilicata	Calabria	Sicily	All Italy
Persons who cultivate, or manage the cultivation of, their own properties	48,813	71,114	114,091	2,583,490
Absentee landlords.............	29,064	53,437	218,753	703,201

They show that actually three-eighths of the landlords of Basilicata, two-fifths of those of Calabria, and even two-thirds of those
of Sicily were to be classed as absentee. It is true that the proprietors of uncultivated lands were included in these figures, but
their number is not great. The habit of living apart from one's
estates has continued to be very common in Italy, and, relatively
speaking, to be from two to three times as prevalent in the South
alone as in the entire country.

On the more significant question of what proportion of the land
is held by absent proprietors, no such precise information is to be
had. In each compartment the experts of the *Inchiesta Agraria*
sought an answer, and the drift of their reports is unmistakable.
At the utmost they conceded that " few " large proprietors lived
on their estates, or that "some" stayed there during certain
months, or that they went there for *villeggiatura*. In other words
the portion of the land held by the absentee owners must have

Sociologia, July–August, 1902, pp. 394 ff.; Colletta, ii, p. 39. An excellent summary is in A. Sartorius Frh. v. Waltershausen, *Die Sizilianische Agrarverfassung
und ihre Wandlungen 1780–1912* (Leipsig, 1913), ch. v.

[1] *Censimento, 1901*, v, pp. cxxi, 135. Domain lands and the lands of companies
do not appear in the figures. Owners of uncultivated lands do, but their number is
not great. A criticism may be brought against the method by which the figures for
fondi rustici were compiled by the census officials. There were added together the
number of persons who owned lands only and the number of those who owned lands
and buildings. Those who possessed buildings only were regarded as essentially
urban and were excluded. This somewhat exaggerates the number of owners of
rural property; but in the light of the Southern tendency to live in towns it only
slightly distorts the picture for the South. For other parts of Italy it makes absenteeism appear greater than it is.

been very great.[1] Twenty-five years later, the testimony of the *Inchiesta Parlamentare* revealed an unchanged situation. Let but one citation suffice (the reference is to Calabria):

> The great proprietors are as a rule absentee. Those of the coast zone, with its extensive cultivation, the rich — the true great proprietors — often live very far from their lands, almost never seeing them. Those of the hill zone are likewise absentee, but their incomes will not let them quit the capital of the province or the circuit; yet from the agricultural point of view it is as if they lived at the other end of the world, for they behold their lands only once or twice a year.[2]

Absenteeism implies cultivation by either an agent or a tenant, commonly the latter. One of the first results of the extensive absenteeism which appeared after the middle of the eighteenth century was the rise of the Sicilian *gabella*, a lease of the large estate, and of the *gabellotto*, the great leaseholder, one of the strangest types which Italian agricultural history has developed. "There had grown up," writes Salvioli,[3] "a class of middle-class persons enriched in the grain trade and in usury, cornerers of products (despite the terrible laws which promised the galley or the gallows), speculators in great herds, secret purchasers of stolen farm animals, persons who had not hitherto been very close to the

---

[1] On Basilicata and Calabria see *Inch. Agr.*, ix, pp. xiv, 57, 116, 208; on Sicily, xiii[i], fasc. i, p. 183, xiii[iii], fasc. i, p. 570. A search through the volume (xiii[ii], fasc. iv) which deals in detail with the several Sicilian provinces reveals an extraordinary situation. The larger proprietors were declared never to live on their estates, or at most to visit them rarely, in the following passages (each page refers to a different region of the province): Caltanissetta, pp. 13, 19, 26; Catania, pp. 47, 56, 67, 80, 92; Girgenti, pp. 116, 123, 134, 143; Messina, pp. 171, 182, 192; Palermo, pp. 216, 227, 236, 263; Syracuse, pp. 280, 293, 311; Trapani, pp. 322, 331, 339. On pp. 201, 302, and 349 more favorable reports appear; on p. 161 is noted an increasing tendency " in the last twenty years " to live on the estates. Probably the situation in the other compartments, for which less detailed studies were reported, was similar. Cf. also Bianchini, ch. vii; G. Alongi, *La maffia, nei suoi fattori e nelle sue manifestazioni* (Rome, 1886), pp. 22, 27; A. Battaglia, *L'evoluzione sociale in rapporto alla proprietà fondiaria in Sicilia* (Palermo, 1895), p. 181.

[2] *Inch. Parl.*, v[ii], p. 182. Cf. Taruffi, pp. 368 f. Out of a large portion of the *latifondi* of Sicily reported to Lorenzoni, five-eighths were cultivated by contract. On the basis of tax lists, he shows that less than eight hundred proprietors own one-third of the area of Sicily, and less than two hundred own one-sixth; two-fifths of the area of Caltanissetta is in latifondi of 200 hectares or more. It is generally the proprietors of such estates who are absent. See *Inch. Parl.*, vi[i], pp. 352, 362.

[3] " Il villanaggio," etc., p. 395.

land."   Not essentially different is Alongi's description.   The great leaseholders were a kind of parvenu, he says, who aspired to be in the class of the born aristocracy.   " The nobles, grown unfit for the exacting contests of labor and trade, were constrained to negotiate with these newcomers, who were energetic, audacious characters and masters of that robber class from which they had sprung and which even then were called mafia." [1]

The gabellotto paid a fixed rent for the estate which he took over for a period of only a few years (six came to be the general term).   Not an ultimate large product, but an immediate large net return was his aim; not organization of production, but a good bargain with the producers. He was, in other words, not an entrepreneur, but a speculator; or as Alongi adjudged him, a parasite. And somewhat a parasite — if we may now describe him in the present — he remains. Sicily, with its large estates, Sicily of the absent landlords, still offers a field for his operations. It is true that he employs capital of his own, but his risks appear to be negligible, disaster is not recorded of him, and his economic function, even if the landlord is accounted inevitably absent, seems tenuous. It is rare for him to manage an estate himself. Generally he sublets to the cultivators, on various contracts, or to other middlemen, who in turn sublet. " If the years are good, he realizes a fat profit at the end of his term; and in bad years he always manages to clear a heavy return upon his capital." [2]

Of what sort were the contracts which the small folk, the actual cultivators, made with gabellotto or proprietor ? They were the survivals of a long antiquity, some having been customary since the days of Rome.   In the mediaeval period they were of great social and economic consequence and generally embraced such terms as an invariable rent, a perpetual or long-enduring tenure (often thirty years, several generations), and the rendering, on the tenant's part, of a multitude of services and dues. Just because they were eminently suited to the stability of the feudal era, they

---

[1] Alongi, *op. cit.*, pp. 21 f.

[2] *Inch. Agr.*, xiii[i], fasc. i, p. 50; references abound in the several volumes on Sicily. See also Wermert, pp. 183 ff.; Sartorius von Waltershausen, pp. 256 ff. Interesting figures on rental and subletting are presented by Professor Passalacqua in *Inch. Parl.*, vi[i], pp. 234 f.

were bound to undergo changes — attenuations — with the decline and abolition of feudalism. Many of the most considerable of these took place before the abolition — in the first great spread of absenteeism — but others came only very gradually afterwards, with the slow readjustment of power in southern society. The break-up of the Church lands greatly increased the extent of contract cultivation.[1]

Consider now the terms of the modern contracts. But let us still, for the moment, postpone the attempt to single out their shortcomings.[2]

In Basilicata, the *mezzadria* (metayer) contract, fairly common in some mountainous regions, as in Lagonegro, is in general not much diffused and not increasing in use. Its terms are recorded only in private writing, or made orally and not recorded at all. It is valid for one agrarian year. The proprietor pays all the taxes, and the final product is, in most things, shared equally between proprietor and mezzadro.

Leases at fixed rents, of small estates in the mountains and large in the plains, are the dominant contract in Basilicata. The term is three to six, sometimes nine years. There is rarely a

---

[1] On the modern changes much has been written. See, *e.g.*, Franchetti, i, ch. ii, esp. pp. 115–121, 131; G. Salvioli, " Gabellotti e contadini in Sicilia nella zona del latifondo," *Riforma Sociale*, January, 1897, pp. 67 ff.; *idem*, " Il villanaggio," etc., p. 399. For a broader view, cf. A. Pertile, *Storia del diritto italiano dalla caduta dell' impero Romano alla codificazione* (2d ed., 6 vols., Turin, 1896–1902), iv, pp. 297–334, 638–643.

[2] The volume, *I contratti agrarii in Italia* (Ministero di Agricoltura, Industria e Commercio, Rome, 1891) brings together the results of three inquiries: (1) a study published in 1874 in *I condizioni dell' agricoltura in Italia*, (2) the *Inch. Agr.* of 1879–83, (3) questions put to the various agrarian societies in 1882–90. These reports, full of regional detail, appear closely consistent. On the South, see pp. 645–723. How slight have been the changes of the years since may be gathered from the reports of the *Inch. Parl.*, representative passages of which are as follows: on the share and mixed contracts, v[i], pp. 47, 133, 187; v[ii], pp. 379, 388, 400, 402–407, 414; v[ii], Note ed appendici, p. 721; vi[ii], pp. 9, 144–146, 180; on the leases, except those of the latifundia, v[i], pp. 42–46, 98, 106, 129–131, 185, 186, 269–273, 296–300; v[ii], pp. 317–319, 354, 359; vi[ii], pp. 185–187, 202; on the emphyteusis and improvement leases, v[i], pp. 134 f., 189, 219; v[ii], pp. 425–442; v[iii], p. 148; vi[ii], pp. 206 f., 229. On the recent situation of the contracts of Calabria, see further the admirable study by Taruffi, pp. 330–390.

written record. The tenants of the large estates (and such are almost invariably rented out) sublet them in small lots to other tenants. The large tenants usually pay a money rent, while the small ordinarily pay in kind. The proprietor assumes the tax charges. It is sometimes contracted that the tenant shall be reimbursed for betterments, but because of the conjectural assessment of their value this provision has been rapidly falling away. The emphyteusis contract, as a form of improvement lease, is found rarely, except in the vineyards of Melfi, and there it survives because redemption has not been found feasible.

In the Calabrian province of Cosenza, the mezzadria exists mainly on the slopes of the Apennines. The contract, which generally depends upon an oral agreement, has a term usually of from one to three years; at its end the tenant often moves to another field. The proprietor pays all the taxes and provides whatever improvements are introduced. The products, except those of the trees (olives especially), are shared equally; but the contract readily shades into one under which different divisions take place, or one which combines the lease and the share.

The lease for a fixed rent in Cosenza is more commonly oral than written. Its duration is one or two years, and it is generally renewed unless expressly terminated. Near the towns the rent has been payable in money. In Castrovillari there are survivals of the emphyteusis contract, but they have lost their character as improvement leases.

In Catanzaro the lease predominates, lasting one year except where cereal culture takes place, when it lasts four or five years, depending on the rotation used. In the mountains and the middle altitudes the lease of great estates is common, and although they are generally without houses or tree cultures, the leaseholder more usually sublets than cultivates his estate. The rental of small plots is commonly paid in produce.

In Reggio, large and middle holdings are generally leased out for a stipulated sum, the contract holds for from two to four years and the proprietor pays the taxes.

In Sicily (to take the seven provinces together) the lease for a fixed rent is the most prevalent form. Something has already been said of the gabellotto and his lease of the latifundium. Sometimes he cultivates a part of the property and gives over the rest to small tenants or mezzadri.

As a matter of fact, these subletting contracts are very harsh. At harvest time the entire product is collected into the magazines of the *padrone* who first takes out the seeds with a 25 per cent premium besides 16 per cent for the so-called *battiteria*, which represents a deduction for the grain taken from the threshing-floor and cleaned and sifted. And for the rent he withholds an amount to the value agreed upon, basing it upon an average of previous prices. In consequence there is often left to the subtenant little or nothing, and in bad years he has often abandoned the field before the threshing and sometimes before the harvesting.[1]

In the aftermath of the sanguinary labor disorders of the nineties, arose the collective lease, fostered sometimes by socialist, sometimes by Catholic, interests. This extraordinary agreement is a device whereby bands of contadini, neglecting the middleman, take over large tracts from proprietors and subdivide them for cultivation.[2]

The Sicilian leases, other than those of the latifundia, run three or six years, and are generally publicly registered. The proprietor pays all the taxes. In the province of Catania there is no compensation for improvements, but in the other provinces compensation is estimated and made at the termination of the lease. The rent is paid quarterly, and sometimes — especially if the proprietor does not reside in the same commune — the provincial and communal taxes are advanced by the tenant and deducted from his quarterly rent.

Contracts providing for a sharing of the product are many in Sicily. For small lots the terms are fixed orally, for the medium lots in writing, and for the large ones a public record is made. The term is three to six years; in very rare instances, recalling a feudal mode, twenty-nine years. The proprietor generally pays the taxes, provides a part or all of the seed, and finally receives as a rule one-half of the product; he makes compensation only for improvements specified in the contract.

[1] *I contratti agrarii*, p. 715.

[2] See Lorenzoni's account, *Inch. Parl.*, vi[ii], pp. 657–681; W. D. Preyer, *Die Arbeits- und Pachtgenossenschaften Italiens*, Jena, 1913; Bruccoleri, pp. 130–145.

II

We have now discussed land ownership and agrarian contracts in regard both to their recent status and their relation to a more removed past. Only incidentally have we considered their advantages and disadvantages for an efficient agriculture. To this critical question we must now turn.

In the first place, is it not to be inferred that many, if not most, estates are either too large or too small? Consider the small estate. The type that is commonest is seldom an economic unit of cultivation. Even when, as rarely happens, an exceptionally good situation encourages a profitable intensive culture, the estate is often too small to occupy the full time of the cultivator; it is an insult to the value of the man. And where extensive cultivation rules — as it does in the South — the almost inevitable absence of farm animals implies an absence of manures, and the need of a crop every year leads to a neglect of fallows. To this must be added the conservatism and general unprogressiveness which a narrow field of operations tends to maintain, if not actually to promote. The small proprietor, a person of scant means, has usually a limited outlook in all directions; and it is upon the small estates that the peasant is most prone to regard the use of machines as an attempt to " go ahead of the Eternal Father, who therefore punishes him with bad harvests." [1]

To say that the large estate is not inherently uneconomical is to say what, though it may be true, has little bearing upon the situation in South Italy. So long as the proprietor regards his property as he might a bond which pays him an income, whether he is versed in the art of agriculture or not, the large estate is for South Italy not an economic form. So stolid has been the indifference of the proprietors in the last century and a half, so little have they made capital improvements in the land, that the large estate has missed its best chance to justify itself.

[1] V. di Somma, " Dell' economia rurale nel mezzogiorno," *Nuova Antologia,* March 16, 1906, p. 307. Cf. *Inch. Parl.*, v[ii], p. 573.

Yet it is sometimes argued that the blame laid upon the great proprietors is not deserved. In parts of Sicily the large estates are cultivated as units either by the proprietors or by gabellotti. Rudinì has pointed out that even where, as by inheritance, a large estate is divided among several owners, it often continues to be cultivated as a whole.[1] His contention that this is necessary and economic rests upon a careful argument, which runs somewhat as follows: Extensive agriculture requires a large unit; fallows and herds are a needful part of it; the small cultivator, even if he could forego a crop for one year in three to six, would be unable to undertake the risks of a one-crop economy; yet extensive cultivation (of grain) is an inevitable consequence of unchangeable meteorologic conditions. "A more frequent and copious rainfall would grow a more abundant forage supply,[2] would so permit the use of stables for livestock, the production of manure, mixed cultures, a radical change in the agrarian rotations, and then the little Tuscan farm or the Piedmontese dairy!"[3]

The reputation for good management which Rudinì's own estate enjoyed — thanks to the deep interest he took in it — has not been general. He himself deplored the gabellotto. And he did not mean that his argument fitted closely the conditions of the large estates of the continental South, nor even of all those of the island. Indeed, in the very heart of Sicily, small estates, intensively cultivated, are to be found in the neighborhood of the centers of population. Irrigation and drainage have in some places wrought wonders. But when all is said, the owner's want of attachment to the soil and his continuing ignorance have held the region in a peculiarly low stage of development.[4]

[1] Rudinì, p. 162. In this connection consider Lorenzoni's observation that it is commoner for one person to own several latifundia than for several persons to own one. *Inch. Parl.*, vi[i], p. 361.

[2] Three or four hectares of land per head of cattle are now necessary; and the supply of milk is meager. The propertyless contadino cannot hope to conduct a large estate.

[3] Rudinì, p. 175. For a similar analysis, cf. a passage in G. Valenti's able essay "Il latifondo e la sua possibile trasformazione" (1894), in his *Studi di politica agraria* (Rome, 1914), p. 276.

[4] Cf. Valenti, p. 281; *Inch. Parl.*, vi[i], p. 404.

The proprietors of medium-sized estates have not been an important group. When mentioned at all in the studies that have been made, they are recorded either as absentee or as making a prosperous living. Were their numbers greater, they could be regarded as a kind of middle class of the population. Undoubtedly they are at far fewer disadvantages in working their properties than the owners either of large or small estates, and when they have true managing ability may be highly successful.

Consider now the defects of contract cultivation. (And let us pass by the emphyteusis; for if, with its term of twelve to thirty years, it was an excellent means of planting hillsides with vines, almond and orange trees, it has ceased to be common.) In the constitution of most existing leases grave defects are plainly evident. Tenure is brief, and renewal by no means customary. Brevity of tenure impels the tenant to exploit the land, a practice hardly to be circumvented by stipulations in the contracts. The benefits of exploitation are immediate; the damage appears late. The proprietor cannot keep a close supervision over the acts of his tenants; more often he does not care to, and if some proprietors visit their estates once or twice a year — unable then to note changes — others again almost never see them. The condition of the property near the end of the lease is proverbial.

A second defect, which is perhaps only the first in another guise, is the circumstance that capital sunk in the soil may be lost to the cultivator. In some regions there is no compensation for betterments. Whenever compensation takes place at all, it occurs at the end of the term, when the proprietor fixes an estimate of the value of the betterments and the cultivator must accept his appraisal or go to the courts (which he rarely does). But the worst fault of the system is that the tenant is discouraged from making betterments at all, and the proprietor is too little interested to make them himself.

The various share contracts represent an attempt to cut the Gordian knot of fixed-rent difficulties. But they are involved in troubles of another sort. The mezzadria system, successful above all other contracts in Tuscany, is not well adapted to a region where extensive cultivation obtains. In its best form it implies the care of live stock, some tree or vine culture, and the growing of a variety of herbaceous plants; and the mezzadro lives upon his land and drafts the services of his family. In much of the South, however, because of the perils of malaria, it is impossible or inadvisable to live upon the estate that is being cultivated, and in the extensive mode of cultivation that natural conditions impose, the labor of a family cannot well be utilized throughout the year.[1]

In practice the mezzadria is not strictly a division of the product into halves. The fertility of the soil is so varied that the contract either requires a division according to a different ratio (in which case the generic name *colonia parziaria* is preferable and commoner), or it is hedged about by many restrictions and compromises regarding the supply of implements, farm animals, and so forth.

One kind of restriction is common to all leases whether for fixed rents or for shares, except the lease for money:[2] the cultivator must agree to cultivate whatever crops, and by whatever rotations, the proprietor is pleased to demand. With his programme thus fixed for a year or several years in advance, he is not in a position to make many experiments, even if tempted. It is true that he might often, if solvent or if likely to be so at the end of his lease, persuade a proprietor to accept a money rent, but the mere fact that traditional ways are so sanctioned as to be stipulated·in contracts must itself operate to repress the desire to introduce new things.

---

[1] See the studies of J. Grizi, *Étude économique sur le métayage en Italie*, Perugia, 1909, and P. F. Serragli, *Un contratto agrario, la mezzadria toscana*, Florence, 1908.

One general defect of the mezzadria must be noted: a special unwillingness of proprietor and tenant to apply capital. " When the cultivator has to give to his landlord half of the returns to each dose of capital and labor that he applies to the land, it will not be to his interest to apply any doses, the total return to which is less than twice enough to reward him." (A. Marshall, *Principles of Economics* (5th ed., London, 1907), p. 731.) As much can be said of course when improvements by the proprietor are in question.

[2] Sonnino (ii, p. 254), in 1876, wrote that the small money lease had been lately increasing. Salvioli in 1894 (" Gabellotti," etc., p. 71) noted that the movement had taken large proportions and that its effect had been to promote absenteeism.

Upon the methods of cultivation — the character of which must have a real dependence upon the facts of ownership and contract which we have studied — it is possible to be brief. When James Blunt travelled through the two Sicilies in 1818 and 1819, he found that the implements and the methods of plowing, mowing, threshing, and wine-pressing answered closely to the detailed accounts in Roman writers. Half a century later, the experts of the *Inchiesta Agraria* were asked to discover how far modern devices had been introduced; with rare exceptions they found that few, if any, changes had occurred; methods and processes were ancient. Quite recently, in Sicily, and on the coast lands of Calabria and Basilicata, some modern machinery has come into use. Yet commonly on the larger estates the ancient plow, *aratro perticale* or *aratro-chiodo*, is still employed; it merely scratches the soil and if the plowing is not done three times over, the land remains scarcely opened. On the smaller estates, the *zappa*, a kind of mattock or hoe, is used, either with this plow, or alone; it requires infinite labor to prepare a field for grain. But it must be remembered that small farms in particular, and the farms of countries where labor is cheap, in general, cannot be expected to use expensive machinery.

Artificial fertilizer long continued to be unknown. Its absence made fallows all the more necessary, with the result that enormous areas of the cultivable land — in Sicily nearly a third — have annually lain unproductive. Although a greater rainfall would be necessary to attain the full efficacy of fertilizer, yet, as Rudinì admitted, an increase in the amount applied would be worth while. Where in the past fallows have not been used or have been infrequent, as often on the small estates, the land has, in a common phrase, become *stanca* — feeble or exhausted. Into the fitness of the systems of rotation employed we cannot enter: though they vary considerably from region to region they always depend much upon fallows; they are traditional and often poorly adapted to their purpose. Seed is not well selected. For much of the reaping a hand sickle is used. Threshing is done by the trampling of oxen on the barn floor, and the chaff is separated from the grain by the wind; or the asses are driven endlessly in circles about a middle pole, treading out the grain as they go — a finely picturesque process, reminiscent of ancient Egypt and Israel, but alas, ill attuned to modern needs! It still happens in places that the olives are heaped so that the vegetable waters may disappear — while the fruit becomes fermented and its oil rancid. Defective processes continue to be used in the manufacture of wine and oil. Hardly anywhere are the rudiments of agricultural bookkeeping to be met, although they are nowhere so necessary as where it is hard to win a profit.[1]

Obsolete methods of cultivation have been so far perpetuated in South Italy that the productivity of the region is low. That is a great general defect. Nature, to be sure, has greatly complicated the problems of agriculture, but it is the controllable conditions of land ownership and administration that have been fatal. Neglect of their interests by the proprietors; contracts which encourage exploitation of the soil; a general failure to return profits to the land and make betterments: these are the fundamental faults. In a word, it may be said that the actual cultivators have too little of the proprietor's interest — whether because the contracts hem in the cultivators, or because, more radically, the cultivating proprietors on estates of a suitable size are too few.

[1] On methods and implements, see, *e.g.*, *Inch. Agr.* and *Inch. Parl.* (numerous passages); Blunt, pp. 208 ff.; Wermert, ch. xiv; Taruffi, pp. 475–593. A work of considerable charm is L. Caico, *Sicilian Ways and Days*, London, 1910; its authoress had lived long in Caltanissetta.

CHAPTER VI

SOUTH ITALY. III. THE PEOPLE AND THEIR EMIGRATION

WHERE the great mass of the population are occupied in agriculture, and where the general productivity has been kept low by cumulative faults, it would seem unnecessary to go further and show in detail what the fortunes of the workers are. Yet I know no other way of making clear how the pressure is felt which seeks its release in emigration. We should like to know what division of the workers into classes can be made, and upon what terms they live their lives.

In Basilicata a quarter of the agricultural population, in Calabria and Sicily a sixth, are persons who cultivate lands of their own. It is a much lower proportion than is found in central and North Italy.[1] Of these proprietors the great majority own small or diminutive plots. Except in certain sections, like the Conca d'Oro of Palermo, where the small proprietor is a rich man, they have not been conspicuously successful. In fact, it has been said that in Sicily very few of them can live by merely working their own lands.[2] In some parts of Basilicata the plots of land are half as numerous as the inhabitants themselves.[3]

Onerous mortgage debts, incurred often in the effort to enlarge the inherited parcel or parcels of land, make impossible the attainment of a comfortable income. Until recently the eighteen-year instalment payments for ecclesiastical lands — although not many buyers, we have seen, had been found on these terms — were a heavy burden upon the shoulders of some proprietors. The fall in prices of agricultural products, a disheartening blow to cultivators who sold their produce, began at a time when they had already become, in the striking phrase of the Director of the

---

[1] *Censimento, 1901*, v, pp. lxxxii, 132–135.
[2] *Inch. Parl.*, vi[ii], p. 9. Cf. vi[i], p. 232.
[3] *Ibid.*, v[i], p. 50.

Inchiesta Agraria, " a proletariate of proprietors." [1]   The evidence, if evidence were needed, for the veraciousness of this phrase, lies in the fact that these proprietors, with only rare exceptions, both on the peninsula and in Sicily, hire out to others for wages.[2] Many lands have been abandoned — too often the allotments of former feudal estates — and the numerous forced sales for failure to pay taxes have been mainly of small properties.[3]

In few districts have the share cultivators been successful. In Sicily, except in some provinces along the coast, they have been among the most miserable of the agriculturists, and as a class have stood next above the common laborers. Undoubtedly a chief reason for their failure has been the unsuitability of the share contract itself to Southern conditions, where a bad year means disaster for an undiversified agriculture. Where the mezzadria prevails, there are few hired laborers, and cultivation is carried on by the members of the mezzadro's family; since these are only partially or irregularly employed, they are glad also to be hired as day laborers.

The tenant who rents a large estate is usually successful, the Sicilian gabellotto markedly so. But the number of such tenants is not great. Where subletting takes place, the undertenants, as we have seen, often fare badly. Most generally those who rent lands are an abject class of cultivators. Particularly numerous in Basilicata, they have found it impossible, year after year, in the mountains, to earn a humble livelihood; and in the coast region

---

[1] *Inch. Agr.,* xv, p. 73. On their decline in the recent period, cf. E. Nathan, *Vent' anni di vita italiana attraverso all' " Annuario "* (Rome, etc., 1906), pp. 192, 261.

It may be noted, as a matter of literary curiosity, that Jacini's famous phrase was used by Robert du Var, many years earlier, in his *Histoire de la classe ouvrière,* iv (1845), Bk. xiii, ch. ii, p. 206.

[2] The census (1901, v, p. lxxxi) qualifies its statistics of cultivation as follows: " When a person declared himself to be a cultivator of property of his own and also a laborer for wages, he was classified with the proprietors and not with the *braccianti,* because the former belonged to a social class in some respects higher; while probably the same person will have received a greater income from labor done on behalf of others than from cultivation upon his own little estate." The volumes of the *Inch. Parl.* show how commonly the proprietors of the South depend largely upon wages.

[3] *Inch. Parl.,* v[i], p. 50; v[ii], pp. 458–462.

two bad years out of six have often been enough to undo the tenant — even where, to be safe, he has rented strips of land in scattered places ! [1]

Half of the cultivators of Basilicata, two-thirds of those of Calabria and Sicily, are hired laborers. They are a passive element in the agricultural economy, determining little, the victims of much; socially despised, a residuum of the population. Whether engaged by the year or the day they are the most miserable group of all; and they are particularly wretched when engaged by the day, which is the usual course with three out of four of them. It is by the proprietors and the tenants of the medium-sized and large estates that they are chiefly employed. At the time of the *Inchiesta Agraria* their wages, still paid largely in kind, ran from 250 to 400 lire in the year, say one or one and a half per working day, with an extra lira daily in the harvest period, and as little as half a lira per day in the slack season. When allowance is made for the fact that these wages were reported by employers, and therefore probably erred in liberality, it is clear that the ensuing twenty or thirty years brought an improvement. But the case is still bad enough. According to a recent study, a usual wage in upper Basilicata is 1.50 lire and food or — following a spreading practice — 2.20 lire without food; but January and February are almost without work, and employment during the rest of the year is inconstant.[2] In interior Sicily, 1.80 lire per day may be earned for 150–200 days (rarely more days), and this rate of 270–360 lire per year is not supplemented by rations; on the coast the situation is better.[3]

On the continent married women engage in exhausting toil, with deplorable consequences; in Sicily, particularly in the interior, a happier age-old tradition has made for the circumscription of women's labor in the fields. Soon after the age of fourteen, boys undertake the work of men, but their bodies are still unfit for it. Savings are few, a trail of debt has been common. Often only the clothes on the laborer's back are his own, and in the winter he

---

[1] *Inch. Parl.*, v[i], pp. 45, 98, 131.

[2] *Ibid.*, v[i], pp. 35 f.

[3] *Ibid.*, vi[ii], p. 136.

may verge on starvation.[1] Dire misery has been the lot of the laborers whose strength has left them. Only recently, in Sicily, has it ceased to be common for them to sell their sons into a kind of slavery in the sulphur mines, receiving from the *piccioniere*, at no interest, a sum of 100–200 lire, while their half-naked boys spent their days carrying heavy loads from the mine's depths to the surface, doomed to baneful toil until the loan should be repaid.[2]

Is only low productivity to blame for the miserable rewards of the South Italian cultivators, whether laborers or tenants? It would be venturesome to suppose so. Certainly the people assert, what doubtless any people in the world so circumstanced would assert, that they are exploited: *sfruttamento* rings in the ears of whoever reads the popular claims. The nonchalance of the proprietor, his readiness to press his advantage in making contracts, the bitter competition of the workers, have convinced the latter that they have substance, not merely semblance, of argument. And the charge cannot be summarily dismissed.

Already we have seen that in the assessment of betterments the proprietor has a bargaining advantage over his tenant. That is but one instance. The gabellotti, though they have vied with each other to get leases, have in turn sought to exact what they could from their subtenants, in rentals, on the one hand, and in the price on the other, at which they have bought the gathered crops. Speaking of the common grain lease of Sicily, Baron Sonnino maintained that the competition of persons who sought to be tenants was so keen that the proprietors were enabled to base the rental entirely upon the returns of good years;[3] and he held that, under the money lease, the tenants were again at the mercy of the proprietors in selling their crops to get cash.

---

[1] For two interesting budgets of families more favorably situated, see *Inch. Parl.*, vi[ii], pp. 138–143.

[2] G. Baglìo, *Ricerche sul lavoro e su i lavoratori di Sicilia, Il solfaraio* (Naples, 1905), on the *carusi, passim*, esp. pp. 184–193, 200–202, 279–282; *Inch. Parl.*, vi[ii], pp. 471–473; Bruccoleri, p. 284. I have based my account of the hired laborers mainly on *Inch. Agr.* and *Inch. Parl.*, the publication of each of which constitutes an epoch in Italian social history.

[3] *Op. cit.*, ii, pp. 253 ff.; he refers also to other writers upon the terratico rent.

In general in a country given over almost wholly to agriculture, a tenant agriculture, the tenants are often in an inferior position for bargaining. Their year's income is precarious, or does not exist, if they fail to get a lease. They must regard the proprietor, on the other hand, as one who could afford to forego a year's rent altogether, or as one who, by the very fact of his ownership of salable land, has a safe margin between himself and want.

When the case of the *giornaliero*, the day laborer, is studied, a more serious situation comes to light. He is unskilled and unorganized. He must take what the competition of his fellows, as hungry as he and as dependent as he upon their day-to-day labor, will give him. He has nothing to fall back upon. It would be absurd to ask whether he could forego a season's labor to induce an employer to come to terms. " In the evening or early in the morning the contadini go to the market place; thither go the proprietors who have work to be done and they bid their wage." The contadini accept when they suppose the wage is as high as they can get. " And since it is a custom to take as many men as are necessary to the completion of one day's labor, both wage and employment remain absolutely speculative." [1] This is written of Calabria but holds as well of Basilicata and Sicily.[2] Looking for laborers before dawn, with a lantern — quite literally ! — instead of through a labor exchange, offers remarkable chances for underpayment and for the suspicion of underpayment.

The tenant cultivators have at times been the victims of that inelasticity of rents which has been generally remarked in agricultural countries. When, after the middle of the century, the prices of grain were rising fast, rents increased somewhat slowly; when prices fell, however, due to international causes, rents continued high for a considerable time. For example, the average price of grain is said to have fallen in the province of Caltanissetta by at least one-third, between 1879 and 1883, while rents stood unchanged; and in the province of Trapani, they even continued

---

[1] Caputo, pp. 1176 f.

[2] *Inch. Parl.*, v[i], pp. 34, 109–111; v[iii], p. 164; v[ii], p. 29. Cf. Sonnino, ii, pp. 264 ff.; G. Baglìo, "Monografia di famiglia," *Giornale degli Economisti*, October, 1912, p. 308.

to rise in 1880–84.[1] Later, however, after the era of lower prices was firmly established, rents also began to decline, irregularly but considerably.[2]

Another complaint has been directed against the proprietors on the ground of usury; not exclusively by the tenants, to be sure, for all classes of cultivators have been involved, and not only against the proprietors, for lenders of other kinds there have also been. Borrowing is common, being sometimes resorted to because the tenant has taken more land than he can cultivate. Usury has flourished in nearly all zones of all provinces. If it is less today than it has been, the past need only be guessed — or can be concretely appreciated in the *Inchiesta Agraria*. Recent studies show rates of 8, 10 or 12 per cent on small money loans, 25 per cent on seed advances, 25–50 per cent on advances of grain, and even much higher rates upon occasion. Sometimes the rates are masked in the prices of goods sold on credit.[3]

Persistently and bitterly the spokesmen of the South have protested against the gradual restriction and abolition of those rights of pasture, of gathering wood, food, stone, and so forth, on communal and feudal lands, which in a friendlier epoch stood between the people and indigence. Many of these lands were usurped through shameful political intrigue, for others an equivalent was rendered. But any equivalent, so the argument runs, benefits only one generation — what of the next ? The law of 1806, according to the indictment, tried to convert the inconvertible, to liquidate the perpetual and inalienable patrimony of the poor, a privilege deriving from the right to life itself.

[1] *Variazioni del fitto dei terreni* (Rome, 1886), pp. 208, 214 f.

[2] No statistics at once broad and precise are available, but the tendency is clear. The reports in *Variazioni del fitto* (pp. 170–215) concur in holding that a decline had taken place. The volume of the following year, *I conti culturali del frumento*, confirms the decline, though incidentally (pp. 198–233). Professors Coletti and Valenti further attested the fact in 1900 in the results of a questionnaire; the depression in rents had been especially great in the South and the islands. See F. Coletti, "La rendita e il valore della terra e la piccola proprietà in Italia nell' ultimo ventennio," *Riforma Sociale*, December 15, 1900, pp. 1164–1171. For other evidence, see *Inch. Parl.*, v^{ii}, pp. 255–259, and v^{ii}, pp. 744–791.

[3] *Ibid.*, v^i, pp. 158 f., 201; v^{ii}, p. 630; v^i, pp. 708 f. Cf. Lori, pp. 437–471.

The world, however, is intolerant of the inadaptable survivals of another age and is chiefly concerned that the transition to a new age should be smooth. Half a century ago, Le Play was still acclaiming the beneficence of these ancient rights; but today there can be no question of reconstituting them nor even of retaining them where they still exist. On the other hand, an important truth lies in the charge that the economic interests of the cultivators have in many places been hurt by the century's changes.[1]

An outcry has been raised against the burdens of taxation, and since these have been often held to constitute a major *causa movens* of emigration, the matter cannot be glossed over. By every standard the taxes of Italy must be adjudged heavy. But only an examination of their character can reveal how far their weight bears upon the emigrating classes.

There is first of all to consider, as a kind of substructure of the entire tax system, the land tax. Its long history we may pass by, except to say that in its modern forms it rests mainly upon the *catasti*, or descriptive land records, of the eighteenth and early nineteenth centuries. The catasti themselves, of which a number often coexisted in one province, had a confusing variety of bases: area, value of product, physical description of the land and its products. Often they erred broadly as originally drawn; in Catanzaro, for example, the cultivable area was represented to exceed the actual area. Their great regional differences gave rise to distressing regional tax inequalities, within compartments as well as between compartments. As the nineteenth century wore on, the inevitable shiftings in crops grown and, presently, the great though varying declines of prices, still further, and notably, accentuated the inequalities. By 1886 the mischief done had already been grievous, and the accusation was common that the larger proprietors were favored. In that year, a new catasto was

---

[1] On the *usi civici* see, besides the references already given on post-feudal land changes, a full essay by E. Carnevale, " I demani e gli usi civici in Sicilia," in *Inch. Parl.*, vi[i], pp. 258–341. See also *Ibid.*, v[i], pp. 136 f.; v[ii], pp. 171–178; v[iii], Note ed appendici, pp. 371–552.

hopefully begun. As, province by province, it advanced, the tax was equalized and substantially reduced. Only, its progress has been at a snail's pace and it has not yet reached the South.

Besides being unequal, the tax has been heavy. What a voracious appetite the new-born kingdom of Italy developed! But a still greater appetite was that of the provinces and the communes, entitled under the law to superadd their tax, their *centesimi addizionali*, to that of the State. The supertax soon became by far the weightier part of the burden. Time and again the investigators of the *Inchiesta Agraria* reported that 30 or 35 per cent of the net income of an estate went into the levies.

Who has paid the land tax? It is insufficient to say that in a relatively burdenless way it has been paid out of a Ricardian rent. Too frequently in this ancient agricultural country, the labor of man has given to the soil its chief value; and the heavy tax easily eats more than an economic rent. However that be, the special fretting of the land assessment turns upon its restless tendency to increase. In the course of a generation most parcels of land change hands, at least once, by inheritance if not by purchase. Since the purchase price will not capitalize the amount of the customary tax, along with the other net income, the purchaser will not feel the burden of this tax; but he will feel the burden of every addition to it.

So it is clear then that every small landowner has had to shoulder every increase of the land tax. It could not be escaped. His land is peculiarly the land whose value derives from invested capital rather than from a pure rent. But what of the great proprietors — can they shift any part of their burden upon their hired workpeople or their tenants? Hardly upon the workpeople, for their wages are independently determined; at the most there might be a generally less liberal treatment by employers. Nor readily upon the share cultivators who likewise make their terms by competition. Sometimes it happens that the tenants who pay a rental for their lands commit themselves to pay the taxes; by such then any new increase in the tax rate would, for the duration of their contract, be felt as a burden. But precisely this situation, in which the tenant pays the tax, we have seen to be an uncommon one. And therefore it must be concluded that the land tax is not easily shifted and that it is felt to be a burden by those only who depend for their living mainly upon the income from their small estates, and then only when, and in so far as, the tax has been increased since their acquisition of the estates.

The remaining taxes, in their aggregate greater than the land tax, may be more briefly considered. The tax upon buildings has attained its great weight principally by reason of the constantly increasing provincial and communal supertaxes; sometimes 25–35 per cent of the taxable income is taken. In theory there is exemption for any building that is indispensable to the work of agriculture (which is independently taxed by the land tax). But in practice exemption is often refused on meager or technical grounds. And no exemption is intended for the town dwellings of agriculturists, so general in the South.

A state tax upon " movable wealth " tries to reach those incomes which do not proceed from land and buildings. Since it exempts annual incomes below 640 lire and daily wages below 3.50 lire, the mass of the wage earners escape its burden. But while a cultivating proprietor pays only the land tax, the tenant who rents land pays a tax upon his agricultural income which is additional to the land tax which the proprietor pays. For tenants whose rental is below 50 lire there is exemption; by other tenants the tax is often seriously felt.

Salt is a government monopoly, upon which the profit or tax approximates as much as eight-ninths of the price of the commodity. It is a most oppressive tax, outraging the canon of proportionality. The burden of the tobacco monopoly can be escaped by those who choose not to smoke. A lighter excise tax on sugar strikes the poor, yet it must be remembered that popular use of sugar is vastly more restricted than in England or the United States. The lottery monopoly and the liquor excises impose heavy burdens, but the provident and sober can avoid them. Duties upon transactions are numerous, unquestionably creating obstacles to business.[1]

[1] For an account of an instance of a large proprietor who wished to break up his land into small plots to encourage small proprietorship and who found that fourteen

Much more important than national tariff duties, whose incidence is not always clear, are the innumerable local duties levied generally by the communes. They survive from a long antiquity. Under united Italy, a portion of the collections has gone to the State, but it has been small compared with that claimed locally. In 1892 the State ceased to be a party to profit from the vexatious bread and paste tax; but the communes, especially in the South, did not generally follow its example. The other taxes upon food and upon other household and construction supplies imported into the communes have shown no tendency to decrease and they bear heavily upon the poor.

The old grist tax, so onerous in the days of the *Inchiesta Agraria* and once an unmaker of ministries, has disappeared; but the tax upon dairy and draft animals persists. It cannot usually be shifted and in the South especially it weighs heavily. Another deplorable charge is the family tax, intended to strike certain forms of income not arising from local real estate or from the remuneration of occupations. Applied in the South, it almost always falls upon incomes already reached by other levies, and despite an exemption of small sums, it is a burden upon many of the families that make up the emigration.

So much for particular levies and their incidence. Fundamentally the great question is not, Are taxes heavy, and must the poor pay them? for in a poor community the necessaries of life cannot escape taxation; but rather, Are the heavy taxes so spent as to ease the conditions of earning and of living? Not a burden, but the lightening of a burden, is the true object of taxes; in other words, a wise coöperative expenditure is their object.

In part such expenditure exists; typical directions are for police, schools, roads, sanitation.[1] But in the case of some taxes

taxes, aggregating 63.25 lire, had to be paid on plots valued at 200 lire, see J. Aguet, " Come l'eccessiva fiscalità impedisca in Italia la costituzione della piccola proprietà," *Riforma Sociale*, January–February, 1917, pp. 122 f.

[1] It is by no means intended that the outlays under these heads are either sufficient or well devised. One of the most reiterated complaints of the contadini is that the roads are inadequate for carrying goods, or are nonexistent, and that all travelling is unsafe because difficult and is therefore so little resorted to that isolation results. In the kingdom of Naples, the capital city was everything — as a matter of

the expenses of collection consume nearly the entire sums received. Many municipal outlays for theaters, festivals, monuments, and the like have been at an extravagant rate. Local political corruption abounds, and many officials render no equivalents for their salaries. A vast amount has been spent on contracts, national and local, for projects beneficial mainly to those who have furthered them. The great State responsibilities — a long-standing national debt, maintenance of army and navy — have claimed much of the tax receipts, and (evil days having come) will claim more. Meanwhile, agriculture and the South have received back, in the more tangible ways, only a part of what they have yielded.

Had it been otherwise, had agriculture and the directer interests of the contadini been advanced, then the great taxation might even have contributed to deter emigration. Strangely, however, it cannot be said that, had the land taxes been lighter, emigration would have been, in any corresponding sense, less. For that tax has been borne mainly by the larger proprietors, by such as, almost as a class, have been spending their incomes otherwise than upon betterment of their estates. Is it likely that alleviation of their condition would have resulted in any more liberal contracts for cultivation or in any substantial increase of care of their estates? All that we know of their ways in the past bids us answer, no.[1]

policy. Railroads were opposed on a thousand pretexts — not least because they made for immorality! A better day has brought the railroads, but the lack of communal and inter-communal roads has continued to be widespread and serious. In *Inch. Agr.* and *Inch. Parl.* are many references to the subject of communications. Cf. G. Malvezzi and U. Zanotti-Bianco, *L'Aspromonte occidentale* (Milan, 1910), pp. 42–58. See also the striking early account by E. P. Rossi, *La Basilicata* (Verona, 1868), Bk. ii, §§ lxiii–lxxi.

[1] The *Inch. Agr.* and *Inch. Parl.* contain much concrete information on rural taxation. Volume vii[iii] of the latter is a monograph by G. Carano-Donvito entitled *Dati sulle finanze locali del mezzogiorno.* The best general treatise on Italian taxation is L. Einaudi, *Corso di scienza della finanza,* 3d ed., Turin, 1916; the previous edition of this work is at some points ampler. See also F. S. Nitti, *Principi di scienza delle finanze,* Naples, 1903. An excellent survey of the changes of taxation is Part ii, ch. vii, of G. Sensini, *Le variazioni dello stato economico d'Italia nell' ultimo trentennio del secolo XIX,* Rome, 1904. An earlier classic is G. Alessio, *Saggio sul sistema tributario in Italia,* 2 vols., Rome, 1883; see especially the first volume.

What are the concrete terms of living in the South ? What is the immediate form of things which the emigrant leaves behind him ? We have dealt so far mainly with the many limitations upon income and have left to inference the ways of expenditure. If we are still dealing principally with conditions having an economic form, let it be remembered that they are conditions so direct and intimate in their pressure that they seem to spell life itself.

The setting is well enough known. Sometimes it is a desolate scene, or a pleasantly picturesque one, sometimes a landscape rising to an association of mountain, sky, and sea in a crystal and incomparable beauty. The houses of the contadini are small and simple, placed generally in a town upon an elevation, those of the more wretched day laborers (which rent for as little as 36 lire a year) being on the periphery. One story is usual. Tuff, stone, brick, mud, and lava are the materials of composition; rarely wood. Washing facilities are meager, drainage is absent. Oil or petroleum may be burned, but many a family has its evening meal in darkness. " The street is the parlor, the resort for gossiping, odes and wooing; it is where the children romp, the women work and the men have their games." [1] On the other hand the house itself, often of only one room, may contain during the night and part of the day, not only the entire family, with a demoralizing collapse of privacy, but the ass, goat, poultry, and other animals, all making assaults upon order and cleanliness; heroic is the rôle of many wives in keeping their households clean. It even happens that several families will occupy one room. When the work-place is far away, the worker may remain in the fields overnight, perhaps throughout the season, resting on the ground, or perhaps on straw, with a straw roof over his head. Worst off is the herdsman, who must sleep lightly. Here and there families live in caves or dens; but in the Matera district of Basilicata, thousands live

The land tax is capably dealt with in M. M. Libelli, *L'imposta fondiaria sui terreni in Italia*, Florence, 1906. Of its chosen theme there is no better discussion than the essay of G. Valenti, *Il sistema tributario italiano in relazione all' esercizio dell' agricoltura*, published by the Società degli Agricoltori Italiani in the volume *L'Italia agricola alla fine del secolo XIX*, Rome, 1901.

[1] *Inch. Parl.*, vi[ii], p. 433.

so, perched upon the hillside, braving the dampness — true troglodites.[1]

During unemployment, whether of a normal sort or exceptional, hunger or at least privation is not uncommon. Otherwise, the food is likely to be sufficient in quantity, even running to seven moderate repasts a day at harvest time, and is likely to be wholesome. Its basis is bread, baked by the wife, and made less often out of maize than when the reports of the *Inchiesta Agraria* were prepared. Dry bread, soaked in oil and salt, is the staple diet of many a laborer. Chestnut bread has become rare. In general meat is seldom eaten, or only on grand occasions, or when a sick animal has died. Women and children never or rarely, depending upon the region, taste wine; men may do so on days of hard work.[2]

Physical robustness is not general and is particularly wanting in the lower districts. In stature the men of the southern compartments rank lowest in Italy, and they have poor chests. Undoubtedly, inferior physique has made for the frequency of malaria, just as it has been a consequence of malaria. Tracoma, as a filth disease, has prevailed in many sections. Tuberculosis and alcoholism are uncommon but apparently increasing; they have had but a brief history in the South.[3]

Life in the South exalts the family. It has been said of Sicily that the family sentiment is perhaps the only deeply rooted altruistic sentiment that prevails.[4] Gallant to his wife, the husband has almost complete power over the members of the family; the wife's affection tends to be slavish. Concubinage is relatively common — is something left of Greek and Saracen traditions ? In marriage, convenience is rarely sacrificed to love, and the parties come generally from the same region. Nearly a third of Sicilian brides are between the ages of fifteen and twenty,

---

[1] The eighteenth century description by Galanti (cited in *Inch. Parl.*, v[iii], Note ed appendici, p. 173) accords with recent conditions. Similar descriptions are in *Inch. Agr.* For the housing situation generally I have drawn chiefly upon *Inch. Parl.*, especially v[i], pp. 144 f., 193; v[ii], pp. 495–505; v[iii], pp. 174 f.; vi[ii], pp. 449–455, and also upon my own more limited observation.

[2] *Inch. Parl.*, v[i], pp. 141 f.; v[ii], pp. 478–480; vi[ii], pp. 456–458.

[3] *Ibid.*, v[ii], p. 516; v[iii], Note ed appendici, pp. 49–60; vi[ii], pp. 559 f., 612–623.

[4] Lorenzoni, in *Inch. Parl.*, vi[ii], p. 462.

on the peninsula probably a larger proportion; the men are generally older than twenty. Four or six children are commonly born, eight or ten sometimes. It is a region where earning capacity demands first of all a strong arm, and where the question of the scattering of a patrimony does not usually arise because there is no important patrimony to scatter. Among the better-to-do contadini children are less numerous.[1]

In this population children have grown to adult life unlettered. Three out of four of the inhabitants six years of age or older, in the first years of the twentieth century, could neither read nor write. It is a situation with few parallels in civilized countries, and a long story lies behind it. Suffice it here to say that under Joseph Bonaparte and Murat, representatives of an ampler democracy, many schools were opened, and elementary instruction was declared obligatory and free. Reaction followed. But while Austria in the North, despite many tyrannies, tried to improve the schools, the Bourbons in the two Sicilies restored the ancestral darkness. It was an era, wrote E. P. Rossi, only six years after it ended, "in which the art of governing lay in neglecting and despising every sort of instruction."[2] Ferdinand II was not anxious that his people should think, and rarely deviated into thinking himself. Even, however, in a liberal era, schools require more than good wishes and toleration. Low as the expenditure for education has been in all of Italy since unification, it continues to be lowest in Basilicata and in Calabria, and very low in Sicily also. Attendance is slight, buildings are inadequate and unhygienic, and the decrease in illiteracy over many years has been much less than in the North.[3]

[1] W. T. Thornton, in 1846, holding that misery augments the birth rate, cited the South Italian laborer as evidence for his theory; see *Over-population and its Remedy* (London, 1846), pp. 158–160. On the family see *Inch. Parl.*, v[1], pp. 65 f., 154, 198; vi[ii], pp. 462–466.

[2] Rossi, p. 258. See the entire § xxvi in Bk. ii, and also §§ xxvii–xxxi.

[3] *Inch. Parl.*, vi[ii], pp. 515–523; De Nobili, Pt. viii, ch. 14; Malvezzi and Zanotti-Bianco, pp. 83–101, 129–132. The last reference contains the results of a direct inquiry. See also G. Salvemini, "Il problema della scuola popolare in provincia di Reggio Calabria," *Nuova Antologia*, February 1, 1910, pp. 521–536. This study contains results of a report on primary schools made by a Florentine society.

Of the implications and accompaniments of the lack of education in South Italy one might speak at length. Tradition and credulity are the masters of the population, impotence to do well and allegiance to false principles of living result. It is the untaught child in the man that sways the destinies of these people; the beauty of the child's impulses is there, but also the inconsequential character of those impulses, their unfitness for comprehensive action. Religion is half festivity and half superstition. The child at play and the pagan tradition of Greeks and Saracens make for the first, the uncriticising and fearing child make for the second. This child's God is anthropomorphic, his saints are in a feudal hierarchy. There is a Church whose secular might is as real and as irresistible as the secular might of sea and burning mountain, as truly a part of the nature of things. The eager control of the priest has reached into the major decisions of the life of the communicant. To understand the tragedy of the result one must remember that the priesthood has been corrupt and immoral and the enemy of educational and economic reform.[1]

Where toil is hard and democratic institutions are few, recreation is likely to take its direction from the elementary dispositions. When the attraction of the numerous religious festivals does not rest upon drama and representation, it rests upon the chance of a frolic. Of popular pictorial art there is little save the splendid decoration of carts in Sicily. One kind of pleasure comes from gambling, which is greatly diffused. Gambling with cards and the like comes nearer to recreation than does the lottery, but the latter, managed by the State for its own profit, has had an extraordinary development in the South. Sexual immorality would appear to be not much less than when the dolorous pictures of the *Inchiesta Agraria* were painted.[2]

---

[1] It is doubtless an evidence of improvement that the accounts of a degraded priesthood are to be found in *Inch. Agr.* rather than in *Inch. Parl.* Lorenzoni (*Inch. Parl.*, vi[ii], p. 514), holding that the clergy are still mostly ignorant and coarse, thinking of themselves rather than of the religious consciences of their people, yet believes that the younger priests are of a more promising type than could have been found in 1885.

[2] *Inch. Parl.*, vi[i], p. 687.

One cannot find in any one circumstance the roots of the unusual record in crime which the South has had. On the continent the rugged country, with its legion hiding places, a sparse and repressed population, a government administratively weak, permitted the great strength of brigandage through the centuries.[1] But brigandage is no more. Of Sicily, however, it cannot be said that the vendetta has disappeared, or the mafia. On the contrary, the principle that each man should settle his quarrels himself has persisted through recent times. A series of alien conquests notwithstanding, Sicily has never been conquered. Its soul is that of a rebel today. Homicides in Sicily are at five times the rate of North Italy, only decreasing somewhat of late years. Other crimes also have been excessively common, with an emphasis upon thefts (as in the fields) and the lesser forms of immorality.[2]

So grave has been the economic maladjustment which has come to rule in South Italy that one need not long ask why it should prompt to emigration. And yet our account is still incomplete. Though we have knit it to sundry remote happenings, a further word regarding historical forces is necessary.

For several centuries a blight has lain upon the South. An ancient greatness there was, under the Greeks, a mediaeval greatness under the Normans; fourteenth-century Frederick made Sicily one of the freest lands of Europe. Under Spaniard and Bourbon, however, the life of the region declined. Neglect, weakness, and oppression in varying degrees characterized the rulers. There was no encouragement of artisanry and bourgeoisie. There was no government which the people could call their own. From the powerful hold of feudalism no relief could come save by external pressure, and such a pressure the Spaniards did not exercise, nor the Bourbon Charles. Though the startling irruption of the French was too short-lived to make a new people out of the old — considering that the old was so far removed from

[1] Cf. Rossi, entire Bk. iii; P. Villari, *Le lettere meridionali* (Florence, 1878), pp. 39–60.

[2] In the period of low wages, 1890–97, stealing became virtually a means of existence in Sicily. See Baglìo, " Monografia di famiglia," pp. 300 f.

modern ways — it effected several momentous reforms which
even the ensuing half century of restored Bourbonism had to
tolerate. " The negation of God erected into a system of government," in Gladstone's phrase, preserved the conditions of the
country much as they had been for three centuries, and when it
gave way to the government of Italy, a stupendous task of reform
was in waiting. But the reform came not. The Mezzogiorno was
promptly regarded more as a conquered region than as a participating entity in the new government. Its people were too backward to count as equals with those of the North. Its deputies in
Parliament were a group to conciliate. The devotion of national
effort to the South, the investment of national money there, could
not be expected to bring such quick returns as in the North, and
the new Italy had the impatience of youth.

So economic ills remained uncorrected. Institutions were suffered to exist which the world in its progress had sentenced to
death. Landed proprietors, who could afford to, kept away from
their estates. No aggressive leadership appeared — how could it
arise when for centuries no social-political ladder was available
upon which the obscure but gifted man could mount to command ? Feudal class lines gave way grudgingly. When the investigators of the *Inchiesta Agraria* inquired into the relations
subsisting between proprietors and laborers, they found everywhere a servile homage on the part of the peasants, the attitude
of the man who appreciates that the gulf between him and another is impassable. In an eloquent article upon emigration,
Professor Villari, after recalling how the communes had made
liberty the privilege of a restricted oligarchy, wrote: "In history
and in legend we have had no rural heroes. . . . Our revolution,
our *risorgimento* were bourgeois achievements. The contadini
never took a notable part in them. They have always been
abandoned by us, entirely outside our national political life, and
such they remain today." [1] Garibaldi, it will be recalled, found
supporters but rarely among the country folk. Gallenga, who had
been in the Calabrian campaign of 1860, wrote: " The population
of the towns was eager for news and all agog with expectation . . .

[1] P. Villari, " L'emigrazione," etc., pp. 54 f. Cf. Franchetti, i, pp. 137 f.

while that of the rural districts maintained its usual attitude of dumbfounded and bothered neutrality." [1]

What Villari asserts of rural political participation is indeed easily borne out. Illiteracy has been (until very lately) a sufficient ground for exclusion from the electoral lists, and in Basilicata the contadini have usually made up only one-tenth to one-third of the names of these lists, and rarely have attained one-half. [2] The voters take a very mild interest in public affairs, and commonly vote according to instructions, venality being frequent and often overt. The *galantuomini*, a genre of gentlemen of leisure, exercise control of the communes and are preoccupied to keep the contadini dependent and uneducated. The latter, in turn, have but little patriotism and resent military service. [3]

An evidence, in many countries, of the extent to which an upper class acknowledges a responsibility for the unfortunate or adherence to the ideal of equalization of opportunity is to be found in the gifts made, as by bequest, to appropriate social institutions. In South Italy no such tradition exists. The rich die, but the call is again, Long live the rich! Whoever is curious may read in the Italian yearbooks what sums are destined to philanthropic uses. He will find that for the entire quarter century ending in 1905 the total of these sums in Basilicata — not the annual average — reached less than three lire per capita, in Sicily less than five lire, in Calabria actually less than one and one-half lire! [4]

We may be spared a summary of this long analysis of production and living in the South. Nature and man together, man most of all, man through the preservation of out-of-date customs and institutions, these have so wrought together that life without a change became unbearable.

---

[1] A. Gallenga, *Italy Revisited* (2 vols., 2d ed., London, 1876), ii, p. 374.

[2] *Inch. Parl.*, v^i, p. 161; cf. v^{ii}, p. 685.

[3] *Ibid.*, v^{ii}, pp. 571, 686 ff.; vi^{ii}, p. 514.

[4] The twenty-five year figures I take from *Annuario Statistico Italiano*, 1905–07, i, p. 227. No later figures appear till those for 1912, when the per capita gifts in Basilicata were only 0.32 lira, in Sicily 1.01 lire, in Calabria 2.08 lire. See *Annuario, 1913*, p. 64. Cf. *Inch. Parl.*, v^{ii}, p. 607.

A lower disaffected class, seeing before it no established avenues of improvement, has often sought its ends by collective force — by revolution or strike. For South Italy the thesis would probably hold that, till recently, the mass of the people were too resigned to their secular misery to be in any very active sense disaffected. A clear-sighted minority had often enough won converts and provoked revolutionary outbreaks.[1] But even the revolution which deposed the Bourbons was no mighty stirring of a mass. If in subsequent decades there has been a labor movement, it has, except for one episode, generally had an aspect of meagerness. On the continent strikes have been few. In Sicily, in the early nineties came the semi-revolutionary outbreak of the *Fasci*, organizations demanding such various things as tax reform, laws on the disposition of communal lands, increase of wages, betterments in agricultural contracts, and subdivision of the latifundia.[2] Blood flowed freely before it was put down, but gradually its main demands in a softened form were urged again by new organizations, commonly called leagues of resistance, with many thousands of members, chiefly in the province of Palermo. These new associations include small proprietors, tenants, and common laborers; and their greatest achievement has been the origination of those collective and partly coöperative tenancies of large estates to which reference has already been made. This has been in Sicily. Even now almost no organization of contadini has developed in Calabria and Basilicata, and the agrarian strike is mainly an affair of the North.[3]

[1] In that treasure house of observations by a learned traveller, *Briefe über Kalabrien und Sizilien* (3 vols., Göttingen, 1787), its author, J. H. Bartels, frequently praised the attitude of those he met. He wrote (i, p. 277) near Nicastro, " I find here people of the brightest intelligence. Under the cruel yoke which hangs upon their necks, it is naturally hard for them to raise their heads. But their means of supporting the yoke, and the courage which constantly animates them, is the most eloquent evidence of their intelligence. You will never find a Calabrian giving way to cowardly sobs. He will complain to you of his burden, but he paints you his picture with such exactness that you are forced to admit that he sees to the bottom, and though he bends under his burden because a sword hangs over his head, he tries at the same time to discover ways and means of freeing himself from the burden."

[2] See the analysis of N. Colajanni, *Gli avvenimenti di Sicilia e le loro cause*, Palermo, 1894.

[3] On the labor movement in Sicily, see the account in *Inch. Parl.*, vi^{ii}, pp. 633–

While the strike seeks a smaller economic gain and presupposes a continuance of patriotic ties, emigration seeks a large economic gain and implies a readiness to sever (or to loosen) patriotic ties. It is simpler and may seem surer than revolution; it is more satisfactory for the individual. It is the method of the outlaw; brigandage in Basilicata and Calabria, it is credibly said, was abolished less by the *carabinieri* than by emigration. But it is also the method of the miserable man whose patriotic or civic ties, being slender, are easily sundered — whose fatherland is whatever country will give him his bread. The act of emigration begins as a renunciation of country, a preference for another land's social ladder. It easily " grows upon itself," because later emigrants find cherished social ties awaiting them in the new country, and because, also, the picture of better things allures more insistently when, through emigrated friends abroad and common rumor at home, it is the oftener presented to the mind.

There have been two fountain heads of emigration from South Italy, Basilicata and Campania. From some communes it has taken its course for half a century or more, and when Carpi's figures began to be collected, in 1869, a rapid increase was under way. Even in these early days — nay, characteristically in them — one of those specialized types was present which stand forth in a certain romantic relief in Italian emigration, the wandering musicians of Viggiano — " so universal is there the art of harmony," wrote Rossi.[1] As the song runs:

> Harp on my shoulder,
> From Viggiano I come.
> All the world is my home.[2]

And indeed they went everywhere, to Spain, France, Asia, Africa; I have talked with them on the boats in Boston Harbor. Often they went as children, too often in the charge of speculators, so

657. On the agrarian strike, see de Rocquigny, *Ligues et grèves de paysans*, Paris, 1904.

[1] E. P. Rossi, p. 65. Even today Viggiano lies some 36 miles from the railway.

[2] L'arpa al collo — son Viggianese — tutto il mondo è mio paese. See *Inch. Parl.*, v^i, p. 82.

becoming one of the chief examples of child slavery developed in this emigration.[1]

From the mountains, as at once the poorest and the most populous part of Basilicata, emigration began and long continued before other sections were aroused. Remoteness of destination was no bar, and Argentina and Brazil were favorite early goals, the United States soon supervening as the goal *par excellence*. It was mainly a permanent emigration, of day laborers, small proprietors, and tenants. Gradually the hill districts of Basilicata and Calabria became involved, and only very slowly the coast zone, with its large estates and meager population. In fact, there are important areas of the coast where emigration is still in its first phases. Once begun, the exodus from Basilicata never appreciably slackened, soon attaining a ratio to population second only to that in Venetia. But this was a permanent emigration, and it did not take long before a sheer decline set in in the population of the mountains, while that on the coast continued to grow. In the first ten years of the twentieth century, the average annual emigration from Basilicata was three per cent of the population, and the region stood forth as the most notable instance in Italy of a decline of population due to emigration. From the start this continental emigration contained many women and children. The phenomenon has been present of the father going first and later sending for his family; so the province of Cosenza, having an old emigration, shows a smaller proportion of men than that of Reggio, which started later in the race. Superposed in the recent period has been the tendency to return home after two to five years abroad, and presently to emigrate again; and this once more has been a movement of men alone.[2]

With surprising slowness, considering its adjacency to Calabria, Sicily became a land of emigration, and when that happened it was upon terms which suggested an independent impulse. The

[1] " More merciful than the heavens and men is the earth which gives them burial," wrote Rossi, *loc. cit.*

[2] See esp. *Inch. Parl.*, v[i], pp. 8 f., 80, 82 f., 136, 139, 166 f., 203, 207, 220, 230; v[ii], pp. 714, 733 f.; v[iii], pp. 87 f., 93, 107 f.; v[iii], Note ed appendici, pp. 581 f.

beginnings were in the province of Palermo, substantially distant from the Calabrian shore; the rest of the island was in the early eighties not yet aroused from its age-long lethargy. From Palermo it continued with vigor, so that of all the Sicilian emigrants of the last quarter of the nineteenth century, nearly half came from that province. Next it began in Messina where probably the contagion of Reggio, across two miles of straits, was more potent than that of Palermo. Only with the twentieth century, however, did the great outburst come. Then all provinces were swept into a resistless current. In their ratio to population other South Italian compartments continued to show a stronger movement than Sicily, but nowhere was its growth so prodigiously rapid as in the island. In the year 1906 the astonishing total of 127,000 Sicilian emigrants was reached. In some regions the annual emigration has been five per cent of the population; these are especially the regions of the interior where emigration began late and the past weighed most heavily. It is significant that emigration should not have originated where misery was greatest. It began where there was the chance of saving enough money for passage fares and has best maintained itself where wages were at a medium level.[1]

In its intensity the movement in Sicily has selected especially the day laborers, next those associated with the mezzadria and rent contracts, lastly the small proprietors. Miners and various operatives and artisans have been numerous also, the first named reflecting the various vicissitudes of the sulphur industry, the rest in part the consequences of the agricultural emigration; and both affected by the contagion of the exodus. Prominent latterly in the secondary emigration — if one may so describe that which seeks escape from the consequences of the primary — have been the small bourgeois proprietors. Once they were a self-sustaining element, often owning estates of 20,000–30,000 lire, but the in-

---

[1] At Caltagirone the contadini said, "We do not emigrate because we still lack the money needful for the journey; but just as soon as we have it we shall go too." *Inch. Parl.*, vi[ii], p. 766. The population of the Matera district of Basilicata, living in the hillside caves described above, has scarcely begun to emigrate.

creased wages cost of working them has consumed their margin of profit.[1]

The Sicilians have gone to North Africa, to South America, and to the United States. From the first and third of these goals many have returned to Sicily, so that it may be said that a considerable portion of the emigration is temporary only. But this is another way of saying that largely if not mainly the emigration has the appearance of being permanent, and only its recency makes hazardous a stronger description.[2]

[1] A proprietor of Termini Imerese said, " I was at Cairo for twenty years. First I was a street vendor, then I set up a small shop and made money. With my savings I returned to Sicily, built a little house and bought land, but with the high price of labor I failed to make both ends meet, so I shall have to emigrate again." It is a typical instance. See *Inch. Parl.*, vi[ii], p. 375. Cf. E. Corbino, *L'emigrazione in Augusta* (Catania, 1914), pp. 17 f.

[2] In general, on Sicilian emigration, see *Inch. Parl.*, vi[ii], pp. 705–730, 761–766.

CHAPTER VII

NORTH ITALY

HISTORY has been kinder to the populations of North Italy than to those of the South. Though battle fields have been in every part and foreign princes have established their rule and their institutions, the buoyant life of the region has withstood all harassings and been ever ready to reassume its autonomy. Feudalism effected an entrance, but its wedge never penetrated so deeply as in the South; the massive opposition of a powerful communal tradition prevented that. An unrivalled situation for foreign trade gained for the region those riches which could allow the development of a staunch and varied civilization. Even in its decay, the republic of Venice showed no such demoralization as did the South in the reign of the Bourbons. Lombardy, under the thumb of Austria, while the victim of abounding afflictions, continued to grow in industry and agriculture. The new Italian kingdom, finally, though it outdid the old régime in the levying of heavy taxes, greatly stimulated and indeed directly aided the industrial advance of the North at the expense of that of the South; its contracts were carried out there, its tariff policy gave to the North a southern market.[1]

In these circumstances an account of the causes of emigration from the North cannot show such profound economic disorders and maladjustments and such extremities of poverty as were described for the South. The picture loses in vivid prominence of line, but at the same time changes in character, presently portraying a type of emigration in many ways different from that of the South.

[1] For an excellent statistical comparison of the well-being and advantages of North and South, see C. Gini, *L'ammontare e la composizione della ricchezza delle nazioni* (Turin, 1914), pp. 277–300. Cf. G. Mortara, " Numeri indici dello stato e del progresso economico delle regioni italiane," in *Giornale degli Economisti*, July, 1913, pp. 17–29; and F. S. Nitti, *La ricchezza dell' Italia* (Naples, 1904), pp. 116–126 and *passim*.

Venetia, Lombardy, and Piedmont are the three major compartments of Northern emigration. Including, as they do, nearly all the territory of the continental North, and displaying a characteristic configuration of hills and high mountains, plain and seacoast, they may serve, for the purposes of this essay, as fairly typical of such adjoining compartments as Liguria and Emilia; and we may therefore confine our study to them. Though their industrial development has been much greater than that of the South, an explanation of their emigration, as of that of the South, is to be found first of all in the ways and circumstances in which agriculture is carried on.[1]

In one important respect the climate is much more favorable for agriculture than that of the South. The number of days in which precipitation occurs is about the same, the amount of precipitation is not much greater, but — a true boon — the rainfall comes generally in the spring and summer. Hence, a wide choice of crops, vigorous growth, a soil responsive to fertilizer, intensive cultivation.

But if this, in general terms, is the situation, other factors, varying according to locality, make for different local pictures. The high Alps lie across the North, and between them and the plains the land is greatly broken. In the heights the cold is intense and the season of enforced idleness long. Much of the soil of Venetia, Lombardy, and Piedmont is invincibly unproductive. As the altitude becomes less, the soil improves, sometimes allowing large herds to graze or encouraging a measure of agriculture. But cultivation is not evidence that the land has independent value; when the return to the farmer does not exceed what a wage earner would be paid for his time, the land is virtually

---

[1] Though there is diversity of recent political history in the North and only one main recent régime in the South before unification (the Bourbon), yet I again assume that it is possible to study the causes of emigration by a procedure identical for the entire region. Whoever studies only the emigration from Venetia and Lombardy runs the risk of overstressing the special abuses of the Austrian régime. Emigration from these regions has pretty constantly increased in the half century since that régime ended, and the emigration from neighboring Piedmont and Liguria has been comparable with that of Venetia and Lombardy.

without independent value and its yield is a wage to the cultivator. This situation has been common in the mountains, but only occasional in the hills.

Much less than in the South of Italy, but seriously enough, deforestation has had an influence upon the conditions of agriculture. Its modern course appears to have begun with the extension of roads, increasing the accessibility of the trees. The forests were largely communal, and the continued exercise of common rights worked for their destruction. Reform legislation of 1811 and 1839, though correct in principle, failed in application to check the havoc which swept away not only deciduous trees, but, what is worse, the evergreens. Inundations became common, yet the plague of malaria continued much less than in South Italy. The presumption is that the humidity decreased; if so, there was accentuation of a natural condition already troublesome.[1]

In fact, in the region of the lower hills and in the plain, the summer is so deficient in rainfall that a veritable drought results. Sometimes, as in the province of Rovigo, the soil is rich; in general, however, as far as a natural element alone is involved, it is only mediocre. And yet this region is luxuriant under cultivation, extraordinarily luxuriant. It is one of the most productive areas on the earth's surface. It yields richly not one crop but a notable variety, in fact, the crops, it might almost be said, of other climates; for rice thrives in subtropical conditions at a few hours journey from the Alps. So eagerly has the area under cultivation been extended that, over great stretches of country, hardly a plant is to be seen that has not been set out by the hand of man — it is not a region that a botanist would love.

What has so effectually overcome the dryness of much of this country is a system of irrigation that has been nowhere excelled and rarely approached in the degree of its perfection. It is in Piedmont and Lombardy that men have drawn the subsoil waters to the surface and taken the streams that flow down from the Alps, especially the waters that come from the reservoir-lakes of

[1] The *Inch. Agr.* contains many references to the course and consequences of deforestation. In particular, see vi[i] (Lombardy), pp. 29–35.

Lombardy, and diverting them into an amazing network of canals adjusted finely to slopes and grade, have spread their blessing over the land. The Cistercian monks it was, of the Chiaravalle abbey, that seven centuries ago began this work, which succeeding generations have developed. Diversity and abundance of crops are a consequence; hay yields several cuttings a year, and dairying thrives — " Whoever has meadowland has everything," says the proverb.[1]

In such diverse physical conditions as prevail in North Italy there could be no uniform scheme of relationship of men's toil to the land. Wherever altitudes are considerable, and the surface slopes, and the soil is reluctant to yield, there the small property comes to the fore. Yet it is again the small property that tends to be synonymous with poverty. In Venetia the greatest subdivision of estates has been in the provinces of Belluno and Udine, the extraordinary situation of which (as indicated in information supplied by the tax authorities in 1878) deserves to be summarized here: [2]

	Belluno	Udine
Number of proprietors having an income from land of 1–1000 lire	62,430	200,590
Number of proprietors having an income from land of 100–1000 lire	1,541	7,016
Number of proprietors having an income from land of more than 1000 lire	175	643
Per cent of proprietors having an income from land of not over 100 lire	97	96
Average number of hectares possessed by each proprietor	4.50	2.40
Number of proprietors in each 100 inhabitants	33	45

The process of subdivision in these provinces has gone forward for a long time, facilitated by inheritance customs, and made possible in many of the more recent instances through savings from emigration. In the nine years 1871–79, nearly two-fifths of the proprietors gave place to others, and more than one-fifth of the

---

[1] *Chi ha prato ha tutto.*

On the canals see *Inch. Agr.*, ii[i], pp. 100–104, and the admirable work — old, but in essentials not superseded — of R. B. Smith, *Italian Irrigation*, 2 vols., 2d ed., Edinburgh and London, 1855.

[2] *Inch. Agr.* iv[ii] (Venetia), p. 305; figures are given for other provinces also.

rural acreage changed hands. This, to be sure, was a period in
which much of the ecclesiastical land was sold, but the whole
amount of such land sold before 1881 was less than two per cent
of the cultivable area of Venetia; what is striking is rather that
the average lot sold in this way was only a little more than two
hectares, the lowest for all Italy. In recent decades, disposal
of communal lands has added greatly to the number of small
properties.

Of the mountainous part of Lombardy, Jacini wrote that nearly
every family owned land and often owned more than one strip.[1]
In such a region the land would not be cultivated at all unless by
its owner. Slight as is the yield of the soil, it would be much less
if the tillers, generation after generation, had not taken out its
rocks, walled up the steep places and with daily care followed the
course of the crops. Even in the hill country of the province of
Milan small properties abound, the large majority of which
extend to less than one hectare in size.[2]

Again in Piedmont, in its mountains and little less in its hills,
given the protection of the Code Napoléon and the general passion
of the people to become proprietors, the land has become greatly
subdivided. Speculators who in the first instance acquired the
lands of the Church and of the towns sold them in small lots. And
when many patrician families were forced by political events to
dispose of portions of their lands, increasing subdivision followed.
It is in the provinces of Cuneo, Torino, and Alessandria that the
process has gone farthest.[3]

In none of these northern compartments does the property of
medium size obtain widely. Historical forces have not made for its
increase. Here and there among the lower hills only, especially in
the vicinity of large cities, it is to be found, the means to its constitution having often come from gains made in industry and
trade.

[1] *Inch. Agr.*, vi[i], p. 43.
[2] A. Serpieri, *Il contratto agrario e le condizioni dei contadini nell' Alto Milanese*
(Milan, 1910), p. 45.
[3] *Inch. Agr.*, viii[i], pp. 441–455; Baldioli-Chiorando, pp. 846–848.

Commonly when land is not in a small parcel it is in a large or a great estate, typically 120–400 hectares in size. Then arises a situation which we have already deplored in South Italy. Many of the proprietors in the hilly country and the plains of Venetia do not cultivate their lands directly. When they do not actually live upon their estates they are particularly unlikely to do so; when they use their estates merely as country seats, as they often do, it is to keep their town habits and avoid what would be helpful contact with their workers. Nor is the case of Piedmont different. When the *Inchiesta Agraria* reported its evidence upon this subject, it might still have used the English words of that competent patriot, Antonio Gallenga, who had written, twenty years earlier:

> Whoever has land enough, or can by any other means eke out ever so wretched an existence in Turin, will hardly think of occupying his house at Ivrea or Pinerolo; and whoever has a house at Ivrea or Pinerolo would be deemed half crazy if he lived at his villa two or three miles — nay, half a mile — away from other habitations. The landlord hastens to forsake the land, and scarcely ever graces the property which supports him with more than a fortnight's or a month's visit in the autumn.[1]

Most of all it is in the lowlands of Lombardy that the large estate, coupled with absenteeism, has become characteristic. Indeed, in Lower Lombardy, absentee proprietors have in recent years held about 90 per cent of the land.[2]

The monks in their extensive establishments of earlier centuries commonly hired others to cultivate for them. In the eighteenth century, especially in the region east of the Adda, there were many small estates whose owners cultivated the grape; more and more these were absorbed by the large estates, and particularly as the system of irrigation was extended. Napoleon's annulment of the *droit de majorat*, and the secularization of Church lands in 1860 brought about great changes in ownership, and, alongside of the old nobility and the charitable corporations which continued to control much of the land, came the new urban industrial classes and the dealers of Milan, Lodi, Pavia, all persons commanding

[1] A. Gallenga, *Country Life in Piedmont* (London, 1858), p. 88. Cf. *Inch. Agr.*, viii[i], pp. 535–538.
[2] F. Rovelli, *Die Agrarverfassung der Niederlombardei* (Karlsruhe, 1908), p. 49.

much capital and able to take the lands for investment. The new classes, however, were not more ready to cultivate directly than the old. It has continued to be the case that, except when they do cultivate, the proprietors, almost as a class, rarely visit their estates; and when they do cultivate, it is to delegate the actual work of supervision and management to an agent. Many, it is even said, have never seen their estates and know not where they are located, who the tenant is, or what the lease price.[1]

To a large extent, taking North Italy as a whole, cultivation rests upon tenancy; and, as elsewhere in Italy, the forms of contract are many. In this survey only the principal ones may be examined. The mezzadria, survival of a notable antiquity, holds an important place today. In Venetia it has persisted chiefly in the provinces of Belluno and Treviso, even there, however, suffering a decline in recent decades; excessive cultivation of grain, insufficient employment of — or scope for — intensive methods, seem to explain its fall from popularity. In Piedmont the contract had a much wider development in the first than in the second half of the past century. It was widespread in the provinces of Cuneo and Torino, least prevalent in the mountains, common in the hills, abundant in the lowlands. At the time when Arthur Young, travelling through Lombardy, described and disprized it, its vogue was great. At one time, in fact, it had been almost alone. But, here too, it declined subsequently, even in the hilly, non-irrigated parts where it had chiefly obtained. The tenants got into debt with the landlords, who appear themselves to have tried to preserve the contract. By a reporter of the *Inchiesta Agraria* its decline was associated with the slow but constant disintegration of the patriarchal family to which it had been best suited. The Countess Martinengo Cesaresco, a witness to many of the changes which the contract underwent in Lombardy, held that it could survive only where there was " an intense power of work and a primitive conception of life."[2] The pure type of the mezzadria, as developed in Tuscany, has been rare in North

---

[1] *Inch. Agr.*, vi[i], *passim*; Rovelli, pp. 45–52; Serpieri, pp. 49 f.
[2] Countess E. Martinengo Cesaresco, *Lombard Studies* (London, 1902), p. 197.

Italy. Sometimes more than half the product, sometimes less, has gone to the tenant, and the form which his own contribution to the production has taken has been equally changeful.[1]

A variable form of agreement frequently to be met in the North is the mixed contract (*contratto misto*). Under it the tenant gives a portion of his product — of wheat, for example — to the proprietor, and a money payment also. Sundry services and dues, survivals of a feudal custom, have also been rendered, but these have in recent years been declining, the tendency being to a sharper separation of landlord and tenant.[2]

The small or medium lease at a fixed rental in product or money has become increasingly common. In lower Venetia are many examples of leases of estates of twenty to fifty hectares, which are sometimes further sublet. Such contracts have not usually been recorded in writing and have been tacitly renewed at the end of the year. Although a change of tenancy has been easy, contracts have generally been renewed, and there are instances in which the same tenant has cultivated for as long as fifty years. In some places, as in the province of Milan, the leased land is a kind of appendage to the laborer's house and is worked by his family while he is employed in the expanding manufacturing enterprises of the region.[3]

In the Lombard plain and in part of Piedmont, the large lease has been usual, corresponding with the large estates above considered. The leaseholder has belonged to the middle class and has brought to bear a considerable though mainly traditional agricultural competence. He makes a contract not essentially different in its terms from one of four centuries earlier. He may

---

[1] On the mezzadria, see *Inch. Agr.*, iv[ii], pp. 444–450; vi[i], pp. 79–81, 133; viii[i], p. 548; *I contratti agrarii* (*cit.*), pp. 46–48, 124–127, 242–245; Gallenga, *Country life*, etc., p. 91; L. Jarach, "Dell' emigrazione delle donne e dei minorenni bellunesi nel Trentino e nel Tirolo meridionale," *Boll. Emig.*, 1912, No. 12, pp. 47–86; Grizi, pp. 63–66.

[2] *I contratti agrarii*, pp. 53–55, 249 f.; Serpieri, p. 309; Martinengo Cesaresco, p. 201.

[3] Serpieri, p. 351; *Inch. Agr.*, iv[ii], pp. 451–468; *I contratti agrarii*, pp. 48–53, 128–131, 245–248; *Variazioni del fitto*, pp. 1–96; G. Cavaglieri, " L'emigrazione dal Polesine (1881–1901)," *Riforma Sociale*, October 15 and November 15, 1902, pp. 1036 f.

not sublet, he may make no betterments except on written power, and he pays an annual rental for an agreed space of nine, twelve, or eighteen years, commonly for nine years, following this term by a renewal for an equal period. Since he is in charge of an extremely complicated system of agriculture, the leaseholder in the irrigated plain has of necessity the qualities of a skilled manager. Mainly to his capacities and energies is due the extraordinary development of this region.

In the course of time such a tenant of the large estate is usually succeeded by his own son. After the agricultural crisis of the early eighties, which induced a substitution of rice culture and fodder for grain, the class of tenants developed a more characteristically capitalist bent, became more genuinely entrepreneurs, and even formed associations of their professional kind.[1]

Such, in bare outline, is the form which the agricultural system of the North takes. On its fitness for accomplishing its own purposes, a word must next be said.

It is possible to write much in praise of the small property as such and yet necessary to point out serious faults in the institution as it has developed in North Italy. In Udine, Sondrio, and the other mountainous regions, with their short season and stony soil, the ordinary small estate cannot yield enough to allow even moderate comfort in living. If such Lilliputian holdings are to be regretted, still more is the irrational mode of their subdivision to be deplored.

"A father," wrote Jacini, "who left to his three sons a property of six hectares, constituted of three equal parts, one of meadow, one of arable land, and one of chestnut grove, could not assign one such part to each son, even though the parts were equal in value, because it would be needful to give to each a portion of field, of meadow, and of grove, in order that each could meet the demands of his own domestic economy; . . . since meadow, field, and grove are in different places, half the day may be spent by the cultivating proprietor in going from one place to another, as he must when different tasks have to be performed at the same time."[2]

Cottage, barn, and the rest are similarly divided. Small wonder then that backward methods of production prevail, even in places

---

[1] Rovelli, pp. 49–78.   [2] *Inch. Agr.*, vi[i], p. 44.

where the soil is comparatively rich. Small wonder that the owners become litigious, accepting the fact of their proverb—in this country of proverbs—"who owns land must fight."[1]

In North Italy, at least, the mezzadria contract, as already indicated, has been in declining favor. For the proprietor it has been insufficiently productive. This has been partly because, as Gallenga long ago pointed out, the master has been unintelligent and has illiberally refused to make improvements.[2] But it has also been because the proprietor, even when his improvements might soon be remunerative, has refused to make them, for the reason that only half their product would go to him. Correspondingly, the tenant would spare his oxen, when the soil was stubborn, rather than yield half the product of the costly extra effort to the proprietor; and he would rarely himself undertake improvements. Heavy demands are made upon the proprietor, who must turn up at all seasons when the crops ripen and find a purchaser. And always, for the smaller crops at least, there is the chance that the tenant will surreptitiously secrete some—it is more than a desire to pun that popularly makes the mezzadro into a *mezzo-ladro* (half-thief). To these difficulties must be added a lack of agricultural knowledge and an insufficient employment of modern implements and machines.[3] While the contratto misto never gives way to the mezzadria, supersession in the opposite direction has been frequent. The proprietor is then encouraged to make larger expenditures for improvement of the soil and the land becomes more productive. Much of the most successful agriculture in North Italy has developed under this contract.

On the small properties, whether worked by their owners or under some form of contract, backward methods of production, it may now be said by way of generalization, have been usual. Absolutely primitive plows, harrows, and other tools have been

---

[1] *Chi ha terra ha guerra.*   [2] *Country Life*, etc., p. 91.

[3] See, *e.g.*, L. Garbaglia, " Intorno alla mezzeria piemontese e alla sua riforma," *Riforma Sociale*, September–October, 1906, pp. 688–698. To realize the defects of this contract in the North, one has only to compare it with the social, economic, and technical conditions of success as they were formulated by the first Congresso Nazionale della Mezzadria, held at Bologna, January, 1913; see *Bollettino dell' Ufficio di Lavoro*, February, 1913, pp. 208 f.

common, though decreasingly so in recent decades. On two-thirds of the land of the Lombard hill district, the plows were reported by the *Inchiesta Agraria* to be primitive, and less than mediocre in accomplishment.[1] " The plow has a colter of iron, but the spade has an edge of gold," it is said; the proverb, how-ever, reflects the poorness of the plow as well as the competence of its rival when managed by abundant human labor. Rotation and fertilizers have been modernized only slowly and only par-tially, and bookkeeping has been absent.

The highest development of agriculture has come under the lease at a fixed rental, where the risk is borne entirely by the ten-ant. It has been successful where only one or two main crops have been in question — as in much of the Lombard plain — and also in the undulating country and where that agriculture prevails which visiting foreigners have so often admired: the utilization of the land for endless rows of mulberry trees, with a diversified agriculture about their bases. Though the saying is not closely true that "the shadow of the mulberry is a golden shadow,"—the shadow being detrimental, and defoliation and other operations hindering the growth below — yet the total production of these areas is much enhanced by such various plainting.

Under the smaller leases, the term of which has commonly been for a year only, the tenant is least willing to apply capital of his own. Where the contract's duration is longest, care of the land is best. Even then, however, the tenant is led to exploit the soil in the later stages of his control. In Venetia much stress has been laid on this fault.[2] Strangely enough, even in Lower Lombardy, a competent accounting system, with the needed regard for depreciation, is rare.

The greatest failing of the tenants on the large estates is that, with a few praiseworthy exceptions, they still concern themselves very slightly with the interests of their workers — a policy from which inevitably the output itself must suffer.[3] Lacking a per-manent tie, they have had no permanent interest. As late as the eighties the extensive lands of the Piedmontese charitable cor-

[1] *Inch. Agr.*, vi[i], p. 70.   [3] Rovelli, p. 72.
[2] *Ibid.*, iv[ii], pp. 451–468; Cavaglieri, p. 1037.

porations were let at auction, a procedure unlikely to insure a wise and sympathetic management. A great farm has been a thing to be exploited, and its workers with it.

It is clear that we face here, as in South Italy, an evil deriving from the fact that those who own the lands do not cultivate them. The proprietor in business, the professions, government service, or simply at leisure, has scorned the country. How trenchantly Cavour put the need for a better-knit rural society!

It is difficult to measure justly how much good can be brought into a community of poor and ignorant cultivators by a family, in easy circumstances, that is conscious of its duties. This good is not noisy or spectacular, does not receive the sounding approbation of the newspapers, is voted no distinction in the academies, yet is non the less far-reaching in its effects.[1]

The few large proprietors who cultivated their estates did so generally without much competence, he indicated; and, being himself an admirable farmer, he spoke with authority.

The indifferent proprietor has only reflected the general attitude of the city towards the country. So it has been in Piedmont, so in Lombardy. Lombard history has been a municipal history, in which the rural classes have never had a real place; the attitude towards them, whether of bourgeoisie or patricians, has been one of condescension and disesteem — whereof a witness remains in the general terms *villano* and *paesano*, common enough throughout Italy.

Circumstances of production which make for a scanty fruitage, or a system of production which yields but slim rewards to many of the cultivators, these largely account for the hardships of living which determine emigration to other lands. In the pictures which have been given us of the conditions of income and living of the agricultural classes, particularly in the period of rising emigration, we can appreciate these hardships. Morpurgo, author of the report on Venetia in the *Inchiesta Agraria*, quoted with approval an earlier comment in these terms: " Happy that family which can end the year without incurring indebtedness; most rare

[1] From a letter, written in 1844, cited in *Inch. Agr.*, viii[i], pp. 536–538. Cf. E. Visconti, *Cavour agricoltore, lettere inedite di Camillo Cavour a Giacinto Corio,* Florence, 1913.

those families which can make any saving, and in these last years
certainly none!" The statement refers not only to the Alpine
proprietors but to the contract cultivators of the plain as well;
and it is further declared that the daily expenditure for each
member of a family, according to a rough average, was only half
a lira.[1] Concerning the Friuli, land of the small property, he
wrote, "From Ampezzo down, all along the mountain, the product of the soil gives a bare sustenance to the population for a part
of the year, less than one-half"; and again, "We are upon a territory the cultivation of which ought at least to keep the cultivator alive. But if all stay there is no pulling through."[2] And
of Belluno similarly, were there no emigration, he held, "the
affirmation is sad but true: here men would die of starvation."[3]
The small proprietors of that province were gradually losing their
hold. "Even those proprietors who, without having been in easy
circumstances, had in the past lived upon the earnings of their
lands, are today reduced to dolorous conditions, and most of their
lands are burdened with mortgages."[4] Not different, except
somewhat in degree, was the situation in the other provinces of
Venetia. For years previously the value of land had fallen.

In Piedmont and Lombardy the poverty of the small proprietors has been little less pressing than in upper Venetia. "Very
assiduous, sober, economical and well-behaved," those of Piedmont were held to be,[5] but the task of making a comfortable
living in the set conditions of poor soil, long winter, and an unen-
lightened technique, lay beyond such qualities.

Unequal conditions have prevailed among those who have
cultivated the soil under contract. Nearly everywhere the share
cultivators have had to accept a pittance; so in Venetia, so in
Piedmont, so in Lombardy — the conditions in recent years being
scarcely less oppressive than those of thirty years ago. Among
those who have paid fixed rentals, a moderate prosperity has in
some regions existed; in others, suffering has followed unless the
profits from good harvests were saved for the stress times of poor

---

[1] *Inch. Agr.*, iv[i], p. 116.
[2] *Ibid.*, iv[i], pp. 103 f. Cf. Cosattini, p. 72.
[3] *Inch. Agr.*, iv[i], p. 20.
[4] *Ibid.*, iv[ii], p. 350.
[5] *Ibid.*, viii[i], p. 620.

years; and sometimes the conditions have been unmitigatedly bad for years on end. Like the small proprietors, the contract cultivators have been among the sufferers from severe blights in the nineteenth century, from the coming, for example, of the oïdium, after 1850, which destroyed all the vines of Lombardy, later from the phylloxera; and, not less seriously, from the appearance of a disease afflicting the silkworm which would have quite destroyed the silk-raising industry had not more resistant breeds been brought to Italy from the ports of Japan, newly opened to trade and civilization.[1]

When the condition of proprietor or contract cultivator is at its lowest it can generally be assimilated to that of the hired laborer. In Friuli, when not merely a harvest hand, the hired laborer is the *sottano* or underling. Paying an annual rental which, in the first years of the present century, ran to about one hundred lire, he receives from his master the use of a miserable hut and of a plot of land sufficient in good years — and then only — to provide his dependents with polenta. He and one or two members of his family must be ready at any time to work for the master for a wage sometimes under a lira per day, which may be credited to rent. His pig is his savings bank, which at the end of the year enables him to pay the balance of his rent. Attached to the large property, he has little liberty of movement, renouncing, in exchange for steadiness of place, the chance to do harvest work at the high wages received by independent workers. In a similar condition is the *boaro*, different only in that no part of his income is paid in money. A sheer insufficiency of food is less common than formerly; and employment is surer, except for the unsuccessful worker to whom it may presently be refused altogether. Morpurgo wrote of the group, that their arms exceeded the demand for them and their mouths the means of subsistence.[2]

Although the name sottano is not current in Belluno, Treviso, and Venetia, the hired class abounds, and is similarly circumstanced, being a kind of permanent proletariat. The unattached

[1] On these blights, see *Inch. Agr.*, iv[i], pp. 60–63; Martinengo Cesaresco, pp. 216 f.

[2] *Inch. Agr.*, iv[i], pp. 14–16; see also pp. 63, 104. Cf. Cosattini, pp. 74 f.

worker is commoner than in Udine. In Rovigo the class was said to be generally in debt until the middle nineties; thereafter, under increasingly felt needs, to be still discontented.[1]

In Piedmont the laborers hired by the day were held to constitute, three or four decades ago, a fifth part of the agricultural population, and its most wretched part. Though wages had risen in previous years, it was still almost impossible to live by work alone; hence frequent abandonment of an employer before advances could be repaid, and many agricultural thefts, and the absence of any relationship of affection between master and worker.[2]

Not otherwise has been the situation in Lombardy. Bread may be got more surely in the plains than in the hills, but even the best paid *contadino obbligato* is always at the beck of his employer and passively obeys orders. He readily changes his abode as the size of his family changes, or for other reasons, and all cordiality toward his employer is lacking. His family is scattered over the fields in the summer, in the winter is housed with other families. Below this group in condition are the unattached day laborers; above it are sundry more specialized types. The dampness of the farmhouses, the unhygienic presence in them of the farm animals, recall the houses of the mountains. " So they have been for two hundred years, so may they stay a little longer," was the proprietors' attitude as recorded by the *Inchiesta Agraria*. The improvements in earning and living conditions which have come in the last thirty-five years, somewhat in response to legislation, have been meager enough.[3]

Much of what has been written of the tax system of South Italy holds of the North. The same heavy land tax has existed, heavier,

---

[1] *Inch. Agr.*, iv[i], pp. 18, 20, 24, 64; Cavaglieri, pp. 1043 f.

[2] *Inch. Agr.*, viii[i], pp. 621, 624, 805, 965.

[3] *Ibid.*, vi[i], pp. 139–143, 151–155; Mosso, pp. 129 f.; Serpieri, *passim;* E. Conti, *La proprietà fondiaria nel passato e nel presente* (Milan, 1905), Pt. ii; Rovelli, *passim*, esp. pp. 78–123. The study by Rovelli, particularly thorough and illuminating, follows competently, despite its narrower scope, upon the classic early work of S. Jacini, *La proprietà fondiaria e le popolazioni agricole in Lombardia*, Milan, 1857, which has been available to me only in the German translation of like date, published in Milan and elsewhere.

it would seem, than any beyond the Alps, and the same great increases in the provincial and communal rates have taken place. At the time of the *Inchiesta Agraria*, the grist tax was deeply resented, while there was rejoicing at the disappearance of the old Austrian *testatico*, a kind of poll tax. Recently the catastal reforms have reduced much of the inequality of burden that had prevailed. Certain specially exasperating taxes, like that on farm animals, and many local import duties, have been abolished. The weight of taxes in general has been much more bearable than in the South, because of the greater well-being of the people and the ampler range of objects of taxation. Not least, the pronouncedly higher level of general intellectual equipment and accomplishment has made for more wisdom in expenditure. To enter upon an examination of the respects in which the taxes constitute a burden upon the classes of people that emigrate would be to repeat essentially the argument detailed above, to which a reference may suffice.

We are concerned with a population that, by and large, stands well above that of South Italy. As regards wages and employment, farm contracts, housing, dress, food, the conditions, low as they are, could be worse. The pellagra has never been comparable with the southern malaria in its ravages. A better clergy, a religion less suffused with superstition than in the South, have allowed the growth of a more liberal spirit. And the school system is better — though gravely defective still, and constituting one of the most vexatious problems of the entire region. In the days of the *Inchiesta Agraria* the rural schools were generally attended only in the winter months, irregularly at that, and with little profit, partly because of the remoteness of the schoolhouses, partly because of the parents' need of utilizing the labor of their children. The newer conditions are better, a little. But even in so favorably placed a region as the province of Upper Milan the communes generally provide only the elementary inferior course, poorly attended after the winter months — indeed from the moment when cocoon raising begins — and taught mainly by women who rarely have less than sixty or seventy pupils. Under these circumstances, in this region, there are few who do not learn to write their names, but many who carry away only a meager knowledge of other things, that is soon forgotten.[1]

What has so far been said points clearly to conditions which many persons must desire to escape. But emigration from North Italy is a complex phenomenon depending upon some things besides an agricultural situation. From the mountains emigration has been age-long; from Carnia, in the Friuli, it has been important since the sixteenth century. Grazing and agriculture do not support many people and other industries are few; even domestic textile working declines when machine-made goods that are pretty and cheap (though they be not durable) can be purchased. Later begins the emigration from the plains. Lacking a tradition, not yet habitual, it commences modestly, acquires momentum quickly, and proceeds feverishly till accumulated pressure has subsided. But such a course is possible only in modern times when receptive and accessible nations exist elsewhere. Consider the amazing rise and fluctuations of the overseas emigration of Rovigo, responsive to the offer of gratuitous passage to Brazil.

Year	Emigrants	Year	Emigrants
1886	70	1891	16,625
1887	1,853	1892	778
1888	13,736	1893	1,601
1889	1,137	1894	4,737
1890	92	1895	11,337

In the three years of most copious emigration there were villages from which nearly half the inhabitants went away; in fifteen years, 64,500 out of an average population of 220,000 departed.[2] This was a permanent emigration, akin in its causes and its developments to that from the southern compartments; the tradition of permanence so started was to continue, while temporary emigration from Rovigo was to begin late and have slight importance.

Farther to the north, in Friuli, has been the greatest source of Italian temporary emigration. Over many years one quarter of

[1] Serpieri, pp. 283, 313.   [2] Cavaglieri, pp. 930 f., 1032, 1045.

the total emigration into Europe came from this region. It is an extraordinary movement and can only be explained if the general account of causes already given be supplemented; for farming folk have not been alone among the emigrants. There are agriculturists who in other countries engage in various sorts of general labor and in small trade. There are also, however, masons, stonecutters, blacksmiths, furnace workers, carpenters, and the like, who have never been in agriculture. Of their sort even a farming community requires a certain number, and since they cannot rise much above the poverty of the rest, they too may be led to emigrate. But the mystifying fact is that in the temporary emigration from the Friuli these more or less skilled workmen, far from being occasional, are a very great part of the emigrants and often indeed the élite of the population. Whence do they come?

It will be time enough to discuss, in later chapters, the opportunities offered to Italian laborers in the countries of Europe. Here suffice it to say that the skilled workmen of Udine have been able to labor abroad upon terms acceptable to their employers and themselves and have found it cheapest to spend the winter in their natal country; they have done better than their agricultural brethren. That is why, counting upon future employment in neighboring countries, the children of Friuli have been trained to the more skilled non-agricultural occupations. As if to prepare themselves to resist the hard toil of later years, boys usually begin with work in the furnaces, in Hungary perhaps or in Germany. A year or two later, drawn perhaps toward the primal trade of all, the mason's, they become hodcarriers, next undertake the coarser forms of masonry and finally the more skilled work with cement and stucco. The winter season may be devoted to the study of a foreign language or attendance at a school where the finer technique of the mason's art is taught.[1] In time many will become contractors, supplying troops of other masons and risking their own capital. By a similar procedure the other sorts of skilled workmen may be developed.[2]

[1] Such schools have various origins. Notable are those maintained by labor organizations and by the philanthropic *Società Umanitaria* (see ch. XXIII below).
[2] Cosattini, pp. 46 f.

What is remarkable in this story is hardly that boys are trained with reference to work in other lands, but rather that as a result of such training a population should grow up which absolutely depended for its livelihood upon employment abroad. Here are scores of thousands of workmen retaining a winter habitat in Venetia who would probably not survive an enforced prolonged stay at home. Indeed, it is likely that they would never have been born, except for the command of sustenance which this temporary emigration has brought into the country. There is here no longer question merely of an outlet for an otherwise starving agricultural population. That exists, but alongside of it is the recurring departure of persons who have never expected to be other than emigrants. And with the passing years of the last quarter century, much even of the agricultural population has become committed to a seasonal emigration, so lessening the strain upon the remaining inhabitants. There is little doubt, for instance, that the annual departure of Bellunese women to the Trentino is to be so explained. In its latest phase, the entire temporary emigration from such a region as Venetia becomes less a movement to assuage hunger than a movement to provide pocket money and a living through the winter.[1]

There is over a great part of North Italy an element absent in much of the South. By the side of a primitive agriculture, or one carried on in unresponsive natural conditions, there is the highly elaborated agriculture in which the workman plays an absolutely essential part and yet is paid scantily. Emphasis is laid in all accounts upon the competition of men against men to secure employment or leases. Sheer numbers press upon each other. Families averaging eight, ten, twelve members, have been common.[2] Where, as in the hill region of Lombardy, circumstances have been kind, there the growing children may secure an eco-

---

[1] This explanation accords with the answers given by emigrants to the question, propounded in 1881 by the Bureau of Statistics, whether they were leaving because of misery at home or to improve their lot elsewhere. To a much greater extent than in the South the second answer was affirmed. On the situation in Udine, see Cosattini, p. 69; on Piedmont, *Inch. Agr.*, viii[i], pp. 766 f. (cf. Mosso, p. 53, on Biella).

[2] Cf. Serpieri, pp. 310 f.

nomic foothold; there every village has its spinning mills able to employ abundant labor. And it happens that the chief industrial section of Italy is in a belt of territory about Milan. Where, however, an alternative and expanding industry does not exist, there, if the population grows, an outlet is possible only through emigration. From Sondrio many depart, and from Cuneo and Torino; for these provinces, or at least their higher parts, offer only agriculture and dairying as livelihoods. Of transoceanic emigration from Piedmont and Lombardy there is today comparatively little, though once a dense current moved to South America; of temporary emigration into Europe there is much. And again, as in Venetia, the phenomenon appears of a specialization of men by trades for emigration, while the women carry on the farm work at home.[1]

For Lombardy, it was noted nearly forty years ago:

In some communes, especially of Como and Bergamo, certain trades are traditional, such, for example, as that of the mason, or stonecutter, or porter, or brazier, or potter; and whoever takes up one of these with the intention of emigrating knows for a certainty that he will have the support of the masters of his place who have preceded him, have already established themselves abroad, have conquered in the struggle for existence and will gladly enrol him in their troop or at least help him and steer him in his first ventures. [2]

Such, then, in its causes and its changing forms has been the emigration from North Italy. That its course has been different from that of South Italy is due first of all to the fact that the conditions of living to be eluded were less wretched than those of the South, and secondly to the accessibility of European labor markets and the quickened growth of industrial activity. The improvement, slight but genuine, which, according to the writers of the *Inchiesta Agraria*, had generally taken place in agricultural conditions over the years 1860–80, is chiefly to be explained by the industrial expansion of that period; and the expansion has since

---

[1] On Piedmont see *Inch. Agr.*, viii[i], p. 608. For the people of Roccabruna, Sig. Baldioli-Chiorando has pointedly written (*op. cit.*, p. 847), "the chief source of wealth is France," whither a third of the population go annually for a six months' stay. Of the emigrants from the province of Cuneo older than twenty years, three-fifths have been between twenty and thirty years of age (*ibid.*, p. 851).

[2] *Inch. Agr.*, vi[i], pp. 44 f.

gone further. Without these labor markets and industrial opportunities, it is reasonable to suppose that in North Italy, as in South, harder terms of living would have come to be and the emigration would have developed a permanent rather than a temporary form. As it is, the dimensions of the whole phenomenon have been the greater because of the maintenance of the custom of large families — but that is a matter to which we shall recur much later in this inquiry.

BOOK III

IN FOREIGN LANDS

CHAPTER VIII

FRANCE

Down from the mountains into the plains the current of men has proceeded from time immemorial. From Alps into lowland has lain the way of the Piedmontese and their neighbors. Generally the lowland has been Italy, but more and more, for a long time past, it has been France.

One current has followed the Mediterranean shore, keeping mainly to the south of the mountain slopes. Another has cut through the Savoyard Alps, by Mont Cenis, and has settled in the east of France; or, passing through Lyons, has followed the Saône and Seine valleys to Paris. The transalpine current has also scattered Italians along the Loire, from Nevers to Angers, and on the southern coasts of Brittany. Though the journey to France has usually been undertaken for a season only, the sojourn there has often been prolonged. In the nineteenth century the temporary immigration of agricultural laborers — men, women, and children — and the establishment of one great city colony, Marseilles, were the characteristic developments. The twentieth has beheld an extraordinary gathering in the mining centers of French Lorraine and a striking expansion of the industrial forms of immigration.

The Italians have come to be the most numerous foreigners in France. In four of the six departments of the country in which aliens most abound, they have been the chief foreign element.[1] In 1851 (when census figures began), they numbered 63,307, or about one-sixth of all the foreigners; in 1886, they were 264,568, or about one-fourth; in 1911, 414,234, or more than a fourth — enough to make a city as large as Genoa and Venice together.

[1] *Résultats statistiques du recensement général de la population effectué le 5 mars, 1911*, i, Pt. i, p. 41. In what follows I have drawn freely upon this work and also, for data involving early censuses, upon an official compilation, *Dénombrement des étrangers en France*, Paris, 1893.

Women have been numerous among them but not many have gone far into France.

With her stationary population and her finely organized industries, France, in the years before the war, had become an outstanding country of immigration. Belgians have long poured over the northern border and for decades led all migrants into France. Luxemburgers, Germans, Swiss, Spaniards in large numbers have penetrated for varying distances into the interior. Yet in nearly every field of labor, the Italians, in recent years, have held a place second to no other foreign nationality. In agriculture and forestry, occupying many immigrants, they have been about 40 per cent; Belgians and Spaniards together, the next largest groups, not much exceeding them. In manufacturing, their chief sphere, they have again been 40 per cent. In transportation they have been nearly two-thirds of all foreigners; in trade more than one-third; in domestic service, a little less than one-third, Germans and Belgians following closely.[1]

A nearer view is perhaps even more impressive. In forestry, besides some 600 persons in charge of operations, the census of 1906 discovered 1700 hired workpeople, actually 6 per cent of all forestry workmen in the country. Since the work places in this industry are scattered, the importance of the Italians could hardly be otherwise inferred than through the census. Some 4000 Italian quarrymen enumerated in the same year were 7 per cent of such workmen in France. In the mines were 6400. Nearly 8000 employed in the chemical factories were 8 per cent of the country's workers. Of 6000 in the textile industries three-quarters were women and girls; nearly all were in the silk mills, for the cotton mills were filled with Belgians. Seventy-seven hundred worked upon the common metals. In ordinary digging and construction were nearly 24,000, more than 7 per cent of the country's supply. So it goes, for these are samples only. Italians engaged on the

---

[1] *Résultats statistiques du recensement général de la population en 1906*, i, Pt. iii, p. 29. In default of later detailed occupational statistics I have found it necessary to rely upon this census. For 1911, I have seen only the collective figures, which show some 31,000 Italians in agriculture and forestry, 124,000 in manufacturing, 29,000 in transportation, 28,000 in trade, 4000 in liberal professions, etc., 19,000 in domestic service.

public works (it is worth noting), before a limiting decree of 1899, were very numerous, averaging nearly half of all employed in the southern departments.[1]

For fifty years past, a diminution of all kinds of agricultural workers has taken place in France. The rural exodus, whatever its compensations, has caused deep concern to the nation; and a rural immigration from neighboring countries has brought only partial alleviation. Among the arriving helpers, the Italians have been second to no other, and probably have been, in number, three-quarters of all.

Only imperfectly has the census revealed their importance. Of small proprietors and tenants — heads of establishments — the 3800 men and more than 4000 women counted in March, 1906, were probably as many as could be found at any other season. Of 8000 isolated workers (*travailleurs isolés*), men and women, the same comment holds. But the 10,000 hired workpeople, of whom three-quarters were men, were certainly only a fraction of those employed later in the year. Belgians were found to be equally numerous with the Italians, and Spaniards about half as numerous, but of these peoples also a later reckoning would have shown more. Still other figures showed Italians occupied in grazing and makers of butter and cheese (present chiefly in the coastal mountains) to be important groups.

To the Alpes-Maritimes some 15,000 a year have come, from Liguria and Piedmont, Umbria and Tuscany. Five or six thousand, mainly women and children, have sufficed for the winter's work entailed by a production of 100,000 hectoliters of olives. Some have later been used for gathering, successively, violets, roses, jasmines, and other flowers, destined to adorn the toilettes of the women of Paris and Berlin. Working in gangs in the autumn and winter, others have prepared the soil for the flowers,

---

[1] Figures are given by L. Rossi, "L'immigrazione italiana nel distretto consolare di Marsiglia," *Emig. e Col.*, 1903, i[1], p. 277. Cf. E. Levasseur, *Questions ouvrières et industrielles en France sous la troisième république* (Paris, 1907), p. 461. On Italian labor on railways (including certain strategic lines), canals, bridges, streets, see, besides L. Rossi (p. 275), the reports of C. Magenta and E. Centurione in *Emig. e Col.*, 1893, pp. 234–238.

and have returned home in the spring. More and more the call for the flower-gardeners has gone forth, and they have been deemed an acceptable labor force, " as far as delicacy and skill are not demanded." [1]

In Var, especially in the harvest season, the Italians have become more and more numerous, the men being employed in digging and the vintage, the women in flower-gardening and in gathering vegetables. After some years of effort they have often bought or rented bits of land, cultivating upon their own account while at the same time hiring out to others.[2] For the other coarser tasks, they have been regarded as indispensable. " When supervised, the men and especially the women, do a greater amount of work than the French. But since they are less intelligent, they cannot be entrusted with tasks demanding initiative." [3]

In that other littoral department of the old Provence, Bouches-du-Rhône, the Italians have been the successors of the mountain folk who once came for the harvest from Aude and Hérault. Many have become permanent residents. Digging, and draining marshes — standing in the water and toiling at all hours — helping in the harvests, they have made themselves almost essential for much of this work. For the vintage they have come by trainloads. " To them," says a French witness, " we owe the transformation of the Camargue into a wine country — a veritable agricultural *tour de force*." In the hilly parts, they have gathered olives, and in the oil factories they have been welcomed as a convenient substitute for French labor.[4]

---

[1] E. Blanchard, *La main-d'œuvre étrangère dans l'agriculture française* (Paris, 1913), pp. 181 f. The general deductions of Blanchard's book rest on a government study of wages (1912) and on evidence gathered personally. Cf. M. Simonetti, "Immigrazione e colonie italiane nel dipartmento delle Alpe Marittime," *Emig. e Col.*, 1903, i^i, pp. 320–325; also A. Souchon, *La crise de la main-d'œuvre agricole en France* (Paris, 1914), p. 49.

[2] Ministère de l'Agriculture. *La petite propriété rurale en France. Enquêtes monographiques (1908–1909)*, (Paris, 1909), p. 259.

[3] Blanchard, p. 183. Cf. P. A. Burdese, "Il dipartimento del Varo e la colonia italiana," *Emig. e Col.*, 1903, i^i, pp. 308–314.

[4] C. F. Caillard, *Les migrations temporaires dans les campagnes françaises* (Paris, 1912), pp. 66 f. Cf. Blanchard, pp. 184–186, and M. Lair, " Les ouvriers étrangers dans l'agriculture française," *Revue Économique Internationale*, March, 1907, esp. p. 555.

To Aude and Hérault, also to Gard, many thousands have come. Though the Spaniards have been the chief vintagers, the Italians, by their arduous labor in grading, drainage, and irrigation, have rendered great services to the viticulture of Languedoc. They have partly taken the place of workers who disappeared during the phylloxera crisis a quarter century ago. Some spend a part of their time in fishing upon their own account off the coast and living in gypsy encampments, while awaiting new work in the fields.[1]

While dealing with the South of France, it cannot be amiss to consider the strange situation of Corsica. To this department, subject to an unremitting emigration of its own sons, many thousands of Italians have come annually for a six months' stay, spreading in gangs over the island. Perhaps as many as 25,000 have taken up permanent residence. Since the native population has no love for toiling in the fields " the sad truth emerges that the cultivation of Corsica is almost entirely the work of foreigners. If the help of the Lucchese and Tuscans were to fail, the position of this department would become truly critical."[2]

In the Basses-Alpes and Vaucluse numerous Italians have found employment. The Piedmontese long migrated into the East of France, even as far as the Nièvre, to carry on the exacting forestry operations of the Côte-d'Or, as well as the general work of agriculture; but they have now ceased to come, preferring the South. In the Savoies, the heavy Italian immigration of former years has been declining.[3]

Most of these immigrants have worked for wages. What of the thousands of agricultural proprietors counted by the census ? Dwelling chiefly in the Alpes-Maritimes and the Bouches-du-Rhône, they were workers who had saved enough to buy and cultivate here and there a strip of land set free by the *morcellement* of a moderately sized estate, or too small for the needs of a French

---

[1] Caillard, pp. 64 f. See also M. Camicia, "Gli italiani nel dipartimento dell' Hérault," *Emig. e Col.*, 1903, i¹, pp. 315–319; Souchon, *loc. cit.;* Lair, *loc. cit.*

[2] Caillard, pp. 68–70. Cf. Blanchard, p. 186, and E. Colucci, " Notizie sulla popolazione italiana in Corsica," *Emig. e Col.*, 1903, i¹, pp. 326–329; *idem*, report on Bastia district, *Emig. e Col.*, 1893, pp. 212–216.

[3] Caillard, pp. 63, 83–107; Blanchard, p. 186.

family, or "abandoned," as our New England farms are abandoned. It is claimed however that they have worked these lands less capably than the French.[1]

Yet in the last analysis, it is not as proprietors but as hired folk that the Italians have been mainly profitable to France. In the oil and wine departments, and where flowers and vegetables are raised, they have been described by French students as " absolutely indispensable " and as " contributing greatly to the agricultural prosperity of southern France." Without them much irrigation would not have been undertaken. Where strength is needed rather than deftness, where a temporary increase of the labor force is asked, where an expansion of agriculture is desired in a population that, apart from the Italians, tends to decline, there they have had a rôle. The employer has found them more manageable than the French workmen and has known that the latter, even when available, would cost him more.[2]

Let us take a glimpse at some of the principal settlements of the Italians in France.

At Paris, in 1911, there were nearly 34,000 of these people, living in half a dozen quarters, and making the largest and the most picturesque of all the foreign colonies in the metropolis.[3] In no other considerable Italian colony of the world has the artistic note been so dominant. Besides the student groups, there have been the literary folk, the musicians, including those of the street; the plaster workers who utilize the labor of their own or others' children in making statuettes and vending them in the streets; the models — not only boys and girls, but their parents often — the father posing as the Christ or an apostle and in the dead season acting for the cinematograph, the mother posing as

---

[1] Blanchard, pp. 195 f.; Min. de l'Agr., *La petite propriété rurale*, pp. 99, 259. In the reports contained in *Emig. e Col.*, 1903, i[1], there is testimony of proprietorship in sundry provinces.

[2] For the quotations, see Blanchard, p. 180 (cf. Caillard, p. 149). See also Lair, pp. 552–563.

[3] Thousands more were in outlying parts. Seventy years ago, Correnti claimed, doubtless with exaggeration, that the Italians in Paris were 20,000, standing well in music, letters, the theater, banking, and the jeweller's trade. (Correnti, *Annuario statistico italiano, Anno I, 1857-58*, pp. 456 f.)

peasant or Madonna; the ballet dancers; the men dressmakers; and those artists of the kitchen who compose menus and devise rare dishes.[1]

The unskilled laborers of the glass works have generally been Italian, preferred to the French because their children work too; and in the earthenware manufacture, the fashioners of stove tiles have, in recent years, nearly all been Italian, because a generation ago the French workmen sought to check competition by limiting apprenticeship, and the Italians invited their friends from Castella Monte to bring their skill to Paris. Finally, there have been thousands of building workmen, a persistently increasing group, evidence that the newer emigration has at last been superposed upon the old. Though the Italians have often brought their

---

[1] Mlle. Schirmacher, *La spécialisation du travail par nationalités à Paris* (Paris, 1908), pp. 140–148. In an eloquent, if curious, work, the fruit of wide searching in books and in life, *Larmes et sourires de l'émigration italienne* (Paris, 1909), pp. 21–186, R. Paolucci de' Calboli treats of certain nomad types that have come to France, as a rule to Paris, over a long stretch of time. Italian models, girls and men, first came in the seventeenth century, when indeed the occupation as such first became recognized; and they soon became numerous as well as prized. In the period 1850–73, while the Roman type declined, padroni brought girls from the South of Italy. A general decrease ensued, a conservative calculation at the time of de' Calboli's writing putting their numbers at 800–850.

Long before bootblacks existed in Italy, before indeed the language had a word for them, Savoyard and Piedmontese boy chimney-sweeps in France, especially Paris, began to use the soot of the chimneys to prepare a blacking. In the eighteenth century many earned their living by polishing boots. In the early nineteenth, they numbered thousands in Paris. After the middle of the century they gradually ceased to come. The 300–400 present in France in the early twentieth century were all in the South, especially at Marseilles.

From Lucca, later from Pisa, Massa Carrara, and Florence, came immigrants, mainly boys, to work as makers of statuettes. Their increase became rapid after 1830.

To France, much more than to any other country, came Piedmontese glaziers, nomadic only with the advent of the nineteenth century. Several hundreds a year came to Paris. From September till April they wandered about in a rather profitable search for broken windows and a chance to repair them. In 1888 the hostility of French workers became pronounced and thereafter the occupation was doomed.

Street musicians, players of various instruments, including after a time many who carried the Barbary organ, came in the eighteenth and nineteenth centuries. In 1867, 1544 were claimed to be in Paris. After 1874 a decline set in, becoming pronounced after the assassination of President Carnot. In recent years troupes singing Neapolitan songs have come.

families to Paris, they have been less likely than other immigrants
to stay there permanently.[1]

How broadly different from this colony is that of Marseilles!
At least 125,000 Italians have been there in recent years, a veritable city in themselves, as large as Messina, and a fifth part —
or more — of Marseilles itself. Add those of the outlying districts
and the total mounts to 150,000. In this colony, the beginnings
of which date too far back to be traced, are found all social classes;
in fact, many of the old families of the city claim a Ligurian
origin. · In the recent decades of rapid industrial progress, the
Italian population has grown faster than the French. Tuscans
and Piedmontese predominate, but more and more South Italians
have come. The annual arrivals have numbered about five or six
thousand, the departures half as many.[2]

It is a rather compact settlement which the Italians have made
in old Marseilles. But semi-rural occupations and suburban
factories have led also to a degree of centrifugal colonization.[3]
In the quarters of Saint-Jean, the Mairie, and two or three others,
unchanged in their characteristics for centuries, live the fisherfolk
and the South Italian element — sellers of fruit, vegetables, fish,
and small wares. Of some 2400 fishermen in Marseilles a majority
have been claimed to be of Italian origin; their number is aug-
mented in the summer by Neapolitans. Many Italians have been
employed as longshoremen, in street paving and maintenance, and
in the salt works. Thousands have engaged in manufactures:
in candle making, in soap making (an old industry, now much
expanded, with factories both in the city and its suburbs), in the
preparation of olive oil (nearly all of 5000 workpeople have been
held to be Italians), in the operations of the potteries and brick

[1] Schirmacher, pp. 129, 136-139; L. Villari, " Gli italiani in Francia, I," *Vita
Italiana all' Estero*, March, 1913, pp. 189-198.

[2] See a study by G. Lelli, chancellor of the Italian Chamber of Commerce at
Marseilles, submitted to the Milan Exposition and published as " Gli italiani in
Marsiglia," in *Boll. Emig.*, 1908, No. 19, pp. 53-69. See also G. Pio di Savoia, com-
munication in *Rivista di Emigrazione*, May, 1910, pp. 59 f. On an earlier epoch,
cf. E. Rostand, *Les questions d'économie sociale dans une grande ville populaire*
(Paris, 1889), pp. 417 ff. On various special aspects see Paolucci de' Calboli, *op. cit.*

[3] On the Italians' distribution over the city, see A. A. Bernardy, " L'Italia a
Marsiglia," *Rivista Coloniale*, July 25-August 10, 1911, pp. 225, 227.

kilns. Most of the shoe workers have been Italians, some employed in the factories, others carrying on a domestic industry, chiefly for their compatriots. Much else that is characteristic, however, like the boy bootblacks of the streets, I must pass by. It may be said in general that the most toilsome tasks of this great city, the most unhealthful, the least well-paid, have been almost exclusively in Italian hands.

Lyons is the center of a district comprising the departments of the Rhône, Loire, Ain, and Isère where thousands of Italians have for many years earned a living. As long as half a century ago the colony was large. Today it is not the men, numerous as general and building laborers and as mill workmen, but the women and children, who give this region its distinction; in the Loire they even exceed the men in number. The silk industry in its growth in the last twenty-five years has utilized ever larger numbers of Italian operatives, and the glass industry, originally derived from Italy, has employed three or four thousand Italian boys at a time — French parents have not permitted their children to do the exhausting work required. The boys employed in the glass works used to travel to France afoot, but the later way has been to come by sea from Naples to Marseilles.[1]

The growth in numbers of the Italians of Toulon accounts in large part for their growth in the department of Var. " At Toulon a goodly portion of the names over the shop windows are Italian. To that nationality belong the servant classes of the hotels, all the nurses, a large part of the workmen. A third of the population of La Seyne (ten minutes' distance from Toulon) is Italian; the 7000 inhabitants of La Londe are nearly all Italian." [2] This was some years ago. At one time they were numerously employed in the

---

[1] E. Perrod, " Immigrazione e colonia italiana nel distretto consolare di Lione," *Emig. e Col.*, 1903, i[i], pp. 222–235; *idem*, " I minorenni italiani nelle industrie lionesi," *Boll. Emig.*, 1902, No. 9, pp. 50–57; V. Ferliga, " L'emigrazione italiana in Alsazia Lorena e Francia," *Rivista di Emigrazione*, October–November, 1909, pp. 22–31; Beatrice Berio (Segretariato Permanente Femminile per la Tutela delle Donne e dei Franciulli Emigranti), *Relazione sull' emigrazione delle donne e dei fanciulli italiani nella Francia meridionale* (Rome, 1912), pp. 7–42; L. Villari, " Gli italiani in Francia, III," *Vita Italiana all' Estero*, May, 1913, pp. 364–368; Paolucci de' Calboli, Pt. ii, ch. i.

[2] Burdese, p. 312; cf. Ferliga, p. 35.

great arsenal, but from it, for many years, all unnaturalized foreigners have been excluded. Once, too, they were a third of the laborers in the naval works at La Seyne, but since 1903 the law has permitted only a fifth to be foreign. The fortifications of Toulon are largely the work of Italians.[1]

The Briey district — to describe it as it was before the German invasion of 1914 — has been nearly everything that Marseilles has not been. Composed of men workers, never women, of men regarding themselves as only temporarily in France, it is a community that has grown with astonishing rapidity, and wholly in recent years; where labor, far from being varied, regular, and relatively light, has been hard, coarse, and exacting.

The Briey basin lies in the departments of Meurthe-et-Moselle and the Meuse. In what became German Lorraine in 1870, great iron mines had long existed. But it was not known that the belt of ore which extends into Luxemburg and Belgium underlies also the meadows of French Lorraine, and it was not until the last years of the nineteenth century that the range of the French deposits was guessed. A decade followed in which the mines were opened with feverish haste, so that they soon yielded three-fourths or more of the total output of French ore. What has been rare in France, the great expansion of the population of a department, happened in Meurthe-et-Moselle. Cities sprang up as if by magic. Tranquil villages burst their bounds and became bustling centers of life. Homécourt, Joeuf, Auboué, Tucquegnieux, Hussigny, Pienne, Longwy, Jasny, Moutiers leaped quickly to importance. But they were not French cities: they resembled rather the mining towns of our own American West. For the French countryfolk held aloof from them, and the miners who came from the coal fields were few. Natives of France were presently (it was claimed) only a fifth of the workers; 15 per cent more were of various nationalities, and all the rest — nearly two-thirds of all — were Italians.[2] In the entire department of Meurthe-et-Moselle,

---

[1] Cf. Berio, p. 59.

[2] According to Dr. A. Vinci, " L'emigrazione italiana nella regione di Briey," *Boll. Emig.*, 1913, No. 12, p. 15.

there had been in 1901 only 6000 of these immigrants. Early in
1910, an estimate put them at 30,000. By the middle of 1913,
they were 46,755 in a foreign population of 74,073, representing
some eighteen nationalities.[1] To these might be added some
1500 living in the department of the Meuse, because it belongs to
the same industrial area.

The Italians came to Briey by way of Metz, after having been
enrolled by their employers while in Switzerland or Italy; ultimately they came from Lombardy, Piedmont, Venetia, Romagna,
Tuscany, the Abruzzi, and Sardinia.[2] Besides settling apart from
other nationalities, they were marked off from each other by dialect and origin. Permanent residence, however, it was soon
clear, did not attract them. Officials of various plants told the
Italian consul that their typical sojourn was of three months, and
that often, after only a few weeks in one place, they would shift to
other employers. A certain capriciousness, a readiness to take
umbrage, was complained of.

By no means all of the Italians were miners. Four or five thousand were railway workers for the Compagnie de l'Est, or general building laborers employed sometimes by Italian contractors.
A great many were occupied in the iron and steel works, and it is
even claimed that most of the blast furnace employees were
Italians. When all is said, however, it is chiefly as miners or
miners' men that they have counted, a group less likely than

[1] According to the count of the subprefecture of the Briey circuit (cited by
Vinci, p. 3). See also the volume by de Canisy, noted on page 537, *infra*.

[2] In an admirable study of the metal industry in Briey Professor Vignes relates
how the companies sought their men outside of France, especially in Italy. First
they utilized foreign agencies at Basel and Chiasso. Then they recruited their
workers directly. But the latter practice came to an end after an amusing episode:
the representative of a leading company was returning through Germany with
some cars of selected men in order to benefit by the reduced tariffs which Germany
accorded to immigrant workers — and he left his men at the Metz station while
he, during the prolonged wait of the train, went to see the town. Upon his return
not a man was left — all had been persuaded to take jobs at the German mills!
Subsequently the common way was for a committee to act in Milan, with the legal
consent of the Italian authorities, the French companies shouldering the transportation charge and a fee of nine francs per man. (M. Vignes, ".Le bassin de Briey,"
Revue d'Économie Politique, five chapters, 1912–13; esp. ch. v, November–December,
1913, pp. 683 f.)

others to go home for the winter; and of such underground workers they were probably a majority.[1]

That the toil of her Italian visitors has contributed in noteworthy ways to the production of France needs now no argument. Even though it is usually the humblest employments and the lowest places of authority that they have held, doing the tasks of obedience and not of command,[2] such has been the reliance placed upon them in the economic system of the country that should they fail, the necessary readjustments would be both difficult and costly. And this the employing classes have recognized.[3]

French workmen, on the other hand, have not received the Italians with open arms. Since they have regarded themselves as sacrificed to their employers' appetite for gain, it is worth while to ask why. An episode in the history of the iron industry illustrates their reasoning. The workers in Lorraine had been unorganized, and all attempts at organization had come to naught. At Thil a strike was called, but when it ended, twenty-nine days later, a third of the strikers, mainly Italians, had gone home, or

---

[1] Vignes, pp. 686 f., 696. In *Boll. Emig.* are many references to the colony. See especially Vinci, pp. 3–31; the author (whose report is dated February, 1913) was a consular agent in Briey as well as an *attaché* of the Emigration Service. See also Ferliga (whose report was made to the Segretariato Toscano per l'Emigrazione), *op. cit.;* " L'immigrazione italiana nei circondari di Briey e di Nancy," *Emig. e Col.,* 1903, i[1], pp. 218–221 (based on information supplied by an official, Bidou, of the Longwy works); G. Reynaud, "La colonie italienne d'Homécourt," *Musée Sociale,* June, 1910; A. Merrheim, " L'organisation patronale en France. I. La métallurgie," *Le Mouvement Socialiste,* July 15, 1908, pp. 5–25; L. and M. Bonneff, *La vie tragique des travailleurs, enquêtes sur la condition économique et morale des ouvriers et ouvrières d'industrie* (Paris, 1914), pp. 93–149; L. Villari, " Gli italiani in Francia, II," *Vita Italiana all' Estero,* April, 1913, pp. 295–302. Cf. the reports of C. Magenta on Cette, and of E. Centurione on Nice in *Emig. e Col.,* 1893, pp. 234–238.

[2] The census of 1906 classified as follows the Italians earning a living: 25,081 heads of establishments (especially in agriculture and trade); 9021 salaried employees (especially in trade; few in manufactures); 61,176 independent workpeople (manufactures, trade, agriculture); 5100 unemployed (especially in manufactures); and 135,543 hired workpeople (numerous in all branches). See vol. i[iii], pp. 58 f.

[3] They have sometimes asked for more immigration. See H. F., " La main-d'œuvre étrangère," *Bulletin Trimestrielle de l'Association Internationale pour la Lutte contre le Chômage,* July–September, 1912, p. 533.

to Luxemburg or Germany. At Hussigny, 350 struck; but two-thirds of them were promptly expelled from France by the authorities and their places taken by newly imported workmen. From Italy a skilled organizer was sent to help, but his efforts to unite the workers failed in turn. Mobile foreigners, the French workmen inferred, particularly if of different races, cannot well be organized. Vignes, whose account is of the industry rather than of the men, and who writes guardedly, does not hesitate to accuse the mine owners of keeping their workers circulating, and expressly of utilizing the temporary home-goings of the Italians to accomplish a change of residence. Hence to trade-union interests the Briey district has been a byword.[1]

As far back as the early eighties, the labor hostility to the Italians became pronounced; at Marseilles, under the stress of the events in Tunis, bloody riots took place. In 1893, at the salt works of Aigues-Mortes, the French miners savagely attacked their Italian competitors, killing fifty and wounding a hundred and fifty. All Italy was kindled and there were serious anti-French demonstrations.[2] At other times, in agriculture as in industry, both before and after the assassination of President Carnot, conflicts have been many, and resentment has been felt even when clashes have not occurred.[3]

What is it, more expressly, that the French have feared in the Italians ? " Despite their native excitability," wrote M. Lair in their praise, "they are infinitely more tractable than the southern

---

[1] Vignes, pp. 695–698; A. Merrheim, " Le mouvement ouvrier dans le bassin de Longwy," *Le Mouvement Socialiste*, December 1 and 15, 1905, pp. 425–482.

[2] The estimate of casualties is that contained in the volume upon Italy (1893) of the report of the British Royal Commission on Labor. Curiously, the accounts are sharply divergent; not improbably a lower figure would be correct.

In Italy there were threats to burn the embassy, pro-German demonstrations, and street troubles that had to be put down with the bayonet.

[3] Tornielli, pp. 70–72, 85–90; Great Britain, *Royal Commission on Labour*, viii (Italy), (London, 1893), pp. 81 f.; P. Gitta, " I lavoratori italiani in Francia," *Riforma Sociale*, July, 1894, pp. 995–1003; Augé-Laribé, "Les ouvriers de la viticulture languedocienne et leurs syndicats," *Musée Sociale*, November, 1903, pp. 266–328; Rostand, pp. 417–442; C. Durando, report on Marseilles in *Emig. e Col.*, 1893, p. 228; Magenta, p. 235; Lair, pp. 554–557; Blanchard, p. 185; Caillard, pp. 62, 135 f.; Souchon, p. 49; H. F., "La main-d'œuvre," etc., p. 534. See also a note in *Bollettino del Lavoro* (serie quindicinale), August 1, 1914, pp. 151 f.

French," and low wages content them.[1] The Italian masons in
Paris have been " attracted by those employers who look for a
less skilful but more docile labor force." [2] The steel workers are
" exploitable and manageable."[3] Messrs. Gide and Lambert,
writing after the Aigues-Mortes episode, declared, " Because of
the strength of their emigration movement, their endurance in
hard labor, their docile obedience to the orders of boss or employer, their sobriety and the native misery which allows them to
accept low wages, the Italians are the Chinese of Europe." To
the workers of France especially, " little disposed to toil so hard
and for so little," they bring " a formidable competition, which is
not supported without bitterness." [4]

The Italians' fault, according to the charge, is that they will
accept lower wages than the French or be content with a rate
which the French would raise. Of certain kinds of labor, however, in some places, they have had almost a monopoly. In such
a case their competition is not obvious: they are in jobs that the
French " refuse." [5] Yet even then the sense of rivalry persists.
Actual acceptance of a lower wage for like work is not held to be
necessary for evidence of effective competition, and readiness to
join in a strike of French workmen would not undo the consequences of their demand for work. A general result of the situation is that the Italians have very rarely, of their own desire,
become members of French trade unions, and that the French,
for their part, have not invited them.

That they are picturesque, sunny, and fond of song is held to be
nothing or little. They are also dirty, ignorant, disorderly, often
criminal; they are parsimonious, and they live ill. In Marseilles,
at Lyons, in Briey, everywhere, they have taken the sort of job

[1] Lair, p. 554. Cf. Blanchard, p. 185.

[2] L. and M. Bonneff, *La classe ouvrière* (Paris, 1912), p. 299.

[3] Merrheim, " L'organisation patronale," p. 16.

[4] C. Gide et M. Lambert, " Les troubles d'Aigues-Mortes," *Revue d'Économie
Politique*, September–October, 1893, pp. 839–841.

[5] Caillard (pp. 135 f.) believes that acceptance of a low wage by Italians occasions the abandonment of a field of employment by the French. He cites a number
of districts where the latter have gradually withdrawn from an employment taken
up by foreigners. Cf. Blanchard, p. 242.

that men associate with inferior capacities. Everywhere, too, they live in groups so that all may see how they are marked off from others.[1] Sometimes they become naturalized, more frequently in fact than the equally numerous Belgians; but their impelling motive is often to get work.[2] They rarely intermarry with the French.[3] Generally the people of France, when not indifferent to their presence, have inclined to sympathize with the labor point of view. Proposals for taxing immigrants and for putting restrictions upon their coming have been rife for more than three decades, repeatedly the subject of debate in Parliament and the press, and undoubtedly an important symptom of opinion, even though they have not yet led to drastic legislation.[4]

What have the Italians earned in France, and how have they lived ?

In agriculture the evidence is clear enough. Throughout the South in recent years (before the war), men received 3–3.50 francs per day in addition to lodging and food, or an extra franc when these were not provided; women a little more than half as much.

---

[1] " The Italian of the people, at Paris, remains very Italian," writes Mlle. Schirmacher, adding " he remains the ' macaroni ' [a popular sobriquet]." *Op. cit.*, p. 129.

[2] It is certain that the naturalization law of 1889 prompted much change of citizenship on the part of Italians. Children born in France, notably the children of the Italian agricultural proprietors of the South, commonly grow up into French citizenship.

[3] In Marseilles about a third of the Italians who marry are said to choose life companions of French citizenship, but these are usually persons of the older Italian stock.

[4] Professor Pic is of those who have held public action to be desirable. See his *Traité élémentaire de législation industrielle* (3d ed., Paris, 1909), pp. 156–165. For another discussion of suggested plans for legislation, see Lair (pp. 559–562) who, on economic grounds, defends immigration. The names of those who have led the discussion in Parliament are given by Levasseur, p. 461. Cf. H. F., " La main-d'œuvre," etc., pp. 529–533.

Chiefly by international agreement and concession, some considerable improvements have come since 1900 in the position of Italian laborers, particularly as regards the victims of industrial accidents. See the excellent account by Professor S. Gemma, *Il diritto internazionale del lavoro* (Rome, 1912), pp. 79–99. For the text of the Italo-French convention of June 10, 1910 for the protection of minors, momentous for its bearings on employment in the glass works, etc., see *Bollettino dell' Ufficio del Lavoro*, July, 1910, pp. 166–169.

What men have been paid in the olive oil mills, four to five francs per day and their lodging, has been a co nmon wage for work requiring little skill. All these earnings have permitted some saving. Woman and child flower gatherers, paid on a piece basis, have received 1.50–1.75 francs per day, but have been able to put by very little of it. In Corsica, out of a wage of about two francs per day, men have saved as much as 200 francs a year and even more.[1]

Yet every centime set aside is a centime purchased by privation. The workmen sleep anywhere, unregardful of personal cleanliness, a dozen or twenty occupying a single room. "At harvest time they throw themselves pêle-mêle upon the straw of their huts, letting pass whole weeks without undressing."[2] When they work in groups one may be designated as a steward to prepare the polenta and other accustomed dishes. But, except when their board is part of their wage, they eat too little. When wine also is a part, they often drink to excess. In passing it may be noted that the men, unlike the women, easily drift away from religious exercises.

In the urban centers the situation is not greatly different. "Taking all the great colonies in Paris," wrote Mlle. Schirmacher, "the labor section of the Italian is incontestably the most primitive."[3] It includes the most illiterate and those that live the most plainly. The Belgian drinks, but not the Italian, who has come emphatically for gain.[4] In the quarter of La Villette soup made of stale bread crusts is currently consumed. "For a Frenchman to buy it would be misery and humiliation."[5] Nine-tenths of the models are said to live in the greatest poverty. Though their pay is good (the women receive more than the men), there is a pernicious *morte saison;* and loose relations of the sexes are general.[6]

---

[1] Berio, pp. 55 ff.; Blanchard, pp. 184, 188 f.; Caillard, pp. 64, 69; Tornielli, p. 106.

[2] Blanchard, p. 190.　　　　[3] *Op. cit.*, p. 130.

[4] Caillard (p. 78) makes the same observation regarding the Belgian and Italian agricultural laborers.

[5] Schirmacher, p. 132.

[6] *Ibid.*, p. 147. Cf. de' Calboli, *op. cit.;* for all the workers he describes, except the glaziers, the record is one of hard terms of labor, the destruction of health and

In Marseilles, 6 francs has been a common rate of pay for irregular work; but in the factories, 3.50 francs for the men and 2.25 for the women. It is very hard, however, to save. The South Italians of the old town " live crowded in houses freshened by little air or sunlight, where — unlike the rest of the city — the most elementary rules of hygiene are still unknown. The streets are alive with troops of boys, many of whom, from the age of seven or eight years, are bootblacks." [1] In the five years 1901–05, when 28,868 Italians settled in Marseilles, 14,513 were repatriated because indigent, infirm, or old, by the Italian consulate or by Italian societies. Alcoholism has been a frequent vice in the great port. Here and at Toulon hundreds of Italian girls have been found in prostitution, more, it would seem, than in any other European center of immigration.[2] Of an interest in forms of solidarity, and a civic sense, the great Italian population of Marseilles has given little evidence.

In the quarter century which has elapsed since Italian children began to work in the glass industry at Lyons, important changes have come. Where ten years was the minimum age for employment, thirteen has become so. Where the *incettatori* once made their arrangements directly with the fathers in Caserta or Basilicata (paying 100–150 lire for the right to hire their boys for two or three years), they have more recently made written contracts with the children; and the latter have oftener been accompanied to France by their parents. While vegetables cooked in water were once the staple food served to the children, macaroni and other substantial dishes are now oftener provided. But the children's ages are still given falsely — a government investigation found 300 under age — and at busy times the eight-hour shift is supplanted by a twelve-hour. Even eight hours, however, and tender years, are too much for the *porteurs* who must carry away the freshly blown glass amidst great heat, humidity, and gas fumes; and whose eyes are hurt by the flashes of light. Boys as

morals, and slight pecuniary gains. The traffic in children is much less than it once was. Florenzano (p. 157) declared that in 1867, during the world exposition in Paris, 1544 Italian begging children were arrested.

[1] Lelli, p. 61. Cf. Bernardy, p. 226; Levasseur, p. 898.
[2] Paolucci de' Calboli, p. 234.

well as adults seek refreshment in alcoholic drinks. Fell diseases are transmitted by lip contacts on tools. Dress, food, light, and air are insufficient for daily living. After a few years the children go back to Italy, uneducated, without a trade, and permanently hurt in health.[1]

In Lyons, the many North Italian seasonal immigrants, who have come as mechanical and building laborers, have been better off than any other group and able to make some savings. On the other hand the South Italian adult workers of the glass factories, living in dirt and ignorance — " in indescribable abandonment," as an observer told,[2] have been despised by the French and ignored by their Northern brethren. The 2000 North Italian girls in the silk mills in recent years were able to save 10–30 francs a month out of their wages of 1.50–3 francs for a ten-hour day. But they have often lived in the very lowest quarters of the city, and when they have married, report is, it has usually been after the birth of a child.[3]

When the Italians first came to Briey — in Nancy, an older field, they were repelled by the French workmen — they found only rural villages. Farmhouses were made over to lodge them and temporary barracks erected; for food and shelter, the large sum of 80–90 francs per month had to be paid. So the better grades of workmen departed, and their ranks were not refilled.

[1] B. Berio, " I ragazzi italiani nelle vetrerie del Lionese," *Rivista Coloniale*, February 16–28, 1913, pp. 124–127; see also pp. 127–130, the report of a discussion in the Italian Parliament. Cf. Ferliga, pp. 28–30; annual report of the Commissioner-General of Emigration, *Boll. Emig.*, 1904, No. 7, pp. 108 f.; Perrod, " I minorenni italiani," etc., pp. 50–53; *idem*, " Immigrazione e colonia," etc., pp. 222–235; G. Sommi-Picenardi, " La tratta dei piccoli italiani in Francia," *Nuova Antologia*, February 1, 1902, esp. pp. 472 ff.; A. A. Bernardy, " L'emigrazione delle donne e dei franciulli dal Piemonte," *Boll. Emig.*, 1912, No. 10, esp. pp. 57–60.

[2] Ferliga, p. 22.

[3] At the beginning of the century, when there were fewer girls, Perrod (*Emig. e Col.*, 1903, i[1], pp. 225 f.) took a favorable view. Cf. L. Basso, report on Lyons, *Emig. e Col.*, 1893, pp. 218 f.; Ferliga, pp. 24–27; Berio, *Relazione sull' emigrazione delle donne*, etc., pp. 1–18. Signorina Berio's account (pp. 30–36) of St. Rambert (Ain), half of whose 4000 people are Italians, of whom in turn 800 are girls, is challenged by the Direttore dell' Ufficio di Confine in Modane, in *Vita Italiana all' Estero*, November, 1913, pp. 372 f.; but the criticism itself admits that the girls live five, six, even eight to a room, where they attempt to sleep, cook, and pass their free hours.

A call for men who would bring wives and children met little response.[1] Such families as did settle in Briey always boarded workmen, sometimes twelve or fifteen at a time, four to six in a room. The hard toil of the mines, the darkness and monotony of the dank galleries, called for contrasts. Wives and daughters among these immigrant families partook in a common immorality, often submitting to a sort of polyandry.[2]

Brawls and crime, turning commonly upon women, were frequent, the harder to repress because flight across the border was easy. The departmental police (no municipal police existed) were intimidated and helpless.[3] Although the victims of crime were usually immigrants, the native inhabitants were led to guard their steps. Religious influences were few. " An atheist and corrupt community," M. Vignes has generalized, " is fatally destined to anarchy and disorder." For many years, the children were suffered to grow up in ignorance; but in 1913 the companies were prevailed upon to make some provision for schools.[4] Various diseases, especially tuberculosis and those associated with loose living, made grievous inroads upon the health of the workers; and the victims of industrial accident were many.

Though the Italians came to Briey to save money, they failed, in innumerable cases, to do so. " If," wrote Dr. Vinci, " you except two or three thousand able and fortunate men who earn high wages and work regularly, so not losing the benefit of their

[1] In 1910, according to an official count quoted by Professor Vignes, eight out of nine of the Italian population were men. *Op. cit.*, p. 688.

[2] There were houses (and inns) owned by the mines, sometimes let at a lower rate if the tenants would take boarders. When, as more usually happened, there were restrictions on this practice, the company houses fell into disfavor. A dominant institution was the "cantine," a kind of expanded boarding house with a downstairs used for eating and drinking, gambling and dancing, and an upstairs used for sleeping. Two men in a bed, beds used day and night, sheets changed rarely, fifteen or twenty beds crowded together, were usual. The "bacana" (housekeeper) and her servants made an income from immorality. At the end of the week dancing girls arrived from other towns.

[3] " The Briey court, despite the relative tolerance of the authorities, is of all French courts that which has to deal with the most crimes and misdemeanors." Raynaud, p. 213.

[4] See two notes in *Rivista Coloniale*, September 15, 1913, p. 144, and October 15, 1913, pp. 204 f.

earnings through unemployment, and who lead a regular life, then the mass of our laborers, I am sure, do not with their present wages realize a sufficient margin to compensate them for their sacrifices in emigration and their daily risks. On the other hand, the thousand temptations offered to these people unused to indulgence are such that the slim savings which might take place in another environment are here not made at all." It was only, he believed, the miners who could profitably come to Briey, for the skilled worker averaged 12 francs a day, and his two men got 6–9 (but the shift was of twelve hours, with weekly turns). Probably, however, those who saved money were more numerous than this statement concedes.[1]

In the social conditions of Briey, the passing years brought some improvements. I have mentioned elementary schools. The police force was got under better discipline. The older shacks were demolished. But the women whose function it was, however blindly, to restore the balance of the sexes, were only licensed in their prostitution. The boarding system, the cantine, overcrowding and the rest continued — until the red torch of the invader was carried into the country.[2]

" If, by way of conclusion to the study I have made and the things I have set forth, one should ask whether or no the Italian movement into France ought to be facilitated or promoted, I incline to think that most persons would reply, no." So, in 1902, wrote the Italian ambassador at Paris at the end of a copious report to his government.[3] Weighing the success or failure of so complicated an adventure as this is sufficiently hazardous, and I am not now even attempting to consider some factors that in the final view must not be ignored. It is clear, however, that the

[1] Vinci, p. 25. Ten years earlier the representatives of local employers claimed that laborers could save half their wage of 3–7 francs per day " by dint of great parsimony " (Bidou, p. 224). Raynaud and Vignes both consider that savings have been made.

[2] On conditions in French Lorraine, see, besides the references given (including Bonneff and Villari), G. Lévy, " En Meurthe-et-Moselle; les bassins de Briey et de Longwy," *Le Mouvement Socialiste*, December, 1912, pp. 341–349.

[3] Tornielli, p. 192; cf. p. 73.

Italian who comes must work hard at tasks that are humble and ill paid, those that Frenchmen avoid in every alternative. Contending against frequent change of employment, the selected victim of every crisis,[1] paying at every step the penalties of ignorance, rolling up losses as he rolls up gains, finding the unexpected along with the expected, he is made over in the end into a different person. Somewhat he safeguards his course by awaiting a summons from his employer of the previous season, or by responding only to the call of a compatriot already in France, or by heeding the warnings available to all who get a passport before migrating. But even such forethought, when it exists and can be applied, has but limited powers of accomplishment. In the scattered colonies and the newer settlements, his mutual aid societies have been few, non-existent or weak; hospital care, except in emergencies, has been proffered only under restrictions; protective agencies, Italian or French, for children and women, have been few. Briey and Lyons are witness to the forces of inertia and self-interest with which reform must contend.[2]

No one can doubt that France has gained by the labor of her immigrants. In Lorraine she was able to provide from her own population only a minority of her workers, and at many other points she has been forced to rely upon aliens. Her gain is a net one, for she insists upon no standard of living and no performance of a civic rôle. She admits no present responsibility for comfort and makes no guarantee of future welfare. Her account is well-nigh complete when a wage has been paid. During the war she drew thousands of swarthy laborers from Algeria to take the places, in vineyards and industry, of the absent Italians. She will not indefinitely be content with such a substitution.

Will Italy after the war again despatch her sons to France? Once, in the twelfth century, she sent great scholars thither —

[1] In 1907, for example, Italians were warned that because of a vineyard crisis, they must not count on employment in the South. *Boll. Emig.*, 1907, No. 13, p. 126. In 1908, because of depression in Longwy, they must expect no work the following spring. *Ibid.*, 1908, No. 7, p. 100. Cf. *Ibid.*, 1909, No. 9, p. 115; 1910, No. 18, p. 249.

[2] Berio (p. 125) claimed that the advantages secured in Lyons by de' Calboli and Professor Schiaparelli some years previously had been well-nigh lost.

Lanfranc, Anselm.   Later, in the fifteenth to the seventeenth centuries, she sent skilled artisans, makers of fine garments, workers in ceramics, glass, the manufacture of scientific instruments, who taught their arts to the French.   In the early nineteenth century, political refugees sought the friendly protection of the northern land.[1]   And now it is the day of the laborer.   The opposition of the French workmen may yet effect some sort of exclusion, but it is also possible that men who have fought together in a great cause will hereafter more willingly work together. Unless restrictive action should yet be taken, and unless the sources of Italian emigration should run dry, the movement of immigration is likely to be resumed — interrupted only, not terminated, by the Great War.

[1] See a study by C. Dejob, " Un bel libro da fare," in *Raccolta di studii critici dedicata ad Alessandro D'Ancona*, pp. 133–143, Florence, 1901.

CHAPTER IX

GERMANY

ALTHOUGH the Italians, bent on settlement or trade, have migrated into Germany for twenty centuries, the modern immigrants are successors of the old only in point of time. Their coming has a new origin, a new character. Its beginning is typified in those Venetian mountain folk who, as itinerant vendors, many decades ago crossed the Alps afoot or with their carts to sell merchandise in the villages of the Rhine and Danube valleys. Of late years — it is naturally the pre-war period of which I write — the mountain peoples have continued their immigration, but their numbers have vastly increased and they have drawn into the current Italians from every corner of Italy, and have scattered over all parts of Germany.

It cannot be said that the movement has had breadth until recently. As early as 1860 some hundreds of Italians worked in the mines of Westphalia.[1] In South Germany there were a larger number: a picturesque collection of braziers, chair menders, street merchants, from North Italy; sellers of marble and alabaster statuettes, from Lucca; men from Caserta who displayed accomplished bears; and the unfailing street musicians. In this early period, however, transportation was still difficult. The St. Bernard Pass had been used since ancient times, the St. Gothard since the Middle Ages, but it required the completion of the railroad over the Brenner Pass (1867) and the St. Gothard (1881) to make travel less arduous and costly. It was, in fact, we are told, the "eisenponeri" (Eisenbahn-eri) themselves whose earnings in the construction of the Brenner railway and similar undertakings stimulated friends and relatives in their native Venetia to emigrate into Bavaria, Wurttemberg, and Baden. In 1872,

---

[1] G. Pertile, "Gli italiani in Germania," *Boll. Emig.*, 1914, Nos. 11 and 15, Pt. i, pp. 21 f.

Wurttemberg contained some thousands of Italians. Before the decade was ended, large numbers had come to Bavaria, Baden, and Alsace-Lorraine; about Cologne they were building fortifications and railways, and in Saxony were working upon bridges, railways, barracks — even such edifices as the royal theater. In the next decade, they reached into the north of Germany; though they were chiefly building workers and general laborers, they also displayed in the cities their characteristic itinerant occupations. In the West, the industrial heart of the country, they increased rapidly both in the decade of the eighties and that of the nineties, and were soon more numerous than anywhere else in Germany. After 1895, and again after the depression of 1901–02, a great and sudden addition to their numbers took place, and finally in 1906–07, a high point was reached which has not since been exceeded.

Only a dim and flickering light is thrown by the censuses upon the numerical strength of this immigration. The Italians are not a population; they are a stream which surges forward and subsides, acknowledging no law but that of change. In 1880, 7841 were counted; in 1890, 13,080; in 1900, after the first great influx, 69,738; in 1905, 98,165; in 1910, 104,204. Here is evidence at least of increase. But the figures all refer to December, when many, if not most, of the Italians were again at home with their families. Of those present in Germany in the summer, no true measure exists, but an estimate of 175,000 for recent pre-war years would not err far from the truth.[1] According to the winter

---

[1] Pertile, Pt. i, p. 40, quoted 90,000 for Prussia in 1906 as a figure reached by the Prussian Minister of the Interior, and he estimated 200,000 for all Germany at that time. S. Jacini (" Die italienische Auswanderung nach Deutschland," *Weltwirtschaftliches Archiv*, January, 1915, p. 128) estimated not less than 175,000. In a German study (" Die ausländischen Wanderarbeiter," *Reichsarbeitsblatt*, March, April, September, 1913, p. 209), the position is taken that the figures from Italian sources are too high. Italians to whom legitimation cards were issued in the year 1911–12 numbered 52,177; but this figure, which in any case touches few Italians outside of Prussia requires " a rather considerable increase " (p. 207). At the Landratsämter, in Prussia alone, registrations in the years 1907–11 ran from 95,000 to 115,000, but these figures, by reason of duplications, are deemed to be 15–20 per cent too high. (They probably correspond to the 90,000 indicated to Pertile by the Prussian ministry in 1906.) In accessible volumes of the *Gewerbliche Betriebsstatistik* (census of June 12, 1907) I have found no particularization by race or nationality. Subsequently, such statistics were published in the *Statistiches Jahrbuch für das*

census of 1910, the Italians were most numerous in Prussia and next in Alsace-Lorraine, Baden, Wurttemberg, and Bavaria.[1]

The industrial census of 1907 found no less than 121,000 Italians, mainly unskilled workers, engaged in manufacturing, mining, and building. In mining and smelting there were 23,000, constituting 3.7 per cent of their kind in Germany. In stone and earthwork there were over 30,300, who formed 5.7 per cent of all those of their occupation. In the building trades were 57,400 — nearly half of the Italians — and they were actually 6.3 per cent of their kind in Germany. Besides these, the predominating types, the census disclosed 4400 workers in the textile trades, of whom three-quarters were women, 600 in the chemical industry, 1100 in machine employments, 1400 in metal working, nearly 900 in commerce, finally, 1400 occupied in inns and hostelries — to name but the larger groups.[2]

In two respects, the immigration of Italians into Germany has been strikingly unlike that into France. It has not colonized in the great cities. Berlin and Cologne have not been centers, like Marseilles and Paris, where Italians have settled to reside and work, spending winters as well as summers. Perhaps a living has been harder to secure in the winter, perhaps the language barrier has been more awkward to surmount, perhaps the temperament, mood, and customs of the people have made adaptation more difficult and failure of adaptation more grievous — whatever the reason the fact is patent. Secondly (and this is scarcely less noteworthy) the Italians have entirely held aloof from farming pursuits. In no other country to which they have thronged have they so generally confined themselves to non-agricultural activities. Difference of crops and mode of production in South Germany; the large families there, with always enough sons to

Deutsche Reich, 1912, pp. 10–15. They show for all Germany 125,520 Italian men and women occupied industrially. For the Italian population there should be added to this figure unemployed children and wives and all the Italians whose immigration had not taken place so early in the year.

[1] Prussia, 42,480 (Westphalia, 10,759, Hesse-Nassau 2384, Rhenish Prussia, 21,135), Alsace-Lorraine, 31,367, Baden, 11,379, Wurttemberg, 6970, Bavaria, 6946 (Upper Bavaria, 3028), Saxony, 2117, Hesse, 1047. See *Vierteljahrshefte zur Statistik des Deutschen Reiches*, 1912, No. 3, pp. 108 f.

[2] *Statistisches Jahrbuch*, 1912, pp. 10–15.

carry forward the work of the fields; in sparser East Germany the readily controllable immigration of hundreds of thousands of Poles, Russians, and other neighboring peoples who have sufficed to the needs of large-estate farming; these conditions may explain an unparalleled situation.[1]

In Germany, as in France, the women and children of the Italians have halted mainly in the South, in parts nearest to their own country.[2] There, however, the resemblance ends. They have not been flower gatherers and vintage hands, but largely workers in the brick ovens of Bavaria, Wurttemberg, and the Rhenish Palatinate. Even before the snow has melted, the proprietors or their agents, or most commonly the *accordanti* (Italian or sometimes German middlemen who contract to produce a season's output of bricks, tiles, tubes, and the like) have been wont to go into Udine and other parts of Venetia to hire their workers. The latter, who include many men also, have commonly entered Germany through Austria by the route of Pontebba-Salzburg or that of Ala-Kufstein. In Upper and Lower Bavaria and in Swabia, there have been perhaps a thousand furnaces, where from the end of March to the second half of September, 12,000 to 15,000 Italians have in recent years found employment, constituting half or two-thirds of the whole labor force. Between Germans and Italians one can draw a sharp line, the former working in establishments using machinery, the latter willing to toil all day long with their hands in the wet clay. It is scarcely too much to say that so far as the establishments using hand labor are concerned — all are small and scattered through the country — the industry has been kept alive by the Italians.[3]

[1] Many years ago an attempt made by agrarian societies and large employers to establish Italian families in certain parts of South Germany collapsed entirely. See B. Lambertenghi, " Gli italiani nel distretto consolare di Francoforte sul Meno," *Emig. e Col.*, 1905, i[iii], p. 22.

[2] Within the state of Baden, it is worth noting, the women have increased as the Swiss border has been left behind. See H. Pfeiffer, *Die Zusammensetzung der Bevölkerung des Grossherzogtums Baden nach der Gebürtigkeit, auf Grund der Volkszählung vom 1 Dezember, 1900* (Stuttgart, 1909), p. 165.

[3] P. Sandicchi, "I fornaciai italiani in Baviera," *Boll. Emig.*, 1912, No. 12, pp. 3-34; A. Cabrini, "Nelle fornaci di Baviera," *Rivista Coloniale*, October 25,

In Baden and in Alsace, girls and women have been operatives in the cotton, silk, and jute mills. From small beginnings in Baden and Wurttemberg this immigration has reached very large proportions, its members staying more and more into the winter. Often entire families have had employment in the factories.[1]

Continuously, since Italian immigration began, men, women, and children have worked in South Germany as models, street vendors — of roasted chestnuts in winter and ice cream in summer — tinkers, street musicians, and the like. Because it has become hard to secure the requisite licenses to carry on some of these occupations, fewer immigrants have in the present century tried to earn their living by them. At the same time a great increase has taken place in the number of building laborers and their kin. Brick and stone masons, stonecutters, hodcarriers, pick and shovel workers, coming in the spring either individually or in groups of thirty to fifty, have undertaken general construction work, railroad building, canalization, and other large enterprises requiring more hands than have been locally available. In the summer thousands have secured employment in South Germany, returning to North Italy after the first frosts. Immigrants from South Italy, rated as poorer workers than their Northern fellow countrymen, have almost ceased to come.[2]

It is into the west of Germany, above all other sections, that the Italians have gone. Here the greatest iron mines of Europe make

1912, pp. 304 f.; Pertile, Pt. i, pp. 103–109; A. De Foresta, G. Pezzani, P. Mondini, and T. Schilling, "La Baviera e la emigrazione italiana," *Emig. e Col.*, 1905, i[iii], pp. 49–75; G. Federer, "La colonia italiana nel Wurttemberg," *Emig. e Col.*, 1905, i[iii], pp. 76–78; report on Munich consular district by E. Cova, *Emig. e Col.*, 1893, pp. 260 f.

[1] Pertile, Pt. i, pp. 116–120; O. Bornhausen, "Gli italiani nel Baden, Alsazia e nel Palatinato del Reno," *Emig. e Col.*, 1905, i[iii], pp. 79–81; Pfeiffer, *loc. cit.*

[2] Pertile, sundry passages; B. Lambertenghi, "Gli italiani in Triberg," *Boll. Emig.*, 1905, No. 8, pp. 42 f.; T. Schilling, "L'immigrazione italiana in Baviera," *Boll. Emig.*, 1904, No. 15, pp. 67 f.; P. Mondini, "L'immigrazione italiana nella Baviera meridionale, *Boll. Emig.*, 1904, No. 2, pp. 10–13; note in *Boll. Emig.*, 1902, No. 9, p. 61; De Foresta, Pezzani, Mondini, Schilling, *op. cit.*; Federer, *op. cit.*; Pfeiffer, pp. 164 f. The industrial census of 1907 counted 15,010 workers in Bavaria, 10,099 in Wurttemberg, 14,579 in Baden; *Reichsarbeitsblatt*, March, 1913, p. 206.

a subterranean state of western Lorraine; the mineral belt is continuous with that of French Lorraine, Luxemburg, and Belgium. Here are the coal fields of Germany; an area about Aachen; another about the Saar, running east to the Bavarian Palatinate, south and west to Lorraine; a third, the most important on the continent, along the entire valley of the Ruhr. Here too are mines of subordinate minerals, stone and lime quarries; textile and other factories; iron and steel mills having an output greater than any save those of England and the United States. All these together, and a network of railways and navigable streams, have constituted the magnet which before the war drew more than a hundred thousand Italians a year to Westphalia, Rhenish Prussia, and Lorraine.

They first came, after the Franco-Prussian war, to demolish and build anew the fortifications about Metz and Cologne. Gradually they overspread the entire district, until, in recent years, they appeared even in the smallest workplaces. Once they came only from Lombardy and Venetia, but subsequently, in heavy contingents, from the middle and even the southern parts of the kingdom. Perhaps as many as four in five, in recent years, had been in Germany before and when they have not gone back to previous employers have at least made for well-known centers. In special trains forty hours have sufficed (where as late as 1900 four days were necessary) to make the journey from Ala to Dortmund. Clad in their characteristic garb of spacious velvet trousers and red belt, a gay shirt and somber coat, with forty or fifty lire in their pockets — enough for the journey — these immigrants used to come in gangs and trainloads. The way was easy, frontier conveniences were many, and at Basel, way station for all who came by the St. Gothard and for most who came by other routes, a special waiting room had been prepared. Some went directly into the northern districts, others scattered from Metz as a center. While a few settled in small growing colonies, more or less permanent, the majority often changed their place of work.

In Lorraine, the Italians have been coal miners in the eastern fields. (The Saar mines, continued in Rhenish Prussia, have been governmental, employing only Germans.) In the northwest, in the Fentsch district and the valley of the Orne, they have mined iron ore for twenty-five years. First from the Alps, latterly from the Apennines, they have come in swelling numbers, and since 1900 have established themselves with their families at Hayingen, at Kneuttingen, at Gross-Moyeuvre. Some have been miners, some their helpers, some (the youths) have assisted in the transportation of material to the mine's entrance. At times they have amounted to a fourth or more of all the miners. A majority of the Lorraine Italians, who are chiefly from Central and South Italy, have been occupied about the iron and steel mills, at Deutsch-Oth, Redingen, Diedenhofen, and other places, some digging, some loading and discharging wagons and cars. Many of these have customarily arrived in the autumn and returned to Italy for the spring planting. Many general laborers have worked on the watercourses, on railway construction, including the building of strategic lines, and such tasks as the demolition and rebuilding of the fortifications at Diedenhofen and Metz. At the last-named place some thousands of Italians were occupied before the war, many upon the construction of the new railway station. Artisans have been few in this immigration.[1]

In Westphalia and Rhenish Prussia, Italians have been present during much of the modern industrial epoch. Before 1850, the local population was sufficient to work the coal mines of the Ruhr. With an enlarged scale of exploitation and the establishment of iron mills, workers were drawn from the farms, from remoter sections of Germany, and from foreign lands. About 1860, as we have seen, a few Italians were present. In December, 1893, about a thousand were on the books of the companies. With the further growth of the industry they maintained their numbers at about one per cent of the working force, exceeded only by natives of Austria-Hungary and Holland. The miners have come from Vicenza, Belluno, and the valleys of Piedmont, and if the years

---

[1] Pertile, Pt. i, pp. 57, 69, 73 f.; P. Röchling, "La Lorena, le provincie di Coblenza e di Treviri e l'immigrazione italiana, *Boll. Emig.*, 1904, No. 15, pp. 3–12; *idem*, " La Renania e la Lorena, e l'immigrazione italiana," *Emig. e Col.*, 1905, iⁱⁱⁱ, pp. 101–111; Ferliga, " L'emigrazione italiana in Alsazia Lorena," pp. 9, 15.

1908 and 1909 may be accounted representative, some two-thirds of them have stayed through the winter.[1]

It is not, however, the few thousands of coal miners who have made of the Ruhr and the lower Rhine the region — after Lorraine — where the Italians have most congregated. The 50,000–100,000 unskilled or low-skilled laborers, largely Venetians and Lombards, who in each of the last fifteen summers before the war came to these states, did their work of excavation, loading, unloading, and the like in manifold connections. All along the Ruhr they worked in the stone quarries, many making stable settlements with their families. Near Cologne they dug peat. Near the Ruhr, the Sieg, and the Saar they did the rough work of the iron and steel mills; but these men were not commonly from North Italy. Many had employment in the textiles. Bricklayers from the Friuli and Belluno and the less skilled sorts of building laborers were numerous. Wherever Italian collectivities became sufficiently large, there retail vendors throve, beginning sometimes as laborers selling Italian food products to their associates. Nor were the street musicians and their kindred absent.[2]

[1] *Wirtschaftliche Entwickelung des Niederrheinisch-Westfälischen Steinkohlen-Bergbaues in der zweiten Hälfte des 19 Jahrhunderts, herausgegeben vom Verein für die bergbaulichen Interessen im Oberbergamtsbezirke Dortmund in Gemeinschaft mit der Westfälischen Berggewerkschaftskasse und dem Rheinisch-Westfälischem Kohlensyndikat* (Berlin, 1904), iii, pp. 36–38, 56. Since 1902 the *Allgemeine Knappschaftsverein* at Bochum has kept statistics of the foreign miners in its membership. On January 1, 1909, the Italians numbered 3890, having reached almost that number in 1907. Depression in industry reduced them by January 1, 1910, to 2814. See F. Syrup, "Studien über den industriellen Arbeiterwechsel," *Archiv für exakte Wirtschaftsforschung*, 1912, p. 264.

[2] On Westphalia and Rhenish Prussia, see Pertile, numerous passages in Pt. i, esp. pp. 56–75, 97–127; *idem*, "Le condizioni degli operai italiani nei distretti consolari di Colonia, Düsseldorf, Saarbrücken e Lussemburgo," *Boll. Emig.*, 1908, No. 19, pp. 3–51; *idem*, "Rapporto del r. addetto per l'emigrazione presso il r. consolato di Colonia," *Boll. Emig.*, 1905, No. 18, pp. 17–27; P. Donadio, "Relazione del segretariato di Bochum," *Rivista di Emigrazione*, September–October, 1911, pp. 434–437; Röchling, "La Lorena, le provincie di Coblenza," etc.; O. Heye, "Gli italiani nel distretto consolare di Düsseldorf," *Boll. Emig.*, 1904, No. 15, pp. 65–67; T. di Oppenheim, "I minorenni italiani nel distretto consolare di Colonia," *Boll. Emig.*, 1903, No. 10, pp. 42–45; *idem*, "L'immigrazione italiana nelle provincie tedesche del Reno e della Westfalia," *Boll. Emig.*, 1902, No. 10, pp. 3–14; *idem*, and P. Röchling, "La Renania, la Vestfalia, la Lorena e l'immigrazione italiana," *Emig. e Col.*, 1905, iiii, pp. 84–111.

The industrial census of 1907 discovered 48,813 occupied Italians in Prussia.

All in all, the Italians concentrated in Westphalia and the Rhineland, outnumbered by only one foreign people, the Austrians, and approached in numbers by no other, have played a large and laborious part in a great industrial development. In contiguous Lorraine, they have far exceeded any other foreign people, and in the Palatinate, Hesse, Hesse-Nassau, and Waldeck, whose industries resemble those of the more western districts, they have likewise been numerous.

Throughout North and East Germany, the Italians, though they began to come soon after 1880, have been far fewer. The railway journey could not be performed for the forty lire that have sufficed to carry a Lombard to Lorraine. Into Hanover or Silesia have gone those chiefly who have expected to stay a long time or who, unemployed in the West, had learned of a job in the North. Street musicians and retail vendors, nomads all, have long come. Girls have worked in the factories of Magdeburg. Earth workers, especially railway and tunnel excavators, have gone everywhere, into Saxony and Thuringia, to Berlin, even to Königsberg. In Silesia the Italians have been coal miners, their women and children toiling at the tasks above ground. Between the late eighties and the middle nineties and more recently again, Italians worked on the Kiel Canal, constituting a veritable colony there. Hundreds helped make the fortifications of Heligoland. In Hamburg and Altona general laborers have had employment. Both masons and unskilled men have worked on the construction of buildings. Hundreds, perhaps thousands, had employment over a long period on the gigantic new union station at Leipsic. Marble and granite sculptors, years ago, ornamented the Reichstag building in Berlin. Workers in stucco and cement, employed by masters who were also Italian, introduced " terrazzo " work into Silesia and Saxony, Berlin, Kiel, and other cities. Generally staying only a little while in one place, most of the immigrants have returned to North Italy at the close of the season.[1]

[1] E. Pasteris, " Una missione sul Baltico," *Rivista Internazionale di Scienze Sociali e Discipline Ausiliarie*, 1913, pp. 44–63, 174–194, and 1914, pp. 195–206, 333–357; extracts from a study by G. Costa, *Rivista di Emigrazione*, August 8, 1911, pp. 377–381; F. G. Krause, " L'immigrazione operaia italiana nella città

In estimating the rôle of all these workpeople it would be preposterous to assert, as the Italian Commissioner-General of Emigration once did, that " they have become essential for large enterprises, the construction of canals and railways, building operations, and the exploitation of the coal and iron mines." [1] Nor can we follow Pertile when he says, extravagantly (in a generally valuable study), that " the iron mines, and the iron and steel mills, especially of Lorraine, would remain largely inactive if stripped of Italian aid." [2] That much less labor would at one point or another be performed if the Italians stayed away, we can, however, maintain with assurance. With her astonishing powers of absorption, Germany in recent years has harbored five or six times as many immigrants from various countries as from Italy alone, and more than any other country of Europe. Either by grade of occupation or by destination in Germany most of these have been marked off from the Italians. The Russians and Poles, for instance, have remained in the East; the Austrians, absent in Lorraine, have been more specialized in their Westphalian tasks than the Italians. It is enough indeed to claim that Germany has found it advantageous to hire thousands upon thousands of Italians for the rougher physical tasks, and that in some districts, she has been glad to leave to them — mainly or largely — certain strata of employment in leading industries. Undoubtedly the landed interests have been grateful for their coming, since the German agricultural population has been the less likely to drift away to the cities.

Few alien immigrants into Germany, of whatever nationality, have performed a service demanding skill or responsibility. It has been precisely the unexampled system of continuation and technical schools which has provided these qualities and left

di Lipsia," *Boll. Emig.*, 1905, No. 8, pp. 44 f.; *idem*, " L'immigrazione italiana nella Sassonia e nella Turingia," *Boll. Emig.*, 1902, No. 10, pp. 15, 18; reports by Krause, Lehmert, Preuss, Molinari, and others in *Emig. e Col.*, 1905, i[iii], pp. 26–48; Landversicherungsrat Hansen, " Deutsche und fremde Arbeitskräfte am Erweiterungsbau des Kaiser-Wilhelm-Kanals," *Soziale Praxis*, May 25, 1911, pp. 1057–1060; reports on Berlin consular district by E. Beccaria Incisa in *Emig. e Col.*, 1893, pp. 255–259 and G. Rossi, pp. 261–267, and on Kiel by R. Lehmert, p. 276.

[1] *Boll. Emig.*, 1910, No. 18, p. 235.

[2] " Gli italiani in Germania," Pt. iv, p. 113.

relatively unclaimed by Germans that whole category of hard manual tasks which modern industry has never dispensed with. Of these the Italians have assumed a large share.[1] For construction work in the open country, for temporary work in large enterprises for which resident labor has been insufficient, they have been gladly welcomed. Unstable they have doubtless been, as a common charge holds, but that is partly because migrants can afford to be mobile; the seasonal turn has been only the largest aspect of their mobility. Their sobriety and endurance have been commended, while their pace has frequently been called monotonous and slow, requiring supervision; the pace in fact of the more southerly Italians has often been slow to the point of uselessness, but apparently has improved after a year or two.[2] The frequent charge that they are capricious and lightly throw up their jobs has not been without basis. Managers have discovered that they can best avoid clashes by acquiescing in the Italians' manifest desire to work with others of their own home region; and wherever small colonies have tended to take root, the same desire has had its way. Yet all these things, though they have limited the productiveness of the Italians or created problems in the utilization of them, have not prevented a substantial and tangible economic gain to Germany.

Nor has any other than an economic gain been contemplated. They have not become German citizens. If here and there a miner or a trader has been naturalized, the case is exceptional. And they have rarely intermarried with the Germans. It has been objected that they are conspicuously dirty, live primitively, and resort readily to revolver and stiletto. They may not come before the courts oftener than the Germans do, but they are unpleasantly characteristic in their crimes.[3]

[1] While the industrial census found the Italians employed in manufacturing, mining, and building to be 1.4 per cent of all such in Germany, it found them to be about 6 per cent of all the unskilled or low-skilled laborers in earth work and in construction, about one-half of all the numerous foreigners in those branches. On the other hand, few Italians were in categories requiring long apprenticeship. For details see *Statistisches Jahrbuch*, 1912, pp. 10–16.

[2] Pertile, Pt. i, pp. 37, 98.

[3] *Ibid.*, Pt. i, pp. 73, 184–201.

The point of view from which Germany has regarded her immigrants is illustrated by the system of legitimation cards (*Legitimations-Karten*) which a number of states introduced some years before the war.   In the immediate interest of employers this device established a sort of control over immigrants which could not be exercised over national workers.   Its assumption, correct for practical purposes, was that the immigrant has only a pecuniary interest in coming and must accept his employers' terms or stay away.   In the agricultural East, immigrants had often broken their contracts to work, and sought hire elsewhere.   The employers, deeming this procedure abusive, organized privately a *Feldarbeiterzentralstelle*, which Prussia, late in 1907, made the agent of a public policy.   All agricultural immigrants were temporarily to yield up their passports (written in various languages) and to receive cards in return bearing their own and their employers' names.   Any discovered seeking work without a due discharge inscribed on their cards were to be expelled from the country.   After the system had been in operation for one year, it was extended (December, 1908) to cover all industry and all immigrant workers, and its name made simply *Deutsche Arbeiterzentrale*.   Each nationality had a card of a special color, the Italian being green.   Gradually several states followed the lead of Prussia.   Since the southern states continued to hold aloof, it remained possible for contract breakers to move into them.   German writers, except the labor press, appear to have approved the institution, while Italian officials and writers have vigorously condemned it.   Italian workmen, of whom 47,700 came under it in the year 1910–11, have generally resented paying the fee of two marks for the useless green card, but otherwise have not been bothered by the system, which was not, as we have seen, directed primarily against them.[1]

[1] An able account of the Zentrale is in C. Willecke, *Die landwirtschaftliche Arbeitsvermittlung in Deutschland* (Berlin, 1912), pp. 92–142. For a French view, favorable, and a good analysis, see E. Schmit, *Organisation des bureaux de placement municipaux et situation des ouvriers agricoles étrangers en Allemagne* (Paris, 1913), pp. 351–433. (France has had a problem not unlike that of Germany.) Cf. Dr. Blumenthal, " Die deutsche Arbeiterzentrale," in *Der Arbeitsnachsweis in Deutschland*, December 15, 1913, pp. 49–53. A bitter condemnation, from the

More directly touched than any other class, the laborers of Germany have viewed the Italians with varying degrees of hostility.[1] The immigrants, eager for gain, have professed no solidarity with German labor. Just the fact that they are competitors makes them acceptable to employers.[2] Intentionally or not, they have on occasion been strikebreakers, as when, some years ago, nearly 700 were shipped to Kiel, and 500 to East Prussia.[3] Twice at least they joined the striking miners in the Ruhr district, but it was not, it seems, from a sense of solidarity, for they were content with the terms of their contract and during the strike lived in retirement.[4] They have been regarded as a factor in the failure or weakness of the organization of building trades workmen in Rhenish Prussia and Westphalia, and in that of the bricklayers in Bavaria, Baden, and Alsace-Lorraine.[5] German workmen have not liked their preference for piece pay.

Perhaps in no other country of Europe have the labor unions made so strong an effort to interest the Italians in organization. From 1898 till before the war, the *Generaldirektion* published *L'Operaio Italiano*, a propagandist journal printed in Italian. In some quarters, Italian secretaries were installed. Agents of German unions have even gone into Italy in the winter to win over

labor point of view, is in *Correspondenzblatt der Generalkommission der Gewerkschaften Deutschlands*, February 27, 1909, pp. 138 f. Cf. E. H. M., " Die deutsche Feldarbeiterzentralstelle," *Soziale Praxis*, May 27, 1911, pp. 1070–1072. For Italian views, varying only in the degree of their denunciation, see Gemma, *Il diritto internazionale del lavoro*, pp. 195–211; G. Mortara, "Le nuove carte di legittimazione prussiane per gli operai stranieri," *Rivista di Emigrazione*, April, 1908, pp. 1–6; Pertile, Pt. ii, pp. 67–72; Jacini, p. 132.

[1] For early references, see E. Beccaria Incisa, p. 258, and E. T. Seifarth, report on Leipsic, *Emig. e Col.*, 1893, p. 277.

[2] C. Conrad, in his excellent study, *Die Organisation des Arbeitsnachweises in Deutschland* (Leipsic, 1904, p. 84), pointed out that the employers' labor exchanges had made a practice of importing Italians and others in order to have on hand an oversupply of men.

[3] Lehmert, p. 29; Preuss, p. 31; Pertile, Pt. i, p. 109. In recent years instances appear to be fewer.

[4] G. Pertile, " Lo sciopero dei minatori nelle provincie del Reno e della Westfalia," *Boll. Emig.*, 1905, No. 8, pp. 39–42.

[5] W. Troeltsch and P. Hirschfeld, *Die deutschen sozialdemokratischen Gewerkschaften* (Berlin, 1905), pp. 109, 113; J. Goldstein, *Arbeiter und Unternehmer im Baugewerbe Deutschlands* (Zurich and Leipsic, 1913), pp. 46–48.

the Italians who regularly visited Germany. Entrance fees have been kept low. In the building trades, German unions have agreed with unions in Italy to give special rights to Italian members working in Germany. Despite these efforts it has apparently been harder to persuade the Italian laborers to organize than any other foreign group.[1] Why? Unskilled workers never organize readily and display little class sentiment. The language barrier is far from negligible. Italians have low standards of living and will accept low wages. They wish to earn quickly and surely, not stopping for strikes, then to return to Italy. They do not favor paying dues in one place if they must shortly go to another. Often deceived and misled, they distrust others' solicitations. And they fear that any unwelcome behavior on their part will lead to expulsion from the country.[2] Hence it seems rather surprising that, in December, 1910, as many as 7000 out of more than 100,-000 Italian workmen in Germany were members of German or Italian unions.[3] But even unionization has not brought equality of working conditions. The leading organized group, the masons, once much given to strike-breaking, have chiefly been employed in connection with railways, roads, bridges, ports, dams, mines, factories, sometimes farmhouses; rarely in cities, for these the German masons have jealously guarded as their own field.[4]

That unskilled Italians have worked for lower wages than the Germans has occasionally been maintained by both Italian and German observers.[5] The only Italians securing full trade-union rates have been those engaged in the building trades and they only, it is claimed, when they have worked in company with Germans.[6] As in France it is the coarser tasks that the Italians have

[1] A. W., " Die Organisierung der Italiener in Deutschland," *Correspondenzblatt*, April 27, 1912, pp. 249–251; note in *Soziale Praxis*, February 12, 1914, p. 574; Troeltsch and Hirschfeld, p. 70.

[2] Cf. Jacini, p. 131; Pertile, *Gli italiani in Germania*, Pt. iii, pp. 101–103; Troeltsch and Hirschfeld, pp. 69 f.

[3] See note in *Rivista Coloniale*, February 1–15, 1913, p. 95.

[4] Pertile, Pt. i, p. 110.

[5] Jacini, p. 131; Lehmert, p. 29. Utterances more or less specific are frequent in *Boll. Emig.* Cf. Goldstein, p. 47; Hansen, *loc. cit.*; *Soziale Praxis*, July 27, 1911, pp. 1334 f.

[6] Pertile, Pt. i, pp. 112 f.

been given to do. By virtue of this demarcation or the fact that humbler employments have in some places been almost abandoned to them, competition with the Germans has often not been obvious. They have then been viewed with a degree of indifference. Let a period of depression come, however, and we are told that Germans want the Italians' jobs. At such times in the past, the public employers of Prussia and Baden have been commanded to discharge their foreign workmen, private employers in Saxony have been urged by the government to do likewise, and other states have followed these examples.[1] It is the fear that immigration, in insidious ways, hurts the interests of German labor, that has made the unions frown upon the Italian influx. They have not believed that any of the economic gain which Italians bring to employers percolates down to them.

The Italians have not asked cordiality of reception. Toleration has sufficed. Above all anxious that their primary aim in coming should not be thwarted, they have incidentally had to accept much that is unpalatable.

Beyond any question, life for the oven workers of Bavaria has been difficult. How often have the accordanti played them false, whose oral contract made in Italy offers a fine opportunity for deceit abroad! The minority employed in the larger works near Munich are not in question, but the thousands are, who are scattered through the upland establishments, where labor laws are harder to enforce. Eleven hours of work, often more, quite apart

---

[1] " Relazione sui servizi dell' emigrazione per il periodo Aprile 1908–Aprile 1909," *Boll. Emig.*, 1909, No. 9, p. 113; note in *Boll. Emig.*, 1908, No. 7, p. 101; Schilling, p. 72; Pezzani, p. 56; Lambertenghi, p. 20; Pertile, Pt. i, pp. 107 f., Pt. iv, pp. 105–112. For a note concerning Prussia, see *Soziale Praxis*, August 4, 1910, p. 1244; concerning Wurttemberg, *Der Arbeitsnachweis in Deutschland*, March 15, 1914, p. 166. See also Kaiserliches Statistisches Amt, *Beiträge zur Arbeiterstatistik*, No. 6, *Die Regelung des Arbeitsverhältnisses bei Vergebung öffentlicher Arbeiten insbesondere in deutschen Städten* (Berlin, 1907), pp. 145–148. A sharp criticism of the Alsatian labor exchanges for not giving employment by preference to Germans is " Die Verwaltung der Elsass-Lothringischen Arbeitsämter," in *Soziale Praxis*, August 17, 1911, pp. 1446 f. For the employers' case see the reply to Hansen (cf. *supra*) by E. Bernhard in *Soziale Praxis*, June 29, 1911, pp. 1206 f.; cf. the same journal, August 13, 1908, pp. 1206 f.

from rests, have been common; and the rests have been less frequent than with German workers. Women have been utilized, like the boys, in the drying and cleaning operations, in loading and unloading the ovens, lifting the sold bricks upon carts, and sometimes even in heavier tasks and upon night work. As to the children, " I asked several fathers," wrote Pertile, "if they felt no compunction in subjecting their sons to such prolonged and exhausting toil. Always their reply was the same, ' We began to work at their age — why should not they begin ? ' " [1]

Boys have received 35–60 marks a month, besides board and lodging, women less. The men who fashion the bricks and manage the ovens have been paid 100 marks. Polenta, a little cheese, and if the contract has specified, a bit of meat on Sunday, have been provided. Lodgings have usually been an integral part of the working establishment, and often unsanitary. The men have developed drinking habits. In a good season, especially where several workers have belonged to one family, the venture has netted them some savings.[2]

In western Germany, the immigrants have generally been grown men, unmarried or with their families in Italy. Consider the miners, who have been the most likely to take their families with them. The skilled men have been paid seven marks or more for an eight-hour shift, their subordinates about three-quarters as much. But the Italians, we have seen, are rarely skilled. Some workmen used to accomplish enough " double days " of sixteen hours to total thirty-five work days a month. The mass, earning little, contending against high costs of living, have been able to lay by even a small surplus only when their families have remained in Italy. Their health has been hurt, as by inhaling

---

[1] *Op. cit.*, Pt. i, p. 106.

[2] Sandicchi, pp. 3–34; Pertile, Pt. i, pp. 103–109, 131, 137 and Pt. ii, p. 25; Cabrini, *loc. cit.*; Mondini, pp. 68–70; Pezzani, pp. 58–60.

Pertile (Pt. i, p. 131) confirms for his day the language used by a Baden factory inspector in 1898: " The places inhabited by these workers are extremely dirty and wholly unfit for human habitation. They are huts put together of planks or boards under the roof of the works. Tables and chairs are absent, daylight often hardly penetrates, the bed is a wooden box with a bag of straw and two coverlets inside. Since there are no cupboards, clothes and valuables are often stolen. Washing fixtures are wholly absent."

powdered rock, which is much more deleterious than powdered coal, and oftener than the Germans they have been the victims of industrial accidents. For their injuries, indemnities have been paid, but there can be no compensation for the condition of exhaustion to which eight or ten years of underground toil have ordinarily brought them.[1] Except for strikes, employment in the mines has been fairly steady; in the Ruhr strike already referred to, the loss in wages to the Italians certainly equalled the possible savings of many months.[2] The building-trades workmen and their kin have received relatively high rates of pay, but as everywhere they have suffered from great irregularity of employment. By freely working overtime, some men have made the ordinary wage of five or six marks an average wage. Substantially the same rate has been received by quarry workers and stonecutters, working by the piece. Accidents and diseases of the lungs have frequently been the lot of these workmen.[3] But, on the other hand, they, like the miners, appear to have had a better diet than was customary in Italy.

Wages of only three to four marks a day have been paid to the mill hands of the iron and steel centers and to the general pick-and-shovel men everywhere. As in all industrial countries, there have been half-day shifts for the mill hands and every week or two a double working day of twenty-four hours. The general laborers, working out of doors, and less desired than more robust men, have suffered greatly through unemployment, those remaining over the winter in Germany having to spend more than their savings. The mill hands have suffered from the same cause, their industry being subject to violent, if non-seasonal, fluctuations. All have had to live as cheaply as possible, in an era of rising prices, in order to save even a modicum of their wages.

Quite the most deplorable living conditions have been in Lorraine, appreciably worse than those of Westphalia and Rhenish Prussia. Wretched lodgings, filthy in the extreme, six or eight

[1] On accidents, see *Wirtschaftliche Entwickelung*, etc., p. 57; Pertile, Pt. i, pp. 58–73; Donadio, p. 436.

[2] See *Boll. Emig.*, 1905, No. 8, p. 42.

[3] Pertile, Pt. i, pp. 109–115, 137; *idem, Boll. Emig.*, 1908, No. 19, p. 3; Donadio, p. 435.

men to a room, two men to a small bed, have been common; the beds sometimes used day and night. The North Italians have everywhere lived better than the South, but it is only when a boarding house has been run by a German family that dirt and overcrowding have been absent. By bunking together and eating under the stewardship of the " boss " who has enrolled them in Italy the laborers have often lived for two marks a day — half their wage. In the attempt to make life tolerable all have been more given to the drink habit than in Italy; the reaction, less frequent than with Germans and French, coming generally on Sundays and holidays. Always under the boarding system, so widely prevalent, moral standards tend to be relaxed. Drinking, gambling, and looseness in sex relations have been by all odds worst in Lorraine and little less diffused than in French Lorraine, across the border, reputed to be the center of infection. Only a more rigorous police system and better discipline in the works have prevented the case from being quite as bad.[1]

No close parallel, fortunately, can be found to the living conditions of Lorraine. Yet the circumstances of the Italians elsewhere have had no roseate hue. After deduction of their railway fares, the general laborers have been able to save little. When an entire family has worked in the textiles, in North or South Germany, good savings have resulted. The pay of women operatives, less than two marks a day, has been inadequate to their needs.[2]

[1] Pertile, *Gli italiani*, etc., Pt. i, pp. 73–75, 97–103, 125–184; *idem, Boll. Emig.*, 1905, No. 18, and *Boll. Emig.*, 1908, No. 19; Donadio, p. 435; Vinci, *Boll. Emig.*, 1913, No. 12, p. 11. On the victims of accidents see an article, " Ausländische Arbeiter und Arbeiterwanderungen in Deutschland," *Soziale Praxis*, November, 1906, pp. 177–179.

Upon the housing situation, Pertile wrote (" Gli italiani," etc., Pt. i, p. 129; cf. pp. 132–135): "Especially in the mineral basin of Lorraine, the houses are with rare exceptions so indecent, filthy, and disagreeable that, compared with those of the local population, they seem pigsties. A pungent and nauseating odor rises from every corner of the house. Oftentimes next the house if not actually in it, pigs and poultry are raised. The floors and walks are covered with a layer of earth or mud. Even the better grade of houses are reduced by the Italians to veritable stables." Wherever in Germany, he held, Italians come together for a considerable undertaking, abominable living conditions arise.

[2] Long hours, low wages, and special abuses have been held to be the lot of the Italians, once nearly 800, chiefly women, in the jute mills of Landsberg an der Warthe. The workers had been enrolled in Munich and Trent. See C. Bartoli,

Though Mädchenheime exist in some places, many girls have preferred to live independently and often have come to grief. The street vendors, exclusive survivors of the circumambulant types, have sometimes fared well. Nowhere have large retail shops been the outgrowth of small ones, but always branches of firms in Italy.

For the Italians to do well in Germany has indeed been a difficult thing. Rarely do we read that any have risen to comfort, and then the condition follows: only after many years of hard work and constant saving. Those ignorant of German — and most have been; those especially who are illiterate — and so it has been with a great many; though they sometimes proceed with almost instinctive sureness, generally grope their way and have to pay for their experience dearly. The consulates know how often the result has been tragic. Stinted living — without a family in Germany — and periodic return to Italy are all that have separated the mass from failure. The fear of being caught by the winter is so great that many have returned to Italy while employment was still good, and sometimes, if reports be credible, the rate of wages has risen after their departure.[1] On the other hand, in their eagerness to get work, they have often arrived too early in the German spring, faring ill at the outset of their season; and both in 1901 and 1908, during industrial depression, they none the less appeared in large numbers — in the second of these periods in spite of warnings issued in Italy.[2]

In non-material ways the lives of the Italians in Germany have not been bright. A difficult situation has arisen when large numbers of foreign men have given a community its character, or when unmarried girls have worked in the factories or sold in the

"Dolori e miserie dell' emigrazione italiana in Germania," *Vita Italiana all' Estero*, April 25, 1914, pp. 55–58.

[1] "Relazione sui servizi," etc., *Boll. Emig.*, 1910, No. 18, p. 238; Krause, "L'immigrazione operaia italiana," p. 45; note in *Soziale Praxis*, November 28, 1912, p. 258.

[2] "Relazione sui servizi," etc., pp. 237 f.; Pertile, in *Boll. Emig.*, 1908, No. 19, p. 42 (cf. *idem, Boll. Emig.*, 1905, No. 18, p. 23); Oppenheim, in *Boll. Emig.*, 1902, No. 10, p. 4; Pezzani, in *Emig. e Col.*, p. 57. In 1912, a warning in the Italian press against emigration into Germany because of building-trades disputes there was judged to have been effective. *Soziale Praxis*, May 8, 1912, p. 932.

streets. Most Italians have been inaccessible to the church. The cathedral at Metz used to hold a Sunday service in their language, but I have learned of no similar instance. The stabler groups have had their priests. In the turmoil of their lives, if we may believe the witnesses, both patriotic and religious feelings have declined.[1]   Undoubtedly radical social propaganda has made headway. Since regional animosities have been keen, the Italians have not organized well in a large way and even mutual aid societies have been rare among them. The latter, though of limited utility in a country having a highly developed system of social insurance, have in other countries done much to maintain or develop social ties. A small-voiced Italian press, seeking out the labor interest, has existed, without exercising much influence. The consular service and especially the *Opera* of Bonomelli have served to guide the perplexed and rescue the failures, but have not touched closely the great mass of the immigrants.

The passing centuries have wrought extraordinary changes. In ancient times the Italians came to Germany as conquerors. Their engineers and architects spanned rivers and planted enduring cities. In the Middle Ages, skilled artisans arrived, teaching the art of building; and merchants came to trade. Latterly the immigrants have come but to beg their bread, willing to toil in the nethermost positions of German industry, not hoping, for they have not dared, that comfort and ease would be the reward of toil.

[1] Jacini, p. 134. Cf. Pertile, " Gli italiani," etc., Pt. i, pp. 144 f.

CHAPTER X

SWITZERLAND

As happens commonly in mountainous countries, the population of Switzerland has grown but slowly — in fifty years by less than one-half. In its composition, however, momentous changes have taken place; for while Swiss families have betaken themselves by thousands to North and South America, foreign immigrants, in still greater measure, have established themselves in the country. The foreign fraction of the population has indeed quadrupled in half a century. That French, Germans, and Italians should freely enter a land where their own languages are all customarily spoken is not to be marvelled at. Whereas, however, natives of France have rarely settled elsewhere than in French Switzerland, and Germans mainly in the German cantons, the great mass of Italians have planted themselves not in the Italian but in the German and French parts. Such defiance of language is a characteristic trait of Italian emigration, and it makes the movement into Switzerland one in kind with the great main currents.

Before the middle of the nineteenth century, few but travellers and refugees came. In the winter of 1860 some 9000 Italian residents were enumerated, in 1870 twice as many, and the great summer immigration had scarcely begun. Into Ticino a stream of such amplitude soon poured that today nearly half the population there may be said to have originated in Italy or been born of Italian parents within the past half century. About 1870, the great era of railway building was inaugurated, and the Italian began to gravitate toward his own. When the St. Gothard tunnel was started, in 1872, Italian laborers undertook the work of construction and, nine years later, saw it completed. In 1880, there was a winter population of 41,500. In the next decade, the Italians hardly increased at all, for it was a slack time in railway work. Again, however, in the years 1890–1900, amid revival of construction work, they resumed their coming, and in the last winter of the century 95,000 were present. In workshops and mines they had increased faster than any other people. Their activities in general had immensely broadened, and a rapidly increasing factory population had gained a foothold. It was soon apparent that there had come to be a rival to the attractions of Germany. Growing industrialization and an ever-swelling tourist business, demanding the construction of factories, power works, railway lines, and hotels, had made of Switzerland one of the great labor markets of Europe.

The half million and more foreigners discovered by the census of 1910 were nearly 15 per cent of the population; in some cantons they were 30 or 40 per cent.[1] So, for this mountainous Old-World land, immigration has had the same proportional importance as for the United States. In the previous decade, in fact, foreign settlers and births in the foreign stock had increased the population more than half as much as it was increased by Swiss stock. The Germans and the Italians together comprised in 1910 four-fifths of the foreigners and were about equally represented, numbering more than 200,000 each. Italian citizens alone were about 6 per cent of the entire population (the *hirondelles* who come for the summer are of course not included in these December statistics). In Geneva they were over 21,000, exceeded only by the French; throughout the German cantons they were numerous; and nearly all the foreigners of Ticino were Italian citizens, that is, about a quarter of the canton's population — in some communes, a majority. In no other country of Europe is Italian immigrant stock so large a factor.

The availability of routes of travel has always governed this immigration. Ticino lies at the very gates of Italy. The Grisons, much higher, have been reached by way of Chiavenna and the Splügen. Until 1906, when the tunnel was completed, Napoleon's road over the Simplon Pass, made in the first years of the nineteenth century, was the natural highway into the Vallais, and indeed into the farther cantons of Geneva, Vaud, Fribourg,

---

[1] *Résultats statistiques du recensement fédéral de la population du 1er décembre 1910*, Berne, 1915. I have at various points drawn upon this census.

and Neuchâtel. Since then, every year, thousands upon thousands of Italians have passed through the little frontier town of Domodossola, lending it a new importance, making it veritably " the western Chiasso." And what is the eastern Chiasso ? It is the town through which pass, on their way to Bellinzona and the St. Gothard—presently to Zurich and Basel—not only the great majority of Italian immigrants destined for Switzerland, but the mass also of those bound for western Germany.

It is no inconsiderable part which the Italians have played in Swiss agriculture. Ten thousand were recorded in 1905, more than 1 per cent of all the workers in this leading industry of the country.[1] Four thousand were farm laborers, mainly harvest hands, who worked in the southern and in the western German cantons; later on in the season more would have been revealed. But the census found also a host of temporary immigrant farm laborers whose nationality it did not determine, most numerous in the cantons where the Italians chiefly went. The Lombard haymowers of Ticino have long been an important class among the immigrants into Switzerland. Six thousand Italians were tenants or owners of land, whose farms, however, were rarely larger than from one to seven acres. In the Grisons and Ticino, the Italian immigrants were, respectively, 11 and 8.6 per cent of the agricultural population. The similarity of farming methods to those used in Italy and the accessibility of these regions make it easy to explain the immigration.[2]

Almost all the foreigners employed in forestry were Italians, nearly 5 per cent of the entire working force. More than half

[1] Many data in this chapter have been taken from *Schweizerische Statistik, Ergebnisse der eidgenossigen Betriebszählung vom 9 August, 1905*, 4 vols., Berne, 1910–12. I have also, for comparisons, drawn upon vol. iii of the general census of December 1, 1900, Berne, 1907.

[2] See esp. *Betriebszählung*, ii, and its supplement. Cf. G. de Michelis, " L'emigrazione italiana nella Svizzera," *Boll. Emig.*, 1903, No. 12, p. 13; L. Silvestrelli, " L'emigrazione e le colonie italiane in Svizzera," *Boll. Emig.*, 1903, No. 11, pp. 14 f. By 1910, many of the " Swiss " agriculturists of Ticino were really descendants of Italian immigrants. Writing in 1893, A. Marazzi (report on Bellinzona consular district, *Emig. e Col.*, 1893, p. 494) claimed that the Italians, taking the places of the emigrated Swiss, had quite saved the agriculture of Ticino. As in the Trentino, the two movements had run parallel for decades. One can almost

were in the Grisons, the rest chiefly in St. Gall, Vaud, and Neuchâtel. The more important industry of mining drew upon them even more strongly, the 6000 and more employed constituting nearly half of all the workers, Swiss or foreign. They were occupied chiefly in the granite quarries, which exist in nearly all the cantons. It is not too much to say that the development of the Ticinese quarries, begun when the St. Gothard railway was constructed, and carried forward with special rapidity after 1890, was accomplished almost entirely with immigrant labor — the labor first of North Italians and later also of men who came from as far south as Tuscany. Their number has fluctuated much with day and season, being always highest in spring and autumn. Hydraulic extraction of lime and cement materials, the quarrying of gravel, sand, sandstone, marble, and slate have also occupied many Italians.[1]

It is, however, in the work of construction and manufacturing, which occupies nearly as many people as agriculture in Switzerland, that the Italians have had their chief place. While citizens of the federation were only three-quarters of all engaged, citizens of Italy were nearly 14 per cent. It is an extraordinary situation. In the economic development of modern Switzerland, more and more during the last thirty or forty years, these immigrants have played a remarkable rôle. In construction work alone, their prime field, they had, when the industrial census was taken, a contingent of 65,000 in a total of 85,000 foreigners, and were actually one-third of all the workers employed, of whatever nationality, including the Swiss. In manufacturing, there were 20,000 more. In the two industries together, Italian wage earners numbered 77,500. The 44,000 of these employed in railway work, on roads and bridges and on elevated and underground structures, were certainly a great majority of all engaged in such work in the country.

hold, says Marazzi, that " the Italian citizens immigrate into the canton because the Ticinese emigrate, and that the Ticinese citizens emigrate because the Italians immigrate."

[1] *Betriebszählung*, ii, pp. 487–537; Marazzi, *op. cit.* in *Boll. Emig.*, 1903, No. 11, pp. 26–28; G. Barni and G. Canevascini, *L'industria del granito e lo sviluppo economico del canton Ticino*, Lugano, 1913 — a particularly careful study.

If one could bring together today a list of the larger enterprises upon which these workpeople have been employed, often almost to the exclusion of others, the result would be impressive. Too meager the record! No diplomatic representative or agent of the Emigration Service writes of his countrymen without general reference to their labor; but only sporadically, as if reflecting an uncommon reach for the concrete and picturesque, does he mention specific undertakings.

One of the earliest of their achievements was the cutting of the Mont Cenis tunnel, begun in 1857 but not completed till 1871, after hand labor had given place to machine drilling. The new passageway was eight miles long. I have alluded to the tunnelling of the St. Gothard, which remains after forty years one of the world's great structures. On the tunnel itself, more than nine miles long, and on the railroad approaches which make a line one hundred and fifty miles in length, thousands of Italians were employed.[1] The first *Bergbahn* to be built, that of the Rigi, was the fruit of Italian toil; so, later, was that of Pilatus. Near the end of the century came the tunnelling of the Albula through three and a half miles of the granite of the Rhetian Alps.

Heralded by manifests in Sicily, Calabria, Romagna, and other parts of Italy inviting workers to enrol in the enterprise, work on the Simplon tunnel was begun in 1898. In the first contingent were some 1900 Italians, including many Piedmontese and Venetians. They and their successors, a labor force fluctuating much during a period of seven years, cut away the crystalline rock over a stretch of more than twelve miles and gave to the world its longest tunnel. Toiling much of the time more than a mile below the surface, in rock temperatures reaching to 130° F., forced to cease their work by voluminous streams of hot water — an obstacle not present, for example, in the St. Gothard — oblivious to the fumes and roar of the dynamite, these men wrought wonders of industry and endurance.[2]

[1] Silvestrelli, p. 16.

[2] F. Gavotti, " Il canton Vallese e la colonia italiana," *Emig. e Col.*, 1903, ii, p. 77; de Michelis, *op. cit.* in *Boll. Emig.*, 1903, No. 12, pp. 71 f.; *idem*, " Gli operai italiani al Sempione," *Giornale degli Economisti*, February, 1899, pp. 138–154; E. Sella, *L'emigrazione italiana nella Svizzera*, Turin, 1899, pp. 40 f.

About the time this tunnel was completed, work began on the Loetschberg railway; a route of immense importance for Swiss internal commerce, and, in continuation of the Simplon passage, replacing the St. Gothard route for Italian-French intercourse. It was to have, when finished, nearly ten miles of tunnel and more than twenty-five of approaches. At the end of four years, there were still more than 3000 Italians at work upon it, including men who had drudged in the Simplon, and even, it is said, some veterans of the St. Gothard. In the most active period there must have been 6000 or 7000 Italians engaged. At one time a troop of 250 Macedonian Turks was substituted for Italians, but the experiment failed. In February, 1912, the tunnelling of the Jungfraujoch, more than 10,000 feet above the sea, was finished. Not till the next year was the Loetschberg railway completed.[1]

In 1914 the first track was constructed of the Brieg-Furka-Disentis line, an extraordinary series of bridges, tunnels, and embankments connecting the Simplon and the St. Gothard routes and the Grisons railway net, running over sixty miles from the upper valley of the Rhône, past Andermatt, to the upper valley of the Rhine. Nearly all the workers, it is said, were Italian, sometimes more than 3000; in the winter they contended with several feet of snow and with intense cold which was little less in the tunnels.[2]

[1] G. de Michelis, " Regio Ufficio della Emigrazione Italiana nella Svizzera, Relazione," *Boll. Emig.*, 1908, No. 10, p. 62; " Relazione sui servizi . . . 1908–09," *Boll. Emig.*, 1909, No. 9, p. 110; " Relazione sui servizi . . . 1909–10," *Boll. Emig.*, 1910, No. 18, pp. 229, 232; E. Mancini, " Dal Loetschberg alla Jungfrau," *Nuova Antologia*, November 16, 1913, p. 280; note in *Rivista Coloniale*, March 25, 1912, p. 220.

[2] A. Carneluti, " La mano d'opera italiana alla costruzione della ferrovia di montagna Briga-Furka-Disentis," *Boll. Emig.*, 1904, No. 9, pp. 51–56.

Other instances deserve to be recorded. Many Italians, largely from the South, helped build the Thusis-St. Moritz railway, about the beginning of the present century (note in *Boll. Emig.*, 1902, No. 6, p. 65; A. Marazzi, " L'immigrazione italiana nella Svizzera Tedesca," *Emig. e Col.*, 1903, ii, p. 92). In the canton of Berne others worked on the Zweisimmen-Saanen-Bulle railway (note in *Boll. Emig.*, 1903, No. 6, p. 111). The Department of Public Works of Ticino told the Italian consul-general that 90 per cent of the men employed on cantonal and communal public works were Italian citizens (F. Lucchesi-Palli, " Il canton Ticino e la immigrazione italiana," *Emig. e Col.*, 1903, ii, p. 44). Many were working on the Martigny-Châtelard rail-

Upon such undertakings as these and upon general housebuilding, a multitude of Italian masons have worked. In 1905 more than 5500 were counted. "Their good work," the census went out of its way to remark, "is known and appreciated everywhere. Upon several occasions attempts have been made in Switzerland to establish schools for the training of skilled masons, but they have failed, unfortunately, and, far from taking the place of the Italian mason, the Swiss workman is content to serve him as a hod-carrier." [1] Italian hodmen, be it said in passing, have, however, also been innumerable. In no other country have masons secured so early and so firm a foothold. Prolific Lombardy, Venetia, and Piedmont provide, we have seen, an extraordinary instance of specialization of skill for an international labor market. Here they have built a substantial railway station, there a hotel, houses everywhere, and they have been busy in every period of building prosperity. A strike by Italian hodcarriers, promptly followed by

way in the Vallais (Gavotti, p. 71). At Kaltbrunn, in 1903, nearly 1000 men were engaged in tunnelling a portion of the Weissenstein on the Solette-Montier railroad; the five or six miles stretch was completed in 1907 (Schiaparelli, " L'opera di assistenza degli operai italiani emigrati in Europa e nel Levante," *Boll. Emig.*, 1904, No. 2, p. 47; de Michelis, *op. cit.* in *Boll. Emig.*, 1908, No. 10, p. 75). In 1906, 2000 gathered at Chippo and Sierre in Vallais for the hydraulic and construction work necessary for an aluminum establishment (de Michelis, " Le istituzioni italiani nella Svizzera per l'assistenza degli emigranti," *Boll. Emig.*, 1908, No. 22, p. 35). In 1909 they were working on a short railroad running from Martigny to Orsières, on another connecting Spiez and Brieg, and were completing the Bodensee-Toggenburg road uniting, through the cantons of St. Gall and Appenzell, lakes Zurich and Constance, — when at its height, in 1908, the last-named task employed about 4000 Italians; 1000 were building the Bernina road; others were altering the channel of the Rhine at Diepoldsau, a task reckoned to last eight years; at Drause a canal was being constructed; in at least eight places large hydro-electric plants were building: these are not half the instances which the Italian emigration commissioner happened to record at one time, many of them promising work for several years (report, *Boll. Emig.*, 1910, No. 18, pp. 232–235; see also E. Pasteris, " Una missione sul Reno," *Rivista Internazionale di Scienze Sociali e Discipline Ausiliarie*, July-August, 1912, pp. 303 f.). Still others were engaged in a four years' task of tunnelling the Grenchenberg for a distance of five miles, and were constructing the Monteau-Longeau road in continuance of the Loetschberg line (F. Calimani, " Condizione degli operai italiani a Granges," *Boll. Emig.*, 1913, No. 5, p. 126). On the construction of the Swiss railways, see F. Tajani, *I valichi alpini*, 2d ed., Milan, 1914; P. Weissenbach, *Das Eisenbahnwesen der Schweiz*, 2 vols., Zurich, 1913–14. Cf. P. Clerget, *La Suisse au XXe siècle* (Paris, 1908), ch. vi.

[1] Betriebszählung, iii, p. 96.*

a strike of bricklayers, made 1907 " a bad year " for building in Basel, many tasks remaining unfinished.[1]

There have been many painters and plasterers, carpenters and plumbers. Of plasterers and stucco workers the 1905 census counted 1500; of cabinet makers an equal number; of plumbers, locksmiths, stonecutters, electric fitters, 600 each. The higher grades of stone sculptor have appeared, coming from Tuscany. Here also mention should be made of 2500 Italians employed in the making of brick and tiles and 1400 in preparing various cement products. Later figures than these would doubtless reveal even more.[2]

In factory employments, the Italians, among foreigners, have stood second to the Germans. After 1895 their increase was particularly rapid, continuing certainly for ten or fifteen years, and probably till before the war. The industrial census counted 2000 in the silk industry, 1800 in the machine-made embroidery trade, 1700 in the cotton mills, 900 in shoe factories,[3] nearly as many in the woolen mills, and 600 in the chocolate factories.[4] Others were in the tobacco, straw goods, and watch factories. In the making of clothing and toilet articles, the 4700 Italians were nearly 5 per cent of all so employed in Switzerland. For these many employments Lugano, Geneva, Basel, Zurich, and St. Gall have been the great centers. In the canton of St. Gall, in 1909 —

[1] Mitteilungen des statistischen Amtes des Kantons Basel-Stadt, No. 12; *Die im Jahre 1907 im Kanton Basel-Stadt erstellten Neubauten* (Basel, 1908), p. 5.

[2] The great increase of the Italians in building appears to have begun around the end of the last century. See Sella, p. 35, on the relation of Italian to other workers. It is certain that the Italians had been becoming numerous for many years previous. Speaking for the Zurich district, F. Lambertenghi in *Emig. e Col.*, 1893, p. 506, declared that in railroad work and masonry the Italians had relatively few competitors.

[3] Doubtless many of the Italian shoemakers of the cities are not included in this figure. Sella, years ago, wrote (*op. cit.*, pp. 29 f.), probably with exaggeration, that in Geneva nearly all the shoemakers were Italian. Some had shops of their own; most worked for a proprietor. They did all grades of work. The employees in the two major factories turning out a machine product were nearly all Italian.

[4] On one occasion at least, the Cailler company brought 200 Italian girls to Fribourg, enrolled by an agent at Pavullo, with the approval of Italian officials. See G. Basso, " I cantoni francesi della Svizzera e le loro colonie italiane," *Emig. e Col.*, 1903, ii, p. 55.

at St. Gall, Rorschach, Affoltern, and other places — were several thousand girls without whose aid some factories would have been in difficult straits. At Birsfelden, near Basel, many girls have worked in a *Lumpfabrik* ("la lompa!") sorting rags; it is an occupation in which employment has invariably been good.[1] In all these occupations, women and girls have tended to predominate. The manufacture of foods and beverages claimed 3200 Italians, 5 per cent of all workers; the paper, leather, and rubber manufacture, nearly 500, or 6 per cent; metal and machine works 3800; printing, over 500.

Italian trade in Switzerland has had a long history. Its modern beginnings are to be found in the itinerant vendors who followed the Alpine passes. When the construction workmen came, retail dealers settled about them; so it was in the St. Gothard, the Simplon, and many other regions. Often their settlements became permanent. Of the 12,000 Italians counted in 1905 more than a quarter were in Ticino, and more than a sixth in the Grisons. Geneva and Vaud had each 1100, 7 per cent and 5 per cent respectively of all there. Engaged in the work of hotels, pensions, inns, and the like were 6700, nearly 7 per cent of all such workpeople in Switzerland. In food and drink shops there were 2500. Ranking only after the Swiss and Germans, the Italians have been over 5 per cent of the entire trading population.

These are the principal groups. To complete the outlines of the picture, it is only necessary to add the employees of the transportation companies (not in construction work) who were 3500 in 1905; and those engaged in the liberal professions, numbering over 1600 — relatively more numerous than in any other country visited by the Italians, the devotees of art being actually one-seventh of all of their kind. Nowhere else, in truth, has Italian immigration been so diversified, nowhere else has so large a factor of skill appeared. The result may be striking, but it is not strange when the nearness of the opportunities of Switzerland to the teeming populations of North Italy is considered.

---

[1] Pasteris, pp. 303–305; M. L. Danieli Camozzi, "L'emigrazione italiana femminile in Germania e in Svizzera," *Rivista di Emigrazione*, May, 1909, p. 56; Bernardy, "Alcuni aspetti . . . Basilea" (*cit.*), pp. 10–16.

Undeniably a tremendous amount of work has been performed by the Italians. Without them the economic advance of the country would have been much less. Is it not astonishing that a European nation should in the twentieth century have come to depend at so many points upon its immigrants?[1] It is not as heads of establishments, officials, technical employees, and the like that the mass of the Italians have worked. In industry some years ago they were about 4 per cent of such persons, whereas of the wage earners, skilled and unskilled, they were 19 per cent.[2] It is for the Swiss then to decide what the Italians shall do, and to supervise and direct their effort. That is the usual situation.

Apart from its well understood limitations, the labor of the Italians has given satisfaction. Even the unskilled have come mainly from those parts of Italy in which vigor and assiduity are best developed. In power of accomplishment the men have compared well with other immigrants who have been used; good words for the masons have been especially frequent. The girl factory workers, though they have sometimes been described as capricious and dirty, and found unacceptable in the more responsible places, have at least been quick-fingered. When all, however, is said, it is clear that fundamentally it is the abundance and cheapness of Italian labor that have made it an asset in Switzerland.

It is in fact as *homo oeconomicus* and not at all as *homo civicus*, as a Swiss eulogist of the immigration has put it, that the Italian is prized.[3] There is no desire to assimilate him. Public opinion has not encouraged naturalization, which takes place only on a

---

[1] With P. H. Schmidt (*Die schweizerischen Industrien im internationalen Konkurrenzkampfe*, Zurich, 1912), we may say, "Swiss industry could not have expanded so greatly as it has in the last ten years nor so fully have utilized the special opportunities of 1906 and 1907, had the assistance of Italian immigrant labor been withheld" (p. 98); but we ought to use cautiously such words as "necessary" or "indispensable" (for instances of which see Schmidt, p. 97, and N. Droz, former president of Switzerland, in his introduction to Sella's book). When the European war shut off the supply of Italians, the pinch was seriously felt; see a note in *Boll. Emig.*, 1916, No. 15, pp. 55-57.

[2] Betriebszählung, iii, 81.*

[3] A. Picot, *Un problème national, La population étrangère établie en Suisse* (Geneva and Basel, 1914), p. 13.

small scale. Now and then Italians marry Swiss women.[1] But there has never been any considerable or general approach to Swiss ways. Though *si* may become *oui, stazione,* '*gara,*' *sciopero,* '*greva,*' these interesting adaptations of the tongue are superficial. The immigrant, wherever he goes, continues to eat the imported food of his own people, bought of his fellow countrymen. And in the cities he goes into his own well-defined colonies. "Italian," as one writer has put it, not unsympathetically, "he remains, body and soul."[2]

Signs of an unfriendly or inhospitable attitude are by no means wanting. The Basel and St. Gall poor-law authorities have refused to aid Italians. In the country as a whole, a considerable burden of poverty, only rarely borne by Italian organizations, is set against the gain from their coming.[3] Probably the people of Vallais are typical enough when, as some one has said, they regard

---

[1] De Michelis, *op. cit.* in *Boll. Emig.*, 1903, No. 12, pp. 51 f.; Gavotti, p. 76; Marazzi, *op. cit.* in *Boll. Emig.*, 1903, No. 11, p. 35; Lucchesi-Palli, p. 44; Silvestrelli, p. 16.

[2] Schmidt, p. 98. Cf. Sella (pp. 17–20, 31) who writes (p. 19): "The aspect of the Italian workman in Switzerland is unlike that of the indigenous workman. And as he differs in clothing and has a coarser exterior, so he is morally and intellectually coarser, and often incapable, not only of comprehending but even of conceiving the existence of moral and social sentiments belonging to the native workers among whom he lives. . . . This is what makes the Italians abroad remain almost isolated from the other workers and constitute, as it were, a people within a people. They feel different because they are inferior." The more intelligent, he adds, if they stay, gradually come nearer to the Swiss.

[3] De Michelis, *op. cit.* in *Boll. Emig.*, 1903, No. 12, p. 89; Danieli Camozzi, pp. 58 f.; Dr. C. A. Schmid, "Das Armenwesen in Oberitalien," *Zeitschrift für Schweizerische Statistik* (Berne, 1907), i, pp. 89, 95. Schmid holds the burden to have increased much in the ten years before his writing. Its origins are excessive frugality, low standards of hygiene, an increasing habit of remaining over the winter, the recommendation by protective organizations in Italy that emigrants in Switzerland should beg aid of Swiss agencies, lastly some development of a pauper spirit. Writing again, seven years later (*Das gesetzliche Armenwesen in der Schweiz*, Zurich, 1914), Schmid holds (pp. 28–30, 35) that in 1911 the public authorities paid 125,000 francs on account of the sickness of Italian immigrants, and the private authorities an equal sum; and that wherever many foreign poor are aided, the care of the Swiss poor suffers. A. Wild, in *Das organisierte freiwillige Armenwesen in der Schweiz* (Zurich, 1914), holds (pp. 267–269, 276) that care by Italian compatriots has been but meagerly developed and that, even where organizations exist, they are often quite inactive. On the existing laws, see J. Langhard, *Das Niederlassungsrecht der Ausländer in der Schweiz*, Zurich, 1913. Nearly half a century ago, the canton of Uri

the Italians as " guests who are necessary rather than welcome." [1]
The names *crispi, macaroni, cinkeli*, popularly applied, are not
marks of esteem. But the spirit of opposition, however varied
the forms it assumes, has rarely led to clashes.[2]

The labor interests have protested against the Italians, but less
vigorously than in other countries. There are, to be sure, the
familiar charges that the immigrants work for lower wages and
displace native labor. Swiss women have been unwilling to work
side by side with Italian women, sometimes, doubtless, avoiding
employment altogether, but more commonly working in different
establishments or at different occupations. The Swiss men have
similarly held aloof. It is not enough to say that they naturally
work in a higher stratum of advantage. I have quoted an official
lament for the small number of Swiss masons. But theirs is an
occupation in which the requisite skill and effort command low
wages — wages that are appreciably lower than they would be if
there were fewer Italian competitors. Although many of the
masons are members of the *Federazione Muraria Italiana*, and
the organized granite cutters of Ticino have successfully waged at
least one notable fight, yet the mass of the immigrants, quite as
in France and Germany, have cared little about organization. In
periods of unemployment, Swiss labor interests have sometimes
asked for the exclusion of the foreigners, but their voices have not
hitherto been powerful.[3]

Whatever the alternative of life in Italy might mean, life for the
Italians in Switzerland is at best a struggle. Those in agriculture,

prohibited the coming of street musicians and exhibitors of animals (Carpi, i, p. 74).
A conspicuous record of blood crime has not helped to create a sentiment in favor
of the Italians.

[1] Gavotti, p. 78.

[2] Sella (pp. 9–11) gives some instances. A memorable rising in Zurich in 1897
was quelled at heavy expense. At Brieg, while the Simplon was building, the authorities had to keep Italians and Swiss apart in their celebrations. For an example
of labor conflict, see de Michelis, *op. cit.* in *Boll. Emig.*, 1908, No. 10, p. 74.

[3] See *idem, op. cit.* in *Boll. Emig.*, 1903, No. 12, esp. pp. 11, 20, 63–68, 72,
111–118; F. Lambertenghi, " L'immigrazione italiana nel distretto consolare di
Zurigo," *Boll. Emig.*, 1903, No. 11, pp. 51 f.; A. Vischer, " Gli italiani nei cantoni
di Basilea e di Soleure," *Boll. Emig.*, 1903, No. 11, p. 55; Gavotti, p. 79; " Relazione
sui servizi . . . aprile 1907–aprile 1908," *Boll. Emig.*, 1908, No. 9, p. 121; Picot,

though they get along, cannot be said to prosper. The excavators, builders, and general construction hands get wages which are only a little higher than those of North Italy. The rates paid about the beginning of the century at the Simplon tunnel were fairly typical for the epoch. Men were there arranged in three shifts working eight hours each, except above ground where the day was of ten hours. Masons received 5–6 francs, miners 4–7, common laborers 3.20–3.80; but the Italians, it is claimed, rarely attained the maximum figures.[1] In the granite quarries at that time men received about 40 centimes an hour for a day varying between eight and a half and eleven hours. A decade later, on the Brieg-Disentis route, masons averaged 6–8 francs, miners 5–7, common laborers 4.50–6; above ground the day was of ten hours, below of eight. The maximum sums were paid at the Furka tunnel which was at two or three days' walk from Brieg, at an altitude of 6000 feet.[2] Probably most Italian men in Switzerland have received wages near the minimum rates I have noted, for a day running to ten or twelve hours, according to season.[3]

Few have had steady hire. They lose much time between jobs. Inclement days halt their work. Even on the great enterprises

p. 11; Sella, p. 120. Cf. Barni and Canevascini (chs. v, vi): the Italian workers, when they came, " seemed to be men who snatched their bread from the mouths of the yet more wretched Ticinese population " (p. 163).

At a Swiss trade-union congress held in Zurich in 1912, delegates from Switzerland, France, and Austria reported their difficulties in organizing the Italians, and vehement language was used. Thus, for example, the representative of the Swiss painters and plasterers: " A chief task that we had to assume was to prevent these people from living like beasts. Where did they live ? Packed together in all sorts of hovels! Out of these they must be driven, in order that they might get used to the ways in which human beings live and in order that they might understand what other laborers must spend for their maintenance. . . . In a word our endeavor must be to increase the scale of needs of these people." A. W., " Die Organisierung der Italiener in Deutschland " (*cit.*), pp. 249–251.

[1] Gavotti, p. 72; cf. Silvestrelli, p. 7. Sella (p. 43), writing in 1899 after the work began, found one mode about 2.80 francs, and one 4; the great majority of Italians received less than 3.

[2] Carneluti, p. 55.

[3] No Swiss official wage statistics exist. A convenient survey is by G. de Michelis, " Salari in uso nella Svizzera," *Bollettino dell' Ufficio del Lavoro*, February, 1909, pp. 209–232.

needing years for completion, they contend with extraordinary fluctuations of employment. Though premiums are often paid to hold the men for a stretch of weeks or months in the uninviting places, the coming of winter generally necessitates a reduction to a fourth or a sixth of the summer's contingent: great, for example, were the month-by-month changes on the Brieg-Disentis line. An aggravated competition has often come from the inpouring cohorts of disappointed workers from Germany, when slack times have begun in that country. Strikes, here as everywhere, have been costly, and especially so to temporary immigrants.[1]   In these and other ways savings are truncated and there is even the failure to earn subsistence. Swiss and sometimes Italian charitable agencies may tide a family or an individual over a hard period. The consuls repatriate rarely less than a thousand Italians a year, sometimes many more, and the Swiss cantons return others.

If members of a family, not themselves earning, have to be supported in Switzerland, all chance of saving ordinarily disappears. But if an industrious man is unaccompanied by his family and makes common cause with other men, he can generally save money. By group travelling he can keep down his railway expenses and by group living the cost of his lodging and food. In eight or nine months of reasonably good employment a man alone, it is said, can save perhaps 300 francs. In the first three years of work at the Simplon, an average of 1600 men employed sent annually 300,000 francs to Italy; one-third of these Italians had their families in Switzerland. Girls and women, if they spend no more than a franc a day, can save six francs a week while employed. This generally implies living in a *Heim*, since most girls who venture independently can save little. By contrasting the postal money-order remittances directed from Switzerland into

---

[1] On such questions of employment as these, see, among many references, Carneluti, pp. 52 f.; " Relazione sui servizi," etc., *Boll. Emig.*, 1910, No. 18, pp. 228, 274, and 1909, No. 9, pp. 110, 116; note in *Boll. Emig.*, 1907, No. 13, p. 127; G. de Michelis, " Ufficio dell' emigrazione italiana nella Svizzera, Relazione," *Boll. Emig.*, 1907, No. 10, pp. 3–38; *idem*, " Il mercato del lavoro in Isvizzera nella prima metà dell' anno 1906," *Boll. Emig.*, 1906, No. 6, pp. 3–8; *idem, op. cit.* in *Boll. Emig.*, 1903, No. 12, p. 89.

Italy and vice versa, the Italian Commissioner-General of Emigration concluded in 1910 that his compatriots annually sent savings of 25,000,000 francs to their homes; and Dr. Zollinger, estimating in addition the savings carried personally into Italy, reached a figure, for the year 1905, of 20,000,000 francs. While the aggregate accumulations are certainly large, as even these rough calculations show, it would be a mistake to argue from them to large individual savings.[1]

When the lives of the Italians are viewed from the standpoint of material comfort and well-being, the picture cannot be painted in gay colors. Their tasks are arduous enough. The day's work is less intermittent than in Italy and the pace quick. Intense cold, dampness in excavation, the stony resistance of the soil, the peril of workplaces, the solitude of the heights, monotony, the ennui that accompanies fatigue, these are the experiences of every day.[2]

The Italians live poorly (less well than any other foreigners in Switzerland), both because they must and because they wish to. Whoever aspires to save must study every penny of expenditure, and will often not have enough to eat nor a decent bed to lie on.

---

[1] See W. Zollinger, *Die Bilanz der internationalen Wertübertragungen* (Jena, 1914), pp. 172–175; V. Valeriani, note in *Rivista Coloniale*, May 15, 1914, p. 265; Bernardy, pp. 26–28, 32, 34, 50; " Relazione sui servizi," etc., *Boll. Emig.*, 1910, No. 18, p. 228; Danieli Camozzi, report to the Consiglio Nazionali delle Donne Italiane, reviewed in *Rivista di Emigrazione*, November–December, 1908, pp. 119–120; *idem*, *op. cit.* in *Boll. Emig.*, 1909, No. 4, pp. 72–74; de Michelis, *op. cit.* in *Boll. Emig.*, 1908, No. 10, p. 62; *idem*, *op. cit.* in *Boll. Emig.*, 1903, No. 12, pp. 23, 71 f., 75–77; Marazzi, *op. cit.* in *Boll. Emig.*, 1903, No. 11, p. 23; Lucchesi-Palli, p. 45. In 1913, the Italian minister at Berne, after a visit to the Italians of the Brieg-Disentis and Loetschberg routes, reported that they were scarcely able to make savings; see *Bollettino dell' Ufficio del Lavoro (ediz. quindicinale)*, November 1, 1913, p. 236.

At the Simplon, Sella observed two diverse phenomena, having, he supposed, a common origin: one, the readiness to spend wages in the freest indulgence for from one to three days; the other, the consistent saving of every possible centime; no middle course appeared to exist (p. 53). At another point (p. 33) he makes the general statement that Italians have saved money while abroad.

[2] During the building of the St. Gothard tunnel, several hundred men lost their lives through accident or sickness. At the Simplon sixty died. See H. A. Carson, article " Tunnel " in *Encyclopaedia Britannica*, 11th ed., xxvii, p. 405. In the first five months 8 per cent had fallen sick or met with accidents (de Michelis, " Gli operai italiani al Sempione," p. 149). One accident at the Loetschberg destroyed twenty-five Italians (Mancini, p. 280).

Prices are found to rise whenever numbers of workers settle in remote and sparsely inhabited places; while the railroad connecting the Rhine and the Rhône valleys was in process of construction, several temporary villages had to be built, in which the lodgings were both unsatisfactory and expensive: and so it had been at the Simplon. In temporary shacks unsanitary conditions are almost the rule. But not alone in them. Whenever, as happens throughout the country, Italian, or sometimes Swiss, families take Italians as boarders, congestion and dirt quickly appear. In some of the cities, the conditions are particularly bad. Basel is one of those centers, numerous in other countries also, where Italians who work in the suburbs prefer to live in a crowded colony in the city. The factory girls who dwell in the *Heime*, of which in 1908 there were thirty-three, live meagerly yet tolerably, but those who live independently, three or four, even six or eight to a room, suffer in health from their economy. Far and wide among the immigrants, toil and self-stinting levy their tax upon bodily capital.[1]

[1] On conditions of living and health, see, *e.g.*, G. E. Palma di Castiglione, " Gli italiani a St. Moritz," *Boll. Emig.*, 1912, No. 12, p. 87; Carneluti, p. 54; Calimani, p. 127; Bernardy, pp. 6–9, 35 (she however believed the conditions of the girls to be less cruel and congested than she had seen among Italians in the United States); Danieli Camozzi, *op. cit.* in *Rivista di Emigrazione*, pp. 57–59; *idem*, article (in *Vita Femminile Italiana*) summarized in *Boll. Emig.*, 1909, No. 4, p. 73; " Relazione sui servizi," etc., *Boll. Emig.*, 1910, No. 18, p. 232; de Michelis, *op. cit.* in *Boll. Emig.*, 1908, No. 10, p. 78; *idem*, *op. cit.* in *Boll. Emig.*, 1903, No. 12, pp. 38–44, 73; Schmid, p. 89; Sella, pp. 31–33, 47; Paolucci de' Calboli, cited by A. Cabrini in *Rivista Coloniale*, January 31, 1914, p. 53.

Here is a passage from de Michelis (*Boll. Emig.*, 1903, No. 12, p. 42): " The most elementary rules of cleanliness, decency, hygiene are unknown. With pain one notes that they are always lodged in the least healthful quarters of the city, in dark houses not penetrated by the sun. . . . Most of the immigrants, in the working season, live in groups, several to a room. Sometimes no bedsteads are there and the workmen sleep on bundles of straw dropped on the floor. Often, as well, there are no pillows and two men stretched upon the same bed are a common case. For the most part these nocturnal Siamese twins were unacquainted with each other the day before. They arrive at the ' pension ' applying for a bed and they lie down where they have been told, without repugnance or complaint. In the morning, having spent the night in sleep, these bedfellows strike an acquaintance.

" So it is everywhere, in the great cities and in the villages. In Geneva the entire old quarter running from the *rues basses* to the Cathedral swarms with ' workmen's pensions ' and taverns. There, next to the brothels, are the houses inhabited by the Italians."

The experiences and moods of the Italians out of working hours are hard to trace, for it is only occasional flashes of light that are directed upon them, and only the externals of change are revealed. New views of the world, the State, social life, grow out of their fortunes and disappointments and out of the civilization about them. The need for recreation and refreshment finds utterance in novel and not always salutary directions.

The children get neither a Swiss nor an Italian school education, often no systematic instruction at all. Their parents, tired with moiling and toiling, worn out by the pain of saving, are not less illiterate nor more schooled than when they came. Rarely do the men's numerous mutual aid societies exceed their primary function of providing a modicum of benefit in sickness, and indeed the entire associated life of the immigrants is insignificant. Between those of different regions of origin, clashes are frequent.[1] The cafe on Saturday and Sunday is an institution. If drunkenness is more than in Italy, it is perhaps less than among the Italians in some other countries. The universal tendency to blood crimes appears. Along with fidelity in sending savings to the home in Italy, yet less commonly, goes a certain weakening of family ties; often desertion, bringing poverty in its train. The girls of the factories, more fixed in their abode than the men who come by the season, frequently, it is held, develop illicit relations with them. Among the men churchgoing greatly diminishes. A large number come to favor the radical movements for social reclamation, but, as commonly happens among those whose life is a routine of toil, not many become active propagandists or even join the more radical associations; the relative weakness in particular of the Italian socialist organization in the Ticino has been remarked.[2]

[1] Sella, pp. 46, 54. Rivalries broke up the *Figli d'Italia* and other societies (pp. 110–116).

[2] On some of these questions, see, *e.g.*, de' Calboli, *loc. cit.;* Calimani, p. 127; Pasteris, p. 457; Bernardy, pp. 58–62; de Michelis, " Le associazioni italiane nella Svizzera, politiche, artistiche, di istruzione, di convegno e di sport," in *Boll. Emig.*, 1908, No. 22, pp. 3–23; *idem*, " La mutualità fra gli italiani nella Svizzera," *Boll. Emig.*, 1908, No. 10, pp. 3–49; *idem, op. cit.* in *Boll. Emig.*, 1903, No. 12, pp. 11, 38 f., 72, 130; Schmid, " Das Armenwesen," etc., p. 90; G. Barni, " La Svizzera contemporanea; gli italiani nel canton Ticino," *Rivista d'Italia*, August, 1914, pp. 223–272, esp. p. 225.

Much of the special sting of immigrant life in France and Germany has been absent in Switzerland, and the welcome of the Italians has been a little kindlier than in those countries. But it is still as the servants of capital — Swiss, and even German and French, not Italian — that they come, and they have rarely risen out of the walk of life in which they began.

CHAPTER XI

AUSTRIA-HUNGARY

In Austria-Hungary, unexampled among countries, the tides of
emigration and of immigration have both run strong. While
from its component states common and agricultural laborers have
set forth for the countries of Europe and America at a rate comparable only with that of Italy, Italian toilers have left behind
them Alps and Adriatic in quest of work in the dual monarchy.
It has been a strange spectacle, for no love has been lost between
the two countries. Only the call of bread has made the traditional
enemy tolerable.

The modern immigration of Italians into Austria-Hungary is
made partly intelligible when we recall that important Italian
settlements have had a long history there. In the thirteenth to
the sixteenth centuries many Italian immigrants established
themselves in the Tyrol — the Italo-German dispute there is very
old. Some Italians had settled on the littoral in the Roman era;
more came in the twelfth century, mingling with a native stock of
different race. The Dalmatian communities likewise began in
ancient times. In the thirteenth century, Italians brought vines
into Hungary to restock the Tokai districts; the Fiume colony is
centuries old. In 1910 not less than three-quarters of a million
subjects of Austria spoke Italian or Ladine. An equal number
spoke Serbo-Croatian; more, in a rising series, Slovenian, Ru-
thenian, Polish, Bohemian, German. In order of diffusion, then,
Italian had come to be the seventh language in Austria.[1]

All of the Italian-speaking subjects have lived in only seven
states, in some of which they have been relatively few. In
Vorarlberg they were, in 1910, 5900, while the great majority of
the population of 133,000 spoke German. In Dalmatia, they
were 18,000; nearly all the rest of 635,000 spoke Serbo-Croatian,

---

[1] My census data are from *Österreichische Statistik, Die Ergebnisse der Volkszählung vom 31 Dezember 1910* (Vienna, 1913–14), esp. i, Pt. ii.

Ragusa, emphatically Italian in the days of its independence, contained only 526 individuals ordinarily speaking Italian, in a population of 39,000. But if Dalmatia, once saved to western civilization by the Italians, has now lost much of its Latin character, the states around the head of the Adriatic have not. In Görz and Gradisca, the Italian-Ladine subjects were 90,000 in a total of 250,000, being chiefly exceeded by the Slovenes with 155,000; in Monfalcone they were 46,000 in 48,000. In Istria they were 147,000 in a total of 387,000, being chiefly exceeded by the Serbo-Croats with 168,000. In Triest, they were as many as 119,000 in 191,000, the Slovenes being next with only 57,000. Here they constituted a merchant and industrial aristocracy. Beyond the Italian Alps, in the Tyrol, the largest Italian community of all, they were 386,000 in 916,000, nearly all the rest speaking German (525,000). But these last figures are decidedly misleading. While in Bruneck and the Bozen district Italians were to Germans as one to five and one to nine respectively, in every other district or city of the Tyrol the population was either almost entirely German or almost entirely Italian. What is more, a line drawn irregularly from the Stelvio Pass in the west to Landro in the east sharply marks off the German or northern portion of the Tyrol from the Italian and Ladine portion; in turn the Ladine portion, involving a people whose Italian association is linguistic only, is sharply marked off from the portion which is Italian in sentiment and tradition as well as unqualifiedly in speech.[1]

Wherever in Austria an Italian-speaking population has continued to exist for generations, there also have been the chief nuclei of permanent immigrant settlement. Triest, the Tyrol,

[1] On the distribution of peoples, see B. Auerbach, *Les races et les nationalités en Autriche-Hongrie* (Paris, 1898), chs. iv, viii, ix, xiv.

For both Austria and Hungary, the census figures of Italian-speaking population are minima. (See the writings, among many, of Auerbach, *cit.*, and of Gayda, referred to below.) The best evidence concerns inconsistencies and intercensal lapses, but these are sporadic only, and suggest that neither a large general increase of the figures nor an important increase in any state's figures is necessary. One cannot go so far, for instance, as a writer, A. Dudan, who holds, in an essay (pp. 65–124) contained in *La Dalmazia* (Genoa, 1915), that the 18,000 Italians of Dalmatia should be 60,000 at least.

Görz and Gradisca, Istria, Carinthia, Styria, these regions have contained nearly all of the unnaturalized Italian population. Lower Austria, with Vienna, has had a modicum, Dalmatia a negligible number (2400). When the Austrian census of 1869 was taken, 29,496 citizens of Italy were reported. They were then half as numerous as subjects of Germany and a third as numerous as subjects of Hungary. In this order, but not quite in this ratio, the three nationalities continued till lately. In 1880, 40,152 Italians were counted; in 1890, 46,312; in 1900, 63,064; in 1910, 79,062. Their increase after 1890 was at a faster rate than that of Germans or Hungarians. Since the censuses were taken in the winter, the figures represent only Italians who had made a fairly enduring stay in Austria; indeed still other statistics show only about one in forty to have been sojourning temporarily and at least one in three to have been resident more than three years. After ten years, when naturalization is possible, a small group — they came to 3785 in 1901–10, about one for each day in the period — disappear wholly from the count of aliens. Consider further that among these immigrants the male element has exceeded the female by only a little, and that to a very unusual extent the men have been married. In fact, nearly 70 per cent of the men above thirty years, and 80 per cent of the women were found to be married.[1]

How diversified have been the industrial connections of this relatively permanent immigration it is worth stopping to note. The figures here given include the members of the worker's family when they too have dwelt in Austria. One thousand Italians were in forestry in 1910, and 7500 in agriculture. In the building trades were 10,800. In work upon stone and earth were 4500; upon wood, and in carving, substantially as many; in the textiles 2400;

---

[1] *Ergebnisse der Volkszählung*, ii, Pt. ii, p. 25.* By residence the 79,062 Italians (of whom 41,921 were males) were grouped chiefly as follows: in Triest, 29,439; in Tyrol, 12,850; in Görz and Gradisca, 8947; in Istria, 6027; in Carinthia, 4637; in Lower Austria, 4199 (of whom, in Vienna, 2502); in Styria, 4127; in Dalmatia, 2425; in Vorarlberg, 1449; in Bohemia, 1317. In no other state did they attain 1200. Since, however, the census was taken on December 31, it makes no allowance for seasonal immigration. In Hungary, in 1900, 9035 Italian subjects were counted.

in the metals 2600; in machinery, boiler making, and the like 1800; in the chemical trades, more than 900, and as many in paper and leather establishments. The clothing industry, including laundry work, maintained 5700; the preparation of food and drinks, 2500. Mining sustained 600; so also the work of illumination and of water conduction. More than 400 depended upon fisheries. To these must be added certain minor groups which reached a considerable total. Broadly speaking, the figures ought to be halved to denote the workers actually engaged in the occupations as distinguished from those dependent upon them.[1]

In the Tyrol and Vorarlberg the Italians have increased with particular rapidity. They doubled between 1870 and 1890, and again between 1890 and 1910. In the winter of the last year they numbered 13,000 in the Tyrol and 1500 in Vorarlberg, the women being almost as many as the men. In the German Tyrol they were half as numerous as in the Trentino. How many besides have come for the summer is partly a matter of conjecture; a computation, resting on sundry important data, has claimed 12,000.[2] Out of the total of about 25,000, certainly several thousands have been masons and building laborers, deriving from Udine and other parts of Venetia.[3] A great many were plain pick-and-shovel men. Indeed, throughout western Austria unskilled immigrants have abounded. In house building and general construction work — the erection of power plants, for example — and in road making many Italians have been employed. The tunnelling of the Arlberg, completed in 1884, was their work; a venture hardly less exacting in its day than the penetration, years later, of the Simplon, and of about the same commercial impor-

---

[1] *Ergebnisse der Volkszählung*, ii, Pt. ii, p. 63.

[2] G. De Lucchi, " L'emigrazione italiana nel distretto consolare di Innsbruck," *Boll. Emig.*, 1913, No. 14, p. 7. In the figure given, no account is made of the Italians who pass through Innsbruck, to and from Germany. Going and coming, these have numbered every year 125,000–150,000.

[3] In the *Rivista Coloniale*, January 1–15, 1913, p. 14, S. Flor, in a report presented to the Congresso dei Segretariati Laici in 1912, held that the masons in Tyrol and Vorarlberg numbered 6000, and that the 5000 Italian hodcarriers and the like in Austria were chiefly in these regions.

tance. Among those who worked on the Arlberg were many who had just come from the St. Gothard.[1] The skilled craftsmen have included carpenters and stonecutters. Until recently the older type of circumambulant artificers, glaziers, scissors grinders, pewterers, braziers, came to the Trentino and the Tyrol; to the Trentino almost exclusively came Brescian rope makers and chair menders. Though immigrants of these sorts had come for forty years—hundreds sometimes in a year, it is said—they had almost disappeared before the war, partly because of new license restrictions.

About 1890 an increase began in an immigration which had long existed and has since become one of the most characteristic. While the men of Belluno were going into Switzerland, Germany, and Austria, the women and children discovered that they could make a better living abroad than by doing simple household work or hiring out at home. Girls chiefly and young wives, of the ages fourteen to thirty, they began to go into the Trentino and even the southern Tyrol. Until before the war, they continued to flock thither, two or three thousand and more a year. Many girls of only ten or twelve have been among them. In their home communes, school attendance almost stops in March. What is chiefly characteristic in this emigration of "*ciode*," as they are called, is its destination for agriculture. To some extent their opportunity has been occasioned by the departure for the Americas of a small but steady annual contingent of Trentine peasants.[2] Enrolled in Italy by Italian women, and mainly in Belluno, the " ciode " have come in late February or in March for an eight-months stay. Until 1908 an outdoor market for their labor was held in the Piazza del Duomo in Trent, but thereafter the public authorities instituted a better organization. The care of animals and other farm chores — of household or field — have been the stint of the younger children, the older ones and the women as-

---

[1] Great Britain, *Royal Commission on Labor*, viii (London, 1893), p. 82.

[2] The Trentines first began to emigrate in large numbers about the middle of the nineteenth century. Those locally specialized in their skill went into the neighboring countries of Europe. In many respects this emigration invites a parallel with that of Venetia and Piedmont. For a word regarding it see the interesting work of C. Battisti, *Il Trentino* (Trent, 1898), pp. 237–239.

suming tasks which in Italy are often performed by men: propping up the Indian corn, spraying the vines (carrying the pumps all day on their shoulders), cultivating with the hoe, reaping and gathering wheat and corn, piling hay, attending to the vintage and, when no other tasks have remained, plucking weeds.[1]

In Rovereto, Riva, and Trent, containing half the more stable Italian population, industry has thrived. Tobacco and silk factories, tile, brick, and pottery works have occupied many Italians; and barbers, tailors, and importers of Italian fruits and vegetables have been numerous. Women too have had employment, not only as factory operatives, but as cooks, nurses, waitresses — a type of Italian emigration which has generally been uncommon in other countries.[2]

In Lower Austria, Styria, Salzburg, Carinthia, Carniola, and Küstenland, masons and general laborers have been numerous. As late as the beginning of the present century, it was claimed that nearly all of the digging laborers of Styria and Carniola were Italian. Before the war, Italians had almost ceased to be employed on the railways: earlier, they had worked on the Triest-Parenzo line, the Triest-Vienna, and, farther north, the Krems-Prein along the Danube, and the Aspang-Friedburg. These are but examples. They helped build for Triest the drinking-water aqueduct of the Aurisina; and that from the Styrian border to Vienna. The Donaugraben (canal) of Lower Austria was largely their work. In various regions they have specialized in the construction of electric power plants. The general laborers have been farm hands from Venetia, who used to leave home after the spring tasks had been completed and return for the harvest. Sawmill hands have been numerous, and workers in cement an important skilled type. In large numbers the immigrants have worked in the naval shops of Monfalcone and Triest; in the latter place also on general

---

[1] Jarach, "Dell' emigrazione delle donne e dei minorenni bellunesi nel Trentino e nel Tirolo Meridionale" (*cit.*), pp. 48–61; De Lucchi, pp. 28–35. Jarach was a special agent commissioned by the Emigration Service to study this movement.

[2] N. R. Bonfanti, "Dell' immigrazione regnicola nel Trentino," *Boll. Emig.*, 1912, No. 12, pp. 42 f.; P. Baroli, "L'emigrazione nel Tirolo e nel Vorarlberg," *Emig. e Col.*, 1903, i[ii], p. 112; De Lucchi, p. 38.

port construction.[1] On public works, except as a rule those concerned with military affairs, they have at various times been abundantly employed. Some tradespeople have come, especially from the South of Italy, to handle oils, wines, and the citrous fruits. Street musicians and their kin were once ubiquitous, but of late years have been discouraged.[2]

No more picturesque, no more characteristic emigrants depart from Italy than the fishermen of Chioggia; perhaps no more venturesome folk. In the very names of their barks romance lives. The Adriatic shines with the redness of their sails and mirrors the strange devices with which these are adorned, a cross, the Madonna, the wings of a butterfly — what not ? Four or five men together, they set forth on long voyages over seas now pacific now tumultuous. Many make four voyages a year. After Easter they depart, to return in mid-August for a month of rest and repairs. When they go again, it is for a trip of eight or nine weeks, their *viaggio magro*, for it yields little. From the end of October till Christmas they are gone again, and make a good catch. Finally, after a holiday week with their families, many set forth once more in the chill winds of January and February, expecting little and therefore not disappointed. Easter every true *Chiog-*

[1] In a generally excellent book, translated as *Modern Austria* (New York, 1915; see esp. ch. i), V. Gayda maintains that Slavic workmen, to the exclusion of Italians, were here employed. My own statement is based on the Italian consular reports. There has been enough — alas! — of the obnoxious in the Austrian handling of the Trentino. One need not, with Gayda, lay stress also on the emigration of the Trentine peasants, for it has been much less than that from Lombardy and Venetia, long redeemed for the government of Italy. Nor should one ignore the readiness of still larger numbers of Italians to immigrate into the Trentino to earn a living. If Croats were introduced there for railway work, immigrant Italians, on the other hand, were much used for construction work. And finally, though Slavic elements have established themselves in Triest, the Italian population there has grown even faster, Italian immigrants into the district having outnumbered all Slavic additions.

[2] Flor, *loc. cit.;* "Relazione sui servizi . . . per l'anno 1909–10," *Boll. Emig.*, 1910, No. 18, p. 251; G. Zannoni, " L'emigrazione e le colonie italiane in Austria," *Emig. e Col.*, 1903, i^{ii}, pp. 95–104; B. Lambertenghi, " La nostra immigrazione e le nostre colonie nel distretto consolare di Trieste," *Emig. e Col.*, 1903, i^{ii}, pp. 105–111; G. Chiap, " L'emigrazione periodica dal Friuli," *Riforma Sociale*, May, 1904, p. 385; G. Prato, "Il movimento d' associazione nelle colonie italiane dell' Austria," *Riforma Sociale*, September, 1899, pp. 870 f.; G. Malmusi and M. Camicia, reports in *Emig. e Col.*, 1893, pp. 83–97.

giotto spends with his family. Unlike all other Venetians, these men are taciturn and reserved; what else could they be, since they are so long sequestered from company and the world's affairs ? Though the Gulf of Triest and the whole northeast shore of the Adriatic is their fishing-ground, they have sold their catch mainly in Triest. Of late years, it has gone for half a million to a million lire, or even more when the sardines and tunny fish have been abundant. Five or six hundred men have so provided from a third to nearly a half of the fish supply of a great city. How long ago their work began no man can say; certainly it was in the epoch of Venetian domination.[1]

In the Balkan West, in Bosnia and Herzegovina, Italians have done pioneer work on the railways. Although almost none came before the Austrian occupation, they were present as early as 1881, binding Zenica and Serajevo by rail. Between 1888 and 1895, six lines were completed, on which Italians have been claimed, with possible exaggeration, to constitute a sixth of all workmen. These were the lines Mostar-Ostrozac, Mostar-Konjitca, Mostar-Serajevo, Lasva-Travnik, Lasva-Bugojno, and Vakuf-Jajce. The tunnel Travnik-Bugojna was built by an Italian contractor. In 1899–1901, in the construction of the Gabela-Trebinje line, cut through the rocky terrain of Herzegovina, parallel with the Dalmatian coast, some thousands of Italians had a part. Other thousands worked on the Serajevo-Ostgrenze line, a succession of bridges, embankments, and tunnels running by Mitrovitza to the Ottoman frontier; only the default of Austro-Hungarians, to whom preference in employment was to be given, opened the way for Italians. And in more recent years, indeed, only the somewhat skilled workmen have come, one or two thousand in the open months. As masons and others they have accomplished much for the modernization of Serajevo. In coal mining and lumbering, many have been employed. In the last-named industry and in agriculture, Venetians are said to have

---

[1] C. Umiltà, " I pescatori chioggiotti nella circoscrizione del r. consolato in Trieste," *Boll. Emig.*, 1910, No. 5, pp. 21–50; S. Milazzo, " La Dalmazia e le sue colonie italiane," *Emig. e Col.*, 1903, i[ii], p. 120.

taken the places of Mussulmans (who had migrated eastward) and to have applied more effective methods in their work. In 1910 the Italian Commissioner-General of Emigration supposed his countrymen here, permanent or temporary in their settlement, to number 6000; but the figure may be excessive.[1]

In Dalmatia, despite its Italian-speaking littoral, Italian subjects have been few. The oldest and most important settlement, Zara, has come to be less than one-tenth Italian. The temporary immigrants have been as likely to hail from Ancona or the Apulias as from Venetia; fourteen hours suffice for the transit from Ancona. To the Dalmatian waters many Chioggia fishermen have come, selling little of their catch, however, in the island and coast markets. Some important railway work has been done. In general, however, the century since Campoformio has marked a decline in the Italian rôle in Dalmatia.[2]

The several thousands of Italians who annually have entered Hungary, and likewise those more permanently there, have rarely been of the unspecialized sort. Before the twentieth century began, many worked on railway construction; since, the opportunity has seldom been offered. Masons, stonecutters, stucco workers have found good employment. At one time, in fact, reports to the Italian Emigration Service claimed that Italians were doing almost all the new stucco work of Budapest, and that many were employed on subway construction. Men from South Italy have imported the staple food products of their districts. In the years after 1880, Venetians established curious agricultural settlements in Croatia and Slavonia, with a nucleus at Pakraz, which have since tended to lose their identity. Other Venetians have mined coal and certain metals. As many perhaps as 1500 immigrants, a fourth of them boys, all deriving from Udine and Treviso, have long found employment in the brick

---

[1] "Relazione sui servizi," etc., p. 252; G. Giacchi, "La colonia italiana in Bosnia-Erzegovina," *Boll. Emig.*, 1910, No. 13, pp. 3–11; *idem*, "Il lavoro degli italiani in Bosnia ed Erzegovina," *Boll. Emig.*, 1906, No. 5, pp. 3–10; note in *Boll. Emig.*, 1903, No. 5, p. 58; V. Mantegazza, *L'altra sponda; Italia ed Austria nell' Adriatico* (2d ed., Milan, 1906), pp. 119–122.

[2] Milazzo, *op. cit.*; Mantegazza, pp. 358, 436 f.; L. Mordini, "La Dalmazia e le sue colonie italiane," *Emig. e Col.*, 1903, i[ii], pp. 121–124.

ovens of Croatia, seventy of which, it was claimed some years ago, they themselves managed. The laborers have commonly made their contracts in Italy in the winter. In recent years, unskilled immigrants have found but limited opportunities in Hungary; and neither they nor the skilled have shown much tendency to stay permanently.[1]

To Austria and Hungary an economic gain has certainly come from the immigration of Italians, and has been recognized. Natives of these lands, however, gradually becoming more mobile, have, for some years past, taken over much of the unskilled work of the Italians, and their governments have protected the movement. This cannot be surprising to anyone who is aware of the backwardness of industry and the abundance of the supply of unskilled laborers, evidenced, if proof were needed, in the great Austro-Hungarian transoceanic migration of the last decade or two. Bohemians in the North, Croats and Slavs in the South have gradually been coming to their own. In some places brick making has been taken from the Italians, and even their work in mines and the forests has been regarded with growing disfavor. More and more, in the central and eastern regions, Italian emigration has assumed a character which it holds neither in the industrial countries of Europe nor in the Americas: it has (in comparison with native labor at least) been largely skilled.[2]

[1] " Relazione sui servizi," etc., *Boll. Emig.*, 1910, No. 18, p. 252; V. Lebrecht. " Inchiesta sulle condizioni degli italiani nelle fornaci di Croazia-Slavonia," *Boll. Emig.*, 1907, No. 5, pp. 36–45; *idem*, " I minorenni italiani nella Croazia," *Boll. Emig.*, 1906, No. 1, pp. 3–13; *idem*, " Fiume, la Croazia, la Slavonia e le nostre colonie in quei paesi," *Emig. e Col.*, 1903, i[ii], pp. 132–141; R. della Valle, " L'Ungheria e l'emigrazione italiana," *Emig. e Col.*, 1903, i[ii], pp. 125–131; Chiap, p. 365; G. De Visart and F. R. Di Villanova, reports in *Emig. e Col.*, 1893, pp. 67–81.

[2] Not less than 90 per cent of the winter population of Italian men aged 20–60 could both read and write; and more than 95 per cent of those 20–40 (*Ergebnisse der Volkszählung*, ii, Pt. ii, p. 26*). In Italy such figures reflect superior quality. Among occupied Italians, 28 per cent were independent, 46 per cent were a substantial grade of wage earner; 11 per cent were day laborers; also, 5 per cent — children ? — assisted others of their families (*ibid.*, p. 28).

The presence of skilled laborers is old. Mantegazza relates (*op. cit.*, p. 122) how in Bosnia, years ago, the government, in order to finish a railroad betimes, by employing superior laborers — miners, masons, stonecutters — gave preference to

Much more than in any other great country of Europe, there has been active political and racial depreciation of the immigrants, but before 1914 at least, their freedom of movement was not impeded. It is impossible to say how far the grounds of the hostility of native labor have been economic and how far political or racial. The Slavs of Triest have sometimes laid violent hands on Italian laborers, but the German workmen of the Tyrol and Vorarlberg are held not to have molested them. The Italians, for their part, large as their economic rôle has been in the past, have shown little tendency (when their numbers are considered) to let themselves be absorbed. Yet it is not an inappreciable number who have become naturalized: in Austria, we have seen, about one a day on the average, and in Hungary, in recent years, more than of any other people save the Austrians.[1] Intermarriage with native peoples has been uncommon, except in the places where the older stock has spoken the Italian language.

Coming chiefly for an economic end, the Italians have met only partial success. Long before the war, the quite unskilled laborers, having deemed the venture unprofitable, had ceased to come (except, to a slight extent, in the western salient of the country). About 1900, unskilled men received only two or two and a half crowns a day, a wage not worth going far to get; years before, it had been higher. About the same time bricklayers secured three to three and a half crowns. Subsequently rates rose, and by 1912 or 1913 unskilled men secured three and a half crowns, masons around five crowns, stonecutters the same, skilled miners a little more. In the same period, swelling costs of food and lodging, almost general in Europe, reduced the margins of saving. Near the beginning of the century, it was reported that workmen who lived together could put by half their earnings, but whenever entire families were present, accumulation was impossible. More recently men have been able to save only if rigid economy has steered their expenditures. The agricultural immigrants of

a thousand Italians over the thousands of Croatian laborers who had come into the region; this, despite the fact that the Italians, partly on traditional account, were bitter enemies.

[1] *Annuaire statistique hongrois*, 1911 (Budapest, 1913), p. 70.

Croatia and Slavonia have done fairly well, many having become proprietors after first leasing their lands or working for hire. With 25–35 crowns a month, in addition to food and lodging, numerous boys of the brick ovens were probably better off as to income than they had been in Italy; but their work of preparing the clay, carrying bricks, and similar tasks ran from four in the morning till half past eight in the evening. The farm workers of the Trentino have been paid at rates current in North Italy: the youngest children, 25–45 crowns for more than seven months of labor; those of fifteen years, about 100 crowns; the older girls, 140–200 crowns — boys and adults (chiefly women) a little more; all have received food and lodging in addition and many have been able to save 150–200 lire in the season. Lastly, the Chioggia fishermen, in the course of a year of contest with the sea, could take to their families a gain of 500 lire.[1]

This is no taste of Eldorado. Moreover, I have drawn only the better side of the picture. There is a darker side which it would be dishonest not to sketch. The " dolorous spectacle " of those who fail to get work in the agriculture of the Trentino, the " misery " of those engulfed in the flood of immigrants returning unemployed from Germany or the United States, these are samples of conditions that stand forth prominently in the consuls' reports. There are those who come too early, those who overstay the fall and suffer in the winter. There are the many caught in the more general depressions. Unemployment worries when it does not destroy: it is an ambushed ogre which threatens to consume in days what has been treasured together in weeks.[2]

[1] De Lucchi, pp. 10–12, 31; Jarach, pp. 62–64, 82; Giacchi, " La colonia italiana," etc., p. 7; Umiltà, p. 36; Lebrecht, " I minorenni," etc., pp. 4, 6; *idem*, " Fiume, la Croazia," etc., p. 137; Zannoni, pp. 98–101; Lambertenghi, pp. 107 f.; Baroli, pp. 113 f.

[2] On the pressure of unemployment, see, *e.g.*, in *Boll. Emig.:* 1913, No. 14, p. 45; 1912, No. 12, p. 55; 1909, No. 9, p. 115; 1908, No. 7, p. 101; 1907, No. 5, pp. 24, 27; 1906, No. 5, pp. 73 i.; 1903, No. 10, p. 60; 1902, No. 4, p. 72; 1902, No. 6, p. 65; 1902, No. 8, p. 76. Cf. *Emig. e Col.*, i^{ii}, pp. 98, 107, 113.

The European war brought new troubles. Payments of 20,000 lire a month due, on account of continuing pensions for accidents, to 800 Italians returned to Italy, were stopped. See " La sospensione del pagamento delle rendite alle vittime di infortunio in Austria-Ungheria," *Boll. Emig.*, 1916, No. 5, pp. 16–18.

But there are other disabilities also. The children have suffered in various ways. Some who would fall within the jurisdiction of compulsory schooling in North Italy have here been engaged in heavy work, and many, especially of the girls, have been hurt in health. Repeatedly illiterate boys and men have been victimized through the contracts they have signed for labor in the brick ovens. In these works boys have usually slept on bags of straw, often with insufficient night covering. In the Trentino sleeping out of doors has been a common practice. When food has not been part of the compensation for labor, when the motives of hunger and frugality have contended, then nourishment has often proved insufficient.[1] The moral situation has given cause for concern. Though abolition of the night market of the " ciode " improved the condition of the girls in the Trentino, other abuses have continued because these workers have been scattered over the country districts and subjected in their tasks to the command of men. Fewer women have in recent years worked in the garrison towns, it is claimed, and in so far one difficulty has been lessened. Finally, an increase of alcoholic drinking has been noted, here as elsewhere.[2]

Has the work of the Italians in the Austro-Hungarian states run its course ? Is their mission completed ? Anyone may see that their immigration had for some years drifted into a precarious position. Living conditions had not improved in the years before the war; industrially, a fresh increment, or a modernization, of skill in the native peoples had become more and more probable. Circumstances have for years been ripening which, even if no war had come, would presently have placed Austria-Hungary and Italy in the same category as regards migration:

[1] Discussing a decade's rise in living costs, De Lucchi wrote (*op. cit.*, p. 12): " In this connection, the interests of our poor workmen are much hurt by the fact that, now more than in the past, the police do not tolerate excessive crowding of sleepers in one apartment, and also by the fact that the modernizing of the principal centers has brought with it, especially on the periphery, the demolition of a quantity of old houses in which our compatriots used to secure reasonable lodging." See also *ibid.*, pp. 32 f.; Jarach, pp. 75, 82, 84; Lebrecht, " Inchiesta sulle condizioni," pp. 36–45; *idem*, " I minorenni italiani," p. 5.

[2] De Lucchi, pp. 36–38, 46; Dominioni, p. 35; Baroli, p. 114.

countries whence workers depart but to which they refrain from coming.   Then the Italian emigration across the Adriatic, modern successor of the old commercial movement from Venice, might have been expected to shrink to comparative insignificance. Who now can say, contemplating the non-Italian parts of the old dual monarchy, what the maelstrom of the after-war time will bring forth ?

CHAPTER XII

OTHER COUNTRIES OF EUROPE. NORTH AFRICA

ITALIAN immigration into Great Britain has had a long and peculiar, if never a broad, development. In the Middle Ages, especially in the thirteenth and fourteenth centuries, Lucchese, Lombards, and Florentines settled in England. Of their eminence then as wool merchants there has never been question, and their bankers have had a perpetual memorial in the name of Lombard Street. In the same early period, Italians came to Dublin. In the seventeenth century, a new movement started, which attained considerable volume in the eighteenth, and soon the types appeared which we associate with the modern era.

Itinerant chimney sweeps of tender years, exploited by older men, were the first modern immigrants. In no other country, be it said, for so long a stretch of time, have the Italians so generally been circumambulant in their trades. By 1750 certainly, the organ grinders had begun to come. Before 1800 monkeys had become the street musicians' adjuncts, and soon birds and bears were exhibited. Contrasting with the old barrel organ were, presently, the concertina, accordion, harp, and violin. For a full century and a half, the street musicians lent color to this immigration, hundreds at a time circulating through the country (not fewer than 2500 were computed by de' Calboli in 1893); and the sufferings of the boy victims of the traffic were beyond all question great.[1]

Street hawkers have been many, a notable *genre* in London. Men and children have sold chestnuts in the winter and ices in the summer. In ramshackle dwellings on Saffron Hill, living crowded

---

[1] " Give something to the pretty little Italian child who comes from the sunny South, and is so poor, and yet sings happily all the day." This characteristic legend under a picture of an amiable organ grinder and his alms-asking child appeared in a paper for children's reading. See W. H. Wilkins, in A. White (ed.), *The Destitute Alien in Great Britain* (London, 1892), p. 166.

together in dirt, they concocted their wares for many years. First, the Italian law of 1873 touching the employment of children, abroad as at home, compelled some improvement in their condition; later, the school board inspectors interfered with some of their practices, and finally the sanitation authorities demolished the hovels where they dwelt, scattering the colony afar. None the less, the census of 1911 counted nearly 1300 costermongers and their like. Though a few ice cream vendors have prospered in Ireland and in Wales (Italians have led all other foreign immigrants into Wales!) it is to Scotland that one must turn for a remarkable development. Some half a century ago, nomad Italians, including Lucchese sellers of statuettes, opened shops there for the sale of ice cream. Having awakened a new desire in the country, they prospered, and attracted others to share their fortune. An estimate in 1911, interesting even if deductions are made, declared that a thousand shops existed in some two hundred places in all of Scotland, especially the Clyde and Forth districts. They sold drinks, candy, bovril, as well as ice cream, finding their mainstay in evening and holiday business. Opposition developing after a while, the immigrants organized a " Temperance Refreshment Traders' Defence Association " and 800 signed a futile petition to Sig. San Giuliano asking for intervention against projected evening and holiday closing ordinances.

In England, and especially in London, in recent years, men and women variously concerned with the provision of food and lodging have been a great majority of the Italians. In 1911, to name but the leading groups, 1200 were in domestic service; nearly 900 men were cooks not in domestic employment; 1400 were bakers and confectioners; 500 kept coffee or eating houses; 1600 were waiters in restaurants, and a thousand were otherwise employed by inns and hotels. Needless to say, these deft and polite workers had usually come from North Italy. And it was their coming, more than any other, that brought about the doubling of the Italian population of England in the period 1890–1901.

Both common laborers and skilled artisans have been few. Long ago, it is said, some helped to build the bridge over the Firth of Forth, but the episode has not been representative. It used to be reiterated in Italian reports that the exclusionist spirit and rules of the English trade unions made all craftsmen unwelcome. To a degree the charge was valid, and disapproval, rather than satisfaction and the enjoyment of the picturesque, has surely been the common note in English utterances. Italian commentators have agreed that most of their compatriots have saved only by privation, and they have put an unmistakable emphasis upon the disabilities of immigrant life in England. The wonder is indeed that more than 20,000 Italians were counted when the census of 1911 was taken.[1]

In recent years before the war, the diminutive grand duchy of Luxemburg must have contained an average of fully 10,000 Italians. Bordering on French and German Lorraine and Rhenish Prussia, it has presented industrial opportunities akin to those of its neighbors. Before 1890 few Italians came. In 1900, 7500 were enumerated, of whom a large majority dwelt at Esch-sur-Alzette, near the French frontier, where they easily created the illusion of an Italian town. In the winter of 1905–06, more than 5000 men were occupied in the iron mines at Dudelange, Differdange, and other places. The annual fluctuations in this immigration have been great and its vicissitudes many. But the labor market of Luxemburg is so much a part of that of the adjacent regions, and

---

[1] F. Catalani, " Fanciulli italiani in Inghilterra," *Nuova Antologia*, February, 1878, pp. 559–586; Wilkins, chapter on " The Italian Aspect " (*cit.*); *idem, The Alien Invasion* (London, 1892), esp. ch. iv; R. Paulucci de' Calboli, *I girovaghi italiani in Inghilterra ed i suonatori ambulanti*, Città di Castello, 1893; G. Tornielli-Brusati di Vergano and E. B. Heath, *Emig. e Col.*, 1893, pp. 288–313; G. Prato, " Gli italiani in Inghilterra," *Riforma Sociale*, July, 1900, pp. 674–703, November, 1900, pp. 1095–1116, January, 1901, pp. 5–35; G. Dalla Vecchia, " Gli italiani a Londra," *L'Italia Coloniale*, January, 1901, pp. 65–79; F. Righetti and F. Sacchi, " La colonia italiana di Londra," *Emig. e Col.*, 1903, iii, pp. 143–169; P. Bainotti and V. A. Montaldi, " Gli italiani nel distretto consolare di Liverpool," *Emig. e Col.*, iii, pp. 170–182; G. Poma, " Gli italiani nel distretto consolare di Cardiff," *Emig. e Col.*, iii, pp. 183–189; G. Breen, " Le colonie italiane in Scozia," *Emig. e Col.*, iii, pp. 190–192; C. Sardi, " I gelatieri italiani nella Scozia," *Rivista Coloniale*, August 25–September 10, 1911, pp. 284–292; Great Britain, *Census of England and Wales*, April 3, 1911, ix; L. Salazar, " Gli italiani in Irlanda," *Rivista Coloniale*, July 10, 1912, pp. 15–17; E. Pépin, *La question des étrangers en Angleterre, L'Aliens Act de 1905*, Paris, 1913; V. A. Tattara, " L'emigrazione italiana nel Regno Unito e nel Principato di Galles durante l'anno 1913," *Boll. Emig.*, 1914, No. 9, pp. 57–59.

what I have written concerning those regions holds so broadly here, that detail is unnecessary.[1]

The Italians in Belgium have been circumstanced much as those in Luxemburg, but they have been less than half as numerous. In addition to working in the mines, they have been retail dealers, glove makers, sellers of ices and statuettes, and street musicians.[2]

Since as long ago as 1870, a not unimportant emigration has proceeded to the Iberian Peninsula. It has most usually been a miscellaneous assortment of street traders, port workers, fishermen. In an ordinary year, apart from an interesting colony in Barcelona, those present in either Spain or Portugal have numbered only hundreds; but special occasions, like the comprehensive harbor work of Lisbon in 1888–89, have induced the coming of many more.[3]

Malta, for centuries in commercial relationship with Italy, especially Sicily, has become the home, more or less permanent, of some 2000 Italians. Most are Sicilians. Strangely enough — for the instance is unique — the colony is almost wholly urban, embracing especially such types as shoemakers and barbers.[4]

In eastern Europe the Italians have had a curious and scattered, yet far from unimportant history.

Few have settled in Montenegro or Albania, the regions most easily reached by sea. A colony of Apulians has been in Avlona.

---

[1] Some references already given on western Germany include frequent mention of Luxemburg. See also G. Weber, " Il granducato di Lussemburgo e l'immigrazione italiana," *Emig. e Col.*, 1905, i[iii], pp. 117–123; note in *Boll. Emig.*, 1906, No. 12, p. 63; " Relazione sui servizi . . . 1909–10," *Boll. Emig.*, 1910, No. 18, pp. 262 f.; note in *Boll. Emig.*, 1916, No. 5, p. 60.

[2] L. B. Longare, A. Gillin de Robaulx, and A. Villa, " La immigrazione italiana nel Belgio," *Emig. e Col.*, 1905, i[iii], pp. 124–130. Cf. a report on Holland: S. Tugini, E. van Dam, and G. Hudig, "Gli italiani in Olanda," *Emig. e Col.*, 1905, i[iii], pp. 131–136.

[3] Carpi, ii, sundry passages; R. De Souza Monteiro, report on Portugal, *Emig. e Col.*, 1893, pp. 401 f.; *idem*, " Il Portogallo e colonia italiana," *Emig. e Col.*, 1903, i[ii], pp. 215–223; A. di Collobiano, " L'immigrazione italiana nel mezzogiorno della Spagna," *Emig. e Col.*, i[ii], pp. 197–208; " Relazione sui servizi," etc., pp. 264 f.; A. Bignotti, *Gli italiani in Barcelona*, Barcelona, 1910.

[4] P. Grande, " Le isole di Malta e Gozzo e la colonia italiana," *Emig. e Col.*, 1903, i[ii], pp. 227–233.

Farther inland, in the old Sanjak of Berat, some hundreds of Italians once had work, chiefly in the bitumen industry. Albania is one of those Balkan regions — the case of Hungary may be compared — in which Italians have made agricultural settlements; but here their projects failed.[1]

Many thousands have gone to Greece. As far back as 1848–49, during the revolution in the Kingdom of the two Sicilies, Apulians settled in Patras. In quieter times, the better-to-do of these returned to Italy; the rest remained as the nucleus of a growing colony of seamen, agriculturists, and general workers. Construction of the port of Patras and of the Peloponnesian railways attracted still more immigrants, and after 1900, the Patras colony was claimed, possibly with exaggeration, to reach 7000 persons, by all odds the chief community of Italians in Greece. Other considerable groups were at Athens, about Laurium, in Corfu, and at Salonica. During the Italo-Turkish war, many came to Greece from Turkey.

Although the Italians of Greece have in many places become less numerous in recent years, yet their past accomplishment is clear. Many were occupied in building the railways of Thessaly and Attica — for example, the line to Salonica — in constructing the Corinth Canal and the port of Calamata, and in draining Lake Copais. In the lead and manganese mines of Laurium, skilled miners were engaged, where once, in an early time, slaves in chain gangs spent their strength for Athens. Apulian fishermen, leaving their families for months-long voyages, have supplied almost the whole market of Patras with their catch and much else of Greece besides. Long ago, Apulian cultivators, now a considerable group, began to improve the swampy areas about Patras and introduced higher standards of agricultural production. The descendants of the older immigrant stocks abound, but in many places, especially at Salonica, have lost much of their Italian character.

---

[1] E. C. Cagli, " L'opera degli italiani nel Montenegro," *Nuova Antologia,* September 1, 1910, pp. 51–73; B. Bollati, " La colonia italiana nel Montenegro," *Emig. e Col.,* 1905, i[iii], pp. 259–262; G. Millelire and A. Anearano, "Gli italiani nel *vilayet* di Janina," *Emig. e Col.,* 1905, i[iii], pp. 363–366; Mantegazza, pp. 358–360.

This immigration has been far from uniformly successful. Fever, unpaid wages (or wages that shrivelled when traded for Italian gold), and unemployment have caused much distress and have made saving difficult for a man alone and impossible for one with a family. Large numbers of Italians were impelled to flee the country by the events associated with the Allied intervention in the fall of 1916. If few should return, and the emigration into Greece should lapse henceforth, it could surprise no one.[1]

Into Serbia, in the epoch of the construction of the Eastern railway, thousands of Italians came. But that work reached its end in 1888, and later years were chary of opportunities. Venetians who came for building may point to the military hospital at Gornia Milanovac as partly the fruit of their exertions.[2]

The forty Italians who in 1865 went into Bulgaria to work on the nearly completed Rustchuk-Varna railway were the heralds of successive regiments that came on similar missions during the next half century. English masters gave way to Turkish, Turkish to Bulgarian, but Italians were absent from probably not one notable engineering enterprise. Contractors and subcontractors, as well as workmen, on railways and allied undertakings, were often Italian. It was about 1896-97 that the largest numbers were employed. After that, the competition of the Macedonian workers became more marked, and disappointments in employment or remuneration became increasingly frequent, to such

---

[1] Reports by A. De Goyzueta di Toverena, V. Thaon di Revel, and V. Finzi in *Emig. e Col.*, 1893, pp. 357-364, 518-520; note in *Boll. Emig.*, 1903, No. 6, p. 113; E. Bonelli and S. L. Rocca, " Il distretto consolare del Pireo e la immigrazione italiana," *Emig. e Col.*, 1905, i[iii], pp. 265-278; E. De Gubernatis, " La immigrazione e le colonie italiane nelle isole Jonie," *Emig. e Col.*, i[iii], pp. 279-292; L. Corinaldi, " Statistica della popolazione italiana nella Turchia europea," *Emig. e Col.*, i[iii], pp. 300-308; V. Thaon di Revel, " La immigrazione italiana in Macedonia," *Emig. e Col.*, i[iii], pp. 341-356; F. Beauregard, " La colonia italiana di Patrasso," *Boll. Emig.*, 1915, No. 4, pp. 3-11; note, "Immigrazione italiana in Grecia," *Boll. Emig.*, 1916, No. 7, p. 86; newspapers, December 11, 1916.

[2] E. Mayor des Planches, " La Serbia e l'immigrazione italiana," *Emig. e Col.*, 1905, i[iii], pp. 236-251; G. E. Di Palma di Castiglione, " L'oriente d'Europa quale mercato per la mano d'opera italiana," *Boll. Emig.*, 1912, No. 11, pp. 119-142; E. Vaina, " Gli interessi italiani e la Serbia," *Vita Italiana all' Estero*, January 15, 1915, pp. 13-29.

effect that in recent years the Italians present have not much exceeded a thousand, mostly artisans and small traders.[1]

At least as important as this immigration, though somewhat different in kind, has been that into Rumania. On the public works undertaken in the years after the new state came to power, Italians played an important part. In numbers they labored at the prolonged construction and improvement of the port of Constanza and the building of the great Cernavoda bridge across the Danube. The canal of Campolungh, the railway lines (among others) of Craiova-Calafet and Barlad-Galatz, the tunnel at Beresti, employed many. Building workmen, always prominent in this immigration, contributed, for example, to the erection of the Chamber of Deputies, the Fine Arts Museum, and the Chamber of Commerce edifice of Bucarest. In the Dobrudja, many have been granite cutters. Lumbermen, with Rumanians in subordinate places, have been numerous about Buzeu and in Moldavia, but have gradually lost ground to the native people. Near Cataloi has been a considerable agricultural colony.

About 1900, the Italians numbered easily 5000. Thereafter a decline set in, the annual temporary immigration — composed of men who year after year, often from childhood on, went into Rumania — especially lessening; and when the war of 1914 broke upon Europe, not many who still counted Italy as their home were left. The riches of the country being first of all agricultural, it is in the periods after good harvests that the immigrants have been wont to arrive. Repeated disappointment in the newer competitive conditions has thinned the annual influx, which had been greater than that into any other Balkan state.[2]

---

[1] Report on Bulgaria by A. Scaniglia in *Emig. e Col.*, 1893, pp. 553–560; G. Silvestrelli, " La Bulgaria e l'immigrazione italiana," *Emig. e Col.*, 1905, i[iii], pp. 206–223; G. Giacchi, " La Rumelia orientale e le sue colonie italiane," *Emig. e Col.*, i[iii], pp. 224–235; "Relazione sui servizi," etc., pp. 254 f.; Palma di Castiglione, pp. 85–107; C. A. Vaccaro, "Gli italiani in Bulgaria," *Rivista Coloniale*, October 25–November 10, 1911, pp. 386–389.

[2] G. Tesi, report in *Emig. e Col.*, 1893, pp. 406–409; E. Incisa di Beccaria and F. Pappalepore, " La Rumania e la immigrazione italiana," *Emig. e Col.*, 1905, i[iii], pp. 187–205; Palma di Castiglione, pp. 7–79; note in *Boll. Emig.*, 1916, No. 5, pp. 59 f.

Even Russia has harbored the immigrants. Only one of the colonies of the great cities, though today it is chiefly a memory, requires mention. Odessa, four or five decades ago, contained a large collectivity of Italians who held a leading position in the grain trade. Even the culture of the city was partly theirs. When presently the great growth of its population set in, the Italian colony was submerged. In the mines of Ekaterinoslaw, many immigrants have been employed. Marble workers have found occupation about Kiev. Into Caucasia, immigration began about the middle of the nineteenth century. In the eighties, Italians worked on the Tiflis-Baku, the Samtredi-Batum, and other important railways; 300 helped construct the Suram tunnel. At Tiflis, Baku, Batum, and Ekaterinodar they have engaged in marble working. Near Kislovodsk, province of Terek, there has been an Italian viticultural colony which has weathered the trials of earlier days. Even into the Caucasus have come troops of wandering musicians.[1]

Turkey, while it still extended across the Balkan Peninsula, contained nearly 30,000 Italians, of whom two in every three were in Europe. When the Balkan wars detached Salonica — next to Constantinople the leading center for Italians — more than 3000 found themselves suddenly in Greece. Nearly all the rest were in Constantinople (about 10,000) and on a belt of land along the Mediterranean. Since the days of Byzantium, there had been a continuous history for some among these groups, and even today a few descendants of the old Venetian and Genoese families are to be distinguished. The great majority trace their immigration to the period of the eighties. In 1885 an Italian chamber of commerce was established, which, despite the prosperity of some of the earlier comers, has run but an uneven course.

[1] Reports by T. Carletti and E. Perrod in *Emig. e Col.*, 1893, pp. 410–418; S. Minocchi, " Gli Italiani nel Caucaso, in Siberia e in Manciuria," *Boll. Emig.*, 1905, No. 6, pp. 7–11; A. Ghersi, M. D. Epstein, " Le colonie italiane in Russia," *Emig. e Col.*, 1905, i[iii], pp. 159–165; E. Spagnoli, " Il Caucaso e l'emigrazione italiana," *Emig. e Col.*, i[iii], pp. 167–170; N. Squitti, " Le colonie italiane nel distretto consolare di Odessa," *Emig. e Col.*, i[iii], pp. 171–184; note, " Gli emigrati italiani nel Caucaso," *Vita Italiana all' Estero*, October, 1913, pp. 300 f.; B. Ischchanian, *Die äuslandischen Elemente in der russischen Volkswirtschaft* (Berlin, 1913), esp. ch. ix.

Those in trade have been fewer than those in general building and the construction of railways, ports, quais, aqueducts, and the like. Skilled artisans worked on the Yldiz-Kiosque, the Sultan's residence. In Adrianople, the bridges and best buildings were largely due to the immigrants. In Smyrna the old Genoesĕ patrician stock is still represented, no longer pure, yet alive to its traditions and retaining the Roman Catholic religion; but the Italian influence here, whether of old or new stocks, is less than the French and the Greek. A notable Asiatic center for construction work is the vilayet of Kastamuni. The coal mines of Zonguldak and the Anatolian railways have employed many Italians. In 1903 contractors and various grades of laborers began to work on the Bagdad railway, some staying several years. Many also worked on the construction of the Damascus-Mecca line. Fishermen from Apulia and Chioggia, finally, have brought their craft even into these distant Mediterranean waters and made a frugal living.

Of the mass of the Italians in Turkey, exception being made of some traders, bankers, and artists, it may be said that, while their conditions have not been bad neither have they been good. Italian citizenship, because of its legal advantages, has been kept long after all semblance of patriotic sentiment has vanished. At the time of the Italo-Turkish war many Italians fled from the country, but most subsequently returned.[1]

[1] P. Sitta, " Gli italiani in Turchia," *Riforma Sociale*, May 15, 1897, pp. 463–475; Rikio, " La colonia italiana di Costantinopoli," *L'Italia Coloniale*, September, 1901, pp. 69–86; Cosattini " L'emigrazione temporanea del Friuli," p. 47; L. Corinaldi, " Statistica della popolazione italiana nella Turchia europea," *Emig. e Col.*, 1905, i^{iii}, pp. 300–308; C. Aldrovandi and C. Fichet, " La colonia italiana nel distretto consolare di Costantinopoli," *Emig. e Col.*, i^{iii}, pp. 309–340; A. Mori, *Gli italiani a Costantinopoli*, Modena, 1906 (this ample volume includes, along with an account of the Italians of the twentieth century, an historical survey and bibliography); C. Poma, " Gli italiani del Levante," *Rivista Coloniale*, September 25–October 10, 1911, pp. 334–337; " Spectator," " L'opera della Commissione pro-espulsi dalla Turchia," *Vita Italiana all' Estero*, January, 1913, pp. 45–49; G. Bevione, *L'Asia Minore e l'Italia* (Turin, 1914), pp. 70–84, 97–122, 136–151; G. Ferretti, " Gli italiani a Costantinopoli," *Nuova Antologia*, March 16, 1915, pp. 257–270; G. Capra, " Gli operai italiani nel traforo dell' Amano (Ferrovia di Costantinopoli-Bagdad)," *Italica Gens (Bollettino)*, January–February, 1915, pp. 40–62; *idem*, " La colonizzazione agraria in Siria e Asia Minore," *Italica Gens*, March–June, 1915, pp. 65–89;

Some of the salient engineering enterprises of modern Egypt have received a characteristic contribution from the Italians. Coming first before 1850, these immigrants soon surpassed in numbers both English and French. By Ismail they were often put into the public service, especially sanitation, where later, to the lament of Italian writers, they were replaced by the English. It was in the same epoch, after the first disastrous experiences in using forced labor for the construction of the Suez Canal, that Italian workmen arrived, numerous in an international throng. Masons, carpenters, and the like, they lent their aid valiantly in this work and had even a small part in its direction.[1] In 1871, two years after the canal was completed, the Italians in Cairo were calculated officially to reach 4500 persons; ten years later 6000 or more; in 1897, nearly 8700; in the early twentieth century, 10,000. Alexandria, also long a center for Italians, had in 1897 nearly 12,000, though the census was taken in May, when many were absent. In all of Egypt, this census showed 24,500 Italians, who were more than a fifth of the foreign population. Only the Greeks — a third of all — were more numerous; the English followed after with 19,500. The census of 1907 showed 35,000, and Italian officials have since claimed 40,000. Included in all these figures are the Levantine Italians, chiefly Jews, established in the country for several generations and a strong group financially. Most of the immigrants were born in Sicily and the South of Italy.

In their work in Egypt, the newer Italians have been true to the tradition of the canal makers. At Assiut, in Upper Egypt, masons and stonecutters helped to build the barrage across the Nile, an open weir over half a mile long. Four years were consumed in this undertaking, which was completed in 1902. At about the same time, a still greater work, the Assuan dam, the

idem, "Adali nella storia e nell' azione italiana," *Italica Gens*, January–June, 1916, pp. 1–38.

[1] For contemporary mention of the Italian rôle, see A. Mangin, "Percement de l'isthme de Suez," *Journal des Économistes*, December, 1866, pp. 448–450; M. P. Borel (of the chief contracting firm), *Conférence faite à l'Athénée le 2 février 1867 sur les travaux d'exécution du canal maritime de Suez* (Paris, 1867), p. 37; M. Fontaine, *Le canal maritime de Suez* (Paris, 1869), p. 130.

chief gift of modern science to Egypt, was finished. The stone-cutters and others who came to labor upon it from North and South Italy had to travel more than five hundred miles south from Cairo.[1] " Without the Italian laborers," the under-secretary of state for public works is reported to have written, " we should not have executed this colossal operation." Numerous Italians worked on the bridges across the Nile at Kafr-el-Zaiat and Behna, the latter a part of the railway route from Cairo to Alexandria.

These are the outstanding examples of Italian effort. Everywhere it is chiefly as masons, stonecutters or miners, rather than as plain navvies, that the immigrants have counted. Lord Cromer wrote, " They are, as a rule, a steady, industrious race, whose presence is very useful to the Egyptians, as it enables the latter to learn various crafts requiring skill in their application." [2]

On the Suez Canal, in the later period, many were employed in rectifications; considerable colonies have been at Port Said and Suez, the source of supply of many Italian pilots in the employ of the Canal company. In the region of Alexandria a host of fishermen, nearly all from Molfetta, in Apulia, have been almost without competitors. There have been clerks, besides, and retail dealers, and a rather motley throng of adventurers, prostitutes, and others. Not less than half the Italians, according to the Egyptian census, are women — it is a unique situation in the countries where the immigrants go! [3]

---

[1] Despite consular warnings diffused in Italy, too many came, including Italians not competent to work in granite, and on two dolorous occasions, hundreds of the surplus had to be repatriated by the government.

[2] Earl of Cromer, *Modern Egypt* (New York, 1908), ii, p. 248.

[3] " La colonia italiana al Cairo," *Annali di Statistica*, ser. II, xxi (1881), pp. 31 f.; the following reports in *Emig. e Col.*, 1906, ii: S. Tugini and C. Arrivabene-Valenti-Gonzaga, " Gli italiani in Egitto," pp. 145–201; O. Toscani, " Il distretto consolare di Cairo e la colonia italiana," pp. 202–212; R. Monzani, " Il distretto consolare e la colonia italiana di Alessandria di Egitto," pp. 213–270; G. Iona, " Il distretto consolare di Porto Said e l'emigrazione italiana," pp. 271–282; L. Deperais, " Suez e la colonia italiana," pp. 283 f. See also E. Bigiavi, " Rapporti commerciali e politici fra l'Italia e l'Egitto," *Rivista Coloniale*, January–February, 1909, pp. 35–44; " Nisi," " Il lato negativo dell' opera dell' Italia e degli italiani in Egitto," *Vita Italiana all' Estero*, April 24, 1914, pp. 258–271.

As far as the past is concerned, Tripoli, unlike Tunisia, might be omitted from a study of Italian immigration. In the future, under Italian rule, the Mediterranean coast of the country may be found to give scope to dry farming, and South Italians will perhaps realize a new career there. In the dramatic developments in Tunisia, some students have found substance for the hope that an agricultural Tripoli might yet be created, when once knotty land problems have been solved.[1]

Six hours and an outlay of five lire suffice for the journey from Palermo to Tunis. Since this northernmost country of Africa is so accessible, and since in its physical traits it has so much in common with the Mediterranean island, we cannot be surprised that Italians should have come to it freely, while the French, as one writer has said, should have deemed the voyage from Marseilles as wild as that of the Argonauts in pursuit of the Golden Fleece.[2] In Tunisia the Italians have put together an intensely interesting community, a true colony in every sense save the political.

The merchants of Pisa, Genoa, and Venice who had dealings with Tunisia in the thirteenth century were the prototypes of those Jews and Christians of Leghorn and Genoa who, early in the nineteenth, bartered manufactured goods with the Arabs for cereals, oil, and wool. Some Sicilian and Neapolitan fishermen and a few laborers also came early in the last century and helped to found one of the oldest of the modern Italian emigrant colonies. When in 1878 construction of the railroad running from Tunis to the Algerian border was begun, it gave a sudden impetus to the immigration of laborers, and thereafter the commercial character of the old population began to lose its prominence. After the French occupation, many Italian interests were taken over by the French, as in Egypt they had been taken over by the English. Especially after 1881, the year of effective French interference in

[1] E. Chicco and A. Medana, " Tripoli e la colonia italiana," *Emig. e Col.*, 1906, ii, pp. 286–296; A. Franzoni, *Colonizzazione e proprietà fondiaria in Libia*, Rome, 1912; Società Italiana per lo Studio della Libia, *La Missione Franchetti in Tripolitana*, Florence and Milan, 1914.

[2] A. Davin, " Les Italiens en Tunisie," *Revue des Deux Mondes*, October 1, 1910, p. 702.

the country, a substantial inflow of Italian labor started. It was the beginning of an era of broad economic development.

Where work was, there the Italian went. To his arms fell the task of laying the railways, of building barracks, schools, hospitals, prisons. The port of Tunis he enlarged and deepened, that of Susa, that of Sfax; Bizerta he fortified. Into northwestern Tunisia he betook himself to carry on the lumber industry, staying five or six months at a time. He found steady employment with the transportation companies. Having built the railways back from the coast into the interior, he reached the mineral country, brought phosphates to the surface and so contributed to the development of a leading industry. Into the coast waters he brought his ships from the ports of the Italian South, staying from three to six months at a time, according to the product he sought — anchovy, sardine, sponge, coral — and no other men equalled him in the extent of this work.[1] He settled in nearly all the cities of the east and north coasts, as merchant and professional man, as tailor, barber, shoemaker, most of all as unskilled laborer and artisan in the building trades. He brought no small amount of capital into the regency for the conduct of his business. And as agriculturist, from small beginnings, made about the year 1890, he spread far over the country, making a tortuous chain of settlements behind the east and north coast lines and southwestward into the interior.

It is this broad achievement, made possible by the unintermittent access of more immigrants, that has given popularity to the saying of an Italian statesman, that Tunisia is an Italian colony guarded by French soldiers. An Italian estimate of 1881 claimed a population of 11,000 Italians, a French estimate 7000. Ten years later, after the Sicilians had come " like ants " (as a writer said), 30,000 were claimed; in 1898, 64,000, a number probably too low. In 1903, 80,000 were estimated (exclusive of 3000 men

---

[1] O. De Boccard, " Le condizioni attuali della Tunisia e della nostra colonia," *L'Italia Coloniale*, April–May, 1904, pp. 469 f.; G. Loth, *Le peuplement italien en Tunisie et en Algérie* (Paris, 1905), ch. viii. Loth's book is one of the best written on any aspect of Italian immigration. See also "Tunisino," " La pesca sulle coste della Tunisia e i pescatori italiani," *Vita Italiana all' Estero*, September 25, 1914, pp. 183–189.

in fisheries and forestry, a group fluctuating much from year to year); three-fifths were men. A census of 1906 found 81,156. Later computations reached results of 105,000 in 1909 and 130,000 in 1915; but these cannot claim to be accurate, and Italians born in Tunisia have been counted along with true immigrants. By contrast, the French, protectors and administrators of the country, have been held to number recently some 40,000 (the 1906 census counted 34,610). Few other Europeans have been present. In Tunis, the largest city, the Italian language is more generally spoken than the French. Outside the cities the French inhabitants are scanty. In some communities the Italians are almost alone.

In its pioneer character the agricultural accomplishment of the Italians has no parallel except in Argentina or Brazil. It is not that they have as yet come to own much land. The most recent figures which I have seen (Department of Agriculture, 1909) grant them command of 83,000 hectares and the French nearly 700,000. Yet Italian proprietors numbered 1167 and French only 2395, and Italian proprietors of estates of less than ten hectares outnumbered French proprietors of such estates — be it said in passing that the native races have no tradition of agriculture and that efforts to enlist their labor have failed. While the French proprietors have large estates which are cultivated by others, there are twelve Italian cultivators for one Italian proprietor. The Italians are sometimes mere agricultural laborers, and sometimes cultivate upon shares. When they plan ultimately to own their land they take it upon an *enzel* contract. The penniless immigrant begins as a hired man, earning sixty or seventy francs a month and saving half of it. In three or four years he lays by a thousand francs, enough to begin the enzel arrangement. Paying commonly about fifteen francs per hectare per year, he secures the right to hold and improve his land in perpetuity, passing the right on to his children. At any time, by making sixteen payments, he may receive the full title to his land. In this way many Italians have already become proprietors or have advanced on the road to ownership; but many also who made their contracts when land values were inflated have since met insolvency. They have cultivated most of all the vine — export prices have been fortunately high in recent years — and, after the vine, the cereals; their household needs of vegetables they have supplied from patches of garden. Gradually the shelter of cave, thatched hut or shack has given way to a house and the farmer has married or has brought his family from Italy. It has been common for the farm laborer's wife to live in the town, working as a laundress or otherwise, and to see her husband only during his week-end visits.[1]

From Sicily, Calabria, Basilicata, Apulia these immigrants have come. Two-thirds or more have originated in Sicily and of them a large majority in the provinces of Palermo and Trapani. They have not grown rich, many have been shiftless and casual. Yet the mass have won for themselves a commendable degree of comfort and well-being (even though their savings sent to Italy have been much overstated). Speaking of the farmer, a French eulogist has written, " The Sicilian is human force contending against an unkind soil. He does not think, for he has not the time; he does not know, for he has not been taught; but he clings to his task as a wild beast to its young."[2] With persistence overcoming the handicap of his want of training, with rigid frugality saving the fruits of persistence, he has indeed made the living that a crowded Sicily has denied him. But it is fair to add that his technical blunders in agriculture have been many, and his capacity for hard work has been much less than that of his occasional Piedmontese rival. In most instances, his wife, as in Sicily, has contributed little to the income of his household. The American type of padrone has sometimes exercised an important rôle.

Tunisia is one of the few countries in which the Italians have had a genuine labor movement. It is true that a competent

[1] On the agricultural situation, see Loth, chs. vi and vii; T. Carletti, " La Tunisia e l'emigrazione italiana," *Emig. e Col.*, 1906, ii, ch. v; U. Sabetta, " Condizioni economiche della Tunisia in rapporto all' emigrazione italiana," *Boll. Emig.*, 1910, No. 2, pp. 47–75; E. Eles, " La proprietà rurale degli italiani in Tunisia," *Boll. Emig.*, 1910, No. 2, pp. 76–90; P. Denis, " Italiens de Tunisie," *Revue du Mois*, June 10, 1908, pp. 686–709; C. Fidel, *Les intérêts italiens en Tunisie* (Paris, 1911), pp. 6–11; O. Pedrazzi, " Gli agricoltori italiani in Tunisia," *Rivista Coloniale*, February, 1915, pp. 70–81.

[2] M. Braquehaye, cited by Carletti, p. 361.

authority could write, as late as March, 1903, " Despite so great a concourse of workmen the idea of a strike has never existed." [1] But even before that year was ended, the Italian masons quit work for higher wages. By quick degrees the carpenters followed, then the harbor workmen, the teamsters, mechanics, and miners. It was almost a general strike, and it accomplished its aim. Under its influence, the burning question of national rivalry sank for the moment to second place. Rising costs of living in the years before and after 1900 seem to have prompted the outbreak, and only unionism could hope to maintain the level of wages against the competition of later immigrants. The young organizations presently, however, came to grief, and their leaders were prosecuted. Next, the masons, held together by their journal, *La Voce del Muratore*, secured wage concessions under the threat of a strike; and the bakers did likewise. In 1907, to protect wages, a decree was secured preventing the immigration of any Italians who had not arranged for employment in advance and who would not be repatriated in case of need.[2] Subsequently, through high costs of living and pressure exerted by the French population, Tunisia, despite its labor movement, lost a part of its attractiveness as a field for Italian immigration.

Both Italian and French observers have borne witness to the intensely nationalistic character of the Italians in Tunisia. The ill-feeling of the Crispi period has passed, but no mutual confidence, no warmth of regard has taken its place. Not only have the Italians lived as in Italy, little assimilated even in external ways; not only have they clung to the language and social organization they have known — so much is only their clear right defined in the agreement of 1896 by which Italy renounced her political aspirations — but they have been enthusiastically patriotic. They have not liked the French, nor the French them. The labor harmony of 1903 was temporary. Although advantages are to be gained by naturalization, less than fifty changed their allegiance in 1914, a typical enough year. They have been a thorn in the French flesh. Much as the question of Tunisia has been discussed, only two paths into the future have been sug-

[1] Carletti, p. 365.   [2] Fidel, pp. 11-13; Sabetta, pp. 18-28.

gested: French immigration may be stimulated — but climatic and economic disadvantages in Tunisia and a stationary population in France have made this way unlikely; or, the Italians in Tunisia may be assimilated — but their excess of numbers, their eagerness to remain Italian and the eagerness of Italy to keep them so, the fresh arrivals of immigrants, the easy coming and going between Italy and Tunisia, these things have made the second way unlikely in the foreseeable future. As long as political overlordship is held by France, a vital matter for the peace of Tunisia must be the continued friendship of France and Italy.[1]

Sharp contrasts accompany the resemblances in the history of the Italians in Algeria and Tunisia. In point of climate, topography, soil and subsoil resources, in point of character of the indigenous population, the two regions have so much in common that any political boundary must serve a human interest only. Even political character, however, is similar in the two regions, for they acknowledge the sway of one country, France. But when so much is said, it is time to turn to the contrasts.

As far back as 1833, 1100 Italians were estimated to be living in Algeria. Among the immigrants of these earlier decades, not yet a part of the great movement of emigration, there were many refugees from justice and deserters from the army. By 1855 some 9000 Italians were resident in a colony where French citizens were ten times as numerous. The great excess of French over Italian population has continued to be one of the most striking differences between Algeria and Tunisia. In 1855 there were also some 42,-500 Spaniards. Their great excess over the Italians has also

---

[1] The general study of Carletti is an enlargement and revision of a report published two years earlier in *Boll. Emig.* In addition to the other works already cited, see Carpi, ii, pp. 146–153; J. Saurin, *L'invasion sicilienne et le peuplement français de la Tunisie*, Paris, 1900 (?); A. di Sandro, " L'italianità minacciata in Tunisia," *L'Italia Coloniale*, July, 1901, pp. 10–16; G. Ricciardi, " La Tunisia e l'emigrazione italiana," *Emig. e Col.*, 1906, ii, pp. 409–417; F. De Velutiis, " La colonia italiana in Susa di Tunisia," *Emig. e Col.*, pp. 433–448; G. Bonacci, " Le scuole e gli italiani in Tunisia," *Rivista Coloniale*, August 10–25, 1910, pp. 250–262; *Inch. Parl.*, vi[ii], pp. 745–749; E. Corradini, *Il volere d'Italia* (Naples, 1911), pp. 114–154; G. Castellini, *Tunisi e Tripoli* (Turin, 1911), esp. chs. iii, ix, x; V. Piquet, *La colonisation française dans l'Afrique du Nord* (Paris, 1912), pp. 305–435.

continued to distinguish the country. Does not Algeria lie near to Spain, quite as Tunisia lies near to Italy ? And is not Algeria much farther from Sicily than Tunisia ? So it happens that Sicilians are much less numerous in the remoter than in the nearer country, and Neapolitans and North Italians relatively more numerous. In 1866 the French official count yielded 17,000 Italians; in 1886, 44,000, but this was the apex of the movement, for the 1896 figures showed only 35,000, and those of 1906 only 33,000. In this substantial decline of the Italian population (presently to be explained) appears still another contrast with Tunisia. The French stock in 1906 numbered 279,000, the Spanish 117,000, naturalized citizens were 170,000. Spaniards and Italians have generally settled apart from each other, the former showing a preference for the province of Oran, nearest to Spain, the latter for the province of Constantine, nearest to Italy. There have been several thousands of Italians in the city of Algiers, even more in Bona, many in Philippeville and La Calle. Rarely is the Italian language so generally spoken as in the cities of Tunisia.[1]

Among those who came earliest to Algeria were the coral fishermen, who developed a most extensive industry. After 1875, discovering more profitable fields elsewhere, they withdrew. The " fishermen of fish " (*pescatori di pesce*) followed and in turn developed a business of broad proportions. At one time there were probably several thousands of them, making their journey periodically from Ischia, Procida, and the coast about Naples generally. The anxious desire of France to have French fishermen off the coasts of her colony, and to have boats manned by crews largely French, led to legal limitations upon Italian marine activities which partly caused the decline in numbers of those registered as Italians after 1886.[2]

In the period of growing population, a potent inducement to come lay in the expansion of public works. On large stretches of railroad, for example that running from Bona to Guelma, in-

[1] On historical aspects, see esp. R. Ricoux, *La démographie figurée de l'Algérie*, Paris, 1880; G. B. Machiavelli, " Immigrazione e colonie italiane in Algeria," *Emig. e Col.*, 1906, ii, pp. 449–460; Loth, *passim;* Piquet, pp. 25–302.

[2] Besides the historical references given, see J. Lenormand, *Questions algériennes — Le péril étranger* (Paris, 1899), pp. 101–104, 155–163.

numerable Italians were employed, who shared their opportunities with fewer Spaniards. Another of the reasons for the decline of Italian immigration was the termination of the great era of construction of railways, roads, canals, reservoirs, and the like. Before 1878 a considerable number of Italians had availed themselves of the chance to take over public lands for agriculture. Statutory restrictions placed on the allotment of farms to others than the French and emigrants from Alsace-Lorraine made still another cause contributing to the decline. As laborers in gardens and fields, and as lumberjacks in the forests of Constantine, Italians have, however, continued to find good hire.[1] An increase, rather than a decrease, has taken place in their employment in the extensive mines, both of the metals and phosphates, in Constantine. In fact, they have been almost alone in this branch of labor. Many have found occupation as marble workers, brick makers, plasterers, masons, even as architects. In the towns, Neapolitan and Palermitan shoemakers have been omnipresent. It is on the whole a rather poor population — economically speaking — that the immigrants have been; a little better off than their compatriots at home, yet in no sense flourishing.

At no point is the contrast between the case of Algeria and that of Tunisia more telling than in the matter of the immigrants' allegiance to country. The Tunisian Italians we have seen to be defiantly nationalistic, robustly resistant to amalgamation. The Algerian Italians have acknowledged a weaker bond. Unlike the *professionisti* of Tunisia, they appear, when economically successful, to regard naturalization as a means of promotion into a more eligible social class. Between 1865 and 1900, more than 8000 were naturalized; in 1906, the census counted over 12,000 who had become French citizens; the decline registered in the Italian population after 1886 being, therefore, through this fact, largely specious. In particular, the restrictive laws governing fishing and the crews of boats induced many Italians to change their alle-

[1] Apart from the indigenous population and some soldiers, most of the agricultural laborers are Italians and Spaniards, "demanding less than the French by way of remuneration." This foreign labor supply is of much greater relative importance than that of Southern France. See P. Raynal, *Le vignoble français et l'Afrique du Nord* (Paris, 1912), p. 80.

giance, so that of late years, notwithstanding these measures, the Algerian fishermen and seamen have continued to be Italians, only naturalized, almost to the exclusion of other stocks.   Again, although the laws of the colony, passed in a period of fear by the French Parliament, prescribe that Algerian-born sons of foreign parents shall be regarded as of French nationality, only a small minority of children born of Italian parents have taken out Italian citizenship, when old enough; this, despite the fact that military service in the French interest is expected of French citizens.[1]

For the greater assimilability of the Italians of Algeria as compared with those of Tunisia, a number of reasons might be assigned. Less homogeneous, they have less in common with each other. Dwelling farther from Italy, they have fewer relationships with that country, commercial or social.   Having never had an ardent hope of political control, they have no surviving hope today. Having never conceded a claim to control, they have never received special privileges by way of indemnification.   Most of all, having never been more than a minor fraction of the total resident European population, they have had only the alternatives of remaining alien or being absorbed.   The way to profit has been the way of absorption, for social and for legal reasons.   Out of the Italian stock of Algeria, it is worth noting in conclusion, has come at least one distinguished servant of France, the premier Viviani.[2]

---

[1] Sig. Machiavelli reported that in three years only twelve Algerian-born Italians had become Italian citizens (p. 456).

[2] On the Italians in Algeria, see, besides the works mentioned, Carpi, ii, pp. 82–84, 91, 108–110; V. Demontès, *Le peuple algérien*, Algiers, 1906; and three reports in *Emig. e Col.*, 1906, ii: G. B. Beverini, " Il dipartimento di Costantina in Algeria," pp. 461 f.; V. Siciliani, " La colonia italiana di Bona," pp. 463–469; D. Palomba, " La colonia italiana in La Calle e l'immigrazione nell' ultimo decennio," pp. 470 f.

CHAPTER XIII

ARGENTINA. I. AN ECONOMIC RENAISSANCE. THE ITALIANS IN AGRICULTURE

ONLY because she is rejuvenated is Argentina today one of the world's young countries. The history of an imperial domain during three of the four centuries which have followed Solis' discovery of the Plata contains little that is edifying and glorious, much that is constrained and illiberal, expressive of an old society and inaccordant with a new. It is the record of the migration of adventurers in quest of treasure, whose expectation of return to their native land was reënforced by the restrictions imposed by their government. The consuming desire to exploit the mines of the Cordilleras, without the competition of others, gives the key to an understanding of Spanish policy in this long period. None but Spaniards might enter the colony, none but them might trade with it. To do so, even they must secure special permission, and their ships must follow rigid prescriptions as to sailing time and route. The introduction of negro slaves in the eighteenth century, under a monopoly conceded to England at the peace of Utrecht, only reflected further the singleness of Spanish policy. Of colonization there was little thought. Only the Jesuits established occasional permanent missions and made some beginnings of industry. But in 1767 they were expelled, while the trade monopolies and general restrictions continued. Because of legal and other impediments to the emigration of Spanish women and the want of any potent sentimental obstructions to union with the Indians, the Spaniards gave themselves readily to miscegenation and started a race which, from this or whatever cause, has since been, in the midst of bountiful opportunities, unprogressive.

Gradually the Spanish crust in America cracked and broke. In 1774, following upon a period of increased smuggling, intercolonial trade was allowed. The partial removal of restrictions by Charles III in 1778, and the stirring revolutions in North America and France, undoubtedly quickened Argentine restiveness under the restrictions that remained. Two elements in the state, creole and mestizo, were democratic. When in 1806 the people, by their own unassisted efforts, terminated the brief English occupation of Buenos Aires, they gained a sense of pride and hope of autonomy. These bore their fruit in the revolution of May, 1810, magnificently starting a movement which in a few years was to liberate a continent from foreign misgovernment, to put a period to three centuries of darkness, a colossal attempt, foredoomed to failure, to impose Old World ways in New World conditions.

Despite this show of capacity, the people failed to inaugurate an era of advance. Whether enduring harm had been done by the absolutist and ecclesiastic régime, or whether the race stock was essentially deficient in commanding and constructive genius, the record was still, for nearly half a century, one of intestine struggle. Not till 1852 did the arch-tyrant Rosas come to grief, and not till ten years later was a federal government born. With the forces of reaction and feudalism spent, the task ahead was to lay new foundations for economic and legal institutions and to make a people out of new elements. Only two years earlier, Austrian dominion had come to an end in Italy. The contrasting task of the *Terza Italia* was to make over old institutions and old peoples into new, but incidentally she was to contribute lavishly to the upbuilding of the new Argentine.

The remarkable physical qualities which fit Argentina for vast contributions to the world's sustenance have been often recited. An unequalled length of country from north to south, torrid at the one extreme, frigid at the other, rainy at both, but moderately dry in the middle; sloping from great mountain heights in the west and northwest to alluvial lowlands in the east; with fertile soil covered in the north with natural growths of extraordinary variety and large usefulness, and in the middle and south with tall grasses or scrub wanting only to be turned down by the plow to prepare for the crops that man desires; these are the gifts of

Nature. The immense pampas lands, while still untilled, served as the roaming grounds of cattle and sheep and horses whose raising constituted the first great industry of Argentina. The discovery of the fitness of the endless plain for cereals dates only from two score years ago. From 1878, when Argentina first began to produce more wheat than was needed at home, to the early twentieth century, when three-quarters of her production is exported, is a romantic step. For among all countries Argentina has become second in the production of corn, second in the exportation of wheat, first in the exportation of linseed. Over such an accomplishment it is reasonable to be enthusiastic.

Of the potentialities of the country the old Spanish population knew little, nor cared to know much. Grazing had occupied it almost exclusively, and grazing requires few hands. Why should a country, thus sufficient unto itself, ask for settlers ?

Here and there, among the public men of Argentina, were those who saw the need of immigration. Long before Alberdi touched immortality with his formula of *Gobernar es poblar*, the clear-sighted Rivadavia, in 1812, persuaded the Triumvirate to decree the special protection of foreign immigrants, above all such as went into agriculture, and in 1824 he appointed a commission to bring " laborers and artisans of every kind " from Europe. The commission did a promising, if costly, work; but its suppression in 1830 by the victorious Rosas ended for many years the attempt to secure immigrants. The tyrant deposed, there sprang from the ashes of despotism in 1853 the Argentine Constitution, noteworthy among the world's fundamental laws for its provision explicitly binding the state to encourage and not to bar European immigration — not, to be sure, so that asylum might be offered, but in the interests of agriculture, industry, the arts and sciences. The provision remains today. For a dozen years from 1857, there operated in the state of Buenos Aires an *Asociación Filantrópica del Inmigración*, sustained by private subscription and state subvention; it issued circulars in Europe, sent its agents there, and could behold a rapidly rising tide of immigration. A similar commission was created in Rosario, Sante Fé, and presently one for the nation. In 1876 a general immigration law was enacted, under which immigrants, upon landing, were received free of charge in a government hotel, with permission to stay a week or even longer; and, besides other advantages, were to be given employment anywhere in the republic. This law still applies.

As early as the mid-nineteenth century, the attempt was made to settle immigrants on the public domain. Each province owned the unsettled lands within its borders, the national government owned those of the territories. In 1850 by far the larger portion of the country was still so held. By a series of laws culminating in 1903, provision was made for the sale, at fixed prices or by auction, or for the renting, or the " conceding," of public lands. Under " concession " an individual or a company received title to the land on the condition, principally, that a stipulated number of persons should be settled on it in a given time. Princely estates were alienated, in too many cases recklessly and illegally.[1] Acting under the land law, private agencies established many colonies, while the provinces and the state established others. That provision of the immigration law of 1876 which ordained that agriculturists be transported to the colonies without charge inspired the province of Sante Fé to grant free transportation to mechanics and others as well.

Though the first coming of the Italians to Argentina antedated all of these measures, the subsequent influx was closely related to them. Before 1860 the Italians could play only a subordinate part. They were present, it appears, at the founding of the city of Santa Fé in 1573 and early made their way into the chief provinces.[2] In Buenos Aires only 10 (all men) were counted in a census of 1744, and 63 in an incomplete census of 1810.[3] In 1832, Sir Woodbine Parish, a credible student, found that the British and French led, among the non-Spanish elements of Buenos

---

[1] A. Pieyre, *Des procédés employés par l'état argentin pour l'aliénation des terres faisant partie de son domaine privé*, Paris, 1905.

[2] G. Parisi, *Storia degli italiani nell' Argentina* (Rome, 1907), pp. 113 f.

[3] Buenos Aires, *Censo municipal de Buenos Aires de 1887*, i, pp. 415, 433. The occupational distribution of these Italians is reproduced from the *Rejistro estadístico del Estado de Buenos Ayres* by E. Zuccarini in *Il lavoro degli italiani nella Repubblica Argentina dal 1516 al 1910* (2d ed., Buenos Aires, 1910), p. 87.

Aires, and that the Italians, Germans, and others made up, perhaps, five to seven thousand.[1]

One of the prouder memories of the Argentine Italians is that in 1852 an exclusively Italian regiment fought and bled in the struggle to maintain the state. In 1854 the Italian Hospital, since grown to imposing proportions, was founded and an Italian newspaper was launched.[2] By 1856, according to the municipal census of Buenos Aires, the Italians there had risen to first place among the foreigners, exceeding even the Spaniards, and numbering 10,276; nearly half the immigrants of that year were Italians. Karl Andree, a contemporary chronicler, said that most of the settlers had come from Piedmont and Genoa. " They work as sailors, traveling vendors, petty shopkeepers and tavern keepers. On the rivers they have eight hundred small craft." At Sante Fé he wrote, " The shipping of this place, like that of other ports, is mainly in the hands of Italians." [3] When a census was taken in Santa Fé province in 1858, it recorded 1156 Italians, of whom four-fifths were males, mostly clustered about the city of Rosario. Yet at this date they were less than 3 per cent of the population of Santa Fé, and the immigration was still to begin which would make them, thirty years later, more than 26 per cent.[4] About 1860, nearly a third 'of the depositors in the Banco de Buenos Aires were Italians and their claim was upon a fifth of the deposits.[5]

But if before 1860 the Italians were only an important minority in the Argentine population, certainly that population and the general degree of development of the country were still so slight as to leave bountiful opportunities for enterprising newcomers. According to guesses of varying credibility, the population had grown from about 500,000 in 1819 to 700,000 in 1837,

[1] Parish, *Buenos Aires and the provinces of the Rio de la Plata* (London, 1839), p. 30.

[2] Parisi, pp. 55, 62.

[3] Andree, *Buenos-Ayres und die Argentinischen Provinzen* (3d ed., Leipsic, 1874), pp. 313, 345. (The first edition, of which the third is a reprint, was dated 1856.)

[4] Santa Fé, *Primer censo general de la Provincia de Santa Fé* (3 vols., Buenos Aires, 1888), i, pp. xxix, liv.

[5] J. A. Alsina, *La inmigración europea* (Buenos Aires, 1898), p. 45.

and to 1,210,000 in 1860 — the last figure based on a rough governmental census of 1857.[1] How much it had accomplished can be not unfairly inferred from a picture drawn by the Director of the first Sante Fé census, which certainly has more than a provincial application. The year is 1852.

The population consisted of only 40,000 inhabitants, and was poor and almost wholly without trade and industry. Agriculture was in a wretched state. Of farming implements there were few, and they were but wooden plows like those used by the Egyptians in the day of the Pharaohs. Insufficient wheat was harvested for bread, and the bread consumed was made of flour that had first crossed the Atlantic or the Pacific. . . . The great majority of the houses had straw roofs and only a few churches of Santa Fé, the City Hall and the houses of a few upper-class persons were of unusual note.

Rosario was a poor hamlet with no more noteworthy building than its little church and four or six houses put up in the last years of this period with substantial roofs of beams and tile. Coronada and San Lorenzo were not so much towns as geographical names; and as for the old places, San Janvier, Sauce and others of which hardly any record remains, they were stagnating in desolation and misery.

Only one activity throve: grazing. The population was essentially pastoral. It had taken on the customs of the desert, living constantly on horseback to drive the cattle, to defend them against the invasions of the Indians, or to be ready to grasp the lance or the saber and quell the invasions of the hostile *gaucho* leaders or to put down anarchy. Yet this industry was insufficient for the progress of the people, since the absence of liberty, as well as of ways of communication, rendered all trade impossible.[2]

After such an era, only a quick growth could achieve the astonishing economic expansion of later days. In the period 1837–60, the annual rate of increase of the population was twice that of the previous period 1819–37, but in 1860–95 it exceeded three times that rate.[3] In fact the census of 1895 showed a population of 4,044,911. No subsequent general count has been made, unfortunately; but partial censuses and estimates yield a figure, about 1915, of at least seven million.

How largely the new Argentina has been made out of fresh stock has not been generally understood. As early as 1869 the 210,292 foreigners in the country were nearly an eighth of the

[1] *Segundo censo de la República Argentina* (3 vols., Buenos Aires, 1898), ii, pp. xv f.

[2] *Primer censo*, iii, p. 120.

[3] *Segundo censo*, ii, p. xviii.

population; but the 1,004,527 of 1895 were more than a quarter. Such a proportion the foreign population of the United States has never approached. Most of all, the growth had been in the eastern provinces.[1] These also had the highest percentage of males, a common result of immigration, and although in 1869 they already had the largest fraction of foreigners, that fraction, in the great population of 1895, was still higher. But if the eastern provinces (as likewise happened in North America) were predominantly those sought by immigrants, such growth as came to the West was even more largely due to them.[2] Spaniards there were in large numbers, and smaller collections of French, English, and other peoples, but the Italians, as a result of the tremendous influx of previous years, were about one-half of all the foreigners. With half a million persons they were actually an eighth of the population of the country — later I shall show that their strain has to be considered much greater. In recent years the foreign-born Italians must have been approximately one million.[3]

If one were to divide the entire history of Argentina into two periods, the first would include the colonial epoch and the major portion of the nineteenth century; it might be called feudal, since socially and legally feudal molds long survived the winning of independence. The second period would date from the firm establishment of agriculture, partly because of the new social forms and ideals to which its development gave rise and impetus. So pervasive are the changes of the new time that it is difficult to think back to an earlier condition. Once agricultural products had to be imported from Spain. Independence, far from promoting home production, merely enlarged the range of countries from which supplies were received. Wheat was brought from

[1] The capital and four provinces increased 197 per cent in population in 1869–95, while the three northern provinces, whose growth stands second in rapidity, increased 61 per cent. *Segundo censo*, ii, p. xxii.

[2] *Ibid.*, p. xl.

[3] For estimates and census figures on the number of Italians in the various provinces and chief cities of Argentina see " Saggio di una statistica," etc., in *Boll. Emig.*, 1912, No. 1, pp. 111 f.

the United States, Chili, and Australia; sugar from Brazil, Cuba, and France; tobacco from the United States, Cuba, and Brazil; oil from Spain, Italy, and France. After the civil wars were ended and railroad building began — ten kilometers were laid in 1857, five hundred were in use a dozen years later — home production started. In 1877, for the first time since Solis' day, the home output sufficed for home needs. But once started, the production grew by leaps and bounds. In 1895 the cultivated area was almost nine times what it had been in 1872.[1] And if in that year the production of wheat attained its apex in one great province, in still other provinces, as the sequel was so abundantly to prove, it had only made a brave start. Year after year, since the seventies, the proportion of exports consisting of grazing products declined, and year after year the proportion of agricultural products mounted. These are but the cold statistical expressions of a veritable transformation of the country.

Where did the Italians stand in relation to this great change ? Were they, in any significant sense, the instruments of it ?

We know that the whole agricultural development of Argentina runs parallel with the rising tide of immigration, in particular the Italian. The only other great industry of the country, the leading one in point of value of products, grazing, was carried on with few workmen, and these, as in Uruguay, were men of Spanish or mixed blood who had grown up to their trade. Further we know that of 845,000 Italians who arrived in the years 1876–97, 564,000 were classed as agriculturists; while, to list the cognate groups, 31,000 others were colonists, 2700 gardeners, 93,000 unskilled, and 75,000 without occupation (women and children mainly, able to lend a hand in farming). Finally, in all the immigrant agriculturists of the period, seven out of ten were Italians. Such were the possibilities of Italian participation in farming.

Let it be recalled that the Argentine government, in its foreign activities, had continually aimed to introduce agriculturists.

[1] 1872, 580,008 hectares; 1888, 2,459,120 ha.; 1895, 4,892,005 ha. (*Segundo censo*, iii, p. xxx.) In 1908 the cultivated area was 16,304,350 ha., of which 7,341,993 were devoted to cereals. Comisión del Censo Agropecuario, *Agricultural and Pastoral Census of the Nation* (3 vols., Buenos Aires, 1909), ii, p. 1.

True, the more modest efforts of the first half of the century had had a broader purpose, Rivadavia for example desiring among others men of science; but the period of successful invitation painted the glories of agricultural settlement. Acquisition of land — *that* was the bait that would lure. The government knew it when it offered tracts to colonizers; the agents abroad knew it when they offered a farm to the colonist. The European agriculturist was self-confident enough to think that tillage would clear him a path to affluence in the New World. To a people particularly whose dream of contentment had ever been the possession of land and who had failed to transmute their dream into reality, any liberal offer must be all but irresistible. Is it strange that Carpi contemporaneously — late in the sixties — should have judged that the circulars of the Argentine government " always act with special efficacy upon the imagination of the Italian country-folk " ? [1]

Though advertisement abroad was largely by governmental agency, the great majority of the colonies were private enterprises.[2] Eager for profit, proprietors of large areas, acquired by inheritance or purchase, or by special " concession " from ambitious governments, looked to the settlement of a grain-growing population upon their idle estates. To capitalists, mainly English as it befell, who would build railways through the colonized sections, public lands were granted freely. Generally the public lands utilized belonged to the provinces, which sometimes, but not very successfully, established colonies directly. The immense domain of the federal government was in the territories, rich, promising, but distant from markets and seaports. Incredible extravagance has characterized its disposition of these lands, which are still speculatively held. Though the territories contain a few colonies, their isolation, together with defective administration, has hindered their development.[3]

[1] Carpi, i, p. 69.

[2] Of those existing about 1885, eight-ninths were private. L. Guilaine, *La République Argentine* (Paris, 1887), p. 134.

[3] See a criticism, resting on records in the Dirección de Tierras y Colonias, by R. Campolieti, *La colonizzazione italiana nell' Argentina* (Buenos Aires and Genoa, 1902), pp. 207 f.

The distinction of establishing the first colony falls to one Dr. Brougnes, who in 1853 made a contract with the provincial government of Corrientes. His guiding ideal, he said, like a good utopian, was " the extinction of European agricultural pauperism." [1] Unluckily his own colony, planted in 1856, itself soon became extinct. The first permanent colony was founded at Esperanza in Santa Fé, in 1856, by A. Castellanos, whose carefully devised contract with the provincial government became a widely followed model.[2] Its success, advertisement abroad, the new constitutional guarantees, and other favoring conditions quickened the pace of colonization. In the next two years were begun San Carlos and San Gerónimo. By 1872 there were 44 colonies in Santa Fé, by 1895, 365. In Entre Rios, San José was founded in 1857, but success, slower to come than in Santa Fé, only followed the establishment of the third colony, in 1871; by 1895, there were 184 colonies in the province. In Córdoba, a little less fertile than its eastern neighbor, Santa Fé, and dependent upon railroads in the absence of such a natural highway as the Parana River, colonization had to wait on the development of Santa Fé. The year 1870 saw the establishment of Las Tortugas; a new colonization law of 1871, generous in its terms, led to the founding of Sampacho in 1875; and by 1895 there were 146 colonies in Córdoba. The settlement of this province was largely the fruit of a westward movement of the population of Santa Fé. In 1895 there were in all Argentina 735 colonies, of which 20 were of national origin. Their combined area exceeded 6,000,000 hectares.[3] For no later date have I seen summary figures, but it is certain that colonization has marched forward.[4]

Buenos Aires has never had a colonization history. Always a region of great estates, always eminently fitted for pasture, it had

---

[1] Citations from Brougnes' writings are made by A. Peyret, *Une visite aux colonies de la République Argentine* (Paris, 1889), p. 116. By 1872 there were 4 colonies in Corrientes, by 1895, 16; but it is a province that has never been broadly colonized.

[2] Its text is reproduced by Alsina, *La inmigración europea*, pp. 160-167.

[3] *Segundo censo*, i, pp. 660 ff.

[4] P. Walle (*L'Argentine telle qu'elle est*, Paris, 1913, p. 480) reproduces an official statement to the effect that the Córdoba colonies had risen to 550, of which perhaps

become the prime grazing province, just as Santa Fé had become the cereal region.   The first result of the Roca campaign against the Indians in 1878 was enormously to increase the area in *estancias*, on which cattle and sheep were raised almost exclusively for meat, hides, and wool, while butter and milk were scarcely to be had.   The success of other provinces in colonization led Buenos Aires in 1887 to enact a law concerning so-called *centros agricolos*, in the hope of developing small-lot cultivation near the railway stations.   Because of its ponderous machinery

100 had ceased to exist. Cf. also, on Santa Fé and Córdoba, A. de Zettiry, *Manuale dell' emigrante italiano all' Argentina* (prepared on official commission and published, Rome, 19-), p. 152.

Numerous works dealing with the foundation and history of the Argentine colonies have been published, among which the following are important: — V. Martin de Moussy, *Description géographique et statistique de la Confédération Argentine* (3 vols., Paris, 1860), ii, pp. 340–384, iii entire — the author, who had lived for eighteen years in Argentina, wrote this book upon an official commission; C. Beck-Bernard, *La République Argentine* (Lausanne, 1865), pp. 190–230 — Beck-Bernard had been the founder and director of the San Carlos colony; Comision de Inmigración de Buenos Aires, *La Republica Argentina, sus colonias agricolas, ferrocarriles, navegación, comercio, riqueza territorial*, etc. (Buenos Aires, 1866), pp. 3–19; R. Napp, *La République Argentine* (Buenos Aires, 1876), ch. xxiv; G. Lonfat, *Les colonies agricoles de la République Argentine, décrites après cinq années de séjour* (Lausanne, 1879), — pp. 53–94 are a description of the colonies and of the condition of the colonists, pp. 95–165 reproduce letters from many colonists; E. S. Zeballos, *Descripción amena de la Republica Argentina* (3 vols, Buenos Aires, 1883), ii, chs. v–xiii; G. Carrasco, *Descripción geográfica y estadistica de la provincia de Santa-Fé* (4th ed., Buenos Aires, 1886), ch. xxi; Guilaine, *op. cit.* (1887), — a valuable detailed survey; Peyret, *op. cit.* (1889), — one of the most useful of all accounts (Peyret was the founder and a director of the San José colony, and the national inspector of colonies); S. J. Albarracin, *Bosquejo historico, político y económico de la provincia de Córdoba* (Buenos Aires, 1889), pp. 143–214 — an admirable survey; G. Jannone, *L'emigrazione italiana nell' Argentina* (Naples, 1891), pp. 13–89; República Argentina, *La provincia de Entre Rios* (Parana, 1893), pp. 371–455, — written under the direction of a commission appointed by the governor of Entre Rios; República Argentina, *Segundo censo*, iii, pp. xxxii–xxxvi; Alsina, *La inmigración europea* (1898), Part ii; M. E. Río, *La colonización en Córdoba en 1898–1899* (Buenos Aires, 1899), — an official publication; M. E. Río and L. Achával, *Geografía de la provincia de Córdoba* (2 vols., Buenos Aires, 1904), esp. ii, pp. 1–191, — an official publication; E. Troisi, *L'Argentina agricola, Cordova e le sue colonie*, Buenos Aires and Córdoba, 1904; República Argentina, Ministerio de Agricultura, *Memoria*, Buenos Aires (annual); A. Franceschini, *L'emigrazione italiana nell' America del Sud* (Rome, 1908), pp. 298–446; Zuccarini, *op. cit.* (1910), pp. 227–273; F. T. Molinas, *La colonización argentina y las industrias agropecuarias 1810–1910* (Buenos Aires, 1910), pp. 45–97.

and its dependence on an inflated credit system, especially created, the experiment collapsed miserably in the panic to whose virulence it had surely contributed.[1]

In quite other ways came the prodigious agricultural development of Buenos Aires. For grazing, the native *pasto duro* served less well than the marvellous alfalfa. Since this crop could best be grown after three, four or five years of other crops, lands were let to farmers who would sow it after the last wheat. Through just this temporary device an enormous cereal output resulted. Incidentally, however, a true competition developed between agriculture and grazing, and over large areas the former prevailed. While the Santa Fé wheat output remained stationary after 1895, that of Buenos Aires, between 1895 and 1908, increased fourfold.[2] In later years has come a small but hopeful breaking-up of the larger estates.

Again, what part had the Italians in the agricultural rebirth of Argentina ? The evidence has many facets. " The first Italian agriculturists who came to the province," wrote the director of the Santa Fé census, " settled in the colonies, prospered, and sent for their relatives and friends; these in turn did the same, and so began the great current of immigration." [3] A decree of 1873 declared: " The Italian immigration which comes to the republic no longer needs to be induced by official agents, since each of the thousands of Italians settled here is a living and eloquent example of the incomparable advantages which this country offers . . ."; it regarded as sufficient the agency in Florence, and established an agency in Alsace-Lorraine, just previously lost to France. Of this decree, the ulterior purpose was " to mix the immigration." [4] But few Alsatians came, and the Italians flocked even more. Estimates made at various times of the population of the colonies to

---

[1] Perhaps the best that can be said for this law was written by G. Godio, in his *L'America nei suoi primi fattori* (Florence, 1893), pp. 466–472. See also A. Gomez Langenheim, *Colonización en la República Argentina* (Buenos Aires, 1906), ch. xv.

[2] For sundry comparisons, see *Agricultural and Pastoral Census*, ii, pp. vi–ix; cf. p. 95.

[3] *Primer censo*, i, p. liv.   [4] Alsina, *La inmigración europea*, pp. 68 f.

which they went reveal the presence of many Argentines. But Argentines of Spanish or mixed stock seldom entered the colonies. Where a hundred Italians settled, there, after some years, might be a hundred Italians and a hundred Argentines — the Italians' children. When we read that in the early eighties there were in the Santa Fé colonies 26,925 Argentines and 25,378 Italians among 64,504 persons for whom particulars could be had, the likelihood is that three-quarters of the colonists were Italian.[1] In 1907 an Italian emigration inspector reported that in a great district about Rosario, including the best lands in Santa Fé, " the agricultural population is made up almost wholly of Italians."[2] In the colonies of Entre Rios, usually passed over in accounts of the Italians in Argentina, Italian proprietors, according to official records of 1896, were about one-sixth of all.[3]

In Córdoba, where figures are available for the heads of families settled in the colonies, three-quarters were found to be Italian, mostly Piedmontese.[4] In 1905, there were in the nine colonized departments of Córdoba, in which the wealth of the province was chiefly produced, 13,435 colonial families, of which 10,291 were Italian, 1737 Argentine (including many of Italian stock), 362 Spanish, 346 French, 244 German, 224 Swiss, 134 Austrian, 45 Russian, and 34 Belgian.[5] In 1906, 948 new families entered the Córdoban colonies and of these " almost all " were Italian. In the department of San Justo, in 1905, were 3508 colonial families of which 3086 were Italian and 191 Argentine. And on the extensive lands irrigated from the San Roque reservoir most of the colonists were found to be Italians.[6]

[1] For the statistics, see Carrasco, p. 238.

[2] U. Tomezzoli, " L'Argentina e l'emigrazione italiana," *Boll. Emig.* (1907, Nos. 16, 17; 1908, No. 3), 1907, No. 17, p. 26. That the wheat production of Santa Fé was mainly in Italian hands was the position taken in 1904 by an Italian parliamentary committee dealing with emigration; see *Boll. Emig.*, 1904, No. 11, p. 33.

[3] Zuccarini, pp. 297–301.

[4] Río and Achával, ii, p. 179. See also Río, p. 120. For still later figures, cf. Walle, p. 480. Troisi estimated that in the 72 colonies which he visited, Italians were 79 per cent of the population (p. 208).

[5] Figures of Dirección General de Estadística; see G. Notari, " La provincia di Córdoba e alcune delle sue colonie agricole," *Emig. e Col.*, 1908, iii[ii], p. 35.

[6] *Ibid.*, pp. 36, 57, 64.

Though relatively few at the incipience of many colonies, the Italians increased disproportionately. To have a number of nationalities well represented in each colony at the outset had been a matter of policy.[1]   But it did not take long to learn that Germany, France, Switzerland, Belgium, and the other countries were less amenable sources of supply than Italy.   As early as 1864 the Italians were two-fifths of all immigrants.   And notwithstanding that the trip from Genoa cost two hundred francs and lasted between sixty and seventy-five days, a swelling throng of Italians deemed the venture worth while.

Some day the historian will fill in the dramatic details of the local settlement of the Italians, which we here may only sketch. The first colonies, Esperanza and San Gerónimo, were begun mainly by Swiss and other non-Italian elements.   When, by 1865, Esperanza had come to have a population of 1627, only 23 of these were Italians; and in San Gerónimo they numbered only 10.[2] In San Carlos, however, founded almost equally early, not only were Italian settlers at the outset extremely numerous, but they were the chief factor in its growth as well, the men being presently joined by their wives and children.   It contained, in 1872, 480 Italian families and soon was the chief colony of Santa Fé.[3] "Thousands" were there when, in the eighties, the sojourning de Amicis drew his charming pictures of its life.[4]   Numerous Lombards and Piedmontese made Las Tortugas one of the most successful colonies.[5]   Guadalupe and Emilia contained many Italians; likewise Italiana, Lago de Como, Nueva Roma, Toscana, Villa Casilda, San José — the latter at one time one of the largest colonies.[6]   In the department of Castellanos important

[1] See, *e.g.*, Guilaine, p. 119.   The Comisión de Inmigración de Buenos Aires (pp. 3-19) gives many detailed illustrations.

[2] Comisión de Inmigración de Buenos Aires, p. 3.   Franceschini (p. 240) errs in claiming that Esperanza was settled by 345 Italian families " which were later joined by a few other families of Swiss and German origin."   The Comisión reported that there were 355 families of six or eight nationalities.

[3] Peyret, p. 175; Napp, p. 489.   Zuccarini (pp. 236–239) reproduces the names of the first colonists.

[4] E. de Amicis, *In America* (Rome, 1897), p. 62.   Guilaine (p. 140) gives its population in 1884 as 3974.

[5] Zeballos, ii, p. 119; Lonfat, p. 59; Zuccarini, pp. 260–263.

[6] Beck-Bernard, p. 203.

groups were at Garibaldi, Iturraspe, Rafaela, and Umberto I.[1]
In Las Colonias, besides San Carlos already mentioned, and
Esperanza, to which in the later period many Italians came,
settlements were made at Bella Italia, Cavour, Franck, Nuevo
Torino, Reina Margarita, San Augustín, and Tunas;[2] but the
entire department is largely Italian. San Pedro, in the department of General López, was founded by Italians; Piamontesa
and Venado Tuerto received many of them.[3] Reconquista, in the
like-named department and its neighbors Avellaneda, Piazza, and
Victor Manuel were largely Italian. So were Ceres in San
Cristóbal, Corondina, Freyre, and Oroño in San Gerónimo; Ale-
jandra and San Janvier in San Janvier.[4] Piamonte and Crispi, in
San Martin, betray their origin in their names. So do Nueva
Italia and Rey Umberto in San Lorenzo; but much larger settlements of Italians were made in Candelaria, Carcarañá, Bernstadt,
and Jesus Maria.

This list of some of the more interesting Italian colonies of
Santa Fé is far from exhaustive. For Córdoba I will name only a
few: Garibaldi, Las Tortugas, San Rafael, Italiana, San Francisco, Iturraspe, Nueva Udine, La Genovesa, Vélez Sarsfeld,
Ricasoli, Caroya, Cañada de Gómez. It is not astonishing that
Troisi should claim that the Italian settlements of Santa Fé and
Córdoba have transformed the country; and Scardin that, in
those provinces, only the uniformity of the landscape prevents the
illusion of one's being in Italy — the Italy of Piedmont, Venetia,
and Lombardy.[5]

In the province of Entre Rios, Libertad was founded by Italians
and surveyed and administered by them, Lombards and Venetians generally, men from the Italian Tyrol. Others founded and

[1] Peyret, p. 146. Troisi (p. 263) says that at Iturraspe Italian families were
223 out of 260. See also A. Rossi, " Note e impressioni di un viaggio nel distretto
consolare di Rosario," *Boll. Emig.*, 1914, pp. 31–33.

[2] Lonfat, pp. 68–74; Parisi, pp. 156 f.

[3] Troisi, p. 269; Rossi, p. 45.

[4] Tomezzoli, p. 26; Peyret, pp. 288, 296, 303; Lonfat, pp. 76 f.; Rossi, p. 30.

[5] F. Scardin, *Vita italiana nell' Argentina, impressioni e note* (2 vols., Buenos
Aires, 1899, 1903), ii, p. 89; Albarracin, pp. 179–207; Troisi, pp. 178–435; Peyret,
p. 311; Tomezzoli, pp. 21–26; B. Sarti, " La colonia italiana di Marcos Juárez,"
Italica Gens, January–February, 1914, pp. 44–53.

mainly developed the colony "3 de Febrero." In Caseros and in Hernandarias were many, and in Crespo, Cerrito, and San José. Villa Urquiza was one of the older settlements. In Municipal, in the department Parana, and in the like-named colony of Negoyá, were important groups. There was the usual assortment of Italian colonial names — Nueva Roma, Garibaldina.[1]

Even in Buenos Aires, despite its lack of a colonization policy, were robust Italian communities. So in Las Flores, in Maipu, in Tandil — once mainly a Danish settlement, but now containing, strange to say, many Calabrians — so in Baradero, Tres Arroyos, Chivilcoy. In the last-named place, Italians are especially numerous; outside the town, " it is very rare to encounter anyone who is not Italian." [2] Chivilcoy is a great grain region, as is the entire district Olavarria, the most important in fact in the province and developed essentially by Italians.[3]

But let us turn again from the trees to the forest. The astonishing development of the broad agricultural provinces of Argentina has been mainly the achievement of Italian toil. The quick bound of Santa Fé when the heavy Italian immigration halted there; the subsequent rise of Córdoba, to the west, when Italians began to remove thither from Santa Fé, and the *récien llegado* also went there; the attainment of primacy in cereal growing by Buenos Aires, after 1895, when Italians migrated there from Santa Fé and Córdoba, and the newer immigrants also chose that province; these changes were largely independent of the activity of the older stocks. Even the more recent agricultural expansion of the Territory of the Pampas has been accompanied by the arrival of Italians.

Not unnaturally it is the Italians themselves who have most acclaimed this performance.[4] But international testimony is not

Peyret, pp. 57, 63, 96, 101; Zuccarini, pp. 299–301; Rep. Arg., *La provincia de Entre Rios*, pp. 381–427.

[2] Scardin, ii, p. 63.

[3] Besides Scardin, see Zuccarini, p. 295; Comisión de Inmigración, p. 19; Kaerger, i, p. 477.

[4] For example, Professor Einaudi: " It may be the vaunt of the Italians if Argentina is today one of the greatest producers of grain." *Un principe mercante* (Turin,

wanting. The German Kaerger, whose study of Argentine agriculture is one of the best, wrote: "It is above all the Italians who, in the newer lands, as renters and share cultivators, are pioneers in farming and who with the little capital at their command make the utmost effort to cultivate the largest possible area. It is to this mania for producing (*Produktionsfanatismus*) on the part of the great masses of immigrant Italians that Argentina primarily owes the rapid development of her agriculture in the last decade."[1] The Argentines Río and Achával, writing officially for Córdoba, ascribe to colonization directly and indirectly the magnificent cereal efflorescence of their province, and recognize, among the colonists, the great preponderance of Italians (chiefly Piedmontese) and their native children.[2] The Spanish Molina Nadal, once himself a colonizer, assigns to Italian labor the most important part in Argentine agriculture.[3] And a French visitor, Huret, attributes the new riches of agriculture to the valiant toil of the North Italians. It is lucky, he says, that they came, for it could not be hoped that the native Argentine would condescend to labor in the fields.[4]

Outside of the cereal and flax provinces, mainstay of Argentine farming, the Italians have counted for less. Yet even in the Chubut and the Chaco they have made important settlements, and in the Neuquèn many have received concessions of vast areas, still little utilized.[5] In Tucumán they have raised sugar. For many years they have been established in the ancient Cuyo

1900), p. 40. Cf. the reports, summarized in *Rivista Coloniale* for July 25, 1910 (pp. 231–233), of F. Martini, who journeyed through the Argentine for the *Corriere della Sera;* also the statement of G. Ceppi, who knew the Argentine well, in his *Guida dell' emigrante italiano alla Repubblica Argentina* (Florence, 1901), p. 49.

[1] K. Kaerger *Landwirtschaft und Kolonisation im spanischen Amerika* (2 vols., Leipsig, 1901), i, p. 924.

[2] *Geografia*, ii, pp. 164, 179.

[3] E. Molina Nadal, *El emigrante in América* (Madrid, 1913), p. 226.

[4] J. Huret, *De Buenos-Aires au Gran Chaco* (Paris, 1912), pp. 441, 447. Cf. also L. Albertini, according to whom the Italians "have been the principal, the first clearers of the land" (*L'Argentine sans bluff ni chantage*, Paris, 1911, i, p. 157); and an English visitor, J. A. Hammerton (*The Real Argentine—Notes and Impressions*, New York, 1915, p. 292).

[5] Fratelli Parato, *Territorio del Neuquèn e la Svizzera Argentina*, Turin, 1911.

provinces. In San Luis a few have grown sugar and tobacco. In San Juan, they own or rent a goodly number of vineyards. But it is in vine-growing Mendoza that true distinction again has come to them.

Although the Mendoza census of 1909 revealed fewer than 19,000 Italians in the province (omitting their Argentine-born descendants), these were about one-eleventh of the population.[1] Largely, while no figures can be given, they own and work the vineyards, seconded by Andalusian Spaniards. In the irrigated section, the grounds they have cultivated are impressive in extent. Viscount Bryce, after a visit, wrote:

> Vine culture is in the hands of the Italians, who have settled here in large numbers, and brought with them their skill in wine making. . . . The wine made here is of common quality, intended for the humbler part of the Argentine population. . . . Nearly all the country is supplied from Mendoza because eastern Argentina is ill fitted for viticulture. The vineyards, interspersed with meadows of bright blue-green alfalfa, give some beauty to the oasis, though the vines are mostly trained on sticks, not made to climb the poplar or mulberry as they do in North Italy. . . . [These Italians] are contributing effectively to the wealth of the country.[2]

They have introduced their own varieties of grape, not, however, to the exclusion of French varieties and a Spanish kind used for eating.[3]   And it is said that, many years ago, when the wine industry was declining because of technical difficulties at the vintage time, a Venetian, one Tomba, devised the means of resuscitating the industry.[4]

Thus far we have regarded immigration into Argentina as the Federal Constitution has regarded it — as a means to national development. But the thronging Italians have had a Constitution of their own, which has pressed them to seek their private

---

[1] *Censo general de la provincia de Mendoza* (Buenos Aires, 1910), p. vi.

[2] J. Bryce, *South America — Observations and Impressions* (New York, 1912), pp. 263, 265. Cf. Walle, pp. 444 f.; Scardin, ii, ch. viii; J. A. Zahm, *Through South America's Southland* (New York and London, 1916), p. 252; Tomezzoli, *op. cit.*, *Boll. Emig.*, 1907, No. 17, pp. 43–47; G. Lombroso-Ferrero, *Nell' America Meridionale* (Milan, 1908), Pt. iii, ch. v; A. de Gubernatis, *L'Argentina* (Florence, 1898), pp. 120–137, 164–166.

[3] Molina Nadal, p. 208.

[4] Lombroso-Ferrero, p. 315.

gain. What fortune have they encountered in Argentina ? What has it meant to be a colonist ?

According as the lands disposed of by private persons or by companies had unusual advantages, natural or acquired, they commanded unusual prices. But the mode of disposal was fairly uniform over most of the country, differing chiefly in such regards as the number of annual payments demanded or the amount of the advances allowed. In a typical instance, the colony of Hernandarias, each " concession " (of 34 hectares) was worth from 400 to 600 pesos ($400–600) and was to be paid for in five equal annual payments, without interest.[1] If a harvest failed, the payment might be postponed, but six per cent interest was then charged upon the unpaid portion. Adjacent to each lot sold, another lot was kept vacant, to be offered to the same buyer by preference and at the original price. The company supplied gratis all the building materials; and advanced tools, instruments, and seeds for one year, to be paid for in annual sums like the land itself. If grazing was suitable, animals also were usually advanced.

The colonist first built his *rancho*, or living house, probably hiring others to help him. Then he cultivated one part of his lot and placed his animals on the rest. Wheat must be sown before the end of August, and harvested in December, Indian corn a little later. Millers would buy the crop directly. Vegetables and fruits would be sold in the towns; and animal products were also easily disposed of. From all direct taxes, for from six to ten years, the colonist was exempt. Not uncommonly he was able to pay off his annual charges and also the advances in as little as three years.

In the few national colonies, the chief differences from the procedure at Hernandarias were that the first hundred colonists received their land free, while later colonists paid a low price, and advances were not made at all.

Whether the immigrant entered a private colony, as usually happened, or a national colony, he required, or at least found most

[1] See Guilaine, pp. 148 ff. For a broader treatment see J. A. Alsina, *Población, tierras y producción* (Buenos Aires, 1903), chs. v, vi.

convenient, a small capital. With the increasing population and development of the country and the rising prices of land, this became an urgent need. And it became indispensable when finally an advance cash payment on the land was required.[1] Not alone the money cost, but other conditions made the acquisition of land and its subsequent retention difficult. A fair previous knowledge of the art of agriculture was desirable; for certainly the special skill needed in the new country would come most readily to experienced cultivators. But among the Italians were many whose deficiency in this regard was serious.

Since a single man could not expect to carry on a farm unaided, he either would have to hire helpers or would need a family. The first alternative demanded free capital, which the Italian usually did not have — and wages are not low in a thriving new country. Nor at the outset was the second alternative typically feasible. Most immigrants were men. Their preponderance is strikingly reflected in the Argentine censuses; for example, in 1858, nine out of eleven Italians in Santa Fé were males; in 1869, three out of four; and in the general foreign population of Santa Fé in 1887, two out of three.[2] These men must either avoid agriculture or enter it otherwise than as heads of establishments. Such precise information as I have come upon confirms the inference that the Italian farmers were not usually proprietors. In Sante Fé in 1887 Italian landed proprietors were 5264, or less than a tenth of the Italian population,[3] — a rate, however, be it noted in passing, half again as great as that of the Argentine element. It is in the northern part of Santa Fé that the largest proportion of the population have been landowners, and the least proportion of the population Italians, while the middle and southern parts, thickly settled with Italians, have had relatively few proprietors.[4] In Córdoba, by 1905, though the Italians were four-fifths of all

[1] Unlike the Italians, the early Germans usually came with capital and bought land. Kaerger observes that such investments were often made before conditions were understood and adds that the Germans often learned the truth of the maxim, " Mutterpfennige bringen im fremden Lande niemals Glück." *Op. cit.*, i, p. 21.

[2] *Primer censo*, i, pp. xxix, xxxiii, lx.

[3] *Ibid.*, i, p. cx.

[4] Kaerger, i, pp. 913 f.

proprietors, the total number who fully owned their lands was only 4568.[1] According to the national census of 1895, somewhat more than an eighth of all Italian agriculturists were proprietors, but their proportion is again higher than that of any other important group.

How then were most Italians occupied ? Argentine estates have been large, larger than a single family could cultivate, even though the method of farming has been adapted to cheap land. From early days a kind of progression has been observed among the Italian agriculturists, and it is observable still.[2] First a *peon* or day laborer, the immigrant may become (especially in Córdoba and Santa Fé) a *mediero* or metayer, then an *arrendatario* or renter, and finally, when his evolution is completed, a proprietor. Generally, says Frescura's wise guide, " one becomes a proprietor only after one has worked hard. Even when circumstances have been propitious, one must first be a day laborer, then a share cultivator, then a renter. And when the immigrant has passed through these stages he will have learned so much of the ways of the country that he will no longer need this guide." [3]

The multitudes of day laborers, wanting capital, need know little of the value of lands, the art of agriculture, the ways of markets. Where they are to perform their services may be information thrust upon them; at work, they have only to obey the behests of their taskmasters. Sagacity and forethought, though counting for little, yet avail somewhat more than for men of their occupation in Italy; for the venture is larger.

Of the diverse types of day laborer, none is more hardy or more picturesque than the *golondrina*, swallow, as the Argentines call

---

[1] Notari, in *Emig. e Col.*, iii[ii], p. 57. Tomezzoli (*Boll. Emig.*, 1907, No. 17, p. 82) holds that in Buenos Aires province only a fifth were proprietors.

[2] I know no better descriptions of the types of agricultural labor than those contained in two guide books for immigrant Italians, both admirable: B. Frescura, *Argentina-guida* (Milan, 1909), pp. 75–88, and de Zettiry, *op. cit.*, pp. 157–163. The former was published under the auspices of the Società Dante Alighieri and the Istituto Agricolo Coloniale Italiano, the latter by the R. Commissariato dell' Emigrazione. Cf. L. Colombetti, " Dati ed appunti sulle condizioni degli agricoltori italiani nella regione di Morteros," in *Emig. e Col.*, iii[ii], pp. 98–106.

[3] Frescura, p. 88.

him, and also — when they are not thinking of compliments — the
" *lingera.*" Upon him, to no mean degree, Argentine agriculture
depends. Bag upon his shoulder containing a few clothes, he
makes his way from colony to colony. " He is no colonist, he has
never put plow to the Argentine soil, he has no house, has nothing
— his sack is his patrimony, fatigue purchases his sustenance, a
modest saving is his hope." [1] Having left Italy in October or
November, the Italian harvest finished, he is likely to proceed
first, as a harvest hand, to the flax and wheat fields of northern
Córdoba and Santa Fé, and next, in December and January, to
the wheat fields of the province of Buenos Aires and of southern
Córdoba. In February, and perhaps till as late as April, he gathers corn in Buenos Aires, thence returns to Italy, by a sea journey
that sometimes is as brief as twelve days, to engage in the spring
planting — has he not aptly been compared to the Laestry-
gonian herdsman of the Odyssey who might earn a double wage by
watching over his charge day and night ? Since his labor is unskilled, he is hired with others in a gang. Food and lodging are
provided for him, perhaps a measure of wine. When the gang's
remuneration is by the hectare — as often in the flax and wheat
fields — the head of the gang pays the wages; but ofttimes there
is a day rate, or a rate per sack of corn collected. Out of the high
harvest wages he may take back to Italy, if the season has been
kind, 350–400 Italian lire, and that is a sum large enough to
tempt away thousands of men annually, including some who have
crossed the ocean a score of times or more.

The farm hands of a second class remain within Argentina.
During the winter (July–September) they may be unemployed
and live poorly, or they may be general unskilled laborers —
porters, hodcarriers, and the like — in the cities and seaports. In
March and April they go to the fields for the plowing, or from May
to July to sow flax and wheat; but most enter the colonies in the
summer months for the harvests and the threshing.

Another group, with their families, live permanently on or near
the fields they cultivate. In the slacker periods they do work of a
miscellaneous, often non-agricultural sort. In the harvesting and

---

[1] Scardin, ii, pp. 108 f. See also Molina Nadal, pp. 229–236.

threshing season, their expertness in handling farm machinery and their habituation to the summer heat give them a place of preference over others. Of this type a variant is the *tantero*. For cultivating one part of an estate he receives, instead of a wage, and in addition to food and lodging, the full title to what he cultivates on another part, allotted to him. If he has a family, his own allotment may be 14–16 hectares, otherwise 5–10; and it may be even less if he reserves the right to hire out by the day at certain times. He may clear 300–600 pesos a year.

When the day laborer, especially the tantero, has acquired a knowledge of agricultural conditions and methods, and saved some money, he may rise a step in the economic scale and become a share cultivator — not yet a renter, for he cannot afford to pay the high sum demanded for the large farms which are here the rule. The advantage to the cultivator is accentuated if he has a numerous family, since then he need hire no outside help. He makes his contract for one year, beginning with March, but sometimes for two or three years. The proprietor supplies the land free of taxes, a dwelling, a well, animals for farm operations and general transportation, tools, machinery, wagons. He advances the seeds, and usually arranges a credit for the mediero with the *almacen* (general store). The mediero performs all the ordinary labor, sustains half the threshing expense, and pays for his living out of his own pocket. One-half the gross product goes to the proprietor. If the harvest fails, the net result of the year may be a debt with the merchant, " as moreover happens in all countries," adds the consoling guide already quoted.[1] But let us suppose that the harvests have been good and the mediero thrifty, or the newly arrived immigrant a man of accumulated savings and superior understanding. Then he enters upon the more speculative course of renting his land. His lease, of one, two, three or more *concesiones*, never runs less than three years, usually four or five, rarely nine. Besides the land, the proprietor supplies materials for the construction of a house and the packing facilities

[1] Frescura, p. 81. On the share contract see also Notari, " La provincia di Córdoba," in *Emig. e Col.* (*cit.*), pp. 77–79.

for his own slice of the harvest (10–30 per cent, according to fertility of soil, degree of improvement, distance from markets). Rarely is a money rent paid — so unpleasant when harvests fail — but its rate is likely to be 2.50–5 pesos paper per hectare. The arrendatario builds the house, cultivates at least two-thirds of his land, harvests his crops at his own expense, and delivers to the proprietor the latter's share of the product. Since the product is usually destined for exportation, it seldom happens that the land is more than thirty miles from a railroad station.[1]

The metayer system used to be more prevalent than it has been of late years. To it and to the fixed rent system, much of the cultivation of Argentina, especially the newer, has been due. A full generation after cereal production in Santa Fé began, three-fifths of all farming establishments were conducted in these two ways.[2]

In Mendoza, apart from their ownership of many vineyards, Italians make contracts with the owners to gather the grapes, being paid for the weight of fruit they pick. In turn they often hire natives for much of the actual work. When a new vineyard is to be formed, the land is let for a period usually of seven years; the renter plants it, receives the product for three or four years, and, for rent, pays the completed vineyard to its owner. Among the numerous Italians employed in the vintage operations are many building workmen, some of whom have come from Rosario and Buenos Aires.

To trace the channels through which an immigrant may steer his way to affluence in Argentina is not of course to show that affluence has been attained. In so complicated a phenomenon as emigration, even the long continuance of a stream is no proof that its course has run smoothly.

Difficulties, perplexities, and disillusionments enough there were in early days. San Carlos and Las Tortugas were not exceptional in having sanguinary contests with Indians. Sometimes for years on end there were droughts. Hailstones devastated the

---

[1] A typical rent-contract is given textually by Notari, pp. 80–83.

[2] F. T. Molinas, *Santa Fé agricola — las cosechas de 1898–99 y 1899–1900* (Buenos Aires, 1901), p. 14. Cf. *idem, La colonización argentina*, p. 142.

crops. The locusts that swarmed irresistibly southward from the recesses of the Chaco left only dead ruin in their path — and did not San Carlos fight their invasions seven times in seven years ? How few must have been the Italians who had not been born among the hills! Here, about them, was a flat, interminable expanse, disheartening above all to the women. "'Ah!', we said in the first days, ' better a crust of bread in Piedmont than to be masters here! We shall not stay long in this land!' And we wept and would have returned to Italy at once, at whatever risk, at whatever sacrifice." So spoke the women to de Amicis, when he visited San Carlos.[1] Yet generally, if the immigrant's foothold was unsteady in the first trials, it presently grew firm. Life was primitive assuredly, but wholesome; most of all, different from life in Italy. Of San Carlos, de Amicis wrote:

> It isn't a village and it isn't a city. We have nothing like it. It is a sketch or plan of a great city, or as it were a page of notes, with words and phrases here and there, separated by great blanks: a single vast rectangle, surrounded with little red and white one-storied houses, among which appear the openings of great streets which do not exist — urban houses, metropolitan streets; a princely waste of space; a primeval simplicity of shapes and colors, light in torrents, and the air of the infinite plain — something, I cannot say what, of youth and adventure, uttering the tones of liberty and hope.[2]

And life was often idyllic. In any one colony it was the people of one part of Italy who predominated. Friendliness there was and festivity. They spoke a single dialect which not infrequently even the Germans and French and Swiss, or whoever their co-settlers were, had to learn! Their ceremonies and songs and dances were those they had grown up with in Italy. If labor was hard, its mead was generous. Their instalments of debt were paid off and they bought more land, while their first holdings rose in value. It was an epoch in which, as fresh settlers came, and railways were built, men touched wealth by a process of increasing returns, and one writer proclaimed that " the desperate theories of Malthus " did not apply.[3]

---

[1] *In America*, p. 116. He also (pp. 105–110) rehearses other complaints of the colonists, particularly against the government.

[2] *Ibid.*, pp. 68 f. Cf. Scardin, ii, pp. 90 ff.

[3] Carrasco, *Descripción geográfica*, p. 239. Accounts of social life in the colonies

The testimony of Lonfat, Beck-Bernard, Zeballos, and others regarding the well-being of the colonists in the earlier period is presently reënforced by statements of various representatives of Italy. When in 1888 the Italian Geographic Society sent a questionnaire to leading Italians of the more considerable colonies, the replies it received were generally comforting. Not always is it possible, in these reports, to separate sharply the agricultural from other careers, but since agriculture is generally named as the chief occupation, the distinction is the less necessary. Wages received were commonly the equivalent of four to seven Italian lire per day. From Rosario it was reported that most Italians tended to become proprietors; from S. Nicolas that they could save half their wages; similarly in the outlying provinces. Their savings were sent to Italy, used to bring over friends and relatives, or invested in land; and from various places there was testimony that, though most Italians came with the expectation of returning, they usually remained in Argentina. Although much was said of the risen and still rising prices of land, the difficulty was not counted serious. Credit could be had, because harvests were usually good.[1]

Four or five years later, the Italian government sent to its agents a similar questionnaire. Though the intervening time had brought panic and depression, whose effects were still partly felt, yet any reader of these reports must regard their general tone as one of satisfaction. In Buenos Aires province, earnings from agriculture were good, few settlers were unable to meet their obligations, labor brought a fair return, only for special reasons were renters of land unsuccessful; but outside of the harvest season, employment might be difficult. Agricultural wages rose after the panic, but the currency was still depreciated. High prices for the cereals kept the share cultivators successful. The consul at

are none too numerous. See Troisi, *passim;* de Amicis, *passim;* Scardin, ii, pp. 89–109, 111–129; J. Ceppi, *Cuadros sud-americanos* (Buenos Aires, 1888), pp. 83 ff.; G. von Stramberg, *Reiseskizzen aus dem unteren La Plata-Gebiete* (Antwerp, 1887). In the Italian consular reports are occasional noteworthy passages. For the later period, see the cited reports of the travelling inspectors Tomezzoli and Rossi.

[1] Reale Società Geografica Italiana, *Indagini sulla emigrazione italiana* (Rome, 1890), especially pp. 88–92, 143–149, 171 f., 207–210, 234 f., 299, 323 f.

Rosario, speaking for a district comprehending several provinces, reported general content; the Italians had made money, and were now resolved to stay permanently. The Santa Fé consul deemed most immigrants prosperous, the agricultural laborers and renters specifically.[1]

After 1900, the indications still for a time continue favorable. In a thoughtful and sane immigrants' guide of the period, the author writes, " If you ask the colonists of Santa Fé province, largely Italians, regarding their way of life, they will reply that they are doing finely." Some have failed, among the immigrants; but many beginning humbly have risen to ownership; and the country is a good one for Italians.[2]   In 1903 a consular report holds both day laborers and proprietors of Santa Fé to be prosperous.[3] The 1904 harvests will justify a further immigration. In 1905 a request for immigration by the Italian Chamber of Commerce is given official approval in Italy.[4] And again in 1905 an elaborate consular report on Córdoba describes satisfactory conditions of labor and wages.[5]

And yet, in these first years of the new century, forces were coming to a head which, for an indefinite and perhaps a long time, were to diminish the attractiveness of the country. Nowhere are the new conditions more pointedly set forth — if also, I suspect, with some excess of pessimism — than in the elaborate reports made to his government by Tomezzoli, a travelling inspector, who in 1905–07 spent some months in Argentina. The evil of evils which he found was the bidding up of land values. In Córdoba and Santa Fé the valuable lands, held in large blocks, only rarely came upon the market, so that newcomers could hardly expect to become owners. If perchance a piece of land was taken to be paid for in instalments, it was found difficult to make payments, and

[1] *Emig. e Col.*, 1893, pp. 18, 29, 41, 45 f., 57, 61.

[2] G. Ceppi, *Guida*, pp. 42, 52, 86.

[3] G. Notari, " Gli italiani nel dipartimento di Santa Fé," *Boll. Emig.*, 1903, No. 7, pp. 3–15. Cf. Malaspina, " L'immigrazione nella Repubblica Argentina," *Boll. Emig.*, 1902, No. 3, pp. 3–24.

[4] Note in *Boll. Emig.*, 1905, No. 18, p. 61.

[5] Notari, in *Boll. Emig.*, 1905, No. 22, esp. pp. 33 f.

presently no money could be saved for further purchases. Since after five years of cultivation the land needed rest, the proprietors required rather large estates, and from the beginning the units settled had been too small. In every five years were two bad, one ordinary, and two good years — it was hard to avoid debt, and often the tradespeople came to own the farms. Share cultivators did not thrive, and renters, paying now an increased share of the net product, and bearing a larger part of the risks, often came to grief. What thousands of cultivators were less well off than they had been in Italy! The peon had to be paid a high wage. " It is curious that the two agricultural classes of farmers and laborers, both Italian, should have interests so diverse that the prosperity of the one can come only by the serious economic sacrifice of the other." By heat and drought the yield of land was reduced. Exhaustion of the soil came in many places after a few years, and migration westward or south had to follow. In Buenos Aires province the nomad Italians must pick up and go after four years, because the proprietors wished to return to grazing. Wherever the Italians went, speculation preceded them and the prices of lands became forbidding. " It is useless to think any longer of the easy acquisition of land in any part of Argentina, especially by the newcomer." And although there were places, like Caroya and Ceres, in which agriculture throve, a pronounced decline of agricultural immigration was to be expected.[1]

Tomezzoli visited Argentina during the culmination of an epoch of prosperity. Beyond doubt the speculative ardor of a peculiarly speculative country was labelling lands with undeserved values and placing its premium upon business shrewdness and unscrupulousness. Some brighter pictures, drawn at about the same time, are not wanting. In the Córdoban department of San Justo, despite years of drought and locusts, the colonists were reported to be doing well, sometimes excellently; but the quick fortunes of 1888 were no longer possible. In the Bell Ville district " all of our colonists have bettered their condition; those here only a year or two are still relatively poor." In the department of Márcos Juárez, the farm hand could still save 1000 pesos

[1] I have only roughly summarized Tomezzoli's copious chapters.

in a good year, and through renting could advance to ownership. In general, all classes of cultivators throve, but less easily and quickly than formerly.[1]

But even these statements are guarded. The tide clearly had begun to recede. A French student, M. Walle, declared that the Golden Age of the cereal provinces had passed; the high land values must check colonization.[2] Still later, an English traveller, Mr. Hammerton, announced that " the roll of those who have turned over the soil of the Argentine and brought it into bearing to the great benefit of its owners and their own non-success is, I am told, beyond reckoning." [3] In 1913, Adolfo Rossi, veteran observer of emigration, journeyed through Santa Fé, Corrientes, and the Chaco. Some of the colonies, he reported to his government, were impressively well off, others more or less in trouble. All the good lands of Sante Fé and Corrientes had been taken up. Nearly everywhere the old first settlers had prospered — had grown rich by the very changes that had made life difficult for the newcomers. The old proprietors and their sons were in a paradise, the renters of land in a purgatory, and the lot of the newest immigrants, struggling against debt and privation, was an inferno.[4]

And here we may leave these immigrants. The unmistakable decline in the eligibility of their condition is a decline from a shining era, to which there can be no return. In some essentials the development, including its latest phase, has a parallel in that of certain states of the northern continent first settled by farming immigrants from northwestern Europe.

---

[1] Notari, in *Emig. e Col.*, pp. 25, 65 f., 70–77, 86, 92, 96 f., 121, 124.

[2] Walle, pp. 96–100.   [3] Hammerton, pp. 292 f.

[4] Rossi's whole narrative deserves to be read. On the newer conditions, cf. also G. Bevione, *L'Argentina* (Turin, 1911), pp. 37, 134, 211; de Zettiry, p. 152; A. Neggia, "La pampa," *Italica Gens*, December, 1912, pp. 384–391; A. Mollo, " Sciopero dei lavoratori della terra nella provincia di Santa Fé," *Italica Gens*, January–February, 1913, pp. 21–38.

It is apparently not the case that any men, by sheer competence in cultivation, have risen to great wealth. The " wheat king " as he has been called, the Piedmontese Guazzone, who after a humble start in Argentina developed the rich Olavarria district in Buenos Aires, appears to have attained his eminence quite as much (perhaps more) by business shrewdness and an understanding of speculative values as by express entrepreneur or technical ability. On Guazzone, see De Gubernatis, pp. 13 f., and Zuccarini, pp. 295 f. (cf. p. 297 for a similar instance).

CHAPTER XIV

ARGENTINA. II. NON-AGRICULTURAL PURSUITS. GENERAL RÔLE AND INFLUENCE OF THE ITALIANS

THE native Argentine of the older stock, Spanish or mixed, had no love for agriculture. The estancia with its less confined life in the leagues of open plain, its semi-feudal social system, and its chances for speculative gain, continued throughout the agricultural period to exercise a strong fascination. Besides, a native population is seldom willing to engage in the same occupations as those of immigrants. Its activities are less " menial," tend to depend much on those wider adjustments permitted by a knowledge of the vernacular, of the physical country, of economic relationships, of social and political traditions. It manifests an eagerness to seem and to be different from the immigrant population. Its income rises, the leisure it enjoys becomes more general and more evident. And the more voluminous the foreign influx, the more abrupt and emphatic is the elevation of the older stock.

In Argentina these changes happened with an intensity rarely to be witnessed. Immigration turned to agriculture and endowed passive lands with fruitfulness and a price — lands, truly, that had often been deemed sterile. Nearly all the lots acquired by the land-avid Italians were bought from private owners or exploiting companies. Still broader areas were cultivated by them as share tenants, renters or laborers. Along with all foreigners they, it has been said, have been desired, not that a prosperous farming class might come to be, but in order that the value of the lands of the great private owners, themselves generally unwilling to sell, might be enhanced.[1] So a leisure class has been promoted and propped up — not created, for its birth was earlier — and sheltered against encroachment.

[1] *E.g.,* " There are two kinds of people," according to an aphorism cited by M. Huret (p. 489), " the foolish and the wise: in Argentina, the wise are those who hold on to their lands and buy more; the foolish, those who sell."

Though Rosario, in the heart of the older cereal country, a kind of Argentine Chicago, is a large city, the actual metropolis of the enriched classes is Buenos Aires. That city, the fourth in size on the American continent and, after Paris, the largest Latin city of the world, holds a fifth of the Argentine population. Had New York the same fraction of the inhabitants of the United States it would contain twenty million. But Buenos Aires is more like New York in harboring also an enormous immigrant population. Of Italians it has nearly as many as the Eternal City itself. It is indeed the great headquarters, if not really the abode, of most of those Italians in the Argentine who are not cultivators of the fields. And their rôle — we have scarcely so far noticed them — is hardly less impressive than that of the farmers.

If we except those first adventurous Italians who made their way into Argentina during the colonial period, then the earliest important Italian settlers were not agriculturists but seamen. What his instrument is to the musician, the sea, it has been said, is to the Genoese. When the demand for sailing ships along the Ligurian coast began to fall, their owners brought them, uninvited, to the promising estuary of the Plate River. This was still early in the century, long before the hand of Rosas had lost its clutch upon the country. They established their routes along the shallow waters of the Argentine coast, skirted both sides of the Plate, and freely moved up and down the Paraná and Uruguay rivers. In navigation they were past masters, from whom the Argentines had everything to learn. Just to the south of Buenos Aires, where the narrow but deep Riachuelo empties into the Plate, these Genoese stationed their craft and — what is more — set to building others. When the Mulhalls wrote, in the seventh decade of the century, this suburb, called the Boca, had a population of five thousand. What Andree had written,[1] years earlier, they found still to be true: the Genoese had a monopoly of the river and coast navigation of Argentina. Their crews at that time sharing equally in the profit, they appointed a commander and traded on their own account, bringing cheese, birds, skins, fruit,

[1] *Op. cit.*, pp. 313, 345.

and other commodities from the upper markets to Buenos Aires and Montevideo.[1] A score of years later, it was estimated that the population of the Boca reached twenty thousand, nearly all Italians. It constituted one of the most animated centers of the province, into which on every holiday the Buenos Aires Italians of the poorer classes poured forth to celebrate.[2] Their primacy in water transportation, won so early, has never been lost. At the end of the century, a computation held that " two-thirds of the crews of the sail and steamboats are composed of Italians and Dalmatians, and the rest, with rare exceptions, of the direct descendants of Italian immigrant seamen." [3]

Out of this teeming population towers the figure of Nicola Mihanovich who, arriving as a poor sailor at the age of eighteen, in 1867, had become the owner, thirty years later, of 125 ships, touching in their courses most parts of the South American coast. He built his craft out of timber from his own colony in the Chaco. Though himself a Dalmatian, he had chiefly Italians for his associates and employees in the greatest shipping company of South America.[4]

It is scarcely astonishing that emigrants from the villages and towns of Italy — not the cities — should have been numerous among the immigrants into Argentina. The general reasons for their emigration we need not repeat. To Argentina they went because they there would have the chance of serving their compatriots and because increasingly, in a new and expanding country, they could expect to make their skill tell in the diversification of its industries and trade. Nothing in the traditions of this

---

[1] M. G. and E. T. Mulhall, *Handbook of the River Plate* (2 vols., Buenos Aires, 1869), i, p. 116.

[2] See the pictures of J. Ceppi, pp. 21–24; of S. Dominguez, *Recuerdos de Buenos Aires* (Valladolid, 1888), pp. 25–33, and, for a later time, of C. Lupati, *Argentini e italiani al Plata* (Milan, 1910), pp. 116–123.

[3] Einaudi, *Un principe mercante*, p. 37. See also Reale Società Geografica Italiana, p. 90; Camera Italiana di Commercio ed Arti (Buenos Aires), *Gli italiani nella Repubblica Argentina* (Buenos Aires, 1898), Parte Generale, pp. 2 f.; and an unsigned article, " The Immigrant in South America," in *Blackwood's Magazine*, November, 1911, p. 611.

[4] See esp. Cam. Ital. di Comm., *Esposizione grafica*, pp. 472–480.

country gave promise that its ascent to a broader civilization could come autochthonously. Tremendous then must be the opportunity for aliens. With large rewards ahead and little competition, a man might climb from humble places to power. How generally such chances were scented by the emigrant before he left Italy no one can say. But we know that the desired success often came swiftly, and must have been bruited in Italy. " The vendor of ices," an Italian consul, for example, related in 1893, "becomes, say, a liquor dealer, the fruit seller a restaurant or hotel keeper, the tailor a cloth merchant, the bricklayer a building contractor." [1]

Even in the first quarter or third of the nineteenth century, such immigrants were numerous in Argentina. They included physicians, artists, engineers, pharmacists, tradespeople, innkeepers, artisans. A writer in the *Revista del Plata* said, " Genoa gives us a world of seamen, together with tavern keepers, sellers of foodstuffs, ship artisans and that succession of shopkeepers who in the Calle Federación clothe and equip our gauchos. From Savoy we get bricklayers, from Lombardy painters, glaziers, figure-makers, etc." Though their architects in this period were unschooled, they began to build numerous small structures of all kinds. The names of many early importers were Italian.[2]

Only in the year 1876 did the immigration statistics begin to specify occupations. Of the 845,000 Italians who came in the period 1876–97 (of whom two-thirds were agriculturists) 13,000 were masons, 23,000 artisans, 10,000 craftsmen, 9000 tradespeople, 2700 gardeners, and 94,000 day laborers. After 1880, the development of the country assumed such a pace that the supply of labor lagged behind the demand. Near the end of this prosperous decade, the inquiry of the Italian Geographic Society, already referred to, was made. The answers submitted showed that in the La Plata region, those next in importance after farmers were, roughly in order, bricklayers, blacksmiths, car-

---

[1] *Emig. e Col.*, 1893, p. 16.
[2] Parisi, pp. 21 f., 30, 36–39. It has seemed right to soften somewhat Parisi's claim as to the extent to which workers of the kinds mentioned, and others, were represented.

penters, shoemakers, tailors, hat makers, furnace workers, cooks and domestic servants, and others; at Rosario, then already a large city, most of the artisan and manual labor class, and most tradespeople, were Italian; in San Juan, masons, carpenters, and blacksmiths came after agriculturists in importance; and so through a considerable list.[1] Thomas A. Turner, who lived for five years in Argentina and deemed the country "swamped by Italians," wrote, with some exaggeration, "All the petty trade of the country is in his hands. The *fondas, almacenes, confiterias,* and many other businesses are almost exclusively carried on by these lean and ill-favored sons of Italy." [2]

The same wide distribution and frequent dominance of the Italians is again abundantly shown in the later consular reports made to the (Italian) Emigration Service. In 1902, Italian masons, carpenters, shoemakers, painters, tailors, street pavers, and unskilled laborers were declared to be "absolutely preponderant" in Buenos Aires.[3] In the Santa Fé district Italians were reported in 1903 to abound as unskilled laborers, tailors, masons, shoemakers, blacksmiths, bakers, mechanics, waiters, retail tradespeople (especially in food), and tanners — hide tanning was claimed to be wholly an Italian industry.[4] In Córdoba City and Rio Cuarto they were blacksmiths, carpenters, tailors, barbers, coppersmiths, hotel keepers.[5] In the provinces of Tucumán and Salta were similar groups; there was only a little agriculture here, but much trade and industry.[6] Their tradespeople and artisans were described as the progressive element in Jujuy. And in Corrientes, Italian commercial houses were among the largest.

[1] Reale Soc. Geog. Ital., pp. 88–92.

[2] Turner, *Argentina and the Argentines* (London, 1892), pp. 123 f.; cf. p. 105. The collection of Italian consular reports published at this time is of the same tenor as the reports of the Geographic Society: *Emig. e Col.*, 1893, *e.g.*, pp. 29, 31, 42, 60.

[3] L. Gioia, "Le condizioni degli italiani in Buenos Aires," *Boll. Emig.*, 1902, No. 8, p. 58.

[4] G. Notari, "Gli italiani nel dipartimento di Santa Fé, *Boll. Emig.*, 1903, No. 7, p. 12.

[5] *Idem*, "La provincia di Córdoba," in *Boll. Emig.*, 1905, No. 22, pp. 13, 18.

[6] *Idem*, "Le provincie argentine di Tucumán, Salta e Jujuy in relazione all' immigrazione italiana," *Boll. Emig.*, 1906, No. 10, pp. 8 f., 28 f.

They establish nearly everywhere the businesses which engaged them at home — here a macaroni factory, there a distillery, here a steam sawmill, there a lime furnace. All industries and trades are successfully carried on by our compatriots, from bootblack to money broker, from blacksmith to jeweler, from gardener to colonizer on a large scale, from stone worker to house builder, from interior decorator to teacher of painting, from mechanic to mill owner.

This was written of Córdoba, the province. Again,

Phenomenal is their fever for work: all wish to get rich, and quickly. . . . The railroad employee has his little foodshop, looking after it as he may, helped by his wife; the school teacher keeps the accounts of five or ten business houses; the shoemaker sells lottery tickets, runs an exchange, or a bootblacking establishment; the type setter maintains a tailoring shop, administered by the women of his house; the *almacenero* sells everything, from wine to dry goods, from pottery and hardware to sausages and liquors. This combination of arts and trades in the selfsame person assumes in the rural districts hardly credible forms. There our immigrant may be at once blacksmith and shoemaker, cook and tailor, porter and bricklayer — willing, gracious, happy, healthy, always content with his lot, always trusting in a better future.[1]

In Córdoba City nearly all the hotels and restaurants have been reported to be in Italian hands, also the principal shops, some large lime furnaces, and the chief establishments for making shoes, wagons, carriages, hats, clothes, preserves, and liquors, and for tanning hides.[2]

In the law and medicine, as university professors, actors, musicians, journalists, they have played no mean part, and have attained to shining places.[3] An overwhelming majority of the horticulturists of Buenos Aires — few cities have made more of the trade of these artists — have been Italians. All these groups we must reluctantly pass by, only because more important ones remain.

As architects, engineers, and builders, they have accomplished a work at once distinguished and comprehensive. Their dominance in architecture over a long period has been unquestionable. A truly extraordinary series of public buildings, theaters, schools,

---

[1] Notari, " La provincia di Córdoba," in *Emig. e Col. (cit.)*, pp. 24 f.

[2] *Ibid.*, pp. 45 f.

[3] Cam. Ital. di Comm., Parte Generale, pp. 243–316; Zuccarini, pp. 451–464. (These by way of example only.)

churches, banks, and private dwellings have been designed by such men as Meano, Tamburini, Aloisi, Pineroli, and Morra. Sometimes, as in the case of Tamburini, they first came to do their work on commission; again, as in the case of Bernasconi, they rose from humble beginnings in Argentina.

Where there was an Italian architect, there also appeared an Italian builder (but much of the work of the builders was independent of that of the architects). " The greater part of the public structures of the Capital and of the other cities of the Republic, almost all the churches, the schools, numerous hospitals were designed and erected by Italian architects, or by their sons trained in Italy," wrote A. Franzoni some years ago.[1] Hence the aspect of these cities today strongly suggests Italian inspiration. The architectural transformation of Buenos Aires, begun by Canale while yet hardly a building of two stories existed, was mainly the work of Italians. Of the houses in Buenos Aires few now standing were built before 1850, and the overwhelming majority have been erected since 1880. Generally in this period, as the municipal statistics of building permits show, the builders, to a preponderant extent, were Italians. The thousands of structures of La Plata, the specially created capital of Buenos Aires province, were mainly put up by them; and these include many beautiful public edifices. At Rosario, Italian building workmen have been four-fifths, or more, of all, and Italian architects have designed many public buildings. Both groups have been prominent also in Santa Fé City and at Paraná, capital of Entre Rios. In Corrientes, totally transformed since 1880, the architects, builders, and workmen were mainly Italian; Italian builders in the like-named province were estimated some years ago to be nine-tenths of all. In Córdoba City, three-quarters of the structures standing at the end of the nineteenth century were their work. In Santiago del Estero, Tucumán, Salta, Jujuy, and Mendoza innumerable public and private edifices were the fruit of their efforts, and a considerable part also of what Catamarca could show.[2]

[1] Cam. Ital. di Comm., p. 6.
[2] *Ibid.*, especially the excellent monograph by P. Moneta, pp. 104–118; Scardin, i, pp. 188 f.

" In particular, building workmen are in constant demand, since every year an abundance of new construction is undertaken in the city," Andree wrote concerning Buenos Aires, half a century ago.[1] At the end of the nineteenth century, it was calculated that an emphatic preponderance of the masons, blacksmiths, carpenters, plasterers, and others who had built and rebuilt the metropolis during the previous forty years had been Italian.[2] A recent generalization holds that " the great mass of the building laborers in the republic are Italians — unskilled men from Apulia and Calabria; masons, marble workers, and the like from the Po valley." [3]

Almost equally impressive is the record in projects of engineering. An Italian, Medici, devised and constructed the sewage system of Buenos Aires and the water supply and sewage systems of La Plata. Others built waterworks in San Juan and the reservoir and filtration system of Tucumán. In addition, the port works of Bahia Blanca, whose harbor is even better than that of the federal capital, and the military port works of Buenos Aires were of Italian construction, designed by an engineer, Luiggi. Some years ago, in the capital, there were, out of seventy-three authorized constructors of private sewers, fifty-seven Italian. Without the great irrigation works of Cipolletti in Mendoza and San Juan the vineyards of those provinces would be much less extensive; the Mendoza reservoir for drinking water is of Italian construction. The San Roque reservoir of Córdoba, head of an extensive irrigation system, is a lake 1600 hectares in area, maintained by a dam 100 feet high. In its construction all of the stonecutters and most of the masons employed were Italian. Others played an important part in the cutting of the Trans-Andine tunnel, many having been enrolled therefor in Switzer-

[1] Andree, p. 322.

[2] Cam. Ital. di Comm., *op. cit.*, p. 104; the author, Moneta, roughly estimates the Italians to have been 85 per cent of these. Cf. Jannone, pp. 132-134. At about the same time, G. Ceppi held that three-quarters of the masons in Argentina were Italians (p. 50).

[3] E. Gérardin, " Les ouvriers du bâtiment au Chili et en Argentine," *Musée Sociale*, July, 1913, p. 196. Cf. also the strictly secondary account of G. Hiller, *Einwanderung und Kolonisation in Argentinien*, i (Berlin, 1912), p. 107.

land. On the railways the inferior grades of work have been theirs; yet an Italian received the commission for the Villa Maria-Rufino line. In 1904 the difficult task of building the Jujuy-Bolivia railroad was begun, to continue for several years. Notari wrote of it, " This enterprise is Italian. The engineers are Italian, the designers, the contractors of the various branches, the foremen, everybody, including the managing heads. They are helped by more than a thousand Italian workmen, who do the more difficult and skilled work, while the mass of the common laborers is recruited from the natives and the Bolivians." [1]

It is a pity that the recent industrial and trade census of Argentina does not specify the rôle of foreigners by nationalities.[2] The general statistics which it offers for the proprietorship of establishments by foreigners as a class reveal a situation that is probably unique even among the newer nations, though it certainly existed in Argentina as early as 1895. Then (in 1895), for some details can be given, the foreign proprietors of food-making establishments (3574) were seven times as numerous as the Argentine, and the foreign employees (18,726) were more than twice the Argentine. In all manufactures of clothing, foreign proprietors (5066) and workmen (22,185) were respectively eight times and more than twice the Argentine; in building (2995 proprietors, 17,817 workmen), they were respectively three and one and a half times the native; in the metal trades (2744 proprietors, 10,613 workmen), they were seven and two and a half times.[3]

In these last years of the century it was claimed that nine out of thirty Italian iron foundries had more than three-fifths the total

[1] Notari, " La provincia di Córdoba," in *Emig. e Col.*, p. 22. See also, on the Italians in engineering, Cam. Ital. di Comm., Parte Generale, pp. 118-144; a subsequent work of a like title, dated 1906, pp. 187-211; Scardin, ii, p. 280; Zuccarini, pp. 76, 348, 350; de Gubernatis, p. 123; " Relazione sui servizi . . . aprile 1906–aprile 1907," *Boll. Emig.*, 1907, No. 11, p. 81; Tomezzoli, in *Boll. Emig.*, 1907, No. 17, p. 41; Rossi, pp. 21-23; Notari, "Le provincie argentine di Tucumán," etc., in *Emig. e Col.*, pp. 141, 156, 167 f. For their emphasis on the Italians as general laborers on streets, railways, etc., see also G. Ceppi, p. 50; Albertini, p. 157; Zuccarini, p. 155; Hiller, p. 107.

[2] *Censo industrial y comercial de la República Argentina*, 1908-14, Buenos Aires, 1915-16.

[3] *Segundo censo*, iii, pp. xcii and 270 ff.

iron output of Argentina.[1] Five-sixths of the makers of iron bedsteads were Italian; nearly all the manufacturers of large clocks
and the owner of the only bell foundry. In brass and in bronze
works they dominated. Of the leaders in the metal trades, many
rose from humble beginnings, for example Zamboni, a former
blacksmith of Domodossola. In the tanneries of the province of
Buenos Aires, Italians have stood high. It is asserted that the
salt meat industry was established by an Italian, one Rocca, and
that his compatriots improved the processes of salting; but, in
the freezing of meats, they have counted only as wage earners.
Many have been soapmakers. The story is told of one Piazza,
an immigrant of 1870, who began to make candles in his own
home, expanded his establishment, gradually added a soap department, a slaughterhouse, a tannery and a shoe factory, ex-
tracted oils, and dried hides for export. In 1898 Italians were held
to own over 600 flour mills, and to preponderate in milling, not
only in the capital but also in the provinces. Of course they controlled the macaroni manufacture! Their distilleries had an output of more than half the alcohol produced in Buenos Aires.
Except in the brewing of beer, where the Germans led, they predominated in making alcoholic beverages. In fruit canning, in
the manufacture of matches, tobacco, paper, and jewelry they
held a respectable or a dominant place. They had great textile
plants, some sugar refineries. All over the country there have
been Italian sawmills, with an output of fine woods and railway
ties. In wood carving, for which the Argentine churches have
created a great demand, they have stood first; and they make
wagons, baskets, furniture. As wage earners in all these industries, they have naturally been numerous. And many are the
wage earners who have set up small establishments of their own;
wherein, I take it, lies the significance of those surprising census
figures which show the Italians to have even a greater excess over
the Argentines as proprietors than as employees. " In the ex-

---

[1] See the monograph on the Italians in industry by G. Grippa in Cam. Ital. di
Comm., Parte Generale, pp. 151–169 (from which I have drawn freely), and pp. 321,
327. The entire 590 pages of the Espozione Grafica are the detailed histories of conspicuous Italians.

ploitation of small industries," wrote Ceppi many years ago, " the Italian has hardly a rival." [1]

From early days, traders have been numerous. The class has not yet disappeared of the *naranjeros*, Calabrian and Basilican, who used to sell fruit in the streets, nor that of the itinerant merchants, Neapolitan and Calabrian, who used to wander all over the country selling their wares.[2] But it is a far cry from the simplicity of these types, once deemed characteristic, to the subsequent many-sided development.

Consider once more the amazing results of the census of 1895. There were then 32,000 foreign heads of trading establishments and 11,000 Argentine; 97,000 foreign employees, 72,000 Argentine. The decade's increase had been very great, especially in the provinces of Santa Fé and Buenos Aires. Four-fifths of the trade in Argentina, reckoned either in number of establishments or of employees, has been in the provision of clothing, food, and lodging. The census ranks the Italians first among the foreigners in trade and grants them especial predominance in the sale of food.[3]

Quite as striking are the results of the municipal centenary census of Buenos Aires taken in 1909: the Italians owned 1890 food and drink shops (large and small), the Argentines only 731. Here are the details: [4]

	Italian proprietors	Argentine proprietors
Coal depots	763	243
Green groceries	192	86
Wine and liquor stores	290	16
Inns	214	116
Dairies	394	74
Barber shops	874	74
Shoe polishing shops	329	16
Dry goods stores	180	174
Vegetable stores	196	26
Shoe stores	650	186

[1] J. Ceppi, *Cuadros*, p. 197. See also Zuccarini, pp. 175, 177; C. Cerboni, *Manuale per l'emigrazione dall' Italia all' Argentina* (Buenos Aires, 1905), p. 83.

[2] Jannone, pp. 129–131.

[3] *Segundo censo*, iii, pp. cxlii–cxliv.

[4] Buenos Aires, *General Census of the Population, Buildings, Trades and Industries* (3 vols., Buenos Aires, 1910), i, pp. 130–134.

Though the Italian share in the trade of the more advanced provinces has not been measured, yet it is clear that in various sections no other element of the population has greater importance. In Córdoba, in a recent time, about half the commercial houses, and in Tucumán and Mendoza an indefinite but large number, were found to be Italian.[1] Indisputably many of these shops were small; modest beginnings, destined often to prove abortive. Yet great establishments have been far from wanting, like the almacenes of the metropolis. Here and there a trader has risen to power. It was in praise of a textile merchant, Enrico dell' Acqua, that Einaudi wrote his enthusiastic *Principe Mercante*, the tale of a merchant prince who by shrewdness, foresight and patience built up a vast trade in Argentina and in all South America, and brought the New World commercially into closer relations with the Old.[2]

What large fortunes the Italians have gained have been in trade and industry, not in agriculture. The owner, it is claimed, of the largest estancias in Argentina is an Italian who is also the president of a bank. Many have accumulated fortunes of a more moderate size.[3] And whoever follows the statistics for real-estate dealings in the cities must conclude that their gains have commonly been invested in that obvious, elementary, and tangible kind of property to which the rising rich everywhere turn. The last census of Buenos Aires showed more Italian male owners of real estate than Argentine; and if Argentine women had not largely exceeded Italian women in ownership — a telling evidence of the native leisure-class status — then the Italians as a class would actually have included more proprietors than the Argentines.[4]

[1] Río and Achával, p. 378; P. Brenna, " L'emigrazione italiana nelle provincie di Cuyo," *Boll. Emig.*, 1914, No. 6, pp. 22–24.

[2] On dell' Acqua, see also Cam. Ital. di Comm., Esposizione Grafica, pp. 1–32.

[3] On individual business successes, see, besides the references on manufacturing and trade already given, Scardin, i, pp. 255–317, ii, pp. 359–588; Zuccarini, pp. 312–314; Parisi, pp. 534–544.

[4] Buenos Aires, *General Census, 1909*, i, p. 103. The annual report on real-estate transfers in Buenos Aires appears in the *Anuario Estadístico* of that city. A convenient summary of data for other parts of Argentina is in Zuccarini, pp. 164 f.

Without the immigration of the past half century the gigantic strides of Argentina would not have been taken.[1] Without the coming of the Italians, the forward movement must have been slow. Yet even their rôle cannot be appreciated without a word of context and setting. Who were their rivals and associates ?

Foremost in some respects were the English. Few in number, they have been occupied in mercantile and banking pursuits, never as mechanics or in the humbler departments of industry. Sometimes they have come to superintend engineering projects, particularly the construction of railways, and often, since the native landlords have turned absentee, they have become the major-domos of the great estancias. Most of all, however, they have counted as investors of capital. Owning the greater part of the railways, they have been indispensable to the Italian agricultural development.

Early comers were the Basques, both French and Spanish. To no other country have they gone as to Argentina. Hardy, industrious, versatile, they have done much in agriculture near the cities, and especially in dairying. Many have entered brickmaking, the saltmeat establishments and miscellaneous trades; many have been common laborers. A few have risen to great wealth.[2]

The French have in recent years settled in the cities, bringing forms of skill they had developed at home. Next to the English, they have invested the largest sums in the railways.

Much more numerous than the French, following next after the Italians and in very recent years actually exceeding them in point of new arrivals, have been the Spanish. They have gone little into agriculture but much into trade. Throughout the country they own many almacenes. In Buenos Aires they have innumerable food provision shops, and as proprietors of dry goods establishments have an extraordinary preponderance, far exceeding the combined Argentine and Italian representation. Many are in tobacco factories. Fluency in the use of the language has been of immense use to them and has given them a place in the pro-

---

[1] It is interesting to read contemporary official opinion of this general tenor. *E.g.*, Buenos Aires, *Census of 1887*, i, p. 533. Cf. Carrasco, p. 275.

[2] An admirable volume is P. Llande, *L'émigration basque*, Paris, 1910.

fessions, in journalism, and in officialdom that no other immigrant group enjoys. For their numbers, they have not been enterprising.

Fewer Germans have come, and these to care for the outposts of commercial houses or sometimes to manage estancias. Once they entered the agricultural colonies, but, like the Swiss, Poles, Russians, and others, they were too few to count for much.

What of the native Argentine — not just the *hijo del país* (anybody born in Argentina except an Indian), but the descendant of the Spanish and mixed stock ? While England has supplied capital and Italy brawn, these people have reaped the rewards of lords of the soil. Both rich and poor have been indolent, scorning labor. Politics, sport, and the speculative mechanism of business have been their major interests; especially, the life of luxury. The *mot* used to be common — perhaps the automobile will antiquate it — that Argentina is the paradise of women, the purgatory of men, and the inferno of horses, — it never had reference to immigrants' families!

The special nature of the contribution which the Italians have made to the life of Argentina is partly to be explained in terms of their own characteristics. These have been often observed and commented upon, and in the recorded opinions there is a large measure of agreement.

To speak first of their deficiencies: in agriculture they have often paid the penalty of ignorance and of the inertia of tradition. Nearly thirty years ago, Peyret drew a picture of the somewhat isolated community in Reconquista which might appropriately have described a village in Friuli — a picture of general unproductiveness, of letting superstition stand in the way of rational cultivation.[1] It is especially the share cultivators and the renters who have been backward and apathetic; the colonists have usually overcome their opposition to machines. An agronomist, Campolieti, writing before the pinch came in Argentine farming, charged his compatriots with stupidly deeming the

---

[1] Peyret, p. 288. Of their inert opposition to machinery, Scardin also, a defender generally, has spoken (ii, p. 104; cf. p. 106).

land to be inexhaustible in fertility and so neglecting to fertilize —
a fault they had had in Italy. Where success was denied them,
the reason could generally be found in their defective adaptation
to new conditions, especially in bad planning and organization.[1]
Failure to select good seeds, to reckon with the conditions of soil
and climate, to try new crops, to utilize chances of profit through
secondary industries, are usual faults noted by Río and Achával.[2]
Tomezzoli, on his disappointing journey, had frequently to dwell
upon the clumsiness of their methods.[3]

What is creditable to the Italians is that they have been able
to overcome by other traits many of the consequences of ignorance. " They are workers of incomparable resistence, robust,
sober, and persevering." And the authors of these words further
speak of their even temper in accepting the fatiguing tasks of the
farm, their plain living, their close application to their work, leaving it only for necessary interruptions, or for the dance and song
of a festival. They are respectful to authority, quiet, keeping
traditional ways, always feverishly anxious to get rich.[4] Huret
speaks of their " admirable endurance," their readiness to shoulder hardships, to sleep on the ground, for example, while they
hastily build a rude hut to live in, to content themselves with
macaroni and corn meal in order to ensure their future.[5] Still
other writers have dwelt upon their frequent versatility; their
capacity (in one or another individual) to get along in almost any
occupation (except grazing, apparently) and to fit their ambitions
to their circumstances; their patience, further, resignation to
the inevitable, and clean morals.[6]

It is most of all the Piedmontese, after them the Lombards, and
finally perhaps the Venetians, who have settled in the agricultural

---

[1] Campolieti, pp. 90, 228, 260. He has much to say on the consequences of the
Italians' ignorance.

[2] *Op. cit.*, p. 180.

[3] *E.g.*, in *Boll. Emig.*, 1907, No. 16, pp. 25, 44.

[4] Río and Achával, pp. 179 f.

[5] *Op. cit.*, p. 467.

[6] Molina Nadal, p. 225; J. Ceppi, pp. 176, 196; Bevione, p. 83; J. A. Wilde,
Buenos Aires desde setenta años atras (Buenos Aires, 1881), p. 115; and the enthu-
siastic opinion of J. M. Ramos Mejia, *Las multitudes argentinas* (Madrid and Buenos
Aires, 1912), pp. 264 f.

colonies. They, primarily, have been the subjects of the praises I have recorded. Though the Piedmontese have also gone into the cities, the characteristic and chief urban immigrants were for a long time the Genoese. To Argentina, the son of the Riviera has been of inestimable value — " the serious and veracious man, enterprising, ambitious, the great merchant," as the skilful Salaverria pithily described him.[1] In the twentieth century, the South Italians have flocked to the cities, increasing the foreign colonies there — especially that at Buenos Aires — to impressive proportions. Without much rising from the humble places, they have been excavators, street pavers, teamsters, porters, barbers, shoemakers, and petty shopkeepers. Their concentration in the vast seaport city is less a reflection of their poverty upon arrival than of their somewhat unenterprising or ignorant dependence upon a great employment market which has lavished its opportunities upon hard-working men of little skill, willing to live meagerly to save.

The accomplishment of the Italians in Argentina is to be explained by much more than their mere numbers, great as these are. For they have been quick and eager workers. They have labored as many hours and days as possible, not, if they could help it, losing time between jobs. Actually, therefore, a hundred Italians might be as productive as two hundred Argentines. Furthermore, at least in agriculture and wherever else the opportunity has been offered, their women and children have much oftener engaged in remunerative toil than have those of the Argentines and some other groups.

Undoubtedly this industriousness of the Italians and, along with it, a keyed-up thrift have been new notes in Argentina. " The Spanish workman does not accomplish miracles as the Italian does, he cannot equal his habits of economy," one Spanish witness has written;[2] and another, that the Italian " is the contrary type of the creole, the opposite pole. . . . The gaucho does

---

[1] J. M. Salaverria, *Tierra argentina — psicologia, tipos, costumbres, valores* (Madrid, 1910), p. 163. Salaverria's entire characterization is at once appropriate and eloquent; see pp. 160–165.

[2] Dominguez, p. 97.

not economize nor reckon with the morrow, while the *gringo* piles up his money one coin after another. Hence the disdain which the creole feels for him." [1] The Italians "will teach us that economy and persistent labor are the sure talisman of fortune." [2]

We have seen that the firm establishment of agriculture in Argentina, mainly by the Italians, was a feat that marked off a new era. The historian may yet hold it even more to the honor of these immigrants that they brought new sorts of moral strength into the fiber of the Argentine nation.

Once more it behooves us to regard the Italians from their own point of view. Into the vicissitudes of their condition in agriculture we need not further inquire. But how have those fared who have sought to make a living by other courses ?

The diligent have had their reward. Artisans and technical workers have done especially well. In trade and industry men have risen high — the tale needs here no repetition. But the path to success, though open, has for many been steep. The quick changes of fortune that mark so rapidly expanding a country as Argentina have often afflicted with disastrous unemployment the humbler workers. In few countries do crop failures require such general retrenchment in expenditure as in Argentina. They may mean that fewer golondrinas can come to harvest the grain and that many industrial workers will be stranded or will deem it best to return home. Particularly in Buenos Aires, there has been a constant and considerable nucleus of the abjectly miserable, plain enough evidence that a foothold has to be won and is not a gift to the immigrant.

Winning a foothold has demanded abnegation, the most careful paring down of the budget of living. A little less economy, and failure has threatened; a little more, and comfort has beckoned. How many immigrants have shortened their years by extreme privation! As long as he has dared, the tiller of the fields has lived in his mud hut, which is sometimes even unthatched, and the urban immigrant in the *conventillo*. Buenos Aires has been a city of large houses, which in many cases have sheltered numerous

---

[1] Salaverria, p. 162.   [2] Dominguez, p. 96.

families. Here the conditions have had much in common with those in the tenement houses of New York. In recent years a centrifugal growth of the city has taken place and now many of the houses are miles away from the workshops.[1] Overcrowding and wretched sanitary conditions have obtained in these dwellings, whether of the old sort or the new. In Rosario, in Santa Fé, and in Córdoba City, quite as in the metropolis, the Italians have inhabited the poorest quarters.[2] Single men have boarded with families, or have lived in groups with one of their number as cook. The concomitants of poverty have exhibited themselves in sundry unwholesome forms. More Italians than Argentines are arrested for drunkenness in Buenos Aires. There are plenty of degraded forms of amusement, and sexual irregularity has been common. The urban social conditions, partly due to the disproportionate presence of men, contrast notably with the rural.

As it became more difficult, some years ago, to earn a living on the land, so it likewise became more difficult to do so in the non-agricultural pursuits. Employment could be had, but the rapid rise in prices made accumulation of savings difficult. The situation, however, was less bad than in agriculture, and after immigrants ceased to enter the colonies they still continued to come to the cities. In the five years beginning in 1912 the greatest difficulty in earning a living appears to have been reached.[3]

Ignorant of the language, the new immigrant has had to contend against fraud and exploitation — not that the older immigrant has been exempt. Corruption and disorganization in the

[1] Cf. Bryce, p. 320: " On the land side, the city dies out into a waste of scattered shanties, or " shacks " (as they are called in the United States), dirty and squalid, with corrugated iron roofs, their wooden boards gaping like rents in tattered clothes. These are inhabited by the newest and poorest of the immigrants from southern Italy and southern Spain."

[2] In Rosario, some years ago, there were 2600 conventillos of from three to forty rooms each; of these 1100 had baths and only 600 had sewer connections. J. A. Alsina, *El obrero en la República Argentina* (2 vols, Buenos Aires, 1905), i, p. 232; see the entire section, pp. 221–255.

[3] See note in *Boll. Emig.*, 1913, No. 5, pp. 121 f.; Società di Patronato e Rimpatrio per gli Immigranti Italiani in Buenos Aires, " Relazione " (1912–13), *Boll. Emig.*, 1913, No. 12, pp. 32–46; Gérardin, p. 198. It was still a favorable situation of wages and prices that Alsina elaborately recorded after the opening of the present century: *El obrero*, etc., i, pp. 221–255, 283–339, ii, pp. 1–418.

Argentine political system have been the source of much unjust discrimination. How many are the Italians, who have cried out against violence gone unpunished, or have complained of venal sentences, of miscarried justice, of despoliation travestying the name of law! Legal guarantees appear to decline as the great metropolis fades into the distance.[1]

Notwithstanding these various maladjustments and disappointments, the life of the Italians in Argentina remains a great fact both for Italy and for the republic. In this life the high hopes of both countries have met, but partly have met in conflict. While the Italians have aimed in divers ways to retain their character, the Argentines have sought to absorb them into the nation.

There has always been a difficulty about the term assimilation. What it implies, the loss of one type in another, is, strictly speaking, an impossibility. In greater or less degree there is reciprocal change. To some extent even, a mechanistic principle holds: the more numerous the immigrants, the greater their effect upon the national stock; and it is only in countries where immigrants are few that the term assimilation, in its one-sided emphasis, has a common sense justification.

In Argentina, the abounding Italians have certainly affected the national tastes and habits. In the ways already pointed out, they have quickened the pulse of the country. They have introduced ideals of industry and economy which are not likely to disappear — though they may decline — when their own generation has passed away. They have established occupations which likewise would persist were no more Italians to come. In architecture and the drama, in music and sculpture, in mural decoration and painting, they have imposed upon the country their own standards of beauty which, whatever the transformation that may take place in a living art, will never be wholly obliterated. These are only the more tangible manifestations of changes due to the Italians. Of the extent and precise forms of still other transforma-

[1] Tomezzoli gives numerous instances. Cf. Bevione, pp. 142–154; "The Immigrant in South America," *Blackwood's*, pp. 612, 614; R. Murri, "Impressioni d'America," *Nuova Antologia*, January 1, 1913, p. 84.

tions we yet know little enough. How many instances might not a diligent search single out![1] And how many may forever elude discovery!

To the forces of assimilation about them, the Italians have opposed a certain resistance. It is not to be found merely in the use of their own tongue, the retention of old ceremonies and customs, but in many patriotic expressions. Nearly three-score years ago, when the news came to Santa Fé that Garibaldi had entered Naples, the Genoese ships in port decked themselves out in flags and garlands, cannon thundered, music played, and the people of the city, unfurling both Italian and Argentine banners, came together in a common enthusiasm.[2] Three years after the death of Mazzini, a monument to him was erected in Buenos Aires; and later, but only after a contentious discussion in the Argentine Congress, a monument also to Garibaldi. Of the latter Rosario likewise possesses a memorial. In Buenos Aires and in Rosario there are Italian hospitals. On the occasion of such national disasters as the Po flood of 1879, the African war reverses, the Sicilian and Calabrian earthquakes, sums of money for the sufferers were gathered; and subscriptions to the recent war bonds were made. Italian theatrical companies and musicians have likewise served to keep Italian sentiment alive.[3] That such nationalistic expressions are broad enough or frequent enough to create very effective opposition to change is not to be inferred; and although a critic [4] has charged that the Italian remembers his country only when it meets misfortune, or on the Twentieth of September, yet these demonstrations by many of the emigrants from Upper Italy probably draw upon some deep roots and are not merely revivals externally promoted.

[1] For example, the Italians, says Viscount Bryce, learn Spanish " while also modifying it with their own words and idioms." *Op. cit.*, p. 322. Cf. Turner, p. 123. In some quarters of Buenos Aires, such as Barracas, Boca, Avellaneda, the Genoese dialect is almost the language of all. Italian is the ruling speech in many parts of the provincial cities and in many colonies.

[2] The story is prettily told by a witness, Mme. Lina Beck-Bernard, in *Le Rio Parana—cinq années de séjour dans la République Argentine* (Paris, 1864), pp. 229–232.

[3] Cam. Ital. di Comm., p. 37; Scardin, i, pp. 45–65, ii, p. 83.

[4] Bevione, p. 190.

Italian schools, maintained by various Italian organizations, and subsidized by the home government, exist in considerable number. They are impotent, however, to reach the mass of the Italian children. The adult immigrants have largely been illiterate, and most are content that their children should receive a modicum only of education, given in the Argentine schools. The cultivated readily become cosmopolitan, and are as likely, it is said, to read French books as Italian. In the public schools the training of the children is intensely nationalistic — to a degree rare in other countries. Italians who read may patronize Italian newspapers in Buenos Aires, but they do so not to the exclusion of the great Argentine dailies.[1]

Of a cultural life among the Italians in Argentina there has been little, and the ties with Italy that would sustain it are tenuous. On the other hand an extensive, if somewhat peculiar, development of the associative life has taken place. In 1861, in Buenos Aires, the first enduring society, *La Nazionale Italiana*, was organized. Fifty years later, its still surviving successors numbered at least three hundred. Some of these have had a charitable character, but most have been mutual aid societies. The latter provide for their members, where possible, hospital care, medical aid — otherwise very costly — drugs, cash, and burial expenses. Many have erected attractive and even beautiful buildings for their headquarters, and in order to protect their property have become incorporated. Even more distinctive than the large number of these societies is their regional character, the emigrant from one part of Italy not being admissible to a society favoring another part. And strangest of all is the frequency of hostile outbreaks, largely personal in their origin, resulting from time to time in schisms. In Chivilcoy, Scardin relates with humor, a society produced by such a schism bore the name " Union and Brotherhood," and because of additional instances he dubs this granary of Buenos Aires the seed ground of Italian discords. Beyond all doubt the personal and regional animosities of the Italians in Argentina, as indicated in their associative experience,

---

[1] On the schools, see de Zettiry, pp. 40–50, 64 f.; Cam. Ital. di Comm., pp. 219–230 (also the volume of 1906, pp. 299–322); Bevione, p. 181; Murri, pp. 86–88.

have been an almost insurmountable block to the rise of effective leadership and a check upon the preservation of Italian sentiment.[1] Not least noticeable is the oft-lamented absence, or meager development, in the agricultural colonies, of those forms of coöperative production and consumption which in North Italy have proved of such great value.

Politically the immigrant generation has played but a feeble rôle. This would be true, even if other things were not involved, because it has shown so little capacity to organize for common action. But it depends further upon the fact that there has been little desire to acquire citizenship. To have reached one's majority and been two years in residence, or to have married an Argentine, confers the right to obtain naturalization. Yet in forty years after 1872, less than six thousand immigrants of all nationalities had been naturalized, and of a paltry 269 in the year 1915 only 121 were Italian.[2] These are astounding facts and suggest the possibility that not only the Italians but also the Argentines have not cared to promote naturalization.[3]

It is not without interest in this connection to observe that the Italians, generally passive politically, have played an active rôle in radical propaganda. Vehemently, as socialists, and still more, it would appear, as anarchists, they, along with the Spanish immigrants, have spread subverting ideas, causing " great alarm to the government." [4] Of very late years radical representatives have

[1] Cam. Ital. di Comm., pp. 231–242; Alsina, *El obrero*, etc., i, pp. 88–101; Zuccarini, pp. 178–182; Scardin, i, pp. 97–104, 125–143, ii, pp. 61–65; Godio, pp. 372–399; E. Spiotti, La Repubblica Argentina, *Annuario dell' emigrante italiano*, Anno II (Genoa, 1906), pp. 221–229; de Zettiry, pp. 65–71; Brenna, pp. 21 f.; Tomezzoli, in *Boll. Emig.*, 1907, No. 17, p. 90; Lupati, pp. 240–246. See also, on associative life, P. Baroncelli-Grosson, *La donna della Nuova Italia* (Milan, 1917), pp. 261–266.

[2] E. Dickmann, *Los argentinos naturalizados en la politica* (Buenos Aires, 1915), pp. 23 f. The Mendoza census of 1909 discovered only 96 naturalized foreigners (*Censo general de la provincia de Mendoza*, p. 30).

[3] A suggestion that satisfaction in the foreigners' not voting is to be justified, partially at least, by the fact that they bring monarchical ideas is made by J. Alvarez, *Ensayo sobre la historia de Santa Fé* (Buenos Aires, 1910), p. 410. A much more explicit and specific study is by A. Saldias, *La politique italienne au Rio de la Plata* (Paris, 1889), esp. p. 32.

[4] Bryce, p. 343. Cf. M. Bilbao, *Buenos Aires desde su fundación hasta nuestros dias* (Buenos Aires, 1902), pp. 124–126.

sometimes exercised a controlling hand in the national legislature. Has the propaganda advanced by the immigrants partly made for this fruition ?

But if the foreign-born Italian has held aloof from the normal political life of the nation, his children have pursued a different course, very freely giving themselves up to their social and political environment.[1] They have perhaps been special bene- ficiaries of the democratic political experience of the rural colonies. Many a son of Italian stock has become the *jefe politico* of a pro- vincial community and now and then has found his way into the national Congress. What visitors from Italy to Argentina have frequently lamented was remarked also by Bryce: that the chil- dren of the Italians " are, perhaps, even more vehemently pa- triotic than the youth of native stock." [2]   Hence the readiness, on various occasions in the history of Argentina, to form Italian regiments; recently, thousands were said to have volunteered to fight in the threatened war with Chili.[3] At one time, Italians like to recall, the son of an Italian engineer and political refugee rose to be president of the republic. Between him and the Italian colony, however, there was little warmth of sentiment, little confession of kinship, for Pellegrini, like every patriotic *hijo del país*, could not reveal sympathy with his immigrant stock nor even speak its language, under pain of being scorned as a *hijo de gringo*.[4]

It may be that some embracing contribution, even of momen- tous consequence to the future, will be made by the Italian blood to the race stock of Argentina.   The ways of heredity are mys- terious enough still, yet the addition of so much North Ital- ian stock, notably Piedmontese, to the Argentine population is likely to be of lasting value.   In no other country to which the

[1] As long ago as 1860, Martin de Moussy (ii, p. 289) noted the rapidity of this assimilation, and many have noted it since.

[2] Bryce, p. 339. Cf. Corradini, *Il volere d'Italia*, pp. 57–59. On the colonial ex- perience, see Troisi, pp. 107 f.; Zeballos, ii, p. 273.

[3] Zuccarini, pp. 184–226; Murri, p. 87.

[4] G. Modrich, *Repubblica Argentina, note di viaggio* (Milan, 1890), pp. 131 f. Cf. Zuccarini, p. 325.

Italians have emigrated have they constituted so large a part of the population. Out of the half million Italians present in 1895 and the 700,000 and more who have settled since (I exclude the repatriated) there may still survive close upon one million — an eighth, perhaps a seventh, of the population of the country.

But that is not all. When Rossi, in 1913, made his journey through Santa Fé, studying the affairs of the colonies, talking with their members, he stopped at the farm of one Pincirolli Aquilino, formerly of Busto Arsizia. This immigrant, twenty-three when he came, had broadened his acres as the years had rolled by and now reached beyond the age of seventy.

" How many children have you ? " asked Rossi.
" By two wives I have had eighteen; fourteen are living."
" And some are married ? "
" Eh, that's another story! Counting daughters-in-law and grand-children, we are more than seventy."

Such, adds Rossi, are the families that are increasing the population of this country.[1] As a matter of fact, families of this size have been uncommon, but families of ten or twelve children have been frequent.[2] The tradition in Italy had been one of large families. But here, much more than there, a wife on the farm, and often in the city, cost less than she earned; and every child, in this country of high wages, was a helper in production. Women married young — in a large proportion of cases, between fifteen and twenty. The span of years from generation to generation was short. The less thrifty Argentine of the older stock married later: if poor, he could not soon afford a wife who would not help him to earn; if rich, he would postpone marriage as the rich do. In either case, his generation span would be larger; and his family was smaller.

It is fairly certain that the Argentines of Italian blood now exceed in number the Italians. So it is reasonable to claim that the Italians, their children and children's children, number today

---

[1] Rossi, p. 8.

[2] I have dealt statistically with this and related topics in an article, "The Italian Factor in the Argentine Race Stock," in *Quarterly Publications of the American Statistical Association*, June, 1919, pp. 347-360.

appreciably more than two million and probably are 30 per cent or more of the population of the country.[1] In Argentina the Italians found a country of small population to which they could come in large numbers and to an important extent they have made it, racially speaking, their own. Of intermarriage with the older stock there has been little, but a half century more must largely fuse the strains. Not to the same extent will the two civilizations fuse, because much that the Italians have brought, such as their language, must be content with fractional preservation, must bow to the sterner standard established and made current before they came. Blood, however, knows no standard save its own. And that is why, if Italian immigration were today wholly to cease, never to be revived, the Italian influence would forever count in Argentina, breathing a characteristic spirit into the political and social institutions of the land. Herein lies the great difference between an immigration of gold and an immigration of men. Some day the millions of English capital, so timely and consequential when they came, may be withdrawn, just as still more millions have in the Great War been withdrawn from the United States; but the Italian contribution of blood to Argentina will remain.

It is not impossible today to detect some of the influences that will play upon the future course of Italian immigration into Argentina. Much of what has made the country attractive in the past will continue.[2] But much also that was attractive has already declined. From July, 1911, to August, 1912, the Italian government suspended emigration to the republic. Ostensibly, and in part actually, this was because it was unwilling to accept an Argentine order which would have put Argentine sanitary inspectors on board Italian immigrant ships. Not so, if one may guess, would the government have reacted a decade earlier. In the interval, for several years before 1911, Argentina had become

---

[1] For the grounds of this claim, see Foerster, *op. cit.*

[2] When the country folk of Calabria were asked what determined their choice of a destination, many replied, the climate. The answer was characteristic of the communes from which emigration had proceeded to Argentina. *Inch. Parl.*, v[ii], p. 723.

less generous to the Italians, Tomezzoli's tale of abuses had been told and more or less confirmed,[1] and no serious loss, it now was felt, could come from vigorous and indignant action.

Perhaps, just as earlier interruptions, such as the Paraguay war and the yellow fever epidemic (when 9000 Italians lost their lives) were temporary, the new interruptions may be. Yet the citizen of the older strains has today little love for the immigrant Italian, and takes him only for gain.[2] Such a law as the anti-anarchist act has apparently been an instrument for class oppression. The Italian is felt to be a person to be assimilated. Much of the opposition against him, quite as in the past, will in the future accomplish nothing. Yet this opposition, though some of its ingredients are peculiar to Argentina, has much in common with a reaction that we have met in other countries, and it may work similar results. In Argentina the first warm protest against stimulation of immigration was coincident with the first workmen's movements in the country. In its initial programme, in 1895, and continuously since, the socialist party has demanded the suppression of all special invitation to immigrants. And a recent law is quite as rigorously selective in its terms as the United States legislation that antedated the literacy test enactment.[3]

As the Argentine nation assumes more definite form, as a larger portion of it rises out of the immigrant stratum, it could not be

[1] It perhaps deserves note that after publication of the reports of Tomezzoli, the subject of Argentina was for two and a half years almost wholly ignored in the special articles of the official *Boll. Emig.*

[2] It is curious to find in a governmental work such a candid statement as the following, which I give in the official English version: " The present-day estanciero, owner of a large estate, such as those of which there are still of 20 to 50 square leagues, at least cordially detests the settler, the husbandman, the people that come in swarms. He uses them for the time being because he cannot help himself, in order to fit his lands for carrying plenty of stock " (*Agricultural and Pastoral Census*, 1908, iii, p. 15). Cf. Salaverria on the golondrina, p. 209. Italian writings abound in expressions of Argentine antipathy: *e.g.*, Murri, p. 85; Bevione, *passim*; P. Micheli, " Gli italiani nell' Argentina," *L'Italia Coloniale*, August and September, 1903, p. 863.

[3] This new law accords fairly with the recommendations made by Alsina some years ago (*La inmigración en la primer siglo de la independencia*, Buenos Aires, 1910, ch. v), but is the fruit of the efforts, particularly, of the socialist Enrique Dickmann.

surprising if the movement for selection were followed by some demand for restriction. But does not the Argentine Constitution still forbid the erection of legislative barriers against European immigration ? Beyond all doubt the spirit of the present law, whether interpreted by its friends or its foes, is strongly restrictionist, and the same spirit may in the future find other effective means — perhaps a literacy test — of constitutionally accomplishing the same result. We cannot foresee, and must remember that in these things there is some swing of the pendulum and that a revival of immigration, resting upon new conditions, may be the next step. But the restrictionist spirit is there and must be reckoned with, since hitherto, in other lands, it has grown and not declined, and since in Australia and the United States, likewise new countries, it has succeeded in making the laws.

CHAPTER XV

BRAZIL. I. THE COFFEE PLANTATIONS

BEFORE 1850, Italian immigrants into Brazil were few. Capuchin missionaries who came in the seventeenth and eighteenth centuries — a type with heroic attributes — were followed in the early nineteenth by Genoese mariners, musicians errant, some painters, decorators and the like, and numerous political refugees.[1] Not least among the last-named was the keeper of a modest butcher shop in the imperial capital, the far-faring Garibaldi, who married a Brazilian bride.

Together these were only the lisping prologue to a mighty movement. The history of the great period of Italian immigration tells of an abruptly acquired impetus, a long and hectic advance with occasional retreat, then a spectacular collapse and a stagnant aftermath. If only because it involved the lives and fortunes of hundreds of thousands of human beings, this history could claim to be heard. For the Italians who arrived in Brazil before the beginning of the twentieth century outnumbered those who in the same time went to the United States. To Brazil and to the world, as it befell, they rendered a service not to be forgotten. If many of them found for their mead only unhappiness and disillusionment, that is still a further reason for trying to understand their unexampled adventure.

For three centuries and a quarter after its discovery, Brazil was not a country of immigration. Portugal, the motherland, not only forbade foreigners to enter her possession, but greatly restricted the travel of her own subjects. Although, by good fortune, these and other checks upon colonial freedom were less galling than those of Spain in Argentina, the growth of the country

---

[1] See M. Napoli and N. Belli, *La colonia italiana di Rio de Janeiro* (Rio de Janeiro, 1911), p. 46, for details of a survey of the Italians made in 1843.

was none the less slow and involved generally the exploitation of only the more obvious resources. The Indians being few and not a satisfactory labor force, negro slaves began to be imported in large numbers, and for three centuries were the principal laborers. Out of a diversity of racial origins there grew up in time a society of amazing heterogeneity: the pure Portuguese were an aristocracy; under them were the Indians, the herds of negro slaves, the *caboclos* (half-breeds), and the mulattoes. In such a society, divided by lines of caste, no great political or economic capacity was likely to arise.

One encouraging token in this otherwise discouraging social state was its partial consciousness of its weakness, its realization, voiced as early as 1808, that some day its universal slave system must give way to a better system and better laborers. In that year a decree of the prince regent gave to the government authority to concede lands to foreigners. From the point of view of our own times, however, the premature and unsuccessful Swiss colony of Nova Friburgo, founded in 1818, seems less a product of the colonial period than a herald of what the independence year 1822 would make feasible. Next, by contract with the imperial government, the Germans established themselves in a colony called São Leopoldo, in the neighborhood of Porto Alegre, but the civil war of 1831–43 blocked their further coming. In the years before 1850, upon imperial or provincial initiative, various colonies were founded, but they came to little. It was not yet an auspicious time for immigration. The entire realm was disturbed, lightly peopled, poor.

As in colonial days, the sluggish life of the country still centered in the sugar-yielding North, about Pernambuco and Bahia. The planting of European colonies had been practicable only in the South. The difficulty of substituting European for dark-skinned labor in the torrid regions was to explain the reluctance with which, later on, the Northern slave owners consented to abandon the slave system. The new colonies which private persons founded after 1840 were, like their governmental forerunners, located in the South. It was a Paulist senator, Vergueiro, of enduring memory, who, as early as 1841, established upon his fazenda ninety Portuguese families; and, not daunted by their failure to stay, brought over, in 1847, eighty German families. The imperial government had advanced the passage money of these immigrants which they, having succeeded, were able to restore in a stipulated three-years time. Vergueiro's estate Ybicaba so acquired the distinction of being the first to employ European labor in coffee production. In the years after 1852, the scheme of this enterprising grower and merchant was widely emulated. It had savored, regrettably — in the importation of families *en masse* and in their establishment in an industry in which slaves were still mainly employed — of the slave-importation tradition itself.[1]

Still another device for securing immigrants, mingling public policy with private interest, was the colonization company. By paying small sums of money, many such companies or societies, during the third quarter of the century, secured large tracts of public land, which they obligated themselves to break up into lots and colonize. The lands were usually near the railways, and were offered on attractive terms: the colonists might receive advances from the company, had six years in which to pay for their allotments, were charged no interest for two years, and thereafter at a rate not exceeding six per cent.[2]

In 1875 there were still in existence twelve colonies established by the imperial government, fifteen by the provincial governments, and twenty-five by private interests.[3] The imperial colonies were often remote and ill-managed and their settlers disillusioned. Of the provincial and private enterprises many were no more prosperous. Although there were outstanding successful instances of each type, the development as a whole fell far short of that in Argentina.

The fifty-two colonies existing in 1875 contained some 48,000 inhabitants. What had become of all the immigrants — six

[1] On the history of Vergueiro's scheme, see V. Grossi, *Storia della colonizzazione europea al Brasile* (2d ed., Milan, etc., 1914), pp. 169–178.

[2] *Ibid.*, pp. 181–185; G. B. Marchesini, *Il Brasile e le sue colonie agricole* (Rome, 1877), pp. 96–106.

[3] See the valuable table of colonies founded since 1812 appended to A. de Carvalho, *O Brazil — colonisação e emigração* (2d ed., Oporto, 1876).

times as many as these — who in the preceding quarter century had entered Brazil ? Many of them were persons who had contracted with the planters to settle on their estates (as at Ybicaba), many others were former colonists who had given up for disappointment or whatever reason and gone to the plantations or the cities, and still others were " spontaneous " immigrants (in the official phrase), not " colonists," who had begun to come in increasing numbers and who went especially to the cities.

It was while these efforts were being made to establish nuclei of European agricultural settlers that it became more and more clear that profound changes were to take place in the exploitation of the country's resources. Of the memorable chapter about to unfold there had begun to be hints. Slowly the economic center of the country had been shifting. The European settlements, all in the South, were only an incidental evidence of this. The province of São Paulo, not long since a thinly inhabited grazing region, where, as late as 1871, there were only 86 miles of railway (owned by an English company), now began to discover unguessed virtues in its endless stretches of violet soil. Coffee plantations there had been for scores of years back. But that there could be more, and more, and still more, no one had had the imagination to see. A railroad was opened into the Northwest, to Ribeirão Preto; immigrants from Europe increased the output of various fazendas; and although, in the entire period from 1855 to 1885, a steady expansion of the harvest of coffee took place, an unperturbed market absorbed it all. Before this time had quite elapsed the notion seemed, of a sudden, to have struck the planters that the limits to profitable production were too remote to be discerned. Were not the fortunate among them reaping gains of 50 or 60 per cent upon their costs ? Not the sugar of the North but the coffee of the South was to be the golden key to the economic future of Brazil. That became dazzlingly clear. *O cafè è ouro* — " coffee is gold " — men said. Surely the new treasure would flow in a steadier, more generous stream than that mineral gold which had been the spent dream of the previous century.

But who was to mine the new gold ? Once the Indians had been slaves, but they were finally liberated in 1755. Now the negroes were slaves, toilers in the coffee fazendas. As early, however, as 1831, the legal importation of negro slaves into Brazil had been stopped, and about 1850 the extra-legal, covert importation likewise ceased. In substituting Europeans for slaves, Senator Vergueiro had been a practical seer. North of the Equator a bloody conflict presently rooted out the most stubborn slave system of modern times — could a civilized country southward hold to a lower standard? A law of 1871 now conferred freedom upon every child henceforth born of a slave mother. The institution was tottering, would next collapse. Who meanwhile was to plant and gather the red berries?

It was an era which those who lived in it knew to be critical. In an elaborate study prepared for the Ministry of Agriculture, Industry, and Public Works at Rio de Janeiro in 1875, the author Menezes e Souza counselled quick action (in a Portuguese style which I have ventured somewhat to deflate!):

> The question which urgently presses for solution is this. Brazil is menaced by an imminent crisis. The gradual emancipation from slavery which the spirit of liberty, favored by Christianity, will shortly render final and complete, has deprived our economic system of its principal labor force. Day by day the cultivation of coffee, chief source of the public wealth, is declining and in a few years it will lie in the paroxysms of a final death agony. The inevitable economic transformation of the country is not to be realized in a short time, but indeed only with slowness. Not for a moment may we hesitate in procuring a substitute for the arms which increasingly fail us, abandoning the fields, the mills, and the factories, and forcing the workers who remain to shoulder difficulties which cannot be avoided and to make sacrifices which cannot be recompensed.[1]

Within fifteen years after 1875 twice as many immigrants entered Brazil as in the previous twenty-five years. But to São

[1] J. C. Menezes e Souza, *Theses sobre colonização do Brazil* (Rio de Janeiro, 1875), pp. 354 f. It is hardly beside the question, at this point, to note the author's opinion of the Italians. They go, he said, to Algiers and the Plata, and are good at gardening, housebuilding, and road making; some pursue small industries in Brazil, or itinerant trading; they are characterized by perseverance, sobriety and thrift, *but:* "They are not useful in agriculture!" *Ibid.*, p. 409. He was not alone. The historian J. M. Pereira da Silva, who in 1865 held that colonization should be regarded as the central and dominating policy of Brazil, believed that only the Germans and the Swiss were suited to the needs of Brazil. See his *Situation sociale, politique et économique de l'empire du Brésil* (Rio de Janeiro, 1865), pp. 104, 108 f.; cf. entire ch. vii.

Paulo, in a dozen years, 1875–86, nearly four times as many came as in the previous years. The practice of many planters in themselves advancing the passage fare of immigrants led the province in 1880 and in 1888 (there had been a somewhat similar act in 1871) to enact laws providing a subsidy for paying the transportation charge to São Paulo.

In the year 1888 slavery was abolished. For years the deaths of slaves, even where treatment had been good, had greatly exceeded the births. The three million slaves of 1850 had been thinned, it was estimated, to two million in 1871 when the law of " the free womb " was enacted. Public opinion had backed Dom Pedro's efforts for emancipation. Understanding what was ahead, the slaves had become increasingly indolent and unmanageable. While the North had remained the stronghold of the institution, the Paulist aristocracy came to desire its termination. Many planters had been virtually freeing their slaves for some time. And the market price of these workers had in anticipation of abolition dropped to almost nothing.

The decline in the quality of slave labor, the expected extirpation of the system, and the coming of foreigners were all inextricably bound up together: all were cause and all were effect, at least in the decade or two before 1888. It is improbable that the foreigners would have come in such numbers, had not abolition been in prospect. In the years between the last two luminous dates in the history of its downfall, 1871 and 1888, two hundred thousand Italians arrived. Abolition could be greeted with more equanimity if such laborers were to offer themselves to the planters. In fact, had immigrants not come, the movement could hardly have made its astonishing headway. In a sense, Ybicaba had been the beginning of abolition. What is more, the resident foreigners had nearly always sustained the efforts of the reformist Brazilians. Of the Italians one careful writer has even said: " They have ever been enthusiastic partisans of emancipation. It was the small Italian itinerant trader, the *mascate*, who went hither and thither on the plantation, who put himself into communication with the blacks, announced to them that the hour of deliverance was at hand, and told them of the efforts which unknown friends were making in their behalf. Sometimes he counselled them to quit their plantations."[1] Even the hope that foreigners would be drawn to Brazil counted. " The most patriotic Brazilians have often said that there could be no serious thought of the coming of European immigrants before slavery was abolished."[2]

After the shock of so stupendous a social change, it was reasonable to expect a period of readjustment. Expectation, however, and precedent were alike flouted, when the country, instead of lying depressed for years, leaped, almost in a frenzy, to a prosperity it had never known before. No check came from the political revolution of 1889, which, having deposed the aged emperor after his half century of reign, instituted in 1892 a federal republic. It was an epoch of numerous measures planned to procure immigrants on a gigantic scale. São Paulo, in October, 1885, had provided by law for the importation of immigrants under contract by companies, to whom the price of their passage was to be reimbursed. Next, the *fazendeiros* organized a *Sociedade Paulista Promotora de Immigração* which received from the province the almost exclusive conduct of its immigration service; through it 126,000 immigrants were imported by 1895 — despite the fact that the naval and civil war of 1893–94, supervening upon the establishment of the new government, had made it difficult for a time to persuade new immigrants to come.

For a climax, in this era of frantic endeavor, the new federal government contracted, in August, 1892, with the *Companhia Metropolitana* for the introduction within ten years of one million immigrants. How soon the unsuitability of this arrangement was to be shown! The company's troubles came in quick order. In 1895, after the interruption caused by the war aforesaid, the cholera suddenly appeared in Espirito Santo, and during a period of months the Italian government suspended emigration to that state. The world-wide business difficulties of these years were

[1] M. E. da Silva-Prado, ch. xvi in M. F.–J. de Santa-Anna Nery (ed.), *Le Brésil en 1889* (Paris, 1889), pp. 489–491.
[2] *Ibid.*, p. 491.

keenly felt in Brazil and accentuated there by violent fluctuations in the exchange ratio of paper and gold. The administrative problem of receiving and placing the masses of immigrants who disembarked took on ever more awkward forms and presently became almost unmanageable. Soon both the federal government and the *Companhia* were glad to retreat from their bold scheme. It was a signal which those states that had embarked on similar projects were ready to follow. São Paulo stood alone in continuing to make contracts for the importation of thousands of immigrants at her own expense. By the terms of a law enacted in 1899 workers on the fazendas could indicate what persons they would like to have come to the state and the *Hospedaria* of the immigration service would offer to pay their way. In that year the practice was begun of stating annually how many persons would be wanted during the year and of enabling their passage. São Paulo in 1902 had agreements with four firms to bring in respectively 14,000, 7000, 7000 and 2000 immigrants. Not being fulfilled within the year, the contracts were allowed to run beyond, but for some time thereafter no new ones were made. A main reason for this is doubtless that, in the same year, the Prinetti decree suspended the emigration to any part of Brazil from Italian ports of all Italian subjects not paying their own passage. The blow struck hard, and was resented. But that it struck justly the state of São Paulo tacitly acknowledged when, at about the same time, it forbade (by means of a prohibitory tax) the further planting of coffee trees.

Between 1888 and 1898 the number of shrubs had tripled.[1] The limits to profitable coffee production, not discernible a decade earlier, had been not merely achieved but exceeded. The flame fed and fanned so persistently had burned itself out. It was realized that, since four years are necessary before a new tree yields berries and six before it touches its maximum flowering, the country was on the threshold of a formidable overproduction — the world price of coffee could not stand the assault. For the planters, the darkness of failure lay ahead. They were prepared to make a desperate effort to prop up the world price. Killing

[1] A. Lalière, *Le café dans l'état de Saint Paul* (Paris, 1909), p. 36.

frosts would be a blessing and were generally desired. Repeatedly, the burning of large parts of the crop was threatened.[1] But what finally came forth from the planters' tribulations was a gigantic governmental scheme of valorization, which, while it strained the credit of the state of São Paulo, did accomplish what was hoped: the withholding of the supply from the world's market until the world's demand could rise to meet it. Truly in São Paulo the fazendeiros are the State. Hence their plan, like the previous subsidization of immigration, has the lineaments of a colossal coöperative undertaking.[2]

According to the Brazilian count, which in the early years was far from trustworthy, 1,227,040 Italians immigrated in the period 1820–1908, constituting nearly half of all arrivals. Before 1875, however, they were a small group. The five Italians recorded to have come to the province of São Paulo in that year were the first enumerated in a half century's immigration of over 11,000;[3] the rest were chiefly Germans and Portuguese. In 1875–86, 20,966 Italians entered São Paulo, outnumbering the Portuguese, and equalling one-half of all comers. In 1887–1906, years which included the boom, the Italians admitted to São Paulo were actually 804,598 or two-thirds of all, the Portuguese once more ranking next. Is it surprising that the inhabitants of that province, later state, should have risen from 1,221,394 in 1886 (a census) to 2,570,000 in 1903 (the Minister of Agriculture's estimate), and in later years to more than three million, and that those of the city of São Paulo should have increased nearly tenfold between 1883 and 1907, attaining a third of a million ? Into Rio Grande do Sul, in 1885–95, Italian immigrants numbered some 56,000, being four-fifths of all. In 1903, more Italians departed from Brazil than arrived, and thereafter increased departures and reduced

[1] It probably did not take place, the statement to the contrary, notwithstanding, of J. C. Oakenfull, *Brazil in 1909* (prepared for the Brazilian Government Commission of Propaganda and Economic Expansion, and published, Paris, 1909), p. 152.

[2] F. Ferreira Ramos, *La question de la valorisation du café au Brésil* (Antwerp, 1907); Lalière, pp. 361–417.

[3] There were probably more, however. See C. Usiglio, " L'emigrazione nel Brasile," *Boll. Emig.*, 1908, No. 7, p. 25.

arrivals became the rule. The stream has continued to flow substantially into São Paulo, embracing, as the record declares, some 24,000 individuals a year in 1912 and 1913, or considerably more than the average of 14,000 for the years 1903–13.[1] Into other parts of Brazil, Italian immigrants have recently numbered but few thousands.[2] More and more they have been eclipsed by the inpouring Portuguese and, in some years, even by the Spanish.

Only guesses exist to tell us how many Italians the provinces, later states, have contained. For the Brazilian censuses have been scant, wild, and unsafe. Moreover, the national government, eager for citizens, regarded as Brazilians all foreigners who did not themselves by a certain date demand the privilege of retaining their nationality. Italian estimates, on the other hand, have commonly embraced not only the immigrants, but also their Brazil-born children, since the members of both groups are held to be Italian subjects. Children born in Brazil must in the earlier years have been few.

In 1892 consular representatives of Italy claimed that there were in São Paulo 300,000 Italians, in Santa Catharina 50,000, in Rio Grande do Sul and Matto Grosso (chiefly the former) 100,000, in the city and district of Rio de Janeiro 20,000, in Minas Geraes 10,000, and in Espirito Santo 20,000.[3] A rough census of 1900 reported 58,466 in Rio Grande do Sul, together with 15,711 Germans and 7051 Portuguese in a population of 1,149,000.[4] By 1906–08, according to new consular estimates, resting upon various sorts of evidence, the Italians in leading states numbered:

Amazonas	2,000	Paraná	20,000
Bahia	3,000–4,000	Rio de Janeiro	50,000
Espirito Santo	50,000	(*Capital alone*	35,000)
Minas Geraes	90,000	Rio Grande do Sul	250,000
Pará	2,000	Santa Catharina	30,000
		São Paulo	800,000

[1] São Paulo, *Annuario Estatistico*, 1912, i, p. 100; *ibid.*, *Relatorio da agricultura de 1912–1913* (São Paulo, 1914), p. 178.

[2] Bryce, p. 407, was misinformed in holding that " most " of the 88,000 immigrants of 1910 were Italians; 14,163 were, of whom 8998 went to São Paulo.

[3] *Emig. e Col.*, 1893, pp. 109, 127 f., 133.

[4] C. M. Delgado de Carvalho, *Le Brésil méridional* (Paris, 1910), p. 392.

For the whole country an estimate of 1,500,000 was made in 1910.[1] It is an oft-reiterated opinion that the Italians in São Paulo are fully one-third of the state's population; and in several of the southern states there are important towns of 20,000–30,000 inhabitants, in which a majority are Italians and their children.

A common error has been to suppose the Italian population of Brazil to have originated in the South of Italy. Actually, to an altogether remarkable degree, as anyone may discover who will glance at the Italian passport figures, North Italians have predominated. In the first years of heavy migration to Brazil fully four-fifths of the emigrants came from the North. It is true that since the collapse of their movement in 1902, numerous South Italians have settled in the cities (as we have seen that they did in Argentina), in São Paulo, in Santos, Rio, Bahia. In the Federal District of Rio de Janeiro they now perhaps even exceed the North Italians;[2] but for no other region of southern Brazil could such a claim be sustained. In the state of Bahia, and apparently in the North generally, they have preponderated over the North Italians.[3] The tropical climate, too hot for the Venetians, and the uninviting agricultural conditions of the North have doubtless made for the result.

The North Italians arrived in families and went directly to the coffee plantations. That São Paulo should have come to produce five-sixths of the Brazilian coffee crop and two-thirds of the

---

[1] " Saggio di una statistica della popolazione italiana all' estero," *Boll. Emig.*, 1912, No. 1, pp. 111 f. Grossi, like most writers, accepts the table given without reserve; *op. cit.*, p. 320. The figure for São Paulo I have incorporated from an informed study by S. Coletti, " Lo stato di S. Paolo e l'emigrazione italiana," *Boll. Emig.*, 1908, No. 14, p. 8. G. Pio di Savoia (" Lo stato di San Paolo e l'emigrazione italiana," *Boll. Emig.*, 1905, No. 3, pp. 18 f.) gives a list of 26 important townships of São Paulo in which, from sundry data, Italians are argued to exceed Brazilians in number, and 12 in which they are held to be less. A municipal census of the city of Rio de Janeiro which I have not seen found 25,557 Italians there in 1906 (Napoli and Belli, p. 124); it doubtless did not include native-born children. A recent estimate by the Secretary of the Interior of Minas Geraes holds the Italians there to reach 96,000; see M. Goffreddo, " La pastorizia, l'agricoltura e la nostra emigrazione nello stato di Minas Geraes," *Boll. Emig.*, 1913, No. 10, p. 23.

[2] Pio di Savoia, p. 5.

[3] L. S. Rocca, " Gli italiani nello stato di Bahia," in *Emig. e Col.*, 1908, iii[i], p. 12.

world's supply is a distinction, it is not excessive to say, which these immigrants have largely made possible. Without them, the prodigious increase in production would scarcely have occurred; for laborers from other countries, despite insistent stimulation — such as the Germans, Swiss, and others who in earlier days were alone hoped for — had been slow to come, had even, by their own governments, been dissuaded from coming.[1] The immigration of the Italians was in part, to be sure, purchased. Half a million of those that came after 1889 received their passage fares from the state of São Paulo, which in twenty-four years after 1880 spent 42,000,000 milreis (over $14,000,000 United States money) in subsidization.[2] Not only in São Paulo but in other states also, in Minas Geraes, in Rio de Janeiro, and in Espirito Santo, great numbers of Italians have been employed in coffee growing.

How extensive the Italians' work has been cannot be shown statistically. When Perrod made his careful report in 1887, about a third of the Italians, he supposed, were in the fazendas, and there they constituted two-fifths of the workers.[3] This was before the great influx. Subsequent consular statements have uniformly held the Italians to be a large majority of the workers. In an Italian publication of 1906, they were claimed to be four-fifths of the plantation hands.[4] But their primacy has been conceded by other than Italian writers also. One French student has declared them to be seven-tenths of the fazenda workers of São Paulo, the rest being chiefly Portuguese and Spanish;[5] and another believes that, beyond a doubt, the expansion of the coffee industry would have been impossible without their aid.[6] Lord Bryce, finally,

[1] Franceschini, pp. 466 f.

[2] *Il Brasile e gli italiani, pubblicazione del " Fanfulla "* (Florence, 1906), pp. 563 f. But the state made a good bargain of their coming, for it taxed the exports of coffee up to some eight times the cost of subsidization! Grossi gives the figures; *op. cit.*, p. 388.

[3] E. Perrod, *La provincia di San Paolo* (Ministero degli Affari Esteri, Rome, 1888), pp. 5, 116. Perrod was vice-consul at São Paulo.

[4] *Il Brasile e gli italiani*, p. 419.   [5] Lalière, p. 265.

[6] P. Walle, *Au Brésil — de l'Uruguay au Rio São Francisco* (Paris, 19–, p. 175). Cf. also the words of an Argentine visitor, M. Bernárdez, *Le Brésil: sa vie, son travail, son avenir* (Buenos Aires, 1908), p. 221; and of P. Denis, *Le Brésil au XX° siècle* (Paris, 1909), p. 170.

wrote, after a visit several years ago, " the labor on the great coffee estates of São Paulo is almost entirely Italian." [1] Such attributions, just because they rest upon a diversity of evidence or are reached from different points of view, get their force from their substantial agreement. Like the cereal development of Argentina, this achievement of the Italians in coffee production has the convenient merit of being at once definite, extensive, and of large consequence. If half the world finds comfort in its cup of coffee on the breakfast table, then half the world is indebted to the Venetian toilers of Brazil.

What, more particularly, has been the rôle of the immigrant plantation workers ? On what terms have they lent their labor ?

In the Rio de Janeiro district, in Espirito Santo, and in the early days likewise in São Paulo, the metayer system was the chief mode of securing laborers. Usually the cultivator received, for his family's labor during the year, one-half the coffee harvested and a varying privilege of growing vegetables for his own use between the rows of coffee trees. While coffee prices were high, this system resulted well for the cultivator. Since the crisis, it has generally implied a low return. In São Paulo it was early given up, because in the good years laborers were forthcoming upon less favorable terms, and apparently because a different contract better fitted the purposes of large-scale production. Today it prevails widely in the fazendas of Minas Geraes.[2]

The *empreitada* system followed the share system in São Paulo. Though it is still maintained, it has suffered a constant and great decline since the late nineties. That is because its essential result was to extend the cultivated area. For the proprietor who had land but little capital it was a convenient system, and it was attractive to the proprietor who had means as well, because it was

[1] *Op. cit.*, p. 406.

[2] On this contract and its workings, see *Emig. e Col.*, 1893, p. 142; Pio di Savoia, p. 32; R. Rizzetto, " L'immigrazione italiana nello Stato di Espirito Santo," *Boll. Emig.*, 1903, No. 7, pp. 24, 27; *idem*, " Colonizzazione italiana nello Stato di Espirito Santo," *Boll. Emig.*, 1905, No. 5, p. 7; F. Mazzini, " Gl' interessi sociali ed economici italiani nel distretto consolare di Rio de Janeiro," *Boll. Emig.*, 1905, No. 13, p. 40; Goffreddo, p. 50 (cf. L. Provana del Sabbione, " Viaggi di ispezione nel distretto consolare di Bello Horizonte," *Boll. Emig.*, 1915, No. 1, p. 40).

inexpensive. The cultivator, for his part, could foresee that after four years of labor he would possess some savings. He had to clear the field, plant the coffee, uproot the weeds that sprang up incessantly, and in general so care for the trees that they could be turned over to the proprietor with the first crop, more rarely the second, ready to be gathered. The cultivator received the use of a somewhat primitive house, a limited right to pasture, the privilege of growing corn and beans freely between the rows of coffee trees for two years, thereafter not more than two rows of vegetables between the rows of trees. For every thousand coffee plants four years old, he received a stipulated sum, in excess of 100 milreis, submitting to a deduction for every hole where new plants had not been substituted for those that had failed to come up. Those colonists who managed their business well and bore clear of debt toward their landlords met success. They promoted themselves to independent proprietorship or they became merchants in the cities. Probably exceptional individual qualities played some part in conducting this minority to a place of command and comfort.[1]

Years before the vogue of the empreitada began to decline, a third form of contract arose which today rules. Its common name, the wages contract, scarcely indicates its character. The colonist, as the cultivator is named, receives the use of a simple house, limited pasture rights, and an advance of food. He agrees to stay a year and takes charge usually of five thousand plants. He keeps them free of weeds, sets in new shrubs for those that fail to come up or die, cuts off the dry or broken branches, and places supports where needed. When the berries are ripe, he cleans the ground under the trees and finally gathers the fruit. He is entitled to a cash wage for every thousand plants that he cultivates and every fifty liters of clear product that he gathers. At his own expense and for his own profit, he may grow two rows of corn between the rows of coffee where the plants are not over two years old — one row where they exceed two years — or he may grow beans and rice. But sometimes, or until the plants are very old,

[1] A good description of this contract is by A. Monaco, " L'immigrazione italiana nello Stato di San Paolo del Brasile," *Boll. Emig.*, 1902, No. 8, pp. 44 ff.

he may grow no vegetables among them. A small lot may be wholly reserved for his use, yielding enough to feed his family. Certain road and fence repair duties he must perform without specific pay. From his wages due at the end of the year fines are deducted for irregularity of work, for allowing animals to leap over his hedges, and for various other offences. Unless the fazenda is near the large centers, he incurs a heavy debt at the fazendeiro's store and this, plus a high interest charge, must also be deducted from his wages. A family normally constituted, avoiding fines, incurring no unusual expenses, as for sickness, has been able to save a fair sum per year.[1]

This contract is obviously elastic. Some changes have been made in it since it began in the nineties almost wholly to displace the empreitada. And the detailed variations from fazenda to fazenda have always been considerable. Unlike the day or seasonal laborers taken on especially at harvest, whose wage rises and falls with the fluctuations of the paper exchange, the year colonists are paid at a fixed rate in paper. Hence serious uncertainties in the amount of gold and commodities which they can command. In general, during the nineties these amounts tended to decline and in the new century to rise. In times of disturbance the rapid fluctuations ran a long gamut.

When the coffee crisis began, many fazendeiros were wholly unable to settle in cash and instituted various species of promises to pay, eventually often worthless. Unpunctuality of wage payment became one of the most serious abuses that led to the Prinetti decree and to its maintenance in force. Likewise, when the crisis set in, the fines deducted often became unreasonable, and those fazendeiros who sold to the colonists through their own *vendas* charged more and more exaggerated prices. Certainly the fazendeiro regarded himself as standing between the devil and the deep sea. Bankruptcy was inevitable if he allowed his colonists to accumulate large wage credits, or if their debts were allowed wholly to eat up their wages, for then they would desert. True, the fazenda police, naturally almost the only kind possible on these

---

[1] The details of the wages contract are set forth by Pio di Savoia, p. 32. Cf. *Emig. e Col.*, 1893, p. 166.

large estates, would try to bring back the deserters, and whipping also availed somewhat — another of the causes determining the Prinetti decree — but the menace was none the less great. Berries were useless without harvest hands; one year's neglect of a plantation necessitated two years work to restore its productivity. In these anxious years, endless properties, with their crops, were mortgaged. Desperate measures, often combined with fraud — both to the colonists and to other fazendeiros as well — were resorted to in the labor emergency. When, in 1902, new plants ceased to be set out, there were already so many young ones in existence that for some years to come climbing harvests seemed inevitable. Then, the price of coffee, sinking since the late nineties, slumped more, till it touched the ruinous level that had been prevalent for a short time in the early eighties. And finally, after an interval, came valorization, bringing relief.

Black pictures have been drawn of the conditions of the Italians in the fazendas. The early era when it used to be said that " the Italians are prospering and sending for their friends "[1] has only in feverish intervals since been recalled. Some of the correspondents of the Italian Geographic Society, in 1888, reported great suffering and privation.[2] Because it was clear that the facilities did not exist for receiving and distributing so many immigrants, the Crispi decree of March, 1889, put a ban upon artificial aids to emigration, including the free passage, and maintained it till August, 1891. When a round of consular reports was asked for in 1892, they revealed frequent skepticism regarding the situation of the Italians: debts were a burden, and the vaunted large sums of money currently forwarded to Italy ceased to be impressive when the size of the Italian population was considered.[3] Although the cholera was the main occasion for the temporary suspension of emigration to Espirito Santo in July, 1895, a consular report from that state had just told of the defects of the transportation system, subjection to various indignities, payment

---

[1] *E.g.*, da Silva Prado, p. 500.
[2] Reale Soc. Geog. Ital., *passim, e.g.*, pp. 237, 290.
[3] *Emig. e Col.*, 1893, pp. 167–169.

in promises, police abuses, and similar matters. In a collection of consular statements made in the late nineties, some bad abuses were recounted, but most colonists were deemed to be fairly well off.[1]

Most of all it was the recital of a travelling inspector, Adolfo Rossi, made in 1902, after the great collapse, which stirred the Italian authorities to action. After three months in Brazil, he drew a crowded picture of frauds and mishandlings, of privation and helplessness. Somewhat the abuses he noted had been perpetrated by Italians themselves, veritable exploiters of their countrymen, but most were the work of the fazendeiros and their overseers. Though he probably wrote when the situation was at its darkest, it is impossible to read his tales of attacks, for example, on women and girls and of floggings of recalcitrant workmen, without believing that something of the old slave system still lingered on in the fazendas.[2]

Light and shadow intermingled and contrasting — more of shadow than of light — appear in the later glimpses we have of Italian life on the plantations. The idyllic moments are there — Professor Bertarelli and Signora Ferrero have painted them — the traditional usages and festivals; the singing, shouting, and music on Sundays; the gay pleasures of the harvest days, recalling the unrestrained jocundity of the vintagers in Italy. But the

---

[1] The questions put by consul-general Gioia and the answers to them are brought together by P. Ghinassi, " Per le nostre colonie," *L'Italia Coloniale*, February, 1901, pp. 24–28; cf. pp. 30 f.

[2] A. Rossi, " Condizioni dei coloni italiani nello stato di S. Paolo del Brasile," *Boll. Emig.*, 1902, No. 7, pp. 3–88. The situation was sufficiently complicated. Brazil in 1901 denounced her commercial treaty with Italy, without so discriminating against France, and roused much feeling in Italy. An inspector visited the state of Minas Geraes, but his report, for whatever reason, was never published. Rossi's findings are unsystematically presented. One can wish that a commission instead of a man had been sent, since the task required balance and perspective, such as might come from mutual checks and criticism. The Rossi mission became a target for Grossi (pp. 489–493), and was bitterly assailed by a São Paulo Italian, F. Canella, in " Le condizioni degli italiani nello Stato di San Paolo," *L'Italia Coloniale*, January (pp. 43–62) and February (pp. 155–181), 1903. Canella, whose criticism is not without a personal tinge, accuses Rossi of exaggerating, of generalizing unjustly, and of securing corroboration of his evidence from the ignorant or prejudiced, and other faults. But he agrees that the suspension of subsidized emigration was desirable.

more usual cast of existence, it seems, is dull, and pleasure shades easily into pain.

Work is monotonous and fatiguing. After the *feitor's* bell rings at sunrise, everyone is busy till sunset. The hardest toil comes in the hottest months, September to March. Relaxation is possible only on Sundays, when the holiday garb and the holiday spirit assert themselves. Food is, fortunately, sufficient in amount and varied in kind, including vegetables, milk, eggs, fowl, and pork.[1]

Dwellings have had a stereotyped form, the materials of their construction being bricks, bamboo, and clay; their floors are usually the earth itself. A row of such houses constitutes a colony; the scattered colonies make up the fazenda. For the families that they must contain the houses are certainly too small, and their hygienic conditions are neglected by both occupant and fazendeiro. Fresh water is often lacking and drainage deficient.

That sickness, in these circumstances, should have been widespread is not surprising. Of trachoma there has been much and in some places fevers have been persistent. The wet, soggy, shaded soil of the fazendas is an ideal propagating medium for the hookworm, which enters the bare feet of the cultivators.[2] Medical aid is absent, remote or costly. Pointedly it has been said (by Dr. Bertarelli) that whoever falls sick in this country of expensive doctors is in danger of losing his money or his life — or both!

The relation of worker and employer has shown improvement since Rossi's day. Wages have still, from time to time, been withheld, either because the employer could not pay or because he wished to retain the worker. Fines have still been excessive, for, textually, the labor contract has always been Draconian and the colonist has had to rely on the planter's spirit of fair play. But such a spirit has by no means generally been wanting. As a magnificent speculation, coffee has attracted the most diverse characters, some spendthrift or unscrupulous, others wise and humane. Especially in that older region about the capital city of

[1] Franzoni has declared that the heavy exports of salt meat from Argentina have gone mainly to Brazil, where they once nourished the slaves and later the plantation workers. Cam. Ital. di Comm., *Gli italiani nell' Argentina*, p. 181.

[2] In 1916 the Rockefeller Foundation added Brazil to the countries where, by education and treatment, it is seeking to stamp out the disease.

São Paulo, where the estates have been somewhat broken up by inheritance and the cultivator has not been dependent on the planter's store, good management has been common; but in the distant centers the ruling circumstances have been less propitious and the state's oversight difficult.

An important enactment of 1907 gave to the colonists a first lien upon the crop, so effectually bettering a situation which a pseudo-benevolent law of 1904 had not improved, a law which virtually confirmed the old practice of allowing mortgage claims on the crop to be satisfied first.[1] In 1911, the state of São Paulo established an Agricultural Protective Bureau for the execution of the federal and state laws, so far as they involve the rights and interests of the agricultural workers. This likewise was an important step forward, but its results will probably come slowly.[2]

By the ordinary tests of civilized countries, the level of wages has surely been low. Though it rose during much of the present century its improved basis left much to be desired, and just before the outbreak of the European war, and in the crisis that next ensued, it sank again. On the one hand, and commonly, there has for years past been the spectacle of the destitute Italian unable to call a penny his own, or of the Italian who has spent the profit of an exceptional year in returning to Italy — in poverty, discouraged, exhausted or sick. On the other hand, but more rarely, and to be discovered chiefly in the older regions about the capital, there has been the nimble accumulator of savings who has bought a plot of land and become an independent cultivator.

Of 57,000 landed estates, which the Secretary of Agriculture of São Paulo counted in 1907, over nine per cent belonged to Ital-

[1] On this episode, see *Boll. Emig.*, 1904, No. 2, p. 44 (gives the text of the earlier law); *Boll. Emig.*, 1904, No. 11, p. 31; Pio di Savoia, p. 53; *Boll. Emig.*, 1909, No. 9, pp. 77 f. There is some indication that the law of 1907 has accomplished less than was expected. See a criticism by Napoli and Belli, *op. cit.*, p. 24.

[2] Guzzini, in *Emigrazione agricola al Brasile, Relazione della Commissione Italiana*, 1912 (2d ed., Bologna, 1913), pp. 235–244; São Paulo, *Relatorio da Agricultura de 1912–1913*, pp. 198–208; A. Tuozzi, " La tutela giuridica del colono nello stato di San Paolo," *Boll. Emig.*, 1913, No. 10, pp. 57–70. The obstacles to assistance are many, as Tuozzi points out: the colonist has no means at hand to insure payment of his wage, his liberty in changing fazendas is restricted, he must get permission to do most things, has little indication of the terminus and mode of his work, must live in the fazenda, whither no one may come save by his master's permission.

ians;[1] and in some coffee regions, as at Ribeirãozinho, there have been more Italian owners than Brazilian. Many Italian properties have been worth 100–150 contos ($32,000–$50,000, United States money), some even much more. Although the owners have sometimes acquired their purchase money in other places or in other industries, yet generally, it would seem, they have done so by dint of hard struggling, incessant toil, privation, and the most scrupulous saving.[2]

Even, however, when the most cheerful aspects are emphasized, when, for instance, it is shown that men have saved money, one evil of broad dimensions remains: the isolation in which the entire fazenda working force lives, its incredibly low civic level. Touch with the outside world is rare. It is not an infrequent thing for the children of a " successful " immigrant to grow up without any elementary schooling; that the parents are not unhappy in the situation rather heightens the force of the criticism. Over all is the baleful influence of a patriarchal organization of industry, which, however necessary it might have been in a society resting upon a slave basis, ill comports with the ideal of free labor.[3]

[1] The figures are reproduced by A. Piccarolo, *Una rivoluzione economica* (Alessandria, 1908), pp. 11 f. See also Bernárdez, p. 222; J. N. Solórzano y Costa, *El estado de S. Paulo* (São Paulo, 1913), p. 18. What proportion of the whole acreage the Italians held is not known; it was certainly less than nine per cent.

[2] A. Cusano, *Italia d'oltre mare* (Milan, 1911), pp. 109–113. In a propagandist booklet, *L'état de São Paulo, renseignements utiles* (São Paulo, 1911), pp. 58–68, are given the names of some 150–175 Italian immigrants who have accumulated riches, together with their residence, the date of their arrival (usually about twenty years previous), the extent of their lands, number of coffee plants and their annual profit from cultivation. Cf. also *Il Brasile e gli Italiani*, p. 842, where the plantations of the Italians are claimed to be worth 28,000,000 lire, and to contain 14,000,000 coffee plants.

[3] On Italian life in the fazendas, see, *e.g.*, E. Bonardelli, *Lo stato di S. Paolo del Brasile e l'emigrazione italiana* (Turin, 1916), esp. chs. iv and vi; Cusano, pp. 85–87; E. Bertarelli, *Il Brasile meridionale* (Rome, 1914), esp. pp. 64–82; Lombroso-Ferrero, pp. 38–61; U. Tedeschi, " Le condizioni sanitarie degli emigranti italiani nello stato di San Paolo," *Boll. Emig.*, 1907, No. 2, pp. 3–58; L. Mazzotti, " Una grave malattia che colpisce al Brasile gli emigrati italiani lavoranti nella coltivazione del caffè," *Rivista della Beneficenza Pubblica*, 1902, pp. 469–476; Dr. Mazzucconi, " Le condizioni degli italiani nello stato de S. Paulo," *Boll. Emig.*, 1905, No. 8, pp. 45–48; Monaco, pp. 35–55; a report by Pio di Savoia to the Consiglio dell' Emigrazione, *Boll. Emig.*, 1908, No. 1, pp. 33–41; and cited writings by Pio di Savoia and S. Coletti.

CHAPTER XVI

BRAZIL. II. PIONEER FARMING. GENERAL ASPECTS OF ITALIAN LIFE

WHEN the best has been said, the experience of the immigrants on the fazendas has been one of broken hopes and vanished dreams. A great work in production has been wrought, some planters — by no means all — have been enriched, but a narrow and stunted life, hedged about with worry, has been the reward of the mass of the cultivators.

If for some time and in good earnest the planters refrained from setting out further trees, then, simply enough, a measure of correction would come from the increase of the world's demand for coffee. And if the agricultural production of São Paulo were more diversified, a steadier utilization of the labor force might be made; for the possibilities of the rich soil of this state are far from exhausted. But it is not even clear that the most economical method of raising coffee is now pursued. Technical advances notwithstanding, the somewhat feudal organization of the fazendas is a remainder of slave days. The operations chiefly requiring capital and a large scale of operations occur in the final stages. Because harvest labor is precious, more families are often taken into the plantation than can be fully occupied during much of the year. It may be that the problem of the planter is partly the immigrant's problem also. The former constantly fears that the latter will desert him before the harvest is gathered; the immigrant, when dissatisfied, is tempted to seek a better connection elsewhere. Could not a harvest reserve of labor be assured to the planter if immigrants were established, at no great distance, on small properties of their own, which they might work with all the interest that ownership inspires and that a traditional worship of the magic of property has especially instilled in the Italians? Though such a solution would not touch the heart of the problem, it might accomplish much. But let us leave the question momentarily unanswered and consider a theme not unrelated, yet also of broad independent interest.

Had coffee not spelt gold for Brazil, the likelihood is that there, as in Argentina, modern immigration would have taken the form of colonial settlement. In the first two-thirds of the nineteenth century, many colonies, we have seen, were started and many sank into oblivion. Even, however, after the virtues of the volcanic soil of São Paulo had begun to be prized, and after the fazendas had contrived to engorge the great mass of the immigrants, the founding of colonies went forward, with some striking results.

The state of São Paulo itself has had a colonization policy, inviting immigrants to make their homes in given centers, called usually nuclei. Paying their way from the port of debarkation to the *Hospedaria*, it has lodged and fed them until their " concession " could be chosen — perhaps a week or more — then has transported them gratis to the colony.[1] There " urban " and " suburban " and " rural " lots have been marked off. Rural lots, commonly of twenty-five hectares, would ordinarily be sold only to heads of families. They paid from four to sixteen milreis (perhaps $1.50–$5.00) per hectare, while purchasers of urban lots paid five to ten times as much. Although a deduction of 6 per cent was made for settlement in cash, most colonists preferred to pay in five annual instalments. After five years an addition, usually 20 per cent, was made to the unpaid amount. If food, seeds, roots, and implements were advanced, the charge therefor became part of the " colonial debt." Service in making roads, which was compensated for, could be required of the colonist.[2]

Such is the form which the colonial policy of São Paulo has taken, and I give it in some detail because it accords closely with that of the other southern states. In themselves the São Paulo

---

[1] Under the existing law, whenever a family of three persons aged twelve or more is in question, the state also pays for the transportation from the foreign port to Santos.

[2] *Emig. e Col.*, 1893, pp. 161 f.

colonies are not in the forefront of their kind. That is largely because the fazendeiros have never heartily supported the small properties movement. The pivot of their interest has been too firmly centered elsewhere, and they doubtless wished to assure the valuable Italian labor supply to themselves. Few Italians have been in the nuclei. In five colonies " emancipated " (dropped from special guardianship) at one time, a few years ago, they were only 50 of 5000 inhabitants. But at Campos Selles, by way of contrast, founded in 1897, they held in early days one-fifth of the lots; and in 1912 numbered (apart from their native children) 327 persons, being a third of the population. At Nova Venecia, in 1912, they were 261, or over half the population. But these were their major centers. In all the unemancipated colonies of São Paulo, the foreign-born Italians have not, at any moment, exceeded some 1200–1500, or 10–15 per cent of the inhabitants.[1]

Of colonization in Espirito Santo the tale may be briefly told. Its pith is that, out of misfortune and out of the colonists' maladaptation to their circumstances, an unhappy result has come. Beginning to arrive about 1875, the Italians rapidly increased, especially in the period before suspension, and if a consular estimate may be credited, there were presently some 5000 proprietors among them. Through the slump in the price of their main crop, an inferior grade of coffee, many lost control of their lands; but these were so disadvantageously distant from the markets that substantial profits were never likely. On the other hand, the colonists have been content with a primitive agricultural equipment (derived, it is said, from the Indians by way of the Portuguese!), and have used no plows. They have lacked an understanding of what their land could do and of what they ought to do, and have pursued their way empirically. Although they and their children have now attained a population of about 50,000, there has been little association among them for the ad-

---

[1] How many have lived in all the agricultural settlements (apart from coffee plantations) cannot be indicated. If such miscellaneous groups as the workers on the sugar plantations of Piracicaba are reckoned in, the total is not inconsiderable.

Current statistics of the *nucleos* may be found in the *Annuario estatistico de São Paulo*. See also Pio di Savoia, " Lo stato di San Paolo," etc., pp. 78, 86–96; Denis, ch. viii; Delgado de Carvalho, p. 213.

vance of their common interests. German immigrants to Espirito Santo, because they antedated the Italians by thirty years, and because they have practised a more varied culture, have been much more prosperous than the Italians.[1]

A distinctly happier lot has been that of the 20,000–30,000 Italians in Paraná, survivors and successors of immigrants who came during some fifteen years before the early nineties. The main influx ended abruptly, and the state government, through indifference or poverty, probably both, ceased to provide for further settlements.[2] Physically, despite a humid coast and a still unexplored West, which is covered with impenetrable forests, the state has offered advantages to settlers. A plateau zone parallel to the seaboard is well suited to human habitation. The soil is good for cultivation — or rather, men have learned to supply its deficiency in phosphates by burning the plentiful timber over it.

Some Italians are at the port Paranguá, but most are still at Morrêtes, one of the first settlements, where they have established themselves in the cultivation of sugar cane and in diversified agriculture. From the somewhat debilitating climate of Morrêtes, fifteen families early sought relief by founding Santa Felicidade, in the fertile plateau country, where now 2500 persons live. Neither language nor dress suggests that this town has not been picked up out of Venetia and dropped into Brazil.

Many settlements have had their origin in the withdrawal of colonists from one or another well-filled center. So in 1896 thirty families of young persons left Santa Felicidade, without means, and started Bella Vista. In seven years all had paid for their lots with the products of the soil — corn and wheat, grapes and wine. Vegetables and tobacco they have raised for their own

---

[1] R. Rizzetto, " L'immigrazione italiana nello Stato di Espirito Santo," pp. 20–32; *idem*, "Colonizzazione italiana nello Stato di Espirito Santo," *Boll. Emig.*, 1905, No. 7, pp. 3–152 (pp. 119–151 give the histories of individual immigrants); G. B. Beverini, " Lo Stato di Espirito Santo," in *Emig. e Col.*, 1908, iii¹, pp. 390–405; L. Petrocchi, " Le colonie italiane nello Stato di Espirito Santo," *Boll. Emig.*, 1915, No. 1, pp. 45–56.

[2] For the text of the settlement law of 1892, see " Legge sulla colonizzazione dello Stato del Paraná," *Boll. Emig.*, 1904, No. 18, pp. 26–31.

uses, corn for polenta and forage; and they have acquired ample stocks of cattle, swine, horses, and poultry.[1] The state leads all others in the production of *herva mate* or Paraguay tea (the powdered leaves of a small tree), which is the South American substitute for the beverage of the East. At Santa Felicidade and elsewhere much of it is produced for export; and at Curityba, the capital, the son of an Italian has established the largest concern for preparing the leaves.

Although some colonists, to their considerable disadvantage, have established themselves too far away from the markets, those in the settlements named, or at such places as Pilarzinho, Agua Verde, and Umbará, have done well, and many have estates worth $10,000–$30,000 (United States money). The chief city colony is Curityba, containing, among others, some 4000–6000 Italians; it is separated from São Paulo city by a rail journey of about thirty hours.[2]

In Santa Catharina, as early as 1836, Genoese families established the colony of Nova Italia. But the great immigration came only after government agents in Venetia had tried to procure settlers of a Latin strain to counterweigh the Teutonic. In all Brazil, as it happens, Santa Catharina has been the region of German predilection and is today the seat of a German population of perhaps 120,000. Without counterbalancing them, the Italians have come to be an important collectivity of 30,000–42,000.

[1] The histories of all these families have been recorded. See G. Silva, " Lo stato del Paraná e l'immigrazione italiana," *Boll. Emig.*, 1903, No. 7, pp. 37 ff.; G. Sabetta, " La colonizzazione e l'immigrazione italiana nel Paraná," *Boll. Emig.*, 1903, No. 10, pp. 17 f.

[2] For some light — not much — upon early days, see N. Marcone, *Gli italiani al Brasile* (Rome, 1877), ch. iv. A particularly useful study is R. Venerosi Pesciolini, *Le colonie italiane nel Brasile meridionale* (Turin, 1914), pp. 201–228. See also Cusano, pp. 177–213; Denis, ch. x; the reports in the volume *Emigrazione agricola al Brasile* (Commissione Italiana, 1912); Silva, pp. 33–40; Sabetta, pp. 3–18; B. Salemi-Pace, " Le imprese di colonizzazione nel Sud del Brasile e specialmente nello Stato di Paraná," *Boll. Emig.*, 1905, No. 4, pp. 3–61; T. Castiglia, " Lo Stato del Paraná," *Emig. e Col.*, 1908, iii[i], pp. 167–211; N. Fortunati, " Condizioni materiali e morali degli italiani nello stato del Paraná," *Boll. Emig.*, 1913, No. 10, pp. 71–73; C. Umiltà, " Il Paraná e l'emigrazione italiana," *Boll. Emig.*, 1913, No. 14, pp. 51–54.

The state is more fortunately provided with a sea front than its southern neighbor, Paraná, but its soil, generally speaking, is less fertile. The colonists have settled between the hot, humid, fever-infested coast, and the upper plateau, which is inhabited by a grazing population of Brazilians. In the more southern colonies, where Germans have been few, the Italians were pioneers. What hardships they suffered in early days they still delight to tell; and of their encounters with the Indians, the cemeteries of Urussanga and Nova Venecia preserve an eternal record.

Azambuja, earliest of the southern colonies, was established on good land and prospered; it now contains 4000 inhabitants. Farther along the railway is Urussanga, Venetian in aspect, founded in 1878 by the imperial government, and in 1901 made a municipality. Its 12,000 inhabitants are still mainly agriculturists who live away from the center. They may be said to have done well, for their farms are worth from four to fifteen times their value of twenty years ago. Bountiful corn harvests serve to fatten hogs, and so to sustain a flourishing lard industry. Grapes are abundantly grown, but only a poor wine is made. Because of mediocre soil conditions, and the want of roads, Cresciuma, like Nova Venecia (the only colony established in Santa Catharina by the *Companhia Metropolitana*), has done less well than Urussanga. At Nova Venecia some settlers have not improved their station in twenty years. Many Italians are at Orleans do Sul, but only a few at Laguna, the home of the immortalized Anita Garibaldi. In all these southern colonies life has the placidity of isolation. Italian is the customary language, and only the merchants need know Portuguese.

The Italians of the northern colonies are but half as numerous as those of the southern — unless some 10,000 Trentines be reckoned with them. At Nova Trento are 4000 Trentines and 1500 Italians. They have not thriven, because their lands are unsatisfactory, and silkworm raising and the making of silk have but little improved their position. Four thousand Venetians and Lombards dwell at Brusque, primarily a German settlement; but their success, too, has been very moderate. Blumenau, established in 1850, is the chief German center, a thriving business and agricultural community, where even the signs in the streets are German, and Italians are few. Rodeio, half Italian and half Trentine, is in a fertile valley, whose products are rice, corn, tobacco, wine, butter, and lard; it has three coöperative associations for the sale of its products.[1] Rio dos Cedros is similarly mingled as to population. In the valley of Pomeranos the Italians have taken the Germans for models in many things — in their style, for example, of house building and in the emphasis they have put upon dairying. The colony at Itajahy, of 3500 Italians, would contain more had not many in past years migrated to Argentina, to improve their fortunes.

All in all, the mass of the Italians in Santa Catharina have become firmly, if modestly, established in farming communities, and generally have risen to proprietorship. They have continued to live apart from the Germans and have not intermarried with them.[2]

When Italians speak with pride of their South Brazilian colonies they usually have foremost in mind neither Santa Catharina nor Paraná, but Rio Grande do Sul, southernmost of all the

---

[1] Venerosi Pesciolini, p. 184, writes: " Nearly all the colonies of Italians in these valleys are in much better economic circumstances than those in other parts of the state; the colonial lots command higher values." Only a little earlier a German traveller who had ridden into the same district (Rodeio) drew this picture: "Very striking in these Italian settlements are the numerous chapels, churches, and crosses on the one hand, and the neglected fields, or rather pastures, on the other. . . . Certainly, where different colonists, for example Germans, settle near the Italians, there is promptly a change of scene." He adds that the men from Pomerania have done better, yet concludes that the Italians are assiduous, industrious, frugal, and could in some things be models to the Germans. W. Vallentin, *In Brasilien* (2d ed., Berlin, 1909), pp. 167 f.

[2] The best account is Venerosi Pesciolini, pp. 115–201. See also Cusano, pp. 217–236; *Emigrazione agricola al Brasile* (Commissione Italiana, 1912), *passim*; G. Pio di Savoia, " Lo stato di Santa Catharina e l'emigrazione italiana," *Boll. Emig.*, 1902, No. 6, pp. 29–64; G. C. MacDonald, " Lo stato di Santa Caterina e la colonizzazione italiana," *Emig. e Col.*, 1908, iii[1], pp. 213–270; L. Petrocchi, " Le colonie italiane nel nord dello Stato di Santa Catharina," *Boll. Emig.*, 1914, No. 6, pp. 49–55; G. Zanluca, " Colonia italiana nella comarca di Blumenau," *Italica Gens (Bollettino)*, December, 1912, pp. 374–383; F. Franzoia, " Condizioni intellettuali della colonia italiana nel sud dello Stato di Santa Catharina," *Boll. Emig.*, 1914, No. 13, pp. 41–47.

states below the coffee belt.   There the survivors and descendants of the immigrants who came in the boom years number about 100,000.

With a temperature rarely rising above 96° Fahr. nor falling below the freezing point, the climate of Rio Grande partly resembles that of South Italy; only — for a difference — rains are ample.   The soil is moderately fertile.   In the North, grazing, still the chief industry of the state, has somewhat fallen back before agriculture; and there it is that the Italians have mainly settled.

The first who came knew only, it is said, that they were going to Brazil and did not guess that they were to be frontiersmen in Rio Grande.   They were quickly abandoned by the agents who introduced them and for a year or more had bitter struggles with Nature which their survivors still recount with emotion.   They were reduced in these days to eating the fruit of the umbrella pine.

Dona Isabel and Conde d'Eu, their first colonies, were both founded in 1875, but patriotically renamed, when the empire fell, Bento Gonçalves and Garibaldi, after the hero of the Rio Grandean revolution and his illustrious Italian companion-in-arms. Of the settlers in Bento Gonçalves a few bought their lots outright from the state.   The rest engaged to pay in five annual instalments, and many received advances besides.   When troubles ensued, the government afterward cancelled a part of the debt. In years more recent, when Italian heads of families came to Bento Gonçalves, they were employed to build roads under a useful arrangement whereby four-fifths of their wage was credited toward their purchase of land.   Italians now number, it is claimed, 22,000 in a population of 25,000, many of them established on lands of great natural fertility.   It is usual to harvest two crops of corn per year.   The growth of Garibaldi, though somewhat less than that of Bento Gonçalves, has been noteworthy and several years ago it was estimated to contain some 15,000 Italians.

To the northeast lies Caxias, " the pearl of the colonies." Founded in 1876, it is estimated now to have a population of 40,000, of whom nine-tenths are Italians.   The city proper presents all the appearance of being the center of a flourishing neighborhood, and boasts electric light derived from water power. It is strikingly Italian, has a *Piazza Dante*, but, as usually happens when a town is reached by the railroad and visited by business folk, the signs in the streets have become Portuguese. The Italian mercantile houses are generally connected with German concerns in Porto Alegre. More wine is made (by Venetians and Mantuans) in the country about Caxias than in any other part of the state: and the whole state's output, second to corn in importance, and greater than the output of any other state in Brazil (Santa Catharina and Paraná following), is mainly the work of Italians. But the reputation which this wine once enjoyed in the trade of Brazil as *vinho nacional* has since been lost through defective methods of preparing for the market. In the country about Caxias are the more modest centers of Nova Trento (with 5000 Venetians and Trentines), Nova Padua, Nova Milão, Nova Vicenza and, further away, Nova Treviso and Nova Roma. Though most colonists have paid their colonial debt, primitive methods of cultivation and (it is claimed) a lack of lime in the soil have blunted their efforts. Hence Caxias and its satellite colonies have ceased to grow. When children marry, they move away and found other centers, and sometimes the older colonists do likewise.

Not only corn and grapes, but vegetables, tobacco, and some sugar are raised. Wheat, long produced in abundance, rose astonishingly in importance when railroad construction was extended, the output of 1912 mounting to five times that of 1908. Italians have introduced the olive — with what success is not yet wholly clear. The crops of one colony are generally the crops of all.

Other Northern colonies are Monte Veneto with its sons of Belluno, Udine, and Treviso; Nova Bassano; Encantado which, founded in 1878, has now 4000 settlers, mostly Italian; Guaporé (1892), containing now 25,000 inhabitants, nearly all Italian; Alfredo Chaves (1885) and Antonio Prado (1886). All of these have flourished. Here also is São Leopoldo, the old German settlement, which somewhat dims the glory of the Italian colonies. Santa Thereza has many Polish settlers, but they are outnumbered by the Italians, whose language they now speak! In the extreme southwest of Rio Grande is Uruguayana, where 2000 Italians, largely engaged in grape growing, are the chief foreign group.[1] In the south-central portion are Silveira Martins and Jaguary (1889). Rio Grande city contains 2500 Italians, Porto Alegre 10,000. At the last-named city and port, the Germans, however, are twice as numerous as the Italians, and much more prosperous and powerful.

Such are the principal colonies of Rio Grande. One cannot read the reports of men who have watched them from near at hand without being impressed by their reiterated criticism of the colonists' methods of cultivation. The immigrants brought with them the semi-antiquated, ill-adapted ways of Venetia, which they have changed since, but only at random and unscientifically. "What this region most needs," wrote an Italian consul, "is some one who can guide and counsel these people of ours. They came from Italy with great hopes and the will to work, but have not the powers necessary for the material and moral development of the colony."[2] In North Italy some of the most admirable types of rural coöperation that the world knows have been developed, but in Rio Grande the promising introduction in late years of coöperative societies for making wine, lard, and dairy products has depended on the initiative of the Federal and State governments. Of subsidiary industries there have been few. The beginnings of silk weaving are hopeful,[3] and baskets, chairs, wickerware, and especially hats, have been made.

The routine of life in Rio Grande is not dull. For worship, for a holiday, and for business, the farmers come to the centers on Sundays. Like the Germans also, they have learned the use of

[1] In 1887, May Frances, a youthful English traveller, noted the attractiveness here of "two estancias owned by Italians, who have planted rows of Lombardy poplars, and whose abodes resemble English farmhouses, they look so much cleaner and more thriving than the Brazilian houses." *Beyond the Argentine* (London, 1890), p. 85.

[2] L. Petrocchi, "Gli italiani nel distretto consolare di Bento Gonçalves," *Boll. Emig.*, 1904, No. 18, p. 4.

[3] The testimony of an English traveller may be noted: "In the colony of Caxias . . . they make some very handsome shawls and scarves, of which I have purchased some fine specimens, also handkerchiefs and other small articles; the thread has elasticity and luster." F. Bennett, *Forty Years in Brazil* (London, 1914), p. 157.

horses " so that on holidays even the women of those races appear on horseback in a way that would startle their peasant cousins left at home in Swabia or Lombardy." [1] It is when sickness shows its face that life seems dark; for doctors and drugs are few, remote, and costly.

When all is said, the accomplishment of the Italians is a bright one. A stretch of wilderness has been redeemed; some trade with the world has been established; and thousands of human beings have satisfied their major needs. After São Paulo and the Federal District, this state is the most progressive in Brazil: the Italians and the Germans have made it so.[2]

So numerous are the Italians of the three southernmost states and in many respects so sharply marked off from those of the fazendas and the cities, that I am loath to leave them without a word on all together. Let us note that they are as predominantly Venetians as the colonists of Argentina are Piedmontese, and that in both countries the Lombards rank second — the Lombards of the hills in Argentina, those of the plains in Brazil.

[1] Bryce, p. 406. Cf. Venerosi Pesciolini, p. 242: men mount a horse to go 200 yards; two or three children, on one horse, ride bareback to school; women go to church or the mill, mounted, often carrying children.

[2] Cf. C. W. Domville-Fife, *The United States of Brazil* (London, 1910), p. 221; Bryce, p. 406. Bryce notes that the Italians live in less comfort than the Germans but work as steadily. More outspoken praise of the Italian qualities is that of L. L. Flores, *Estado do Rio Grande do Sul* (Rio Grande do Sul, 1897), p. 30.

In general, on the Italians, see Venerosi Pesciolini, pp. 13–113; Cusano, pp. 239–274; Denis, ch. xi; *Emigrazione agricola al Brasile, passim;* E. A. Lassance Cunby, *O Rio Grande do Sul* (Rio de Janeiro, 1908), pp. 209–278; E. Ciapelli, " Lo stato di Rio Grande del Sud e l'immigrazione italiana," *Boll. Emig.*, 1903, No. 4, pp. 48–59; Petrocchi, pp. 3–13, and his other contributions to *Boll. Emig., viz.,* 1904, No. 13, pp. 11–19; 1905, No. 8, pp. 3–15; 1906, No. 5, pp. 11–31; E. Ciapelli, " Lo stato di Rio Grande del Sud," *Boll. Emig.*, 1905, No. 12, pp. 3–83; U. Ancarini, " La colonia italiana di Caxias," *Boll. Emig.*, 1905, No. 19, pp. 3–30; F. De Velutiis, " Lo stato di Rio Grande del Sud e la crisi economica durante l'ultimo quinquennio," *Emig. e Col.*, 1908, iii¹, pp. 283–359; G. B. Beverini " Nella zona coloniale agricola del Rio Grande del Sud," *Boll. Emig.*, 1913, No. 10, pp. 3–20. For the text of the colonization laws, etc., see *Boll. Emig.*, 1906, No. 11, pp. 13–34. Some useful passages are also in Delgado de Carvalho, pp. 385–521; Walle, pp. 312–351; and the observations of a former president of Colombia, R. Reyes, *The Two Americas* (tr. by L. Grahame, London, 1914), pp. 135–165 — a section dealing with the southern states generally.

They are never hired farm hands, but all are proprietors and most are secure in their possessions. The crops they grow partly resemble those of Italy. Some they have introduced;[1] others the Germans or Brazilians had first grown. How far their cultivation of Italian crops — fortunate for Brazil — has depended upon inertia, how far upon enterprise, is not easily said. Certainly they have manifested no enterprise in learning to use machines, though they live in a country where horses and mules are cheap, and where, therefore, machines may be inexpensively employed. Nor have they to any extent, unlike the Germans, undertaken to raise cattle or sheep, contenting themselves with pigs and poultry as they had done in Venetia. They have put their profits into land, and some have by now acquired twenty or more lots of 20–25 hectares each; it is common to present a lot to the newly married child. Coöperative societies have made a start in Santa Catharina, just as in Rio Grande, but in both states it has been under government leadership.[2]

In all three states trade has been handicapped by distance from markets, the lack of railways or the high tariffs, the want or the badness of wagon roads. In trade the Italians have counted for much less than the Germans, and in industry — despite interesting beginnings — for less than both Germans and Brazilians.

Few are rich, few poor. Abject poverty they do not know. Though world events touch them — a small crisis came with the outbreak of the European war — they are nearly self-sufficient and are protected by their isolation. Their houses are small, generally of wood, but in some places are of masonry; and travellers have often remarked the orderliness and cleanliness inside. Food is abundant and varied, not including a daily portion of meat, yet pork and fowl upon occasion. The routine of life is healthful; but unlucky are those who fall ill, for medical facilities — not in Rio Grande only — are wretched. Great hardship is experienced where the hookworm and malaria prevail; and pro-

---

[1] Bertarelli (p. 56) mentions the cucumber, asparagus, melon, and tomato.
[2] For a clear statement of the forms of coöperation, see Guzzini in *Emigrazione agricola al Brasile*, pp. 257–288.

longed and widespread suffering of the women has resulted from the absence of obstetrical care.

The traditional religion clings tightly.

"I do not know," writes a priest who diligently visited nearly every colony, "any other country in which the priest has equal authority. This derives from the fact that he is generally the only schooled person and the only one who disinterestedly busies himself with the colonists' affairs. He is their counsellor in all things, even material. When a colonist falls sick, he is sought before the doctor is called. Nothing is done without his opinion. With difficulty may a stranger be heard in a colony unless with the priest's approval. When latterly commissioners came to Rio Grande from the Brazilian government to rouse an interest in coöperative schemes, they had no success whatever until the priests had spoken." [1]

Some loosening of parental authority there has been, such as in many countries takes place among immigrant families. Yet it is a little surprising that it should occur in these rural states, where distractions are few. And the children secure but a skimped education, in Italian or Brazilian schools.

If the Italians had come to these states with the capital, the supple agricultural knowledge, the trained leaders of the Germans, they would be much better off than they are. But neither Germans nor Brazilians have yet learned how best to cope with and to coöperate with Nature. Once soil and climate have been subjected to that close study which in some lands has quite transformed the routine of agriculture, a new day may dawn for the Italians.[2]

The time will come when, through the growth of population and the multiplication of highways, the Italian farmers will reap the advantage that the world grants to first settlers. Their lands will rise in value and they will attain some of that status of ease which the Germans have already reached. Here is one supreme advantage which ownership has over wage earning, and since these southern states are rich in the gifts of Nature, it will surely count for much. Mines and manufactures are also destined to develop, and an active general trade.

[1] Venerosi Pesciolini, p. 266.
[2] On recent governmental attempts in Brazil to extend the knowledge of agriculture, see A. Ledent, "Le Brésil et l'enseignement agricole," *Revue Économique Internationale*, March, 1910, pp. 509–537.

It is difficult to believe that a well-conducted settlement of Italian immigrants in small properties in São Paulo and Minas Geraes would interfere with the work of the coffee plantations. The planters, we have seen, could manage with fewer laborers during the year, if assured of a supply of harvest hands. If Italians lived as independent proprietors at no great distance, still perhaps paying off their land, some would surely migrate to the fazendas for the harvest. Every further development of the means of communication makes the suggestion less fanciful. In recent years São Paulo has offered free land transportation for harvest workers, and many hundreds have responded. The stream flows in from Minas, from Paraná, even from Santa Catharina; the return reaches as far as to Argentina, even to Europe. So simply learned are the final operations that even townsfolk undertake them, coming from the various cities of São Paulo.

Such a plan, advantageous for the independent farmers, would somewhat relieve the pressure upon the Italians established in the fazendas. But still another plan might help. Brazil is no exception to the rule that in new countries the large estates of early days tend to break up. Already in the older districts the fazendas are smaller. It is only the last stage in production, that of transforming the harvested berries into commercial coffee, that requires a scale of operations beyond the reach of the small proprietor. If the Italians, instead of being wage earners, were to become independent proprietors, as some already are, they might coöperatively undertake the last stage. What they have done farther south in making grapes into wine, hog fats into lard, cream into butter, they might repeat in drying berries for coffee. So would stability replace an irregular swelling and depletion of the labor force, and a more enterprising race of laborers arise. Already at Morro-Cipo a considerable group of Italians own and, unaided, cultivate small plantations, some with less than a thousand plants, some with more than twenty thousand; they take their berries to the city where, for a share of the product, a company performs the machine operations. And at another point near Ribeirão Preto, a coöperative society was organized with the plan of gradually acquiring ownership of the needed machinery.[1]

Although the Italians have in no other country given themselves in such numbers to agriculture as in Brazil, yet their work in other occupations there is so important that we cannot pass it by.

They have been railway construction hands. On the important line which runs from São Paulo through Paraná and Santa Catharina into Rio Grande do Sul, not to speak of smaller projects, large numbers of Italians were employed. It was work on the railroads of Paraná in 1876 that started the immigrants there on their path of success. The stretch of line seventy-five miles long connecting Paranaguá with Curityba, rising from sea level to a height of 2700 feet along a treacherously steep mountain wall, consisting of a succession of trestles and tunnels, was one of the most arduous railway enterprises in South America. An Italian engineer directed its construction and the great majority of workers, it is claimed, were Italian. By the state of São Paulo they have often been employed. Recently they have helped cut the road through the forest to Matto Grosso, and on the line into the state of Goyaz most of the laborers are said to have been Italians.[2]

Much other construction work, public and private, has fallen to them. In the agricultural colonies, they of necessity undertook to build roads. They have done an important part of the street work of São Paulo and Rio de Janeiro, and much of the harbor work of Rio. Most commonly these construction laborers (and the railway builders may be included) have been South Italians. Hence, by their origin, as well as by their careers, they

---

[1] On these experiments, see Denis, pp. 170 f.

[2] On railway builders, see, e.g., Venerosi Pesciolini, pp. 126, 160, 209 f.; *Emig. e Col.*, 1893, p. 112; Fortunati, p. 73; Umiltà, p. 54; Napoli and Belli, pp. 27 f.; P. Guerra, *L'emigrazione italiana e gli Stati Uniti dell' America Latina* (Rome, 1910), p. 70; H. Stephens, *South American Travels* (New York, 1915), pp. 574–593; and these passages in *Boll. Emig.*, 1902, No. 11, pp. 52 f.; 1903, No. 7, p. 32 and No. 10, p. 9; 1905, No. 7, p. 4; No. 12, p. 73; No. 18, p. 276; 1908, No. 16, p. 5.

are to be marked off sharply from the plantation hands and the farmers.[1]

Merchants, artisans, operatives — townsfolk generally — have been a numerous throng. None of the 260 Italians reported in Matto Grosso a quarter century ago were in agriculture; all were successful craftsmen and tradespeople; and of their sort there were many in other southern states.[2] Then already had arisen the instance, soon to become a type, of the Italian wholesaler serving as a center for numerous petty traders who tramped venturesomely about the country, as far even as Bahia. These roving merchants were usually Neapolitans who took up their business soon after arrival in Brazil. When a North Italian entered trade, it was usually after he had accumulated a small property in agriculture and then moved to the city. Yet innumerable South Italians have also kept to the cities, especially Rio, selling fish and fowl, vegetables and fruit, and small wares, in the streets or in shops. In recent years the small street dealers of the Federal Capital have been almost routed by competing Syrians, who have even opened their own wholesale houses.[3]

Italians of the South, especially from Basilicata, have long been bootblacks in the cities, not only in Rio, but in São Paulo, Santos, Campinas, even in northern Pernambuco. In the capital, over a long stretch of years, they were almost without competitors. Theirs has been a strange monopoly indeed, but often the first step out from the ranks of the humble.

In Rio, again, many building artisans have made a living, and innumerable tailors, cobblers, barbers, cooks, and waiters. Many have been tramway employees, or occupied in the public cleaning and lighting departments, or as harbor workmen. A minority of these workers have been Venetians, Lombards or Ligurians; the

---

[1] Reale Soc. Geog. Ital., p. 125 (cf. pp. 149–151); *Boll. Emig.*, 1904, No. 14, p. 11; 1905, No. 3, p. 55 and No. 13, p. 7; 1907, No. 18, pp. 273, 276.

[2] *Emig. e Col.*, 1893, pp. 109–111, 145, 160, 171 f.

[3] " Victory came easily to the Syrians, since this race is content with the lowest gains, living, abjectly of course, upon a few pennies of expenditure, toiling like beasts of burden." Napoli and Belli, p. 97. Familiar words, these, but they have generally been directed against the Italians!

great majority have come from Calabria, Basilicata, and Campania. Here and there among them, men have risen to distinction in the arts and in business. The Calabrian Jannuzzi, an immigrant of 1872, became a well-reputed designer and builder, and erected more than a thousand structures. Such an example shows what is possible but does not even remotely suggest what is usual. In the comprehensive municipal improvement works undertaken in Rio some years ago, a host of Italians, some in the high places, but most in the low, participated.[1]

Not Rio, however, but São Paulo City, is the metropolis of the Italians, as it is the metropolis of interior Brazil. They are (all estimates agree) at least a third of the population; and in its busy life — no city in South America is more active — they have counted for much. Somewhat they control the large enterprises — textiles, hatmaking, food establishments, brick and cement making, leather tanning — but principally they crowd the middle and lower strata of employments. Shoemakers, tailors, barbers, bakers and grocers of Italian origin are everywhere; so are drivers of vehicles. Innumerable drinking saloons, well fitted out with marble counters, are owned by Italians, and countless fruit stalls — the two often in conjunction. Itinerant vendors are many, but fewer than they once were. Sellers of newspapers abound. Numerous are the employees of the large manufacturing and trading concerns, and the building workmen. Nearly all the marble cutters of the state as well as of the city are Italian; and innumerable are the common laborers. In the professions, the architects have stood highest, and the good taste that has found its way into the buildings of the city is largely of their bringing. In one way or another, the Italians have made a most substantial contribution to its life, those from the North, however, more than those from the South. Needless to say, they are in São Paulo the leading foreign group, while the Rio Italians are outnumbered by the Portuguese.[2]

[1] *Il Brasile e gli italiani*, pp. 752, 851–875; Napoli and Belli, pp. 51–53, 72–75, 83–96; F. Mazzini, " Gl' interessi sociali ed economici italiani nel distretto consolare di Rio di Janeiro," *Boll. Emig.*, 1905, No. 13, pp. 3–69 (cf. No. 11, pp. 45 f.).

[2] Besides many references in the consular reports and in the volume *Il Brasile e gli italiani* (esp. pp. 746, 857–936), see the reports of visitors: Bryce, pp. 376 f.;

In the coffee port, Santos, Italian is the language of thousands whose occupations are almost as varied as those at São Paulo. At Ribeirão Preto a rough census of 1902 gave the Italians 21,765 inhabitants, nearly half the city's population. In 1887 there were already said to be 3000 Italians at Campinas, of whom a fifth were in trade.[1] They are to be found in all the smaller centers of São Paulo. Here an Italian runs the chief hotel, there he controls the shops; here he leads the band and there he is the only doctor. Finally, far to the north, in hot Bahia, westward in the cities of Minas Geraes, southward in Curityba, Florianopolis, Porto Alegre, the same city types appear, and generally with the same South Italian predominance.

Whoever would understand the life of the Italians in Brazil, and particularly the shadow of failure that has tinged the careers of so many, both on the fazendas and elsewhere, should recollect the melancholy condition in which they arrived. They brought into the country little of capital or of personal accomplishment. When the first great influx began, Marchesini declared that without the help of others the emigrants fresh from Italy would starve, and he cited a report of the chief executive of Santa Catharina to the effect that while the Germans arrived with clothing, baggage, and implements the Italians came in rags.[2] The more casual Marcone who also visited Brazil in the middle seventies pictured the thousands of Italians whom he saw as " all covered with rags, disheartenment writ upon their brows," and by these tokens they could anywhere be quickly recognized.[3] In 1887 Perrod wrote that there was no such poverty in his own poor Val d'Aosta as about him in São Paulo; rare were those who could make modest savings except by painful sacrifices.[4] Incessantly the warning is

Bertarelli, p. 54; Stephens, pp. 556–563; Bernárdez, pp. 220–222; Lombroso-Ferrero, pp. 30–38; J. Burnichon, *Le Brésil d'aujourd'hui* (Paris, 1910), p. 228. Cf., for the comprehensive services of the Italians, the testimony of a Brazilian, B. de Magalhães, *O estado de S. Paulo* (Rio de Janeiro, 1913), p. 25.

[1] Perrod, pp. 39–62; he reports also on the other urban centers of São Paulo.
[2] Marchesini, pp. 132, 135 f.; cf. pp. 159 f.
[3] Marcone, pp. 66, 93.
[4] Perrod, p. 34.

repeated that the feeble will fail in Brazil; and this, if true of the fazendas, holds all the more of the colonies, where the forest must be cleared away and the soil bared. Yet when the initial hardships of the colonies had been overcome, many there, as we have seen, rose to relative comfort.

The more fortunate, the stronger, the sharper-witted everywhere made their foothold secure. The mass, over much of the country, found their task in varying degrees too formidable. It is not a bad living which many have made in the cities, yet there too they have suffered, and over broad districts of Rio and of São Paulo the crowded houses, ill-suited to human living, still reflect their stinted fortunes. A small group of technical workers have done well in industry and building; in trade and in industry, superior qualities have carried other men to heights they might not have reached in Italy; but all these are exceptional men.

Culturally, the immigrants have lived upon a humble plane. Probably a majority of the North Italians of the great influx were illiterate and doubtless most of the South Italians have been so. Many of their children in the fazendas and in the colonies have grown to manhood quite untaught. And although two hundred schools or more have been moderately subsidized by the Italian government, it is a meager education that they provide. Corradini wrote: " I personally visited some 80 of the 120 or 150 schools in São Paulo. With few exceptions — judged on pedagogical and on sanitary grounds — they are a horror and a shame to the name of Italy." [1]

Societies for mutual aid and other purposes are relatively far less numerous and strong than those of Argentina. But if the comparison be omitted they must still be called numerous! Many once dominant have become defunct, and many are weak. Petty personalities and the regionalist spirit have split them and kept them in contention.[2]

[1] *Il volere d'Italia*, p. 68. Pp. 796–810 of *Il Brasile e gli italiani* list the subsidized schools. See also Bonardelli, pp. 114–116; Umiltà, p. 52; Franzoia, pp. 42–46; Petrocchi, in *Boll. Emig.*, 1914, pp. 53 f.

[2] *Il Brasile e gli italiani*, pp. 811–839; Napoli and Belli, pp. 101–117; Bonardelli, p. 124; Venerosi Pesciolini, p. 213; Bertarelli, pp. 80 f.; Umiltà, p. 51. On some interesting women's organizations, see Baroncelli-Grosson, pp. 269–281.

If the Italians had cohesion they might count politically. Except in the colonies, where many have yielded up their native citizenship, naturalization has been uncommon. When in 1889 aliens were given a term in which to demand to be allowed to retain their citizenship, the Italians in São Paulo flocked to make their claims. They have shown no interest in the question of change of allegiance, and their names rarely appear in the official reports on naturalization.[1] It must be remembered, however, that Brazilian politics have been less of parties and issues than of personalities. Some inclination toward socialism they have shown, even enough, it is claimed, to constitute an important influence in the state. To them, in fact, the transition has been ascribed, in the cities of São Paulo, from an era of vague discussion about the new doctrine to the formation of a workmen's party.[2]

Touching Italy, too, the collective spirit of the Italians has been weak. The purse opens to an appeal to help the flood sufferers of the Po, the victims of the eruptions of Vesuvius, of the cholera in Naples, of the earthquakes in Calabria, Sicily, the Abruzzi; the heart is stirred to commemorate, upon their deaths, Victor Emmanuel II, Garibaldi, Humbert, or it cheers to the celebration of the Twentieth of September or the anniversary of Garibaldi's birth; but when these occasions are past, apathy reigns again. Race pride cannot be counted on to perpetuate Italian influence in Brazil, for it is not even maintained. Fresh arrivals of immigrants are few, and the children acknowledge a new country.

But if the ideal influence of modern Italy is not kept alive in Brazil, the attributes we call Italian are fairly tenacious. In the southern colonies and the many embryonic social communities of the southern states, the Italian tongue, and much even of the Italian dress, will endure long after patriotic sentiment has cooled. In the metropolis, it is true, speech and dress retreat before the assaults of custom and fashion, but, even there, pressure cannot obliterate essential traits, and what seeks to change is itself

[1] *E.g.*, São Paulo, Secretaria da Justiça e da Segurançe Publica, *Relatorio*, 1913 (São Paulo, 1914), pp. 166–171.

[2] *Il Brasile e gli italiani*, pp. 773–778, 843; Napoli and Belli, pp. 31 f.; Umiltà, pp. 51, 54.

changed. Italian words find their way into Portuguese, and Portuguese into Italian, and these are the symbols of mutations too numerous or too subtle to count and discern.

Brazil cannot lose her Italian strain. It is too sturdily rooted. For every Italian who goes back to Italy, some arrive and many are born. The birth rate, here as in Argentina, is high, whether one inquires in the colonies, or in the fazendas; and every child past toddling earns more than its current cost.[1] In São Paulo, the most progressive state in Brazil, the Italian strain now amounts to one-third at least of the population. In the three states to the south it is perhaps a tenth. In Brazil as a whole, it may be seven per cent. But in the civilization of the country the Italians, like the other foreigners, count for much more than their fraction of a population of twenty million, in which Indians, negroes, and various mixed stocks are included.

For the energy, application, and economy in living which these immigrants have shown, they have generally been welcomed by the Paulist aristocracy and the Portuguese stock. Of personal disprizal of the humbler types there has been a good deal, but never a feeling that the immigration was not in itself a boon, conferring great advantages upon the country.[2] Once the fear obtained in some quarters that the Italians might become overpowerful in the state, and it prompted the endeavor to set off against them colonists of other nationalities. But the fear has long since subsided and in its place there is unmistakable regret that the Italian stream has slackened. There is even the thought that resort to Asiatic laborers might be necessary to maintain the great activity of the fazendas.

[1] There are no useful statistics, but innumerable comments. I submit one only: " In the Italian colony, however [Curityba], I observed that the families were larger, with a closer union among them than in the others." Reyes, p. 146. He tells of one man who, having immigrated thirty years previously, had had ten children of whom all were married and all had in turn had children.

[2] There is little indication that in São Paulo the Italians are an admitted social burden of any consequence. Few are in the asylums for the insane, or the orphanages, and in 1913 only two were among the offenders sent to the correctional colony. *Annuario estatistico*, 1912, pp. 264, 269; Secretaria da Justiça, etc., pp. 181–183.

CHAPTER XVII

UNITED STATES.[1] 1. COMING OF THE ITALIANS. SOME SPECIALIZED TYPES

THROUGHOUT the nineteenth century, the immigration of Italians into South America exceeded that into North America. In the twentieth, although the current has poured much more copiously into the northern continent than into the southern, the difference has not yet been made up. Any attempt to find in the history of the Italians in Argentina and Brazil a clew to their fortunes in the United States is bound to fail, partly because the Italians who came were mainly of a different sort and partly because their destination was a broadly different country. It needs a knowledge of the Italian experience in the United States to complete an understanding of the work and fortunes of the emigrants from modern Italy.

That part which the Italians played in Argentina during the second half of the nineteenth century is one which in the United States fell to immigrants who preceded the Italians and to natives of the seaboard. With opening up the country, geographically speaking, they had little to do. The early westward movement was accomplished by Easterners who, to the number of half a million, entered western New York and Virginia, Tennessee and Kentucky, between the American Revolution and the year 1800. A score of years later Americans had settled the Ohio Valley; by 1840, the cotton states of the Southwest, and Illinois and Indiana; by 1860, the eastern portion generally of the Mississippi Valley. The tumultuous settlement of California in the years of gold discovery was followed by the gradual development of the entire Pacific coast, coincident, in great part, with the peopling of the western portion of the Mississippi Valley.

This swift course of migration and settlement was hastened, if it was not indeed made possible, by two momentous forces. One

---

[1] In these chapters I have incidentally referred to the Italians in Canada. In 1901, 10,834 were enumerated there, and in the fiscal years 1901–16, according to Canadian statistics, 119,346 came.

is the improvement in transportation. The twenty-five years in the course of which the steamboat was proved practicable, the Erie Canal opened, and the Baltimore and Ohio Railroad begun, constitute an epoch. Rapidly thereafter the mileage of railways was redoubled, pushed into the West even faster than settlers would go. In the first ten or twenty years of the century, pressed on by political and military contingencies, the factory had crowded out the domestic system; but the incessantly ripening chances of securing cheap land in the West tended, by abstracting the population, to limit the expansion of manufactures. This tendency was itself, however, partly held in check by the second momentous force of the period. The immigration of European settlers, never, since colonial days, wholly arrested, but fluctuating with the years and fed by shifting currents, supplied the places of many Americans who moved West. At times, as in the decade 1810–20, the population of some important eastern cities and states was hardly more than maintained; but as the stream of immigrants became heavier the places of those who went West were more than filled.

Between 1840 and 1890 (while Italians were going to South America) fifteen million immigrants entered the United States. They were mainly English, Scotch, Irish, Welsh, Swedes, Norwegians, Danes, and Germans. By predilection they established themselves in the cities and states of the seaboard; for then, as now, the immigration was of persons whose means were slender and who sought an easy adaptation to the country. A courageous minority, Swedes and Norwegians largely, made pioneer settlements in the agricultural West and Northwest, displaying much of that independence of character that had marked the Easterners who went West. Only in the most indirect way—the contrast with Brazil is emphatic — could it be shown that the collapse of slavery had anything to do with the coming of the foreigners.

Yet even the movement of these immigrants into the West depended first of all upon the railway building of the country. In a few years after the Civil War the length of the rail course doubled, touching 52,000 miles in 1870; after a great boom it was 93,000 in 1880, and 166,000 in 1890. Almost wholly this great saddling of the continent, an indispensable means to the rearing of a great nation, was the performance, as to common labor and largely even as to skilled, of the incoming foreigners. Digging and constructing, in the opening country, they received something at least of that harsh contact with a virgin natural environment which in earlier years had conferred upon the frontier settlers some of their most valuable traits. The first results of the extension of the railways were quick to appear. To the riches of cotton and tobacco were added the astounding harvests of wheat and corn.

In the early years of the century the men who created the country's wealth were, characteristically, self-dependent owners of their farms and shops. Such they could be because the acquisition of a farm on the public lands was a universal alternative to employment by others. Of the arriving immigrants, however, most found that they could make their start with the greatest security not by independent ventures but by entrance into a hired class. The creation of an opportunity for them was the outstanding accomplishment of the second half of the century. In the first half, manufactures had unfolded slowly but had found an expanding market in the opening West, and after the Civil War received a tremendous impetus. Coincidently, mining developed. No longer was agriculture the country's one great industry. By 1880, 30 per cent of the entire population were of foreign birth or were the children of foreign parents. The sixfold increase in the capital invested in manufactures between the outbreak of the Civil War and the year 1890, a period in which the population of the country doubled, was largely made possible by the inpouring immigrants. Now social classes could be discerned. They were the fruit of the modes of employment that modern industrial systems impose and were the surest sign that a primitive phase of the history of the United States had come to an end, bringing a modern state. Rich as are still the untouched resources of the country, the land frontier — which as late as 1860 was the Mississippi Valley — could not be said to exist after 1890. Henceforth, to do well by himself, a man must meet the tests laid down, not by Nature, but by his fellows.

The days of turnpike and stagecoach were only a memory when the Italians began to come. In all the time before 1850, their immigration had none of the marks of a mass movement. Between 1820 and 1850 less than 4500 were counted and a third of these came by way of unexplained exception (or statistical error) in one year, 1833. When the census first distinguished nationalities, in 1850, 3645 were in the country. To these in 1850–60, 8940 were added by further immigration — the merest ripple compared with the mighty wave then sweeping in from western Europe — and in 1860 those still alive and in the country numbered 10,518. In 1861–70, 12,206 disembarked in our ports; in 1870, 17,157 were living here. In 1871–80, 55,759 came and in 1880, 44,230 were still in the United States.

Before 1860 the immigration appears to have been of persons who desired permanent settlement. That could be readily explained, without going further, by the difficulties of transportation. Chiefly the arrivals were North Italians, and they included, besides traders, many Lucchese vendors of plaster statuary and street musicians with monkeys — fantastic vanguard of the brawny army to follow. Because they were few, they escaped the attention, certainly the ire, of the anti-immigrant agitators of the time. In the miscellany of the Italians were a slight but precious group of political refugees, and it is a fact still enshrined in the bosoms of Italians that chief of these was the ubiquitous Garibaldi who lived on Staten Island while he made candles in a shop on Bleecker Street.[1] Some sprinkling of Italians there had been in the cities of the eastern seaboard since early colonial days. Although a few individuals came to the western coast as early as 1830, larger numbers were drawn by the gold fever, to their very mediocre profit.[2]

---

[1] The experiences of one refugee are described in the anonymous "Letters of an Italian Exile," *Southern Literary Messenger*, December, 1842, pp. 741–748.

[2] Some recollections of the Italians of the early fifties are in C. Dondero, "L'Italia agli Stati Uniti ed in California," *L'Italia Coloniale*, June, 1901, pp. 9–22. C. Gardini relates a romantic legend — with doubtless a basis in fact — of how in 1858, 300 Italian miners gaily went nine miles, with gifts, to greet the first Italian woman who came to California. *Gli Stati Uniti* (2 vols., Bologna, 1887), ii, p. 224.

Between 1860 and 1880, as the fresh arrivals increased, the immigration assumed a much more definite character. Where before there had been individuals there were now types and classes. From small beginnings the contingent from South Italy had swelled to substantial proportions. After 1870, for the first time, it became evident that, following a somewhat indeterminate stay, many repacked their chattels and went home again. No previous immigrants into this land of promise had done that!

The New York colony was passing through a curious phase. To the Genoese merchants who had come in earlier years were added, after 1860, Palermitan merchants who dealt in the citrous fruits and oil. But still other immigrants, of a startling sort, had perched and nestled in the section called Five Points. Not so much the novelty of the type as the number and persistence of those who embodied it made it conspicuous even in the cosmopolis. In large tenement houses these everlasting organ grinders and sellers of statuettes dwelt — how, is authoritatively described by that rare spirit in American philanthropy, Charles Loring Brace:

In the same room I would find monkeys, children, men and women, with organs and plaster-casts, all huddled together; but the women contriving still, in the crowded rooms, to roll their dirty macaroni, and all talking excitedly; a bedlam of sounds, and a combination of odors from garlic, monkeys, and dirty human persons. They were, without exception, the dirtiest population I had met with. The children I saw every day on the streets, following organs, blackening boots, selling flowers, sweeping walks, or carrying ponderous harps for old ruffians. [They did not, he adds, go to school and rarely went to church, and many were indentured to masters.] The lad would frequently be sent forth by his *padrone* late at night, to excite the compassion of our citizens, and play the harp. I used to meet these boys sometimes on winter nights half-frozen and stiff with cold.[1]

About 1870 there was a considerable diversity of types in the United States. They were largely North Italians, it would seem, and were perhaps more evenly scattered over the country than their people were ever again to be. Some were grocers, or keep-

---

[1] C. L. Brace, *The Dangerous Classes of New York* (3d ed., New York, 1880), pp. 194 f. The first edition was in 1872. In 1855 Brace helped to establish a remarkable school among these Italians; he relates its vicissitudes before 1867. Florenzano (pp. 154 f.) gives the text of an agreement made in 1866 between a Viggiano father and an exploiter who took his boy to New York; see also, on the situation of such boys in New York, pp. 161–164. Cf. Carpi, ii, p. 121.

ers of barrooms and restaurants — mainly Ligurians who had settled in New York. Some were in market gardening, especially about New Orleans, or in other branches of agriculture. Many were successful stonecutters; others were masons. In the South and West, fishermen had established themselves. In many cities were waiters, street musicians, and sellers of casts. There were sundry important groups of Sicilians (they had a settlement in Alabama, for instance) and Neapolitans were numerous. Though many disappointed miners had departed from California, other sorts of workers had stayed there.[1] Generally, however, in the western states where " the inhabitants live armed to the teeth to fight Indians and wild beasts," as a contemporary wrote,[2] Italians were few.

A decade later the New York colony numbered 12,223 — including the children, possibly 20,000. So it was materially larger than before, though otherwise not greatly changed. In one of the few pictures we have of the time, Charlotte Adams noted " the child musicians and the wandering minstrels . . . who pass their summers playing on steamboats and at watering places," the adult organ grinders, and the makers of macaroni, of art things, confectionery, artificial flowers. The Genoese girls studied needlework at night schools. The North Italians repudiated kinship with the Neapolitans and Calabrians. Italian workmen of the unskilled sort were " everywhere," but that is Miss Adams' only pronouncement touching a group that was every day becoming more prominent. One sentence was prophetic: " That the Italians are an idle and thriftless people is a superstition that time will remove from the American mind." [3]

Adolfo Rossi, who came to the United States in this period, was an adventurous youth, with keen powers of observation and a capacity for vivid, even poignant, narrative. The South Italians he found to be the dominant type. Country folk they had been in

---

[1] Carpi, ii, pp. 131, 225–267. Carpi followed a consul's lead in estimating at 55,000 a population that the census presently figured at 17,157. Even though it doubtless included American-born children, the estimate was much too high.

[2] Florenzano, p. 311.

[3] C. Adams, "Italian Life in New York," *Harper's Monthly*, April, 1881, pp. 676–684.

Italy but now they inhabited the dirtiest part of New York City, dwelling often more than one family to a room. " Men, women, dogs, cats, and monkeys eat and sleep together in the same hole without air and without light." They buy stale beer at two cents a pint from a rascally Italian in a basement, and they break into endless brawls. During the summer they work on the railroads and in the fields; " in the winter they return to fill the streets of New York, where the boys are bootblacks and the men either are employed at the most repulsive tasks, scorned by workmen of other nationalities — carrying offal to the ships and dumping it in the sea, cleaning the sewers *et similia* — or they go about with sacks on their shoulders rummaging the garbage cans, gleaning paper, rags, bones, broken glass." The Five Points are the center of that species of slavery exercised by Italian bosses or *padroni*. These fellows know English, hire workmen in herds (being paid by the employers), charge them enormous commissions, having already advanced to many their passage money for the journey from Italy, sell them the necessaries at high prices, and deduct heavy commissions from the savings which they transmit to Italy. " And while the workmen fag from morning to evening, the bosses smoke tranquilly and superintend them with rifles at their sides and revolvers at their belts. They seem — and are — real brigands." Whoever tells these natives of Avellino, of the Abruzzi, of Basilicata, that they are being cheated, loses his words. " *Signorino*," they reply, " we are ignorant and do not know English. Our boss brought us here, knows where to find work, makes contracts with the companies. What should we do without him ? " The Camorra flourishes as in the worst Bourbon times and " the Italian, illiterate, carrying the knife, defrauded and fraudulent, is more despised than the Irish and the Chinese." Rossi made a journey across the continent with a squad of Italians, two-thirds of them from the South, who were engaged in New York by the Denver and South Park Railway. To them fell the gang tasks while the Irish and the Americans wielded authority.[1]

[1] A. Rossi, *Un italiano in America* (3d ed., Treviso, 1907). My citations are drawn more especially from pp. 65–71, 80, 217 ff., 301. Comparison with Jacob

By 1880 the formative years of Italian immigration may be said to have been completed. Then its main characteristics were apparent. It was largely from South Italy, was increasingly disposed after a time to return to Europe, had taken up a certain range of vocations in the United States, and had developed the institution of the padrone, unknown previously among immigrant peoples. In later years no new elements appear, but the old assume many forms, of deep significance. If some of the newer immigrants came while yet the country had a frontier, it retreated westward before they could reach it. A heavy immigration after 1880 left a population of 182,580 in 1890. Henceforth, those who came were to find a full-grown nation, with all good lands preëmpted.

In 1900 the Italians were a population of 484,027, or nearly three times their number of ten years before. This increase is impressive, not only because it was exceptional, but because it took place during a period disturbed by industrial collapse. It is partly explained by the fact that in South Italy the decade had been one of intensified hardship and of desperate desire to escape. But why should the South Italians come to the United States ? Perhaps the knowledge prevailed that South America was the hunting ground of the North Italians; more likely, it seemed most natural to follow in the footsteps of those South Italians who had done well in the United States. Whatever the reason, the influx was heavy.

In 1900–10, years of prodigious industrial expansion in the United States, 2,104,309 Italians arrived. So many, however, had gone home again that the enumeration of 1910 found only 1,343,125. But these were nearly three times the number present a decade earlier. Having been less than 5 per cent of the foreign population, they had become 10. Together with their American-born children they now numbered 2,098,360. Their stock had increased faster since 1900 than that of any other large group, except the Russians. Among the foreign-born Italians two in three were men, a proportion not nearly approached by any other

Riis' picture in *How the Other Half Lives* (New York, 1890), chs. v–vii, suggests that no advance had taken place in ten years either in occupation or mode of living.

important group in the country, and reflecting better than any other circumstance the fact that they had come to earn.[1]

After the initial stage of settlement of any immigrant nationality at its chosen destinations, some scattering, however gradual, invariably ensues. Thus one expects subsequent censuses to show less geographical concentration. As the Italian immigration, however, increased in volume and the predominance of the Southern element became greater, its concentration became actually more marked. In 1850 just half the Italians were within the area included in the census of 1790, but in 1900 three-quarters were.[2] And in 1910 they were distributed as follows, in the several groups of states:

New England	13.2%	East South Central	0.7%
Middle Atlantic	58.6	West South Central	3.0
East North Central	10.8	Mountain	2.4
West North Central	2.6	Pacific	6.0
South Atlantic	2.6		

It is a strange result.[3] In the state of New York were about as many Italians as the whole country had contained ten years earlier. Two out of five of all the newcomers, in some recent years, have gone thither. Of those in the state in 1910, nearly two-thirds dwelt in its metropolis, 340,770 — such a number as would make one of the largest cities in Italy; and if their children were added, the colony would exceed in population every Italian city, except possibly Naples. No two cities of Basilicata to-

[1] The statistical data for these observations, and those that follow, are available in *Thirteenth Census — Abstract of the Census* (Washington, 1913).

[2] The percentages are 49.6 and 74.9. In the New England states, in 1850, were 7.2 of all the Italians, in 1900, 12.7. In the Middle States the percentages were 28.2 and 60.3; and in the Southern, 14.2 and 2.0. Bureau of the Census, *A Century of Population Growth, 1790–1900* (Washington, 1909), p. 131.

[3] In the states where the Italians chiefly went, they numbered in 1910: —

New York	472,201	Michigan	16,861	Oregon	5,538
Pennsylvania	196,122	Colorado	14,375	Vermont	4,594
New Jersey	115,446	Washington	13,121	Florida	4,538
Massachusetts	85,056	Missouri	12,984	Nebraska	3,799
Illinois	72,163	Minnesota	9,669	Kansas	3,520
California	63,615	Wisconsin	9,273	Maine	3,468
Connecticut	56,954	Texas	7,190	Utah	3,117
Ohio	41,620	Maryland	6,969	Delaware	2,893
Rhode Island	27,287	Indiana	6,911	District of Columbia	2,761
Louisiana	20,233	Montana	6,592	Alabama	2,696
West Virginia	17,292	Iowa	5,846	Oklahoma	2,564

gether, to make but one further illustration, contain so many natives of that province as does this American city. And in New York no foreign people, save only the Russians, are so strongly represented.

In New Orleans, in 1910, the Italians exceeded all other foreigners. But in no other large city except New York were they either first or second in rank among the immigrants. Philadelphia and Chicago each had about 45,000, Boston had 31,000 — subsequently (by the Massachusetts census of 1915) 43,000. Newark in 1910 had 20,000, San Francisco 17,000. The other large centers were, in order, Pittsburgh, Jersey City, Buffalo, Cleveland, New Orleans, St. Louis, Detroit, Baltimore. About four-fifths of all the Italians were classed by the census as urban, twice as high a proportion as that for the country's population as a whole.

The emigration of Italians into the countries of Europe has for the most part been specialized according to the understood requirements of those countries. That into Brazil and Argentina has aimed either to fulfill a need or to take advantage of unexploited resources and opportunities. What likelihood has there been that the great outpouring from South Italy would find itself suited to the conditions of the United States? By what occupations have the immigrants tried to earn a living? And what has been their accomplishment?

That some notion of fitness to prosper in the future articulately or inarticulately precedes the decision to emigrate, might be inferred from the action of that "professional proletariat" which so abounds in Italy. Because of the language barrier and the specialized nature of their training, such persons can ordinarily expect to serve only their fellow countrymen. Hence they have been few, relatively far fewer than among immigrants from English-speaking countries or from those nearer to the United States in institutions and ways.

To this rule there has been one very notable exception. With the musicians, training, where it exists, is of advantage, and language does not matter since their art is universal. Training may indeed be absent; and if there is only an inborn love of music and the impulse to play, then the *organetto* and the tambourine, the resonant voice and the rhythmic legs, contribute all that is needful. Gains do not depend upon length of residence in America; a too facile assimilation to established ways may even make profit less easy. So it happens that musicians have been plentiful among these immigrants, constituting about half of all Italian professional persons in the United States. With the lapse of time, they have undergone some changes. In city and suburb the hurdy-gurdy has displaced the harp, violin, and old-time hand organ. The street types as such are less than they once were, and the band players in the great cities more. But all together, humble types, high, and highest, they contend for the primacy in numbers among foreign musicians.

Less favorably circumstanced, the physicians, lawyers, teachers, actors, priests, and their kin have had to contemplate taking one of two courses. Either they must settle in some " Little Italy " or an isolated cluster of Italians anywhere, or they must sink into unskilled work. Let such persons avoid this country, an Italian consul-general at New York recommended a quarter century ago. " Hardly have they landed when they discover that America is not for them. Wanting knowledge of the language, and every other resource, they come to the consulate to ask succor in repatriation. How many think themselves lucky if they can find employment as waiters on board a vessel bound for Italy!"[1] A colony must have attained a certain size and stability before it can maintain a priest. Teachers may find posts in parochial schools. Doctors, when they have duly passed examinations or had their diplomas validated, can still only secure a patronage among their compatriots. On the other hand, where the demand is meager, the supply may also be meager. Among a thousand Italians in Richmond in 1909 there was said to be not one professional person.[2] And in 1882, when the first Italian daily paper

---

[1] G. P. Riva in *Emig. e Col.*, 1893, p. 438. Cf., on the same period, G. Conte, *Dieci anni in America* (Palermo, 1903), pp. 58–61.

[2] L. Villari, " Gli italiani negli stati di Virginia, Carolina del Nord e Carolina del Sud," *Boll. Emig.*, 1909, No. 8, p. 58.

was started, " not only," says Rossi, its first news-gatherer, " were
there in New York no Italian reporters by vocation, but it was
extremely hard even to find an Italian who could write his own
tongue with accuracy." [1] The consuls have not ceased to discourage professional immigration. In the most prosperous epoch
of the Italian coming, the Labor Information Office, with its seat
in New York, said of teachers, under-officials, accountants, and
others in liberal professions: " All of them meet bitter disillusionment and are often forced to take up humble and arduous occupations, not always well paid." [2] Despite many fluctuations a
persistent decrease in the professional element has taken place.
In the immigration of 1910 it had relatively only one-fifteenth the
importance it had had in 1875.

A vastly broader place has been occupied by those who are conveniently styled skilled workmen and by certain types that have
successfully defied our statisticians' capacity in classification and
been dubbed " miscellaneous." These together have not necessarily either more intelligence and skill or less than the professional immigrants; but they satisfy different wants: they provide
generally the material things of life and the physical services, and
if they touch aesthetic or liberal interests at all it is incidentally.

The proportion of skilled workmen — leaving aside for the
moment the miscellaneous group — has risen appreciably in the
last thirty or forty years, and recently has been about an eighth of
all.[3] The percentage is lower than that of the immigrants from
western Europe — the Germans, Irish, English, Scotch, Scandinavians, French — but is much higher than that of the Croatians
and Slavonians, the Slovaks, Lithuanians, Magyars, and Balkan
peoples. One recalls that North Italian skilled emigrants have
played some part in the countries from which these eastern immi-

---

[1] Rossi, p. 179.

[2] Note in *Boll. Emig.*, 1907, No. 2, p. 116. Cf. *Boll. Emig.*, almost at random,
e.g., 1903, No. 4, p. 47; No. 5, p. 45; No. 11, p. 12; also G. Preziosi, *Gl' italiani
negli Stati Uniti del Nord* (Milan, 1909), p. 40.

[3] By quinquennia, beginning with 1876–80 and ending with 1906–10, the percentages were 7, 9, 6, 8, 14, 13, 11. Since no figures are to be had for 1896, I have
made the fifth period cover four years only.

grants come. Yet our Italians are of the South, where skill is less than in the North; hence the proportion of skilled among them approaches more nearly the low ratios of the eastern peoples of Europe than of the western, and it has actually, in most years, been less than the proportion for all immigrant nationalities together.

What is peculiar in the Italian contingent can be brought out by some simple comparisons. In 1907, for example (a year when the immigration from all countries was very heavy, and when that from Italy was one-fourth of the total, and when Italian skilled workers were a fifth of all skilled immigrants), Italian plumbers were one in 150 arriving plumbers, locksmiths one in 74 of their kind, milliners one in 48, painters and glaziers one in 16, clerks and accountants one in 23, plasterers one in 26, saddlers one in 18, machinists one in 38, tailors one in 8. Extremely few likewise were the butchers, bookbinders, iron and steel and other metal workers, hat makers, woodworkers, and wheelwrights. And generally these immigrants originated in North Italy.[1] In a different group of occupations, the Italians have been much more numerous. Of blacksmiths, bakers, millers, in some years miners, their representation has been near the average for all peoples. It fell but little below such an average in 1907 in the case of cabinetmakers, carpenters, dressmakers, gardeners, and metal workers (other than in iron and steel), but in some years has exceeded the average.

The peculiarities of representation are in no sense fortuitous. In one or two instances, the grounds are wanting for such heavy emigration as other countries show. Tailors and locksmiths seem few chiefly because in the Russian Jewish exodus they abound — the consequence of centuries of trade specialization. In some occupations language creates a difficulty. Others have in Italy had no material basis for growth; hence, iron and steel workers, for example, come rather from Germany and England. Since bakers and carpenters exercise trades as universal as they are

---

[1] The figures are compiled from statistics in the *Report of the Commissioner-General of Immigration for the Fiscal Year 1906–1907*, but the reports for other years are of similar tenor.

ancient, nothing in the Italian rate of their coming is characteristic. Miners are mainly from North Italy, where their history has been long.

Unique interest attaches to those trades in which the Italian representation is high. Here fall the stonecutters, mechanics, mariners, masons, barbers, seamstresses, and shoemakers. Commonly one-half or more of all arriving masons are Italian, and in some years a third to a half of all the stonecutters. In deforested Italy, with its rocky vertebrae of Alps and Apennines, stone and cement are used to an exceptional degree in building. It is the countries from which in general many skilled workmen come — Germany, Great Britain, Scandinavia — and not the eastern countries, that chiefly rival Italy in sending masons and stonecutters. Mariners have always been numerous — the Genoese maintain an old tradition. Were the Hebrew seamstresses excluded, the Italian portion, now commonly a fourth to a third of all, would rise substantially. The prominence of this type argues at once the Italian women's need of earning and their proficiency with an implement universally manipulated by women. The amazingly heavy representation of shoemakers reflects the persistence in South Italy of a traditional village craftsman, working by hand. In the United States, the *calzolaio* must change. Strangest of all, Italian barbers and hairdressers are actually one-half to two-thirds of all arrivals of such workmen! Indeed, these artists have long stood forth prominently in our immigration from Italy and over many years have increased in number. They derive largely from South Italy, where in truth men's beards grow heavy and where the narrow range of possible employments has made for concentration in the standard sorts.

Consider some other types. Italian fishermen are often half of those who come from all countries; for Italy is bordered by fish-abounding seas, supplying, in a country where meat is expensive, one of the most valued of foods. Draymen, teamsters, and their allies are often a third to a half of all who come; for Italy is a land of few railroads and fewer navigable streams. Did not England and Germany, and still more the Jewish populations of central Europe, send extraordinary numbers of merchants and dealers, those that flock from the simple communities of South Italy, the more numerous because of the small scale of their operations, would eminently stand forth. Many immigrants have been servants at home, but their general proportion in the whole shrivels because very great numbers have come from two or three other countries. In particular, there have been many farm servants. Farmers, finally, that is, persons who have had an independent position in agriculture and have not been mainly hired by others, have been few. From Germany, in the days of her great emigration, which was yet materially inferior to that from Italy in recent years, five to ten times as many farmers came annually as have come from Italy in the years of amplest immigration; and even several other western countries have sent more. In late years while immigration from these countries has been dwindling, their farmers have still exceeded or have nearly equalled those from Italy. For this strange situation the explanation is first of all that the innumerable Italian proprietors of farm land have also been laborers; and at one time it was true that our officials did not carefully distinguish farmers from farm laborers.

Passing by for the moment the more purely industrial types, let us scan more closely the careers of the rest. In part these people work for wages, in part they are made independent, each man a center unto himself, by the circumstances of their trade. Training and apprenticeship may be necessary for some, for others reliance is mainly on personal resources, even upon qualities that one is encouraged to call social.

The bootblacks, humblest of all, have not, save in rare instances, plied their trade in Italy. But they found it open to them here (or occupied mainly by negroes) and they brought to it a pride in neat work which is in some sense a national attribute. In goodly numbers they entered the trade very early, at the time in fact when the street musicians, with their bears and monkeys, and the rag pickers, were still the conspicuous types; and they were one in sixteen of all bootblacks counted five years after the Civil War had ended.[1] Twenty years later, in those quarters of

[1] *Ninth Census*, iii, p. 833; later censuses have ignored their vocation.

New York where the foreign population dwelt, 473 out of the 474 foreign bootblacks enumerated were Italians — and the native workers numbered 10![1] Subsequently, though no statistics exist, the frequent references to their kind in Italian consular reports fortify the opinion that in the cities they were exceedingly numerous.[2] Especially in early days they patrolled the streets, carrying their implements; but the evolution of their industry has brought to the fore the chair and stand, sometimes the shop, whose owner now and then is self-styled " professor " or " artist." In New Orleans, they appear to have outgrown their trade some years ago, being superseded by negroes.[3] In the great eastern cities, Greeks, Jews, and others have cut into their dominance. This is not surprising, for while men past middle life often are bootblacks, the majority are youths, who expect to turn to other things.

Of the barbers and hairdressers, few abandon their vocation here, while many for the first time enter it. In 1870 only the French had a higher proportion of barbers.[4] In 1890, when the Italian population was still small, the actual number of Italian barbers exceeded the total of British, Irish, Scandinavian, and French, and was nearly a third the number of all German barbers, although German workpeople in general were twelve times as many as Italian.[5] In 1900, the 12,289 Italian barbers were half

[1] Seventh Special Report of the United States Commission of Labor, *The Slums of Baltimore, Chicago, New York, and Philadelphia* (Washington, 1894), pp. 188 f.

[2] The following references touch different parts of this country and Canada. V. Manassero di Castigliole, *Emig. e Col.*, 1893, p. 451; G. Marazzi, *ibid.*, p. 478; A. Dall' Aste Brandolini, " L'immigrazione e le colonie italiane nella Pennsylvania," *Boll. Emig.*, 1902, No. 4, p. 6z; R. Michele, " L'immigrazione italiana in . . . Connecticut," *Boll. Emig.*, 1902, No. 5, p. 11; G. P. Baccelli, " Gl' italiani in . . . Albany," *Boll. Emig.*, 1902, No. 5, p. 16; Serra, "Gl' italiani in California ed in altri stati della costa del Pacifico," *Boll. Emig.*, 1902, No. 5, pp. 45, 51; E. Rossi, " Delle condizioni del Canada rispetto all' immigrazione italiana," *Boll. Emig.*, 1903, No. 4, p. 9; L. Villari, " L'emigrazione italiana nel distretto consolare di Filadelfia," *Boll. Emig.*, 1908, No. 16, p. 26.

[3] G. Saint-Martin, " Gli italiani nel distretto consolare di Nuova Orleans," *Boll. Emig.*, 1903, No. 1, p. 12.

[4] *Ninth Census, loc. cit.*

[5] *Eleventh Census*, ii, p. 485. Among the Irish, barbers were amazingly few — one in a thousand occupied males; among the Italians one in thirty-four.

as many as the Germans; they were one in twenty-five occupied males — a rate nine times as great as that for the entire country.[1] In New York today they may be nearly as numerous as all other barbers together. Before their numbers and their proficiency the negroes and Germans have in many centers lost command of the trade.[2]

Figaro must learn American styles of hair cutting and the use of American instruments. That is not difficult. The system by which in Italy customers often pay by contract is rare in this country, a less personal relationship being the rule. In the great cities the barber patronizes one of the numerous towel supply houses (often Italian) instead of washing his towels himself. Quick fingers and a sense of neatness and finish are dependable natural assets which he brings with him. American requirements and a bit of English, the fresh immigrant learns in an established shop. Presently his wage is $9-14 per week. What his next and final fortune will be depends on his skill and his proficiency in English. Innumerable are the one-chair or two-chair shops using a basement or narrow room, serving mainly Italian or other immigrants, and charging rates much lower than those of the established shops, whether union or non-union. In the more flourishing concerns six or eight competent men are employed; and the ablest of all can count on being welcomed in the great hotels.

Italian shoemakers and shoe repairers were found to be very numerous both in 1870 and 1890. In 1870 the Germans were relatively much more numerous, but in 1900, after the great South Italian influx, their proportion was only a third that of the Italians.[3] Makers of shoes though they had been in Italy, they became in this land of machine-made shoes chiefly repairers, invading the patronage of others. Many of the residents of our

---

[1] *Twelfth Census, Special Report on Occupations*, pp. ccii, 65. The *Thirteenth Census* unfortunately did not give occupational statistics by nationality.

[2] Cf. New York, *Report of the Commission on Immigration* (Albany, 1909), p. 134; J. Daniels, *In Freedom's Birthplace* (Boston, etc., 1914), p. 324; F. G. Warne, *The Immigrant Invasion* (New York, 1913,) p. 174.

[3] *Twelfth Census, Report on Occupations, loc. cit.* I shall not, in the remainder of this account, detail my references to the Ninth, Eleventh, and Twelfth censuses.

cities have beheld the German repair shop disappear — through the death of the cobbler or transformation by his children into a store — and the Italian, humbly beginning, take its place. More, apparently, than the barbers, the shoemakers have courted a general patronage, reaching out into the suburbs and into parts of cities where Italians are scarce, and managing their affairs with the barest knowledge of English. In one person or in one family bootblack and shoemaker may be united. Expensive machinery is sometimes used, electrically propelled. But the Italians who have successfully undertaken the general sale of boots and shoes are still few.

Traders and dealers, like barbers and cobblers, have not been wont to abandon their vocations after arrival. As early as 1870, dealers in groceries, wines, liquors, and other commodities, and hucksters, were one in nine of all occupied Italians. Then the Italian consul-general estimated, I suspect rather liberally, that in New York three-fifths of all street sellers of peaches and pears — or in the winter, of apples and chestnuts — were Genoese or Sicilian; and in the larger and stabler forms of trade, some considerable fortunes were said to be in the making.[1] Twenty years later there were over 10,000 dealers. As hucksters and pedlars, only the German and Russian Jews were more numerous. Many were wholesalers, and a goodly number, for the most part Sicilians, imported lemons and other fruits and wine. In 1892 the consul-general in New York reported to his government that Italians owned most of the fruit stands in the metropolis and ran them profitably; in Boston also were many. In the Far West, during the period of the gold excitement, the dealers had more success trading in the camps than their brethren had digging in the mines. Subsequently they rose to considerable importance in San Francisco and elsewhere in the coast states, selling wines and liquors, groceries, fruits, and vegetables — in the last two departments, apparently unrivalled. In New Orleans, long a center for trade with Sicily, the Sicilians had achieved a leading position in the sale of fruit, vegetables, and oysters. In part their specialty

[1] Carpi, ii, p. 231.

grew out of their prior employment, as seamen and longshoremen, in unloading fruit from Italian sailing vessels. In the face of the operations of the United Fruit Company, the Italian shipping was destined to decline, but the retail trade was to continue long in Italian hands. In Texas, Alabama, and Mississippi, in Colorado and the adjacent parts, and in the Central States, sellers of fruit and other commodities were reported to be numerous in the nineties.[1]

The new century has brought a still more extensive field of operations, with substantial outposts even in Canada, and has set the general characteristics of Italian trade into sharper relief. In 1900, retail dealers numbered 17,640, wholesale dealers 369, hucksters and pedlars 7209 — with the German and Russian Jews in relatively much the same position as ten years earlier. The tremendous increment of the immigrant population since 1900, all unmeasured statistically as to occupation, has certainly boosted the Italian participation in trade. For we must remember that many general laborers, miners, and others are tempted to enter " bisinisse," and that they can do so by learning fifty words of English and buying a fruit stand. Sometimes the wife manages the shop or stand while the husband continues at his work. In New York many men have begun with a pushcart, then got the privilege of a stand, then a concession to sell garden produce in connection with a grocery store, and finally have set up a shop of their own.[2] In small towns and at railroad stations many Italian fruit stands are now to be found. The Italians' love of their trade, bringing an eagerness to have fresh fruits and to display them in comely arrangements, has undoubtedly somewhat stimulated the fruit consumption of the American people. In recent years, the

[1] See the reports in *Emig. e Col.*, 1893, pp. 442, 449–453, 462, 464, 475–479. Note the prominence of dealers in the directory of Fratelli Metelli, *Guida Metelli della colonia italiana negli Stati Uniti per l'anno 1885* (New York, 1884), pp. 265–311. See also C. Ottolenghi, " La nuova fase dell' immigrazione del lavoro agli Stati Uniti," *Giornale degli Economisti*, April, 1899, p. 381; Saint-Martin, p. 4.

[2] H. B. Woolston, *A Study of the Population of Manhattanville* (New York, 1909), p. 94.

Greeks and Syrians — the latter already met as competitors in Brazil — have challenged the Italian dominance in the fruit trade, not merely in New York, but as far away as Galveston.

A common type in our foreign communities is the coal and wood or coal and ice dealer, observed half a century ago in San Francisco. In some places he has been the successor of the Jews, as these have succeeded the Irish. The business is simple enough: one rents an unused basement, constructs crudely in the rear a bin or bunk, then hangs out a sign or peddles small portions in the tenements.

In the specifically Italian districts are many shops providing a single class of wares, such as Italians are likely to seek. Nothing sells so well as food. A sufficiently modest shop is styled, in Italo-English, a "*grande grosseria italiana.*" Here a window displays voluminous round cheeses, or strings of sausages, or tinned eels; there are loaves of bread thirty inches from end to end, or great round loaves with holes in the center like gigantic doughnuts. Confetti or macaroni tempts one in another window. Dealers in alcoholic and soft drinks are many. Here, in combination, are a "*caffé e pasticceria,*" there a bank sells coal. Some shops become so diversified as to approach the " general merchandise " stores of our rural districts. Capitalizing the timidity which the Italian often shows about trusting many people with his affairs, a versatile fellow will be at once a barber, banker, undertaker, wholesale and retail dealer, perhaps also a real estate and employment agent — yet even such a grotesque association of activities can hardly be incomprehensible to American patrons of tourists' agencies abroad!

Powerful firms and individuals have arisen. New York, Chicago, and San Francisco have their Italian chambers of commerce, composed, to an extraordinary degree, of bankers, fruit and wine merchants, and importers of fruits, wines, oil, and raw silk. The heavy Italian importations into New York and into New Orleans are mainly in Italian hands. In passing, it may be noted that the California fruit trade has cut deeply into the trade in Italian fruits. Of the large firms many are outgrowths of firms previously successful in Italy, while others have sprung from small beginnings here.[1]

Other city types are prominent, little less so in the inland centers than on the seaboard (east, south, and west). Sometimes the restaurant keeper had exercised his vocation in Italy, but as often, I suspect, he has first sold only to customers who took their purchase home; so wine merchants come to sell for consumption on the premises. The many cooks, almost always North Italians, were conspicuous as early as half a century ago. Genoese, in the early days, and many others recently, have been waiters, finding a haven often in the largest hotels. It is not necessary that they should have learned their calling in Italy. Nimble hands they may count upon, also such courtesy and deference as centuries have wrought into their fiber — centuries of abounding state and religious ceremony, maintained in an old civilization. Before the influx of Italian and other white waiters, the negroes have lost their former prominence. Confectioners are many, from northern and central Italy, and bakers have been a leading South Italian type. Dressmakers and tailors have been innumerable.

Of Italian fishermen there has been a wide scattering. In Boston is an old colony which used to moor its gaudy craft along time-honored " T Wharf." At several points in Florida, notably at Tampa, there have been settlements, the men sometimes owning their ships, sometimes manning those of other persons; most are from Sicily, but many are from Tuscany and the Marches. An old colony — it can count fifty years — is at New Orleans. The fishermen of Galveston, who sell their fish under contract, have been chiefly from the isle of Elba. On the Pacific coast are several collectivities, one for instance in Oregon (Astoria), but all shrink in importance before that at San Francisco.

As early as 1870, the Italians were supplying much of San Francisco and part of the adjacent interior with fish. In the

---

[1] The chambers of commerce (subsidized by the Italian government) have issued various publications. On trade see a contribution by G. Rossati to the comprehensive volume *Gli italiani negli Stati Uniti* (New York, 1906), pp. 54-59; I have drawn freely upon the consular reports.

early eighties it was said that a majority of the resident Italians were fishermen or fish merchants. Generally they came from North Italy, but their successors have been largely Sicilians. About a third of all the emigrants from Augusta (province of Syracuse) have been fishermen. And they have gone chiefly to California and Alaska. Still others of the San Francisco colony have come from the Isola delle Femmine or from the Sicilian settlements in Tunisia. Mending their nets or returning with their catch, they have made a considerable part of San Francisco picturesque by their presence. Their industry was not abated after the earthquake. On the Sacramento River, not far from San Francisco, there is an Italian fishermen's town. Some 1250 a year, it is said, go to Alaska for the April–September season, during the rest of the year fishing from motor boats owned by themselves or by companies. For the Alaska campaign they are enrolled by half a dozen South Italian " bosses," who make a pretty pile in pay from the salmon companies, in commissions from the fishermen, and in their profit on the sustenance they provide. The fishermen make their catch with nets at the mouths of the streams on Kodiak Island, in Bristol Bay, and on the west coast of Alaska Peninsula, receiving for the season $100 in " run money " and $3\frac{1}{2}$ or 4 cents per head of fish caught, say $450 for five months.[1]

---

[1] Carpi, ii, pp. 132, 225, 237; *Guida Metelli*, p. 183; *Emig. e Col.*, 1893, pp. 462, 464, 478; Ottolenghi, p. 381; G. B. Cafiero, " Gli italiani nel distretto consolare di Nuova Orleans, III, Florida," *Boll. Emig.*, 1903, No. 1, p. 21; Fara Forni, " Gl' interessi italiani nel distretto consolare di Nuova Orleans," *Boll. Emig.*, 1905, No. 17, pp. 6, 16; G. Moroni, " L'emigrazione italiana in Florida," *Boll. Emig.*, 1913, No. 1, p. 73; Corbino, p. 24; F. Daneo, "I pescatori italiani nell' Alaska," *Boll. Emig.*, 1915, No. 4, pp. 39–44; H. A. Fisk, "The Fishermen of San Francisco Bay," in *Proceedings of the Thirty-second Annual Conference of Charities and Correction*, 1905, pp. 383–393; E. Patrizi, *Gl' italiani in California* (San Francisco, 1911), *passim*.

CHAPTER XVIII

UNITED STATES. II. THE WAGE-EARNING MAJORITY

In a modern society, it is upon the men engaged in the primary operations of production, rather than upon the retail traders, servant types, and others that the major risks of industry fall. This the Italians have understood. Holding aloof when enterprise has been slack, they have rushed forward in the intervals of growth and expansion when entrepreneurs have had a fever for organization, when capital has been freely offered and the normal increase of the country's population, from its own loins, has left unsated the desires of the industrial leaders for labor. Telltale evidence of their intention is the heavy dominance of males and of adults. The censuses have successively shown a proportion of occupied males in total males seldom equalled in the rates of other immigrants and commonly far in excess of them. Not less striking is the fact that, in the statistics of arriving Italians, the percentage of males has risen rapidly (as might be shown in a curve) with every pronounced spurt in immigration.[1] And at each resumption of the upswing the percentage of skilled workmen has increased, only to decrease again afterwards, as if to show their perception of the fact that only during a time of heightened demand for labor can foreign workmen, ignorant of the country, its language, and its ways, be absorbed into its industrial life. Whoever further studies the month-by-month fluctuations in Italian immigration must infer that many workmen — we call them " birds of passage " — have taken advantage of the fact that there are seasonal periods in industry.

The unspecialized farm and day laborers have given to Italian emigration an all but unique character in the world's history. The same individuals, had they lived two thousand years ago,

[1] The absolute numbers have moved independently for, in its growing period, Italian immigration has sometimes ignored the general tendencies of the country.

would not have been harnessed to tasks materially different from those they toil at today. Not only have they lacked all specialized training, but they have even reached adult years without an elementary inculcation of reading and writing — it is not an accident that printers are few in Italian emigration! They have worked out of doors, betaking themselves wherever a strong back and compelling arms were needed, and so far have tended to develop into muscular and healthy men. But the uncertainty of their employment, the long hours of their labor, their slender wage, and the slim purchases it allows, have held back and broken their development. To the rest of the world it has fallen to utilize them as they are.

During the last forty years, laborers have been a higher proportion of the Italian immigrants into the United States than of any other important immigrating people. In 1882, for example, when the immigration from western Europe was at its zenith and more persons reached our coasts than ever before, one-seventh of the German immigrants (speaking roughly) were laborers, and one-third of the Irish, but of the Italians one-half. Rarely less than a third, usually a half to two-thirds, of a year's Italian immigrants have been general laborers. The percentage in five-year periods since 1876 falls generally between 45 and 60.

In some respects (but only in some) a more truthful showing of the relative place of the laborers is given in the censuses. In 1870, one-seventh of all occupied Italians were general laborers, and only the Irish and the East Asiatics had a higher proportion. By 1890 the laborers had increased to 38,976 and were more than a third of all occupied Italians, the Irish, their leading rivals, having an unchanged rate of only a fourth; but unskilled railroad laborers were 10,280 more (at a very high rate again) quarrymen were 1687, coal miners 3889, other miners 4132, and in special fields many others had unskilled employment. By 1900, the last year for which census data can be had, the general laborers had become actually 93,864, again a third of all occupied Italians, making a rate now twice that of the Irish, nearly four times that of the Germans. Besides, unskilled railroad workmen were 17,485, quarrymen and miners were 25,915 and further thousands were in lesser fields, there too having a representation far above that usual in the immigrant stock. Do the laborers here seem fewer than in the annual immigration reports? The censuses reveal the conditions which several years have brought to existence. They are decennial cross views of a shifting and irregular current, rather than indices of an orderly progress — which does not exist. Swelling in the plenteous seasons and years, shrinking with the approach of the leaner times, the armies of general laborers come and go; and oftener than the case is with other classes, the same men appear twice, thrice or more times in a decade's immigration. The laborers, *par excellence*, are the true temporary immigrants.

To trace with any fullness, above all in a brief space, the multifarious industrial connections which the Italians have made in this country is quite impossible. We can deal with them only in the large, and can hope only to convey an impression of diversity and broad scope, and to emphasize what is typical. Let manufactures have our first attention.[1]

[1] What follows is based mainly on these works: United States, *Reports of the Immigration Commission* (41 vols., Washington, 1911), viii-xii, xiv, xv, xvii, xx; New York, *Report of the Commission on Immigration* (*cit.*); New Jersey, *Report of the Commission on Immigration*, Trenton, 1914; New York, *Preliminary Report of the Factory Investigating Commission* (3 vols., Albany, 1912), esp. i; and *Fourth Report* (5 vols., 1915), esp. ii; United States, Bureau of Labor, *Report on the Condition of Woman and Child Wage-Earners in the United States* (19 vols., Washington, 1910-11), esp. i, ii, iv; Connecticut, *Report of the Special Commission to Investigate the Conditions of Wage-earning Women and Minors in the State*, Hartford, 1913; United States, *Reports of the Industrial Commission* (19 vols., Washington, 1900-02), esp. xv; United States, *Report on Strike of Textile Workers in Lawrence, Massachusetts, in 1912*, Washington, 1912; M. H. Willett, *The Employment of Women in the Clothing Trade*, New York, 1902; J. E. Pope, *The Clothing Industry in New York*, Columbia (Mo.) 1905; M. van Kleeck, *Artificial Flower Makers*, New York, 1913; E. B. Butler, *Women and the Trades*, New York, 1909; A. M. MacLean, *Wage-Earning Women*, New York, 1910; Women's Educational and Industrial Union, *Industrial Home Work in Massachusetts*, Boston, 1915; S. H. Clark and E. Wyatt, *Making Both Ends Meet*, New York, 1911; L. C. Odencrantz, *Italian Women in Industry* [New York City], New York, 1919; Rossati, p. 56; M. M. de' Rossi, *Le donne ed i fanciulli italiani a Buffalo e ad Albion*, Rome, 1913. Among the many reports to the Italian government, the following have been the more useful: E. Rossi, *op. cit.*; G. Moroni, " Lo stato dell' Alabama," *Boll. Emig.*, 1913, No. 1, pp. 34-66; G. Moroni, " La Louisiana e l'immigrazione italiana," *Boll.*

The metal trades have attracted many Italians, but not into their primary operations. Unlike the Slavs they are rare in the rolling mills, whether because of their physical lightness, or as has sometimes been said, of a lack of nervous strength. But many have been employed outside the mills, in Birmingham, in Pittsburgh, and in the Maritime Provinces of Canada. Many have worked in the foundries, as for instance in Detroit. There and at Racine and Kenosha they have been occupied in the automobile factories; at Kenosha, in the iron-bed works also. In various centers they have made cutlery and tools, gas and electric fixtures. In the metal-working shops of Connecticut several years ago, the Italian women were nearly a tenth of all women employed. In all these trades dexterity and celerity count, but those who lack them have still some place.

As lumber and sawmill hands, Italians have been employed in Canada, in California and, especially, in Louisiana and the South generally. Many have worked in the paper and wood-pulp manufacture; others in the rubber factories of the East. In growing numbers they have entered the brick and tile works of New Jersey. In the Middle States, Sicilians and Calabrians have become prominent as employees in the glass manufacture, but not in glass blowing, for which they seem ill-adapted. Their coming, and that of the Greeks, have been concomitant with the declining importance of boy labor in the glass industry. " The predominance of these two races has been in part the result of chance, but much more largely the result of the better adaptation of these races to the work." [1] It is for their quickness and carefulness that they are wanted. In the cigar and tobacco industries in the region east of the Mississippi, the South Italians have been one of the leading foreign groups employed; in Tampa, Florida, several thousands have been engaged in the work. In the oil and chemical industries of New Jersey, Italians (and some others) have been displacing the German and Irish workers. In the Middle West

---

Emig., 1913, No. 5, pp. 31–53; G. E. di Palma-Castiglione, " Vari centri italiani negli stati di Indiana, Ohio, Michigan, Minnesota e Wisconsin," *Boll. Emig.*, 1915, Nos. 6 and 7, pp. 7–46 and 11–62, respectively.

[1] *Woman and Child Wage-Earners*, iii: *The Glass Industry*, p. 168.

and in Massachusetts (especially Brockton) South Italians, men and women, have been prominent among recent immigrants employed in the making of boots and shoes. Some of these, working in small groups in regular workshops, are taking the places of the disappearing old New England turn-shoe men, who did home work on hand-sewed turn shoes.

The Italians have played an important part in the textile industries, except the cotton manufacture. They are to be found in the cotton mills of fewer localities, and in smaller numbers, than any of several other immigrant groups. Why this has been is not easily said, particularly since mill owners in Germany have found them satisfactory.[1] In the silk manufacture, North and South Italians have been more numerous than any other recent immigrants. They have been employed in New Jersey much more than in Pennsylvania and mostly in the city of Paterson, the leading center in the country. In New Jersey, where in recent years they have been perhaps a sixth of all the operatives, more than half have been weavers, warpers, or twisters-in, which are the most highly skilled and best paid categories of labor; many work at silk dyeing. Frequently a whole family is employed. In a hundred families of North Italians, a Bureau of Labor investigation found, on the average, 250 workers; of South Italians 280. The latter did the less skilled, more poorly paid work. The North Italian families earned $933 per year, the South $829. Some Italians, it may be noted in passing, have been the owners of silk mills, presumably men who had been previously associated with the trade in Italy. Among the makers of woolens and worsteds, in New England, notably at Lawrence, some thousands of South Italians have had unskilled employment. The same may be said of the workers in the rope, twine and hemp mills of New England and New York.

---

[1] By way of explanation the Bureau of Labor ventures that "they are regarded with less favor than other races employed in the same pursuits. This disfavor may be attributed rather to a prejudice against their low standard of living at their homes than to any particular lack of efficiency in their work in the mill." They began to enter the mills especially after 1904, and more in Rhode Island than in Massachusetts, yet mostly in Waltham. *Woman and Child Wage-Earners*, i, pp. 116 f.

What the Italians have done in the clothing industry might serve for an important chapter in the history of labor in America. In point of number of employees, the making of men's clothing has in normal times been the seventh of our manufacturing industries, and, in the number of women engaged, it has come after the cotton industry. Almost entirely it has been carried on in some half dozen of the great cities, and by foreign operatives. Nearly a third of the women aged sixteen or over, when the Bureau of Labor studied the industry, were Italian, the rest being mainly Hebrews, Germans, and Poles. In New York and Philadelphia Italian women were respectively two-thirds and one-half. In point of number of men employed the Italians have come after the Jews only. It was about 1890 that the Italians first invaded this stronghold of the Jews, and they have since continuously rivalled them. Unlike Germans and Bohemians, they have rarely been machine workers, which may be due to their later arrival in the trade — in our labor history, such lines of cleavage, however created, have often tended to persist. The Bureau of Labor study found the Italian men to be earning $7–$10 per week, averaging in New York $8.30 — about three-quarters as much as Germans and Hebrews — while the women earned $5.42, the lowest of any class of workers.

As early as 1902, Miss Willett could write of the Italian woman that she had " secured a complete monopoly of part of the work, the felling and finishing of ready-made clothing."[1] After the machine work, or "operating," and the basting have been done, only plain sewing is necessary to fell the lining to the cloth of the garment. The materials can be taken into the tenement and the work performed there, at any hours, on all days of the week, and with or without the aid of helpers, who are often children. Of the home finishers, in New York at least, the Italian women have for many years been about seven in eight of all workers, earning $50–$125 a year. No wonder that a Rochester manufacturer could say of their kind, " They are as cheap as children and a little better."[2] Except for such experience as the women had had in

---

[1] Willett, p. 38.
[2] *Woman and Child Wage-Earners*, ii, p. 305.

their homes in Italy, they — and the men also — have entered
the trade unskilled; yet both have proved themselves industrious
and deft.   Besides men's clothing, many Italians have made
cloaks and children's apparel.

The South Italians, along with the Jews, constitute a large
part of the glove makers in the state of New York.   In the hosiery
and knit-goods manufacture many are occupied.   The New York
Factory Commission, in a comprehensive investigation, found the
Italians, mostly women, to be about a sixth of the employees in
the shirt trade, and a seventh of those in the button industry.   In
large numbers they have entered the curtain manufacture and in
smaller numbers the wholesale branches of the millinery trade.
Several years ago, the making of willow plumes was carried into
the Italian tenements, to the great cheapening of the product and
the collapse, within three years, of the fashion.   They made a
much more permanent entry into the artificial flower trade of
New York, " driving out," as employers and workers both admitted or charged, the other nationalities; for the fingers of Italian girls are delicate and nimble and the newcomers have not
scorned a low wage.   In this little trade, as so often elsewhere,
they have manifested a characteristic pride in craftsmanship.

In several states, Italians of both sexes work at candy making.
In New York, as the Factory Commission discovered, they are a
large part, perhaps three-eighths, of the workers.   Though the
occupation is mainly for girls and women, yet a third of the
workers are men and of these three-fifths were found to be Italians; the girls and women receiving generally $5-$7.50 per week,
the men $10-$14.   Numerous Italians, mainly men, have worked
in the paper-box factories.   In Massachusetts many home workers
have made celluloid goods.   The steam laundries of New York
city have employed German women first of all, but Italian next,
who are followed by Poles and lastly by Americans; Italians are
specialized in mangle work.   In those New York piano factories
which turn out an inferior grade of piano, the Italian workmen
have largely outstripped all other nationalities, even counting the
German and German-Americans as one group; the industry was

once a stronghold of the German mechanic. In the canneries of various parts of the country, for example in Pittsburgh, the region about Buffalo, and in California, a great deal of seasonal labor has been performed by Italian men, women, and children.

Of such breadth has been the work of the Italians in manufacturing and allied pursuits. Natural aptitudes have counted in it, trained skill only a little, and physical strength to but a moderate degree. Not much knowledge of the country's speech has been necessary. Chiefly the work has taken place in the East, where the principal factories have been located and most Italians have settled. New York State, the Connecticut Valley, and New Jersey — where the Italians are now the second immigrant group in point of numbers — have been preferred regions. If Italian women seem prominent in the recital, the reason is that they have been exceptionally eager for employment and yet have held aloof from domestic service and commercial pursuits.

In mining, as in manufacturing, the inflow of immigrants in the past half century has been accompanied by technical changes which make possible the utilization of large numbers of unskilled workers. Once every miner undercut the coal, drilled his own holes, fired his shots and, with his helper, loaded the coal upon the cars. Now a machine and a skilled shot firer can provide work for a number of unskilled men. It is a change that has brought an opportunity to the Italians.

When they first came they were skilled miners from the North of Italy, but gradually also farm laborers, both Northern and Southern, offered themselves, and in our own day have attained an important post in the industry. In 1870 there were 831 Italian miners of all sorts; in 1890, 3889 coal miners, 4132 other miners and 1687 quarrymen; in 1900, 25,915 miners and quarrymen; and the great increase, which cannot be shown statistically, was still to come. The miners of 1900 were one in twelve Italian workmen, a rate far exceeding that of the Irish and Germans, and, in general, of the foreign population. In bituminous coal mining alone, the broad survey of the Immigration Commission found them to be one-eighth of the entire working force, little less numerous than Slovaks and Poles.[1]

To Pennsylvania the Italians came early. For a long time, in the anthracite fields, they specialized in the stripping operations, shunning the underground work.[2] Gradually they assumed other tasks and also increased in number. By 1910, the anthracite counties — primarily Luzerne, Lackawanna, and Schuylkill — contained 28,650 persons born in Italy, most of whom lived upon miners' earnings.[3] In the southwestern counties — Allegheny, Westmoreland, Fayette, and Washington — the Italian miners of bituminous coal have been still more numerous. Beyond doubt, in this greatest coal-mining state of the Union, the Italians have constituted one of the chief groups upon which the operators have counted for the successors to the Irish, German, Welsh, and other miners who once dominated.

To the bituminous mines of other states they have gone in ever increasing numbers — to Virginia and West Virginia, Ohio, Indiana, Illinois, Alabama, Tennessee, Texas, Oklahoma, Kansas, New Mexico, and even (in large numbers) to British Columbia. To the Birmingham district they went in three successive cur-

---

[1] On the Italians in mining, see *Immigration Commission*, vi, vii, xvi; *Industrial Commission, loc. cit.;* P. Roberts, *The Anthracite Coal Communities*, New York, 1904; Warne, ch. viii; *Emig. e Col.* 1893, esp. pp. 436 f., 452, 454, 464, 478; F. J. Sheridan, *Italian, Slavic, and Hungarian Unskilled Immigrant Laborers in the United States, United States Bureau of Labor Bulletin*, No. 72 (Washington, 1907), pp. 403–486; L. Aldrovandi, " Note sulla emigrazione italiana in Pennsylvania," *Boll. Emig.,* 1911, No. 3, pp. 3–51; Moroni, in *Boll. Emig.,* 1913, No. 1, pp. 52, 73; *Idem,* " Il Texas e l'immigrazione italiana," *Boll. Emig.,* 1913, No. 5, p. 25; *Idem,* " L'emigrazione italiana nell' America del Nord," p. 55; *Idem,* "Il British Columbia," *Boll. Emig.,* 1915, No. 1, p. 74; *Idem,* "Le regioni delle Provincie Centrali del Canadà," *Boll. Emig.,* 1915, No. 2, pp. 43–71; F. Tiscar, " L'emigrazione italiana nel distretto della R. Agenzia Consolare di Scranton," *Boll. Emig.,* 1913, No. 13, pp. 25–42; A. Castigliano, " Origine, sviluppo, importanza ed avvenire delle colonie italiane del Nord Michigan e del Nord Minnesota," *Boll. Emig.,* 1913, No. 7, pp. 3–22; F. Daneo, " Condizioni delle colonie italiane a Stockton e nelle Contee di Sonora, Jackson ed Amador city," *Boll. Emig.,* 1915, No. 4, pp. 45–47; *idem,* " L'emigrazione italiana in California," *Boll. Emig.,* 1913, No. 14, pp. 55–57.

[2] They were held to be timid, unwilling to incur danger. *Industrial Commission,* xv, p. 419.

[3] Even allowing for subsequent additions to the Italians' numbers and for their children born in America, it is difficult to reach the figure of 87,000 proposed by Tiscar, p. 30.

rents, first Genoese and Emilians, then Lombards and Pied-montese, lastly Sicilians, especially from the province of Caltanis-setta. The North Texas community, at Thurber, is also of Sicilians. The Illinois coal counties contained, in 1910, 18,489 North and South Italians, one of the largest concentrations. According to the findings of the Immigration Commission, more than two-fifths of the Italians employed in mining bituminous coal had been in the country less than five years. We are dealing again with a group that comes and goes between Italy and the United States. Italians of the North, who have been two-thirds of all, have been stabler than those of the South.

In the metalliferous mines, the work of the Italians has been of almost equal consequence. In the early days of the Calumet exploitation, half a century ago, some Piedmontese and Tuscan miners were employed; a recent estimate, which I take to be somewhat exaggerated, places at 8000 the number of Italians in the copper region of northern Michigan.[1] Miners of copper and silver are, or have been, numerous in the Cobalt district of Ontario, in Montana, Utah, Arizona, New Mexico, Colorado, and in several counties of California. In all these regions, their numbers have fluctuated much, a circumstance not unfavorable in an industry whose workplaces are isolated and for whose product the demand varies broadly. In partial explanation of the decline of Italian miners in the Calumet district in the years before the war, it has been suggested that they have been unwilling to work amid the perils of the ever deepening mines.[2] Iron miners have long been established on the peninsula of Upper Michigan, in Marquette, Dickinson, and Gogebic counties. The Iron Mountain colony follows after Calumet in age and importance. In the Mesaba Range of Minnesota, thousands of Italians have had employ-ment. The Neapolitan and Calabrian open-pit miners of this district work for eight months and then hibernate in the cities.

These are the principal kinds of Italian miners and their dis-tribution. Two others may not be passed by. To South Caro-lina, Italians came to dig phosphate rock a quarter century ago, and to Florida somewhat later they came for the same purpose,

---

[1] Castigliano, p. 6.   [2] *Ibid.*, p. 7.

but in both states their numbers have fallen in recent years.   In the Middle and New England states, with an important center at Quincy, Italians in large numbers have entered the granite and other stone quarries.   It is a work for which they have shown predilection and which they have performed with consummate success.

The outstanding importance which the Italian skilled building-trades workmen appear to have in the statistics of disembarking aliens is somewhat diminished when they are regarded after arrival in the country.   The reason is only that, unlike the types we have so far considered, they exercise a calling in which men of the older stocks are numerous.   Rarely do they abandon it or change it for another.   At the least their skill is easily adapted to the circumstances of the country, and sometimes it is of a superior order, and is prized.   From Venetia and Tuscany, for example, workers in mosaics and stucco have brought a special training, a traditional aptitude of which Americans have been glad to avail themselves.   Still more does this hold of the marble and stone-cutters — only 72 in 1870, over 4000 in 1900, when their proportion among Italian workmen was thrice that among foreign workmen in general.   It is common to find them at work on the most exacting tasks, insuring the neatness of appearance, or the beauty, of the most ambitious public and private structures.

The carpenters and joiners, woodworkers, painters, plasterers, and some others have each been represented by fewer individuals, at the censuses, than the stonecutters, yet of all the workmen of of their sorts they have been no unimportant part.   Because of the fact that they engage in work as individuals, not under a foreman's eyes, and the fact that only a few are assembled on one undertaking, or work together for a limited time only, it is difficult to record their accomplishment.   A larger class than any of these are the brick and stone masons, 67 in 1870, 5582 in 1900 — no one can say how much they have since increased.   Twice as large a proportion of Italians have been masons as that of men in the general foreign population.   They are numerous not only in the cities, but in the open country, finding employment upon temporary and isolated enterprises.[1] A still larger group — but now we approach the realm of the unskilled — have been the hod-carriers. Here the Italians stand prominently beside the Irish. From their ranks men rise occasionally to be masons. Lowest in the scale of building workers are the excavators, reckoned quite unskilled men, and among the South Italians they are an innumerable throng. Of the character of their work it will be better to speak in another connection.

From early days one of the broadest fields of employment of the Italians has been the creation and maintenance of public works, including public buildings, and the construction of the plants of the privately owned public utilities. Since the forms of their work vary greatly, many skilled men are utilized, but the mass are men without skill. Sometimes, in the great cities, they are street cleaners, snow shovellers, or scavengers; in San Francisco, for example, the hundreds of Italian street sweepers were said, some years ago, to enjoy a virtual monopoly of their labor.[2] But chiefly their work has been in excavation, surfacing and grading streets, laying pipes for gas and water, digging sewers, and constructing harbor works, bridges, dams, canals, and subways (of their work upon the railways, more anon). In varying degrees, but extensively always, these are tasks on which unskilled men have worked in gangs, eager for employment, however low the wages.

Even in the last decade or so of the nineteenth century, before most Italians had come, their work in these departments had assumed astonishing breadth. In 1890, the Inspector of Public

[1] To the New York Commission on Immigration (*Report*, p. 134), union officials declared: " The Italian race is gradually getting control of our line of work in the outskirts and are working their way into the center of the city." Because references to the rôle of the building-trades workers in the Italian and in other reports are generally brief and scattered, as well as numerous, I have not attempted to prepare a list of authorities. Twenty-five years ago, to give but one example, the volume *Emig. e Col.* (1893) referred to the skilled workers on pp. (among others) 442, 448, 451 f., 455, 463, 478.

[2] G. Ricciardi, "Le condizioni del lavoro e l'emigrazione italiana in California," *Emig. e Col.*, 1909, iii^iii, p. 248. See also Serra, p. 51 and F. Prat, "Gli italiani negli Stati Uniti e specialmente nello Stato di New York," *Boll. Emig.*, 1902, No. 2, p. 24.

Works of New York stated, during a Congressional investigation, that 90 per cent of the employees on the public works of New York were Italians (some 8000); of the older workmen, only a few Irish-Americans, he said, were left. During the ten years previous, machinery had been coming into use for quarrying rocks in roadways, and steam shovels were taking the place of hand drills. " All reputable contractors use steam machinery today . . . but the Italian contractor finds it cheaper to use the men in the old-fashioned way." [1] At the same time Italians were claimed (with superfine precision!) to be doing " 99 per cent " of the street work of Chicago.[2] When natural gas was discovered in Indiana the labor of laying 250 miles of pipe for its conduction was performed by Italians.[3] In the early nineties, many were employed in constructing the granite dam across the Colorado River, near Austin, Texas, and others in widening the port of Galveston. In the states of the Far West, South Italians were numerous in street work, and many were employed on the grounds of the Chicago Exposition.[4] In Massachusetts, in these years, while the cities still hired English and Irish workmen directly, contractors were more and more making use of Italians, particularly when unskilled men were needed for work of an exceptional character; so it was, for example, with the construction of the Brockton and Beverly sewers, and of a reservoir at Northampton.[5] Before the century was out, on the two-years enterprise of enlarging the Erie Canal, 10,500 Italians were employed in a working force of 12,500.[6]

At the beginning of the new century, the Industrial Commission inquired of the mayors of Eastern cities what was the nationality of the men employed on waterworks, street cleaning, and related undertakings. From the replies it appeared that, even when citizenship was a condition of employment, Italians led or were

[1] House of Representatives, *Report of the Select Committee on Immigration and Naturalization* (Washington, 1891), p. 546; see in general, pp. 540–547.

[2] *Ibid.*, p. 623.

[3] O. C. McCulloch, discussion in *Proceedings of the* [16th] *National Conference of Charities and Correction* (Boston, 1888), p. 430.

[4] *Emig. e Col.*, 1893, pp. 450, 454, 464.

[5] Massachusetts, *Report of the Board to Investigate the Subject of the Unemployed*, Part III (Boston, 1895), pp. 43, 94, 102 f.

[6] *Industrial Commission*, xv, p. 159.

prominent; so at Baltimore, Bridgeport, Buffalo, Pittsburgh, Providence, Erie, Hoboken, Newark, Schenectady, Springfield (Mass.), Syracuse, Utica, Yonkers, and other places.[1] After the devastation of Galveston by the hurricane in 1900, large numbers of Italians assisted in clearing the city;[2] and after the earthquake and fire of San Francisco in 1906, other thousands were among the first, as common laborers, to contribute to the rebuilding of the city.[3] An examination of the workmen sent out from New York City by employment agencies in that year indicated that the Italians were maintaining their very conspicuous position in excavation and construction.[4] In the cities of the northern states they appeared to have an undisputed monopoly in street grading.[5] On the building and maintenance of the street railway lines of all the large cities of the East, countless Italian unskilled laborers have been employed, often almost to the exclusion of other nationalities. In a large sense the subways of New York and Boston are their work. Many were employed for the building of the filtration plant of Washington, D. C.[6] Somewhat later, in the Catskills, they were prominent among the workmen engaged in constructing the great Ashokan Dam.

So the record goes. Or rather, these are but hints of the kinds of entry that might be made in the record innumerable times over, if those who knew were to write. In the life of a nation such a chronicle would have much more than an episodic interest. For us, even these few fragments may serve to fix what has been characteristic in the Italian contribution to the country.

An important class of Italian laborers whose form of activity is only defined after their arrival in this country is the longshore-

[1] *Industrial Commission*, pp. 437–440.

[2] According to information kindly supplied to me by consul Nicolini.

[3] G. Naselli, " Il terremoto di San Francisco di California e la colonia italiana," *Boll. Emig.*, 1906, No. 12, p. 40.

[4] Sheridan, p. 420.

[5] *Ibid.*, p. 421. On similar employments in Rhode Island, see Rhode Island, Bureau of Industrial Statistics, *Some Nativity and Race Factors in Rhode Island* (Providence, 1910), p. 335.

[6] A. Ravajoli, " La colonia italiana nel Distretto di Columbia," *Emig. e Col.*, 1909, iii^iii, p. 159.

men.   Perhaps the oldest group is at New Orleans, where Sicilians unload the fruit that comes from the Antilles and Central America. Another is at Jacksonville, Florida.   In the North, at Duluth, these workers help start the prodigious ore shipments on their way and at Buffalo they have a hand in the immense Great Lakes traffic.   At Boston, it is only in connection with the coastwise traffic that they have managed to get a foothold.   But at the greatest of all American ports, they have come to be a third or more of the men employed.[1]

South Italians almost entirely, they first found employment on the New York waterfront about 1887.   Between 1890 and 1892 they increased, and by 1896 promised to threaten the supremacy of Irish and Irish-Americans.   By 1912 they had become a close second to these older groups, and had forced them to speculate, or even confidently to predict, that within ten years the Italians would stand first.   By 1912 they were a majority of the men employed by the American Line (Chelsea piers) and were increasing on the Hoboken and East River piers; the Bush Terminal of Brooklyn employed Italians mainly; the California Line had one-half Italians; the Lloyd Brazileiro employed them almost exclusively.   These are leading instances.   On the Hoboken piers in 1917, the discharge, for military reasons, of German and Austrian employees, left the Italians there almost supreme.

In its swiftness, this substitution of the Italian longshoremen for others is one of the most striking examples of racial displacement in American industry.   It is by reason of their increasing numbers and not by superior qualities that they have come to the fore.   In discharging Mediterranean fruit they may have a special fitness; but generally they have been ordinary coal shovellers and pier men, sometimes hold men, only rarely deck hands.   They have had less strength than the Irish, if common opinion and some rough experiments may be accepted in testimony.

The Scandinavian-American Line, Hoboken, once worked a gang of Irish in one coal boat and a gang of Italians in another at the same time, and

---

[1] E. Mayor des Planches, *Attraverso gli Stati Uniti* (Turin, 1913), p. 159; Moroni, in *Boll. Emig.*, 1913, No. 1, p. 76, and other passages in *Boll. Emig.*   I have relied much upon an admirable work, C. B. Barnes, *The Longshoremen*, New York, 1915.

found by actual count that the Irish brought up two bucketfuls to the Italians' one. [Again.] A foreman . . . told of once having put Italians to work piling sugar. It had been the custom to pile it four and five bags high, but when they got it three bags high they had reached their limit. Another stated that he had seen Italians sink helpless under bags of sugar which the Irish handled easily. A third said there is a knack in the work which the Irish possess. He had seen two Irishmen grab a bag of sugar by its ears and swing it up, after Italians had tugged at it for some time without moving it. [1]

It is worth noting that they have been inducted into the industry by contracting stevedores of their own people, who have usually withheld a part of their wages by way of commission. Because of this deduction and because their employment has commonly been less regular than that of the Irish, their earnings, in the period about 1912, were generally as little as $10 or $12 a week.

What is characteristic in the labor of Italian men in North America is nowhere so apparent as on the railways. Both relatively and absolutely, the South Italians, as construction and repair workmen, have there achieved a foremost position. The censuses are but blind aids to tracing these elusive armies. It is true that the category of general steam-railway employees gives to the Italians an altogether exceptional place, but it embraces only a part of them, while the others are mainly and indistinguishably collected in the group of general laborers. What is more, there has been no census since 1900. The circumscribed studies of the Immigration Commission of 1907 found the Italians to be 15 per cent of the workmen examined in steam railroad transportation and 44 per cent of persons engaged in construction work; but its figures reveal only an interesting cross-section view and the section runs only partly across. Without specifying nationalities the census of 1905 found 311,000 track laborers employed by the railroads of the United States. Mr. Sheridan's subsequent questions discovered that those of the New England states (11,271) and those of New York, Pennsylvania, New Jersey, Delaware, and Maryland (60,543) were " largely Italians "; those

[1] Barnes, p. 9.

of Ohio, Indiana, and Michigan (42,530) and of Illinois, Wisconsin, Minnesota, and Iowa (59,265) were " largely Italians and Slavs, with some others," while they were present in the " mixed races " of the western states and less common among the workmen, " largely negroes," of the southern states.[1]

The Italians have succeeded the Irish as the predominant unskilled railway laborers of the country. Other peoples have played important parts — the Chinese, Germans, negroes, Slavs, and Hungarians, more recently the Mexicans and Japanese — but Irish and Italians, in successive epochs, have led all. Thirty odd years ago, when rag pickers and street musicians still seemed to many the very quintessence of Italian immigration, the pick-and-shovel laborers were silently being carried to the remoter places and set to work on the railways. A decade later, a contemporary non-statistical view held that " the Irish have ceased building railroads and doing the hard work of constructing public works. The Italians have taken their place." [2]

It was in fact in the nineties that they first came to be employed extensively. They were scattered over much of the country, as appears from their engagement in these years by the Bangor and Aroostock, Maine Central, Pennsylvania, Central of New Jersey, Union Pacific, Colorado and Southern, and " Big Four " roads.[3] In the early years of the decade there had come to be at New York a constant demand for Italian railway labor,[4] and Chicago had become a great center of distribution.[5] Later the Maine Bureau of Labor reported to the investigators of the Industrial Commission that Italians had quite displaced railroad labor in Maine, adding, " It would be a difficult thing at the present time to build a railroad of any considerable length without Italian labor." [6]

---

[1] Sheridan, p. 434.

[2] G. F. Parker, " What immigrants contribute to industry," *The Forum*, January, 1893, p. 602.

[3] These facts and others detailed below I take from letters which I have received from the officials of a number of important roads. I have below referred to the source as *Letters*.

[4] Riva, in *Emig. e Col.*, 1893, p. 439.

[5] Ottolenghi, p. 379.   [6] *Industrial Commission*, xv, p. 441.

In the new century the utilization of Italian labor has continued apace. A few years ago, the Union Pacific was employing with some constancy 500–1000 Italians, the Great Northern 1500, and the Pennsylvania 10,000.[1] The Wabash reported that it had employed at one time over 800, the Chicago and Northwestern 1100, the Chicago, Milwaukee, and Puget Sound 1500, the Union Pacific 1500–2000, the Great Northern 9000, the New York, New Haven and Hartford 10,000, the Pennsylvania 13,500.[2] These are samples only. On the other Eastern, Central, and Western roads the scale has been similar; but on the Southern roads Italians have been fewer.[3] Even the most distant parts of Canada have received a great supply of Italian railroad labor, sometimes importing it directly through Italian employment houses, sometimes receiving it from the United States. In 1902, consular agents claimed that the Canadian roads were employing 6000 Italians. In 1903 the Canadian Pacific alone employed over 3000,[4] and the Grand Trunk Pacific has in recent years used large numbers in its extensive construction work.[5]

[1] *Letters.* Vice-President Atterbury of the Pennsylvania wrote (August 26, 1911): "On nearly all the important work we have done in recent years there has been a large percentage of Italian labor, and this applies to work done directly by the railroad or by contractors."

[2] *Letters*, except for N. Y., N. H. & H., concerning which see Michele, p. 11. Thousands of Italians were employed by contractors, in which case they did not generally appear in the figures given.

[3] *Letters.* See also *Boll. Emig., passim; e.g.:* G. Banchetti, "Gli italiani in . . . Buffalo," 1902, No. 5, p. 20; P. Ginocchio, "Gli italiani in . . . Louisiana," 1902, No. 11, pp. 14 f.; Saint-Martin, p. 5; C. Nicolini, "Gli italiani nel . . . Texas," 1903, No. 1, p. 20; "Relazione sui servizi . . . aprile 1907–aprile 1908," 1908, No. 9, p. 46; L. Villari, "L'emigrazione italiana nel distretto consolare di Filadelfia," 1908, No. 16, p. 27; "Relazione sui servizi . . . 1909–1910," 1910, No. 18, p. 85. Cf. Ravajoli, p. 160. In 1906, 56 per cent of the Italians sent out of New York by various employment bureaus went as railroad laborers; Sheridan, p. 421.

[4] Canada, Royal Commission on the Immigration of Italian Labourers to Montreal and the Alleged Fraudulent Practices of Employment Agencies, *Report* (Ottawa, 1905), p. xi.

[5] E. Rossi, pp. 7, 9; D. Viola, "Le condizioni degli operai italiani nel distretto minerario di Cobalt," *Boll. Emig.*, 1910, No. 13, p. 13; B. Attolico, "Sui campi di lavoro della nuova ferrovia transcontinentale canadese," *Boll. Emig.*, 1913, No. 1, pp. 3–26; G. Moroni, "Le condizioni attuali dei lavori sulla grande Transcontinentale del Canadà," *Boll. Emig.*, 1914, No. 9, pp. 45–50.

Neither exceptional strength nor exceptional carefulness is essential to the performance of the railway tasks of the Italians. Upon occasion there is unusual hazard.[1] Generally the salient characteristic of their work is routine: groups of men — a few or many — are directed by an " interpreter." The gangs toil at the construction and repair of track and roadbed — laying and replacing ties and rails, ballasting and surfacing — and in ditching, grading, quarrying rock and tunneling. They are sought for the removal of soil and rock after washouts, and are found willing to stand in wet and muck. While some immigrants welcome work with timber, the Italians avoid it and specialize in rock work, including blasting. Sometimes they undertake masonry operations, or are employed on work trains, or, less commonly, as dock laborers in unloading coal and cleaning pits, and in general building with its attendant excavation (as for example on the Union Station at Washington or the Grand Central Terminal in New York). Whatever their tasks, skill, judgment, and responsibility are but an insignificant element, and they fulfill their function when a number together contentedly and unintermittently ply shovel and pick. Next to lifting loads, this is perhaps the most elementary form of human labor.

Because Italian workmen have done so much to make and maintain the American railway net, and because so many who have not entered transportation have yet been similarly circumstanced as regards both skill and pay, I inquired further, several years ago, into the traits they have exhibited. From railway vice-presidents in charge of operation, chief engineers, division superintendents, and others in a position to watch Italian workmen, on the larger railways and many of the smaller ones, I obtained statements aiming to show what measure of steadfastness, strength, endurance and other qualities the Italians have manifested. Somewhat, and inevitably, the personal equation affects all of these opinions, yet their general drift may be credited.

---

[1] They were singled out for employment on dangerous cuts by one Western road. See V. S. Clark, " Mexican Labor in the United States," *Bulletin, U. S. Bureau of Labor*, No. 78 (1908), p. 500. Cf. Moroni, in *Boll. Emig.*, 1914, No. 9, p. 50.

In not one letter is there unqualified praise of both South and North Italians. On one Northern road their persistence during the season of mild weather is commended and they are said to be less given to the excessive use of alcoholic drinks than most American laborers. In various statements their "regular habits " are noted and they are described as economical and fairly industrious — how industrious depends partly on the character of the interpreter or supervisor. But let the letters speak; each numbered excerpt refers to a different road.

1. They are probably the best immigrant labor we are able to procure in any quantity at the present time. They do not, of course, compare in efficiency with the Irish labor employed by the railroads fifteen or twenty years ago.

2. Their bad qualities are low efficiency and inability to withstand cold weather, consequently leaving the service in winter. (Their good qualities are those just stated with regard to a Northern road.)

3. With rigid supervision they are able and desirable employees, but with the relaxing of such supervision their efficiency decreases.

4. Work which they understand is satisfactorily done. They are not as desirable as Irishmen.

5. They have no special qualifications; in fact they are usually paid somewhat less than so-called white labor.

6. We further find that after a few weeks employment, the interpreter starts a row in the gang by which the gang quits work, and we immediately find that they have gone to work for some other company; the interpreter thus collecting another fee. . . . Where a few can work together in taking out rock they do very well, both as to the character of their work and the rapidity with which they do it. . . . But for general railroad work I prefer any other nationality. (Mexicans, Japanese and some others had in the previous two years been supplanting Italians on this road.)

7. Some of our Division Superintendents report that they consider the Italian track laborers better than other nationalities for the reason that they seem to live and take care of themselves better and are better able to perform their duty and work more regularly. Some report that they find many of them slow to understand what is wanted but after they once learn the work they are very fair laborers, steady and reliable, but not good for any work requiring much skill or care. One Division Superintendent reports that he does not consider the Italians any more desirable workmen than the Greeks.

8. Our opinion is that generally the amount of work done per Italian laborer per day is not equal to the amount of work done per laborer per day by our other white laborers or by negroes.[1]

[1] Unfavorable comparison with the negro, on physical grounds, has led, I am informed, to some substitution of negroes for Italians in the unloading of vessels at New Orleans.

9. The Division Superintendent of — division says, " I am unable to say very much in favor of Italian labor. We would prefer to employ Huns [Hungarians], Slavs or Poles if we could get them. The dearth of other foreign labor has compelled us to introduce Italian labor." The chief difficulty with these laborers appears to be that they are easily influenced, very superstitious, quickly dissatisfied, and therefore, under the circumstances, for the most trivial cause will seek other employment. Other classes of foreigners are also generally more brawny and better fit for the work. The Huns, Slavs, and Poles will not live in bunk cars, or even bunk houses. . . . Italians live in bunk cars for from $5 to $8 per month for all the food that they consume, part of which is for beer, and they naturally do not have the strength and vitality that the other classes referred to have. It has been our experience that it takes a larger number of Italians to do any piece of work than natives, or even the other foreigners referred to. . . . Our superintendent of — division reports that . . . the Sicilians prove good laborers, provided they are in charge of a foreman of a different nationality, who will keep close watch on them and see that the work is properly done, but without a competent foreman they are of very little value. . . .

In an actual test made by this company to determine the efficiency of Italian laborers, they were shown to have performed in a given time only from 35 per cent to 50 per cent of the same work done by native laborers.

10. From our experience it is generally agreed that [Southern] Italians run below Americans as to strength and efficiency. . . . It is the general opinion that the Northern Italian, together with the Austrian, is the best foreign laborer. The Southern Italian is a poor worker of low efficiency; and the Sicilian is a very poor, undersized laborer, incapable of heavy work.

What clearly emerges from this study is that the Italians are employed in great numbers partly because they are to be had, while other workmen are not, and partly because, in certain kinds of work especially, and with due organization and oversight, they produce good results. While demonstrating less power in accomplishment than some of their harder-fibered predecessors, they have been willing to fag in isolated places for many hours in the day.

CHAPTER XIX

UNITED STATES.   III. THE AGRICULTURAL SITUATION

WHOEVER reads the expansive signs that glare from the façades of the endless Bowery employment houses cannot fail to understand why Italians are to be found in the occupations we have discussed.   Whoever further stops to recall what has been the industrial phase of the country during the quarter century past cannot fail to understand why such signs should appear.   The Italians have grasped at opportunities held out to them.   " Here I am," they have said, being humble folk, "use me where you will, only give me my daily bread."

No one, however, who has followed the history of the Italians in South America can fail to ask one question: Have not the Italians become farmers ?   Agriculture is still the principal industry of the country.   It employs more hands than any other.   A glance at the census shows that its output has continued to increase by leaps and bounds.   Farms are for sale, workmen are in demand, and every year brings hosts of Italians to our shores — men and women, from the most agricultural parts of one of the oldest agricultural countries of the world.   What have the Italians done as farmers ? [1]

[1] An invaluable study is by Dr. Cance in *Report of the Immigration Commission*, xxi and xxii. See also ch. vii (by E. Lord) in E. Lord, J. J. D. Trenor, S. J. Barrows, and others, *The Italian in America*, New York, 1905; A. H. Stone, " Italian cotton-growers in Arkansas," *American Monthly Review of Reviews*, February, 1907, pp. 209–213; E. F. Meade, "'The Italian on the Land" [Hammonton] in *United States Bureau of Labor, Bulletin No. 70* (1907), pp. 473–533; L. Mathews, " Tontitown," *Everybody's Magazine*, January, 1909, pp. 3–13; A. Pecorini, " The Italian as an Agricultural Laborer," *Annals of American Academy of Political and Social Science*, March, 1909, pp. 380–390; F. Ferrero, " A New St. Helena," *The Survey*, November 6, 1909, pp. 171–180; A. Moore, " A Safe Way to Get on the Soil " [Tontitown] *World's Work*, June, 1912, pp. 215–219.

In *Boll. Emig.*, see Serra, pp. 38 f., 46 f.; Banchetti, p. 22; " Delle condizioni della Virginia dell' Est [sic] rispetto alla colonizzazione," 1902, No. 11, pp. 19–22; A. Ravaioli, " La colonizzazione agricola negli Stati Uniti," 1904, No. 4, pp. 3–49; G. Rossati, " La colonizzazione negli stati di Mississippi, Louisiana ed Alabama,"

They have not held aloof. They have even — unless the heterogeneous peoples of Austria-Hungary be admitted collectively to rivalry — been more numerous than any other recent immigrants. Measured, however, by plausible expectations, they have been few. In 1870 they numbered 1443 and were one out of seven occupied Italians; it was a much higher proportion than any they have since touched. In 1890, they were 7902, perhaps one in fifteen occupied Italians. Ten years later, they were 19,194, reckoning all persons who had at least one parent born in Italy; say, one in sixteen of the class. But among Germans, Norwegians, and Swiss, one in two, at least one in four, were in agriculture when the present century began.

If the Italian agriculturists in the United States have sometimes undertaken their work very soon after arrival in the country, they have quite as commonly engaged first in a different occupation. They may even for an indefinite time alternate employment in two callings, as several thousand Italians are reported to have done when they quitted railroad work in the North and moved to Louisiana for the sugar harvest between December and March.[1]

1904, No. 14, pp. 3–30; G. Fara Forni, "Gl'italiani nel distretto consolare di Nuova Orleans," 1905, No. 17, pp. 3-17; C. Quairoli, "La colonia italiana di Vineland," 1908, No. 16, pp. 51-57; G. E. di Palma Castiglione, "Dove possono andare gli immigrati agli Stati Uniti?" 1909, No. 18, pp. 3–26; G. Moroni, 1913, No. 5, pp. 3–53; 1913, No. 12, pp. 47–55; 1915, No. 2, pp. 41–72, and his other articles, viz., "Il Texas e l'emigrazione italiana," 1909, No. 18, pp. 27-56; "Gli italiani in Tangipahoa" (Louisiana), 1910, No. 7, pp. 3–6; "Censimento delle famiglie italiane nelle piantagioni di cotone della vallata del fiume Mississippi," 1913, No. 5, pp. 122–124; "Condizioni attuali delle colonie agricole italiane di Daphne, High Bank e Hearne," 1913, No. 8, pp. 70–72; B. Attolico, "L'agricoltura e l'immigrazione nel Canadà," 1912, No. 5, pp. 3–36; L. Villari, "Gli italiani nel distretto consolare di New Orleans," 1907, No. 20, pp. 3-46; and idem, a report with a similar title, in Emig. e Col., 1909, iii[iii], pp. 202–221.

See further Gli italiani negli Stati Uniti, pp. 20-48; V. Mantegazza, Agli Stati Uniti (Milan, 1910), pp. 119–125; Mayor des Planches, passim; A. Starace, Articoli, lettere, discorsi, New York, 1913; G. Chiesi, "La nostra emigrazione agli Stati Uniti e la colonizzazione italiana nel Texas," Rivista Coloniale, March-April, 1908, pp. 177–194; P. Pisani, "La colonia italiana di Chicago, Ill., e la nuova iniziativa di Marconiville," Italica Gens, May 1910, pp. 155–178; P. Bandini, "Il ritorno ai campi," Italica Gens, June–July, 1911, pp. 258–279; Almanacco enciclopedico italo-americano I (New York, 1913), pp. 143–150.

[1] Saint-Martin, p. 5; G. Moroni, "L'emigrazione italiana nel distretto consolare di Nuova Orleans," Boll. Emig., 1908, No. 16, p. 24. Such cross-country seasonal

To some extent the many settlements of independent farmers in Louisiana were begun by railway laborers who invested their surplus earnings in land and devoted their available time to improving it. The colony at Fredonia, New York, composed chiefly of emigrants from Valle d'Olmo (province of Palermo), was established by common laborers who had been working in the vicinity; and the South Italian colony at Cumberland, Wisconsin, is a pronounced instance of the same sort. In a broad survey of the Italians in agriculture made by the Immigration Commission, it was discovered that one-half had previously been engaged in some industrial labor; for the South Italians a higher percentage than for the North. Not only the denizens of the rural colonies (like those mentioned), but also the cultivators of lots outside the large cities, generally South Italians, have been day laborers. After all, the transition to the farm, by way of common or industrial labor, has in it nothing surprising, as will presently be made clearer; in Brazil, and especially in Argentina, the procedure has been common enough.

In one capacity or another, the Italians as agriculturists are present in nearly every state. Three distinct types exist. The commonest is the laborer, often a resident of one of the larger cities, who goes out to some sort of encampment to pick berries or, in the canning season, to gather vegetables and fruits. He is found in the Eastern and Southern states and, to some extent, in the Far West. The second type is the market gardener or truck farmer, usually a South Italian, who has acquired a piece of land in the suburbs of the larger cities or who turns to account some vacant lot. He may sell to his compatriots in the cities or to the general markets. Though he is to be found in a wide range of states, his important settlements lie between the Mississippi and the Atlantic, and on the southern edge of San Francisco. The

migrations, recalling the seasonal movements within Italy, are perhaps more frequent in the United States than they are known to be. Attention has already been called to the winter movement from the copper camps to the cities, and to the disappearance of the railway laborers from the northern tier of states on the approach of winter. There is also, during the winter, a movement from the construction camps and their kind, of upper New York and elsewhere, to the water front of New York. Barnes, p. 90.

third type is the proprietor or tenant of a plot of land in a fairly isolated rural community. Such communities exist in some fifteen states, in the East and South of the country. They come nearest to being counterparts of the South American colonies. In 1909, when nearly all were studied by the Immigration Commission, they contained about 22,000 Italians of foreign or American birth.

A signal instance of the Italian colony is at Canastota, in western New York. In 1897 a laborer bought and cleared some muck land and sent for his family. Gradually other settlements were made, chiefly by Neapolitans who had been in the United States for from ten to twenty years. On their farms of from five to ten acres they raise onions and other vegetables, utilizing to the full the labor of wife and children, and making a good profit. Near Hartford, Connecticut, in the hills about South Glastonbury, to take another case, a North Italian laborer squatted in 1892, clearing land of the relatively infertile sort that Americans had ceased to care about. Soon other men followed, who had been farm laborers in Piedmont, Lombardy, and Liguria and had saved money as common laborers in the United States. These Italians have prospered, raising peaches and berries, some grain and forage, on farms generally of less than eighty acres.

In Wisconsin, again, at Genoa, along the Mississippi, a few men from Piedmont and Lombardy settled as far back as 1860, and most of the others as lately as 1890. They cut away the hardwood forests, and slowly developed a successful general farming, despite a temperature that in winter reaches 38° (Fahr.) below zero. Such cleanliness and neatness as their houses show are rare in our Italian colonies, contrasting sharply for instance with those at Cumberland, Wisconsin, an important South Italian settlement. Men from the Abruzzi and Sicily, railroad workers and the like, bought lands in this place from real estate speculators in the eighties and later grew hay and potatoes, and kept some "scrub" cattle; but they have not generally raised wheat or corn, and have done little dairying in a region finely fitted therefor. At Cumberland it is still largely the wives and children of laborers who cultivate.

Most important of all the northern colonies are those of New Jersey. With the help of one Secchi de Casale, North Italians began to come in 1873 to the pine barrens of Vineland. They bought their lands of the American owner who took an initial payment and allowed liberal time — and extensions of time — for the payment, with 6 per cent interest, of the remainder. South Italians have recently come also, for the colony has a wide area; but the first comers' farms are still the larger and better. Sweet potatoes and berries are the chief crops, but grapes, peppers, corn, and forage also are important. Though slow to discover the cheapness of machinery and horse labor, and relatively unsuccessful in growing peaches and pears where Nature has offered many inducements, the Italians have otherwise learned, and successfully used, an American technique. In the seventies, some Sicilians, at first only from the town of Gesso, began to come to Hammonton, also in the pine belt. Many had been berry pickers, living in Philadelphia, and they set to growing blackberries, strawberries, and red raspberries in the sandy and gravelly loam, and grapes and sweet potatoes. Though indebtedness is still common and their houses often are poor and dirty, the colony has grown greatly and many of its members have saved money.

In North Carolina are two noteworthy settlements. To the wild heights of Valdese, directly from the mountains of the province of Turin, there came, in 1893, a number of selected farming families, literate, skilled, possessed of some money. They paid $5 an acre for land, and soon emerged from debt. As general farmers they quickly proved themselves superior to the Americans about them, whom they have stimulated, in turn, to more productive methods. St. Helena was settled in 1905 by farmers who had been brought by a land company straight from the province of Rovigo. They also purchased their lots on instalments, and as growers of truck crops and fruits have prospered. In Alabama, Daphne (1890) and Lambert (1893), founded by the enthusiastic Mr. Mastro-Valerio, and composed of a few North Italian families previously resident in the United States, have done considerably less well.

Justly well known is the colony of North Italians at Sunnyside, Arkansas, located on rich Delta soil. Established in 1895 by the landowner, Mr. Corbin, it all but came to grief in 1898. Revived, with cotton factors in charge, it climbed to success. Unlike the negroes, the Italians have been unwilling to rent on shares, paying instead about $6–$7 per acre per year. In their yards they grow vegetables, while the negro buys them at the store, paying credit prices. They work incessantly, planting every corner and, as repeated comparisons have shown, secure a crop half again as great per acre as that of the negro. As cultivators they are emphatically superior to the black folk.[1] In the northwest of the state, high in the Ozark mountains, is Tontitown, a remarkable instance of the success that springs from capable leadership. Father Bandini chose the place and brought to it some of the dissatisfied first settlers of Sunnyside, to whom other North Italians added themselves. Fruit and early vegetables have won them good profits and they have introduced the grape into the region. They possess fruit evaporators, canneries, cider and vinegar factories. Their lands have risen greatly in value, they have neat and clean houses and a good school, and have dissipated the prejudice of the Americans. Through it all, Bandini has been a sage counsellor and administrator.

Louisiana is one of the chief strawberry producing states in the Union. And in Louisiana a leading center is Independence, a town whose economic life has been revived by Sicilians. Farm laborers, hired to come there in 1890, stayed and invited friends and relatives. They bought lands on an instalment basis and now have come to own many. How to raise berries they learned from their predecessors, and today their capability is indisputable. They have organized a powerful marketing association and in refrigerator cars send every year several hundred carloads of berries (in 1910, 264,000 crates) to the cities of the North.

[1] To Mr. A. H. Stone, the first historian of these comparisons, one surprised negro said, " Fo' Gawd in Heaven, dat Dago en his wife en fo' chillun wuz pickin' cotton by de moonlight. I do' 'no' how it looks to you, but I calls dat er underhanded trick myse'f." (" Italian Cotton-growers," p. 213.)

There are other important colonies in Louisiana and a number in Texas. Of the latter I will mention only Bryan, the largest Italian colony in the South. Thither came railroad laborers and others till a population of two thousand has been reached. They raise buckwheat, cotton, and corn on the rich bottom lands of the Brazos River, which they have made valuable by their labors. They cultivate sometimes by a sort of metayer system, sometimes for a money rent, but often — as all aspire to do — as proprietors.

Of the thousands of North Italian agriculturists in California, a large part have grown grapes and made wine for the Italian-Swiss Colony. Started in 1881 under the leadership of A. Sbarboro, a man of entrepreneur ability, this colony, after early reverses, rose to a place of national importance. Asti is its center and claims to have the largest wine tank in the world. Elsewhere in the state still other vineyards and wineries have supplied a product sold throughout the country. At its incipience the colony issued 2250 shares, which were paid for in sixty monthly instalments of one dollar each ($135,000), but by 1910 it claimed assets of nearly $3,000,000.[1]

The Italian venture in farming has now proceeded far enough to allow certain generalizations to be made. Agricultural labor for wages attracts these immigrants only at certain seasons or in times of transition from one employment to another. They have been acceptable enough as farm hands — excelling the negroes, for example, on the sugar plantations — but they find farm wages low. It has been estimated that in eight months of construction work, an Italian can save a fifth more than in twelve months of farm labor.[2] While some have been content to be mere " croppers " on the cotton plantations, most have wished to own land.

---

[1] These details I take from a personal letter from Mr. Sbarboro, who adds with pride, " The Italian farmers are very industrious, patient and sober, and although we furnish them with wine at their meals *ad libitum*, during the past thirty years we have never had an intoxicated person at the Colony." For many years he strove to promote the moderate drinking of wine and to check the agitation for prohibition.

[2] " Memorandum degl' istituti italiani di patronato per gli emigranti in New York sulle cause che ostacolano l'avviamento all' agricoltura degl' immigranti italiani negli Stati Uniti," *Boll. Emig.*, 1909, No. 8, p. 9.

Purchasing on time, they have often been ready to take uncleared land, and then have performed pioneer operations and worked incessantly to pay their debt. When that has been accomplished, they have invested their further savings in more land.

The North Italians have more usually possessed qualities necessary to success than the South Italians, and, relatively speaking, have oftener taken up independent agriculture. But not even they have been disposed to enter diversified farming. This is not, as some writers have supposed, because wheat is not raised in Italy — on the contrary, it is actually the most important Italian crop. Rather it is because American extensive farming requires many acres and costly equipment. There are instances in which the Italians live so far apart that sociability is difficult, but these are few. Generally they live in colonies, or near the cities, even in the cities; many agriculturists have lived in the North End of Boston! In most cases they have small farms, which they till by hand intensively. Whereas the colonists in southern Brazil have generally had few or poor models about them, the farmers or truck gardeners in the United States have learned much from their neighbors; the strawberry growers have apparently acquired their entire technique in America. They exercise economy wherever possible, and an uncommon loving care over their crops, and they cultivate the last corner of the cleared land. Nearly always, however, their buildings and grounds look less well than those of their neighbors — a stinted penny makes a penny saved. In Louisiana and in California they have resorted to coöperative associations for buying and selling with a degree of success that is infrequent in American rural economy.

They have in only the rarest instances made considerable fortunes, but they have made a living for themselves, created a surplus, and rendered some service to the country. As in Argentina, they have often taken up lands held to be unproductive and have given them a value — to be sure, by extraordinary exertion and penurious living. But the lands which they have reclaimed, whether from Nature or from man's neglect, have been maintained in such good condition that the circumjacent lands have substantially appreciated in value. As a farm class they have shown indubitable superiority over the negroes, in the several respects that really count. As the proprietors of lands which they have brought under cultivation they will some day win the rewards that come to owners of valuable acres which others would like to acquire.

Despite the difficulties and disasters which sometimes clouded their earlier days, the Italians have done fairly well by themselves and the country. Why do not more enter agriculture? Is it because of ignorance of their prospects? Scarcely. No opportunities have been so published in Italy, at least by the government. The consular reports dwell upon details of procedure that in the case of other occupations are ignored. Though the Italian Labor Office in New York has advertised farming opportunities widely, its director, several years ago, announced his failure to persuade his countrymen to avail themselves thereof.[1] Climate is a factor which will doubtless always deter the South Italians from settling in numbers upon northern farms, but there its disadvantages end.[2] The cost of land is a much more serious matter. The public strips that still remain are poor or require costly working. Abandoned farms and uncleared areas of a promising sort require heavy initial outlays, $500–$1000, ofttimes. It is an old cry in the Italian reports that all good lands have to be paid for! Increase in acreage value partly explains why the old colonies grow so little by immigrant accretions. While day labor brings an immediate wage, the returns in agriculture are slow, and, what is worse, are speculative. Advances may be necessary, even to the cotton "cropper" who otherwise needs little capital. While wage earning commonly allows a home among Italians, the farm is often isolated. Not previous vegetable growing in Italy but the fact that the truck farm has neighbors explains the importance of this form of agriculture among the United States Italians.

In Argentina the Italians had the advantage of being first settlers, with none but each other for competitors. In the United

---

[1] G. di Palma-Castiglione, " Ufficio del lavoro per gl' immigranti italiani in New York, Relazione," *Boll. Emig.*, 1909, No. 8, p. 24.

[2] Cf. Professor Ravaioli, in *Boll. Emig.*, 1904, No. 4.

States, long established agriculturists have worked out the suitable ways of procedure which new competitors must master, a task the harder when capital is scarce and grasp of English slight. It is, after all, much the same situation as in manufactures, mining, and the rest. There too the independent start is difficult and hire for wages is far the commoner lot.

It is not enough to point out that the crops and methods that promise well in the United States differ from those of Italy, but it must be recalled that the emigrating classes are highly deficient in an understanding of technique — of machines, fertilizer, rotation. From being farm laborers in old agricultural Italy, the transition is far easier to digging sewers in America than to independent farming. It takes a better Italian immigrant than the average to master his besetting inertia and ignorance enough to carry him to success. Half a century ago, and less, the Scandinavians and Germans, with more of self-reliance than the Italians have shown, made their way directly to the remote interior of the country, to the frontier often enough, learned the use of machinery and became model farmers. Like the Italians in Argentina, they measured out and fixed the pace which later comers must follow. The North Italians — witness Argentina and the colony at Genoa, Wisconsin — seem better fitted for general and diversified farming than do the South Italians, and if they predominated among our immigrants from Italy, the problem of agricultural adaptation would be much lightened.

Although it is far from clear that in the present circumstances of the United States a diversion of Italian labor from industry to the farm would be of advantage, yet colonization companies or philanthropic persons or associations have still an opportunity for interesting experiments. Inexpensive land — so that the poor can buy it; land situate in healthful parts of the Atlantic, Middle and Southern states, and California — so that a rigorous winter may be avoided; cultivation upon small plots of ground — so that neighborly association may be possible; intensive cultivation, or instruction and guidance in extensive methods — so that tradition may count or ignorance be overcome; these are desirable and more or less essential. Settlement must be by families, such as have not yet caught the glitter of American city life and are composed of individuals more than usually valid in body and mind. Direction and oversight must be good. Tontitown succeeded because it had a true leader, New Palermo failed because it had not.[1] Those, finally, who enter the colonies must belong to that minority of Italians who have made up their minds not to return to Italy.

A century ago manufactures lagged because free land was an alternative to employment. Today, let us be reminded, agricultural colonies may thrive slowly because industry is a vociferous alternative which tempts away from the farm even the long established American-born whites and negroes, and may in future tempt away the American-born children of the cultivating Italians.

---

[1] On the collapse of New Palermo, see A. Rossi, " Per la tutela degli italiani negli Stati Uniti," *Boll. Emig.*, 1904, No. 16, pp. 74–80.

CHAPTER XX

UNITED STATES. IV. THE ITALIAN EXPERIENCE

ONLY incidentally or by indirection have we so far dealt with the question which most of all interests our immigrants, Have they profited by coming ? Has the game, for them, been worth the candle ? In the continuance and expansion of their immigration, as of all immigration, Americans have been wont to read but one answer — it is Eldorado that lures and is found.

In truth there are impressive evidences of success. Consider alone the remittances of money to Italy, mute testimony to the accumulation of a surplus. They aggregated in 1907, according to a widely quoted estimate by the Immigration Commission, $85,000,000.[1] I cannot believe, however, that this figure — which may serve as an example — justifies the inferences commonly drawn from it. Like 1906, the year 1907 was one of extraordinary prosperity, when wages were high and employment was constant. With irregular work and lower wages the margin beyond expenses must shrink. Of the $85,000,000, the best ascertained part was some $52,000,000 transmitted by the correspondents of immigrant banks. In 1908 this part shrank to $23,000,000 and during the first six months of 1909 to $8,000,000. Clearly, again, the *per capita* remittances of nearly two million persons were not high. When, further, the large proportion of males and the still larger proportion of adults among the immigrants are borne in mind, it becomes patent that the remittances are mainly not sheer savings but go to pay for the current maintenance of families dwelling abroad. The best that can be said for the procedure is that maintenance in Italy is at lower prices than in the United States: the birds of passage are canny birds.

[1] *Immigration Commission*, xxxvii, pp. 261–288. Cf. C. F. Speare, " What America Pays Europe for Immigrant Labor," *North American Review*, January, 1908, p. 107; for earlier periods, Ottolenghi, p. 382; and *Emig. e Col.*, 1893, p. 444. Annually the *Boll. Emig.* records the amounts sent via the Banco di Napoli's agencies.

What is saved by Italians who have made this country their home would seem to be better indicated in figures of property ownership. Unluckily such as exist are few and ill-based, and are more likely than most estimates to be exaggerated. In 1902, for instance, it was claimed that the Italians of New York owned $60,000,000, about $400 for every man, woman, and child enumerated in 1900; but the estimate, made almost without scientific criteria, was surely an exaggeration.[1] Of the total, $15,000,0c0 was said to be in savings banks, but the popular Italian Savings Bank had in 1915 only $4,500,000 in deposits.[2] At the same time, two-thirds of the houses in the Little Italy section of Philadelphia were supposed to belong to Italians;[3] and their compatriots on the Pacific coast were held to be worth $22,600,000.[4]

It is not alone the fact that such statistics as these do not generally rest on itemized appraisals that invalidates them, or that they generally say nothing of offsetting indebtedness, which is common when real property is in question. It is even more the fact that they are indiscriminate in lumping together the investments or the gains of both great and small, so conveying to many minds a misleading notion of average well-being. In the grand total are the costly investments in real estate and plant of successful American branches of Italian firms. There are also the riches of the broadly successful immigrants, an interesting group observable even in early days, as witness the cases of Delmonico (a Ticinese Italian) of New York, of Ghio of St. Louis, of Lonato of New Orleans;[5] and also for later days one could name Saitta, once of Palermo, who has been called the " lemon king " of New York, Di Giogio, the "banana king,"[6] and Sbarboro of San Francisco,

---

[1] Prat, " Gli italiani," etc., in *Boll. Emig.*, 1902, No. 2, p. 28.

[2] See note in *Il Carroccio*, August, 1915, p. 58. Some 637 houses, mostly tenement, were registered in Italian names and worth $19,301,110, according to P. Acritelli, " Il contributo degli italiani alla prosperità materiale della città di New York," *L'Italia Coloniale*, January–February, 1904, p. 39. Real estate is the chief form of Italian investment.

[3] A. Dall' Aste Brandolini, " L'immigrazione e le colonie italiane nella Pennsylvania," *Boll. Emig.*, 1902, No. 4, p. 63.

[4] Serra, p. 51. On Rhode Island, see Michele, p. 14. For a decade earlier, cf. *Emig. e Col.*, 1893, pp. 443, 449, 451–453.

[5] Carpi, ii, pp. 238–241.   [6] See *New York Times*, November 2, 1913.

let us call him the "wine king"! (Wherever Croesus lives, though the mass go naked, the average wealth, strictly speaking, is high.) In trade the largest fortunes have been made, and many persons have risen to comfort.[1] But innumerable tradespeople have had to be glad if, year in and year out, they could make both ends meet; and a heavy majority of all the Italians have worked for hire at wages that could never bare a primrose path to riches.

It is no view of general comfort that the history of the Italians reveals. The pictures that cut across the years are somber. If brightness and cheer show in them, it is as candles scattered, impotent to make the darkness day. Something has already been said of the living conditions of the Italians in the earlier period.[2] Until the final decade of the century not much description appears; the situation then recorded can hardly have been worse than what went before. Giuseppe Giacosa published in 1892 a poignant recital of the life of disillusion and misery lived by the Italians of New York and Chicago.[3] New York, Chicago, Philadelphia, and Baltimore contained in 1890, as they have since contained, about a third of all the Italians in the country. In an elaborate statistical study of their slum populations made by the United States Commissioner of Labor, the Italians were shown to be living in deplorable poverty;[4] and not many had yet been

---

[1] Most of the volume *Gli italiani negli Stati Uniti, cit.,* is devoted to ample accounts of the successful. For California alone, see Patrizi, *op. cit.* Many evidences of success can be read in the *Italian Business Directory,* 5th ed., 1911–12, New York, 1911; and, for a date nearly three decades earlier, in *Guida Metelli,* pp. 317–344.

[2] Cf. also, for 1879 and 1880, *Industrial Commission,* xv, pp. 472 f.

[3] "Gli italiani a New York ed a Chicago," *Nuova Antologia,* August 16, 1892, pp. 618–640; and "Chicago e la sua colonia italiana" in the same journal, March 1, 1893, pp. 15–33. See also his volume, *Impressioni d'America,* Milan, 1908.

Some cursory consular reports made in these years, though they found the artisan and trade classes to be doing well, and common labor to be in demand in some places, discovered a slack or very low demand for common labor in other places — in Louisiana, for example, the Italians could hardly earn a living. See *Emig. e Col.,* 1893, p. 463.

[4] United States Commissioner of Labor, *Seventh Special Report, The Slums of Great Cities,* Washington, 1894.

able to move into better districts. Presently began a prolonged period of depression, bringing a halt especially in those kinds of work that the Italians performed. When the Commissioner of Labor undertook a detailed study of the Italians in Chicago, it was to make disheartening exposures regarding their wages and general conditions of employment and living.[1] After the revival of industry, the Industrial Commission made a report (1901). Italian tradespeople were making progress, but the common laborers, though thrifty, were not advancing. It was mainly " the compulsion of extreme poverty " that led parents to take their children from school.[2]

These are only the briefest indications of some of the pictures that reveal the more general aspects of Italian life at or before the turn of the century. I do not believe that the situation of most Italians in the twentieth century can be called a happy one, though it may have been better than what went before. Let us try to single out some of its principal elements.

All irregularity of employment is a problem. We found it not to be of crucial consequence in agricultural South America, but it is so in a land where the mass of the immigrants are in industry, mining, and construction work, employed at wages. For the common laborers and building-trades workers the winter is a season of much idleness; if the South is an exception, it is also that part of the country whither few Italians, relatively speaking, go. Many return to Italy, but most stay. They shovel snow, pick up casual jobs of whatever sort, and mainly live upon saved earnings, often the fruits of a summer's privation. Southern railroad contractors, unable to compete with Northern roads in engaging Italian laborers during the summer, have sometimes got them for lower wages in the winter, the more readily because Italians have no love for the chill North.

---

[1] United States Commissioner of Labor, *Ninth Special Report, The Italians in Chicago*, Washington, 1897. Of this report a reviewer, A. Bertolini, wrote in the *Giornale degli Economisti* for June, 1898, " it seems a cry of anguish and entreaty that our brothers send to the mother country from which only greater misery has expelled them."

[2] *Industrial Commission*, xv, pp. 474 f.

But the winter's unemployment is only one kind. There is the cyclical depression, which gives often but a faint forewarning, little heeded. The difficult thing about such a time is that, unless it comes with a thunderclap as in 1907, nobody, least of all the humbler workman, knows whether it will be merely transitory or will make a sojourn. Those immigrants who can set their affairs in òrder scamper homeward. What an outflocking was seen in 1907 and again in the war year 1914! Too often the path to Italy is blocked. One must suffer mutely in America. Unemployment is worse than for one's American neighbors. Two-thirds of the appeals for aid made by Italians in the cities were found by the Immigration Commission to be for unemployment — a high proportion. In its fiscal year 1914–15 the Associated Charities of Boston dealt with 40 per cent more new cases than in the previous year; but in the principal Italian district the increase was 300 per cent. Notably in the first war year, but time and again in the previous dozen years, Italian consuls reported to their government that unemployment was grave, or they recommended that emigration to particular regions, or to all, be discouraged, or even suspended. How serious an effect upon earnings even a normal idleness may have can be inferred from the fact that in the coal mines of Illinois, Indiana, and Ohio, in the three fairly typical years 1911–13, the annual workdays averaged only about two hundred. In the silk mills, the Bureau of Labor found the South Italians to be unemployed more than any other group.[1]

Since the great mass of the Italians work for wages, the rates which they receive are in some sort an index of their success. It is, however, neither possible nor necessary that our survey of rates should be highly inclusive, particularly since not many grades of workpeople are in question. Home workers in the clothing trade have received about five cents an hour; men workers in the same trade, perhaps $8 or $9 per week. Shop operatives in confectionery, artificial flower making and allied trades have been paid in recent years $5–$7 a week, in the case of girls and

---

[1] Report on *Woman and Child Wage-Earners*, iv, p. 271. It is scarcely necessary to detail the numerous references in *Boll. Emig.* to fluctuation of employment. Cf. Odencrantz, pp. 114–124.

women. Half the boy and men confectioners received less than
$10 a week. Common labor in the Eastern states, for years be-
fore the war, was given $1.50 per ten-hour day, a little more or
a little less, sometimes $1.25. In the cities construction work-
men might secure $2. Unionized hodcarriers have been paid $3–
$4, non-unionized, $2–$3 for a longer day. Miners' helpers have
made $2–$3. Skilled miners (the minority) have been paid $3–$4,
and other skilled workmen the same or more. These are samples
only, selected from the more characteristic trades and supple-
menting various figures given in the narrative above. Though the
rates have been higher in recent years than fifteen or twenty
years ago, they contend with strikingly higher prices of food and
other necessaries.

What can be saved ? Much depends upon the year's income
and that, limited by unemployment, is hard to gauge. Only the
Immigration Commission has made the attempt. In more than
a thousand families of South Italians in the cities it found the
male heads to average $390 per year; more than half earned less
than $400, and only 2.4 per cent earned $800 or over. But of
course the husband's earnings were often supplemented. In
another study by the Commission of households of South Italians
employed in manufacturing and mining, the earnings of the entire
family averaged $569; half of the families earned less than $500,
a sixth less than $300. The South Italian average was the lowest
in twenty-two nationalities; the North Italian was much higher.[1]
At best, the remuneration for unskilled and factory labor is
almost incredibly low. American minimum-wage commissions
have put at $400–$450 the sum necessary to the decent maintenance of a single girl worker living independently; and a pre-war
estimate carefully prepared for the New York Factory Commission put at $876 the amount needed in New York City to main-
tain a normal family without any savings, and in Buffalo, the
city where maintenance was cheapest, $722.[2] Living upon less
than these incomes, a family may be assumed to be spending its
human capital.

[1] *Immigration Commission*, i, pp. 412, 767.
[2] *Fourth Report of Factory Investigating Commission*, iv, pp. 1668, 1671; cf. pp.
1609, 1619.

By Italian students it has been estimated that a single worker, unencumbered by a family, can save as much as $40 in a month's pay of $50; but this is without allowing for expenditures on such items as clothing, beer or travelling. In a full year such a worker is more likely to save less than $150–$250 than he is to save more, and many a one has spent his treasure by the time he has regained his Italy.[1] Earning more than the South Italian, the North Italian worker spends more, and often saves even less. For the South Italian especially, saving nearly always involves pinched consumption. Our cities vie with each other in bidding for the entertainment of fraternal or business organizations assembling in convention; but no small town gains by the arrival in its neighborhood of the Italian construction gangs. The Southern storekeepers, the Immigration Commission reported, prefer the negro in agriculture to the Italian.

No one can be said to understand the economic conditions of this population who fails to note the important rôle played by the women. The wives of the South Italian men, the Immigration Commission found, are more likely to be gainfully employed than are any others.[2] As workers and economizers they are indefatigable. In the anthracite districts they gather coal on the culm banks, or pick up brush in the woods. On the farm, they work from morning till evening. In the cities they toil for hire. Not marriage, it has been said, but only child-bearing interferes with their work. In the manufacture of men's clothing, three-eighths of the Italian women workers have been found to be married, a rate nearly four times that of other peoples; in the silk manufacture Italian married women were three times those in the general rate; in the metal trades they held a similar place. In the men's clothing manufacture, three out of four married women employed were Italian, sometimes women of sixteen or seventeen, expecting to stay in the trade for years.

[1] For the estimates see di Palma-Castiglione, in *Boll. Emig.*, 1915, No. 6, p. 30, and 1915, No. 7; Castigliano, p. 17.

[2] *Immigration Commission*, i, p. 414.

Their wages are low, probably the lowest paid to any women. Why do they work ? Often because their husbands are idle. After five to seven months of common labor, a job is hard to find, or the cold deters. A Pole is more likely to work twelve months than a Sicilian is, braving and enduring the cold; in Buffalo the contrast of the two nationalities has been marked. The low wages received by the men are a second factor in the wives' working, and a third factor is the overweening desire to save. These all together exert tremendous pressure.

That the wives so often toil in the home is partly because they would turn to account odd moments, but often it is because the husbands are unwilling (in a non-farming country) that their wives should go forth to earn. There is here a manifestation of that traditional reluctance to have their wives work which, earlier in this volume, we observed to prevail in Sicily. There is also a conception of family living in which privacy and intimacy are deemed quintessential. The Italian girl's life, for instance, is inseparable from that of her family. She takes over many of her mother's tasks. Her wedding becomes, what her christening was, a great family event. That she should enter a factory at all is a concession to American conventions, but the factory is certain to lie near her home. What the girl earns is of course a welcome addition to the family income. And both married women and girls are ready to work for wages, indeed to underbid others, in order to be sure of having employment.[1]

It is in the housing of our Italians, more perhaps than anywhere else, that their characteristic impulses show. Their task is to earn, to live, and to save. All three may be juggled somewhat, and the evidence of the juggling — though uncontrollable elements are also involved — is in the house that is inhabited. Consider first the cities, since there the mass live. New York has several Italian centers: about Mulberry Street on the East Side,

[1] On the lives of the Italian women, see cited volumes of *Immigration Commission*, report on *Woman and Child Wage-Earners*, Willett, van Kleeck, de' Rossi, and Odencrantz; also a chapter by Josephine Roche in R. S. True, *The Neglected Girl*, New York, 1914, and K. Anthony, *Mothers Who Must Earn*, New York, 1914.

t Bleecker Street in the lower West, around Jefferson Park in
.......m, in the Bronx about 150th Street and Morris Avenue, near
Bedford Park and 200th Street, in Brooklyn between Atlantic
Avenue and Hamilton Avenue, in Flatbush, in Williamsburg, and
other places. In Philadelphia there is one great square-shaped
district. In Boston there is the North End and part of East
Boston. In Chicago there are the 17th, 19th, and 22d wards.
Let these suffice for examples of an extraordinary degree of concentration in the Italian settlements. Although a secondary
migration may carry the more successful Italians elsewhere, the
first halting places are generally the old, even the oldest sections,
where the houses are superannuated or in poor repair, sometimes remodelled, and generally ill-adapted to the demands
made upon them by a people accustomed to living largely out
of doors.

Who that has sauntered through these colonies can forget
them ? Who, since they are unique, can describe them ? An
ant hill is like them or a beehive — but too soon all analogies
break down! Where East Houston, Mott, Prince, and Elizabeth
streets come together in New York, making one block, fairly
long but very narrow, dwell 3500 people, 1100 to the acre. It
disputes with few other blocks the dismal honor of being the most
populous spot on earth. Its tenements rise four or five stories into
the air but each story bursts, as if the inward pressure were too
great, into a balcony. The street below is at once playground
and place of business: one threads one's way betwixt push carts
and stands, past little children and quite as little old women,
whose black eyes scintillate above their bronzed Sicilian cheeks.
Here doctor and midwife might make a living while scarcely
leaving the block. (One child in nine dies before the age of five.)
On each floor, as a rule, are four " flats," often of two rooms: one
room serving as kitchen, dining room, and general living room, the
other as bedroom. " There is not," says a government report, " a
bath tub in this solid block, unless there be some in the Children's
Aid Society Building, and only one family has a hot water range.
In one of the buildings there are radiators in the hall, but the furnace has never been lighted in the recollection of the present

tenants. All halls are cold and dirty the greater part of the time, and most of them are dark." [1] Neither bath tub nor stove is an institution which these immigrants have known in Italy, but in America both climate and the perils of crowded living make their omission costly.

Twenty-five years ago, it is worth recalling, Jacob Riis opened an attack upon these houses in New York. He said then that the Italians sought out the cheapest — the oldest and worst — tenements. Wherever they went, as in Harlem, the houses sank to the Italian level. They were content with a pigsty and let the rent collector rob them, so were acceptable tenants. In the Mulberry Street Bend were the most squalid tenements; once cow bells tinkled there, but now the bells announced the home-coming rag-pickers' carts. In a single block, in a specimen year, there had been 155 deaths of children under five. " Stale bread was the one article the health officers, after a raid on the market, once reported as ' not unwholesome.' " The Italian's stale beer dives were his worst social offence, for there he made a profit out of human wrecks. His universal vice was his dirtiness; he was dirtier than the negro, and the Bend was " scarce dirtier " than the Little Italy of Harlem.[2]

Today the occupations are different, but the crowding and the dirt remain. Who shall say that they are less ? Most tenements hold ten to thirty families. Many families take boarders. A whole family, or eight or ten men, may sleep in a room. On hot nights every fire escape becomes a bedstead. In the winter the windows are shut in the unheated rooms. The distinction between workrooms and living rooms vanishes. " You may find work in a kitchen where lodgers sleep; on the bed mixed with the family's soiled bedding and clothing — and even loaves of bread and other food in the bed, too — or on the dirty floor, on greasy tables with food, on chairs — anywhere. Nothing could be added to or taken from many of these homes to increase

---

[1] *Woman and Child Wage-Earners*, ii, p. 263.

[2] J. A. Riis, *How the Other Half Lives*, esp. chs. v–vi; *The Children of the Poor* (New York, 1892), esp. ch. xi. I cannot forbear to add his book of tales, *Out of Mulberry Street*, New York, 1898.

their squalor." [1] It is not surprising that ten years ago the Italian government subsidized the New York Exhibit on Congestion of Population.

To observe how many of the New York conditions are reproduced in other cities is almost startling. Philadelphia has the same crowding of families, the same dark rooms, only the tenements are smaller. In Boston there has been much congestion. An investigation into the Lawrence strike found the South Italians to be living in the most crowded places, almost always with no other heat than that of a kitchen stove, and a third of the members of their households were lodgers or boarders; sometimes two to four families maintained one household. In two blocks in the Seventeenth ward of Chicago, containing 877 people, the municipal Department of Public Welfare, two or three years ago, found only two bath tubs. Darkness and dirt were plentiful. One apartment of less than 350 cubic feet held three adults and three children; the instance is extreme but others approached it. Kitchens were used as sleeping rooms, by many families. So one might go on, with Paterson, Buffalo, Milwaukee, St. Paul, Pittsburgh, and other places. In the smaller centers the houses are of one story or two, but congestion and dirt are ever the Italian badge—not their badge exclusively, for other groups wear it also, but none by a better title.

In the cities, the Immigration Commission found nearly a quarter of the South Italian households to be occupying two rooms each, and nearly three-eighths, three rooms; a palpably lower allotment than that of other immigrants. Its investigation into the households of persons engaged in manufacturing and mining found 262 South Italians in each 100 sleeping rooms, and only slightly fewer North Italians; the latter were twice as commonly owners of their homes as the former. More than a third of both sorts received lodgers or boarders. Of the quality of shelter purchased an index may be found in the fact that the average rental per person per month was about $1.50.

An immigration so mobile as the Italian and containing so many men either without families or separated from them must often

[1] *Woman and Child Wage-Earners*, ii, p. 296.

be unconventional in its housing. Partly because of expense but more because of the human desire for the sociability, or at least the presence, of a normally constituted family, the single man avoids a hotel and becomes a lodger. He pays, maybe, $3 a month for a bed, the necessary personal laundry, and the use of the kitchen. He buys his food, but may pay the *padrona* to cook it. How can he do otherwise than invade the privacy of the family ?

In construction work there must be the willingness to utilize many temporary devices. Sometimes the men sleep in railroad cars, or improvise the season's domicile out of boards. The shanty bunk house is typical; usually 25 cents is paid as a weekly rental to the " boss " who also sells food and liquor. Or a kind of coöperative arrangement arises, the workmen choosing one of their number, in rotation, to be the commissary and cook. In its best form this system suggests a little the camp life which the youths of our better-to-do classes welcome for a summer's recreation. But the analogy quickly ends. For the day's toil is fatiguing, the night's quarters are crowded, the season is long, and cold and damp impair the health of the workers. In berry and vegetable picking and the canneries, when the work is not only seasonal but deals with perishable things, men, women, and children, sometimes babies, are often huddled closely in quarters loosely put together and unsanitary.[1]

[1] So much has been written on the housing of Italians that selection, apart from a few main references, like the *Immigration Commission* and the report on *Woman and Child Wage-Earners*, is difficult. I have of course drawn somewhat on my own observation. See the cited works of Sheridan, Butler, de' Rossi, Palma-Castiglione (in *Boll. Emig.*, 1915, No. 6), Castigliano, and A. Bernardy, "Sulle condizioni delle donne e dei fanciulli italiani negli Stati del Centro e dell' Ovest della Confederazione del Nord-America," *Boll. Emig.*, 1911, No. 1, pp. 52–85 (cf. her *Italia randagia*, Turin, 1913, pp. 49–55, 205–214). See also Massachusetts, *Report of the Commission on Immigration*, Boston, 1914 — pp. 69–73 are on the construction camps; R. W. De Forest and L. Veiller (ed.), *The Tenement House Problem*, 2 vols., New York, 1903; T. J. Jones, *The Sociology of a New York City Block*, New York, 1904; F. A. Craig, *A Study of the Housing and Social Conditions in Selected Districts of Philadelphia*, Philadelphia, 1915; M. de Biasi, " Colonie italiane d'America: Filadelfia," *L'Italia Coloniale*, January–February, 1904, pp. 48–58; Chicago, *First Semi-Annual Report of the Department of Public Welfare*, Chicago, 1915 — pp. 74–94 deal wholly with an Italian district; G. P. Norton, " Chicago Housing Conditions: Two

Somewhat the defects of housing are the inevitable result of low wages, somewhat they follow from the desire to save or from sheer ignorance of alternatives. The same factors, and one besides — the preference due to custom — determine the diet of the Italians.

Not many years ago, Mr. Sheridan wrote, in his careful comparative study of unskilled workmen: " The bills of fare of the Italian laborers at their commissaries in the United States, in variety, quantity and cost, do not equal those of the Slavs and Hungarians in the labor camps and boarding houses, and are far below the standard of laborers of other nationalities, native and foreign born." [1] It is certain that the Italians, at least in the early years of their residence, when they are trying hardest to save, eat less than the day's toil demands. They often have but one warm meal a day. Of meat they eat little, and an insufficiency of nitrogen is a common defect of their diet. They consume plenty of vegetables; and therein their diet is more wholesome than that of many other laborers in America; only, it easily runs to an extreme. Everywhere, even in the agricultural colonies, imported spaghetti and macaroni are freely consumed. The use of milk is somewhat restricted, and olive oil is a common but expensive substitute for butter. Large quantities of beer are drunk and it is given even to the young children. When all is said, however, the Italian diet, insufficient in quantity, ill constituted as to the cost of its elements, and defective in variety, compares not unfavorably with that usual in Italy. But life in Italy is on the other hand less active, and the climate is warmer.

When the lightness of the Italian's physique is considered, and the conditions of his labor and living, impairment of the body would seem bound to result. The subject is vast and our knowledge limited, yet certain facts stand forth in sharp relief.

Italian Districts," *American Journal of Sociology*, January, 1913, pp. 509–542; F. O. Beck, *The Italian in Chicago* (Chicago, 1919), pp. 13–18; R. Crawford, *The Immigrant in St. Louis* (St. Louis, 1916), esp. pp. 19–22; D. Ciolli, " The Wop in the Track Gang," *Immigrants in America Review*, July, 1916, pp. 61–64.

[1] Sheridan, p. 477. Cf. Commissioner of Labor, *The Italians in Chicago*, pp. 44–48.

Except for gardeners, some tradespeople, and some artisans, the day's work is generally exacting. Even under the best conditions, it has been said, nine or ten years in an American foundry suffice to ruin the health of the Italian.[1] In the consular reports are abundant references to the exhausting character of the work performed. The Italians arrive healthy, " but when," wrote Luigi Villari, " they have been here a few years they and their children appear pale and used-up." [2]

" As a class the home workers visited in New York," an American official investigator has stated, " are anemic, poorly nourished individuals. . . . Rearing large families in the most depressing surroundings, the women give their entire time to their ' finishing ' work and household duties. . . . A rosy, robust home finisher was never encountered in this investigation. . . . Some of the pathological conditions among these people, however, are such as result from constant sitting in a faulty position, confinement, and close concentration. The most apparent disease symptoms common to women doing this work are badly nourished bodies, pallor, anemia, catarrh, poor appetite, lack of animation, bad teeth, curved spine, stooped shoulders, hollow chests, and lack of suppleness, in general poor stamina." Heavy bundles are lifted and carried often to the day of the baby's birth. " After the baby is born, while such a woman is working — sewing — she nurses her child every time it cries and does not wean it for several years. This is to her the cheapest and most convenient method of feeding her infant." [3]

Such words cannot of course describe the career of every Italian woman. The home finishers (what an appellation it is!) are a fraction of the collectivity. Yet they are a symptomatic fraction, and could not exist in isolation. Other classes of workers press upon them — and what is there in the preparation of these other classes that fits them for a materially different lot ? The lined faces, for that matter, with many a confession of past beauty,

[1] Such statements are common. See, *e.g.*, G. La Piana, *The Italians in Milwaukee, Wisconsin* (Milwaukee, 1915), p. 28.

[2] *Op. cit.* in *Boll. Emig.*, 1908, No. 16, p. 29. Cf. A. Pecorini, " The Italians in the United States," *Forum*, January, 1911, p. 17; and *Industrial Commission*, xv, p. 497. In 1914 and 1915 the Metropolitan Life Insurance Company studied some 10,000 children who had received employment certificates. The Italian boys and girls (nearly a fifth of all) were the shortest in stature; the girls were the lightest in weight of any group; the boys the lightest of all but one; the children born in America were shorter and of lighter weight than those born in Italy. See L. K. Frankel and L. I. Dublin, *Heights and Weights of New York City Children 14 to 16 Years of Age*, New York, 1916.

[3] *Woman and Child Wage-Earners*, ii, pp. 295 f.

and the frail forms that have never been free to grow, anyone can see who will observingly visit the Italian settlements. There is no girlhood, some one has said, among the Italians; womanhood follows upon childhood.

Pneumonia and broncho-pneumonia have taken a fateful hold upon these people, who are in general victims of the infectious maladies, and of rheumatism, but seldom of gastro-intestinal diseases. In the children enteritis is common — evidence of ignorant or careless feeding — and diphtheria and measles. In Boston and New York the death rate of Italian children under five has been very high. Young and old fall a ready prey to tuberculosis; women, it would seem, oftener than men, though among other peoples men come first. Tubercular men and women may continue at their work — making candy, pastry, cigars — but since the belief that the air of their native land will cure them is widespread, they often sell their belongings and make for their native towns. Hence the death rate in New York is not high, except for children under fifteen — their rate is exceeded only by that of the negroes. The Italian government physicians who accompany the emigrant-carrying ships testify to hundreds of cases of tuberculosis per year, but not to all, since the patients with more moderate cases, which do not require treatment, escape their detection, and many sufferers in the most advanced stages seek the comforts of the first or second cabin, outside the physicians' jurisdiction.[1]

[1] On the problems of health, see La Piana, pp. 26–37; R. C. Cabot and E. K. Ritchie, "The Influence of Race on the Infant Mortality of Boston in 1909," *Boston Medical and Surgical Journal*, February 17, 1910, pp. 199–202; W. H. Davis, "The Relation of the Foreign Population to the Mortality Rates of Boston," a paper read at the 37th annual meeting of the American Academy of Medicine, June, 1912; W. H. Guilfoy, *The Influence of Nationality upon the Mortality of a Community* (*Monograph Series, Department of Health of the City of New York*), New York, 1917; P. R. Eastman, "The Relation of Parental Nativity to the Infant Mortality of New York State," *American Journal of Diseases of Children*, March, 1919, pp. 195–211; and several statements by Dr. A. Stella: "The Prevalence of Tuberculosis among the Italians in the United States," reprinted from *Transactions of the Sixth International Congress on Tuberculosis*, 1908, pp. 429–453; "The Effects of Urban Congestion on Italian Women and Children," reprinted from the *Medical Record*, May 2, 1908, pp. 3–26; *La lotta contro la tubercolosi fra gli italiani nella città di New York ed effetti dell' urbanismo* (*VII Congresso Internazionele contro la*

A constant source of bodily impairment or death is industrial accident. The occupational concentration of the Italians is precisely such as to subject them to risk; for few are in agriculture or the commercial callings, and many work in an environment of rocks, heavy machinery, sharp implements, and the ĕlemental motive powers. Blasting, concrete mixing, coal gases, and the dangerous seams of coal mines dispose, typically, to many accidents. Ignorance of spoken English, inability to read, fatigue, that uncultivated intelligence which, after a mishap, is only too easily called carelessness, complicate the risk. In 1912, in California, a non-industrial state, report was made of some 600 accidents to Italians, including 26 deaths and 35 cases of permanent incapacity to work. The death rate in bituminous coal mining is about four per thousand persons each year; but for ten years of work, one in twenty-five. In the Pennsylvania mines, the deaths of Italians have exceeded 100 per year, say, one in every three days. In 1908 — an off-year, industrially — the Italian consulate heard of more than 100 deaths of Italians on the railways of Pennsylvania, this number covering only those instances in which no heirs survived in the state. Now and then, as at Cherry, Illinois, and Dawson, New Mexico, a single accident may destroy a hundred or more Italians. No one can say how many industrial injuries or deaths take place each year in the length and breadth of the land. No one can say how many of those who escape injury in one year will not meet it in five or ten years, or twenty. Once it happened commonly that the worker was known to his employer only by number, so that identification was impossible, and friends were uninformed; and even today this occurs, or Pasquale suffers a sea change into Pat! Under American lia-

Tubercolosi), Rome, 1912; and a statement before the New York Factory Commission, *Preliminary Report*, iii, pp. 1939–1944. In *Boll. Emig.* annual statistics appear of the morbidity of returning Italians.

When the Emigration Council was asked to approve an appropriation of 300,000 lire for the Italian Hospital in New York, Senator Bodio recommended affirmative action but considered that " in view of the great number of sick poor to be counted daily in the Italian population " it could render but a limited service. See " Rendiconti sommari delle adunanze del Consiglio dell' Emigrazione," *Boll. Emig.*, 1907, No. 1, p. 14.

bility and compensation laws, indemnities for accidents to the Italians have been meager or often lacking altogether.[1]

An unwholesome situation which Italian writers have repeatedly stressed is that produced by the long separation of the sexes, married or unmarried. Two-thirds or more of the immigrants are male. It is an abnormal existence which the gangs lead, secluded for long periods, so that the restraints collapse after a while. The savings which are faithfully sent at first to the wife in Italy become less frequent and then cease; a new wife is supported here. The boarding-house system gives a special spur to immorality. Innocently or illicitly, venereal disease is acquired and is transmitted, women and children becoming frequent victims. It is not clear that the Italians are in a worse plight than some other immigrant groups similarly circumstanced, but it is certain that disease is more prevalent among them than it was in Italy.

Not to speak of the exploitation of the Italians by their countrymen would be to convey a false notion of their experience. It is an extraordinary chapter, the like of which would not need to be written in a history of the Scandinavians, Germans, and Irish. Mr. Ross has ascribed the difference to the lack of mutual helpfulness among the Italians,[2] but he does them serious injustice. When business troubles appear, friends and relatives are quick to help. In many small ways the Italians are to an uncommon degree coöperative. They are the only people, an inquirer has found, for instance, who make no charge for watching over a neighbor's child while its mother is away at work.[3] No, the indubitable basis of exploitation is the ignorance and credulity of these immigrants, sometimes a mercenary drift. Given these traits to play upon, the way of the exploiter is easy.

[1] Casual references to accidents abound in the consular reports; but see especially Aldrovandi, pp. 48 f.; " Il distretto vice-consolare di Pittsburg," *Emig. e Col.*, 1909, iii[iii], pp. 182–186; F. Daneo, "Gli infortuni sul lavoro in California nel 1912," *Boll. Emig.*, 1913, No. 14, pp. 59–64. Cf. Bernardy, *Italia randagia*, pp. 161–189. Our state reports do not generally supply details of nationality.

[2] E. A. Ross, *The Old World in the New* (New York, 1914), p. 294.

[3] Anthony, p. 140. See also Odencrantz, p. 25.

Of the great abuses, only that virtual slavery of children, already described, has quite disappeared.[1] Despoliation of newcomers by hotel keepers has been frequent, and the calculated exactions of notaries and quack doctors have persisted.[2] But the greatest depredations have touched the matters of employment and savings.

The immigrant walks through Mulberry Street and sees a crowd around a bar in a basement. He enters the basement and finds a man employing men for a company. He adds his name to the list without knowing anything about the work he will be called upon to do, or about the place where he is to be transported, or about the terms of his engagement. Perhaps, however, he passes a banker's establishment and stops to read on a paper displayed at the window a demand for two hundred laborers, supplemented with the significant assurance that the place of work is not far distant. He enters, enlists, takes his chances, and falls in the snare set for him. [3]

So it was and still partly is. And the snare ? Wages may be lower or employment briefer than expected; payment of wages may be delayed, so that idleness becomes the alternative to unsatisfactory terms of labor; transportation charges turn out to have been merely advanced; unavoidable expenditure at the company store consumes the wages due; return to the city or transportation to a different employment annihilates savings. The boss who accompanies the gang, perhaps providing shelter and food, cuts off a slice of the wages and is brutal. The greatest abuses follow when employment is slack. The padrone may rise to wealth. Often retention of the job depends upon a faithful silence concerning the fact of a commission paid. It is only in a fairly recent period that the padrone system has suffered a decline, but the boss persists — because he is indispensable — and abuses are frequent still.

Remarkable has been the rôle of the banker. He is generally a *paesano* — from the immigrant's village — and it used to be said

[1] At one time, a consular estimate, which I suspect to be somewhat wild, placed at 8000 the number of such children in the chief cities; Florenzano, p. 156. Cf. Carpi, i, pp. 233–235.

[2] Miss Wald has called attention to the difficulty had in establishing a nursing service in the Italian parts of New York, because of the quack and the secrecy of his methods. L. D. Wald, *The House on Henry Street* (New York, 1915), p. 37.

[3] S. Merlino, "Italian Immigrants and their Enslavement," *Forum*, April, 1893, p. 185.

that there were as many in Mulberry Street as there are regions in South Italy. " The newcomers," wrote Mr. Villari succinctly, " cannot even go about in the streets without a guide always at their side. They need some one to write their letters, to supply paper and stamps, to send their letters, to accompany them while they make their purchases and go to the station, to find lodgings for them and an eating-place and work, to safeguard their savings and transmit them to Italy, taking care even of sums so small that no serious bank would handle them." [1] The banker sells tickets and coal, writes letters, finds employment and lodging, acts as a lawyer, and renders many other services. At the time of the Messina earthquake, while Americans flocked to the newspaper bulletins, the Italians collected about the bankers' quarters for news. The very humbleness of the establishment is in its favor — one mistrusts the costly fronts of the American banks. One fears even the impersonal Banco di Napoli, delegated by the Italian government to transmit emigrants' savings. But one pays a price for the comprehensive service of the small banker, partly in the high commissions but more in the risk that is run. Recent protective legislation in Massachusetts and in New York came only long after the history of abscondings had begun to unfold its crowded pages. What pathos is in this chronicle! Much has been uttered about it, in passion or in prayer, and every episode electrifies the Italian colony; but, lesson unlearned, the immigrant takes his next savings to still another *paesano*.[2]

---

[1] Villari, in *Boll. Emig.*, 1908, No. 16, p. 33.

[2] On exploitation see, among innumerable references, J. Koren, " The Padrone System and Padrone Banks," *Bulletin U. S. Bureau of Labor*, No. 9 (1897), pp. 113–129; Conte, pp. 115–132; C. Cianfarra, *Il diario di un emigrante* (New York, 19—), pp. 56, 84, 122 f., 168–170; Carpi, i, p. 72; anon., " I lavoratori italiani nel West Virginia," *L'Italia Coloniale*, August–September, 1903, pp. 858–861; Canada, Royal Commission . . . the Alleged Fraudulent Practices of Employment Agencies (*cit.*); Sheridan, pp. 435–456; A. Franzoni, *Gli interessi italiani in New York* (Rome, 1908), ch. ii; New York, *Report of Commission of Immigration*, pp. 24–47, 111–128; A. Vinci, " Banche e banchieri italiani negli Stati Uniti," *Rivista Coloniale*, December, 1909, pp. 1139–1156; G. Preziosi, *Gl' italiani negli Stati Uniti del Nord* (Milan, 1909), pp. 69–78; L. Villari, *Gli Stati Uniti d'America e l'emigrazione italiana* (Milan, 1912), pp. 245–253; and the full report on " Immigrant Banks " in *Immigration Commission*, xxxvii, pp. 203–350.

The coöperative or fraternal spirit of this population takes peculiar forms. As in other lands also, the chief type of Italian organization, a type comparatively uncommon among other nationalities of immigrant, is the mutual aid society. In 1910 an Italian census discovered 1116 societies in thirty-five states, and half of them were held to contain 78,000 members. But the census did not pretend to be complete; in Chicago for instance, where two years later 400 mutual aid societies were estimated to exist, only 10 were reported. Not only are many of the societies weak, but federation is rare — an instance in Upper Michigan and the *Figli d'Italia*, composed of local lodges, probably stand alone. The comparative absence of federation and the multiplicity of organizations arise from that remarkable spirit of regionalism of the Italians, which we have elsewhere noted. How often are the societies even named after the village whose sons are their members, or after the patron saint of that village! [1]

Inter-society hostility is constant, and is the greater the more intense the clan feeling within the society. Indeed, the fundamental phenomenon is rather the inter-regional hostility, and that, where it is not acute, is at least clearly conscious of itself. Regional lines have had a long history in New York where emigrants from one village may occupy one street, those from a different village another. The tale is repeated in the other centers, great and small. It has been said that in some of the agricultural colonies of Texas only Sicilians can get a foothold. Even in the church going of the women regionalism has been remarked. And in the field of industry it leads to those clashes between groups which have so often perplexed foremen and contractors. In praise of Mexican laborers, a Western trackmaster once said, " They don't have feuds and disorders like the Italians, who are always fighting unless the whole gang is from the same

---

[1] " Le società italiane negli Stati Uniti dell' America del Nord nel 1910," *Boll. Emig.*, 1912, No. 4, pp. 19-54; L. Provana del Sabbione, " Condizioni della emigrazione nel R. Distretto consolare in Chicago," *Boll. Emig.*, 1913, No. 1, pp. 27-33; di Palma-Castiglione, in *Boll. Emig.*, 1915, No. 6, p. 35; Villari, *Gli Stati Uniti*, etc., pp. 239-241. For an earlier date, cf. *Guida Metelli*, pp. 124-131.

town in Italy." [1]   Only years can be expected to attenuate this
trait, before which the efforts of Americans to help the city Italians have often collapsed in futility.   Even when the immigrant
seems wholly " Americanized," a trifling incident may uncover
the regionalist impulse.

What few Italians understand before they come to the United
States — and I speak especially of those who will linger or stay
permanently — is that a mysterious process of unmaking and
remaking will take place in them.   In the older persons the
inevitable resistance is greater than in the young.   But all have
come a long way, and their die is cast.   Children of circumstance,
they are under a spell of suggestion which makes them fertile
ground for the seeds of assimilation — to good elements of our
life or bad.   America would " Americanize " them.   But " Americanization " is a two-edged sword.   Some the prodigious conflict
will strengthen, others it will weaken.   All that moral support
that men derive from religious and social ties with the group they
have grown up with is imperilled when they find themselves in the
maelstrom of a strange land.   The Italians are rural dwellers
dropped into the unaccustomed brutal parts of great cities.   The
fascination of the new home may be unwholesome but it is
keen.   For many the destiny is one of loneliness, disappointment, demoralization, sometimes transitional in its stay, but
often enduring.   The immigrant has pressed his steps into a
" one-way street."   " The number of those who are unhappier
than I is great," cries the buffeted immigrant of Cianfarra's
diary, " and unluckily for many of them, there is no hope of
better days." [2]

There is question not merely of moral change and economic

---

[1] Clark, *Mexican Labor*, etc., p. 477.   My own railway correspondents testified
in the same vein.   On the general subject, see, *e.g.* (besides the references on
societies), *Industrial Commission*, xv, p. 474;   Fara Forni, in *Boll. Emig.*, 1905,
No. 5;   Villari, in *Boll. Emig.*, 1908, No. 16;   Mayor des Planches, p. 159;   A. Bernardy, *America vissuta* (Turin, 1911), pp. 322 f.

[2] Cianfarra, p. 95.   Only those, he says in his preface, will disbelieve his tale who
are but newly arrived in the country.   Cf. Conte, pp. 101–113.

loss. The new life about the immigrant may be rich and full, but it is imperious in its injunctions. He must make the discovery that America exacts for all that she gives. She applies tests, imposes conventions, demands compromises, stipulates concessions to her very practical ways, and the deep provincial emotional nature of the Italian must undergo atrophy or metamorphosis. For many it is even as one perspicacious observer has said: " To be happy in America one must have a certain mechanical ability, a practical and opportunist spirit, a nature that is sharp in business but in other things narrow and matter-of-fact, with a tendency to conventionalism and the literal following of approved standards, a great interest in whatever is American and a high disdain of all that is Latin or that glorifies the Latin life." [1]

It is the children who most easily make concessions. Their plastic bodies and impressionable minds have less of the Old World to discard and they move so much faster than their progenitors that either a breach ensues or parental indifference arises. " The standards are different in America," they assert and their elders cannot gainsay them. Less is learned by the children in their homes than was usual in Italy, for many things are now bought ready-made that there would be contrived by the mother with the help of her growing children. More, relatively, is learned in the bristling outside environment, in the street and the school. To the school every child is forced by law to go, but with rare exceptions it does so only until it has reached the minimum age at which work is permissible, and probably the exceptions are more than balanced by instances in which the father's false oath as to the child's age liberates the child prematurely. It should be noted that only the public school is ordinarily in question, since parochial teaching has little counterpart in Italy.[2]

[1] Bernardy, *America vissuta*, p. 308.

[2] A striking contrast appears in some results of an inquiry made by the Immigration Commission (ii, p. 71). In 37 cities, 81,265 South Italian children were 4.5 per cent of all pupils in the public schools, the Irish slightly exceeding them with 4.8 per cent. In 24 cities, 10,640 South Italian children were only 0.8 per cent of all pupils in parochial schools, the Irish having 26.2 per cent. On the promptness with which the children leave school at fourteen, see, *e. g.*, Crawford, p. 45.

The ability to read and write, what is more to read and write in English, gives to the child a powerful instrument for adaptation which his parents lack. And his growth toward American ways rouses in him some of that contempt for his origin which has so often brought sadness to his parents.

Liberal influences may tantalize, but they perhaps less often benefit, the illiterate parents. The admirable work of Miss Moore with the Italians in construction camps was as a drop in an ocean; and the urban night schools are little more. It is strange that a country, whose president vetoed the literacy test bill on the ground, largely, that immigrants had been denied schooling opportunities in their own countries, should itself have taken hardly a step to provide schooling for those adults who are four in five of all immigrants. Many Italians, of course, are literate when they come. For them there are bookshops in the great centers whose selection of volumes is miserable and disheartening, a reminder of how far literacy may fall short of cultivation and training. For them also there are now many Italian newspapers, including a half dozen dailies in New York alone, some of which are said to dispose of 25,000 or more copies per day. Editorially these journals are weak, and I do not believe that they seek to foster the best interests of the immigrants. Among the leading ones I have repeatedly found as much as a fifth of their space devoted to medical advertisements, commonly of quack doctors and nostrums. Theirs is surely a shameful exploitation of the ignorant.

Profound changes take place in the recreations of the Italians. What the open country or the little village allows has scant place in the American city, and anywhere else has scant opportunity. Much gambling persists. The saloon, though far less widely patronized than among a number of other nationalities, acquires a strong hold. Beer was hardly known to the Italians in Italy. In the strange land it is a solace which terminates the strain of the day's hard toil. The theater is a favorite institution, accessible even in the small centers. In New York, San Francisco, and Boston the marionette used to display and recite the deeds of knighthood. But the deeds, alas, have lost their flavor, or the imagination needed to enjoy them has been jaded or found other delectation. In the United States, the stage must exhibit in full more than the imagination can be trusted to conceive, and even the immigrant becomes sophisticated. The burlesque theater has always welcomed an immigrant patronage, and as in turn the German, the Irish, and the Jew have been the protagonists of its febrile comedy so now the Italian has begun to dance and sing and break his English for the diversion of others. There are indeed theaters in which short plays are enacted in Italian, or where every "variety artist" speaks only the language (adapted!) of Dante. To the moving picture show, a tremendous and deserved vogue has come and more than any other institution it has superseded the marionette theater. Since it requires little or no knowledge of spoken or written English, it may bring its educational or moral force to bear upon even the newly arrived immigrant. Until I found it in Catanzaro and other South Italian communities, I had supposed it to offer a new experience to our immigrants in America; yet to most it doubtless is novel, and few can previously have had the habit of visiting it.

One of the deepest changes which the Italians experience is in religion. A nucleus of the faithful there is to be sure in every important collectivity. In New York City alone there are probably a hundred Italian priests. Commodious churches have been built, some now counting two-score years and more. On saint's days an altar may be erected in the street, the image of the saint is displayed out-of-doors, brilliant lights and vivid colors are everywhere. The festive result is striking in its contrast at once with the American community about and with the historical background of Protestantism, even of Puritanism. That is half the story.

In the scattered places, however, amid diversity of sects, under stress of the chill winds of indifferentism and irreligion, far removed from that complex of conditions which in the Italian village sustained the priest in even a species of temporal power, the spirit of the immigrant changes. Is a local church lacking? Then the church may be deemed unnecessary, and many are the immigrants who have long lived and toiled beyond the reach of priest or church. In a coal community of Indiana, where four thousand Italians lived, neither church nor priest was to be found.[1] Everywhere Italians have fallen away from that religion whose earthly capital is still the Italian capital. A Milwaukee Catholic organ, in 1913, estimated (loosely enough!) that a million Italians had already been lost.[2] Those who abandon the church altogether are the majority, but an impressive minority go over to the various evangelical denominations, forming Italian congregations even in many small communities of the country. This extraordinary movement away from a secular religion is proceeding as quietly as it is extensively, and most of what we would like to know about the psychology of it is still enshrouded in darkness.[3]

Unschooled, scattered, mobile, sundered by regional rivalries, the Italians have in the past given few indications of the presence of a national spirit. Several monuments, including at least two to Garibaldi, have been erected. Support, but not general enthusiasm, played a part in furthering the Columbus Day movement. The earthquake catastrophes of the Abruzzi and Sicily have evoked financial sacrifices for succor of the stricken. At the outbreak of the Italo-Austrian war, demonstrations of loyalty were many: substantial subscriptions were made in New York to the *prestito della vittoria*, thousands of reservists responded to

---

[1] Di Palma-Castiglione, in *Boll. Emig.*, 1915, No. 7, p. 59; cf. No. 6, p. 35. The case of the granite-cutting colony at Barre, Vermont, where the Italians are even more numerous, is perhaps even more striking; see A. Mangano, *Sons of Italy* (New York, 1917), p. 30, and Villari, *Gli Stati Uniti*, etc., p. 229.

[2] See an article, " Catholic Italian Losses," reproduced in *Literary Digest*, October 11, 1913, p. 636. The defection runs to " 60 per cent," according to E. C. Sartorio, *Social and Religious Life of Italians in America* (Boston, 1918), p. 104.

[3] What little has been written on the religion of the Italians is much scattered. On the Catholic phase, see J. De Ville, " Italians in the United States," *Catholic Encyclopedia*, viii (New York, 1910), pp. 205 f.; *Venticinque anni di missione fra gl' immigrati italiani di Boston, Mass., 1888–1913*, Milan, 1913; Rev. P. Capitani, *La questione italiana negli Stati Uniti d'America*, Cleveland, 1891; and sundry articles in the bulletin of *Italica Gens*. On the Protestant phase, see Mangano, pp. 149–194; Sartorio, ch. 4; A. Clot, *Guida e consigli per gli emigranti italiani negli Stati Uniti e nel Canada* (2d ed., New York, 1916), pp. 44–55 (a list of Italian evangelical churches); W. P. Shriver, *Immigrant Forces* (New York, 1913), pp. 206–212; A. McClure, *Leadership of the New America — Racial and Religious* (New York, 1917), pp. 153–166.

the call to return to Italy, and a characteristically warm reception was given to the members of the Italian mission to the United States.[1] Undoubtedly the war served greatly to intensify national feeling, but it is still too early to say in what degree. Certainly some plain limitations upon the feeling also asserted themselves. The great mass of reservists did not return to Italy, but worked in the United States for unprecedentedly high wages, and the Italian newspapers, whether selfishly or reflecting their readers' sentiments, were unfeignedly glad when, in 1917, the American effort to secure from Italy consent to enrol immigrants for war service came to naught.

When the Italian takes political action in the United States, it is either because he holds by certain strong convictions or, much more generally, because after a prolonged residence the expansion of his interests gives to naturalization a special value. A small but not inconspicuous group have held aloof, professing radical principles. Some are anarchists, but the name is often falsely applied to them. In the summer of 1917 several anarchists were killed or wounded while resisting the authorities. Fourteen of thirty-six radicals deported in June, 1919, were Italian. The number who in spirit are socialists substantially exceeds the thousand members recently claimed by the Italian Socialist Federation.[2] Yet these radicals and the syndicalists, of whom more anon, are the least part of the argument. Expecting to return to Italy, the Italians generally avoid naturalization. In the study which the Immigration Commission made of foreign-born persons who had satisfied the age and residence requirements for naturalization it was found that one-third of all immigrants (of all nationalities) had become citizens, and of the North Ital-

---

[1] See G. C. Speranza, " The 'Americani' in Italy at War," *Outlook*, April 12, 1916, pp. 844–864. In the monthly *Carroccio* (New York) many of the principal doings of the Italians of the United States are recorded. See also the monthly *Corriere Italo-Americano*, New York, 1915–.

[2] Mr. John La Duca, secretary of this association, writes me (August, 1917) that the illiteracy of the Italians makes their organization difficult, but that, once members, they become ardent propagators of socialist principles. Cf. P. Brenna, *L'emigrazione italiana* (Florence, 1918), p. 252. On Italian radical movements a score of years ago see P. Ghio, *L'anarchisme aux États-Unis* (Paris, 1903), ch. iii.

ians in particular only a quarter, but of the South Italians less than a sixth only.[1] On the farm it is the ownership of property and the obligation to pay taxes that stir the desire for naturalization. In the cities, besides this factor, stimulation by political parties and, latterly, by patriotic organizations, has been a powerful factor. An initial preference for the Republican party, due doubtless to its name, has in some large centers been overcome by the greater pressure applied by the Democratic leaders. We have even had the spectacle of an Irish politician reading to an Italian throng a prepared speech rendered into Italian! Undoubtedly the naturalized Italians, already many thousand in the great cities, are often volatile and easily confer their support where eloquence is greatest or latest. The American-born Italians seem to be especially ardent in their patriotism. In the older colonies of several states, particularly where the North Italians have settled, election or appointment to public office occasionally takes place. Often it is the second generation which so rises to importance, and generally, as might be expected, it is the minor offices which are involved — police captain, clerk of the city hall, justice of the peace; more rarely, treasurer, member of the school committee, judge, or representative in the state legislature. In national affairs, the Italians have so far been all but negligible. By their delegations and newspapers they have opposed the enactment of legislation restricting immigration, but in this regard, though they are especially involved, they have shown much less pertinacity than some other groups.

It is difficult to indicate in brief compass what the sojourn of the Italians in the United States has meant to them. I have tried to present a particolored picture, for no other, I believe, can be true.

---

[1] Among those who had taken out first papers, the South Italians had a rate of 14.4 per cent, the North Italians 20.5, and all nationalities 16; the showing of the Italians seems better, but the reason is that, among other nationalities, so large a proportion had already become fully naturalized. *Immigration Commission*, i, p. 484. A recent investigation in Canada found that only 19 per cent of men born in Italy had been naturalized, the lowest rate for any except certain minor immigrant peoples. Census and Statistics Office, *Special Report on the Foreign-Born Population* (Ottawa, 1915), p. 18; cf. p. 27.

Legion is the number of writers and speakers who innocently or intentionally have ignored the ills which afflict this immigration, but the ills are there and, taken together, are portentous. In the lot of the immigrant what is not foreseen is always more than what is, and it is far less simple.

How have the people of the United States received this many-sided immigration ? In the latter part of the nineteenth century they threw open to aliens in general, we have seen, extensive industrial opportunities. If the workers who have come had been only a mechanism adjusted to certain tasks there could be no further question touching them. But they have been human, members of the body politic, actors as well as instruments; and because they fall into complicated social relationships within the country they cannot be judged from one point of view alone.

The Italians have generally been held in favor by the employing classes. While a low wage, to be sure, implies that any one worker could be dismissed without serious loss, the mass who receive the wage are not conveniently discarded. Like a low-grade ore deposit, they have value in the large. Work that demands training, responsibility, discretion, is not for the great majority. But work that is simple and monotonous, that exhausts through duration rather than from concentrated application, that can be performed by men disposed in a gang, under the more or less military supervision of a foreman, so that the worker becomes himself like a part of a machine, set in motion only when other parts are active, such work the Italians, helot-like, have performed satisfactorily.[1] Their workplace is often dangerous, dirty, and wet, and their tasks are of the unideal sort that students of utopias and socialisms have feared men would universallyseek to avoid. To secure such employment the Italians have been willing to go to remote places, to give up all thought, for the time, of a fixed home, or have been ready to toil long hours at a wheel for

[1] " The Italians are driven like so many dogs by the foreman. . . . I do suppose you can rush an Italian gang more than others," said the city engineer of Brockton, some years ago. Massachusetts, *Report of Board to Investigate the Unemployed*, Part IV, p. 43.

a wage that allows only a pinched and stunted living. Prodigies of labor have resulted. The capital equipment of the country has grown. Less robust than the Slav, less hardy than the Irish, the Italian has contributed largely to the country's economic expansion.

The non-immigrant laborers similarly have a point of view, which, like that of the employers, is echoed by many persons in the general population. The Italian is a competitor, because of his numbers and his qualities deemed unwelcome. His saving grace is that he often enters trades in which his competition with Americans is not apparent or direct. He takes a low wage; even, according to a charge that is common and, I believe, sometimes well founded, a lower wage than others would require for equivalent work. Such is his tractability that strikes for increase of wages and all bargaining for better conditions are through his presence less likely to succeed, and so the general condition remains poor.[1] That employers make capital out of racial rivalries, playing off " Wop " against " Hunkie," for example, and so preventing a united labor front, is well enough established. To American laborers the procedure has naturally been obnoxious, and they have perhaps been more willing to regard the Italian as blameworthy than as victimized. Equally they dislike the Italian's readiness to pay commissions for jobs and to accept a loss from a loose calculation of time served — for example, to take pay for $29\frac{1}{2}$ hours when the work has lasted 30.

Italians have often been strike breakers. They helped to defeat the Pennsylvania coal strike of 1887–88. A few took employment during the longshoremen's strike of 1887, and their increasing numbers became the employers' means of preventing further trouble. The immediate cause of the introduction of Italians into the New York clothing industry is declared to have been the employers' desire to escape trade-union demands. With other workers they helped to break the Chicago meat packing strike of 1904. During the cigar makers' strike in Florida the

---

[1] For instances of the common charge, see, *e.g.*, Report on *Woman and Child Wage-Earners*, iii, p. 169; Massachusetts, *Report [on]* . . . *the Unemployed*, p. 101; Barnes, pp. 8, 12; Clark and Wyatt, p. 194; Warne, p. 312.

Italian operatives refrained from work, but their interest in its outcome was so slight that a large part permanently abandoned the region.

The Italian women, like the men, have not been interested in labor hostilities. Visit a Jewish flower maker, said a student of some of the smaller trades, and she will plunge at once into a discussion of her trade, its wages, the shop treatment, and the like; but the Italian girl thinks only of displaying her work, grateful for the interest shown.[1] In 1909 while thousands of non-Italian workers in the New York shirt-waist trade struck for three months, the Italian women stayed at their posts, and additional hundreds of them stepped into the empty places.[2]

To some extent the Italian's eyes have been opened to the effect of his actions. Where the existing unions have been strong, he has been ready to enter them; so in some of the mines, so too, in certain quarters, in the building trades — and one son of Italy has risen to important office in the International Hodcarriers' Union. In the anthracite strikes of 1900 and 1902 the Italians were won to participation; their leaders, the Irish, in actually overcoming for the time their regional factionalism, did what the Italians themselves and their employers had often failed to accomplish. In 1907, in New York, six thousand organized Italian longshoremen and many others who were unorganized played an important rôle in a great six weeks' strike which involved thirty thousand workers; as it happened, the strike failed and keen resentment at the union was felt. Under American or English-speaking leaders, the bituminous coal miners of a portion of the western Pennsylvania fields struck for sixteen months, beginning in 1910; but again discouragement over the failure of their efforts was acute. Upon many counts memorable, a strike was started by Poles and Italians in the textile mills of Lawrence in 1912; the conditions protested were not unlike those in innumerable immigrant occupations, but the publicity given them stirred much of that general sympathy which became a factor in a

---

[1] Van Kleeck, p. 35.

[2] See an account by Adriana Spadoni, " The Italian Working Woman in New York," *Collier's*, March 23, 1912, pp. 14 f.

settlement favorable to the workers. In this strike, the Italians and Poles were the most active belligerents and to an exceptional extent did the picketing. Though most of the leaders were English-speaking, one Italian organized the strike for the quasi-syndicalist Industrial Workers of the World, which in other centers also has found support among his countrymen.[1] During the war years, with the tremendous enhancement of the bargaining power of labor, Italians have frequently participated in strikes and at times, as in the case of the coal heavers of the New York piers in 1917, they were the first to quit work.

Yet it is still but a fraction of the Italians who are members of unions. Only one in ten of the South Italians was found by the Immigration Commission to be organized (among the less numerous and more skilled North Italians the rate was nearly four times as great). In many quarters their early strike breaking history still condemns them and their competition is feared even when it is not detected. That the employer cannot at any moment discover enough Americans to engage is held to be no argument.[2] Sometimes, where the unions are powerful, the aspiring Italians are elbowed out; witness various San Francisco trades and the longshoremen of Boston in the transoceanic service.[3] Inspired always by labor interests, many cities and some states have long forbidden or restricted the employment of aliens in public work and have even sought to limit their employment in private undertakings. For more than ten years, American labor organizations have aimed to secure national legislation restricting the coming of such immigrants especially as the Italians.

Disproportionately, perhaps, yet surely, some part of the American attitude toward the Italians has been determined by their record in crime. If this history had in it less that is char-

---

[1] On this strike and the preceding, detailed accounts exist. *Report on Strike of Textile Workers in Lawrence, Mass., in 1912* (a United States Senate document of 1912), and United States Bureau of Labor, *The Miners' Strike in the Bituminous Coal Field in Westmoreland County, Pa.*, Washington, 1912.

[2] See, *e.g.*, O. G. Cartwright, *The Middle West Side* (New York, 1914), p. 41.

[3] Ricciardi, p. 209; Barnes, p. 181. Cf. di Palma-Castiglione, in *Boll. Emig.*, 1915, No. 7, p. 55.

acteristic it might indeed count for less. For it is not so much the number of offences that has fashioned public opinion as the evidence they appear to give of an uncanny and fearsome disposition. Elemental natures seem to be at work. Abduction, kidnapping, rape, stand forth, and the newspapers glory in the details. The knife is used by men in their senses, by sober men; and a startling record of homicides or of attempted homicides appears. It is the Old World way. That the victims are themselves Italians, and that the roots of the dispute often lie in the past or in a misadventure of love, is insufficiently realized.

The strangest manifestation has been in the "Black Hand" outrages, which in their frequency and power of terrorization — but little else — recall the "Molly McGuire" doings of the Irish period of immigration. A man of means receives a scrawled missive bearing the sign of the black hand and the inexorable demand that a stated sum of money be privately conveyed to the nameless writer. The robber is as good as his word. Death by the knife or bomb, the blasted home or store, is the proof which comes too late. In the first seven months of 1913, there were sixty Italian murders in New York. The perpetrators of such crimes may have been members of the Camorra or Mafia and may have followed their chosen prey to America; or, in a country of defective police administration, and dazzled by the success of others, they have been led by imitation to choose the short, if speculative, road to wealth. Any Italian trader or shopkeeper, sometimes an opera singer, is the recipient of a letter. With a more complicated motive it is sent to a judge or it prevents a concert scheduled by an orchestra which had discharged Italian musicians. Although few attacks have been made upon others than Italians and most have been in New York, yet the terrorization has affected a larger circle. Since no "Mano Nera" exists in Italy, we may say that the whole development has been conditioned by imported criminals or by criminals bred in the American environment — assimilated, if you will, to bad elements rather than to good — and by the presence of a large community of aliens. The constant unwillingness of the Italians to act as witnesses in the courts has made the suppression of Black Hand crime, as of Italian crime generally, all the more difficult. Yet some diminution has of late years taken place, thanks, first of all, to an improved police system.

Other sorts of crime or misdemeanor need but brief mention. Of drunkenness there is less than among some nationalities in the country. The abundant gambling is more or less clandestine. Violations of city ordinances are indeed beyond number; but generally not serious. Easily escaping from parental checks, the Italian child often runs a career of idleness and crime which pains the hearts of his more restrained, if less assimilated, parents, and may lead them to regret the day of their coming.[1]

In the matter of dependency, the burden, thus far at least, has been less than low earnings and unemployment might lead one to expect. I believe it to be true that the breaking point is reached later by the Italians than by many other groups in our population. Though starving, they often continue at work — at any work they can find. That distress which is often the lot of new arrivals various Italian organizations seek to prevent: in New York, the Society for Italian Immigrants watches over their debarkation, helps them to find employment, and otherwise assists them, while the *Casa per gli Italiani* supplies beds and food. If collapse comes later, American agencies are likely to give succor. In the first half of the year 1916 more Italians than persons of any other nationality were aided by the Charity Organization Society of New York. It is when their families are with them in the United States that they appeal for aid; the exhausted or starved bodies, stricken with illness, need repair. The very frugal ways of the

[1] A statistical analysis of Italian crime is in *Immigration Commission*, xxxvi. See also Massachusetts, *Report of Commission of Immigration*, pp. 104–106. Among many secondary accounts see N. Colajanni, " La criminalità degli italiani negli Stati Uniti," an essay (pp. 115–192) in a composite volume, *Gl' italiani negli Stati Uniti*, Rome and Naples, 1910. On the Black Hand see, besides the files of the newspapers, F. M. White, " How the United States Fosters the Black Hand," *Outlook*, October 30, 1909, pp. 495–500; and *idem*, " The Black Hand in Control in Italian New York," *ibid.*, August 16, 1913, pp. 857–865; S. Reid, " The Death Sign," *Independent*, April 6, 1911, pp. 711–715; A. Woods, " The Problem of the Black Hand," *McClure's Magazine*, May, 1909, pp. 40–47; and the *Statuto* and *Regolamento* of an interesting, if rather impotent, counter-agency, *Società Italiana La Mano Bianca*, Chicago, 1908. According to a report published by Carpi (ii, p. 244) forgery and the coinage of money were characteristic crimes forty-odd years ago.

unmarried or of those whose families are abroad enable them to tide over most personal difficulties out of savings, but often, no doubt, the pinch is communicated to the dependents in Italy. There are indications that the repugnance to asking aid which exists among the newcomers wears away somewhat with the lapse of time, and it is quite possible that when a larger fraction of the Italians have reached old age they, like so many of their predecessors in immigration, will frequently fall a burden upon charitable institutions. If that should happen, the reason would lie, not in such thriftlessness as the Irish and some other groups have manifested, but contrariwise (in addition to low wages) in that blind economy which often sacrifices physique and earning power.[1]

When the American people are not swayed by the industrial or the labor argument or by such manifestations as delinquency and dependency, their attitude may take any of various turns. Sometimes it is one of indifference — why should one bother about the Italians at all ? Sometimes an ideal principle is applied, such as that the movement of men must be free, and for this principle a traditional basis may be found in the practice of the United States; or it is argued that the country should offer an asylum for the oppressed and a democratic home for those who seek equality of opportunity.

More generally, a direct personal reaction overshadows or excludes an ideal. By his tongue and his ways, the Italian is felt to be a " foreigner," and even employers sometimes avoid him on that account. He has a low standard of living, and that is ever an unpleasant consideration to those who wish to live better. His crowding and dirt are assumed to be of his own choice; in any case are unlovely and to be avoided. His children are too numerous, and perhaps his low standard of living shows nowhere so

---

[1] *Immigration Commission*, xxxiv, xxxv. Less about the nationality of immigrants aided is to be found in public records than in private. See a chapter (x) by Barrows in Lord, Trenor, and Barrows. In *Boll. Emig.* are frequent references to situations calling for aid. See also B. Attolico, "La 'Society for Italian Immigrants' e la *Casa per gli Italiani* in New York," *Boll. Emig.*, 1912, No. 3, pp. 36–48. An earlier but broad discussion of the work of various agencies is in Conte, pp. 133–185.

plainly as in that pressure of baby cart upon push cart which makes the Italian streets of New York picturesque. Contempt, or at best contemptuous tolerance, prompts the vernacular epithets "Wop," "Guinea," and "Dago." In a country where yet the distinction between white man and black is intended as a distinction in value as well as in ethnography it is no compliment to the Italian to deny him whiteness, yet that actually happens with considerable frequency.[1]

Depreciation in its intenser forms may be feared by the Italian and lead to clashes. A few years ago an Italian consul advised those of his countrymen who objected to such an attitude to stay away from c ̣ain parts of the South.[2] Sometimes a trivial incident converts opposition into acts of hostility. The memory still lives of the New Orleans episode of 1891 when the lynching of Italians — reports say of eleven — strained the relations of Italy and the United States. Accused of shooting the Chief of Police, three of these immigrants had just been condemned by a jury and eleven acquitted, while others were yet untried, when the cry "Kill the Italians!" prevailed.[3] The case is by no means unique. Late in 1914, in southern Illinois, when race antipathy and economic competition had gone before, some Italians were lynched for killing Americans.[4]

It is always hazardous to try to guess the drift of argument and desire in a great country. But the ruling attitude on immigration now stands fairly clear. Fortified by a steady access of support during many years, the Congress of the United States, in 1917,

[1] See the account (p. 361) of the qualities of the railroad laborers. "One 'white man' is as good as two or three Italians!" has been said on some piers in New York; Barnes, p. 9. Ambassador Mayor was startled to overhear, in the South, the words, "It makes no difference whom I employ, negro, Italian or white man"; Mayor des Planches, p. 144.

[2] Moroni, in *Boll. Emig.*, 1913, No. 1, p. 65.

[3] See the study by Professor Pierantoni, *I fatti di Nuova Orleans e il diritto internazionale*, Rome, 1891; also his article, "I linciaggi negli Stati Uniti e la emigrazione italiana," in *L'Italia Coloniale*, April–May, 1904, pp. 423–447, and July, 1904, pp. 37–52. In the United States the episode increased the pressure for restriction of immigration; see H. C. Lodge, "Lynch Law and Unrestricted Immigration," *North American Review*, May, 1891, pp. 602–612.

[4] Di Palma-Castiglione, in *Boll. Emig.*, 1915, No. 6, p. 41.

succeeded in enacting over the President's veto — a very rare occurrence — a law prohibiting the admission of aliens who fail to pass a simple literacy test. No other important group of immigrants is so broadly affected by the new law as the South Italians. And today (1919) still further restriction is proposed.

What of the future ? It is not difficult to discern some of its ingredients. The North Italians will probably be a larger fraction of our Italian population than they have at any time been save in the early years of their coming. For the good name of Italy, that is hardly a disadvantage. Even where the distinction is popularly blurred and all are called just " Italians," those of the North by reason of their qualities are in better repute.[1]

Undoubtedly those South Italians who stay in the country will, as they take on American ways, rise in estimation. When they lose their sobriety, habits of economy, devotion to their customs and traditions and attachment to their kind, one student has ironically observed, they tend to come more into favor! It is surely so, for their neighbors then find them less inscrutable. The little changes, it must be conceded, come quickly. The advent of a linen collar soon brings an altered speech. The newly arrived youth in the theater clamors for " musica," violently anglicizing the " u." " All right " he transforms to " oraitte "; " yes " to " iesse " — and so through the whole essential vocabulary.[2] Giovannina becomes Jenny, Domenica, Minnie, while Giovanni and Giuseppe, luckier, become John and Joe; and illustrious family names, like Aquinas and D'Adamos, have been known to change, by a process surely of magic, into Quinns and Adamses![3] It is precisely such changes as these, trivial to all appearances, that make the Italian feel himself to be an American and the American to regard him as no longer quite an Italian. By schools

[1] Thirty years ago, in California, Gardini wrote (ii, p. 223), " I was very happy to hear my compatriots spoken of with so much praise and such sympathy, a thing I had not heard in New York."

[2] Cf. Bernardy, *America vissuta*, pp. 318 f. She notes that whiskey becomes " vischio," which is good Italian for " birdlime "!

[3] Roche, p. 110.

and philanthropic agencies ever greater momentum is given to the transformation of the immigrants. Through the teaching of English or of the requirements for citizenship, somewhat broadly conceived, through classes for the women in cookery and the care of children, the evangel of " Americanization " makes itself heard; yet in its magnitude the task of conversion is stupendous and so far as the mass are concerned can never reach far nor deeply. It is for those of the second generation that the hope is best based. Handicapped though they be by many of the parents' handicaps, enjoying a precocious independence, they are yet amenable to a wise steering, and could they receive it, would surely rise well above their parents' fortunes.

Unless the American birth rate should greatly decline and the Italian immigration and birth rate be not only maintained at high levels but extended, the Italian stock will one day lose its identity in the United States. True, the more immediate showing is one of persistency. Census materials of 1900, only recently made available, show that in Rhode Island Italian women aged less than forty-five and married for from ten to twenty years had an average of five children each, or twice as many as native women of a corresponding class, and that children followed one another twice as rapidly among Italian families as among native.[1] In 1915, roughly, 22 per cent of the children born in Connecticut, 20 per cent of all born in New York state and in Rhode Island, nearly 12 per cent of all born in Massachusetts, and 9 per cent of all born in Pennsylvania had an Italian father.[2] We are plainly concerned therefore with a stock that has taken a tenacious hold upon the country. But it is a hold that must relax, for the Italian stock has arrived too late to lend its traits perceptibly to the mass of the population. Such a situation as has come about in Argentina will never be even approximated in this country. In 1858,

---

[1] *Immigration Commission*, ii, pp. 462–464; other data also are in this report.

[2] U. S. Bureau of the Census, *Birth Statistics for the Registration Area of the United States, 1915, First Annual Report* (Washington, 1917), p. 56. Intermarriage of Italians with those of other stock has certainly not yet gone far. On some tendency of Italians in New York to marry Jewesses, see a summarized report in *Immigration Journal*, September, 1916, pp. 88 f.

we have seen, the foreign-born Italians of Santa Fé province were already 2.8 per cent of the population, and only beginning to increase, but in the United States the year 1910 had come before the Italians, foreign-born and native together, two million and more strong, had attained a somewhat similar fraction (2.3 per cent) of the whole.

BOOK IV

ITALY AMONG THE NATIONS

CHAPTER XXI

THE EMIGRANTS — A STUDY OF MOTIVE AND TRAIT

OF the externals of the emigrant's life much has been written. How he thinks and feels, however, what kindles and what chills him, what his deeper moods are and the springs of his action are matters mainly hidden, guarded, and unconfessed. A Cellini, a Rousseau, a Goethe bares the record of his life's course; but the emigrant, besides lacking the faculty of literary expression, accepts the fact that for the world he is a supremely unimportant person. What is more, he is less to be thought of, after all, as an individual than as a composite. Hence he cannot speak. And we can only guess.

Out of fragmentary pictures of the emigrants' lives in Italy and abroad, I have tried to weave together some of the tissues of this composite, to reach out from the single experience to a generalized character. Some qualities and traits, because they are common to many more emigrants than are others, I have freely emphasized; still others, particularly if they have stood forth sharply in the chapters dealing with the Italians abroad, I have here touched only lightly in passing. Moreover, the process and appraisal are alike personal, much more so than the long narrative that has preceded. Only the circumstance that the result in general accords with the conditions there set forth gives it some claim to objective validity.

Let us begin quite at the beginning, with the very motive to emigration itself. That assuredly must govern much that follows. Speaking of the importation of negro slaves into South America, Signora Ferrero once asked whether all emigration were not involuntary.[1] Has the Italian been so? Is the meaning of those conditions described in the earlier chapters of this book that

---

[1] Lombroso-Ferrero, p. 101.

the mass have been banished ?   Behind the departure of the negroes from Africa was the physical constraint exercised by their captors.   Behind the departure of Garibaldi, of Fanti and a long line of their kind [1] was the threat of death if they stayed.   Behind the departure of the emigrants has often been the threat of that slow decline, that death in life, which may make the act of emigration, at a critical juncture, almost like a simple reflex action or obedience to an inexorable behest.   " We should have eaten each other had we stayed," the peasants have sometimes been reported to have said.

But imminence of disaster has not been usual.   The morrow and the morrow's morrow have been fairly discernible ahead. Emigration is no device of emergency relief.   There is time and to spare for making one great rational inference: so irksome are thé terms of living that flight is desirable.   All else may be non-rational, the decision, for instance, to go to one country rather than another; but not this primary reaction.[2]   On the other hand, there is in all agricultural folk, or at least in those that possess even a bit of land, so great an inertia, such an identification of the whole content of existence with home and habitat, that the decision to flee can come only slowly: and with the mass it has been as with the individual.   That is why, as late as half a century ago, men were led (for example, Adolf Wagner) to regard the Italians as a people not given to emigrate — a people as attached to the soil, some one has said, as an oyster to its rock.

The notion of flight is rudimentary, without doubt, yet of itself too simple to explain what happens.   Rarely if ever does it alone govern the man's conduct.   Companioned with it in his consciousness is the notion, however vague, of a tangible positive gain to be secured, a notion that generally depends upon the evidences of others' success.   There must be here a whole gamut of combinations, the idea of flight paramount at one extreme, that of gain paramount at the other.   For any individual the promise of gain

---

[1] They form a large part of the numerous warriors, literary folk, and others individually described in a valuable if curious work by F. F. Carloni, *Gl' italiani all' estero dal secolo VIII ai dì nostri*, 2 vols., Città di Castello, 1888, 1890.

[2] The local and special variations and accompaniments of this reaction are finely described by F. Coletti, *Dell' emigrazione italiana* (Milan, 1912), secs. 40-51.

must be felt to be more or less indirect. In the most elementary case, he wills to emigrate because the mass do, accepting the rationality of their quest; [1] and the contagion may extend so far as to lead him to follow the same occupation abroad that the others do — four-fifths, it is claimed, of the emigrants from Laurenzana (Basilicata) became bootblacks in cities of the United States.[2] He may gaze forlornly at the houses erected by emigrants who have returned, and himself depart because such an emblem of success has impressed itself on his mind.[3] He may pause to envy the coat and cigar displayed by them — " they come back arrayed like *signori* " has been a common observation.[4] He notes that they send back money, and coming home, buy land. Or he listens to the recitals of emigrants returned, who asseverate that America is better than Italy, or to the sanguine words of agents of the steamship lines. Or, himself venturing abroad once, he may return, complete his comparison, and decide to sally forth again; it is a common case.[5]

Assurance of well-being ahead he can rarely have. He must take a chance, and if there were not implanted in every man some readiness to do so, emigration might not take place. Particularly among the younger men the disposition may assume a very active form, even dominating all other impulses. The stock exchange, the race track, in South Italy the lottery, are institutional testimony to the power of the risk-taking motive, which is usually coupled with an egoistic expectation of selection of oneself for fortune's favors. (How finely Samuel Johnson, in one of his *Rambler* papers, painted the mood!) The stage, the law are familiar instances of occupations in which great prizes so allure that the mass of the competitors are actually underpaid for their sacrifices. Perhaps emigration is another instance. There is question here not merely of the symbolic influence of those who turn out to be better off abroad than they had been at home, or

[1] For a crude statistical measure of the strength of the factor " imitation," see *Inch. Parl.*, v[ii], p. 714.

[2] A. Rossi, " Vantaggi e danni' dell emigrazione nel mezzogiorno d'Italia," *Boll. Emig.*, 1908, No. 13, p. 16.

[3] Cf., *e.g.*, *Inch. Parl.*, v[ii], p. 507.

[4] Rossi, p. 25, and *passim*.   [5] *Ibid.*, p. 13.

who come back to live comfortably, but of those who after only a few months send home a thousand lire, or after ten or twelve years return with ten to twenty thousand lire, of several far-famed men—speaking provincially—whose amassings have run into the hundreds of thousands. The compelling force of such examples upon the popular imagination can hardly be overdrawn. They provide the bacillus which produces what has sometimes been called the fever of emigration.[1]

The affinities of the emigration movement with the phenomenon, universally observed in modern countries, of migration from rural into urban districts have been curiously ignored.[2] In Italy, while the cities have grown in recent decades by accretions from the country, there has simultaneously been a tremendous movement from the farming community to the foreign city, let us say chiefly the North American city. Doubtless the stories related by those who had returned to Italy, especially in the earlier days, the vivid tales told by the musicians errant and their kin, served to fire the imaginations of the people; much as the fame of Paris or London filters out into the remoter countryside. A deep human need, a welling gregarious impulse, has only in the nineteenth and twentieth centuries found its clearest expression, for these centuries have brought an era when more cities and larger cities have been economically sustainable than ever before. The opposite migration, from city to country, is universally rare; and correspondingly there has been no movement from the Italian cities to foreign rural regions, nor even, in any noteworthy sense, to foreign cities; and all attempts to dislodge Italians from the American urban centers have encountered emphatic resistance. For living and acting with others, for watching the human drama in its intenser moments closely at hand an equivalent is not

---

[1] On the influence of exceptional success see many passages in *Inch. Parl.;* also Rossi, *passim,* esp. pp. 19 f., 25.

[2] But Carpi, nearly half a century ago, quoted A. Caccianiga in a significant passage: " The first departure of a son usually aims at better earnings; the second often adds to the motive of profit a love for the pleasures already tasted in the unbridled life of the great cities, and aspirations toward an existence diverse from rural modes." (i, p. 66.)

easily to be had, and for the Italians even less so, assuredly, than for many another people.

Those who have studied the exodus from country to city have generally averred that it is the more active spirits that participate. In a large view the affirmation must apply as well to a general emigration. To venture one's all — even if that be little — amid incalculable perils and the friendlessness of differing peoples requires a certain staunchness of soul that many men lack. In energy and prowess the emigrant must run well ahead of his sessile neighbor. " His is the life of the conqueror compared with that of the citizen content to count his life's days upon his calendar." [1] Small wonder that other lands sometimes speak of immigrant "invasions." It of course does not follow that those who do not emigrate are devoid of the necessary qualities. They may indeed lack them wholly, or the qualities may be latent. And sometimes those who go are so sheltered at every stage that in the first instance they may be the veriest weaklings. But in those who made pioneer settlements in Argentina and South Brazil, in those who have gone into the outlying parts of Europe and Asia, as far as the mines of Mysore, in those Sicilian fishermen who, after the Suez Canal was opened, betook themselves to Australia, in those wandering minstrels who have carried their traffic in music into a large part of the cities of the world, in all of these, by way merely of example, the persistence, the tireless verve of the conqueror has been present. They are of the race of Columbus still. In those who have journeyed far or made their journeys repeatedly — like the " swallows " who go to Argentina for the harvest — a certain superiority to circumstance appears, a ripeness and robust self-assurance, an urbanity even, qualities not infrequently encountered among far-travelled men of leisure or position but till now met rarely among humble folk.

One of the commonest opinions expressed in both North and South American writings holds that immigration is primarily a tribute to a country's democratic institutions and liberal civilization. The immigrants are idealists; they thirst for freedom, and

---

[1] Barni, "La Svizzera contemporanea," etc., p. 241.

have come where they know it can be tasted. Often, undoubtedly, the opinion has had a deep basis in truth, but at least in its emphasis it has too often been self-flattering. Not only can the Italian immigrants not approach closely to the characteristic life of the Western countries to which they go, but much the same types have entered countries like France, Germany, even inimical Austria into whose institutions they have not pretended that they would fit themselves. As for those who have come to the United States, I have sometimes heard it said that they have desired to pursue ideal ends and would do so more freely, did not their families impose on them a burden of poverty; yet single immigrants, as any one may observe, live as meagerly and as much in isolation as their married brethren.

Rooted much more deeply in the characters of the emigrants is that pecuniary motive which I have been led to stress even in the first chapter of this book. Nothing could be more striking than the frequency with which ideas of economic well-being and of country are reconciled by identification. At Goeschenen Professor Villari (whom I have already cited in a similar context) asked some workmen, "Are you Italians?" and they replied, "We were born in Italy but are not Italians, because we have had to seek our bread elsewhere." [1]   And thirty years earlier, to take another striking example, a Belgian sojourner in Italy, Émile de Laveleye, recorded the dramatic language of a manifesto by which the peasants of Lombardy replied to a ministerial decree urging them not to emigrate:

> What do you mean by a nation, Mr. Minister? Is it the throng of the unhappy? Aye, then we are truly the nation. . . . We plant and we reap wheat, but never do we taste white bread. We cultivate the grape but we drink no wine. We raise animals for food but we eat no meat. We are clothed in rags. . . . And, in spite of all this, you counsel us, Mr. Minister, not to abandon our country. But is that land, in which one cannot live by toil, one's country? [2]

It is a sentiment sufficiently ancient, *Ubi bene ibi patria*, Greek even before it became Roman, reuttered and rephrased, sung with changes, made to live again by millions.

---

[1] P. Villari, " L'emigrazione," etc., pp. 53 f.

[2] *Lettres d'Italie, 1878–1879* (Paris, 1880), p. 350.

Neither love for the new country nor hatred for Italy is necessarily involved when the emigrant sallies forth to satisfy his primary needs. A discreditable materialism cannot be imputed to him, for he has not risen high enough to be justified in disciplining his material desires. Economic redemption cannot wait for other redemption. He will go to that country which his special circumstances and the chance for gain make most inviting. It may be, like the United States, a country of liberal laws; but he will avoid a country of liberal laws if its offer of material rewards be slight. It may be an illiberal country, like the Brazil of the fazendas; yet he will go there, if the prospective reward be seductive. The innumerable guidebooks for Italian emigrants in the countries to which they go never assume that any other aim than the pecuniary is central.[1] And from liberal and illiberal land alike the emigrant will return when making money becomes difficult. So powerful is this aim that it has led to a defiance of language barriers more general and more emphatic than can be found in any other great emigrating people, unless the Chinese be so considered. The English and the Irish have gone almost exclusively into the English-speaking countries, the Germans mainly into countries whose tongues stand related to theirs, the Italians quite as frequently into Anglo-Saxon, Germanic, and other lands as into Latin countries.[2] As the professional soldier of a past age rendered an impersonal service to whatever nation would pay him his hire, so the Italian laborer has looked no farther than his wage and what it will buy. For this modern Hessian the world is a labor market and that country stands first in his favor

[1] One example will suffice (G. Ceppi, p. 56): "The principal, almost the sole aspiration of the emigrants who arrive in the Argentine Republic, is to make much money, the greatest possible amount of money, in order to enjoy it at home."

By a curious custom which prevails in some parts of South Italy a young man will be married by a legal ceremony, in order to secure the dowry that will pay for his emigration, but postpone the religious ceremony until his return.

[2] G. Ferrero has overstated the tendency of the Irish and Germans to establish themselves in lands of diverse tongues, and understated that of the Italians; the latter, however, had not at his writing shown their characteristics so explicitly as they have since done. What he says, however, of the Germans' relatively greater tendency to be assimilated in the countries to which they have gone still holds. See his *L'Europa giovane* (Milan, 1897), pp. 116–118.

which bids the highest wage. The economic principle once so established in his mind, he will often be led to migrate even when his wage at home — in such a region as the Marches, for example — is yet sufficient to a comfortable subsistence.

It used to be said that the Italians are the Chinese of Europe.[1] That is, to make clear the comparison, they were held to be devoid of a sense of solidarity with the labor groups about them. While other workers would demand that toil should be paid for in comfortable living, the Italians would live miserably in order that their toil might be somehow paid for. " It is solely the dullards and the *strikers* who come back without savings," said a contadino of Cosenza,[2] and only incessant pressure by organized labor in the immigrant countries has reduced somewhat the opprobrium in which the striker has been held by the Italians. Only gradually, and today still far from perfectly, has the Italian learned to steer clear of strike breaking. He continues generally to deplore a strike, and rather than wait for the contest to end he betakes himself to a different labor market, or returns to his home in Italy. To regard him as deliberately hostile to other laborers would be puerile. His traits are rudimentary still and a sense of oneness with other toilers has simply not found a place among them. In another sphere, that of politics, the same economic motive — the desire for a job or for privileges — and not a generous solidarity, or a new allegiance of sentiment, has often led to his naturalization.

Not cardinally the passion to earn but the passion to save is the form which the economic motive assumes. Here is one of the clearest traits of the Italians, in its definiteness sharply marking them off from most other emigrant peoples. They stand, for example, at the opposite pole to that of the Irish. Near them, in the United States, are the Austrians. And everywhere the Italians of the South save more eagerly than those of the North — do they not also more commonly prefer those occupations which remunerate more promptly and frequently ?

[1] The phrase has had much currency. For an essay taking its cue from it, see V. Spångberg, *Europas Kineser*, Stockholm, 1897.

[2] Rossi, "Vantaggi e danni," etc., p. 11.

This passion colors the details of the Italians' lives. Everything must be done cheaply, directly, without waste. They are in all things bargain hunters. Among the nationalities in Lawrence, Massachusetts, it was found upon investigation several years ago that they peculiarly were without account books, not following the practice of trading exclusively with one firm.[1] When it is necessary to move, family and friends do the work, a cartage fee being rarely paid. Sobriety and frugality rule the routine of their living. Always too little rather than too much is their principle. They must be abstemious. Perhaps one reason why the South Italians at home and abroad partake more sparingly of alcoholic drinks than do other peoples is that their constitutions and temperaments require no excitant, but it is still more broadly true that Italians, Northern and Southern, unless already demoralized, drink less than other peoples for the reason that indulgence in the habit nibbles away their potential savings. In Italy sobriety is often a necessary of existence; in the countries of immigration it is only little less than that.[2]

Everywhere the incessant beaver-like industry of the Italian has been remarked. He works much more and much harder than many other immigrants. He is up and about early in the day, and nightfall does not seal his labors. Under his touch the Argentine prairie or the New York abandoned farm blooms. The fruit vendor or small merchant of California or Peru presently builds himself a substantial shop.

Yet the tale is not ever so. As an employee the Italian has often been described as lazy, shirking, tricky, a time server; the foreman who watches over him has no perfunctory task. He does indeed work hard and apparently with great powers of endurance, but he does not work willingly. In truth, what he loves is not labor as labor, for he is but human; he loves, first of all, and eagerly, accumulation. Effort which does not make for accumulation is half-hearted, or performed without zeal. Sometimes men

[1] *Report on Strike*, etc. (Senate document, *cit.*), p. 182.

[2] A half century ago Florenzano wrote (p. 330): "The Italian is patient, resigned, sober, economical — qualities that stand forth as well about the ice of the Alps as at the base of the volcanoes." Amid the great diversity of historical antecedent, such are really the common qualities.

have observed in him a characteristic docility or amenability to their wishes, and employers have made capital of the quality. Partly it is to be explained by the century-long domination of church and foreign prince in Italy, or of feudal lord. Partly it is the effect of an overpowering and unyielding environment, both natural and social; the patience which knows no alternative, resembling the resignation of the beast of burden. But chiefly, I believe, it is to be explained, much more directly, by the emigrant's reluctance to imperil the job that yields savings, his recognition that for him acquisition is everything. He asks few favors. Lacking physical strength, he must get his price by long hours of hard, monotonous toil.

It is possible to follow out numerous striking manifestations of the hunger for savings. Time and again, at the point of departure for America, emigrants have shown themselves more eager to get there cheaply than to acquire a clear notion whither they would turn after arrival.[1] They have moved into houses so congested and unsanitary that only a miracle might avert costly consequences to health and morals. They have, in all the major countries of their destination, formed the practice of taking boarders, with its many deplorable results, a thing they had never done in Italy. When beauty and utility have come into conflict, they have sacrificed beauty: witness their cutting down the shade trees at Vineland, New Jersey, the general absence of lawns and flowers and any aspect of homelikeness both in their North and their South American farms.[2] Self-denying or negligent of dress as of lodging, they have incurred the dislike of people about them: of the workmen, because they seem content with a low wage, of shopkeepers because they avoid trade. And as they sacrifice comfort and beauty so also they are jealous of learning. For themselves and for their children — even as was their way in

---

[1] Cf., *e.g.*, De Michelis, in *Boll. Emig.*, 1907, No. 10, p. 16.

[2] See the reports on *Immigrants in Agriculture* of the United States Immigration Commission. De Amicis, observing the Italians in Santa Fé province, wrote (*In America*, p. 99): "While the houses of the German and English colonists, even of those less well off, are whitewashed and adorned in some fashion inside as well as out, those of the Italian colonists have coarse exteriors and interiors and are in every non-essential thing neglected."

Italy — they desire only that minimum which will promote their earning. Their children must not go to school for a day longer than the law requires, and if a false word can affirm that a child's years excuse him, that word will often be spoken. It is scarcely irrelevant to add that a money motive has prompted a characteristically large fraction of Italian crimes, most of those, for example, that are associated with the Black Hand.

In a powerful tale of Tolstoi's, Pakhóm the peasant, offered as much land as he could encircle by walking in a day, strained every fiber to the utmost and encompassed a great tract, but as the night descended upon his completed journey, fell dead. The passion to save may be, philosophically speaking, the Will to Live, but like every other passion, it is often blind. On the Italian immigrant's farm, visitors have remarked the gaunt and overworked horses. In thousands upon thousands of Italian homes, the women and children have borne the marks of a drained vitality, a spent beauty. The men themselves have been reported to decline prematurely, their famed " endurance " being often but a shortsighted or unescapable expenditure of the reserved strength of youth. The physical body, its plasticity departed even before the moment of emigration, has been asked to make a difficult adaptation to novel requirements, and it breaks under the strain. Pakhóm perhaps does not fall at the day's end; but he bows his head ever a little more as the days pass.

A character so bent upon saving as the Italian cannot fail to develop strongly a practical side, or to accentuate any previously existing tendency of the sort. The Italian is indeed a prudentialist. Ideas do not fascinate him. He reflects, and evolves ideas, but all cogitation which does not quickly and surely bring the wished-for gain, generally a personal gain, he terminates and abandons. A realist, cold and calculating, he submits every idea to an acid test of fact.[1] He often speculates, we have seen, when

---

[1] " The Italian who occupies himself with things which do not directly touch him is an Italian who has yet to be born " (A. Pelligrini, cited by De Boccard, p. 5). The view is of course extreme, but in its tenor otherwise just. Compare the emphatically objective character of Italian philosophy, the absence of sustained reflection in Italian music, indeed the relatively meager development of any but dramatic music.

he decides to emigrate. But his is most commonly a speculation that takes place under provocation; abroad he avoids hazards where he can, economic as well as physical, and seeks independence through saving daily a fraction of his wage. He is not an adventurer. Though he often finds himself in a place where work is not to be had, he never goes to a place unless he has been led to believe that work will offer itself. He may smother his personal inclinations if thereby he can live more cheaply and save more; but he is less willing than many other workers are to incur risks likely to imperil his chance of savings; in fact he has sometimes been said to feign sickness in order not to have to work in bad weather, reporting himself well again when rubber boots or other protection had been provided. Partly it is the Italian's sense of the practical and the expedient which determines his attitude, already discussed, toward strikes. He is an adherent of few causes, of those only in which his interest is visibly involved, and he has little wish to make converts. His enthusiasm, though it may attain a high pitch, quickly again subsides. He has taken to heart the lesson of deception and intrigue at home and is suspicious of those who would make advances to interest or help him. All alliances, he fears, tend to become entangling. The same distrust of others leads him to preserve silence at many moments when persons less prudentially constituted would freely uncover their thoughts.

The keenness of the Italian's desire to earn and to save, overriding so much else that the world deems wholesome, cannot be understood without reference to his ulterior philosophy of life, and this in turn cannot be understood without inquiry into his relation to the land of his birth. Of patriotism as a Frenchman, for example, knows it, a proud devotion to the traditions and ideals of his nation, he has little. *La terza Italia* is of recent birth. What is magnificent in an earlier age is unknown to the lower classes, remote, or thought of as not representative; or it is simply blended in the much acuter memories of secular, even millenary, alien conquest and oppression. Below Rome especially, there is a history of governments, but not a political history of the people.

The State has meant a hated rule, and distrust, even into the era of better governmental intentions, has been its sure reward.[1] The distrust becomes one of governments as such and easily is transferred to the country of immigration. It is certainly one factor, and a strong one, in making for that susceptibility to subversive propaganda which sundry chapters of this book have recorded.

Abroad the Italian's sentiment of patriotism, such as it is, may be reanimated. Thrown among men of other nationalities, put upon the defensive, the critic may find in himself a pride like that which other men show, and he may regard his own countrymen in a new light. I recall sitting of an afternoon in a popular Italian theater in Boston during the first year of the European war, when at intervals, in the progress of a song, the flags of the nations were displayed on a screen, Belgian, British, Russian, and the rest. Each won its round of applause, which was heightened when the Stars and Stripes appeared, but was redoubled and prolonged when finally the Italian banner flashed forth. Beyond doubt, I reflected, the response was greater, under this contrast, than when on other occasions the Italian flag alone was presented. The change of which this episode was symptomatic is so far spontaneous or unconscious. Under leadership and stimulus it further happens that a national holiday like the Venti Settembre is honored in a celebration, and support has upon occasion been found in America for erecting in public places statues of those household gods — as they have become to many — Garibaldi and Mazzini. Patriotism again certainly played a part in the return to Italy from European countries and America of Italians who planned to fight in the Libyan and European wars. On the other hand such patriotic organizations as other peoples maintain in

---

[1] One striking instance of such distrust, pertinent to our study, was given to the Senate, June 30, 1909, by Sig. Reynaudi, Commissioner-General of Emigration (see *Boll. Emig.*, 1909, No. 12, p. 112). Some sixty workmen, he said, clandestinely enrolled at Naples to go to Brazil, had been warned by the emigration officials that they would be defrauded. In vain. Again at Genoa the officials declared that the Brazilian wage would be insufficient, the work hard, the climate bad. Yet they departed. At Lisbon the officials offered to pay their way back if they would return. One accepted. Scarcely had the rest reached their destination when the consul cabled for permission to repatriate them, which was given, involving an expenditure of 10,000 lire.

foreign lands have been few or weak among Italians, lacking sustained strength, continuance of effort. Aptly was it observed by Corradini that only in *Italia Irredenta* had his compatriots presented a firm patriotic front,[1] and there, it might be added, the elements most outspoken had been, not the newcomers, but those longest established.

And here a paradox. Far from being an eager patriot in the land of his birth, seeking his Italy in whatever country will give him his bread, not fervid in his patriotism abroad, the Italian, like no other emigrant, aspires to return to his home. This hope he bears in his heart when he departs, as opinion universally witnesses; he keeps it warm and pulsating in foreign lands, where it contributes tellingly to that aloofness from others or clannishness which his neighbors there have noted in him; and as our formal statistical study has suggested, it is potent in directing him back to his Italy. It carries him thither indeed from all countries, whether their governments be liberal or illiberal, and it by no means always awaits the oncoming of depression in business.

"He abandons the niggardly soil as the swallow forsakes the inclement skies; he returns to his familiar and cherished hut as the bird repairs to its old nest."[2] The Italian, when he emigrates, has in a notable sense already attained his growth, is a fully fashioned character. His affections are warm and deep, attaching him to his family and the scenes of his childhood. When he breaks from these tugging intimacies it is conditionally, not absolutely, he must live in them again, and he departs only that he may live in them more richly than before. Life abroad is a strange and difficult thing to the unsheltered Italian, who tolerates it only for the promise of the return to Italy. Where contrasts glare upon him from every angle, a homesickness appears and the *animus redeundi* becomes restless and impatient. Yet he stays and sacrifices, rounds out his purgation, putting aside as many lire as he may to realize his master passion, the assurance of a house and land and comfort for his family in his native *paese*. At bottom,

[1] *Il volere d'Italia*, p. 95.
[2] E. Morpurgo in *Inch. Agr.* (1882), iv[1], p. 95.

and quintessentially, this is the meaning of his parsimony and saving in other lands, this defines his prime and paramount motive in settling in them, this is his idealism.[1]

One journey abroad may not suffice to make the dream real. Some emigrants pass many times between Europe and America. When their migration is periodic — the true " bird of passage " sort — they doubtless are carrying out a plan. But it must happen very often, especially when periodicity is absent, that their lives are an incessant contest, wholly unplanned, between the desire to live at home and the desire to earn abroad. They return with money — it is not enough. Forth again, therefore, and back again. But their developing tastes have surpassed their savings. Once more the course is repeated; but now perhaps adversity strikes, and renovation of fortune must begin anew.

He who embarks upon so great an adventure knows not whither it may lead him. Be his heart never so steadfast at parting, yet he must reckon with the wide world's wooing. As abroad there is a strife between the desire to continue to earn and that to return to Italy, so there arises a contest between the old home and the new — the one calling, the other seducing. How deeply the trouble stirs must vary much from individual to individual. It may pass quickly, a thing of a day, because excess of pain accompanies the memory of the old home, or because bitterness and disillusionment are the main gift of the new, or again because fullness of success in the new land may convert sentiments and sympathies to a fresh allegiance. Instances of such faring are easily verified, and endless nuances of them as well. Discontented in America, the emigrant may go back to Italy only to find it less beautiful than it appeared in the gleaming delineation of his

---

[1] Italians much occupied with their dream are less successful abroad than others. See, *e.g.*, Carpi, ii, p. 133, and G. Ceppi, p. 43. Ceppi has written: " These vacillations . . . enormously hurt the emigrants, impeding their activity and their initiative, holding them always in disquiet and uncertainty. Those who from the first reckon with what is best and decide to regard the Argentine Republic as the field in which to deploy all their aptitudes win an immense advantage over those who waver and who think only of returning." They are led, he adds, to exhaust their lands.

memory (one recalls the blind couple in Synge's play whose restored vision shatters their happiness) and the experience may send him definitively forth.[1]   Or he may be treated in Italy as a parvenu by bourgeoisie and aristocracy alike — " What was he before he became rich ? " they may unpleasantly ask, and again he must sally forth.[2]   Gradually the country of secondary allegiance — or of none whatever — may supplant its rival and become primary; and this even when naturalization is neither acquired nor sought.   Indeed in nearly all countries the readiness of the Italian actually to change his citizenship, unless for business reasons, has emerged tardily or not at all.   When children have been born abroad, they become the most powerful of all forces to sever the tie with Italy.[3]   For the dream of the return to Italy has rested largely on the love of family and home; and the new births, especially when the children have so far grown up as to recognize a tie of their own, create a new home.   Very rarely do these foreign-bred children seek out Italian citizenship.   And if, on the contrary, as happens abundantly in Argentina and the United States, the children become infused with the demonstrative patriotism of the new nation, then the parents too may come to regard Italy as a country without a morrow, and America as the country of strides and grandeur.   So at the last the bright colors of the dream may fade and the dream itself be forgot.

The connection subsisting between the Italian's attachment to the scenes of his early life and his hunger for savings while abroad is now sufficiently clear.   But the precise form which his patriotism assumes in other lands has still to be determined.   Directly or indirectly, for instance, through that national amalgamation which comes with the Italian method of military training, he has learned to respond to the name of Italy, and he kindles to the glory of Garibaldi and the Risorgimento satellites.   But his nationalism is still a veneer, thick and substantial often, but rarely

---

[1] Cf. de Amicis, *In America*, pp. 111–115.

[2] Cf. Troisi, *L'Argentina agricola*, etc., p. 107.

[3] *E.g.*, " To the question ' Shall you return to Italy ? ' ' God willing, but how can I ?   How should I live there ?   And all my children born here ? ' — so they all replied."   Venerosi Pesciolini, *Colonie italiane nel Brasile Meridionale*, p. 278.

if ever the deepest aspect of his social experience (perhaps the War of Wars will make it otherwise).[1]

A great nation tends to have a great capital, a pulsating heart. So France has Paris, and England, London. But in Italy life centers as surely in Naples or Milan or Palermo as in Rome. The powerful traditions are mainly regional and they include even the memory of passionate regional hostilities, now doubtless attenuated but still deserving the name of animosities.[2] Each region has its dialect, and even its dialects within a dialect, all difficult for the unaccustomed to understand.[3] Communication has till recently been slow, and in many places still is; not many decades have passed since eight days were required to go from the Valtellina to Milan. Marriage outside the *paese* is rare. Deeper trust is lodged in a fellow townsman than in the general government.

In foreign countries this regionalism persists. Observers have reported that they do not find Italians but rather Venetians, Calabrians, and so forth.[4] Even the smaller unit, the village, clings to its identity. In Briey, in New York, in Buenos Aires, something like a street-by-street separation of the immigrants according to origin has been recognizable. Partly this cohesion

[1] Bonardelli (*Lo stato di S. Paolo*, etc., p. 120) has succinctly expressed the nature of Italian patriotic sentiment abroad: "For the mass of them, ignorant and illiterate, the idea of country reduces itself to the indelible recollections of youth, of family, of home, the confused tales of the glorious deeds of our history, of our illustrious men; excellent sentiments which yet do not rise to a high idealism of country."

[2] Le Bon is a severe critic, but if his words apply somewhat to the general population they apply *à fortiori* to that lower tier which emigrates, a tier least versed in the history of the third Italy. He says: "A country like Italy may suddenly succeed, through exceptional circumstances, in forming a single state, but it would be an error to believe that it thereby, at one and the same stroke, acquires a national soul. I observe clearly in Italy, Piedmontese, Sicilians, Venetians, Romans, etc., I do not yet see Italians." *Les lois psychologiques de l'évolution des peuples* (8th ed., Paris, 1907), p. 16.

[3] The story is told of an Italian consul who, disembarking at Buenos Aires, found himself among workmen noisily speaking a language strange to him. Inquiring of their nationality, he was told that they were Italians. See Ghinassi, "Per le nostre colonie," *L'Italia Coloniale*, February, 1902, p. 68.

[4] E.g., see di Palma-Castiglione, in *Boll. Emig.*, 1915, No. 6, p. 36 and Bertarelli, *Brasile Meridionale*, p. 81.

rests upon a timidity felt in the presence of strangers, partly it is a variant of this, like the friendliness noticeable among tourists of a single origin who meet in a European pension. But most of all it is a thing so characteristically Italian that it is best denoted by the Italian name *campanilismo*: a loyalty to that which falls within the range of the village bell tower. This it is which spurs the immigrant to entrust his savings to his fellow townsman, rather than to a chartered but foreign bank, or to marry an immigrant girl deriving from his own neighborhood, or to write home asking that a girl from his village be chosen to traverse the seas to be his bride.[1] But with this loyalty also goes marked hostility — at the least, indifference — to the immigrants from other parts of Italy. While conflicts of a sanguinary nature are one result of the curious situation so produced, a larger consequence is a patent disunity of the Italian population as such, mute evidence of the weakness of nationalist sentiment. Most clearly of all, the disunity shows in the schisms and dissensions among Italian societies. When Enrico Ferri was called upon, as a distinguished guest, to speak at a celebration of the Venti Settembre at Rosario, Santa Fé, he declared to his hearers that in maintaining their organizations upon a regional basis they were inharmonious with the spirit of the day they were honoring, for its exclusive significance was the oneness of the Italian nation.[2] As much as anything else, the regionalist temper has further been responsible for the general limitation of the Italians' societies to those forms which serve the more urgent needs of life.

[1] Endogamy is perhaps still commoner when the emigration is merely overland. Of the girls of Cuneo, immigrated into France, it is written (Baldioli-Chiorando, p. 857): " They do not marry the French, few marry Italians who are not from the province of Cuneo, and at the most they marry other Piedmontese; even their love-making is usually in the same circle, and so they end by marrying men of their region almost as if they had stayed at home."

[2] See his address to Parliament June 22, 1909, reported in *Boll. Emig.*, 1909, No. 12, p. 7. On the societies themselves the testimony of a widely travelled Italian is worth adducing: "In my long experience I have found very few Italian societies whose corporate existence has not been constantly corroded and menaced by the same evils, in every country, in every climate, in every environment: excessive individualism, excessive decentralization, the separatist and regionalist spirit." Brenna, *L'emigrazione italiana*, p. 160.

Why it is that Italian societies are more commonly described as innumerable than as large or strong cannot however be fully understood by reference only to the workings of regionalism. Another trait is in play, one which determines a great deal in the behavior of the emigrants. Individualism, since its presence in a people is usually accounted a virtue, has been claimed — has it not ? — for nearly every people, and so for the Italian. In this last association it has attained to such striking and characteristic manifestations that it may be said to be almost pervasive of the national character.

Individualism presumes the State to be a more or less artificial society. It dislikes most forms of collective action. It resents coercion and discipline. One form of it thrives readily in those countries in which governments have succeeded each other, or in which governments have been weak, non-representative, and through their errors and vices mistrusted. So it has thriven in most of Italy. Such an individualism declines when governments tend to become benevolent and efficient. So it has declined in most of Italy, but only a little, for its roots run deep, are tenacious, and give up their hold only after long coaxing. Nowhere has it such strength as in South Italy. The endless denial of State justice in Sicily, even through the first years of United Italy, has elevated into a system the private vendetta. The intense affection of the Sicilian for his family, coupled with the conception that each man must take vengeance into his own hands, privately, not even telling the authorities of his wrong, has fostered a spirit of self-reliance which is elsewhere not common. It is a somewhat ferocious self-reliance, resembling in degree but not at all in kind that of the American frontiersman of a day now gone by, who battled singly, not with the State, but with Nature. Success in the vendetta may require that the idea of revenge be nursed for years, by an implacable memory, pending the right moment to strike. Fitness to steer clear of trouble may depend upon a certain promptness to take umbrage.[1] Hence — partly to be so explained at least — that sensitiveness which every one who has

---

[1] See Lorenzoni's fine analysis of a complex of Sicilian qualities in *Inch. Parl.*, vi[i], pp. 676–680.

known Italians has remarked; that sudden coming of a moment when something must be pardoned or reconstrued. For what has been said here especially of Sicily is in varying degree representative of many parts of Italy.

The same temper which, in the conduct of his affairs in Italy, keeps the Italian from depending upon the State may lead him to seek the rehabilitation of his career by his own instrumentality in other lands. No other emigration has embraced so large a representation of the itinerant types, like the hawkers and the street minstrels; among Irish emigrants, by way of extreme contrast, they have been all but absent. These are perhaps a special incarnation of the individualist impulse for self-redemption. Whatever his type, however, the Italian goes forth to achieve his independence, and generally by saving. He must be a sovereign. Bit by bit, from his low, irregular wages, he lays the foundations of his freedom — how romantic, seen from a complacent angle, is the million times repeated project! He may collapse in his endeavor but, outside the pathological realm of pauperism, he is slow to beg. Yet he does beg if so he may, without obligation, improve his economic status. What he deeply detests is being in another's debt, for that imposes a limit upon his cherished independence.[1] A debt to make emigration possible he freely incurs, but that is a step toward independence and he seizes an early opportunity to repay. The individualism of the South Italian is not of the kind which makes a good pioneer in opening up a country to farming — herein the comment of the investigator of the United States Immigration Commission is justified; yet something even of that individualism has been shown by the North Italians in Argentina. Rather, the Italian's individualism presupposes a social world. In such a one he will struggle to rise and will suffer the inevitable with serenity.[2] He has stoicism, and none but an individualist becomes a stoic.

[1] *E.g.*, " If an Italian has no money and can get none, he will not call a doctor, no matter how ill he may be." Mangano, p. 127.

[2] Cf. Riis' remark: " Neither poverty nor hard knocks has power to discourage the child of Italy." *Children of the Poor* (New York, 1892), p. 21. Bertarelli declares that he has on several occasions compared the Italians on shipboard, during

It is safe to say that the individualism of the Italians shows in even bolder relief abroad than in Italy. Partly this is because the act of emigration itself selects the more enterprising spirits, partly it is because experience in faring for themselves accustoms men to self-dependence. The self-made man develops a certain egoistic belief that the man of quality will surely rise above the mass unaided; and he is therefore none too solicitous about the mass. Of a true civic life, it can surprise no one, there is little in the Italian colonies. There are too many shades of opinion, too many personalities always breaking loose from one allegiance, setting up little kingdoms of their own. There is irreconcilable fretting under discipline and control. Musical as few other peoples have been, the Italians have never developed much interest in choir singing. It is only the readiness to pay the necessary price for a job that makes the worker seem docile; when the readiness is imperfectly maintained, he is called capricious; in the sphere of free decision he is anything but tractable. The difficulty in Italy of holding him to continuous allegiance in the " leagues of resistance " (their best Southern strength is in Apulia, but there too it succumbs to individualist rivalry) is paralleled by the feebleness abroad of his labor-union development. The endless splits of the Italian political parties, again, are paralleled by the division and multiplication abroad of the mutual aid societies, associations for the protection of arriving immigrants and the like, all resulting in a pulverization of competence.

In close association with the Italian's individualism is a certain love of show. It is bound up also with that high regard for aesthetic effect upon which no essay on Italian emigration need dilate. What spectators at a play universally tend to do, namely, to

storms, in seasickness, etc., with Spanish, Portuguese, Arabs, and Poles and noted their superior serenity and strength (*op. cit.*, p. 238; cf. p. 239).

In de Amicis' masterpiece, *Cuore*, which hundreds of thousands, perhaps millions, of Italian children have read, is a story, " Dagli Apennini alle Ande," concerned, idealistically, with this same spirit. Its first sentence shows its drift: " Many years ago a Genoese boy of thirteen years, son of a workman, went from Genoa to America, alone, to seek his mother." And the peregrination it tells of only ends in Tucumán.

identify themselves with the actors, the Italian inclines to do with special urgency. His sensitive personality merges itself in the actor's, and now weeps now exults as the example bids. His approval or disapproval partakes almost of vehemence; to him, how the actor carries his part is no negligible matter. That he should merely sit by, content to gaze and listen while others perform, is already a concession; what he will do if he can is to act in the spectacle himself — compare those religious representations and pageants which make of an entire village in South Italy a stage. It is in harmony with the impulse here under scrutiny that, as some one has said, the municipal expenditures in Italy are, to an unusual extent, munificent rather than provident and every town wants a statue to some *valoroso concittadino:* for so one may stand forth vicariously. When the Italian of the fruit stand in a New Hampshire village or on a New York by-street exhibits his wares dressed in such neatness of design that the customer almost hesitates to disturb the picture, the same proud individualism — commendably proud, we say — is in play.

Much of the life of the Italians in their foreign settlements is organized about this trait. Many a mutual aid society has come into existence largely because of the chance offered for pomp and paraphernalia, and has been held together by its picnics, excursions, and parades.[1] Through the narrow streets of such a colony a funeral procession may take its way, an endless succession of carriages smothered in flowers, followed by an endless line of men marching single file, plumed, decorated, in uniform, carrying gorgeous banners — is it all for the deceased or the living ?

Particularly when a man has won his independence, become a sovereign, he desires that others should respect his success. The colonies have their " prominenti," men who are avid of tribute. Sometimes the successful return to Italy and when they buy land it may be in part to gratify a sort of vainglory.[2] The money which they send home for religious festivals and the like is "partly

---

[1] A leading Italian newspaper of New York prominently advertises that it supplies societies with their printed stationery, seventeen different items, at a price, for minimum quantities, of nearly $50.

[2] Cf. Rossi, " Vantaggi e danni," p. 33.

sent by reason of true devotion, partly for pride in their district and partly to display their own affluence." [1] And de Amicis, from his vantage point on board an emigrant carrying ship bound for Argentina, has remarked how those who have been in America hold forth to the rest, " what a burning desire they feel to become known, to make for themselves a pedestal even in so poor a throng, in order to show how superior they are to the wretchedness to which they are reduced and by which they are surrounded." [2]

In our study of the causes of emigration it was pointed out that in many things the Italian has the mind of a child. In our survey of the emigrants abroad we have repeatedly had to note a certain helplessness, parent of innumerable maladventures. And in the present chapter it must often have been plain that, along with the qualities particularly under discussion, went a certain tentativeness of comprehension or shortness of vision, without whose aid even the illustrations given could not wholly be explained. We cannot longer forego to speak explicitly of this persistent *tertium quid*.

What marks off the mature citizen of the world from the child is a certain fitness for dealing with the world's revolving facets, with the changing demands, contingencies, and conjunctures it presents. This capacity is the result of the activity or the transformation of original powers and impulses, the special result often of methodical schooling, such as our educational systems afford, or of the imitative acquisition, out of a rich social environment, of its heritage of manners and modes of behavior, or finally of the direct experience of life in its ampler ranges. Such a fitness the Italian emigrant lacks. Various are the origins of this deficiency, and numberless the points at which it is revealed.

Sometimes what is impressive is a sheer lowness of standards, a state of contentment with those modes of living which civilized people, as much by metaphor as by knowledge, surely, call primitive. " Dirty " — the Italians are " dirty," personally and in

---

[1] *Inch. Parl.*, viii, p. 58.
[2] *On Blue Water (Sull' oceano*, tr. by J. B. Brown, New York, 1897), p. 85.

their mode of living — how endlessly the charge is reiterated! In the old days there were no baths for emigrants aboard ship. De Amicis complained that for fifteen hundred people in the steerage of the ship that carried him to Argentina there was not one bath.[1] By the Italian law of 1901, two must be provided on each ship. Yet in 1910, when Dr. Madia reported upon the thirty-nine voyages he had made as medical inspector, he could write, " The wise foresight of the law and the best intentions of the government commissioners find a primary obstacle in the ignorance of this mass, which will not let a blow be struck at its venerated century-old traditions of dirt." [2]   The greater part of the emigrants, he further declared, not only make no renewal of linen during the long voyage but even pass the night with their clothes on. Whatever the changes — seemingly not great — which the emigrants abroad undergo, with respect to habits of personal cleanliness, the direction of change is in some environments at least not upward.[3]

The low intellectual development, which has so frequently had for a concomitant neglect of person, has been accountable not only for many of the most grievous blunders of the Italians in foreign lands but also for one element in their success: a stolid indifference to circumstance. To be a helot is assuredly not to have an enviable place. But if one must be a helot one insures best against discomfort by acknowledging few needs, making few demands, discriminating and refining little in one's emotional

---

[1] *On Blue Water*, p. 180.

[2] E. Madia, " Relazione su trentanove viaggi in servizio di emigrazione," *Boll. Emig.*, 1910, No. 15, p. 42. He adds (p. 43) that if at least the children were to be given a bath, the royal commissioner had personally to see to it. That the aversion of emigrants to bathing amounts to a kind of phobia was maintained by Dr. T. Rosati, " Il servizio igienico-sanitario nell' emigrazione transoceanica per l'anno 1908," *Boll. Emig.*, 1909, No. 16, p. 55. In his report for the following year, however (*Boll. Emig.*, 1910, No. 16), he recorded (p. 47) a perceptible increase in the readiness to bathe, under the contagion of example.

[3] Cf. S. Coletti (" Lo stato di S. Paolo," etc., *Emig. e Col.*, 1908, p. 378): " The level of personal cleanliness of our colonists, low in Italy, sinks by several degrees in the fazendas, because the environment is rougher than at home and because the contadino lacks the incentive which he had in Italy of appearing neat at least on holidays, taking part in religious exercises, or merely stopping for gossip in the village square — even those simple social forms disappear in the fazendas."

content.[1] People and affairs touch one not closely, for a haze keeps their reality low. The hard-handed man is not even aware of the prick from which the soft-handed man recoils, and with his physical callousness goes a certain mental callousness; melancholy and neuropathological developments are far less common than many persons have supposed. There is here still another partial explanation of that quality of " endurance," universally noted, which has been discussed above from another angle.

In the unschooled character, illiteracy is only the most immediate of disabilities; it signifies not so much the absence of schooling as the absence of even a little schooling. The Italian's deeper impulses are untransformed, weakly inhibited, and now and then stormily break forth. The passions show uncommon strength, the fervor of love rises to a kind of fierceness. Hate is implacable, vengeance unswerving from its path. For a score of years the intended victim may succeed in living a normal life, augmenting his income and comfort, only to be suddenly shot or stabbed, so mysteriously that the police will listen to no accounting but suicide. Both the intensity of the emotion and the directness of revenge are more familiar to primitive than to civilized societies. Jealousy arises and prompts to many a crime, even to a special crime deriving from emigration: " So-and-so," the newspaper relates, " who returned last week from America, yesterday slew his wife whom he accused of having cohabited with a neighbor in his absence." Or perhaps it is the neighbor who was slain.[2] Unpremeditated blood crimes, such as issue from brawls, are com-

---

[1] Sella (p. 25), makes a striking observation touching the time sense of the Italians in Switzerland: " They speak of things that happened a month ago as of remote things. They speak of events of a year ago as of events that scarcely anyone can remember, as if a current of oblivion had swept over them. Finally, they speak of things that occurred five, six, ten years previously as of things so remote that memory no longer suffices to keep their record, as if not one but ten generations had supervened upon them."

[2] Of this type of crime the Final Report of the *Inch. Parl.* held (viii, p. 57) that " the popular conscience almost always absolves it; . . . The emigrant, often married but a few days, deems it just and natural that he should conserve his bachelor freedom while abroad; no pity, however, for his young wife who, tired of his long abandonment, constrained by continual siege or driven by poverty, yields to seduction or to violence."

mon; only little less, the more deliberate crimes for money. The net result appears in that extraordinary rate of homicides which is so characteristic of Italy, above all of South Italy, and of Italian communities, especially when they contain South Italians, the world over.

The emigrant is highly superstitious. His religion we have seen to be imbued with superstitions.[1] The Sicilian will pray, it is said, indifferently for rain and his family's health and for the lucky outcome of a vendetta or homicide. Events of the past century have contributed to reduce the hold of religion as such upon the Italian, but the element of superstition, become second nature, has been harder to dislodge. It brings with it sometimes a kind of fatalism which again is a frequent attribute of primitive natures.

Toward woman and marriage the emigrant has once more an attitude which harks back to an older time. Marriage takes place while the parties are young. If the circle of the bride's horizon is even narrower than her husband's, that circumstance is for him not disastrous. She may help him in the work of the fields and look after his interests while he earns and saves abroad. He expects of her only that she should be home-loving, industrious, and obedient to his will. With her numerous children (so numerous in Italy and abroad that, as an epigram holds, child bearing and child burying must go hand-in-hand) she becomes for him the center of a small world, or perhaps a retreat from the greater world. She does not ordinarily go back and forth much over the bridge that binds with that larger world. Such a responsibility is her husband's. He it is who decides the major questions of family policy, commonly, for example, making purchases for the household, leaving to her their adaptation to home needs.[2] Per-

---

[1] On the retention of some of these in the United States, see Sartorio, pp. 100 ff.

[2] It is this meagerness of the wife's responsibilities which creates what Mrs. Simkhovich, from the point of view of the social settlement worker, chooses to regard as "the most serious problem in connection with our Italian immigration." See her *The City Worker's World in America* (New York, 1917), p. 102. Lilian Betts had the same situation in mind when she wrote: "The Italian woman is not a good housekeeper, but she is a home-maker." ("The Italian in New York," *University Settlement Studies*, October, 1905–January, 1906, p. 94.) By 758 in 884 Italian working women who reported to Miss Odencrantz "the pay envelope was turned in unopened to the manager of the household." (*Op. cit.*, p. 21.)

haps the feeling of jealousy is never so strong as among those who conceive their wives to be a species of property, deeply prized, no doubt, but yet not free to make decisions, and therefore to be rather guarded and feared than trusted.[1]

Plenty of testimony exists to show that loose living on the part of male Italians abroad is common. Our witnesses, who are generally also critics, affirm that there is often a ready frequenting of prostitutes, a class of persons all but absent from the Italian countryside and village. Still another anomaly is that of wife desertion. Just as the Italian's affection for his native land sometimes declines, and he renounces his plan to return to it, so his affection for his wife, however intense, may decline or in time wither, while a new affection springs up. Such a snapping of the tie is common, and thus emigration may take the place of a divorce court. Both loose living and desertion, however, must be ascribed much more to the abnormal conditions of living which emigration occasions than to a lack of training for life.

Whoever wishes to understand the transformation of the emigrants in foreign lands and whoever in particular wishes to promote it must begin by appreciating the strength of the resistance to change which, intentionally or unintentionally, every emigrant opposes. Even when the conscious aspiration to change is fervid, the unconscious or physical reluctance may be so puissant as to nullify it. That whole assemblage of traits and habits, partly inborn, for the rest accumulated and solidified in the growing years of life — the great majority of emigrants, we must never forget, are adults when they first depart — blocks the path to change, censors and repels what is novel. All true growth is organic, and however the will may welcome expansion or development in one or another particular, the physical context may refuse to budge or may move but haltingly. Change being difficult to the relatively inflexible or inert, as many things as possible will be kept unchanged. Herein lies the meaning, to take a striking

---

[1] Coletti declares (*Dell' emigrazione*, etc., p. 185) that in some parts of South Italy men who marry just before emigrating sometimes, by way of precaution, leave their wives immaculate.

example, of the persistent demand of the Italians, wherever they go, for Italian viands. It is not that Italian dishes are the best — by a similar argument, or want of argument, Greek or German or French dishes are the best — but they best fit the ingrained habits of the partakers. Macaroni, cheeses, polenta, olive oil, wine — if they are not imported they are made after the ancestral models, to the prosperity of maker and retailer. And the Italians, having stressed vegetables in their diet in Italy, will again stress vegetables, though the sorts be different, in foreign lands.

For the mass of the emigrants the rule holds, at the outset at least, that they will change only where all alternatives are closed. They must live in such houses as they can find, having regard for their means; they must consume such food as the country affords; and so forth. Inevitably, migration entails a certain minimum of change, and the expectation, further, of return to Italy sometimes prevents any considerable exceeding of the minimum. Economic need or desire, on the other hand, may dictate a wider range of modification. Some one has said that the language of Dante yields abroad to the language of Calderon, Cervantes, and Shakespeare. It is a picturesque saying, but untrue. A dialect, often one which Dante would not have comprehended, gives way to a hybrid tongue which meets the elementary demands of communication but has ordinarily far to go in accent, grammar, and vocabulary to be merged in the language of the new country. And as the emigrant's language changes piecemeal, so, for the sake of greater gain, he modifies his occupation, when he can. A field hand in Italy, he becomes a miner or a construction hand abroad — it is a theme with endless variations.

Like a violent drug, or an evangelist's eloquence, or war, emigration produces a shake-up of the individual, and the resulting changes may take all manner of surprising forms. He may be quite bowled over and see life as from a new center. He may discover new sources of moral strength or unsuspected aptitudes, winning and justifying a fresh confidence in himself. Or the change may assume mainly a destructive form. Most characteristically, a break from traditional religious doctrine and with church and priest ensues. These simply cease to be necessary, or to count. In their place a more positive freethinking may appear, which is probably not broadly constructive; or even, under stress of propaganda in the United States, attachment to some branch of evangelical Christianity.

Another development that often takes place after the great shake-up is adherence to the radical social philosophies. Its elements are clear enough. A proletariate emigration is from the first in question. The emigrants are at the social bottom in the countries which receive them. The instincts of many are balked by abnormal living. They behold in the new countries the contrast of rich or poor as they never perhaps dreamed it to be possible in Italy. Could anything be better calculated to astound the imagination of struggling indigence than the stupendous show of wealth of New York or Buenos Aires, seen in all its glare from the immigrant vessel as it steams into the harbor ? The countries of immigration are by selection richer countries than Italy. The socialism or anarchism of the Italians departs from the usual types. These toilers spin their doctrines coarsely and care naught if the mesh be loose, so it be strong. They stand as remote as possible from all those who contemplate and speculate in order that they may write books. They would act. In this they simply illustrate again, and forcibly, the realistic and practical and individualistic traits discussed above. And since these intrepid social free lances also, as we have seen, waste no love upon government and the state, the police of all lands have come to take careful notice of their presence.

When the immigrant once converts the presumption of future return to Italy into the presumption of permanent residence in the new country, his step is likely to signify that the change to new ways has already gone far. As a consequence or a cause of taking this step he may marry some daughter of the new country. Not much is known about such intermarriage, except that it is still uncommon. Generally it is the Italian man who marries a foreign woman; that is, doubtless, among other reasons, because Italian men are more numerous than women.[1] A large portion of the

---

[1] G. Capra maintains (" Gli italiani in Australia," *Boll. Emig.*, 1911, No. 2, p. 52) that in Australia the Italians occasionally marry Irish girls. It is to be regretted that we know so little of the facts of intermarriage in the United States.

intermarriages in Argentina and possibly elsewhere are unions of immigrants with the native daughters of other Italian immigrants.[1] Whatever the circumstances, however, the result is bound to be, for the Italian, a more competent grasp of the new country and the means to still further change.

In general, the younger the emigrant at the time of his arrival in a foreign country and the more favorable for his activity the new country, the more profound will be the change in him as time passes. After many years, indeed, recognition of the worker as the farm hand of Italy may be difficult. In Genoa, Wisconsin, for example, one of the older Italian agricultural settlements in the United States, the farmers have quite ceased to be deemed Italians by their neighbors. There has been, in all such cases as this, no catastrophic change, no caterpillar-pupa-butterfly progression, but gradually, in the clearest instances, such an awakening of personality, such an unfolding of competence, specialized or general, as fills observers with wonderment.[2] The old habits and predispositions, borrowed from a long social ancestry, seem outgrown. And the deeper traits, the instinctive ? He would be a bold man who with present knowledge should speak positively of them. The deepest mysteries of the New World populations concern the extent to which these older traits have been preserved in the continuing stocks, whether in the pure strains or in those that have been fused in the crucible.

---

[1] Cf. Foerster, esp. p. 357.

[2] Let de Amicis, sojourner at San Carlos, Argentina, speak again (*In America*, pp. 93 f.): " Accustomed to the lamentations, the everlasting discontent of our people, timid or servile before *signori*, constrained somehow and shut in, ignorant or indifferent to whatever does not touch their immediate interest, I was amazed to see these workmen deal with each other as peers with a cheerful and courteous self-assurance, to hear them discuss administration and politics, make toasts at banquets, expound projects for reforming the elementary schools, and put such questions to me concerning their districts of origin as not one of them, in Italy, would have uttered or dreamed."

CHAPTER XXII

ITALY ONCE MORE — CONSEQUENCES AND REACTIONS OF EMIGRATION

WHEN a birth or a death takes place in a family, profound changes ensue in the careers or relationships of its members. For any one person there may be more or heavier work to do; a cherished advantage — school, music lessons, marriage — may lie open or be blocked; old desires may lose their potency, new ambitions spring up; dependency or its opposite, self-reliance, may arise. And as with the family, when members are lost or gained, so with the larger community.

What changes immigration — a kind of birth — brings into the life of a country the chapters of this book have amply illustrated. Emigration, the abstraction of people — a kind of death — brings changes equally great. So far-reaching are they, in truth, that one must despair of following them into their remoter courses; and, in the case of Italy, they visibly touch so many aspects of national life that there is ever an insidious danger of ignoring the action of other and independent forces. Some changes are the direct or indirect consequence of the abstraction or diminution of certain groups or classes of the population, while others proceed from the return of the emigrants or from the advent of their savings. Because of the vast importance which the economic system of Italy has in causing emigration, we must ask first what the economic reactions of emigration have been. But we must be prepared to find effects of other sorts not less momentous.

Just such a fascination as has long pressed economists to trace the course of the new gold which poured into Spain after the opening of America attends the effort to measure and follow the savings introduced into Italy by her emigrants. These gains come through divers channels. Sometimes money is carried in, foreign or Italian — who has not found an Argentine copper in his lira's change at a shop ? Sometimes Italian paper is bought in the foreign country and sent registered into Italy. It is a safe and a very common method, and when the letter is insured, we have an index to the amount of its contents. Often a postal money order is dispatched — there seems to be little distrust of the financial departments of governments. By recommendation of the Italian authorities, transmission is through the Banco di Napoli; but only gradually has this institution drawn away a large part of the patronage of the small and often fraudulent private concerns.

How much money altogether passes through these principal channels can be only imperfectly estimated; for against the exact figures possible in one or two instances must be set, for others, sheer conjecture. Some students, utilizing various sources of information, have attempted merely to say how much money most emigrants of a particular sort bring back, or with what savings the ordinary emigrant from a district returns. So Dr. Cosattini estimated that seasonal emigrants from the Friuli brought 250 lire; [1] and the girls of Cuneo, to take another example, after five or six months in the fields, have been said to bring 50–80 lire each, the men 100–200 lire.[2] Some years ago, the Commissioner-General of Emigration inferred from local reports that a much larger sum, 300–500 lire, was annually brought back by the emigrants who had gone into Europe, and that 1000–5000 lire, or even more, depending upon country and length of stay abroad, was commonly saved by those emigrants overseas who subsequently returned to Italy.[3]

Still other students have made investigations that are more reliable than those described, partly tending to confirm them and partly differing, since they seek to show the total sums remitted. For the year 1907, Dr. Lorenzoni made a careful local study of the transoceanic remittances into Sicily and Dr. Jarach a similar one

[1] *Op. cit.*, p. 83.
[2] Baldioli-Chiorando, p. 855.
[3] " Relazione sui servizi," etc., *Boll. Emig.*, 1910, No. 18, p. 46.

for a part of the Abruzzi. Generalizing upon the results of these researches the author of the final report of the oft-cited parliamentary study of the contadini estimated that the remittances into all of Sicily and the South amounted in the same year to the impressive total of 350,000,000 lire.[1] Finally, Professor Coletti, partly utilizing these computations and estimating the sums carried back personally by transoceanic emigrants and the sums returned from European countries as well, computed that for all of Italy, in 1907, the receipts were 550 million lire, or, with sundry deductions, 500 million.[2] Regarding the ultimate details of his computation there is necessarily much uncertainty. It is the more noteworthy therefore that Bonaldo Stringher, making an independent study for the Banca d'Italia, of remittances in the same year, should have reached the same general total, 500 million. Stringher's method, admirably applied, was to resolve the payment for a growing and continuing excess of imports over exports into tourist moneys and emigrants' savings.[3]

Not enough, probably, has been made of the inevitably great annual fluctuations of the remittances. Just such a year as 1907 must be rare, for not only were employment and earnings then abnormally, perhaps unprecedentedly, high, especially in the United States, but the panic occurring in its last months provoked extensive liquidation, in order that the savings of years might be securely preserved in Italy. How drastic such liquidation can be is shown by what happened in 1915 — *not* a good industrial year — when Italy entered the war, and her sons came helter-skelter homeward; the Banco di Napoli received 162 million in immigrant remittances, against 85 million in 1914 (already a year of regurgitation of emigrants, especially from the countries of Europe), and 38½ million in prosperous 1907 (when, however, the patronage of the bank was less widespread).[4] What

---

[1] *Inch. Parl.*, viii, p. 52.   [2] Coletti, *Dell' emigrazione*, etc., pp. 239–244.

[3] B. Stringher, "Sur la bilance des paiements entre l'Italie et l'étranger," *Bulletin de l'Institut Internationale de Statistique*, xix[iii] (1912), pp. 93–123. For 1907 at least we may claim that these figures supply a fairly accurate idea of the dimensions of the flow of remittances.

[4] See excerpts from the report of the Director-General of the bank, "I risparmi degli emigranti trasmessi in Italia dal Banco di Napoli nel 1915," *Boll. Emig.*,

first melts away in a bad year is the surplus of earnings over expenses.

Notwithstanding their irregularity, the sums, in the aggregate, year in and year out, are large. It is scarcely wonderful that emigration is sometimes called a leading Italian industry, and the emigrants commodities, or exports. But it is more accurate to say that labor services are exported and are traded against goods, for that is the meaning of the excess of import-values over export-values which the statistics of commerce show. An achievement of the remittances has been to improve the value of the lira in foreign exchanges. And in 1916 and thereafter, during the Great War, one indubitable factor in the astonishing decline in the lira was precisely the lessened export of labor services, the shrunken stream of remittances. In Italy, before the war, the savings must have contributed, however slightly, to that reduction in the rate of interest which has meant so much for the invigoration of Italian industry and which, as Coletti has taken occasion to observe, enabled the conversion of the public debt in 1906.

The rapidly swelling deposits in the postal savings banks are an index of the accruing gains through emigration. Even in Basilicata, while the population was declining, the increase in deposits was from nine million lire in 1900–01 to fifteen million in 1905–06. In Sicily, in Venetia, wherever emigration has been, a similar tale may be told.[1] It is true that postal savings accounts have expanded generally in Italy, but their increase has been much more accentuated in the South than anywhere else. The postal banks are peculiarly institutions for the poor; in the provinces of little emigration, other savings banks have grown faster. What is more, the postal banks are a witness, in South Italy, to the comparative absence of channels of profitable investment. The moneys deposited are lent to further numerous enterprises of public utility throughout Italy, and so contribute to the general good.

1916, No. 5, pp. 19–23. From the United States came 117 million, against 66 million in 1914; from New York alone, 72 against 26½; from Argentina 26½ against 7.

[1] See, *e.g.*, *Inch. Parl.*, v[ii], pp. 758 f.; v[iii], Note ed appendici, pp. 586–604; De Nobili, p. 853; Cosattini, p. 84.

Of all the effects of emigration none stand forth in such definite outline as the local diminution of the supply of labor in agriculture. When that diminution is slight, as for example in Tuscany, it may even bring a sense of relief.[1] Commonly in the South, though not at all uniformly, it is great, so blighting large districts or neighborhoods, and producing effects which have been officially compared with those of a pestilence. Here are villages all but abandoned, the houses uninhabited and in decay, grass growing in the streets, and in the gardens weeds choking whatever vegetables come up. Far and wide, it is the aged, the women and the children, who constitute the labor force, all valid men being as rare as when the existence of a state is imperilled at its frontiers. Tremendous over many a countryside has been this limitation of labor; and so, of the productivity of agriculture.

The effects of this draught upon workers are to be specifically noted in the conditions of cultivation. To the mayors of the communes of Calabria and Basilicata, and to many proprietors, the question was put, in 1909, Has there been abandonment of lands ? Of the mayors, 318 said yes, 75 no; of the proprietors, 633 yes, 98 no. More than five-sixths of 425 communes for which details were secured embraced within their limits abandoned lands.[2] In Basilicata, the phenomenon has till now gone farther than in Calabria, and in Calabria much farther than in Sicily. Over much of these regions grain had previously been cultivated, under the not very happy *terratico* contract. More often than not, it is the less fertile or accessible lands that have been sacrificed, but in the localities of intense emigration, or in those where the streams from the mountains have broken their bounds, the better lands too have been involved. In Sicily it is the latifundia that have suffered.

Various are the implications of abandonment. Those communes in Calabria and in Basilicata in which the desertion was absolute have been approximately equalled in number by those in which pasture has succeeded tillage; and indeed there has been

[1] Cf. Mori, " L'emigrazione dalla Toscana," p. 78.

[2] *Inch. Parl.*, v[iii], Note ed appendici, pp. 606–616. The answers, considering their source, are probably somewhat biased.

an extension of pasture in many other regions of emigration. What was a cause of migration from the rural districts in the England of Thomas More is here its consequence, and the economic change that then spelled higher profits here, in the first instance at least, spells lower. Not always, be it said in passing, is increase of pasture accompanied by increase of dairying. There are still other kinds of abandonment, which are not equivalent to the desertion of a piece of land or its conversion into pasture, and which therefore do not figure in the reports of prevalence. Some sorts of cultivation may disappear quite; so it is said that the growing of saffron has ceased in the province of Catanzaro, and that of flax on the Sila.[1] Or there may be a restriction of the more intensive forms of cultivation, as of vegetables and the grape. It has been said that the reconstitution of the Calabrian vineyards, after the ravages of the phylloxera, went forward tardily because of the emigration of laborers. In general, the plants with woody stems, which require much attention, have in many places been neglected, to their cumulative detriment, or have been grievously abandoned. Or, finally, the operations of tillage and after care have been performed less thoroughly or often than formerly.[2] It is in devious ways, hard to follow and record, that many of the effects of emigration have manifested themselves.

Day laborers being scarce, it has been necessary to pay them a higher wage. Emigration has wrought in Italy what once the Black Death wrought in England. But let us for the moment ignore the meaning which this may have for the wage earners themselves, and note its other bearings. For the whole class of small proprietors, the mass of the landed bourgeoisie, who depend on hiring a few workers, the new requirement has been critical. Over much of the South, it is indeed usual to speak of the crisis of the small property. These landowners are forced to cultivate less intensively, or to sell their lands, entering trade perhaps or politics. As a class they have played a varying and often minor part in the cultivation of their estates, so that in their

---

[1] De Nobili, p. 842.

[2] Cf., on the cultivation of wheat in the hills above Milan, Serpieri, p. 229.

decline they are themselves the chief sufferers.[1] The proprietors of medium and large estates have withstood the higher wage costs much better. Their incomes have been greatly reduced, but not to the vanishing point, partly because — unlike the small proprietors — they have been able and willing to resort to machinery and other expedients. Whenever an intense emigration has been unrelieved, there land values have fallen. So often has the return of emigrants brought relief to the situation created by the drain of population, that in many places a right-about-face shift of land prices has ensued. No aspect of this entire history has deeper interest. Why panic has seized the hearts of the proprietors when a permanent emigration has got started and why cheer has come to them when emigrants have returned, gold in pocket, may need no special explanation, but it certainly deserves a word of amplification.

More than three decades ago, when emigration was still mainly from the North, Count Jacini, in his summary of the work of the *Inchiesta Agraria*, held that the maintenance of the institution of the small property was owing to the land purchases made (at high prices, it happened) by the returned emigrants.[2] With some reservations, a similar statement can be made today. Wherever the land has already been much fractioned, in Venetia, in Piedmont, and in much of the South, the returned emigrants have simply bought out the existing small proprietors. As the price has mounted, the subdivision has gone further, and sometimes, as in northern Friuli and in interior Sicily, some middle or large estates have been broken up.[3] In both the North and the South, and in Sicily, the business of buying and selling land has become established, shrewd speculators acquiring vacant parcels at low prices, in anticipation of the return of emigrants, then breaking them into cultivable units, and selling them at advances.[4] The tendency to split up estates has so far, however, not been common, and it is conspicuously rare in one compartment, Cala-

---

[1] Naturally they are outspoken against emigration. For a defence of them, see C. Palombella, *L'emigrazione nella provincia di Bari* (Bari, 1909,) pp. 53 ff.

[2] *Inch. Agr.*, xv, p. 88.　　[3] Cf. Cosattini, p. 85; *Inch. Parl.*, vi[1], p. 395.

[4] " Relazione sui servizi," etc., *Boll. Emig.*, 1910, No. 18, pp. 47 f.

bria, where innumerable purchases of land have been made by the *americani*, as those who return from overseas are called.[1] In the Marches, in Apulia, nearly everywhere, but far less in Basilicata than in other important regions of emigration, the purchase of small lots has proceeded; and often truly diminutive bits of land are purchased, as if the emigrant were anxious chiefly to invest his savings; for he may have to sally forth once again to earn enough money wherewith to cultivate his lot. What is of largest social importance is the fact that the titles to land often pass from the non-cultivating small proprietors to those who cultivate; and so, in some places, is the tragedy of " the crisis " of the small property relieved.

What the landless generally buy is land. But those who have it will often devote a portion of their savings to ancillary forms of agricultural capital, especially buildings and stock. In some provinces of Piedmont, in the Valtellina and in Venetia, about a third of the savings brought back, it is said, have been used for raising cattle.[2]

And here perhaps too a word may be spoken concerning usury. It is a weed that grows in sheltered places unevenly fructified by gold. It implies the absence of a really general and elastic money market. The writers of the *Inchiesta Agraria* frequently noted how the gold brought back by the temporary emigrants of the North reduced the capital needs of men and also added to the offering of capital.[3] Recently, the writers of the parliamentary study of the rural South have set the same effect into sharp relief. The payment of long-standing debts, secured often by mortgages on land, and, less frequently, of new debts incurred to make emigration possible, has been common, though its extent is all indefinite; in the Abruzzi and Molise certainly it amounts almost to a specialty.

Is the state of agriculture improved by the changes which emigration has ushered in ? Wages, we have seen, have risen — a

[1] *Inch. Parl.*, v[iii], pp. 26, 127 f.
[2] " Relazione sui servizi," etc., p. 48. Cf. Cosattini, p. 86.
[3] *E.g.*, see, on the Lombard mountain district, *Inch. Agr.*, vi[i], p. 45.

third, a half, twice or thrice, according to locality and period, loosely following in the wake of emigration; but the increase has had no reference to improved quality of labor. At the same time the landowner has undoubtedly been spurred to introduce machines, in parts, for instance, of Calabria and Sicily and of the Abruzzi and Molise. Yet even upon occasion where wages are low — and here one cannot say whence the prick has come — some proprietors have deemed it worth while to resort to machines.[1] It is a token of progressiveness in the landed class for which students of the South have long yearned.

But does not the returning emigrant, he who has lived in the progressive countries, lead or at least follow the way to a better agriculture ? The homely story is told of a contadino of Lombardy who through his experiences in a Swiss dairy, now hard, now pleasant, tempered with instructions and admonitions, learned such matters as how to raise a cow's yield to its maximum, how to minister to the beast's health, how to adjust its surroundings to the demands of sanitation, and then returned richer by vastly more than his savings.[2] It is an animated autobiography — fictitious, for aught I know — disseminated as a tract to open the minds of emigrants, but also somewhat generally representative, of a surety, much more as regards the transalpine emigrants of the North than the transoceanic emigrants of the South. For the latter, with rare exceptions from the Argentine, have had little to do with agriculture abroad. And when they return and hearken — if they do — to the call of the fields, it is once more, as a writer has said, to take up " the hoe of Columella and the plow of Triptolemus." [3] In truth, it is a matter for regret, as one turns

---

[1] " The use of machines is enlarging also in the western part of the circondario of Gallipoli, where emigration may be said not to exist. It happens that the use of machines lowers the cost of production even where wages are relatively low." *Inch. Parl.*, iii[i] (Apulia), p. 686.

[2] Cattedra Ambulante d'Agricoltura per la Provincia di Sondrio, *Il viaggio e la vita di un contadino di Valtellina nel paese di Goldstein*, Sondrio, 1909. In this connection, however, an observation of Jarach may be recalled (" Dell' emigrazione delle donne," etc., p. 12) that the *cattedre ambulanti* of Belluno and of Feltre had had difficulty in making their instruction effective because emigration had withdrawn so many of the more robust farming people.

[3] De Nobili, pp. 875 ff.

the pages of the parliamentary report upon the Southern contadini, to find how general the tale is that improved methods of production have not been introduced by the returned emigrants.[1]

Here leaving the more special study of the reactions of emigration upon agriculture, so important because it is the conditions of farm industry that initially prompt to emigration, let us turn to the changes that have come in the conditions of living and the outlook upon life of the people of Italy. Has progress come or retrogression ? What of those left behind and of the emigrants who return ?

Wages, to repeat, have risen. They have risen in all of the compartments from which there has been emigration. Local studies have generally explained the result as due to the rarefaction of the labor supply. But the rise, over many years (before the war), has been more general in Italy than emigration, and the prices of commodities have risen almost simultaneously. It is certain that only a part of it is to be ascribed to emigration; but also that in some places, especially where agriculture and other industries have languished, that part is large. Employment has, however, it is maintained, become less steady in the places where industry has declined. Partly for this reason, but more largely because of the rise in prices, incomes expressed in terms of what they will purchase have not risen at all, have risen but little, or have risen considerably only in some districts (for instance, in Apulia and the Abruzzi). Hence, generally speaking, the laborer who has stayed at home has benefited only slightly in an economic way by emigration.[2] Like the wages of field hands, the wages of artisans have

[1] In the Abruzzi and Molise, by way of exception, the americani are said to be among the first to turn to better methods. *Inch. Parl.* ii[ii], p. 257. But for Campania we read that the land purchased is regarded as a savings bank account. " In few places have agricultural changes extensive enough to be perceptible been brought about by the money of the emigrants, while the contrary has happened in the case of urban properties. Rather, where such changes have occurred, they have mostly been the work of those left behind and not of the returned, and indeed the zones where they have chiefly occurred are the first and the second, which have supplied the least contingent to emigration." *Ibid.*, iv[i], p. 613. For earlier observations, see Taruffi, pp. 121 f. and P. Villari, " L'emigrazione," etc., p. 49.

[2] Lorenzoni, writing about Sicily, considers that the gain from emigration has

risen, but if exception be made of such a special increase as followed the Messina earthquake, then it is doubtful whether these workers too, oppressed as they have been by higher prices, have materially bettered their status.

Agricultural contracts have commonly improved. Rents, to the joy of proprietors, in those parts of Venetia and of the South where there has been a large stream of returning emigrants, have risen; but more commonly, as in Calabria generally, they have fallen, so that it becomes more feasible than in the past to supplement an income from hire by working on leased land. Although even the cultivator upon such land must contend with higher prices, some gain doubtless remains for him, one of the few gains that the folk of the mountains of Basilicata, for example, can count.

What influence upon well-being have the savings of emigrants? When the husband is abroad, his family in Italy, however they may strive in his absence, cannot earn the equivalent of his wage. Therefore a large part of his remittances, sometimes nearly or quite the whole, must be applied to sheer current maintenance.[1] There is question not only of the family still resident in Italy, but of the emigrant himself, who spends his winter there; he is idle precisely because the season is customarily, or for climatic reasons, one of idleness, or because industries supplementary to agriculture have not been developed.[2] An indeterminate part, however, is surely applied to raising the standard of living. We know that shoes and stockings and other comforts of habiliment which once

been essentially of another sort: " It has given leave to the contadino abroad to save a little capital, with which upon his return he could become the proprietor of a bit of land, or a mezzadro or small renter; and so it has given him a chance to enlarge his sources of income, now no longer limited to labor for hire." *Inch. Parl.*, vi[i], p. 137.

[1] Curiously, in the Final Report of *Inch. Parl.* (viii, p. 55), where the use made of foreign savings is discussed, there is no mention of this factor. Sundry factors are listed (*e.g.*, the payment of old debts) and a (residual) fourth of the remittances is held to be devoted " to *elevating* the scale of life of the respective families."

[2] Cf., *e.g.*, Jarach (" Dell' emigrazione," etc., p. 83): " On the other hand the savings of 150–200 crowns which on the average are made in the Trentino do not afford much economic relief to the families, since they do not always go to increase the family account, but are consumed by the person who has laid them by, for the satisfaction of his own desires."

graced their wearers chiefly on holidays have arrived at daily use. We know that meat is a commoner dish than it was, that there is more wheat flour in bread, that the *paste alimentari* are more generally eaten, that sweets have lost in part their holiday connotations, that tobacco comforts more men than it did, and that sewing machines are in wider use. We know that the returned emigrants turn to such things and we infer that in varying degree the stay-at-home population has also risen to them.

The circumstances of the emigrants who come back are not without sharp contrasts. In the earlier days particularly, the reports about them conceded little gain. Morpurgo, author of the report upon Venetia for the *Inchiesta Agraria*, wrote, " It may be said that some emigrants alter their existence for the better; but most, up to the present, certainly do not." [1] In subsequent years a greater measure of success came to the Venetian temporary emigrants, but even the more recent writers hold that a large part of those who return, the unskilled men above all, make a desolate picture.[2] Those who came back from Brazil were in general either penniless or when their travelling expenses had been paid, had but little left.[3] In reports touching especially the recent period, and more particularly the South, there is a strong tendency to represent the instances of success as in the majority: nearly every one who comes back from the Americas can show a little, sometimes a big, nest egg.

Not many emigrants certainly can live quite without working after their return, particularly not many in Basilicata. Some buy farm lands, but though they constitute a most interesting class, they are a minority and seldom acquire enough land for independence (partly because the land is too dear, partly because many of the emigrants who have made money lack the qualities which fit for independent cultivation). Some enter trade in the towns or lend their money to others — often usuriously. And

---

[1] *Inch. Agr.*, iv[i], p. 102; cf. the previous pages.

[2] See Cosattini, p. 63. Cf. G. Smaniotto-Dei Roveri, " L'emigrazione delle donne nella provincia di Belluno," *Vita Italiana all' Estero*, March, 1913, pp. 218–223.

[3] Cavaglieri, pp. 1050 ff.

some buy or build houses in the towns, a striking group, whom we must pause for a moment to consider.

Building or buying a house is one of the first steps which the emigrant takes when the desire to live on a higher plane wells up within him. His penury gone, he is ready to enjoy existence, and he adopts the same method in town or village which the newly-made American millionaire adopts when he plants himself in a residential city. A good house confers a measure of social distinction which the returned emigrant is glad to claim, rightful recompense for his strivings in foreign lands. It does not necessarily preclude his cultivating a small farm near the town; but he certainly generally prefers it to a farm, for the number of those who acquire houses is everywhere much larger than the number who purchase farm lands. The additional fact must be borne in mind that the emigrant who has been abroad, not less often than the country boy who has lived in the city, is thereafter satisfied with nothing less than a town life.

These new houses are readily enough recognizable. Not generally in the older part of the communes — though money sometimes is spent on extending or refurbishing an old house — they are erected commonly in the outskirts. Not hugging each other closely, like the houses that line the well-trodden narrow town streets, they stand separate, cottage-fashion, with a broader road before them. Unlike the houses in which many of the emigrants were born, these rise commonly to a second story, and if there are animals a partition separates them from the family. The houses are substantial, with a sufficiency of doors and windows; hardly decorative in architecture; regrettably deficient from a sanitary point of view. Plastered in white, or with the uncovered brick showing against a hillside, they possess a certain picturesqueness, but rarely charm. Sometimes, as in a number of communes of the Abruzzi and Molise, there are entire quarters that have grown up with the new abodes of the americani.[1]

[1] Numerous references to the new houses and telling illustrations of them are in the volumes of *Inch. Parl.* At the epoch of the *Inch. Agr.* such houses were few and chiefly in the North.

The same aspiration that is revealed in the acquisition of a
house may lead to liberal expenditure upon dress and ornament.[1]
Indulgence of a love for finery is often self-defeating and after an
interval may give way again to more modest modes of living. In
those communes of the South, however, in which the number of
returned emigrants is considerable, house, dress — an element
of luxury in all expenditure — and leisure become the tokens of a
newly conditioned bourgeois class. Its affinities on the one hand
are with the new economic group of cultivators or tradespeople
who have achieved their positions with the aid of American gold,
on the other hand and chiefly, with the old hereditary class of
galantuomini, with its inseparable ideal of *otium cum dignitate*.
Is it strange that those who have cared enough about the country
of their upbringing to return to it should pay their court to the
ideal of which their youth dreamed ?

Touching the mentality and character of the returned emigrants a certain disparity of opinion is noticeable. This is due
partly to the fact that the aspects fixed by the observer differ and
partly to the circumstance that the phenomena noticed are never
at rest; but further it sometimes arises because one man describes a mass effect while another infers general importance from
individual evidences of change.

" It must be confessed," wrote Professor Bordiga in his report
on Campania, " that the great majority of the emigrants depart
illiterate and return so, and at home have no influence on the
spirit of the country, the course of public affairs, and so forth." [2]
In other compartments as well, such a statement doubtless holds
of the great majority. It is perhaps a graver thing that many of
the returned live in idleness upon their savings; in the volumes
of the *Inchiesta Parlamentare*, in the chronicle of Rossi's southern
journey and in minor records, there is frequent reference to this

---

[1] Corbino (p. 70) tells how the women sometimes go about heavily clad in costly
silks, displaying hundreds of lire worth of jewelry—bracelets, chains, crosses, and
the like. " It is sad to see spent upon a stupid gown a considerable part of the man's
savings accumulated bit by bit through great sacrifices in a foreign land."

[2] *Inch. Parl.*, iv[1], p. 613.

condition, indefinite as its bounds remain.[1] Abroad the emigrants often cannot but accept the bad opinion in which they are held, retaliating with carelessness of dress and living; and these traits many exhibit after their return — is it not natural that they should ? Abroad too no moral training comes to them; is it strange that its signs should be wanting among the returned, or that, here and there, newly acquired vices should appear among them ? They do often assume abroad, and manifest at home, a certain self-assurance, a challenging disposition, even a sort of vainglory, which contrasts sharply with their former servility and has among its many consequences, some good, some ill, one of sterling, epochal value: a more resolute attitude toward the employing landlord. Even among the women who have returned, commonly those of the North, a growth in independence has been remarked.

These are general considerations. Nitti has said that emigration is a distribution of scholarships. It is not possible to measure the gains in knowledge or the inferences from experience that emigrants bring back. They have seen the world and lived in it and have grown indefinably in stature; something that has been dormant has come to awakening; where blankness was, positive wisdom has surged forth. " Many of our women," wrote Pertile, " have learned, in the German fashion, to scrub the floors and pavements every two weeks, which they certainly never did in their whole lives in Italy." [2] To this sufficiently humble instance, many others could be added, but none more plausible than those of a propagandist tract, circulated to tell how a Valtellinese peasant stayed in Germany long enough to discover what the words " schmutzig," " Schwein," meant as applied to him, and how he, as a strike-breaker, learned from a striker what sinning against labor solidarity implied.[3] In Apulia, it has been claimed, the returned emigrants show increased readiness to join leagues of

---

[1] It figured in an indictment by Pasquale Villari in the Senate, June 30, 1909 and a defence by Giustino Fortunato. See *Boll. Emig.*, 1909, No. 12, pp. 98, 108.

[2] " Gli italiani in Germania," Pt. i, p. 129; cf. p. 136.

[3] Ufficio del Lavoro e dell' Emigrazione di Tirano, *Mezza pagina di vita d'un emigrante (corrispondenza famigliare)*, Tirano, 1911.

resistance.[1] Some gain in technical equipment surely appears, but probably it is limited, for the most part, to those who have had previous training, and if it is such as to lead to the emigrant's success abroad, he is likely to be kept from returning to Italy at all. What gives to all these gains their social importance is the circumstance that, by contagion, they must presently spread among the general population.[2]

Does not emigration give a great impetus to popular schooling ? Those who go abroad do not, we know, first equip themselves for the journey; but do not those who return chant the virtues of knowledge ? No plain answer of yes or no can be given. Directly at least there is pejoration of a bad situation. Children are torn from the schools to emigrate, so in Campania, so in Venetia, for example: in one province of the latter compartment early examinations are even provided for children who expect to emigrate. Or, as in Calabria, they are sent into the fields, especially for the olive gathering and the harvests, because their fathers are abroad. Or they are left at home to look after the still younger children, while the mothers take the absent fathers' places in the fields. These are all common cases. And among those emigrants who return from abroad, indifference to schooling is often only one token of a general, long-standing indifference to many immaterial things.

Yet, abroad, unguessed influences are at play, conspiring to stir up in many emigrants a new attitude. Letters must be written. They never before, in Italy, had to be written, and now it is inconvenient and awkward to ask or purchase the help of others in writing them. Where no paths are beaten, where faces, things, events, the law's demands are all strange, even to make a plan, and to carry it out, are tasks difficult often to exasperation for whoever cannot read. And such a one may also come to feel a sense of inferiority not unmixed with shame. He is cheated, and

---

[1] *Inch. Parl.*, iii[i], p. 545.

[2] Some proselytism even occurs. Italians converted in America are said to have given a spur to Protestantism in Italy. See Mangano, pp. 91–94; E. A. Steiner, *The Immigrant Tide, its Ebb and Flow* (New York, 1909), pp. 176 f.

his wage is lower than another's. " Send our children to school "
is his message to his wife; and returning, he adds his pressure, or
even himself goes to an evening school. No one can say how frequent is this new educational orientation, but its existence and
importance have been attested by many observers. Besides, in
those regions where the well-being of the people has risen, school
attendance has increased; so first of all in the Abruzzi and Molise,
next in Sicily and only thereafter in Calabria and Basilicata.[1]

Important though it is to inquire what changes in the health of
the population have resulted from emigration, it is difficult to
measure them or do more than particularize their kinds. Among
the emigrants who return are many who have lived in comfort
abroad, well sheltered and nourished, and many who, here and
there, through employment in a modern factory, have learned its
standards of hygiene. A ship's physician tells us that after he had
himself bathed the infant of unwilling parents and restored it to
them clean and aglow, other infants were brought to him for a like
transformation. Invaluable for Italy must be the home-coming
of all such families! We can further understand that every family
that lives better because of earnings remitted or brought from
abroad fortifies its resistance to the inroads of disease or, if any of
its members succumb to illness, can make a prompter and surer
claim upon the physician's aid. So we can readily believe those
students of malaria who report that in various regions a factor in
the lessened ravages of the scourge is the more robust constitu-

---

[1] Coletti (pp. 259 f.) shows that illiteracy among new recruits for the army declined much between 1872 and 1901 and at the same annual rate, or a lower rate
(we should expect a higher), between 1901 and 1907. So far, however, as increased
literacy is due to emigration we should expect it to show most in the later years. As
a matter of fact the improvement is even greater for the whole of Italy than for
just the southern compartments. Among the contadini alone, as Coletti points
out, the decline in illiteracy has been notable for central and upper Italy, but
meager in the southern compartments, and in Basilicata there has even been an
increase. This strange result Coletti explains on the ground that it is the literate
who especially depart for America, and the explanation doubtless has much truth;
in view, however, of the known high rate of illiteracy among the South Italians who
arrive in the United States — we are unlucky in not having figures by compartment of origin — it would seem easy to overrate the explanation.

tions of people dwelling within the charmed circle of a successful emigration.[1]

But the question of health has another aspect which no one who has read the record of the Italians abroad is likely to ignore. To quench his thirst at the alluring cascade of gold, the emigrant skimps sustenance, toils in perilous, congested, unsanitary workplaces, braves all unfit the rigors of alien climates, and in the decline of his health pays the price. It is a tale of every day. By no means every such emigrant returns to Italy. But no one who reflects that the eastward journey overseas is made much less often than the westward can fail to be impressed by the far greater numbers of sick Italians reported by the ship physicians for the eastward journey, especially that from the United States. In 1910, for example, 857 persons ill of tuberculosis were counted on the ships, of whom 841 on the return trip; and of these 700 came from North America.[2] In 1901–08 more than 2500 tubercular patients were repatriated from overseas, of whom three-quarters went to Sicily, Campania, Calabria, the Abruzzi, and Molise.[3] Women are especially numerous among these victims. In a broader view it is not, however, the numbers of those reported sick who measure the reduced health of those that return, for they are but an index of collapse. Unquestionably there is a much greater throng of those who, though not broken in body, have yet spent their vitality. For them no measure at all exists and even a guess is hazardous. Many also are the emigrants who have been permanently, and more or less seriously, maimed by accident in industry.

Such diseases as tuberculosis and syphilis have been introduced by returned emigrants into regions previously all but exempt. Deaths from the latter disease have been more numerous in the province of Udine, where nearly every one is an emigrant or of an emigrant's family, than anywhere else in Italy. Such, however,

---

[1] Cf., *e.g.*, A. Sergi, " La malaria in Calabria (Bruzzano Zeffirio) durante il 1904," *Atti della Società della Malaria*, vi (Rome, 1904), pp. 441 f.

[2] F. Rosati, " Il servizio igienico-sanitario nella emigrazione transoceanica per l'anno 1910," *Boll. Emig.*, 1912, No. 8, p. 14.

[3] G. Candido, " La tubercolosi polmonare in rapporto all' emigrazione," *Boll. Emig.*, 1910, No. 14, p. 99.

have been the advances of medical skill in a quarter century past that death is much more rarely the outcome of illness than formerly, and therefore the death rates for many diseases have ceased to be a gauge of their prevalence. It is entirely possible that in Basilicata and Calabria, where the deaths from tuberculosis are fewer than formerly, the prevalence of the disease has increased. The doctors of the South have asserted a connection between various maladies and emigration. In the North, the emigrants have brought much disease from transalpine lands, which, as in the case of the tuberculosis of the Venetian stonecutters, is sometimes closely associated with their occupation, but is more commonly the fruit of constrained or irregular living. The deleterious effects of emigration upon the Italians of the North have undoubtedly been more serious than upon those of the South; not by reason of any comparative immunity of the South Italians — the reverse being more probable — but because the Northern emigrants, in much greater proportion, customarily return to their country, and only the more successful of the Southern return.

The wives and children who stay at home, though in the long run often the gainers by emigration, are not infrequently, in the first instance, touched adversely, and their loss may be of an enduring sort. The young, I have already pointed out, often undertake tasks beyond their powers; and the women by their excessive labors, sometimes complicating the problems of maternity, develop anemia or other impairment of health and too early show the signs of general decline. These things lie beyond statistical measurement but have been repeatedly emphasized by careful observers.

What has here been said concerning health does not readily lend itself to summary. There is always a danger lest particularization of this or that difficulty give it overimportance. On the other hand there exists no general index to show what has been the effect of emigration upon the health of the population. Some persons (writing before the war) have pointed out that rejections from the army on account of low stature are fewer than formerly, and this circumstance doubtless reflects some general improvement of health, but it cannot show that emigration has been alone or even mainly responsible therefor.

That increased readiness to partake of alcoholic drinks which we have found among the Italians abroad has had its repercussions in Italy. Beer is now consumed in parts of the South where a few years ago its name was scarcely known. Immoderate drinking is still rare there, particularly among the countryfolk, but where it exists, the americani lead. In central Italy, likewise, an increase in drinking has been noticed in the emigration centers. But it is in the North, most of all, that alcoholism, still without in any sense becoming the rule, has spread and caused grave concern. In many a village there, wine, whiskey, and beer have been consumed in large quantities in the emigrants' attempt to counteract the dull monotony of an idle winter; the tavern has become an institution which those who have not yet emigrated patronize more and more.

In various ways, by no means pointed in the same direction, emigration has reacted upon the commission of crime in Italy. Sometimes there is less, because the active and discontented spirits have quit the country; so homicides have declined in such regions as Apulia and Sicily, and thefts are fewer. Or there is more, because the returned emigrants have acquired new impulses or adopted new practices abroad; so resort to the revolver has, it is said, increased in the North. The expansion of affairs connected with the process of emigration has undoubtedly encouraged certain common forms of fraud or even given rise to new forms. The disorder in which some regions have been left has incited more than the ordinary number of agricultural thefts, an old problem in Italy. Quite generally the prolonged or frequent absence abroad of one or more members of a household has produced a weakening of family ties, variously manifested. The aged may suffer neglect. The wife may give herself to others; infanticide may follow upon adultery and the returned emigrant may take a bloody revenge. For by tens of thousands at any one time, in many provinces, must be reckoned the wives whose husbands are earning abroad. Prostitution has not increased in these provinces, since there has been neither the anonymity of the large center nor the corrupting influence of the garrison town and its like. On the other hand, in certain provinces, as in Cuneo, for instance, young women who as waitresses or in kindred exposed occupations in the countries of Europe, especially France, had been led into prostitution, have after their return continued the new way of life. We have seen that emigration has brought to various regions material economic improvement, so tempering some of the forces that in any society make for disorder: field thefts, by way of example, have on the one hand declined; on the other, illegitimacy has fallen off and subsequent recognitions of parenthood have increased. Looking at the complete picture of misdemeanor and crime, as it is pieced together from many sources, the North, it may be said, is the region in which the reaction of emigration has chiefly been deplorable and the South the region of net gain. Outside influences have counted in the one case, alleviation of old troubles in the other.

How has emigration reacted upon the military power of Italy, which has been for many years a matter of deep concern to her? The facts of the situation are plain enough; whether they are to be viewed with optimism or pessimism depends primarily upon one's expectations; wearers of both sets of spectacles have been plentiful. The provisions of the law are such that anyone may escape military service by emigrating before the age of sixteen. As Villari has emphasized, this constitutes an inducement to emigration.[1] Older men, when their class is called, must present themselves for examination wherever they are — if abroad, then to the consular or diplomatic officials. Failing to do so, within a reasonable time, they are accounted *renitenti alla leva* and are answerable for their default. In those provinces where emigration has been slight, they have been less than 1 per cent of all

---

[1] " What does it signify? It signifies the encouragement of emigration! When one thinks of the superhuman efforts — and many of us certainly remember them — which General Govone had to make to introduce military conscription in Sicily, to what trials he had to subject the country, it is sad to see this same people, which so exerted itself to establish compulsory service, open the way to escaping the compulsion." P. Villari, in Senate, June 30, 1909, *Boll. Emig.*, 1909, No. 12, p. 100.

called to the colors. In North Italy they have been about 6 per cent, but most of these, absent in Europe at the time, have within a year or two, upon their return to Italy, regularized their position. In South Italy and Sicily they have averaged above 12 per cent and sometimes, as in Calabria, have exceeded 20 per cent. In 1906, of 27,000 recruits of the class of 1886 living abroad, only one-sixth presented themselves for service. The emigrants in America have rarely regularized their position. In the last decade of the nineteenth century and the first of the twentieth the annual average of defaulters was 33,000. Though a large part of these were still living abroad in 1907, barely 3 or 4 per cent came forward in the amnesty granted that year in celebration of the birth of Garibaldi. More recently (but before the war) the defaulters have numbered 50,000 a year.

Nor do these losses tell the whole story. Although it is the healthiest Italians who go away, the percentage of recruits who need physical rehabilitation before being fit for the army is particularly high in those centers, like Udine, whose male population has toiled much abroad; and in the foreign countries themselves, in Europe, North and South America, from 25 to 40 per cent of the registrants have needed rehabilitation. At all times there is, by way of still further loss, a considerable group of actual deserters from the army, largely clandestine emigrants. And finally there are the reservists themselves, living abroad.

In 1915 Italy entered the Great War. Indubitably the homegoing of reservists from the countries of Europe was great, but from the Americas it included only a modest fraction of those stationed there. Some purchase of Italian war bonds took place. In Italy, as could only be expected, the emigration provinces of the South were relatively least represented among the purchasers, both in amount taken and in number of buyers. Abroad, the subscriptions were at a much lower rate than in Italy, and much less spontaneous; in the case of the 5 per cent loan of 1916 the subscriptions in Argentina amounted to half again as much as those in the United States, and even those of Brazil were substantially higher.

The conclusion is clear. If gain comes to the Italian military strength from emigration, it must be indirectly, through such increase in health or wealth as this chapter has examined. Against this must be set extensive losses, which turn mainly upon the fact that emigration has brought a great decline in effective citizenship.[1]

Many years ago, Carpi held that it was only the transportation of emigrants which made possible, without government subsidy, an animated navigation between Genoa and the Plata.[2] Actually, however, during the years in which the overseas emigration was still of modest proportions, a subsidy was paid to the merchant marine without sufficing to lend it robustness. It was only, as one writer has put it, when the oxygen of abundant passage fares was applied that the marine began to draw its breath more freely.[3] The new business enabled the great expansion of Italian ports, most of all Genoa and Naples, and it gave a tremendous impetus to the building of more ships, until the Italian fleet, in the years 1907–15, carried over three-fifths of all the emigrants. One of the great marines of the world, its craft in all waters, thus owes its existence, in no mean degree, to the emigration — the great migration, back and forth — of the people whose country it serves.

To the increase of trade which has accompanied the increase of Italian shipping, emigration has tangibly contributed. Wherever Italians have gone, they have been followed by supplies of fruit, wine, oil, olives, garlic, cheeses, macaroni, and other products. The heavy cheese production at Moliterno, to cite but one instance, has been purchased largely by Italians in America, and at

[1] See, besides the *Annuario Statistico*, an article, "L'emigrazione e la sua influenza sul reclutamento dell' esercito," *Boll. Emig.*, 1908, No. 23, pp. 57–64; C· F. Ferraris, " Il movimento generale dell' emigrazione italiana: suoi caratteri ed effetti," *Boll. Emig.*, 1909, No. 5, esp. pp. 37 f.; Rossi, " Vantaggi e danni," various passages; *Inch. Parl.*, viii, pp. 97 f.; an article, " Contributo degli italiani residenti all' estero al prestito nazionale 5 per cent," *Boll. Emig.*, 1916, No. 7, pp. 93 f.; E. Cesari, " Nota sui risultati complessivi e sulla participazione regionale ai prestiti nazionali," *Giornale degli Economisti*, November, 1916, pp. 453, 458.
[2] *Op. cit.*, i, p. 57.
[3] L. Fontana-Russo, "La marina mercantile e l'emigrazione," *Rivista Coloniale*, May–June, 1908, p. 425. A relevant discussion with the situation in the afterwar time is by M. Pantaleoni, *Note in margine della guerra* (Bari, 1917), pp. 143–154.

increasing prices. Far and wide, also, the people of the countries where Italians have settled have learned to prize their products — not merely because Italian houses have striven to win a new market, but because the people, in restaurant and shop, have experimented and been satisfied. Sometimes competitors have arisen to threaten the import trade: Italians or others have discovered that macaroni can be made in America. But in the case of many products competition is difficult, unprofitable, or impossible, and the new international trade has acquired a permanent basis. Undoubtedly a favorable exchange rate, resting upon emigrants' remittances, itself stimulates Italian importations from foreign countries; but whether the demands of the repatriated have or have not much to do with setting up new sorts of trade it is hard to say with confidence, though conjecture is easy. It is scarcely irrelevant to record the fact — for the example may be somewhat representative — that phosphates dug by Italians in Tunisia have been shipped to Milan to be made into fertilizer for use in Italy.[1]

A blow that strikes so near to the root of the tree may fell more than has been intended. If emigration may be said to have any aim with regard to the population of a country, surely it must be to remove an excess. Actually its consequences, in any case manifold and hard to trace, are certainly other than those foreseen.

Whether absence from Italy shall be enduring or temporary rests largely with the individual. When women depart overseas they generally stay away permanently, and some persons have gone so far as to read in their departure an index to the permanence of the general emigration. In our statistical chapters we have seen that, during a half century past, four million persons have been permanently lost to Italy and twice as many temporarily. To convert the temporary absences into an equivalent

---

[1] See A. Visconti, *Emigrazione ed esportazione*, Turin, 1912, and V. Nazari, " I nostri vini nei paesi di immigrazione italiana " (to name but one recent study of its sort) in *Atti del Primo Congresso degli Italiani all' Estero*, i, pp. 279–384. Cf. a treatise published by the Italian government, P. Trentin, *Manuale del negoziante di vini italiani nell' Argentina*, Buenos Aires, 1895. On the phosphates of Tunisia, see Davin, p. 692. The general statistics of trade are easily accessible.

of permanent adult lifetimes would be an interesting mathematical speculation, but is not vital to our argument. The loss is comprehensive — has it brought a cure to a state of overpopulation ?

It is arguable that the population of Italy is not less than it would have been if emigration had not taken place, and perhaps is greater.

In the first place the death rate has fallen. To ascribe its decline primarily to a marked improvement in economic conditions, such as emigration is assumed to have wrought, is, however, a mistaken course. After the unification of Italy, the system of public sanitation was reorganized, and the discoveries of modern pathology in the field of endemic diseases were applied to regions where the harvest they had recurringly reaped had been high. With the better training of doctors and surgeons and the incessant improvements of medical knowledge, death became ever more rarely the consequence of impaired health. Over several decades the lowering of the death rate appears to have been greatest in just such emigration districts as Calabria and Basilicata, for here the infectious diseases had been most rampant. But in addition here, as elsewhere, the recent improvement in living, due to the gains from emigration, has undoubtedly counted for much; and were it not for other adverse reactions, such as the increased labor of women in the fields, the improvement would have counted for much more.[1] For us, however, let it suffice that, from one or another cause, a material decline in deaths has taken place throughout Italy.

We are mainly concerned with regions whose denizens have been given to early marriage and where the man of forty has a son earning a man's wage. It is only very lately that the general marriage rate of Basilicata and Calabria has shown a real decrease, due to the absence of eligible men. In Sicily, it is still as high as the average for all Italy; on the continent south of Rome it is

[1] The leading countries of emigration, Italy, Austria, and Hungary, are the only great European countries having a higher death rate of women aged 15–45 than of men. See G. Mortara, "Tavola di mortalità secondo le cause di morte per la popolazione italiana (1901–10)," *Annali di Statistica*, Ser. v, vol. 7 (1914), p. 71.

higher than the average. Widowers are prompt to remarry in these districts. But the broadly significant fact is that, despite emigration, and in part no doubt because of it, the marriage rate has maintained a high level.[1]

In Italy as a whole the rate of births has greatly fallen in recent decades. Partly the decline has gone hand-in-hand with the lessening of infant mortality, and partly it reflects those aspirations to comfort which in other modern democracies have had like consequences. It has been more emphatic in the cities than in the rural regions and so far has no obvious connection with emigration. But one considerable emigration district has supplied an impressive exception to this statement: Piedmont, whose sons and daughters return from France with the conception of the two-child family — has a more remarkable instance of the effects of emigration been discovered ? [2] Thus far the decline in births in the South has been relatively slight, and the rate of births there still ranks with the highest among European peoples. This is a fact lost sight of by those who quote the census to show that South Italian families are small: their four to six members are the survivors of more births (the deaths in particular of young children have only recently grown fewer) and they take no account of persons absent in foreign countries.[3] Death rates are always the

[1] " The average annual number of bachelors (1900–01) who marry is 103 per 1000 censused in Basilicata and 85 in Calabria, while in the entire population of Italy it is scarcely 67. Even more pronounced, relatively to the country's average, is the nuptiality of widowers: in Basilicata per 1000 censused, 82 marry in a year, in Calabria 62, in all Italy only 37." G. Mortara, " Basilicata e Calabria secondo le statistiche demografiche," *Giornale degli Economisti*, 1910 (April, pp. 435–462, June, pp. 659–676), p. 663. The census of 1911 found a larger proportion both of males and of females to be married than the censuses of 1872, 1882, and 1901.

[2] A. Necco, " Il problema della popolazione in Italia: Perchè la natalità declina più rapida in Piemonte e Liguria," *Riforma Sociale*, June–July, 1913, pp. 433–475. Some writers believe that emigration is a force tending to lower the birth rate for the whole country; cf. C. Gini, *I fattori demografici dell' evoluzione delle nazioni* (Turin, 1912), p. 105.

[3] " The number of those who die without having entered upon the period of economic productivity is very high, and, among males, the number also of those who die without having completed it. . . . At almost all ages the probable further duration of life is lower in the two southern regions than in Italy as a whole." Mortara, " Basilicata e Calabria," p. 443.

first to respond to new conditions of living and of knowledge; birth rates, in comparison, are inert, yet what has happened in Piedmont may possibly, given time enough, have a parallel in other regions.

Not only has the total population of Italy not been lessened by her prodigious emigration, but it has increased annually even in the great period of emigration (1880–1910) and then actually at a faster rate than before. The expanding cities have been able to absorb their increase, but the mountain and farm lands have not; hence, from them, emigration, which in the first instance is a kind of substitute for death, and subsequently, in many places, a means of allowing a larger population to subsist. With a less fecund population, the first great exodus might have brought enduring relief; rather it appears to have been a means of maintaining a high fecundity. In the somewhat technical sense, it has therefore not lifted the standard of living. Sicily, which in 1871 had a population of 2,580,000, had in 1901, 3,520,000; between 1872 and 1905, its excess of births over deaths averaged annually nearly 11 per 1000, while that of all Italy was little more than 6. Calabria and Basilicata had a much greater annual excess of births over deaths in the period 1892–1908 than in the seventh and eighth decades of the past century.

Although emigration has not prevented an increase in the inhabitants of the whole country, its tremendous action has led to a thinning of the population of particular localities. The first fear that the South might prove another Ireland was given support when it was revealed that between 1882 and 1901 the population of Basilicata had declined some 3.4 per cent. This was the only instance in these years of a decline for an entire province or compartment, but even before 1882 and in the years since there have been numerous instances of decline in the population of circondarii. The population of Basilicata has continued to shrink since 1901, and that of the Abruzzi and Molise has followed suit. In the other southern compartments the rate of growth was only much slackened in this extraordinary decade. When the population of particular communes is considered, there are numerous cases of drastic reductions.

These then are the consequences of emigration as regards the size of the Italian population. When its composition is studied, those changes appear to which more or less explicit reference has already been made. Wide currency has been given to figures compiled in 1901 showing that, as a result of the previous twenty years' emigration, one man in eight aged 21–50 had been lost to the nation and in some compartments a much higher proportion. Relatively speaking, the aged — those 65 or more — are half again as numerous in some compartments as formerly, and the children are more numerous. Women, who in all Italy exceed men but little, are in a pronounced majority in the great emigration provinces.

An old moot point with students of migration has been the question, What is an emigrant worth? What loss does he bring to the old country, what gain to the new? In Italy the matter has been discussed with more than usual competence, and the issues clearly discriminated. First, Professor Pareto, a quarter century ago, applied to the figures for Italian emigration Engel's reckoning of the cost of bringing up a child, and inferred that the loss to Italy due to the emigration of those who had not paid back in productive labor the cost of their rearing ran into hundreds of million lire per year. A decade later, the question came into open controversy. The computation of economic loss now was led into minutiae and the details of a balance sheet were presented. But the propriety of discussing such a loss was also vigorously questioned. Professor Coletti argued, that, as the family grows, the older children go to work and sumptuary expenditure is reduced; that mothers increase their care; that in some sorts of economic activity — notably under the mezzadria contract in agriculture — the young children have a precocious value; that cost of production for that matter never does determine the value of men; and that in any case all statistical reckoning of cost is impossible. Professor Pareto in a later work reiterated that, whatever the interpretation, it would be false to ignore the primary evidence of loss.[1]

[1] Professor Pareto's argument first appeared in his *Cours d'économie politique* (2 vols., Lausanne, 1896–97), i, pp. 151–153. See also A. Beneduce, " Capitali

With a computation of money loss we need not be here concerned. And if the emigration of the eighties had finally relieved of a burden those who remained, then only a gain might be in question. But we have just seen that through forty years of emigration the population has generally increased, and the inference is that the new additions have generally not been better able to thrive than the older elements had been. Where a great temporary emigration has been developed, as in Udine, it is as if the boundaries of the country had been enlarged and more people could live than before. Somewhat too the transatlantic remittances are an evidence of such an enlargement. But the great fact remains that in the emigration centers of Italy only a very gradual or a very recent, and in any case a far from adequate, improvement in living conditions has occurred. The country has taxed itself to supply new contingents of emigrants. Protection and training urgently needed by the first-born have been withheld from them in order that others might be born, reared, and sent forth. Not that the emigrants were planned for their careers from the first. They resemble rather an unfulfilled purpose, a resolution given up. In an older time (and somewhat it is so still) death would have removed these children of poverty; now they are sold to a higher bidder, Emigration, and what is received must often not pay their cost.

sottratti all' Italia dall' emigrazione per l'estero," *Giornale degli Economisti*, December, 1904, pp. 506-519; F. Coletti, " Il costo di produzione dell' uomo e il valore economico degli emigranti," *ibid.*, March, 1905, pp. 260-291; V. Pareto, " Il costo di produzione dell' uomo e il valore economico degli emigranti," *ibid.*, April, 1905, pp. 322-327; Beneduce, " Capitali personali e valore economico degli emigranti," *ibid.*, July, 1905, pp. 33-44; Coletti, " Ancora del costo di produzione dell' uomo e del valore economico degli emigranti," *ibid.*, August, 1905, pp. 179-190.

CHAPTER XXIII

PHASES OF OPINION AND POLICY IN ITALY

Tot capita tot sententiae an Italian Foreign Affairs Minister once affirmed, speaking of the emigration question. But if diversity of opinion is at any one moment paramount, the history of opinion in Italy admits easily of classification into three periods. That they overlap goes without saying. As evidence of tendency they stand clear. In the first, men deplored emigration; in the second they deemed it necessary and, upon some grounds, positively advantageous; in the third, regarding it as not the less necessary, they accumulated concrete evidence of gains at home and discerned it to be a manageable instrument to expansion abroad. In the first period they sought to curb it, in the second to protect and encourage — without stimulating — it, in the third to cherish it and give it direction. But having thus absolutely stated the course of opinion, let us, in fairness, examine its content more narrowly.

THE FIRST PERIOD: UNTIL ABOUT 1895

As early as January, 1868, a deputy, Lunaldi, began a discussion in Parliament in which he lamented the fact of emigration and recited its evils. In May, 1872, another deputy, Tocci, sounded an alarm which Minister Lanza minimized; but Lanza by the following January changed his opinion and then maintained that not only should all illicit emigration be put down, but even voluntary and legal departures should be somewhat checked. The writers of the time held similar views, Carpi inferring from the reports of " nearly all the consuls " that the evils due to emigration equalled if they did not exceed the benefits,[1] and Florenzano concluding that emigration is " a very grave evil for the country." [2]

---

[1] Carpi, i, p. 29.

[2] Florenzano, p. 297. Almost identical language was used twenty years later by Godio (p. 104), who recalls the contemporary phrase, " the open sore of emigration."

Among the countries of Europe, Italy, in these years, was almost alone in having no law on emigration. In 1876–87, incidental provisions of one sort or another came through Nicotera, Depretis, Giudice, and Minghetti. In December, 1887, Crispi introduced a bill for a general emigration law, which, largely through the eloquence of De Zerbi, was enacted in the following May.

" Emigration," this instrument began, " shall be free save for such duties as the laws impose upon citizens." But its inspiration had been the unhappy fortunes of the Italians abroad and the drain upon the home land; hence its special aim, apart from a small measure of control over ticket agents, was restrictive. For a soldier to depart before the age of thirty-two was all but forbidden, and many a man who had sought the hospitality of another land found himself virtually exiled. It was a law, like so many another, prompted more by fear than by a supple understanding of its theme.[1]

The Second Period: about 1895–1908

Emigration was not curbed, but stubbornly went its way. Here, it would seem, was a phenomenon more apt to make laws than to obey them. Men began to believe that all violent interference with its course must only precipitate evils greater than those that had come in its train. Of the new view, no clearer spokesman is to be found than Senator Bodio, who said before the Fourth Geographic Congress:

" Emigration is for Italy grounded in necessity. Two or three hundred thousand persons a year must go from us in order that those who stay may find work. . . . Migrations are ordained by Providence. In the social order their task is analogous to that of the ocean and air currents in the physical, which spread movement and life throughout the earth." [2]

---

[1] C. Festa, *L'emigrazione nella legislazione comparata*, Castrocaro, 1904; A. Brunialti, " L'esodo degli italiani e la legge sull' emigrazione," *Nuova Antologia*, July, 1888, pp. 96–114.

[2] L. Bodio, " Dell' emigrazione italiana e dell' applicazione della legge 31 gennaio 1901," *Boll. Emig.*, 1902, No. 8, pp. 9, 21.

In 1896 Nitti wrote (and he subsequently had many occasions to repeat his thought):

" Emigration, in a large view, is not only no artificial phenomenon, but is irrefragably necessary. It alone can provide a powerful safety valve against class hatreds. It is a masterful school, and the great and sole avenue to salvation for a country wanting in material resources but fruitful of men." [1]

Repeatedly too that staunch protagonist of his native South, Senator Fortunato, has uttered a kindred sentiment, for example:

" Emigration is a good or an evil according to point of view; at all events an evil, I should almost say, of a Providential sort, if it frees us, as undeniably it does, from even greater woes." [2]

A recent chief of the Emigration Service, Di Fratta, once instructed recruits to his department in these words:

" The history of mankind is the history of migrations, of successive human displacements and adaptations. . . . Emigration is peaceful, is continuous, and has a rhythm easily discovered. Actually, even in its present form, it is produced by the same elemental motives that have caused the great historical displacements of peoples. It cannot be judged in the usual categories of good and evil, of advantage and disadvantage." [3]

The Roman Catholic view, finally, has established the necessity of emigration in the sovereign behest, Increase and multiply, which man must obey till his mission on earth is completed. In the words of Bishop Bonomelli, whose ideals and work have become familiar in several lands:

" Emigration is demanded by Nature and by the Author of Nature. To proceed to limit it or to suppress it would be both stupid and wrong." [4]

---

[1] F. S. Nitti, " La nuova fase della emigrazione d'Italia," *Riforma Sociale*, December, 1896, p. 748. Cf. his words before the Chamber of Deputies, June 21, 1905, *Boll. Emig.* 1905, No. 15, p. 37. Bodio spoke in a similar vein before the Second Geographic Congress, cited by A. Brunialti, *Le colonie degli italiani* (Turin, 1897), p. 251.

[2] G. Fortunato, *Il mezzogiorno e lo stato italiano* (Bari, 1911), ii, p. 504.

[3] P. Di Fratta, " La tutela degli emigranti," *Boll. Emig.* 1912, No. 3, p. 4. The speech is translated in *New York Evening Post*, March 2, 1912, p. 4.

[4] G. Bonomelli, *L'emigrazione* (2d ed., Rome, 1912), p. 9. For a view concordant with this and not less authoritative, see " Un intervista con monsignor Scala-

Besides being necessary, so runs the argument, emigration is beneficial. In the later nineties a new economic reckoning began to be made, revealing valuable gains, earnests of still greater rewards, if emigration were allowed a free course. Einaudi's spirited recital of the *Merchant Prince*, written in admiration of Anglo-Saxon traditions, showed how Italian capital and enterprise might transform " Little Italy " into " Greater Italy." Trade, it declared, should follow the emigrants. Were not these humble folk, as Bodio held, Italy's best travelling salesmen ? Defence of emigration became popular as men counted the savings dispatched home by the wayfarers, beheld the foreign markets of Italy grow, and discovered a new era in the coming of an international exchange rate favorable to Italy.[1]

With these newer views the law of 1888 was harshly out of accord. It left the emigrant to his own devices. The epoch-making law of 1901, inspired largely by Luzzatti. " the most important of our social laws " as Pantano called it, rests upon a different basis. In Di Fratta's words, it presumes " that the emigrant, by the very fact of his social condition and his character, is an incapable . . . is now too credulous, now too shy, in general ignorant, and as such is readily outwitted and defrauded." [2] Tittoni's phrases are even more expressive: " These great currents of our workers who go abroad resemble the currents of birds and fishes; the fishes are pursued by sharks seeking to devour them, the birds by

brini," *L'Italia Coloniale*, August–September, 1904, pp. 167–172. Cf. the argument of a modernist priest, G. Preziosi, *Il problema dell' Italia d'oggi* (Milan, 1907), pp. 28–37.

[1] Baron Tittoni, in the period of his earlier ministry, had occasion now and then to dwell upon these gains. See *Italy's Foreign and Colonial Policy, a Selection from the Speeches Delivered in the Italian Parliament by the Italian Foreign Affairs Minister, Senator Tommaso Tittoni* (London, 1914), pp. 155, 210. But the exportation of capital he held to be a dream (p. 205 — Deputies, 1909): " Every time I have been urged to use my influence in favor of some important undertaking abroad in which the investment of Italian capital would have been desirable, I have made every possible effort to secure it, but these Italian capitalists willing to take into consideration such investments are not to be found, and if by chance one of them turns up who is disposed to risk his capital, it is only upon condition that the Government guarantee the interest on the money invested."

[2] *Op. cit.*, p. 5.

falcons and other birds of prey seeking to ravish them, the emigrants are accompanied by a troop of exploiters eager to pounce upon and despoil them." [1]   What such persons need is protection, and the law which provides it has a more emphatically paternal character than any modern emigration law enacted previously or since, though some recent laws (the Spanish for example) have taken their cue from it.   The machinery which it sets up aims to exclude entirely from participation in the commercial sides of emigration persons who cannot supply guarantees of honesty; to prevent all misdirection of emigrants to disappointing destinations; to provide positive assurance that those seeking to emigrate shall readily find responsible persons to deal with; to assist the emigrants, wherever they may be, without expense to them, to maintain their rights.   Such are the general principles of the legislation. In turn they are the means of rendering effective a policy which, on the platform and in the press, men in authority and private citizens have frankly held to be: holding the emigrant as closely united as possible to the Mother Country.   Emigration must be protected, Pantano has said, to take but a single instance, so that it " shall not be miserably lost to our country, our nationality and our economic and political future." [2]

To the Minister of Foreign Affairs the law gives power to suspend emigration to any place, not merely in the public interest, but whenever " the life, liberty and property of the emigrant are at stake."   This power, as we know, was exercised on a famous occasion in the case of Brazil, and subsequently in the cases of New Orleans, Uruguay, and Argentina.

The most elaborate creation of the law is the office of Commissioner-General of Emigration, depending upon the Ministry of Foreign Affairs.   It is the center of all the public protective institutions, and stands in a definite relationship with the private as well.   From this office, ably held in the past by such men as Bodio, Reynaudi, Pantano, Di Fratta, and L. Rossi, the *Bollettino dell' Emigrazione* is published, a rich mine of information.

[1] *Italy's Foreign and Colonial Policy*, p. 117.
[2] *Boll. Emig.*, 1904, No. 11, p. 40; cf. p. 43.   See also Tittoni in *Italy's Foreign and Colonial Policy*, p. 200.

The Commissioner-General is a member of the Emigration Council, a broadly representative organization of twelve persons who meet in at least two sessions a year to discuss the larger problems that call for action. A high level of competence has characterized the Council's membership and its deliberations have carried weight.

No company may sell passage tickets to emigrants unless duly licensed by the Commissioner-General as an emigrant carrier, and the rates for passage are fixed every three months by the Commissioner-General, after consultation with a variety of interests. In the effort to protect emigrants, needlessly favorable terms were at first made with foreign carriers. The charges for passage have mounted substantially, but the poorer types of vessel have been gradually eliminated. It cannot be said that all incitement to emigration has disappeared, for the twelve or fifteen thousand ticket agents in all Italy have abundant scope for solicitation. The tax of eight lire which the law requires every carrier to pay in respect of every ticket sold, and also all license fees and other sorts of income, are credited at once to an Emigration Fund, administered by a permanent Parliamentary Committee. From this Fund, so largely contributed by those whom Luzzati has called " the flower of our unhappy people," no expenditure, however noble in intent, is allowed unless clearly for the entire and exclusive advantage of the emigrants.

It is the aim of the Commissioner-General so to enlighten prospective emigrants that they may avoid the pitfalls that lie in the path of the ignorant; hence — besides the *Bollettino* — innumerable free popular circulars, notices, instructions for emigrants who select particular countries. Some years ago, for example, he issued a first edition of 50,000 copies of a collection of rules for the avoidance and treatment of tracoma, for use both in Italy and Brazil. When quick action is necessary, he may turn to the public press to discourage men from setting forth for work in some countries — as, for example, when the enterprise of the Panama Canal was begun. When, early in 1916, a colliery near Nancy asked for Italian laborers and offered them good terms, the Commissioner replied that laborers would be sent only if the terms were applied also to the Italians already there; the condition was not met, the laborers were not sent.[1]

To furnish information on the general problems of emigration, in particular to aid in executing the latest suggestions of the Commissioner-General, there is a widespread system of local committees (*comitati mandamentali o comunali*), several thousand in number, composed of official and other persons, in no way interested in the business of emigration. When, a number of years ago, employers in the southern United States, who could not offer satisfactory working conditions, entrusted prepaid tickets to their agents in Italy to induce laborers to come, the Commissioner-General issued a circular to all the committees (among other bodies) exposing the practice; it is one instance among a great number. It must be confessed, however, that these committees as a whole have never functioned successfully, partly because mayor, doctor, and priest do not combine well, partly because philanthropic zeal, as we have seen, is rare, especially in the South, and because people trust the beaten paths of emigration, or the very helpful ticket agent, more than they trust the government, particularly when they suspect that it wants to keep them at home.[2] Upon occasion, the Commissioner-General's advice, supplemented by advice from potent independent sources, has had conspicuous effect, as when, in the spring of 1910, wide publicity was given to an extensive building trades lockout in Germany.

Every ship authorized to carry emigrants must have on board a military doctor who must both see to the maintenance of sanitary standards and treat disease. On the outward journey such a policy is primarily aimed at the protection of the emigrants themselves; on the return, it is largely concerned with safeguarding the health of the Italian people. The annual reports of these physicians have not shown any material decline in the amount of sickness on board ship.[3]

---

[1] See a report by Cabrini to a trade-union congress in Paris, *Boll. Emig.*, 1916, No. 6, pp. 72–75.

[2] Rossi's report " Vantaggi e danni " was the fruit of an attempt to discover why the committees did not work well. Cf. also *Boll. Emig.*, 1905, No. 14, pp. 28 f.

[3] Besides the reports themselves see further, E. Fossataro, " Il servizio igienico e

An extensive personnel watches over the emigrants abroad. Besides certain travelling inspectors and travelling commissioners who study the welfare of the emigrants from many points of view — we have had to cite their testimony time and again in this book — the entire diplomatic and consular staff is utilized. As a class, the consuls are certainly not above the average of those of other great countries, their jurisdictions are often of enormous extent and perforce scantily visited by them, and their manifold duties may leave little room for general helpfulness. Yet competent men have shone among them. One of their powers is that of engaging legal aid in the interest of the emigrants — most commonly to collect indemnities for accidents — and they are supplied with funds for the repatriation of the indigent.[1] In 1908, a special fund of 10,000 lire was put at the disposal of the consul at Panama to enable the return of idle Italians there, and in 1914, we have seen, official repatriation from the countries of Europe assumed a prodigious character.[2] In 1905, the Commissioner-General, upon recommendation of the Emigration Council, appointed two emigration attachés (*addetti*) for the industrial region in West Germany, and one for Switzerland. These depend upon the consulates and give their entire time to watching over and helping the emigrants — studying the labor market, visiting workplaces, advising when there are strikes, helping to secure accident indemnities. Although the attachés have functioned well, they have never been introduced in the transatlantic countries, not because there would be no scope for their activity but because, as Baron Tittoni once put it, addressing the Senate, " the people of the United States will look on us with suspicion," not understanding why consuls are not sufficient.[3]

Appropriations of money are made for many purposes besides publication and the salaries of such officials as have been named

sanitario sui piroscafi da emigranti," *Boll. Emig.*, 1909, No. 17, pp. 11-23, and G. Mortara, " Emigrazione e sanità pubblica," *Giornale degli Economisti*, January, 1913, pp. 39-45.

[1] In this connection see a report to the Emigration Council, " Organizzazione del servizio legale nel nord-America," *Boll. Emig.*, 1914, No. 2, pp. 88-161.

[2] Read the vivid account, for example, of T. Tittoni, " Assistenza degli emigranti in Francia nei primi mesi della guerra del 1914," *Boll. Emig.*, 1915, No. 1, pp. 7-20.

[3] *Italy's Foreign and Colonial Policy*, p. 165.

and their expenses. Exhibitions have been aided both in Italy and abroad, when they might help toward a better understanding of the emigrants or lessen prejudices. Employment bureaus have been established, less to assist individuals than to enable the movements of masses, but so far their accomplishment has been small. In various parts of the world, and with telling effect, Italian hospitals have been subsidized. Requests for loans or for guarantee of interest in aid of colonization companies have hitherto failed of approval by the Emigration Council. In aid of schools very considerable appropriations have been made, " one of the most powerful means . . ." said Baron Tittoni, the father of important legislation in the matter, " of maintaining alive and propagating ever more the language, the ideas and civilization of Italy in other States, of affirming her political and moral influence which should open the way to her commerce." [1] In the countries about the Mediterranean the schools have been entirely maintained by the Italian Government; in North and South America they have only been subsidized; in South America alone they have numbered several hundred. Into the rural parts of Brazil " teacher agents " have been sent, men who besides instructing pupils perform certain of the functions of consuls. Finally, philanthropic societies of many sorts, engaged in the assistance of emigrants, have been given large subsidies. But these organizations — not all are subsidized — are of such independent importance that a separate description of their work is necessary.

One of them is the *Società Umanitaria*, or Humanitarian Society, with headquarters at Milan. The subsidy it receives is small compared with its income from the munificent bequest of its Hebraic founder. Venturesome, willing to experiment, maturing its plans well, it has in no department of its activity performed a more admirable work than in its Emigration Office. Quite independent beginnings had been made in the organization of " emigration secretariates," representing local labor interests in the great reservoir regions of temporary emigration. The democratic character of these, and their large possibilities of action, the Society was quick to recognize, and it has steadily worked to

---

[1] *Italy's Foreign and Colonial Policy*, p. 200; cf. p. 203.

introduce higher standards into their activity, and to bring still other secretariates into existence. Their stated objects are to provide legal aid for emigrants when the labor contract and social legislation are in question; to advise concerning working conditions, in general and at the moment, in the countries of emigration; to take the initiative in securing special schools or training for persons about to emigrate; to provide an employment bureau service, utilizing the devices instituted by the Commissioner-General; to maintain a live relationship with the latter's office and all other protective organizations. These are also the objects of the Emigration Office of the Society itself. The secretariates, of which some two-thirds (the older established) are in the North, receive financial support from the *Umanitaria*, the Commissioner-General, the interested communes, the provinces and sundry credit institutes, besides the emigrants themselves. Some forty of fifty existed at the outbreak of the European war and there were also correspondent secretariates outside of Italy. Chiefly on the Society's initiative, they have held congresses; and their affairs are currently reported in the national *Bollettino dell' Ufficio del Lavoro*.

The Society has also set up frontier stations for the assistance of emigrants. It had long urged the provision of courses of training in the major centers of emigration to fit men industrially and otherwise for emigration, and it has beheld the fruition of its efforts. Indeed it has itself instituted training schools for teachers of such courses and for the officials of secretariates; and as I write I have before me a carefully compiled pamphlet programme for the instruction of masons.[1] Several editions have been published of a *Calendario per gli emigranti*, which are at once guides, in separable parts, for continental and for transoceanic emigrants. And every week an issue appears of *Corrispondenza dell' Ufficio Centrale di Emigrazione*, a journal intended primarily for the secretariates but also abundantly clipped, as it happens, by the local newspapers; in 1917 it published valuable lists of refugees.[2]

[1] Società Umanitaria, *Programma per corsi d'insegnamento a favore di operai muratori nei centri d'emigrazione*, Varese, 1912.

[2] The *Umanitaria* issues annual reports and many special publications, the latter including, for example, the reports of the Consorzio per la Difesa dell' Emigrazione

For many years more extensive in its ramifications than the Humanitarian Society, yet now somewhat overtaken by this acknowledged rival, is the *Opera di Assistenza agli Operai Italiani Emigrati in Europa e nel Levante*, founded by the late Bishop Bonomelli, and enjoying a subvention from the Commissioner-General. Avowedly religious in its general character, it has aimed at the manifold protection of emigrants. At such main sluices for the continental currents as Chiasso and·Domodossola, it has provided night abodes, cheap kitchens, and other aids. It acquaints men with the condition of the labor market and with the best routes of travel. In France, Germany, Switzerland, and Austria it has maintained secretariates, and sometimes, in connection with them, schools for women and children, cooking classes, savings banks, circulating libraries, and the like.[1]

What the Opera Bonomelli has been for the Italians in the countries of Europe, that, in a minor sense, the *Italica Gens* has been, or has aspired to be, for the Italians overseas. An outgrowth of a missionary organization associated with the name of the ardent and enterprising Scalabrini, its headquarters in Turin, it has invited Italian priests everywhere to enter its membership. While it seeks to give help of many sorts in entirely secular matters, its principal aims are moral, to be furthered by church and school. " It is beyond a doubt," said the first number of its monthly *Bollettino* (February, 1910), " that the chief course of action to follow is moral, the development of the latent intellectual energies of our emigrants in order to make them efficient citizens and rouse in them the national spirit "; again, " we have put among the first of our aims the conservation of the national sentiment." It has sought to further compact collectivities, in city and agricultural colony, and the number of parishes and

Temporanea in Europa (which it has absorbed). The Director of the Emigration Office, A. Cabrini, has published widely. The interest roused by the *Umanitaria* in neighboring countries is exemplified by occasional reports in the *Correspondenzblatt der Generalkommission der Gewerkschaften Deutschlands.*

[1] The *Boll. Emig.* has many accounts of the *Opera's* activities, but see also Opera di Assistenza agli Operai Italiani Emigrati in Europa: *Primo Congresso Italiano dell' Assistenza all' Emigrazione Continentale, Milano, Maggio 1913, Relazioni* (Milan, 1913), and *Rendiconti delle sedute* (Milan, 1914).

priests now comprised in its organization is large, in both North and South America.[1]

Here general mention should be made of the numberless independent societies of many sorts existing in the emigrant communities and mainly original there. " Whatever their individual aims," an official summary concluded some years ago, " it is comforting for us to note that they always and everywhere exert a commendable action, since they have inestimable value as factors of civilization and progress and admirably serve to tighten the bonds between those who compose the colonies, and between the colonies and the mother country." [2] Some societies, for specific aids to emigrants, secure subsidies from the Commissioner-General. Some have founded hospitals, many have maintained schools. They have gathered funds for the relief of the victims of disasters in Italy, have managed patriotic celebrations, have entertained distinguished guests, and in the Great War have in endless ways served their country.

One among these many societies, its headquarters in Rome, its branches in all countries where Italians go, deserves a special word. This is the *Dante Alighieri,* founded in 1889 under the presidency of R. Bonghi, and subsequently headed by P. Villari, L. Rava, and others. It has aimed to avoid every partisan character, religious, political or class, and has sought by means of annual congresses to keep fresh and efficient its instruments for attaining its central purpose, that of protecting and disseminating the language and culture of Italy. At home it has kept alive in the national Parliament the question of schooling the Italians abroad. In France it has established some institutions of charity; in the Levant, North Africa, and America it has arranged celebrations, provided lectures, diffused tracts, and set up libraries. Needless to add, its influence has been generally above the stratum of the unskilled and manual labor class.

[1] See a volume *Nel XXV anniversario dell' istituto dei missionari di S. Carlo per gli italiani emigrati fondato da Mons. Giovanni Batt. Scalabrini, 1887-1912,* Rome, 1912. The studies of Venerosi Pesciolini in Brazil were made under the auspices of Italica Gens.

[2] " Le società italiane all' estero nel 1908," *Boll. Emig.,* 1908, No. 24, p. v.

Still other organizations seeking to secure the welfare of the emigrants have risen or flourished in this Second Period in the history of Italian opinion. But either they have been born in the latest years, or what is most characteristic in their work has developed subsequently, and therefore they are best considered with the Third Period.

THE THIRD PERIOD: SINCE ABOUT 1908

How the emigration question was somewhat forcibly drawn out from placid waters into the tumult and stress of a particularly tumultuous epoch of politics makes the dramatic theme next to be unfolded. The faithful historian must confess that the period contains nothing which could not be found, in germ at least, in the previous periods. But these recent years have taken what earlier seemed insignificant or inert and have painted a canvas of large figures in action. While such a policy of protection as had been evolved in our Second Period could be so carried out as not to startle or harm other peoples, the policies in question in this Third Period were calculated to touch very deeply the interests and desires of other nations. It is entirely possible, if one wishes, to minimize and gloss over the international character of emigration; but in the recent period it is precisely that character which men have chosen to make the basis of their action.

The new attitude is related to the striking revival of imperialism in Italy. It is also bound up with the development of a conception of Italian citizenship. Only when these two are understood — and I will deal with the question of citizenship first — will the special drift of the emigration argument be plain.

The new view of citizenship rests upon the fact, now familiar to readers of this book, that the Italian who goes abroad expects some day to return, changes little in his new environment, and often does return. It renders affection in return for affection and desires that the emigrants should rear the edifice of a Greater Italy. It is particularly unwilling that they should be lost to the country whose traditions they have shared in common — as unwilling, one sometimes infers, as Northerners of the United States were to allow the South to secede in 1860. " May they and their children never forget Italy! " exclaimed Pantano in a report to Parliament as long ago as 1904, " This is our aspiration, this must guide our every action." [1] The best emigration then is that which is undisguisedly temporary.[2] But the hand of Italy would keep its hold on those also who seem to abide permanently abroad, and on their children. De Zettiry's *Manual*, an official gift to emigrants to Argentina, pointing out the duties of sons when they reach the age of seventeen, has these words:

Perhaps you have taken children with you to your new home; others may have been born to you there. Our country, Italy, regards all these your children as its subjects. This mode of conceiving nationality, which moreover is common to all civilized nations, will some day come in conflict with the laws of the country where you reside. But do not let that trouble you: the two governments will amicably settle each instance as it arises.

This occurs especially in regard to the obligation of military service. . . .

Educate and bring up your children in manly ways, see to it that they be courageous, broken to the great discomforts of life and of toil, respectful of the constituted order and if you can, also good horsemen and able marksmen. . . .

Further: But this reconciliation of conflicting duties will be neither easy nor complete, unless you shall have taught your children, along with a full and sincere affection for the Argentine country, a similar affection for the country overseas. Therefore speak to them often of the dear and beautiful Italy which cradled you, of its struggles, of its triumphs, of its glories, of its great destiny, and having done so you will have educated them to that very devotion to a noble patriotism which today makes Argentina proud of the sons of her brave colonists.[3]

Sometimes the suggestion has been made that Italy should allow her emigrants abroad to vote, at the consuls' offices, in the national elections, but it has never won substantial adherence.[4]

[1] " Relazione della Commissione Parlamentare di Vigilanza sul Fondo per l'Emigrazione," *Boll. Emig.*, 1904, No. 11, p. 119; cf. p. 123.

[2] Cf. the words of the Commissioner-General, *Boll. Emig.*, 1910, No. 18, p. 157. A similar conclusion, with a somewhat different argument is that of the Final Report of the *Inch. Parl.*, viii, pp. 96 f.

[3] De Zettiry, pp. 183-187.

[4] Yet see A. Cabrini, *Manualetto per l'emigrante in Europa* (Milan, 1910), pp. 33 f., and a parliamentary discussion reproduced in *Rivista di Emigrazione*, July-August, 1912, pp. 245-253. More than twenty years earlier, Italians in Montevideo made proposals that they (and their compatriots everywhere) be allowed to elec representatives in Parliament to be styled " colonial deputies "; Saldias, p. 44.

Frequently the emigrants are urged to refrain from naturalization abroad; or satisfaction is taken in the circumstance that they commonly do refrain. Indeed the whole structure of protection, mainly reared in what I have called the Second Period, exists largely in order that the national traits and the loyalty of the emigrants may be strengthened rather than suffered to decline.[1] As if in sheer contradiction of this view, emigrants are sometimes urged to become naturalized. But the reasons therefor destroy the force of the contradiction: for it is not so that the new citizens may whole-heartedly serve their new commonwealth. " We ought to instruct, to organize these phalanxes of laborers," said Sig. Nitti in Parliament, June 21, 1905.

It is a thing that the officials of the State can not and ought not to do, but private agencies can accomplish it easily. To us it matters not that our fellow citizens should be for this or that party, it interests us only that they should be a real and live force, and that their aid should be sought and they should not dwell always as strangers in the land that fosters them. If I may say so, we ought at one and the same time to develop in them the national culture and love of Italy, and to confer on them the political power they now lack.[2]

The agitation for some form of double citizenship had its beginnings in the previous century, but did not acquire force until the first years of the Third Period. Then Minister Scialoja recommended that Italian nationality be suspended, not lost, by Italians naturalized abroad, and restored to validity (save where a contrary desire is declared) by the fact of return to Italy; quite as cohabitation annuls the legal consequences of separation. Senator De Martino, the president of the Colonial Institute, other members of Parliament, and many journalists urged some such measure. Enrico Ferri, back from Argentina, told his attentive listeners in the Chamber:

[1] Cf. the words of a deputy, R. Murri, " We assist the emigrants, not so that they may become good New Yorkers or good citizens of the Port, but so that, at New York or in Buenos Aires, they may continue to be, just as far as is possible, good Italians," in his article, " Gl' italiani nell' America Latina — impressioni di viaggio," *Nuova Antologia*, April 1, 1913, p. 440.

[2] *Boll. Emig.*, 1905, No. 15, p. 53. Such a course, Nitti believes, would leave them not the less good Italians after their return to Italy. The view in general is a very common one. On its prevalence as regards Argentina, see A. Franzoni, " Italia ed Argentina," *Rivista Coloniale*, November 25–December 10, 1910, p. 408.

I said to the Italians down there: If Italy passed a law amending our Civil Code in such a way that when an Italian citizen accepted foreign citizenship he could reacquire Italian citizenship by merely reëntering Italy with the intention of ending his days there, would the difficulties be removed? Would you be content? Yes, they replied, for we should no longer be considered renegades, we should be citizens of Argentina or of Brazil but, reëntering Italy, Italian citizens once more.[1]

And the Final Report of the *Parliamentary Inquiry into the Condition of the Southern Contadini* held:

Most frequently the new citizenship is asked for by the emigrant under pressure of necessity or economic advantage, to the end that his status before the law may not be inferior to that of native born or naturalized. Such an act on his part, however voluntary, today involves the loss of his original nationality and this thought weakens in him his affection for his native land. . . . When the emigrant shall be able to say: " I am an Argentine in Argentina but an Italian in Italy and I always retain my place in the ranks of the regiment to which I was assigned," then he will be proud of a country which does not disown him and he will love it because he will feel himself to be loved.[2]

The situation came to a head in 1912. A bill for the amendment of the law of citizenship, in essentials unamended since 1863, was introduced into Parliament. In the discussion, double citizenship was not seriously pressed for; it seemed too visionary. On at least two previous occasions the Italian Government had opened negotiations with the United States and Argentina, but they had failed to lead to the adoption of any fixed rules. *Duarum civitatum civis esse nemo potest* — the new legislators could find no way out of an old Ciceronian dilemma. They put the case also in biological terms: a cell cannot be a member of two organisms. And they reflected that the naturalization law of the United States requires the renunciation of previous allegiance, and noted that

[1] Session of June 22, 1909. *Boll. Emig.*, 1909, No. 12, p. 23.

[2] *Inch. Parl.*, viii, pp. 97 f. On double citizenship see various addresses before the first and second Congressi degli Italiani all' Estero; N. Samama, *Contributo allo studio della doppia cittadinanza nei riguardi del movimento migratorio*, Rome, 1910; M. Vianello-Chiodo, *La cittadinanza del nostro emigrato*, Rome, 1910; G. C. Buzzatti, " L'Italia, l'America Latina e la doppia nazionalitá," *Rivista Coloniale*, January-February, 1908, pp. 3–21, and *idem*, " La doppia cittadinanza studiata nei rapporti fra l'Italia e la Repubblica Argentina," *Rivista Coloniale*, July-August, 1908, pp. 547-575.

general opinion in the United States favors naturalization of immigrants. It was recognized that one sort of double citizenship already exists, but pathologically only, by a conflict of laws. This very conflict, however, such as it was, they now reënacted. Holding that those shall lose their Italian citizenship who spontaneously acquire a foreign citizenship, or who have established their residence abroad (the Government may dispense with this rule) or who accept military or other employment with a foreign state, Article 8 of the law of June 13, 1912, declares that such loss of citizenship shall not exempt them from the duties of military service. Would not any other rule have opened a wide gate to an exodus of Italian citizens? But consider the new measure further. Article 7 holds, as the previous law had done, that the foreign-born son of an Italian, even though claimed by the foreign country (as in the Americas), shall be deemed an Italian citizen, but on attaining his majority or civil rights he may renounce his Italian allegiance. Most of all, however, it is Article 9 that commands our interest. This provides the way to an easy reassumption of Italian citizenship, in its main lines enacting a proposal made three years earlier by Tittoni. Those, it holds, who, by the provisions of Articles 7 and 8, have lost their citizenship may reacquire it (a) by rendering military service to Italy or accepting government employment, (b) by renouncing foreign citizenship or foreign military employment and taking up a residence in Italy, or (c) by residing for two years in Italy, provided loss of citizenship was due to acquisition of foreign citizenship, or even, by permission, by residing two years in another country and not there assuming citizenship. Let me only add that Article 13 declares that there shall be no taxes or costs for the acquisition or reacquisition of citizenship.

Here, then, is a law enacted at the very apogee of the emigration movement, with the aim, not of establishing double citizenship, but yet of facilitating the rapid resumption of citizenship by repatriated emigrants. It assumes, what doubtless is true, that there must be many emigrants whose naturalization in other countries is primarily for personal convenience, and not the sign of a new allegiance of the heart. It does not desire to discourage such naturalization and it does encourage the wandering children of Italy to return to the mother.[1]

Italian imperialism has had its inspiration in much more than the example of other nations. In a country which had been the center of the Ancient World, its colonies scattered far and wide, and which in a later time could " hold the gorgeous East in fee," dreamers were bound to arise who would demand a revival of such greatness. The stones of Rome and the stones of Venice were alike eloquent. So Mazzini, while yet modern Italy seemed only a radiant hope, foresaw a great Mediterranean rôle for his country, the mistress-to-be, he pictured, of Tunisia and Tripoli. C. Negri in 1863 portrayed the Argentine as an Italian Australia. The purchase of Assab in 1870 was the modest beginning of an attempt to bring the vision to earth. Preachers of colonial expansion became more numerous, the voices of such men as C. Correnti, A. Amati, L. Carpi, being heard. Soon after the occupation of Rome, Carpi, the first student of his countrymen's peregrinations, wrote that, in order to derive the full benefit from her emigration, Italy should have true colonies overseas.[2] A major hope was blasted when the French seized Tunisia. But the dream went its way, becoming grander and more vivid. Crispi delineated a great African empire, not unmindful however of the Mediterranean coasts as well. Hearts beat faster when Abyssinia was invaded, but a terrible reversal to the Italian arms scattered the dream's fabric and left blank disillusionment in its stead. Crispi fell and the di Rudinì cabinet began to renounce. Italian imperialism had come too late. Benadir, Eritrea, these wastes must content the ambitious.

Meanwhile, after Adowa, the great current of human emigration became ever thicker. A non-political empire was being founded. Could not Italy be proud of her colonies *sans drapeau* ? There were even those, however, like Professor Grossi, who felt that the proper way of dealing with such colonies would in time

---

[1] The speeches and reports on the new law make interesting, if lengthy, reading. They are reproduced in *Boll. Emig.*, 1913, No. 3, pp. 13–222.

[2] *Op. cit.*, i, p. 64.

enable the Italian nation to spread its civilization and its language over two continents.[1]

Although the incumbents of the newly established office of Commissioner-General of Emigration were undoubtedly enterprising and from the first gave free rein to the desire to espy in any continent new habitations for Italian emigrants — the Congo, Australia, Chili, what not — yet they lacked the freedom which a private organization might have. In 1906, to fill a need, the *Istituto Coloniale* was founded, presently to be subsidized by the Government. " Its aim is to further and develop Italian colonial action, whether public or private, to make studies and researches abroad, to constitute itself a permanent bond between the mother country and the compatriots who live abroad, and to represent collective interests." Its membership has included the officials of government and of the great non-governmental associations. Its organ, the *Rivista Coloniale*, has been given over, in about equal parts, to the discussion of colonial and of emigration problems, all from the point of view of creating a stronger, more influential Italy, taking a lead, for instance, in the discussion of double citizenship. To the Foreign Affairs Office the Institute has been of great service in providing new, non-official, sources of colonial information. When disaster came to Calabria and Sicily by earthquake, it at once sent appeals to all Italian collectivities, asking for help. It arranged a visit of young Turks to Italy and a centennial celebration, in Italy, of Argentine independence, and it sought to federate the various Italian societies in the United States. But its principal achievement has been its organization of two impressive emigrant congresses. To the first of these, held in Rome in October, 1908, the delegates who came from European countries numbered 110, those from America 107, those from Africa 36. It revealed, as the president of the Institute later said, material and moral energies till then unsuspected in Italy. The discussion turned upon such questions as citizenship, schools, trade. It was voted that the Government be recommended greatly to increase the subsidies to schools abroad, that measures

---

[1] V. Grossi, " L'insegnamento coloniale in Italia e nei principali paesi d'Europa," *L'Italia Coloniale*, November, 1901, pp. 37–52, December, pp. 48–84.

be taken to promote the unity and harmony of the Italians in the foreign settlements, and that the Government be asked to call an international conference on emigration. The delegates visited the monuments and attended a performance of d'Annunzio's irredentist play, *La Nave*. In 1911, in connection with the semicentennial celebration of the birth of Italian freedom, the second congress assembled, a fit symbol of the Greater Italy that had come to pass. Its thronging delegates again discussed such matters as double citizenship, the protection of emigrants, trade, culture; and the votes passed either reaffirmed those of the first congress or called for still more extensive action. The resolution, for example, which followed the debate on double citizenship anticipated the most important provisions of the law enacted in the next year.[1]

The successful launching of the Colonial Institute was only one sign — and the less important of two — that time was healing the Abyssinian wound. A new generation was coming to manhood, keen of vision, fresh in hope, bold and urgent. When some of its more alert representatives became conscious that their thoughts had a common drift, they called a congress for December, 1910, which, all but unnoticed at the time, can never be forgotten. Dubbing themselves "Nationalists," they held that Italy must be roused from her servility and apathy; that only war, a glorious source of greatness, can rouse her; that her rulers must be firm imperialists, bold in their foreign policy, prepared to strike; that a main object of war must be to provide lands whither emigrants might go. Not a regional life, but a collective national soul, was the need of Italy, as Scipio Sighele, the philosopher of the movement, put it. And Sighele also declared that the doctrine first took form as a reaction against the Austrian seizure of Bosnia-Herzegovina; but anti-Austrianism soon became a submerged issue. After the congress, committees were appointed all over Italy and a propagandist journal, *L'Idea Nazionale*, began to be

---

[1] Istituto Coloniale Italiano, *Atti del Primo Congresso degli Italiani all' Estero (ottobre 1908)*, 2 vols., Rome, 1910, and *Atti del Secondo . . . (giugno 1911)*, 2 vols. in 4 parts, Rome, 1912.

published. The first votaries of Nationalism, despite its stress upon war, were not of the military caste, but intellectuals, largely literary folk.[1]

Not unfairly Enrico Corradini, the novelist, has been claimed to be the founder of the movement. Certainly he was its chief propagandist and he sets forth more eloquently than any other writer the connection of Nationalism with emigration. Even in his novels, the doctrine is foreshadowed. Buondelmonti, for example, tells his compatriots in Brazil, as he is about to depart to fight for Italy, that he seeks to make a better world for their kind:

> They will not need to do what you have had to do, to emigrate into foreign lands, equipped only with brawn and patience, but they will be free to choose lands that their country will have conquered. Italy will then not be only where Italy is today, but it will be wherever there are Italians, just as today England is wherever the English are. And then the Italians will no longer speak the language of their masters, but will speak their own language.[2]

Consider however his frankly political writings. In a recent essay he says:

> Study and reflection on these lines led me in 1908 to travel among the Italian colonies in South America. . . . I examined into the labor done by them, the benefit accruing to those regions, and the inadequate reward of the hard-working colonists. I came home with ideas clean contrary to the opinion held in Italy which at that time favored emigration. All alike had taken a sort of pride in the achievements of our brethren . . . oddly enough, gloried in their mission to cultivate the globe while others reaped the harvest.[3]

In another work, *The Will of Italy*, he declares, "Emigration is, after death from starvation, the worst of necessities." The " detestable optimism " in which it is viewed must be destroyed. " Italian individuals cannot do otherwise than emigrate, and

---

[1] Sighele's chief works dealing with Nationalism are *Pagine nazionaliste*, Milan, 1910, and *Il nazionalismo ed i partiti politici*, Milan, 1911. He died in 1913. An admirable objective study is E. Flori, " Nazionalismo e individualismo," *Rivista d'Italia*, March, 1916, pp. 309–350, and April, 1916, pp. 502–536. Cf. P. Romano, " Nazionalismo e valore nazionale," in the same journal, December 15, 1914, pp. 781–803.

[2] *La patria lontana* (Milan, 1910), p. 255.

[3] " Italy from Adowa to the Great War," *Nineteenth Century*, May, 1917, p. 1017.

woe to them if they should be prevented from emigrating! But the Italian nation, if it is content with that and lauds it, is morally base, is immoral, and the limit of its immorality is only marked by its ignorance." Again, " Let us boast of the fecundity of our women, but not of the dispersion of their children." The emigration of Italy " is the main condition of the circumstance that she is forced to have a foreign policy," and from that policy she should aim to secure the greatest profit. " Emigration is one of the points of departure of Nationalism, one of the very determiners (*capisaldi*) of its character, perhaps indeed the first." [1] Returning to his theme in still another work, he says, " It should be understood that emigration signifies the abandonment of Italian labor to itself throughout the world, whereas conquest of colonies signifies Italian labor accompanied through the world by the other forces of the Italian nation, by the nation itself." Again, " Too large a population in too small a country. And when it is so, either men must conquer colonies or emigrate or must become neo-malthusians. But the last course is vile, emigration is servile, and only the conquest of colonies is worthy of a free and noble people." [2] Once more, " There are proletariate nations just as there are proletariate classes." That is, they are inferior to others. Such a nation is Italy — " for all arguments let her emigration suffice." She should become nation-conscious, nationalistic. Nationalism is a reaction against socialism — class-consciousness, the class struggle — which it fights tooth and nail. It is a reaction against a false international idealism; all balance of power represents but a transitory adaptation. The aim of Nationalism is *la guerra vittoriosa* — in labor, in trade, in morals, in culture. [3]

Corradini and Sighele are only the best known of the Nationalists. Others are G. De Frenzi, F. Carli, L. Federzoni (a prominent journalist and deputy), R. F. Davanzati (who came from socialism), G. Bevione (correspondent of the Turin *Stampa*),

---

[1] *Il volere d'Italia (cit.)*, pp. 63 f., 75, 178; his most explicit work. Earlier (Florence, 1907), he had published *La vita nazionale.*

[2] *L'ora di Tripoli* (Milan, 1911), pp. 21, 30.

[3] *Il volere d'Italia*, pp. 163–177.

L. Villari (writer and former consular official), and G. Castellini (a brilliant journalist). The *Idea Nazionale* from having been a weekly became a daily. Presently not only the Turin *Stampa*, but the Naples *Mattino* and the *Giornale d'Italia*, became imbued with the new spirit. Yet, though an apostolic fervor marked the utterances of the leaders, few can have guessed how soon the seed they scattered would itself come to fruit. The " hour of Tripoli " was at hand.

To ascribe to the Nationalists the seizure of Tripoli would be excessive. The issue harked back farther. Di Rudinì was the spokesman of all Italy when in 1881 he cried out his resentment against the French for occupying Tunisia, with its Italian population, and so disturbing the Mediterranean balance of power. As everybody knows, the political consequence of this act was to make Italy a member, the next year, of the Triple Alliance. Step by step the vision of an Italian empire had been narrowed. England was in Cyprus and in Egypt, Austria fastened her hold upon Bosnia and Herzegovina, France next became assured of the possession of Morocco. These events were mainly recent. Indeed after Italian claims upon Morocco had been yielded up, or, as one writer put it, after the " tunisification " of Morocco, there could be left to Italy in North Africa only Tripoli. But much earlier, when Tunisia, held to be geographically a prolongation of Sicily, had become *terra perduta*, Tripoli became *terra promessa*. In 1890 Crispi got Salisbury's assurance that some day Italy should have Tripoli. Historical destiny, based upon a conception of prior right, pointed her finger the same way — had not Tripoli and Cyrenaica been colonies of the Roman Empire ? Men spoke of the region as bound to become Italian again. Ricciotti Garibaldi kindled imaginations when he declared that eight or ten million Italians could live there. Presently came the celebration of the first half century of Italian unity, with its quickening of patriotism, its heightening of the pride of the people. Conscious of their own abounding population, they resented the further acquisition of colonies by nations that had room to spare. They were tired of being, in a common phrase, the Cinderella of the nations. And only Tripoli could keep them from being prisoners in the Mediterranean.

In 1905 the Foreign Minister Tittoni had deplored any effort to take Tripoli while friendly relations existed with Turkey. Five years later, the Foreign Minister San Giuliano declared it to be a fundamental of his policy also to maintain the status quo in the Mediterranean and he more than once rebuked those who attacked the Turks, or who urged that America might close her doors to Italian emigrants who therefore ought to be free to go into a conquered Tripoli. Early in June, 1911, further agitation developed in Parliament, one speaker alluding to articles published in the preceding two months in *La Stampa*, " the most authoritative journal of Piedmont," and in *La Tribuna* of Rome, showing the need of raising Italian prestige in the Mediterranean. To all San Giuliano replied, on June 9, that the integrity of the Ottoman Empire must be preserved, that even then the Turks feared the expansionist aims of Italy and indeed had been given some ground therefor.[1]

Three months later the Italian expedition was virtually decided upon. What had happened ? Hand in hand, the balance of power argument and the argument for an outlet for the nation had swept Italy. Just at what moment the propagandists ceased to be regarded as visionaries and were deemed advocates of a desirable course is hard to say. Seven months before war was declared, Castellini wrote his *Tunisi e Tripoli*, the first Nationalist book directly inciting to the expedition. " Every day," he said, " which passes is, politically, a day lost." [2] The Austrian war he declared could wait; sentiment was ripe for Tripoli. In the spring, the *Tribuna* printed the enthusiastic exhortations of G. Piazza (later editor-in-chief of the *Rivista Coloniale*), and his book, *La nostra terra promessa*, was issued in July. In the spring likewise appeared Bevione's letters in the *Stampa*; in September he declared " It is now or never." In the spring once more, Cor-

---

[1] On some thirty years of Parliamentary debate see *La Libia negli atti del Parlamento e nei provvedimenti del Governo*, issued by the Collegio di Scienze Politiche e Coloniali, 2 vols., Milan, 1912–13.

[2] *Tunisi e Tripoli* (Turin, 1911), p. 193.

radini lectured, and through the summer published his letters in *L'Idea Nazionale.* The question of South Italy, he maintained, is an African question. " I mean to say that the South is as it is mainly because it is near to Africa. The principal cause of all the differences between North and South is the difference between Europe and Africa." To europeanize Africa is therefore to help the South.[1] Increasingly the newspapers championed the project, often dwelling upon the emigration argument. It was urged that men would doubtless leave Tunisia and other countries where they were not wanted, to settle in Tripoli.[2] As the summer drew to a close there was no longer any doubt that the preponderance of opinion enthusiastically favored the expedition.

Corradini has stated the opposition of Nationalism and socialism. Did the socialists yield ? A left wing under Turati, and the Emilian socialists generally, opposed the expedition; the rest favored it, including the Labriolas, P. Orano, A. O. Olivetti, A. Cabrini, A. Berenini. It must be remembered that Italian socialists are largely from the South, and the Southern populace in general approved the war. Arturo Labriola counselled not to confound this venture with imperialism, since Nature had granted to Italy freedom of movement in the Mediterranean. In the *Idea Nazionale,* the staunch Antonio Labriola held that the expedition would give a spur to Italian initiative, a quality necessary to socialist ends. It was not, he asserted, anti-democratic to employ military force to carve out a region whither the Italian people might go to settle for centuries — never could there be an independent life for them in Argentina and Brazil.[3]

Needless to say, the authorities of the Colonial Institute ap-

---

[1] *L'ora di Tripoli,* p. 227. Later he wrote (" Italy from Adowa," etc., p. 1019): " Progressive communities may be said to fulfill the law of productive possession. They have a just claim to the territory they occupy. . . . Not so the undeveloped or the decaying peoples. Of these it is right to say that they are colonies awaiting the European, who shall extend to them and for their advantage the science of production which he has mastered. That is his title to dominion."

[2] Cf. D. Tumiati, *Tripolitania* (Milan, 1911), p. 288. As early as 1904, Tumiati wished the conquest of Tripoli to be undertaken.

[3] On the socialists, see G. Podrecca, *Libia-impressioni e polemiche* (Rome, 1912), esp. pp. 5–51, where the socialist argument appears. Cf. A. Dauzat, *L'expansion italienne* (Paris, 1914), p. 91.

proved the expedition, as the columns of its organ illustrate.[1] Its
first president, in fact, had written an expansionist book about
Tripoli. The cross being superior to the crescent, the Roman
Catholic clergy likewise approved and publicly prayed for the
success of Italian arms.

By February of 1912 the main burden of the fighting was over.
Peace terms were signed in October. The ultimatum precipitat-
ing the war had threatened " military occupation," but annexa-
tion was its outcome. The entire diplomatic procedure leaves a
dark page in Italian history, for which the best that can be said is
that a Moslem power and a supposedly inferior race were in
question.[2] Whether the natural conditions of the new colony can
ever be so managed as to provide a haven for Italian emigrants
has not yet been determined. Hopes have certainly run high, and
emigrants in various parts of the world were presently declared to
have made plans to go there.[3]

When the war for Tripoli was ended, Sighele declared that the
Nationalist party had no further reason to exist. Its aim was accomplished. Yet its special aim, in this seer's eyes, had been to
awaken and unite Italy. And that was now accomplished.
" Have you ever noted the light in the face of a girl in love ? "
Such a light, he held, radiates from Italians' faces now — they
love Italy.[4] Something had been done to bring North and South
together. And Italians the world over felt an access of pride.

[1] See the article by R. Paoli, " Tripoli nostra," *Rivista Coloniale*, September 25–
October 10, 1911, pp. 317–322.

[2] On the procedure see Sir Thomas Barclay, *The Turco-Italian War and its Problems*, London, 1912.

[3] Cf. L. Villari, " Italy a Year after the Libyan War," *Fortnightly Review*, November, 1913, p. 936.

On the Tripoli venture a considerable literature, largely Nationalistic, was quick
to blossom forth. Among the important books of 1912 are these: G. Piazza, *Come
conquistammo Tripoli* (Rome); G. Bevione, *Come siamo andati a Tripoli* (Turin);
E. Corradini, *La conquista di Tripoli* (Milan); G. Castellini, *Nelle trincee di Tripoli*
(Bologna); G. Coen, *L'Italia a Tripoli* (Leghorn); V. Mantegazza, *Tripoli e i
diritti della civiltà* (Milan); G. Mosca, *Italia e Libia* (Milan); V. Cottafavi, *Nella
Libia italiana* (Bologna). An important later work is Società Italiana per lo Studio
della Libia, *La Missione Franchetti in Tripolitania*, Florence, 1914.

[4] S. Sighele, " La nouvelle psychologie irrédentiste depuis l'expédition tripoli-
taine," *La Revue*, March 15, 1912, p. 151.

The imperialist dream had been quickened, not ended, by the step toward empire. The East still lured. During the Libyan war Rhodes and the Sporades had been occupied, and the Italians, welcomed with enthusiasm, hoped to stay.[1] In 1913 Italian capitalists received a concession to build the Adalia-Burdur trunk line in Asia Minor. Promising to print articles dealing with the region, the *Rivista Coloniale* said editorially, " now that European Turkey is liquidated, the appetites and rivalries of the European powers are directed toward the territories of Asiatic Turkey." [2] Adalia is the port of Anatolia, the land nearest to Rhodes. When Turkey entered the European war the prospect of disintegration became still brighter, and the Colonial Institute's journal, which hitherto had published little on the war, printed a leading article on the opportunity created by the new turn of events.[3]

The Irredentist movement, which in the passing years had lapsed (as Sighele put it) into a form of patriotic romanticism, did not require the outbreak of the Great War to be revived. " At Tripoli we all felt that the spectacle of energy and victory given by Italy in Africa was not without meaning and without the hope of other displays of energy and other victories." Sighele refers to the Trentino and Trieste.[4] These the Nationalists had only for the moment neglected.[5] With the entrance of Italy into the war, the recovery of them became primary aims. In Switzerland, the fear was spurred (it is still strong) lest the ardor of the cause be extended also to the absorption of Canton Ticino.[6] From Austria, full control of the Adriatic was to be secured. Albania

[1] Read Corradini's recital of events, *Sopra le vie del nuovo impero*, Milan, 1912.

[2] *Rivista Coloniale*, November 30, 1913, p. 277.

[3] E. C. Tedeschi, " La fatale crisi risolutiva turca e l'espansione italiana in Oriente," *Rivista Coloniale*, February, 1915, pp. 61–69. See also in this connection the jubilant article by G. Capra (a Salesian priest), " La nostra guerra," printed in the *Bollettino* of Italica Gens, March–June, 1915, pp. 145–148.

[4] " La nouvelle psychologie," p. 145.

[5] Many advocates of the Tripoli expedition now wielded their pens for Italia Irredenta. A characteristic instance is G. Castellini, *Trento e Trieste*, Milan, 1915.

[6] In 1911, while the desire to take Tripoli was being spurred, A. O. Olivetti published articles in Ticino urging that the canton be absorbed by Italy. There was alarm in Switzerland, Olivetti was expelled, and his paper suppressed. See Barni, *La Svizzera contemporanea*, pp. 271 f.

was hoped for and a road into Asia Minor. All these regions could be peopled. So the Italy of the future would be made by the emigrants.

Such has been the recent history of expansionism in Italy in relation to emigration. In other countries the desire for colonial aggrandizement has been fully as strong as in Italy, but in no other country has the argument for an outlet for redundant population counted so heavily or in so wide a circle of the nation, and in no other country surely has it been so cogent and practical an argument. What lands shall we develop with our abounding capital ? Whence shall come our raw materials ? Where shall we find a market for our goods ? These are the questions asked by the imperialism of the rich. But the imperialism of the poor, as Corradini called it, asks, Whither shall we send our sons and our daughters, who have no place at home ?

CHAPTER XXIV

CONCLUSIONS. THE LARGER TASKS AHEAD

A WAVE which breaks upon many shores, Italian emigration is not to be appraised from any one angle alone. Like every world phenomenon, it so closely touches many different interests that here an Italian, there an American, have each felt warranted to pronounce separate judgment. Whether we will or not, however, we must not leave out of account any great interest that is touched — not the emigrants themselves, not Italy, not the lands to which they go. And we must assume that our powers of action or of suasion exceed the bounds of any one country, and must be willing to contemplate some sort of coördinated policy.

Only the blindest historian will hold that what exists is independent of ourselves and is best. The complexion of affairs will change, and largely what we decide will determine what will next follow. New emigration policies will rule, and, in the era we are now entering upon, they will not be complacent ones.

Since this entire book has been an attempt to lay bare the grounds for a policy, only a few words are here necessary to gather together separate strands. One thing stands forth plainly. So mingled with all success is failure, so balancing all happiness is disillusionment, that those who would fling wider the gates for emigration cannot be the spokesmen of the mass. That emigrants who return to Italy are generally better off than when they departed, or better off than those who stayed at home, is not to be doubted: at least two government investigations have so concluded. But those who returned were mainly a somewhat select group in emigrating, and were among the more successful abroad. At the other extreme, some thousands of indigent Italians every year are repatriated by charitable organizations, yet most of them and the mass who just manage to escape indigence enter into the calculations of few persons. It is impossible to construe the impressive totals of remittances sent home as evidence of general success: they are too irregular, or too small, or represent too extensively the surpluses of individuals not supporting families abroad. The houses of the " americani " on the Riviera about Genoa were built with remittances, but they tell us nothing of those toiling thousands who were only the stepchildren of fortune in the New World and whose voices of protest cannot be heard. Fraud and deceit are at every turn, too elusive to be more than speciously checked; like beetles that infest a tree whose robustness is gone, these are competent to find out the emigrant wherever he is. The padrone who trafficked in children in the early days was succeeded by the padrone who trafficked in men; if today the name is fading, the function, though more diffused, is still there. " Le peuple a besoin de rire," was said of the singing and dancing children, but the same impersonal exploitation of the Italian's humble competence exists today wherever he goes.

" Among ten illiterate emigrants, only two perhaps will succeed in clearing themselves a path to moderate gains," Sig. Franzoni once declared, and he recommended that the illiterate be prevented from emigrating.[1] But illiteracy is only one evidence of ill preparedness. The tragedy of emigration lies precisely in this, that it exacts energetic and well directed effort of a mass generally ill fitted therefor. The fact that a man wishes to sally forth is no proof that all is well. There is no one "emigration" by which he can gauge his chances of success; there are emigrations — to Buenos Aires, to Delaware, last year, this year, by one kind of person or another — and the variability of circumstances, according as one year or country or collection of personal attributes is taken, makes any inference from others' fortunes difficult. Italy, we have seen, has recognized the blindness to which the emigrant masses are heir by so far assuming responsibility for their decisions as, from time to time, to suspend emigration to particular regions. But it is by no means certain that the responsibility should not be exercised oftener and in more diverse ways.

---

[1] *Atti del Primo Congresso degli Italiani all' Estero*, ii, p. 140. Cf. Brenna's similar inference and recommendation in his *L'emigrazione italiana* (1918), ch. xiii.

No one can follow the fortunes of the Italians abroad without being struck by a sort of contempt in which they are often held. " Dago," " gringo," " carcamano," " badola," "cincali," "macaroni " — how long the list of epithets might be! " Italy feeds nobody and is everybody's guest " was the widely quoted utterance of a Frenchman. Whether such names and such opinions originate in the laborer's resentment of competition or in the citizen's easy association of objectionable or misunderstood personal attributes with the idea of the foreigner, they but emphasize the discomfort of the Italians and stir up a sense of shame in Italy.[1] In the Parliament at Rome frequent reference has been made to the dislike in which Italians have been held in the United States, and such men as San Giuliano and Tittoni believed there were reasons for it. Those who have most lauded the Greater Italy of the emigrants have realized its circumscriptions. Money confers a respect and an influence (that of England for example in Argentina) to which toil cannot attain. The Greater Italy is an empire — but a proletariate empire. It bestrides the world like a Colossus — but a Colossus arrayed in rags.

In nearly every country which they enter, the mass of the Italians, at least for a period of years, are at the social bottom. This derives not merely from their economic status, their manifold helplessness, their all but inevitable retention of foreign ways. It derives from the fact that their traits unpleasantly or too plainly suggest the hybrid. For good or ill, the old, more homogeneous stock, priding itself on its harmonious manners, its political cohesion, and often on its pure blood, resents intrusion. Only in such a region as the Ticino is the Italian regarded as the representative of a purer strain and a higher civilization. He may take out the citizenship of the country which he has entered, but to his new compatriots he is still a naturalized Italian. Naturalized or not, on the other hand, if he returns to Italy after a sojourn overseas he is classed with the americani; yet this appellation, it must

---

[1] This, for example, from de Amicis, watching his countrymen debark: " I felt a humiliation which made me shun the regard of foreigners who were on the ship with me and whose affected exclamations of surprise were only so many reproaches to my country." *On Blue Water*, p. 375.

be granted, does not forget that at bottom he is still a sort of Italian. In truth he is neither an Italian nor an American, but a denizen of some Third World. Cabrini tells of a recruit who, after failing to understand instructions given by a corporal in Italian, became a party to a lively dialogue when a sergeant, back from America, addressed him in English. That perhaps is the humor of the situation. But there is deep pathos too. In the foreign settlements, visiting Italians of culture have often regretfully pointed out that the emigrants seem lost, half absorbed, unable any longer to speak their own language; yet these same immigrants the people of the new country regard as foreigners, seeing ten points of difference for one of achieved resemblance.

Italians in Italy have often deplored the fact that the emigrants are not pioneers but wage earners. The surplus value, in the language of socialism, which they create is neither for themselves nor for their country. What is more, their toil in the past has gone largely to strengthen their enemies, has even gone to further military preparations later directed against them. But this, perhaps, is less an argument than an indictment of fate.

Vastly more momentous is the reasoning as to nationality. Grant that the political sense is weak in most emigrants, yet that which makes the best foundation for its upbuilding, the love of country, if only a campanilismo, is tremendously rooted. The Italian abroad does not want to be absorbed, he wants some day to return home. The Italian at home desires him still to remain an Italian. A parental — not a crudely imperialistic — desire is there. Italia is the mother. To become naturalized abroad is to give up what one dearly loves, is even, as a writer has held, to be treacherous to one's country. Yet not to become naturalized abroad is only to accentuate one's Third World character, is to be " an individual only, not a citizen — that is, half a man," as Corradini put it.[1] To press naturalization upon such persons, as is sometimes done in the United States, is a one-sided idealism, and may be the reverse of kindness. The Third World dilemma has yet to be solved.

[1] *Il volere d'Italia*, p. 154.

One honor indeed Italy enjoys upon which little or no stress has been laid. Her blood makes its contribution to the great world races. Her sons die, but their sons live on. As generations of plants succeed one another, there is here an immortality of race stock. The Italian blood will count in the remotest future of Europe and North Africa, of South and North America, and in some important countries it will count for a great deal. What the natural historian of emigration here sees is no barren distinction to Italy. But, also, what he sees fails to send a thrill through the heart of the patriot in the Mediterranean, who beholds only the price that has inevitably to be paid: political and cultural discontinuity and sacrifice.

What shall be thought of the mountains of labor performed by the Italians in the countries where they go ? A poet might make an epic of it. It is a tale which deserves never to be forgotten, a tribute to hardihood and energy. Generally, however, those who praise the labor, seeing only the shining result, have made little reckoning of its true cost in terms of human strain and privation. The Pyramids inspire the beholder with awe — do they inspire him enough with pity? We live in an age which has increasingly given the worker a voice, made him a brother in society; and we are asking, as men have never asked before, whether such conditions of toil and of living shall be tolerated as these of the Italians. For, if exception be made of the stagnant pools of sunken humanity which our great industrial nations have developed here and there in their cities, then these emigrants can be said to lead more irksome lives than any other modern class of workers, not themselves emigrants, of an equal racial endowment.

The economic value of their achievement to the nations concerned is not to be denied, even though that of the single emigrant be deemed slight (as it must). It cannot be argued, however, that a corresponding world gain also arises. Rather, on the contrary, the exportation of unskilled laborers, shopkeepers, and the rest, along all the pathways of the globe is a most costly procedure. That adaptation to environment which comes almost incidentally to the growing child, the knowledge for example of the vernacular, is largely useless abroad and must be done over again and this time by an organism that has lost its flexibility. Could anything be more luckless ? In all time, doubtless, it will prove advisable to make economic readjustments through the emigration of skilled men, or of men with special aptitudes, and in all time cultural enrichment will result from such movements, but more and more men will question whether the unskilled, because fit for so little and the sport of every wind that blows, should be encouraged to migrate.

In Tunisia, South Brazil, and Argentina, mass settlements of Italians have largely made the race stock of the country or have built a state within the state. In other countries most citizens have generally deemed them a foreign body. Far from providing any of that " cohesive force " which Mr. Graham Wallas has eloquently claimed to be needful in the Great Society, they are a force for disunion. Everywhere employers of labor want them, but laborers want them not, and everywhere the conflict of employers and laborers waxes a little sharper through their presence. It may be true that the " marginal productivity " of the laboring classes is heightened a peg by their coming, but that is an intangible gain, whereas the conflict in the labor market and propinquity in domicile — the assault upon the standard of living — are felt exasperations; and certainly for some classes of laborers the standard of living is really adversely affected. The temporary comer, the kind most approved in Italy, is generally disliked, for it is realized that he is *homo oeconomicus* alone, and remains quite outside the body politic. On the other hand, if the immigrant becomes naturalized, his new country declares it must not be for business reasons, but because, heart and soul, he wishes to substitute its interests and traditions for those of the land of his birth. To citizens of the United States, for example, nothing could be more repugnant than the thought that any Italian should profess a new allegiance in order to make more dollars, while inwardly reserving to himself the presumption that, when the pecuniary motive is satisfied, he will return to Italy to avail himself of the law for the quick restoration of his former citizenship. All true allegiance of the heart changes with difficulty. The Great

War, exercising tremendous pressure and putting a premium upon gigantic coöperation, seems to bring into line a large part of the foreigners of all nationalities in the United States, and some of its accomplishment will surely endure; but when the united front is no longer necessary, many of the immigrants will again show themselves, as Mr. Wallas would say, " resistant to the dissolving force of national consciousness." [1]

Dr. Brougnes, aspiring, through the colonization of Argentina to extinguish pauperism in Europe, was only one rather interesting adherent of a theory that fifty years ago held many thinkers in thrall. It is a theory which today has not a leg left to stand upon. Probably, also, the conditions which made the last half century a dynamic era without parallel, when, for example, the great railway nets of the newer countries were laid down, will not rule in the next half century. It is clearer now than it has ever been that, as Dr. Bertarelli once put it, emigration is a sort of conquest, and, if it is to bring success to the individual, he must be strong physically and variously fit and resistant for a hard task. And it must be manifest to whoever fairly surveys the whole breadth of the emigration sequence that most of the emigration from Italy, far from voicing any hope common to men normally situated, is a protest, vociferous yet unheard and unheeded, against conditions that must some day be made over. Emigration does not itself change these conditions, or it does so but slowly, at great cost, imperfectly. It is not a stream that carries away flood waters (for the general population has not been diminished), but rather a costly means of holding the flood in abeyance. It acts, not by checking the water at its source, but by systematically providing for its partial removal. To sanction it is to evade an issue.

The reigning philosophy of emigration in Italy is rudimentary. Expand and multiply, the Catholics have said, but they have ignored the circumstances and standards of living. We find you multiplying and poor, the non-Catholics have said, we will open a way out for you; but they too have underestimated the possibili-

---

[1] *The Great Society* (New York, 1914), p. 10.

ties of internal social amelioration. Even Bodio, whose words on
the necessity of emigration have been so widely echoed, could
write, " The excessive increase of our population is a product of
the ignorance of the people and of their misery," but these factors
he feared would inevitably change slowly.[1] Whether a state of
overpopulation shall or shall not exist in a country depends, as a
matter of fact, upon conditions that human decision, acting
through the institutions of government, is largely competent to
control. Italy, with her remarkable law for the protection of her
emigrants, has been less watchful over her children at home. For
Italy to leave to her emigration itself the task of the redemption
of her people, as many persons have recommended, is a method as
cruel as it would be bungling. Specific steps of reform must be
taken, and to that end a new point of view must rule, resting upon
a new philosophy, and requiring unprecedented coöperation. The
old apathy must go. The unqualified notion that emigration is
necessary must likewise go, for it is wrong and leads to an over-
drawing of benefits derived; and the discovery be made that
self-confidence, even when the social heritage is feudal, may be
justified.

How strangely persistent the old view has been that poverty is
inevitable! Kings, as the historian of South Italy knows, made
their trusted alliances with the organized poor, the *lazzaroni*.
After the South was somewhat brusquely incorporated into the
kingdom, the statesmen of United Italy and the people generally
failed to see how special was her problem. Villari's *Lettere
Meridionali* impressed thinking minds when they appeared in a
newspaper in 1875, and two years later Franchetti and Sonnino's
remarkable study of Sicily deepened the impression. Yet greater
landmarks even than these, in the development of study of the
South — immensely significant for the North as well — were the
mighty volumes of the *Inchiesta Agraria*, a seven-years' project
begun in 1877. Had these volumes, as they severally appeared,
been carefully studied, instead (as Jacini complained) of being
ignored by the press and deemed an unprofitable undertaking, the
misery of masses could have been vastly lessened. But it re-

---

[1] " Dell' emigrazione italiana," p. 9.

quired a similar undertaking, instituted precisely two-score years later, the invaluable *Inchiesta Parlamentare*, so often cited in this book, to rouse a response and breed a desire for reform. (I would not ignore the brave efforts made in certain laws of 1904 and 1906.) Yet the active friends of the South have still been chiefly Southerners, men like Zanardelli, Nitti, Fortunato, Villari. The time has surely come when the special conditions that have made at once for misery and for emigration, in South and North together, should be deemed national problems, and the best resources of the country directed to coping with them.

Argument in Italy has too often taken a mercantile turn. The South, it has held, is a poor region; it cannot pay for the costly improvements it needs. But the retort is plain enough. Five or six per cent may indeed not be earned, but greater losses will be avoided. The poverty of a region supplies the best reason why, decade after decade, children should not be raised to be sent forth as soon as they have attained their growth. The lessening of strain and misery should be a main object of the expenditure of wealth and effort; in positive terms, the creation of the conditions that make for happiness should be a primary aim of statesmanship.

Some of the improvements required are material, some moral. In the history of peoples like the Scandinavian, Swiss, and German, whose emigrations have been greatly diminished, the direction of needed reforms is prefigured. Economic changes apt to give freer scope to the activities of men, cultural changes that enable the individual to utilize economic opportunities and to raise the level of his existence, these are the great agencies. They imply as well a better-knit society, a social organization in which the aloofness and passivity of the possessing classes are brought to an end.

Many needed improvements are such as in better situated societies would naturally be promoted through local initiative and at local expense. The error in Italy has been to assume that the South, if left to itself, would act. Rather, the first steps must be taken by the State, either alone or in conjunction with the local authorities. Consider the matter of public safety. Were the countryside reasonably secure, were it unnecessary to pay an annual tax to thieves, many proprietors who now dwell in the cities would be ready to return to their estates. Consider the forests. Were the hillsides reafforested, much land that lies waste and unproductive could be made to yield, and those floods which now devastate farms and increase malaria could be reduced.[1] The task is one for both forestry experts and engineers, but since the gains to be secured are general, the State should either give the money therefor or lend it (with the forests as collateral). Consider the question of roads. The century old absence of them (the Bourbons feared they would be instruments of conspiracy) is largely to blame for making the men of neighboring towns as strange to each other as men of different countries. With the construction of needed highways, not only would all marketing be facilitated but the spirit of campanilismo, which pulverizes political competence, would decline. Consider the problem of malaria. Analysis of the blood, where necessary, to detect infection, the cure of every case, the careful screening of both infected and uninfected, the drainage or oiling of standing water — these means of preventing the spread of the disease and of eliminating the mosquito or the germ that it carries can only be effective if there is a centralized and costly campaign. Here again the State must lead, and possibly must bear the chief burden.

Difficulties bristle in the path of agricultural reform, so neglected during the struggle for unification and for consolidation; but much can be done to lessen them. Some one has said that the task of the South is to utilize every drop of water that falls. What the English have done in Egypt (nay, it was partly the Italians!) can be done in a small way many times over in South Italy. Irrigation, which is possible in many sections, would make the latifundium less necessary. One difficulty about the system of large estates is that they rarely come into the market, so that

[1] In a period of forty years the amounts spent on reafforestation and other preventive measures were utterly insignificant compared with the cost of flood damage repairs. See E. Branzoli-Zappi, " Conseguenze economiche del diboscamento in Italia," *Giornale degli Economisti*, May, 1903, pp. 409–422.

even if men had money wherewith to buy land, their dreams must be unfulfilled. While it is true that the ownership of land by the cultivator is not inevitably good, the ownership of medium-sized estates has far the best chance of bringing economical exploitation. A hopeful provision of the law of 1906 aimed to restore the improvement lease, which has had an honorable history in Italy. The collective lease likewise deserves to be spurred. In the long run it is desirable that cash rentals should supplant share rentals. On the technical side of agriculture and arboriculture a vast field for improvement lies open. Deeper plowing would alone accomplish much. More and better fertilizer is needed. Machinery, a device for saving labor rather than land, could be more extensively employed; though the individual ownership of many machines cannot be afforded, coöperative ownership and renting are possible.

The development of British land legislation will suggest ways of bringing the cultivators into better control of their lands. Of the public domain little that is good is left. It might be advisable for the State to buy lands and resell them (companies, under existing laws, are recommended to do so, but have done little). The entire credit situation is unfortunate. It perhaps does not much matter which of several possible ways out is utilized. In any case the remittances of emigrants should to a larger extent be made available for local credit purposes.[1]

Emigration has resulted partly from the growing competition of the newer countries in agriculture and partly from the increase of the people at home. The agriculture of Italy can be bettered and specialized, but it cannot be expected to support so large a fraction of the whole population as it once did. When over half the population is engaged in agriculture, and yet not enough grain is produced for home consumption, it is obvious that other industries must supply the means for purchase. Manufacturing and trade have progressed but slowly in Italy. In many regions

---

[1] See A. Vita, " Sulla ripartizione territoriale del risparmio in Italia," *Giornale degli Economisti*, September, 1914, pp. 161–188; and G. Nicotra, " Fabbisogno e disponibilità di capitale agricolo circolante per la Calabria," in the same journal, October, 1914, pp. 245–256.

the domestic industries have decayed faster than modern forms have been introduced. Probably the confusion resulting from the abolition of internal tariffs, after the unification of Italy, did much to depress industry in the South, while stimulating it in the North. Yet not the North alone, but the South also, have valuable supplies of water power, as yet but slightly utilized. In the working up of the products of agriculture and fishing there is a good opportunity for trade. The fact that foreign capital, especially English, has been introduced into South Italy is a comment both upon the absence of a spirit of enterprise, and upon the backwardness of business methods. Well organized, the production, for example, of the citrous fruits in their salable forms might win a wide market. Industry should have the effect of employing more hands and of diversifying local life, and so providing a chance to rise in the scale. What it has accomplished in checking emigration from the mountains of Switzerland it can accomplish in Italy. Indeed examples of its action there are already to be found.[1] But as Montemartini once urged, in comment upon Nitti's ideal of the industrialization of the South, such an exodus of the valid population as has taken place in Basilicata is the wrong way to prepare for industry.

Physical remaking of the country, land reforms, and the encouragement of trade and industry are only part of the necessary programme for redemption. The essential institutions of democracy must be more firmly planted. Steadily, until May, 1912, when the Libyan war made men reflect upon the loyalty of laborers and soldiers, the Governments had blocked the way to suffrage reform, and the vote was actually more accessible to Italians in some great foreign countries than in Italy. Steadily, until then, when a new law was enacted, the mass of the taxpayers, and of men held to military service, were denied the franchise. But the

---

[1] " Five or six years ago there was a strong current of the emigration of women from Biella into France (Meurthe-et-Moselle); now it is much less. The reason is that the local factories, besides being both more numerous and more important, and offering more employment to women, tend to move into the cities, and so all the more attract the factory hands after them." Bernardy, " L'emigrazione delle donne e dei fanciulli del Piemonte," p. 11; cf. p. 22.

vote in Italy is even now more restricted than it is (legally) in the United States, and much must still be done to render effective the new modes of representation and the new path to leadership.

But the institution that more than any other can fit men to utilize the projected economic and political opportunities, and indeed to assist with initiative and intelligence in establishing them, is the school. " If I could read I should have four eyes, but now I see naught," a peasant in Cosenza said.[1] Seeing, they would cease to be, in all countries, the children they have continued to be. So great is the handicap of illiteracy that, even were unlimited emigration to become permanent, every country should acknowledge its obligation to give those born within its borders the great primary preparation for living. Here is a reform which both those who would keep the Italians at home, and those likewise who would have them go forth, are bound to support. It has been approved by the imperialist elements (compare their support of the *Dante Alighieri*), for it tends to make more successful and more united the Italians abroad. It has been urged by many returned emigrants. The want of it has for years immemorial been almost the sum of the indictment which all observers of the Italians abroad have made. Yet in the responsible circles of Italy interest in popular education has been all too mild. The clear-seeing Villari advocated it as early as 1872, the volumes of the *Inchiesta Agraria*, a few years later, repeatedly asked for it, but through the entire period, Parliamentary reference to the matter, in arguments dealing with emigration, have been few. By enactments of 1904, evening and holiday schools were established, with State aid, especially in the most illiterate districts, but what these provisions accomplished was much less what had been hoped for. In 1906 a similar but more systematic provision was made in the South and Sicily generally, and in a few years some three thousand schools were established, the State quite taking over the function of education in some of the poorest communes and spending a million lire a year on new schools, generally upon new buildings. But since the schools were excessively modest affairs, and since many had later to be shut because of a lack of money for

[1] Rossi, " Vantaggi e danni," p. 58.

paying teachers and for other purposes, it is clear that a much more extensive provision is now necessary. Until ten or a dozen years ago, the average annual expenditure per inhabitant on education in the South was under two lire, and this, perhaps more than anything else, explains the extraordinary figures for illiteracy which even the most recent census has been forced to confess.[1] Besides overcoming illiteracy, the schools must go further. On the one hand they must provide trade and technical education, so facilitating industrial reforms, and on the other those liberal branches of learning which mean so much for the training of valuable leadership and which a war-worn world, overstressing material things, will so imperatively need.[2]

One universal factor in problems of sickness and health is the community, and in Italy, if the local community will not take the initiative, the State should. I have spoken of a malaria campaign. Further, there should be resanitation of all dwelling houses and none should be erected unless with the expert approval of sanitary authorities — what ignorance of hygiene has characterized the planning of the houses of the americani!

I have proposed that the State should shoulder the main responsibility of rehabilitating the backward regions, especially those of the South. If an emigration is large after fifty years of new government, not the old but the new is mainly answerable therefor. The family injured under the previous régime is scattered, dies. Where the blood of the patriot fell, the corn blooms again in the fields. An obnoxious tax can be removed, a system of oppression repealed, tariffs revised, the vote given, schools opened. If the old economic order persists, it is because a half century of new government has sanctioned it, even though un-

---

[1] In 1911, 37.6 per cent of the population of Italy over six years of age were illiterate; in the Abruzzi, Sicily, Basilicata, and Calabria, the percentages were respectively 58, 58, 65, 70. *Censimento*, iii, p. 230.

[2] Villari's (P.) early article is " La scuola e la quistione sociale in Italia," *Nuova Antologia*, November, 1872, pp. 477-512. Among recent writings see D. Samminiatelli, " Sulla istruzione delle masse emigratorie," in *Atti del Primo Congresso degli Italiani all' Estero*, i, pp. 407-427, and a comprehensive governmental study, *L'istruzione primaria e populare in Italia*, Turin, etc., 1911.

wittingly. And what it has sanctioned, if it be wrong, it can now unsanction. The demolition of reactionary governments that blocked the way to progress is not enough. It must be followed by that further effort which alone can make over old institutions or create new ones.

How shall the expense of an elaborate programme of rehabilitation be met ? Are these times in which to throw new burdens upon State treasuries ? Is not rather the lightening of taxes one requirement of the new day ? Some equalization of taxes is assuredly needed, and removal of the more obnoxious ones, but even though a kinder future may make unnecessary the support of a great army during peace, the general burden will enlarge rather than shrink. Somehow the North must contribute to the South and somewhat the rich must pay for the poor — the last, in all countries, is an inexorable demand of the transitional era that will follow the war.

But will not a scheme of State paternalism weaken the moral fiber of the people ? Of a well-considered paternalism history shows few examples, but those few no one would retract. The greatest, of course, is popular education. Coupled with democratic opportunities to rise, education has nothing to fear and much to hope. Only through a right education of their younger members can the possessing classes in South Italy be led to a full understanding of *noblesse oblige*. Many of the returned emigrants now bring an education got by experience, and where they are numerous in a town they may count for much.[1] But in general it is the young who will make Italy. What the children of Italian parents have accomplished in Argentina and the United States they will accomplish in Italy when good schools give them training, and when the circumstances and institutions of their own beautiful land tempt their initiative, an initiative which the spirit of feudalism will not long withstand. When the liberation of Italy has been followed by the liberation of the Italians, a great work will have been done.

---

[1] Many instances exist of towns whose population fell sharply through emigration and later, as emigrants returned, exceeded their old levels. See, *e.g.*, A. Fraccacreta, *Le forme del progresso economico in Capitanàta* (Naples, 1912), pp. 4 f.

One consequence of the coming of democratic institutions, unless all signs fail and experience elsewhere be disproved, will be a decline in the birth rate.   Then it should be all the easier to absorb at home such increase of population as will come.   There is much to suggest that European countries will generally, in this regard, drift in the direction of France.   But such a consequence will take many years to run its course, and meanwhile a further diminution of the death rate will tend for a time to make the annual increase of the population greater, or at least to maintain its level.   No one can discern the future, but it is justifiable to expect that, as the fruit of the changes suggested, Italy will in time become a country of few emigrants and those few of specialized, trained sorts; for such has been the course of several great emigrating peoples in the past.[1]

The great external problem of emigration remains.   It cannot be left to its own hazards.

No diminution is desirable in the programme of protection of emigrants to which the Italian Government so extensively committed itself in 1901.   Foreign labor leaders have often and advisedly criticised that programme, holding its inevitable effect to be a stimulation of emigration, and Senator Villari has vigorously insisted that such provisions as those governing the military service of emigrants are particularly likely to act as an encouragement to migrate.   But these wholly just criticisms will lose their force when substantial internal reforms have been instituted in Italy.   Then indeed the protective policy may be widened.   Advice touching transoceanic labor markets, labor disputes, and the like should be as freely provided as that concerning European countries.   The representations of ticket agents should be still further controlled or duly counterbalanced by unbiased accounts of foreign conditions.   The too extensive consulates of North and South America should be subdivided.   These are but examples.   Pantano's recent bill, for putting the Emigration Service under the

---

[1] It is worth noting that in the years before the war Denmark, Norway, the Netherlands, and Prussia were countries having an annual excess of births over deaths considerably higher than that of Italy in the same years.

control of the Ministry of Industry, Trade, and Labor, denotes increasing realization that the problems of protection are largely technical.

Within narrow yet important limits, Italy is in a position to compel the adoption of certain standards of protection on the part of foreign countries. The suspension of emigration to Brazil by the Prinetti decree was the sequel to vain efforts to persuade that country to safeguard her immigrants. When, several years later, attempts were made to have the ban lifted, but no guarantees were offered, the Emigration Council, upon Bodio's recommendation, voted to keep the restrictions in force. Later, as we know, the state of São Paulo, eager for plantation hands, established a system of protection.

Quite as interesting is the reaction upon Italy when it is the country of immigration that has the higher standards. Tremendous has been the influence exerted by the United States through its ever more selective laws. It is widely realized that the emigrant must have or acquire certain qualifications for admission to this country, and the lawmakers of Italy have been constantly watchful to fit their compatriots for departure, all the more since emigration is deemed necessary. Here is a lever that may yet work great internal reforms.

Let me cite a striking example and episode. So much had the literacy test bill, finally enacted in 1917, been assailed by idealists in the United States — it had likewise been vetoed by three presidents — that the repercussions in Italy of its many vicissitudes in Congress deserve to be noted. When enactment seemed likely in 1903, the Minister of Public Instruction asked the Commissioner-General of Emigration for a subsidy of 50,000 lire — meager to be sure! — toward an appropriation of 150,000, to help instruct illiterates in one thousand communes. The Committee of Vigilance, convinced that the United States would act, sanctioned the proposal. But the American Congress voted in the negative. At a session of the Council of Emigration, in March, 1904, Sig. Luzzatti, presiding, said: " For the present we are not threatened by the law; but the danger may return, hence we ought to be forehanded in preparing this rapid-fire instruction." Sig. Bodio agreed that " Now the danger is less pressing," and the Council voted not to grant the appropriation.[1] In February, 1904, the Council reversed its decision and in that year, as we know, a very modest measure was enacted establishing schools iñ certain regions whose people emigrated mainly to the United States.[2] In the following year the special appropriation for illiterates in emigration centers was omitted. Agitation in America continued. In July, 1905, the Minister of Foreign Affairs declared to the Senate, " It is now certain that, in one form or another, defensive action will be taken against undesirable immigration . . . therefore we should not neglect to diffuse schooling in those provinces which send illiterate emigrants to America." [3]

In 1913 the bill again seemed likely to pass in the American Congress. Again the Italian emigration authorities were asked to make an appropriation and again the vote was affirmative. And this time the American Congress accepted the literacy test bill, but Mr. Taft promptly vetoed it. " Hence the Commissioner-General no longer had to concern himself with the matter," reads an Italian report.[4] The Italian newspapers in the United States jubilantly hailed the President's action.[5] But the following year the bill was again before Congress, and in the Italian Emigration Council the necessity was again urged of freeing the people of Italy " from a danger which will not always remain in a state of mere threat " (C. Corradini), and the shame of Italy was pointed

[1] See "Rendiconti delle sedute del Consiglio dell' Emigrazione tenute nell' anno 1903," *Boll. Emig.*, 1904, No. 9, p. 64.

[2] "Rendiconti sommari delle sedute . . . nell' anno 1904," *Boll. Emig.*, 1904, No. 10, pp. 34–36; cf. *Boll. Emig.*, 1906, No. 13, pp. 20 f.

[3] T. Tittoni, *Boll. Emig.*, 1905, No. 16, p. 30.

[4] " Proibizione dello sbarco negli Stati Uniti agli stranieri analfabeti," *Boll. Emig.*, 1915, Nos. 10–12, p. 126.

[5] *Ibid.*, p. 119. An editorial of the *Rivista Coloniale* (February 16–28, 1913, p. 113), noting that only five votes were lacking to pass the measure over the veto, urged the government to keep in mind this " threat," so that if enactment came, the harm to Italian emigration would be reduced to the smallest proportions. Cf. G. Preziosi, " La proibizione dello sbarco agli analfabeti negli Stati Uniti dell' America del Nord," *Vita Italiana all' Estero*, February, 1913, pp. 99-114. More enlightened views on the ulterior effects of education are those of L. Villari, *Gli Stati Uniti*, pp. 304 f., and Starace, p. 45.

out in allowing her illiterate emigrants to the United States to be
as numerous relatively as those from Turkey (A. Cabrini), and
was voted that the Commissioner-General take any measures
ᵉssary to overcome illiteracy.[1] Then came the war, paralyzing
all action.

Mr. Wilson's two vetoes of the bill were followed by its final
passage over his veto in 1917. Is it not likely that earlier enactment would have given the greatly needed spur to the extension of
popular schooling in Italy ?

The essential problems of emigration and immigration are very
old. The *termini* of migration have ever had to deal with such
matters as the retention of necessary kinds of labor or of soldiers,
the costs of looking after newcomers, supporting the poor, protecting resident workers, and avoiding large sudden increases of
population. In the Middle Ages the towns put formal impediments in the way of migration, or exacted taxes, like the *gabella
emigrationis* or the *detractus personalis*, and so far they acted much
as modern governments have done. But sometimes, also, the towns
had recorded agreements which amicably exchanged advantage
for advantage or set off disadvantages against each other.

The method of agreement has had numerous modern applica-
tions also, though generally very restricted in their scope. Italy
herself has been a party to various conventions and some men in
Italy (notably Luzzatti) have warmly championed them. There
have been, for instance, the Italo-French agreement of June 9,
1906, giving to Italians in France and to Frenchmen in Italy
equivalent rights to compensation for industrial accident injuries;
the Italo-French convention of June 10, 1910, for the protection of
child workers of the two nations, requiring consular certificates or
parental permission for work and setting up committees in the
major industrial centers, on which the children's countrymen are
represented, to see to the enforcement of general labor laws; and
the Italo-German convention of July 31, 1912, providing for the
compensation of workers disabled through accident, invalidity or

---

[1] " Rendiconti delle adunanze del Consiglio dell' Emigrazione," *Boll. Emig.*,
1915, Nos. 10-12, pp. 17–33.

age.[1] Generally these treaties have had no other object in view than the protection of laborers, but in some quarters, proposals have been rife that Italy should act somewhat as a gigantic trade union, selling her labor to the highest bidder, and especially should aim to serve her political ends.[2]

Here indeed a large question is raised, bringing us face to face with the whole post-bellum situation. What, in the years to come, are to be the tendencies of emigration ? What will be the needs of countries ? What chances of clash will arise ? And what should be done ?

There will be reconstruction, slow doubtless rather than fast, of most areas devastated by war; and some fairly extensive new regions may be opened for settlement. If not at first, certainly later, Italy will again have a great emigration (it will at best take many years for internal reforms to check the flow substantially). The probability exists that here and there among the other belligerent nations, people will seek homes or wages in other lands, perhaps on a far-reaching scale.

Even, however, if these portentous new forces, vaguely as they must be defined today, had not come into being, enough ground has existed in the ante-bellum situation to warrant the calling of an international conference to suggest legislation by the great countries.[3] The discontent roused by immigration in various

[1] L. de Feo, *I trattati di lavoro e la protezione dei nostri lavoranti all' estero*, Milan, 1916 (an excellent discussion, with various texts); G. Valentini-Fersini, *Protezione e legislazione internazionale del lavoro, prodromi di un diritto internazionale operaio*, Milan, etc., 1909–10; L. Luzzatti, " Nota sul trattato lavoro tra l'Italia e la Francia," *Nuova Antologia*, January 16, 1916, pp. 169–179. For certain texts, see also *Bollettino dell' Ufficio del Lavoro*, July, 1910, pp. 166–169; *Boll. Emig.*, 1913, No. 5, pp. 81-88, No. 8, pp. 42-48.

[2] Ferri so argued in 1909. A fairly typical recent discussion of its sort is G. E. di Vallelonga, " La politica dell' emigrazione italiana dopo la guerra," *Vita Italiana*, May 15, 1916, pp. 404-410.

[3] The idea of international regulation of migration is not new, but I do not know that it was proposed before 1897, when the International Law Institute of Ghent met at Copenhagen. It has been often suggested since, but never with much backing until our own Congress, rather mildly, in 1907, and the Italian emigrant congresses sponsored it. See also J. D. Whelpley, *The Problem of the Immigrant* (London, 1905), ch. 2, and Preziosi, *Il problema dell' Italia d'oggi*, pp. 195-199.

countries is the first reason for calling such a conference. But also the desire of the nations, prompted by humanitarian considerations, further to protect emigrants and immigrants, tends to increase emigration, and so intensifies the discontent with which immigrants are regarded. Such a conference could neither legislate nor dictate. Single states would still act independently, being governed by their special interests, and agreements between two countries would still be sought in order to secure mutual advantages. But in many matters, single states are helpless; and two cannot come to agreement, one having a favor to grant, the other being a beggar. When all, however, act with regard to each other there is a chance of so reordering the sum of advantages and disadvantages that an improved general arrangement may result.

The topics of international consequence which such a conference would discuss — and I assume that the laboring classes themselves would be prominently represented in it — are four:

(1) *The adoption of standards of fitness for emigrants.* What bodily, moral, and educational or other restrictions should be put upon the freedom to migrate? The answer to this question measures the extent to which a nation shall be deemed to have obligations towards those born into its fellowship. It is, for example, not desirable that Italians, found unacceptable to the medical officers at the ports of embarkation, should yet depart clandestinely and be admitted elsewhere, nor that individuals debarred from one country on grounds of health should find their way to other countries. The costs of properly safeguarding emigrants in the countries where they go should help to determine the standards.

(2) *The distribution of fit emigrants.* What facilities should be created for enabling men who seek homes or wages to discover the most suitable destinations? There is question here not merely of preventing such congestion in special centers as has so often been the object of complaint in the United States, but of performing a true international labor exchange function. Greater economy in the employment of birds of passage might result and better conditions for them. The construction of public works in distant and undeveloped places could be facilitated, and that agricultural

emigration disciplined which utilizes the seasons in both the Northern and Southern Hemispheres, or which moves between neighboring countries — like that which during the Great War arose between Brazil and Argentina. It is possible, too, that a world which during that war performed such prodigies of experiment will take more kindly to certain adventures in the matter of emigration. When once the whole emigration movement is brought under control, various countries which now chiefly desire to stem the tide may be willing to try experiments (for example, in a conditioned agricultural colonization), so developing a new accommodation of aptitude and skill to environments where they are lacking. An invaluable statistical organization might grow up in connection with such an international service.

(3) *Citizenship.* What shall be the rights of emigrants in the matter of allegiance to country ? In the special sanctions which an international labor exchange office might provide there is some chance of reconciling such conflicting desires as that of the Italian who merely wishes to earn abroad and the American who wishes him to be absorbed. Yet this is but a single aspect of the problem. Italy is not the only country which exacts certain duties from her sons naturalized abroad and their children born to another citizenship. The conflict in its present terms is an absurd one, provocative of much worry on the part of individuals already much harassed; and the means to at least its partial extinction are unquestionably within the reach of debate.

(4) *The protection of emigrants.* What action, public or private, shall the states take in sheltering the emigrants from the dangers that surround them ? It is clear that a certain minimum of police aid is indispensable and yet is lacking today. By internationally coördinated arrangements a vast deal can be done. Above all, control is needed over the routes and conveyances of travel. The journeys which in every year of peace many thousands of emigrants make to the United States and other countries, only to be refused admission, should by due administrative devices be rendered less frequent. The simple scheme some years ago of stationing United States medical officers at Naples saved innumerable needless journeys. Again, the means must be found of assuring

certain rather primary kinds of protection of emigrants in the countries where they go. No citizen of the United States can take pride in the situation revealed a decade ago in the Maiorano case, in which compensation for the death of her husband, employed on an American railway, was refused to a widow because she was residing abroad — notwithstanding the contention of the Italian Foreign Minister that the decision of the United States Supreme Court violated treaty stipulations. As a rule the more adequate the protection provided, the more costly it is; and many dangers will long elude our efforts. The more costly the protection in turn, the more we shall be led to restate the minimum standards of fitness for emigrants.

What finally shall be thought of those who wish to transform the Italian emigrant empire into a political empire ? Does not the world today stand surfeited with imperialism ?

For those schemes of State aided emigration and colonization which the classic world knew, much of a surety can be urged. They gave an opportunity for the organic extension of the commonwealth. If in truth a new era were now to be at hand in which national aspirations would find no opportunity for exaggerated developments into imperalism, it would none the less — but perhaps rather the more — be true that the principle of nationality should be encouraged, for nothing else can take its place as a bulwark against the commonplaces of cosmopolitanism. The immigration of the people of one country into another breeds grave problems and ultimately means absorption, without even any considerable and palpable legacy from the disappearing nationality. The Italian people are one of the priceless assets of the world. What the world may gain by making Italian emigrants and their children into citizens of other countries is as nothing compared with what it may gain from continuing in a Greater Italy their language, their traditions, their finest spirit as it breathes in the arts of civilization.

Here is not an aspiration to be put down. So much of the world is now given over to peoples whose contributions to human history, however treasurable, are certainly less rich and less promising than those of the Italians, so much also is given over to development by peoples of other European nationality who leave no corner which emigrants from Italy can call their very own, that a claim for a larger Italy, whether in North Africa or western Asia, deserves to be heard. Tripoli is not likely to meet the need. Tunisia, hardly necessary to stationary France, and already mainly peopled by Italians (except for African stock), would serve admirably. (May the means yet be found of conveying it to Italy!) There is here no argument for conferring a great empire. There is only question of providing an outlet for that population which will not, if the most be done, be quite adjusted to its own peninsula and islands for many years to come. This is that *imperialismo della povera gente* which no well-wisher of humanity can begrudge such a people as the Italian.

APPENDIX

APPENDIX

MEMORANDA SUPPLEMENTARY TO BOOK I

1. INTENSITY OF EMIGRATION

AVERAGE ANNUAL NUMBER OF EMIGRANTS PER 10,000 INHABITANTS,
ACCORDING TO THE POPULATION CALCULATED FOR THE
MIDDLE OF EACH PERIOD

(Data of the Bureau of Statistics compiled by the Commissioner-General of Emigration. See *Boll. Emig.*, 1910, No. 18, p. 5.)

	1876–1886	1887–1900	1901–1909
Piedmont	96	85	162
Liguria	59	43	60
Lombardy	53	53	113
Venetia	134	324	298
Emilia	23	50	133
Tuscany	40	57	117
Marches	10	42	204
Umbria	0.5	10	144
Latium	0.5	10	98
Abruzzi and Molise	31	102	337
Campania	34	96	222
Apulia	3.9	17	104
Basilicata	108	184	305
Calabria	44	115	308
Sicily	7	44	210
Sardinia	1.5	7	62
All Italy	47	87	179

2. AGE, SEX, AND DEPARTURE UNACCOMPANIED BY MEMBERS OF FAMILY

(Compiled from the official summaries in *Boll. Emig.*, 1910, No. 18, pp. 490-495, and from *Statistica della emigrazione* for 1910 and 1911, p. xv.)

In 10,000 emigrants, there were:

Periods for which annual averages are computed	Males	Persons not older than 15 years	Persons younger than 14 years	Persons not accompanied by members of their families
1876–1878	8641	921	....	7659
1884–1886	8263	....	1078	6924
1894–1896	7717	....	1618	5932
1904–1906	8230	....	1059	7967
Years				
1907	8152	....	1025	8093
1908	8271	....	996	8134
1909	8116	1029	....	7903
1910	8154	1067	....	7869
1911	8073	1038	....	7868

3. OCCUPATIONS

NUMBER OF MALES AND OF FEMALES IN EACH OCCUPATION PER
10,000 EMIGRANTS OF EACH CLASS ABOVE THE AGE OF 15

Periods for which annual averages are computed		Workers employed in agriculture, dairying, gardening, forestry, and related undertakings	Common day laborers employed in excavation and in road and waterway construction	Masons, hodcarriers, stonecutters, furnace workers, and others employed in the building trades	Workers employed in other industries (mining, metallurgy, glass, textiles, etc.) and artisans (carpenters, shoemakers, tailors, barbers, etc.)	In the liberal professions (physicians, apothecaries, lawyers, engineers, teachers)	In other and unknown or indefinite occupations
1878-1880	Male	4181	2133	1624	1186	71	595
	Female	5774	1287	65	1089	73	1712
1884-1886	Male	4893	2284	1413	780	59	571
	Female	5754	1417	103	1047	54	1625
1894-1896	Male	4471	2564	1735	623	63	544
	Female	6330	1482	112	610	76	1390
1904-1906	Male	3587	3221	1312	1166	32	682
	Female	3183	1376	95	1446	35	3865
Years							
1907	Male	3477	3195	1361	1227	37	703
	Female	2775	1343	95	1656	48	4083
1908	Male	3297	3473	1507	1081	42	600
	Female	2464	1559	162	1510	39	4266
1909	Male	3618	3512	1161	1026	37	646
	Female	2656	1355	141	1447	32	4369

For this table I have drawn upon a compilation made by the Commissioner-General of Emigration and published in *Boll. Emig.*, 1910, No. 18, pp. 504–511. The figures for 1884–86 and 1894–96 are for emigrants above the age of 14.

The annual reports of the Bureau of Statistics do not give the occupational classification according to sex, but they do give the occupational groups in greater detail. The agricultural and day labor groups, taken together, were in the years 1910 and 1911 respectively 62.4 and 59.9 per cent. The building trades workers were 12.0 and 13.6 per cent. In miscellaneous industries and crafts were 11.3 and 11.8 per cent. Hotel and restaurant keepers, and dealers in food, were each 1.0 per cent. Waiters and the like were 1.2 and 1.3 per cent.

Itinerant traders were .6 per cent in each year, numbering about 3000 a year. In domestic service were 2.5 and 2.9 per cent. See *Statistica della emigrazione* for 1910 and 1911, p. xiv.

A good discussion of some of the bearings of occupation is by L. Marchetti, " L'émigration dans ses rapports avec l'occupation des travailleurs," *Bulletin de l'Institut Internationale pour la Lutte contre le Chômage*, July–September, 1912, pp. 553–573.

4. THE INTERNAL MIGRATION OF ITALY

The internal movement depends upon the extraordinary agricultural differences that obtain between even neighboring regions of Italy. These in turn follow natural diversities of altitude, slope, soil, and season.

The first period of migration runs from January to the end of April. Central and southern Italy are involved. The operations are pruning grapevines, loosening the ground about their roots, caring for olive trees, sowing grain, and preparing the soil in the rice fields. At the same time brickmakers go to the ovens of Piedmont, Lombardy, and the outskirts of Rome. Masons and hodcarriers go from Varese and Biella to Milan and Turin. In 1910 the migrants of this period numbered nearly 100,000.

A second, the chief, period extends from early May to mid-August. Agricultural work abounds and is of a kind requiring many hands. The soil must be turned over for the grains, the vineyards irrigated, the first hay mown, the mulberry trees stripped and pruned, silkworms raised, barley and bean crops harvested, wheat and oats reaped and threshed. Especially do the cultivation of rice and the reaping of grain demand new labor.- Between May 10 and May 20 throngs of workers of both sexes descend from Alps and Apennines to the lowlands of the Po for the silk growing. Late in May the rice huskers complete their tasks. In 1910 the May migrants numbered 100,000, the June migrants 150,000. By June 20, fully a quarter of a million people are at work in other communes than their own. They begin then to go home; so do others who had left their homes in fall or winter. July calls a special contingent to the mountains for the grain harvests. Many of those who return in July and August have been absent for ten months. The brickmakers stay through September, the masons till November.

The third period begins at the end of August and lasts through December. The mowing calls, and the rice harvest, with its threshing and drying operations. To North and South go the vintagers. In Sicily and the South emigrants go to harvest olives, oranges, and lemons. Woodcutters and charcoal burners go into Sardinia and the Roman and Tuscan maremmas. The herdsmen take their summer charges down to the plains. There is an agricultural emigration to certain great malarial districts (the maremmas, the Apulian plain, the Ionian coast of Calabria) not worked in the warmer season. Some of the emigrants of this period go home for Christmas, either finally or for a respite; others tarry till the spring.

In 1910 the emigrants officially recorded were 559,434; in some years there have been more. Apulia accounts for a fifth; Sicily, Piedmont, Lombardy, Emilia, Latium, Campania, Abruzzi, Tuscany, Calabria are other great sources. Of the rice weeders in Novara and Pavia three-fourths are young women. In 1912 they cleared about 90 lire each, in forty workdays of ten hours. The 41,741 rice cultivators in Novara and Pavia averaged less than 100 lire in forty days. Of these workers 17,062 came by train, 17,860 by train and cart, 4376 by cart only, 3541 afoot; the mode of coming was not recorded for 6902.

There is no indication that this migration is coming to an end. The greater use of machinery may some day diminish it, but till now machinery has often been hard to apply — as, for example, on the uneven *agro romano* — or has encountered too rigid a tradition.

On the whole subject see the admirable study by Dr. L. Marchetti, "Die inneren jahreszeitlichen Wanderungen der Landarbeiter und die landwirtschaftlichen Stellenvermittlungsämter in Italien," *Zeitschrift für Socialwissenschaft*, September and October, 1914, pp. 605–617, 683–693. In the publications of the Ufficio dell' Lavoro are various contributions, especially *Le correnti periodiche di migrazione in Italia durante il 1905*, Rome, 1907.

INDICES

BIBLIOGRAPHICAL INDEX

Since a large majority of the works utilized have mainly a specific interest, the footnotes of the separate chapters may take the place of a classified bibliography. This index is essentially a reference list, the first page cited under an author or a title supplying the full bibliographical detail.

Where the authorship of a work has not been given or is not clear, the title, commonly abbreviated, has been utilized instead. But if, in such a case, the work has been published in a magazine, the name of the latter has alone been given. Anonymous articles and official studies of an occasional nature, published in the *Bollettino dell' Emigrazione*, especially when they have been referred to only once in this book, have not been listed at all.

General works. Only those that have been found useful for my purposes have been referred to in the text. Two others of some scope may be named here: R. Le Conte, *Étude sur l' émigration italienne,* Paris, 1908; P. E. De Luca, *Della emigrazione europea ed in particolare di quella italiana,* 4 vols., Turin, 1910.

Guide books for emigrants. An extremely interesting series has appeared. Besides those referred to in connection with the text, others deserve mention as being typical of their class: D. G. Curti, *La chiave della fortuna ossia manuale pratico dell' emigrante e dell' emigrato italiano in America,* 2d ed. Turin, 1908; Ufficio del Lavoro della Società Umanitaria, *Guida degli emigranti nella Lombardia,* Milan, 1909 (for internal seasonal migrants); J. F. Carr, *Guida degli Stati Uniti per l' immigrante italiano,* New York, 1910 (an English version was published in 1911); Anon., *Consigli agli emigranti — vade-mecum per gl' italiani agli Stati Uniti,* Florence, 1912; P. A. Sardella, *L' emigrante,* 3d ed., Lecco, 1912.

Italians in France. An admirable monograph has come to my hands too late to be referred to in the text : A. C. de Canisy, *L'ouvrier dans les mines de fer du bassin de Briey,* Paris, 1914.

GENERAL INDEX

Abandoned lands in South Italy, 57 ff., 449; France, 134; United States, 366, 370.

Abruzzi and Molise, emigration from, 38, 139, 326, 529; reactions of emigration in, 452–454, 457, 461, 462, 471.

Absentee landlordism, 70 ff., 78, 79, 93, 99, 111 f., 117, 451.

Abuses of Terms of employment in Brazil, 293 ff., 296 f.; United States, 391. *See also* Defrauding of Italians.

Abyssinian war, 271, 491, 493.

Acqua, dell', 262.

Adams, 325.

Agrarian contracts in South Italy, 72 ff., 79 f., 84 f., 86 f.; North Italy, 112 ff.; Italy generally, 455, 512. For other countries, *see* Agriculture, Italians in.

Agricultural laborers in South Italy, 83, 85 ff., 99, 450; North Italy, 116 ff.; Italy generally, 39 f., 454. For other countries, *see* Agriculture, Italians in.

Agricultural methods of Italians in South Italy, 61 f., 64, 77 ff., 453 f.; North Italy, 112, 114, 115 f., 118; France, 131 ff.; Switzerland, 173; the Trentino, 193; Tunisia, 216 f.; Argentina, 265 f.; Brazil, 291 ff., 301, 302, 307, 308, 310; United States, ch. xix *passim;* Italy generally, 450, 452 f., 512.

Agriculture, Italians in, in Italy, 51 ff., 449 ff., 531; France, 129, 130, 131 ff., 143 f.; Germany, 153; Switzerland, 173, 182 f.; Austria, 191, 196, 199; Albania, 207; Greece, 207; Rumania, 209; Tunisia, 215, 216 f.; Algeria, 221; Argentina, 230 ff., 256, 265 f.; Brazil, 289 ff., 299 ff.; United States, 325, 334, 363 ff., 424, 425, 434. *See also* Dairying.

Albania, Italians in, 206.

Alberdi, 225.

Alcoholic drinking in South Italy, 95, 423; France, 144, 145, 147; Germany, 166, 168; Switzerland, 187; Austria-Hungary, 201; Argentina, 269; United States, 361, 362, 369, 380, 386, 396, 406; significance of, 423; increased in Italy, 464.

Algeria, Italians in, 5, 10, 21, 219 ff.

Algerians in France, 149.

Aloisi, 258.

Alongi, 72 f.

Alsace-Lorraine, emigration from, to Algeria, 221; Argentina, 234.

Amati, 491.

" Americani," 452 ff. (*passim*), 503, 515.

Amicis, de, 236, 247.

Andree, 227, 259.

Annunzio, d', 493.

Anselm, 150.

Apulia, emigration from, 38, 197, 206, 207, 211, 213, 217, 259, 529; reactions of emigration in, 452, 454, 459 f., 464.

Arlberg Tunnel, 192 f.

Argentina, Italians in, 5, 15 ff., 18 ff., 30 ff., 37, 103, 223 ff., 305, 329, 365, 370, 372, 410 f., 419, 421, 429, 431, 434, 444, 466, 487, 489, 498, 507, 516.

Argentine-Paraguay war, 277.

Art, Italians in, in South Italy, 97; France, 134 f.; Switzerland, 179; Turkey, 211; Argentina, 255, 257 f.; 270, 271; Brazil, 315.

Asia, Italians in, 10, 211, 419.

Assimilation of Italians in Switzerland, 180 f.; Greece, 207; Turkey, 211; Tunisia, 218; Algeria, 221 f.; Argentina, 270 f., 276; Brazil, 318 f.; United States, 394 ff., 405, 406, 409 f.; abroad generally, 441 f., 505, 506 f., 524.

Attitude of employing classes toward Italians in France, 132, 134, 140, 146; Germany, 160 ff.; Switzerland, 180: Brazil, 319; United States, 401 f., abroad generally, 424, 507.

Attitude, general, toward Italians in France, 149; Germany, 161; Switzerland, 180 ff.; Austria-Hungary, 199; Egypt, 213; Tunisia, 218; Algeria, 222; Argentina, 252, 273, 274, 277 f.; Brazil, 319; United States, 325, 380, 401, 407 ff.; abroad generally, 504 f., 506, 507 521 f.

Attitude of labor classes toward Italians in France, 140 ff.; Germany, 163 ff.; Switzerland, 182; Austria-Hungary, 198 f.; Great Britain, 205; Argentina, 277; United States, 402 ff.; abroad generally, 504, 507, 517.

Austria, rule in North Italy, 96, 106, 107, 108, 121; territories of, desired by Italy, 493, 496, 497, 500.